NEW PERSPECTIVES ON

The Internet

9th Edition

COMPREHENSIVE

NEW PERSPECTIVES ON
The Internet
9th Edition

COMPREHENSIVE

Gary P. Schneider
Jessica Evans

COURSE TECHNOLOGY
CENGAGE Learning·

Australia • Brazil • Japan • Korea • Mexico • Singapore • Spain • United Kingdom • United States

COURSE TECHNOLOGY
CENGAGE Learning

New Perspectives on the Internet, 9th Edition, Comprehensive

Vice President, Careers and Computing: David Garza

Executive Editor: Marie L. Lee

Associate Acquisitions Editor: Amanda Lyons

Senior Product Manager: Kathy Finnegan

Product Manager: Leigh Hefferon

Product Manager: Julia Leroux-Lindsey

Director of Marketing: Elisa G. Roberts

Marketing Manager: Valerie A. Hartman

Associate Marketing Manager: Adrienne Fung

Marketing Coordinator: Michael Saver

Developmental Editor: Kim T. Crowley

Senior Content Project Manager:
　Jennifer Goguen McGrail

Composition: GEX Publishing Services

Art Director: Marissa Falco

Text Designer: Althea Chen

Cover Designer: Roycroft Design

Cover Art: Image Copyright Lukáš Hejtman, 2012;
　used under license from Shutterstock.com

Copyeditor: Suzanne Huizenga

Proofreader: Camille Kiolbasa

Indexer: Rich Carlson

For product information and technology assistance, contact us at
Cengage Learning Customer & Sales Support, 1-800-354-9706
For permission to use material from this text or product, submit all requests online at **www.cengage.com/permissions**
Further permissions questions can be emailed to
permissionrequest@cengage.com

Some of the product names and company names used in this book have been used for identification purposes only and may be trademarks or registered trademarks of their respective manufacturers and sellers.

Microsoft and the Office logo are either registered trademarks or trademarks of Microsoft Corporation in the United States and/or other countries. Course Technology, Cengage Learning is an independent entity from the Microsoft Corporation, and not affiliated with Microsoft in any manner.

Disclaimer: Any fictional data related to persons or companies or URLs used throughout this book is intended for instructional purposes only. At the time this book was printed, any such data was fictional and not belonging to any real persons or companies.

Library of Congress Control Number: 2012935733

ISBN-13: 978-1-111-52911-6

ISBN-10: 1-111-52911-6

Course Technology
20 Channel Center Street
Boston, MA 02210
USA

Cengage Learning is a leading provider of customized learning solutions with office locations around the globe, including Singapore, the United Kingdom, Australia, Mexico, Brazil, and Japan. Locate your local office at:
international.cengage.com/global

Cengage Learning products are represented in Canada by Nelson Education, Ltd.

To learn more about Course Technology, visit **www.cengage.com/course technology**
To learn more about Cengage Learning, visit **www.cengage.com**

Purchase any of our products at your local college store or at our preferred online store
www.cengagebrain.com

Printed in the United States of America
2 3 4 5 6 7 8 9 16 15 14

Preface

The New Perspectives Series' critical-thinking, problem-solving approach is the ideal way to prepare students to transcend point-and-click skills and take advantage of all that the Internet has to offer.

In developing the New Perspectives Series, our goal was to create books that give students the software concepts and practical skills they need to succeed beyond the classroom. We've updated our proven case-based pedagogy with more practical content to make learning skills more meaningful to students.

With the New Perspectives Series, students understand *why* they are learning *what* they are learning, and are fully prepared to apply their skills to real-life situations.

About This Book

This book provides complete coverage of using the Internet and its technologies, and includes the following:

- Hands-on steps for searching the Web and evaluating the available resources to determine their validity, credentials, timeliness, and accuracy
- Hands-on steps for using Microsoft Internet Explorer, Mozilla Firefox, and Google Chrome, and for creating and using a Windows Live Hotmail email account
- In-depth and expanded coverage of social networks, wireless technology and networks, security countermeasures for various types of threats, and protecting individual privacy and avoiding identity theft
- E-commerce coverage updated and revised to reflect the consumer's perspective of buying and selling on the Web, Internet advertising and marketing, PayPal and digital wallets, consumer concerns, and international issues
- Updated and new case problems at the end of every tutorial

New for this edition!

- Each session begins with a Visual Overview, a new two-page spread that includes colorful, enlarged graphics with numerous callouts and key term definitions, giving students a comprehensive preview of the topics covered in each session, as well as a handy study guide.
- New ProSkills boxes provide guidance for how to use the Web in real-world, professional situations.
- Comprehensive ProSkills exercises at the end of Tutorials 5 and 9 integrate the skills students learn in the tutorials with one or more of the following soft skills: decision making, problem solving, teamwork, verbal communication, and written communication. These comprehensive exercises provide an opportunity for students to complete more challenging, thought-provoking assignments that reinforce the critical thinking skills taught in the tutorials.

System Requirements

This book assumes that Microsoft Internet Explorer 9 (or higher), Mozilla Firefox 5 (or higher), or Google Chrome, and Windows 7 are installed. (Students using Internet Explorer 8 (or lower) or Firefox 4 (or lower) and Windows Vista or XP can still complete the steps in this book, but they might encounter some differences.) Note that the figures and steps in this edition were written using Windows 7; therefore, Windows Vista/XP users might notice minor differences in the figures and steps. This book assumes that students have a complete installation of the Web browser and its components, an Internet connection, and are able to create an email account. Because the Web browser or email account students use might be different from those used in the figures in this book, students' screens might differ slightly; this difference does not present any problems for students completing the tutorials.

> "The clear step-by-step instructions, real-world data files, and helpful figures make New Perspectives texts excellent for courses taught in the classroom, the hybrid/blended format, or entirely online."
>
> —Sylvia Amito'elau
> Coastline Community
> College

VISUAL OVERVIEW

PROSKILLS

INSIGHT

 TIP

REVIEW

APPLY

REFERENCE

GLOSSARY/INDEX

The New Perspectives Approach

Context
Each tutorial begins with a problem presented in a "real-world" case that is meaningful to students. The case sets the scene to help students understand what they will do in the tutorial.

Hands-on Approach
Each tutorial is divided into manageable sessions that combine reading and hands-on, step-by-step work. Colorful screenshots help guide students through the steps. **Trouble?** tips anticipate common mistakes or problems to help students stay on track and continue with the tutorial.

Visual Overviews
New for this edition! Each session begins with a Visual Overview, a new two-page spread that includes colorful, enlarged screenshots with numerous callouts and key term definitions, giving students a comprehensive preview of the topics covered in the session, as well as a handy study guide.

ProSkills Boxes and Exercises
New for this edition! ProSkills boxes provide guidance for how to use the software in real-world, professional situations, and related ProSkills exercises integrate the technology skills students learn with one or more of the following soft skills: decision making, problem solving, teamwork, verbal communication, and written communication.

InSight Boxes
InSight boxes offer expert advice and best practices to help students achieve a deeper understanding of the concepts behind the software features and skills.

Margin Tips
Margin Tips provide helpful hints and shortcuts for more efficient use of the software. The Tips appear in the margin at key points throughout each tutorial, giving students extra information when and where they need it.

Assessment
Retention is a key component to learning. At the end of each session, a series of Quick Check questions helps students test their understanding of the material before moving on. Engaging end-of-tutorial Review Assignments and Case Problems have always been a hallmark feature of the New Perspectives Series. Colorful bars and brief descriptions accompany the exercises, making it easy to understand both the goal and level of challenge a particular assignment holds.

Reference
Within each tutorial, Reference boxes appear before a set of steps to provide a succinct summary and preview of how to perform a task. In addition, each book includes a combination Glossary/Index to promote easy reference of material.

Our Complete System of Instruction

Coverage To Meet Your Needs

Whether you're looking for just a small amount of coverage or enough to fill a semester-long class, we can provide you with a textbook that meets your needs.

- Brief books typically cover the essential skills in just 2 to 4 tutorials.
- Introductory books build and expand on those skills and contain an average of 5 to 8 tutorials.
- Comprehensive books are great for a full-semester class, and contain 9 to 12+ tutorials.

So if the book you're holding does not provide the right amount of coverage for you, there's probably another offering available. Go to our Web site or contact your Course Technology sales representative to find out what else we offer.

CourseCasts – Learning on the Go. Always available...always relevant.

Want to keep up with the latest technology trends relevant to you? Visit our site to find a library of podcasts, CourseCasts, featuring a "CourseCast of the Week," and download them to your mp3 player at http://coursecasts.course.com.

Our fast-paced world is driven by technology. You know because you're an active participant—always on the go, always keeping up with technological trends, and always learning new ways to embrace technology to power your life.

Ken Baldauf, host of CourseCasts, is a faculty member of the Florida State University Computer Science Department where he is responsible for teaching technology classes to thousands of FSU students each year. Ken is an expert in the latest technology trends; he gathers and sorts through the most pertinent news and information for CourseCasts so your students can spend their time enjoying technology, rather than trying to figure it out. Open or close your lecture with a discussion based on the latest CourseCast.

Visit us at http://coursecasts.course.com to learn on the go!

Instructor Resources

We offer more than just a book. We have all the tools you need to enhance your lectures, check students' work, and generate exams in a new, easier-to-use and completely revised package. This book's Instructor's Manual, ExamView testbank, PowerPoint presentations, data files, solution files, figure files, and a sample syllabus are all available on a single CD-ROM or for downloading at http://www.cengage.com/coursetechnology.

SAM: Skills Assessment Manager

SAM is designed to help bring students from the classroom to the real world. It allows students to train and test on important computer skills in an active, hands-on environment.

SAM's easy-to-use system includes powerful interactive exams, training, and projects on the most commonly used Microsoft Office applications. SAM simulates the Office application environment, allowing students to demonstrate their knowledge and think through the skills by performing real-world tasks, such as bolding text or setting up slide transitions. Add in live-in-the-application projects, and students are on their way to truly learning and applying skills to business-centric documents.

Designed to be used with the New Perspectives Series, SAM includes handy page references, so students can print helpful study guides that match the New Perspectives textbooks used in class. For instructors, SAM also includes robust scheduling and reporting features.

Content for Online Learning

Course Technology has partnered with the leading distance learning solution providers and class-management platforms today. To access this material, visit www.cengage.com/webtutor and search for your title. Instructor resources include the following: additional case projects, sample syllabi, PowerPoint presentations, and more. For students to access this material, they must have purchased a WebTutor PIN-code specific to this title and your campus platform. The resources for students might include (based on instructor preferences): topic reviews, review questions, practice tests, and more. For additional information, please contact your sales representative.

Acknowledgments

Creating a textbook is a collaborative effort in which authors and publisher work as a team to provide the highest quality book possible. We appreciate the many contributions of our Course Technology team, including Marie Lee, Executive Editor; Amanda Lyons, Associate Acquisitions Editor; Kathy Finnegan, Senior Product Manager; Leigh Hefferon, Product Manager; Julia Leroux-Lindsey, Associate Product Manager; and Jennifer Goguen McGrail, Senior Content Project Manager. We also would like to thank Christian Kunciw and his outstanding team of Quality Assurance testers for their many contributions in error-checking and fine-tuning this book's content throughout its development, and Marisa Taylor, Senior Project Manager at GEX Publishing Services, for guiding this book through the production process. Words cannot express our gratitude for the outstanding work of our Development Editor, Kim Crowley. Throughout this book's development, Kim has provided limitless and much appreciated encouragement and support, and her many excellent suggestions have significantly improved this book. Finally, we offer our heartfelt thanks to Robin Romer, for her substantial contributions to this edition of the book; to Katherine Pinard, who has contributed to this book in the past and also authored the book's adaptation for other markets; and to Janice Jutras, for her exceptional skill and diligent efforts to secure permissions for this text.
–Gary P. Schneider
–Jessica Evans

Dedication

To the memory of my brother, Bruce. – G.P.S.
To Hannah and Richard. – J.E.

www.cengage.com/ct/newperspectives

BRIEF CONTENTS

INTERNET   **Level I Tutorials**

Tutorial 1 Browser Basics . . . . .WEB 1
Using Web Browser Software

Tutorial 2 Basic Communication on the Internet: Email . . . . .WEB 73
Using Email and Sharing Files

Tutorial 3 Searching the Web . . . . .WEB 131
Using Search Engines and Directories Effectively

Tutorial 4 Information Resources on the Web . . . . .WEB 183
Finding Specific Information Online

Tutorial 5 User-Generated Content on the Internet. . . . . .WEB 243
Evaluating Different Methods of Internet Communication

Level II Tutorials

Tutorial 6 Internet Security . . . . .WEB 297
Managing Common Security Threats

Tutorial 7 Wireless Networking . . . . .WEB 351
Using and Securing Wireless Networks and Devices

Tutorial 8 Creating Effective Web Pages . . . . .WEB 397
Creating HTML Documents and Understanding Browser Extensions

Tutorial 9 Electronic Commerce . . . . .WEB 455
Doing Business on the Internet

Appendix A The Internet and the World Wide Web . . . . WEB A1
History, Structure, and Technologies

Additional Assignments 1–4 . . . . .ADD 1

Additional Assignments 5–8 . . . . .ADD 9

Glossary/Index   **REF 1**

TABLE OF CONTENTS

Preface. v

INTERNET LEVEL I TUTORIALS

Tutorial 1 Browser Basics
Using Web Browser Software . . . . **WEB 1**

SESSION 1.1. . . . .**WEB 2**
Microsoft Internet Explorer

The Internet and the Web. . . . . .WEB 4

Hypertext Markup Language and Hyperlinks. . . .WEB 4

Starting Microsoft Internet Explorer . . . . .WEB 5

Customizing the Internet Explorer Window . . . . .WEB 6

Navigating Web Pages .WEB 7

Entering a URL in the Address Bar . . . . .WEB 7

Clicking Links . . . . .WEB 10

Moving Among Visited Web Pages . . . . .WEB 11

Returning to Internet Explorer's Home Page . . .WEB 12

Using the Page Tabs . . . . .WEB 13

Using the Favorites Center . . . . .WEB 15

Creating and Organizing Favorites. . . . . .WEB 16

Deleting Favorites and Folders from the
Favorites Center . . . . .WEB 20

Navigating Web Pages Using the History List . .WEB 21

Managing Cookies. . . . . .WEB 22

Private Web Browsing . . . . .WEB 24

Getting Help in Internet Explorer . . . . .WEB 25

Saving Web Page Content . . . . .WEB 27

Saving an Entire Web Page . . . . .WEB 27

Saving an Image from a Web Page . . . . .WEB 28

Copying Text from a Web Page . . . . .WEB 29

Printing a Web Page . . . . .WEB 30

Session 1.1 Quick Check . . . . .WEB 33

SESSION 1.2. . . . .**WEB 34**
Mozilla Firefox

The Internet and the Web. . . . . .WEB 36

Hypertext Markup Language and Hyperlinks. . .WEB 36

Starting Mozilla Firefox .WEB 37

Customizing the Firefox Window . . . . .WEB 38

Navigating Web Pages .WEB 39

Entering a URL in the Location Bar. . . . . .WEB 40

Clicking Links . . . . .WEB 42

Moving Among Visited Web Pages . . . . .WEB 43

Returning to Firefox's Home Page . . . . .WEB 44

Using the Page Tabs. . . . . .WEB 45

Using the Library . . . . .WEB 47

Creating and Organizing Bookmarks . . . . .WEB 47

Deleting Bookmarks and Folders from
the Library. . . . . .WEB 53

Navigating Web Pages Using the History List . .WEB 53

Managing Cookies. . . . . .WEB 55

Private Web Browsing . . . . .WEB 57

Getting Help in Firefox .WEB 59

Saving Web Page Content . . . . .WEB 60

Saving an Entire Web Page . . . . .WEB 60

Saving an Image from a Web Page . . . . .WEB 61

Copying Text from a Web Page . . . . .WEB 62

Printing a Web Page . . . . .WEB 64

Session 1.2 Quick Check . . . . .WEB 66

Review Assignments . . . . .WEB 67

Case Problems. . . . . .WEB 68

Tutorial 2 Basic Communication on the Internet: Email
Using Email and Sharing Files . . . . **WEB 73**

SESSION 2.1. . . . .**WEB 74**
How Email Works

What Is Email and How Does It Work? . . . . .WEB 76

Common Features of an Email Message. . . . . . . .WEB 77

To, Cc, and Bcc. . . . . .WEB 78

From . . . . .WEB 79

Subject . . . . .WEB 79

Attachments . . . . .WEB 79

Message Body and Signature Files . . . . .WEB 80

Internet Etiquette (Netiquette) . . . . .WEB 81

Email Programs . . . . .WEB 83

Common Features of Email Programs. . . . . .WEB 84

Sending Messages . . . . .WEB 84

Receiving and Storing Messages . . . . .WEB 84

Printing a Message . . . . .WEB 84

Organizing Messages . . . . .WEB 84

Forwarding a Message .WEB 85

Replying to a Message .WEB 86

Deleting a Message . . . . .WEB 87

Managing Your Contacts . . . . .WEB 87

Protecting Your Computer from Viruses . . . . .WEB 88

Dealing with Unsolicited Messages. . . . . .WEB 89

Session 2.1 Quick Check .WEB 91

SESSION 2.2 . . . .**WEB 92**
Message in Hotmail

Webmail Providers. . . . . .WEB 94

Creating a Windows Live ID . . . . .WEB 95

Accessing Your Windows Live Account. . . . . .WEB 99

Sending a Message Using Windows Live
Hotmail . . . . .WEB 102

Receiving and Opening a Message . . . . .WEB 106

Viewing and Saving an Attached File . . . . .WEB 107

Replying to and Forwarding Messages. . . . . .WEB 109

Replying to an Email Message . . . . .WEB 109

Forwarding an Email Message . . . . .WEB 110

Filing and Printing an Email Message . . . . .WEB 112

Deleting a Message and a Folder . . . . .WEB 113

Maintaining Your Contact List . . . . .WEB 115

Adding a Contact to the Contact List . . . . . . .WEB 115

Creating a Category . . . . .WEB 117

Using SkyDrive to Share Files . . . . .WEB 119

Signing Out of Your Windows Live Account . . . . .WEB 122

Session 2.2 Quick Check. . . . . .WEB 123

Review Assignments . . . . .WEB 124

Case Problems. . . . . .WEB 124

Tutorial 3 Searching the Web
*Using Search Engines and Directories
Effectively* . . . . **WEB 131**

SESSION 3.1. . . . .**WEB 132**
How a Search Engine Works

Types of Search Questions . . . . .WEB 134

Finding Answers to Specific Questions . . . . . .WEB 134

Finding Answers to Exploratory Questions . . .WEB 135

Formulating Effective Web Search Strategies. . . .WEB 137

Web Search Tools . . . . .WEB 139

Understanding Search Engines . . . . .WEB 139

Using Directories and Hybrid Search Engine
Directories . . . . .WEB 148

Using Metasearch Engines . . . . .WEB 154

Using Web Bibliographies . . . . .WEB 155

Session 3.1 Quick Check .WEB 157

SESSION 3.2. . . . .**WEB 158**
Evaluating Web Sites

Using Logical Operators and Filtering Techniques
in Complex Searches. . . . . .WEB 160

Logical Operators. . . . . .WEB 160

Other Search Expression Operators. . . . . .WEB 161

Wildcard Characters . . . . .WEB 162

Search Filters. . . . . .WEB 163

Performing Complex Searches . . . . .WEB 163

Using Exalead to Perform a Boolean Search . .WEB 163

Filtered Search in Google. . . . . .WEB 164

Using Search Engines with Clustering
Features . . . . .WEB 167

Exploring the Deep Web. . . . . .WEB 169

Evaluating Web Research Resources. . . . . .WEB 170

Authorship, Expertise, and Objectivity . . . . . .WEB 171

Web Site Ownership and Objectivity. . . . . . . .WEB 171

Accuracy, Relevance, Scope, and Objectivity
of Content. . . . . .WEB 172

Form and Appearance .WEB 172

Evaluating the Quality of a Web Page . . . . . . .WEB 173

Evaluating Wikipedia Resources. . . . . .WEB 175

Session 3.2 Quick Check. . . . . .WEB 177

Review Assignments . . . . .WEB 178

Case Problems. . . . . .WEB 178

Tutorial 4 Information Resources on the Web
Finding Specific Information Online . . . .**WEB 183**

SESSION 4.1. . . . .**WEB 184**
Types of Information on the Internet

Finding Current and Specific Information on
the Web. . . . . .WEB 186

Finding Recent Information . . . . .WEB 186

Getting Current News .WEB 189

Finding Up-to-Date Weather Information . . . . WEB 193

Obtaining Maps and Destination Information. . . . WEB 196

Finding People and Businesses . . . . WEB 200

Finding Products and Services Online . . . . WEB 203

Session 4.1 Quick Check . . . . WEB 207

SESSION 4.2. . . . . **WEB 208**
Web Page Citation Guidelines

Understanding Copyright . . . . WEB 210

    Determining Fair Use . . . . WEB 210

    Works in the Public Domain . . . . WEB 211

    Understanding Plagiarism. . . . . WEB 214

Citing Web Resources . . . . WEB 215

Accessing Text-Based Resources Online. . . . . . . WEB 217

    Online References. . . . . WEB 217

    Periodical Databases . . . . WEB 221

    Online and Virtual Libraries . . . . WEB 222

    Government Sites . . . . WEB 225

Multimedia on the Web. WEB 228

    Finding Graphic Images on the Web . . . . WEB 228

    Finding Audio Files on the Web. . . . . WEB 229

    Finding Video Files . . . . WEB 233

Session 4.2 Quick Check . . . . WEB 236

Review Assignments . . . . WEB 237

Case Problems. . . . . WEB 238

Tutorial 5 User-Generated Content on the Internet
*Evaluating Different Methods of Internet
Communication* . . . . **WEB 243**

SESSION 5.1 . . . . **WEB 244**
Pull Technologies

Push and Pull Communication. . . . . WEB 246

Web 2.0 . . . . WEB 246

Email-Based Communication . . . . WEB 247

Getting Information from RSS Feeds . . . . WEB 249

Podcasting. . . . . WEB 252

Mashups . . . . WEB 255

Session 5.1 Quick Check . . . . WEB 261

SESSION 5.2. . . . . **WEB 262**
Push Technologies

Internet Chat Communication. . . . . WEB 264

    Voice over Internet Protocol . . . . WEB 266

Online Social Networks. WEB 268

    Connecting with Friends. . . . . WEB 268

    Advertising Revenues from Social Networks . . WEB 269

Online Business Networks. . . . . WEB 270

Sharing Pictures on the Web. . . . . WEB 272

Sharing Videos on the Web. . . . . WEB 274

Blogs . . . . WEB 276

Microblogs. . . . . WEB 279

Protecting Your Privacy and Identity on Social

Networks . . . . WEB 283

Protecting Your Reputation . . . . WEB 284

Session 5.2 Quick Check. . . . . WEB 286

Review Assignments . . . . WEB 287

Case Problems . . . . WEB 288

ProSkills Exercise: Decision Making. . . . . WEB 292

INTERNET LEVEL II TUTORIALS

Tutorial 6 Internet Security
Managing Common Security Threads. . . . . **WEB 297**

SESSION 6.1. . . . . **WEB 298**
Physical and Logical Security

Security Basics. . . . . WEB 300

Using Encryption to Protect Against Secrecy

Threats. . . . . WEB 300

Protecting the Integrity of Electronic Data . . . . . WEB 302

    Phishing Attacks . . . . WEB 303

Protecting Copyrighted Materials Using Digital

Watermarks . . . . WEB 307

Preventing Denial-of-Service Attacks . . . . WEB 309

Recognizing and Preventing Identity Theft. . . . . WEB 311

Security Concerns for Social Network Users. . . . WEB 315

Session 6.1 Quick Check . . . . WEB 319

SESSION 6.2. . . . . **WEB 320**
Enhancing Security

Web Client Security. . . . . WEB 322

    Active Content: Java, JavaScript, and

    ActiveX . . . . WEB 322

Detecting and Removing Malware . . . . WEB 327

Blocking Tracking Devices in Electronic

Communications . . . . WEB 333

Blocking Communication Using a Firewall ......WEB 334

Communication Channel Security.............WEB 335

   Digital and Server Certificates ....WEB 336

   Assurance Providers ....WEB 339

Secure Sockets Layer (SSL) and Transport Layer
Security (TLS)..............................WEB 341

Session 6.2 Quick Check....................WEB 344

Review Assignments ....WEB 345

Case Problems ....WEB 345

Tutorial 7 Wireless Networking
*Using and Securing Wireless Networks and
Devices* ....**WEB 351**

SESSION 7.1...........................**WEB 352**
Wireless Device Timeline

The Evolution of Wireless Networks ....WEB 354

Wireless Local Area Networking.............WEB 356

   Wireless Mesh Networks ....WEB 360

Personal Area Networking..................WEB 362

   Infrared Technology ....WEB 362

   Bluetooth ....WEB 362

Wireless Wide Area Networking.............WEB 365

Metropolitan Area Networking..............WEB 366

   Worldwide Interoperability for Microwave
   Access (WiMAX).......................WEB 366

   Long Term Evolution (LTE) ....WEB 370

Using Wireless Devices to Access the Internet...WEB 372

Session 7.1 Quick Check ....WEB 375

SESSION 7.2...........................**WEB 376**
Wireless Security Concerns

Security Concerns for Using Wireless Networks .WEB 378

Methods for Securing Wireless Networks.......WEB 378

   Wireless Encryption Methods..............WEB 378

   MAC Address Filtering ....WEB 380

   Disabling the SSID Broadcast.............WEB 381

   Changing the Default Login ....WEB 381

   Using Software to Protect Wireless Networks .WEB 382

Understanding Security Threats to Wireless
Devices ....WEB 384

   Security Concerns for Bluetooth-Enabled
   Devices..............................WEB 385

Security Risks with Smartphone
Applications ....WEB 386

Methods for Securing Wireless Devices ....WEB 388

Session 7.2 Quick Check....................WEB 390

Review Assignments ....WEB 391

Case Problems ....WEB 392

Tutorial 8 Creating Effective Web Pages
*Creating HTML Documents and Understanding
Browser Extensions* ....**WEB 397**

SESSION 8.1...........................**WEB 398**
Understanding HTML

Understanding Markup Languages ....WEB 400

Understanding Tags and Attributes ....WEB 401

Planning an HTML Document ....WEB 402

Creating an HTML Document ....WEB 405

   Creating the HTML Document Structure .....WEB 406

   Adding a Comment to an HTML Document ..WEB 408

   Inserting and Formatting Headings ....WEB 408

   Inserting and Formatting a Paragraph ....WEB 410

   Creating a List........................WEB 412

Using Images in an HTML Document ....WEB 414

Using Anchors ....WEB 417

Adding a Link to a Web Page ....WEB 418

Session 8.1 Quick Check ....WEB 421

SESSION 8.2...........................**WEB 422**
Creating a Web Site

Evaluating Web Site Content ....WEB 424

Using a Web Site Management Tool...........WEB 425

Choosing Other Development Tools ....WEB 429

   Programming with JavaScript..............WEB 429

   Creating Animated Content ....WEB 433

   Choosing Image Editing and Illustration
   Programs.............................WEB 436

Choosing a Web Hosting Service ....WEB 439

   Understanding Types of Web Servers ....WEB 439

   Understanding the Site's File Size and
   Transfer Requirements ....WEB 439

   Evaluating Other Services Offered by a
   Web Hosting Service ....WEB 440

Publishing a Web Site ....WEB 444

Search Engine Submission and Optimization . . . . WEB 444

Session 8.2 Quick Check . . . . WEB 447

Review Assignments . . . . WEB 448

Case Problems . . . . WEB 449

Tutorial 9 Electronic Commerce
Doing Business on the Internet . . . . **WEB 455**

SESSION 9.1 . . . . **WEB 456**
E-Commerce Categories

Buying and Selling over the Web . . . . WEB 458

    Buying and Selling Goods . . . . WEB 459

    Buying and Selling Subscriptions . . . . WEB 462

    Buying and Selling Services . . . . WEB 464

Advertising and Marketing on the Internet . . . . . . WEB 468

    Advertising . . . . WEB 468

    Affiliate Marketing . . . . WEB 469

Paying for E-Commerce Purchases . . . . WEB 471

Consumer Concerns . . . . WEB 474

    Transaction Security Concerns . . . . WEB 474

    Privacy Concerns . . . . WEB 475

International E-Commerce Issues . . . . WEB 477

    Cultural and Language Issues . . . . WEB 477

    Legal Issues . . . . WEB 480

Session 9.1 Quick Check . . . . WEB 481

Review Assignments . . . . WEB 482

Case Problems . . . . WEB 482

ProSkills Exercise: Written Communication . . . . . . WEB 486

Appendix A The Internet and the World Wide Web

History, Structure, and Technologies . . . . **WEB A1**

Computer Networks . . . . WEB A2

Connecting Computers to a Network . . . . WEB A3

Understanding IP Addresses and Domain Names . WEB A5

    IP Addressing . . . . WEB A5

    Domain Names . . . . WEB A6

Origins of the Internet . . . . WEB A7

    Connectivity: Circuit Switching vs. Packet
    Switching . . . . WEB A8

    Open Architecture Philosophy . . . . WEB A10

    New Uses for Networks . . . . WEB A10

    Interconnecting the Networks . . . . WEB A11

    Network Use in Business . . . . WEB A12

Growth of the Internet . . . . WEB A12

The Evolution of the Web . . . . WEB A15

    Origins of Hypertext . . . . WEB A15

    Evolution of Web Browsers . . . . WEB A16

Businesses That Provide Internet Access . . . . . . WEB A20

    Bandwidth and Types of Connectivity . . . . . . WEB A20

Additional Research Assignment 1

*Locating and Evaluating Health Care Information
on the Internet* . . . . **ADD 1**

Additional Research Assignment 2

*Evaluating Encyclopedia Resources on the
Internet* . . . . **ADD 3**

Additional Research Assignment 3

Advances in Distance Learning . . . . **ADD 5**

Additional Research Assignment 4

The Future of the Semantic Web . . . . **ADD 7**

Additional Research Assignment 5

*Using a Web Site to Translate Business
Correspondence* . . . . **ADD 9**

Additional Research Assignment 6

Using Short Message Service . . . . **ADD 11**

Additional Research Assignment 7

Evaluating the Use of Blogs in Business . . . . **ADD 13**

Additional Research Assignment 8

Reintermediating Travel Services . . . . **ADD 15**

GLOSSARY/INDEX . . . . **REF 1**

Browser Basics

Using Web Browser Software

OBJECTIVES

Session 1.1
- Understand the Internet and the Web
- Customize the Internet Explorer window
- Navigate Web pages
- Create and organize favorites
- Access the history listing
- Manage cookies
- Use InPrivate Browsing
- Get help in Internet Explorer
- Save and print Web page content

Session 1.2
- Understand the Internet and the Web
- Customize the Firefox window
- Navigate Web pages
- Create and organize bookmarks
- Access the History list
- Manage cookies
- Use Private Browsing
- Get help in Firefox
- Save and print Web page content

Case | *Danville Animal Shelter*

The Danville Animal Shelter is an organization devoted to helping improve the welfare of animals, particularly unwanted pets, in the local Danville area. Trinity Andrews, the director of the shelter, is always looking for ways to improve the services it offers to the community.

The shelter is a charitable organization that is supported mainly by contributions from the local community. Trinity budgets the limited funds that the shelter receives to do the most good for the animals. One of the most important functions of the shelter is to let people in the community know about the pets available for adoption. Advertising in the local newspaper or on television stations is very expensive. Another problem is that the pets available for adoption change from day to day and, by the time a news story or ad runs, the pet that is featured often has been adopted. Although newspaper and television advertising and promotion can be a good way for the shelter to get its general message out to the community, these outlets are not the best way to let people know about specific pets that are available for adoption.

You have volunteered at the shelter for several years, and Trinity heard that you were learning to use the Internet. Trinity wants you to help identify ways to use the Internet to let the community know about the shelter and, in particular, about specific pets that are available for adoption. To do this, you need to learn more about using a Web browser.

Note: If you are using Microsoft Internet Explorer as your Web browser, you should complete Session 1.1. If you are using Mozilla Firefox as your Web browser, then skip Session 1.1 and complete Session 1.2.

STARTING DATA FILES

SESSION 1.1 VISUAL OVERVIEW

The **Navigation bar** is used to open and move among Web pages as well as access favorites and commands for saving and printing.

Internet Explorer is a **Web browser**, which is software you run on your computer to make it run as a Web client, allowing it to locate and display Web pages.

The **Refresh button** loads a new copy of the Web page in the browser window.

The **Favorites bar** includes buttons that provide links to saved shortcuts to Web pages (called **favorites**) that you visit frequently.

You type the **Uniform Resource Locator (URL)**, or the address for a Web page, in the Address bar to open that Web page in the browser.

You use the **Favorites Center** to organize and display links to your preferred Web sites, RSS feeds, and recently visited sites.

A **Web page** is a document that has been created using **HTML**, a programming language used to format documents containing text and images so they can be viewed in a Web browser.

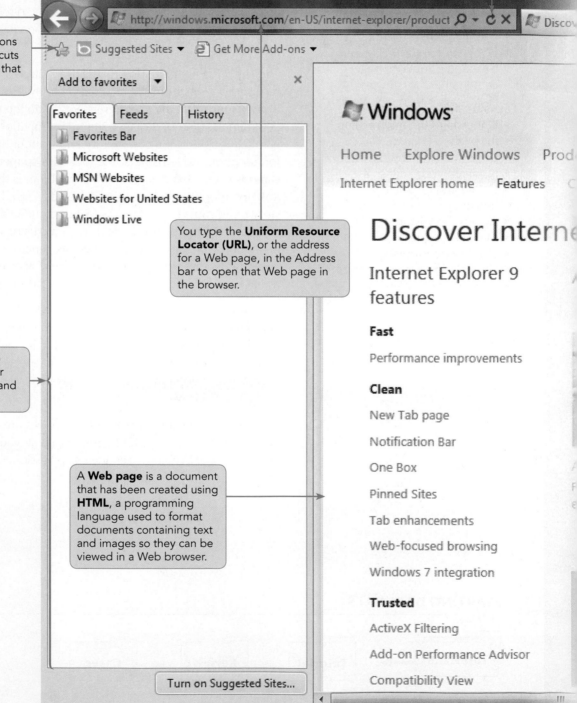

Courtesy of © Microsoft

MICROSOFT INTERNET EXPLORER

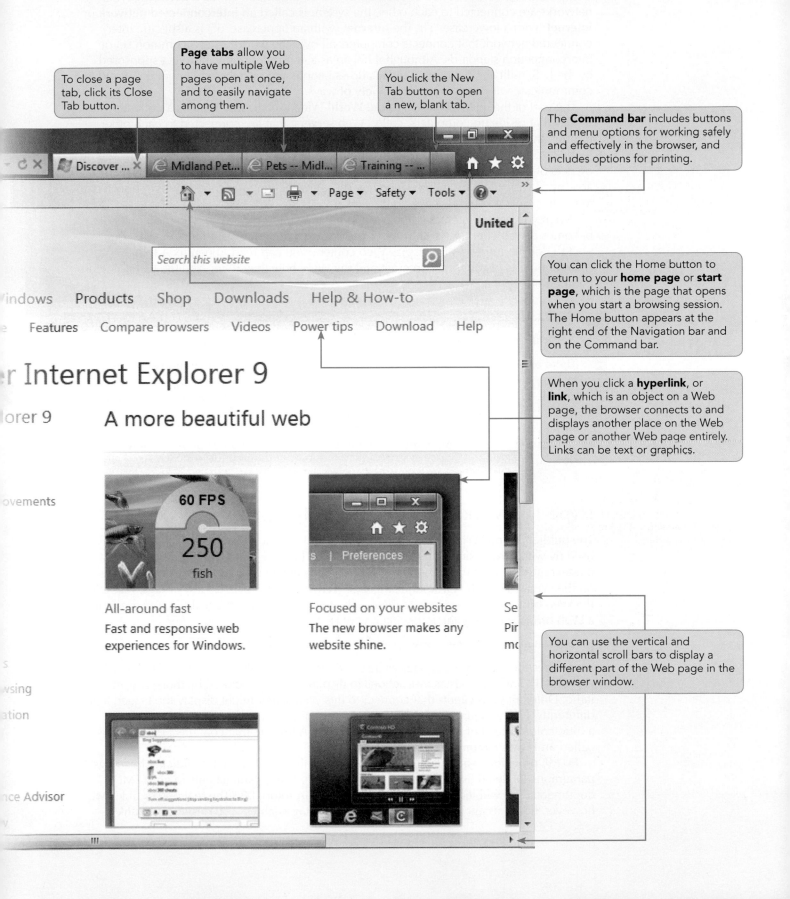

Page tabs allow you to have multiple Web pages open at once, and to easily navigate among them.

To close a page tab, click its Close Tab button.

You click the New Tab button to open a new, blank tab.

The **Command bar** includes buttons and menu options for working safely and effectively in the browser, and includes options for printing.

You can click the Home button to return to your **home page** or **start page**, which is the page that opens when you start a browsing session. The Home button appears at the right end of the Navigation bar and on the Command bar.

When you click a **hyperlink**, or **link**, which is an object on a Web page, the browser connects to and displays another place on the Web page or another Web page entirely. Links can be text or graphics.

You can use the vertical and horizontal scroll bars to display a different part of the Web page in the browser window.

The Internet and the Web

Computers can be connected to each other in a configuration called a **network**. When networks are connected to each other, the system is called an **interconnected network** or **internet** (with a lowercase "i"). The **Internet** (with an uppercase "i") is a specific inter-connected network that connects computers all over the world using a common set of interconnection standards. Although it began as a computer science project sponsored by the U.S. military, the Internet today allows people and businesses all over the world to communicate with each other in a variety of ways.

The part of the Internet known as the **World Wide Web** (or the **Web**) is a collection of files that reside on computers, called **Web servers**, that are connected to each other through the Internet. Most files on computers, including computers that are connected to the Internet, are private; that is, only the computer's users can access those files. The owners of the computer files that make up the Web have made the files publicly avail-able by placing them on the Web servers. Thus, anyone who has a computer connected to the Internet can obtain access to the files.

When you use an Internet connection to become part of the Web, your computer becomes a **Web client**. A **Web browser** is software that allows your computer to con-nect to, locate, retrieve, and display Web content. You can read Appendix A to learn more about the history of the Internet and the Web, how they work, and the technologies behind their operation.

Choosing a Browser

There are a variety of Web browsers available. Some of the most common are Microsoft Internet Explorer, Mozilla Firefox, Google Chrome, Apple Safari, and Opera. You can download and install these browsers for free, enabling you to choose the one you want. All Web browsers have similar features, but some are more robust and others are more streamlined. To help evaluate and decide which Web browser you want to use, you can read reviews, explore the product pages, take tours or demos of the browsers, and download and try them.

Hypertext Markup Language and Hyperlinks

The public files on Web servers are ordinary text files, much like the files created and used by word-processing software. To enable Web browser software to read these files, the text must be formatted according to a generally accepted standard. The standard used on the Web is **Hypertext Markup Language (HTML)**. HTML uses codes, or **tags**, that tell the Web browser software how to display the text contained in the text file. For example, a Web browser reading the following line of text

```
<B>A Review of the Book <I>Wind Instruments</I></B>
```

recognizes the <B> and </B> tags as instructions to display the entire line of text in bold and the <I> and </I> tags as instructions to display the text enclosed by those tags in italic. Different Web clients that connect to this Web server might display the tagged text differently. For example, one Web browser might display text enclosed by bold tags in a blue color instead of displaying the text in bold. A text file that contains HTML tags is called an **HTML document**.

HTML provides a variety of text formatting tags that can be used to indicate headings, paragraphs, bulleted lists, numbered lists, and other text enhancements in an HTML document. (You will learn more about HTML tags in Tutorial 8.) The real power of HTML, however, lies in its anchor tag. The **HTML anchor tag** enables Web designers to link

HTML documents to each other. Anchor tags in HTML documents create **hypertext links**, which are instructions that point to other HTML documents or to another section of the same document. Hypertext links also are called **hyperlinks** or **links**. The linked HTML documents can be on the same computer or on different computers. These computers can be anywhere in the world if they are connected to the Internet. When a Web browser displays an HTML document, it is often referred to as a **Web page**.

Starting Microsoft Internet Explorer

Microsoft Internet Explorer is the Microsoft Web browser; it is installed with all recent versions of the Windows operating system software. In this session, you will use the Internet Explorer Web browser to do your work for the Danville Animal Shelter. This introduction assumes that you have Internet Explorer installed on your computer.

To start Internet Explorer:

1. Click the **Internet Explorer** button on the taskbar. The Internet Explorer browser window opens.

   Trouble? If the Internet Explorer button does not appear on the taskbar, click the Start button on the taskbar, point to All Programs, and then click Internet Explorer. If you cannot find Internet Explorer on the All Programs menu, ask your instructor or technical support person for help. The program might be installed in a different location on the computer you are using.

2. If the program window does not fill the screen entirely, click the **Maximize** button on the title bar. Your screen should look similar to the Session 1.1 Visual Overview.

   Trouble? Your computer will open to the home page for your installation of Internet Explorer, or no page at all.

   Trouble? The Session 1.1 Visual Overview shows the Internet Explorer program window with the Command bar, Favorites bar, and Favorites Center displayed. Some or all of these may be hidden on your screen. You will learn how to customize the program window later in this session. In addition, other programs can add icons and toolbars to the Internet Explorer program window. So if you are using a computer that has been used by other people or your own computer on which other software has been installed, you might see icons and toolbars that are not shown in the Session 1.1 Visual Overview.

   Trouble? The Session 1.1 Visual Overview shows the Favorites Center open on the left side of the browser window. Your Favorites Center might not be open on your screen. This is not a problem; you will open the Favorites Center later in this session.

The very first time Internet Explorer starts, only the Navigation bar is displayed in the program window. The Navigation bar contains the Address bar for opening Web pages; the Back and Forward buttons for navigating among previously visited pages; the tabs for open Web pages; and the Home, Tools, and View favorites, feeds, and history buttons to access the most common Command bar functions. This streamlined version provides more screen space for viewing Web pages.

You can, however, display additional toolbars, including the Command bar and the Favorites bar, which are shown the Session 1.1 Visual Overview. You can also customize the toolbars by deleting icons and adding new icons. Internet Explorer allows you to change the toolbar settings because some people like to have many commands available on the screen, while others prefer to have more space available for displaying the Web page. Also, other software programs installed on your computer can place icons on the Internet Explorer toolbars so that you can use these programs from within Internet Explorer. As a result, your Internet Explorer browser window might have different toolbars displayed or the toolbars might contain icons not shown in the Visual Overview.

Customizing the Internet Explorer Window

In Internet Explorer, you can display or hide the menu bar and toolbars as needed. The menu bar and toolbars are hidden by default. When they are hidden, more of the Web page is displayed in the browser window. To display the menu bar or a toolbar, right-click a blank area of the Navigation bar, and then click the corresponding option on the shortcut menu. If the Command bar is displayed, you can click the Tools button on the Command bar, point to Toolbars, and then select or deselect the corresponding option to display or hide the menu bar or a toolbar.

At any point, you can switch to **Full screen mode**, which temporarily hides the program window—the title bar, the Navigation bar, the menu bar, and any toolbars as well as the Windows taskbar—leaving only the Web page visible on your screen. You can select the Full screen option by clicking Tools on the Command bar, and then clicking Full screen. When the window is in Full screen mode, you can display the hidden toolbars by pointing to the top of the screen. When you move the pointer away from the toolbars, they will become hidden again. To exit Full screen mode, point to the top of the screen until the toolbars appear, click the Tools button on the Command bar, and then click Full screen to remove the check mark and deselect this option.

REFERENCE

Hiding and Restoring Toolbars in Internet Explorer

- To switch to Full screen mode, click the Tools button on the Command bar, and then click Full screen (or click the Tools button on the Navigation bar, point to File, and then click Full screen, or press the F11 key).
- To temporarily restore the toolbars in Full screen mode, point to the top of the screen until the toolbars appear.
- To exit Full screen mode, point to the top of the screen to display the toolbars, click the Tools button on the Command bar, and then click Full screen (or click the Tools button on the Navigation bar, point to File, and then click Full screen, or press the F11 key).
- To display or hide individual toolbars, right-click a blank area of the Navigation bar, and then click a toolbar name on the shortcut menu. If the toolbar name is already checked, the toolbar will be hidden when you click the name. If the toolbar name is not checked, the toolbar will be displayed when you click the name.

Next, you will customize the Internet Explorer window by displaying and hiding the toolbars. In these tutorials, you will use the Command bar and Favorites bar, so you will leave them displayed.

To display and hide toolbars in Internet Explorer:

1. Right-click a blank area of the Navigation bar. A shortcut menu opens, listing the available toolbars. A check mark appears to the left of each toolbar that is displayed.

2. Click **Menu bar** on the shortcut menu to select this option and place a check mark next to it. The menu bar appears below the Navigation bar.

   Trouble? If the menu bar disappears, it was already displayed. Continue with Step 4.

3. Right-click a blank area of the Navigation bar, and then click **Menu bar** on the shortcut menu to uncheck this option and hide the menu bar. This on-off, or toggle, function works for all of the toolbars on the shortcut menu.

4. If the Favorites bar is not displayed, right-click a blank area of the Navigation bar, and then click **Favorites bar**. The Favorites bar appears below the Navigation bar.

5. If the Command bar is not displayed, right-click a blank area of the Navigation bar, and then click **Command bar**. The Command bar appears to the right of the Favorites bar. You can temporarily hide these toolbars.

6. Click the **Tools** button on the Command bar, and then click **Full screen**. The Web page fills the entire screen.

   Trouble? If the toolbars do not immediately roll up out of view, move the pointer away from the top of the screen.

7. Point to the top of the screen. The toolbars scroll back down into view.

8. Click the **Tools** button on the Navigation bar, point to **File**, and then click **Full screen** to deselect this option and redisplay the toolbars.

TIP
Another way to switch Full screen mode on and off is to press the F11 key.

Now that you are familiar with the tools in the browser window, you are ready to navigate to a Web site.

Navigating Web Pages

To identify a particular Web page's exact location on the Internet, Web browsers rely on an address called a Uniform Resource Locator (URL). The URL is the address of a specific Web page. Every Web page has a unique URL. A URL is a four-part addressing scheme that tells the Web browser:

- The protocol to use when transporting the file
- The domain name of the computer on which the file resides
- The path for the folder or directory on the computer in which the file resides
- The name of the file

So in the URL *http://www.nytimes.com/pages/sports/index.htm*, the *http://* is the transfer protocol, which is the set of rules that computers use to move files from one computer to another. The two most common protocols used to transfer files on the Internet are Hypertext Transfer Protocol (HTTP) and File Transfer Protocol (FTP). The second part of the URL, the domain name, is *www.nytimes.com* and this references the location of the computer on which the Web page resides; *www* indicates the computer is connected to the Web, *nytimes* is the name of the Web site, and *.com* identifies the Web site as being a commercial organization. The */pages/sports* portion of the URL provides the path for the folder in which the Web page file is located, and the last portion of the URL, *index.htm*, is the filename.

Entering a URL in the Address Bar

You can use the Address bar, which is located on the Navigation bar, to enter a specific URL and go directly to that Web page. For example, you can enter the complete URL for a Web site, such as http://www.cnn.com, to load that Web page in the browser. As you begin to type, a list opens, displaying pages you have previously visited that begin with the letters you are typing; you can select a URL and press the Enter key to return to that Web page. Also, Internet Explorer will try to complete partial URLs that you type in the

Address bar. For example, if you type cnn.com, Internet Explorer will convert it to http://www.cnn.com and load the Web page at that URL.

If you don't see the URL you want in the Address bar list, you can enter a partial URL or a search word; Internet Explorer will open the search engine selected for your browser. A **search engine** performs a search based on the text you type in a search box—in this case, the Address bar—and displays the search results. You can click any link in the search results to go to that Web page. You will learn more about search engines in Tutorial 3.

INSIGHT

Understanding Home Pages

The term "home page" is used at least three different ways on the Web, and it is sometimes difficult to tell which meaning people intend when they use the term. The first definition of home page indicates the main page that all of the other pages on a particular Web site are organized around and link back to. This home page is the first page that opens when you visit that Web site. The second definition of "home page" is the first page that opens when you start your Web browser. This type of home page might be an HTML document on your own computer. Some people create such home pages and include hyperlinks to Web sites that they frequently visit. If you are using a computer on your school's or employer's network, its Web browser might be configured to open the main page for the school or firm. The third definition of "home page" is the Web page that a particular Web browser loads the first time you use it. This page usually is stored at the Web site of the firm or other organization that created the Web browser software. Home pages that meet the second or third definitions are sometimes called start pages.

Trinity wants you to start your research by examining the Midland Pet Adoption Agency's Web site. She has provided the URL for the site's home page.

To load the Midland Pet Adoption Agency's home page:

1. Click in the **Address bar** to select the URL, and then type **www.midlandpet.com**. This is the URL for the Midland Pet Adoption Agency Web site.

   Trouble? The Address bar might display a list of suggested URLs as you type; ignore these suggestions and continue typing.

2. Press the **Enter** key. The home page of the Midland Pet Adoption Agency Web site loads, as shown in Figure 1-1.

Figure 1-1	Midland Pet Adoption Agency Web page

URL

graphic image

hyperlinks are underlined and a different color

Courtesy of © Microsoft; © Cengage Learning

PROSKILLS

Written Communication: The Importance of Organization in a Web Site

Web sites are written communications media just as printed brochures and newsletters are. When visiting a Web site, you can learn a great deal about how to create a Web site for your organization, just as you can learn to design brochures by reading brochures produced by other organizations. The writing that appears on a Web site's pages must be organized to reflect the organization's communication goals for the site. For example, the Midland Pet Adoption Agency's main page includes links to information that it believes Web site visitors will be seeking, such as:

- Pets available for adoption (including their names and pictures)
- Training programs offered
- The agency's emergency clinic
- Directions to the agency and contact information

The Midland Pet Adoption Agency's Web site is organized so that each of these information sets appears on its own Web page. The links are organized on the home page in order of importance, from left to right. For example, the first link next to the Home page link is the Pets link, which opens a page of information about pets available for adoption. This is the agency's primary mission and is the most important set of information it wants to convey to site visitors.

Another important point in organizing the Web site is that the navigation tools (in this case, the links) should appear in the same place and in the same form on every page. This consistent structure reinforces the site visitors' knowledge that the site is well organized and tells them that they are still on the same Web site. For example, the Home page link appears in the upper-left corner of all the site's pages, providing the visitors a consistent means to return to the site's main page. The use of common color combinations and consistent headers and graphics (for example, the use of the same two graphics at the top of each page, along with the reminder to "Take me home today!") reinforces the primary message of the Web site, which is to encourage visitors to stop by and adopt a pet, and conveys a sense of urgency regarding doing so.

Good written communications are clearly organized around a theme that conveys the message while guiding readers to the most important information in a direct way. You can accomplish this in a Web site by understanding what your site's visitors will be looking for, and structuring your site to organize that information and make it easy to find.

Clicking Links

Most Web pages include links to other Web pages. A link might open a Web page that is related to the original Web page, such as the Pets link on the Midland Pet Adoption Agency home page, which opens a page listing pets available for adoption. A link could also be a link to a company, such as the Course Technology link at the bottom of the home page. Other times, a link could open a Web page with related information or an advertised product or service. The easiest way to move from one Web page to another is to click a link on the open Web page. You'll use links to open the Training Programs and Pets Web pages.

To use links to navigate the Midland Pet Adoption Agency Web site:

▶ **1.** On the Midland Pet Adoption Agency home page, point to the **Training Programs** link, as shown in Figure 1-2. The pointer changes to the shape of a hand with a pointing index finger, and a ScreenTip listing the URL to which the link points appears near the bottom of the browser window.

Figure 1-2	Using a hyperlink

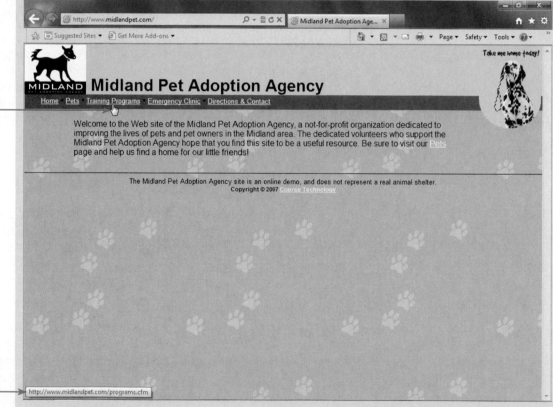

pointer shape changes when positioned over a hyperlink

ScreenTip shows the URL to which the hyperlink points

Courtesy of © Microsoft; © Cengage Learning

▶ **2.** Click the **Training Programs** link. The Training Programs Web page opens in the browser window.

▶ **3.** On the Training Programs Web page, click the **Pets** link. The Pets page opens in the browser window.

▶ **4.** On the Pets Web page, click the **Meet Maxie** link. The Web page with information about the cat named Maxie opens in the browser window.

Moving Among Visited Web Pages

The Back and Forward buttons on the Navigation bar let you navigate among the pages you have just visited. When you first start Internet Explorer, these buttons are grayed out. After you visit more than one Web page in a browsing session, the Back button changes to blue, indicating that it is active and available. Clicking the Back button returns the browser to the previous Web page you visited. You can continue clicking the Back button until you reach the first page you viewed when you started Internet Explorer. Once you click the Back button, the Forward button changes to blue, and you can click the Forward button to return to later pages you have visited.

As you move among the pages you visited, you might want to reload, or refresh, a Web page you return to. The Refresh button on the Navigation bar loads a new copy of the Web page that currently appears in the browser window. Internet Explorer stores a copy of every Web page it displays on your computer's hard drive in a Temporary Internet Files folder in the Windows folder. Storing this information increases the speed at which Internet Explorer can display pages as you move back and forth through the Web pages you have visited because the browser can load the pages from a local disk drive instead of reloading them from the remote Web server. When you click the Refresh button, Internet Explorer contacts the Web server to see if the Web page has changed since it was stored in the Temporary Internet Files folder. If it has changed, Internet Explorer gets the new page from the Web server; otherwise, it loads the copy stored on your computer.

You'll use the Back, Forward, and Refresh buttons to navigate among the Web pages you visited on the Midland Pet Adoption Agency Web site.

To navigate among visited pages on the Midland Pet Adoption Agency Web site:

1. Point to the **Back** button on the Navigation bar. A ScreenTip appears, listing the page that will be displayed if you click the button, as shown in Figure 1-3. In this case, the Pets page will be displayed.

Figure 1-3	Using the Back button

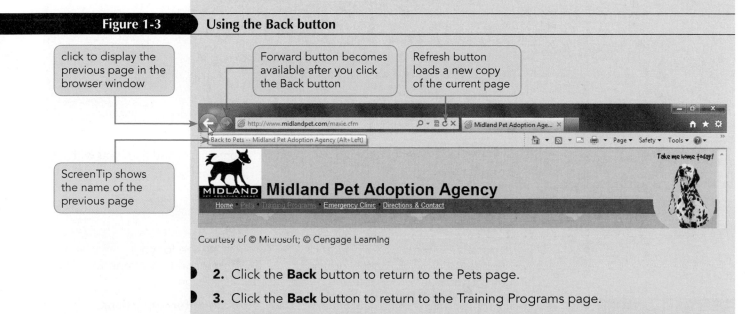

Courtesy of © Microsoft; © Cengage Learning

2. Click the **Back** button to return to the Pets page.

3. Click the **Back** button to return to the Training Programs page.

4. Point to the **Forward** button on the Navigation bar. A ScreenTip appears, listing the page that will be displayed if you click the button. In this case, the Pets page will be displayed.

▶ **5.** Click the **Forward** button to return to the Pets page.

▶ **6.** Click the **Refresh** button in the Address bar to load a new copy of the Pets page. Because the content on the page hasn't been updated, you won't see any differences on the refreshed page.

Returning to Internet Explorer's Home Page

When you click the Home button on the Navigation bar or the Command bar, the browser displays the home (or start) page for your installation of Internet Explorer. You can select one or more pages to display as the default home page. If you select multiple pages, each page opens in a separate tab when you click the Home button. You can set the page or pages you want to use as the default home page in the Internet Options dialog box, which you open from the Tools button on the Command bar. You can also open a Web page and then set it as your home page or as one of your home page tabs in the Add or Change Home Page dialog box, which you open from the Home button arrow on the Command bar.

REFERENCE

Changing the Default Home Page in Internet Explorer

- Click the Tools button on the Navigation bar or Command bar, and then click Internet options to open the Internet Options dialog box.
- To use the current page, use Internet Explorer's default page, or use a blank page as the home page, click the corresponding button in the Home page section on the General tab.
- To specify a home page, type the URL of that Web page in the Home page box. To open multiple home pages on separate tabs, type the URL for each home page on separate lines in the Home page box.
- Click the OK button.
  or
- Open the Web page you want to use as your home page.
- Click the Home button arrow on the Command bar, and then click Add or change home page to open the Add or Change Home Page dialog box.
- Click the Use this webpage as your only home page option button or the Add this webpage to your home page tabs option button.
- Click the Yes button.

You will use the Home button to return to your browser's home page, and then you will view the home page settings.

To view the settings for your browser's home page:

▶ **1.** Click the **Home** button on the Navigation bar. The home page for your browser appears in the browser window. This is the same page that opened when you started your browser at the beginning of this session.

▶ **2.** Click the **Tools** button on the Navigation bar, and then click **Internet options**. The Internet Options dialog box opens, displaying the General tab, which provides options for specifying your home page, or a series of home page tabs. See Figure 1-4.

TIP

Many organizations set the home page defaults on all of their computers and then lock those settings.

| Figure 1-4 | Internet Options dialog box |

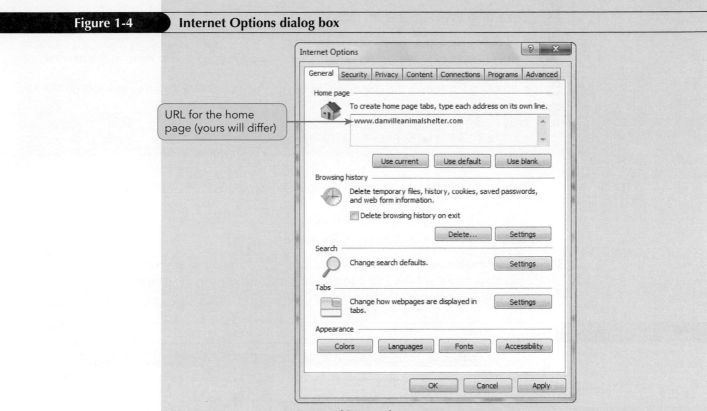

URL for the home page (yours will differ)

Courtesy of © Microsoft

To use the currently loaded Web page as your home page, you would click the Use current button. To use the default home page that was installed with your copy of Internet Explorer, you would click the Use default button. If you do not want a page to open when you start your browser, you would click the Use blank button. If you want to specify a home page other than the current, default, or blank page, you would type the URL for that page in the Home page box.

▶ 3. Click the **Cancel** button to close the dialog box without making any changes.

Using the Page Tabs

So far, all the Web pages you have visited have been displayed on the same tab. You can open additional page tabs on the tab row next to the Address bar and load different Web pages on each tab instead of opening additional Web pages in separate browser windows. This tabbed browsing technique is especially useful when you need to open many pages or move frequently back and forth among multiple Web pages.

There are several methods for opening a Web page in a new tab. You can click the New Tab button on the tab row, and then open a Web page as usual. You can right-click a link on a Web page, and then click the Open in new tab command on the shortcut menu. Or, you can press the Ctrl key as you click a link. To close a tab, you click the Close Tab button on that page tab. If you have only one tab open, closing that tab also exits Internet Explorer. Conversely, if you try to exit Internet Explorer when you have more than one tab open, a dialog box opens, asking whether you want to close the current tab or all open tabs.

REFERENCE

Opening Web Pages in Tabs

- Click the New Tab button on the tab row.
- In the Address bar, enter the URL for the Web page you want to open in the new tab.

or

- Right-click a link on the displayed Web page, and then click Open in new tab on the shortcut menu.

or

- Press the Ctrl key as you click a link on the displayed Web page.

You'll use page tabs to open and navigate among multiple Web pages.

To use page tabs in Internet Explorer:

1. On the tab row, click the **New Tab** button. A second tab appears in the browser window and the New Tab page opens, displaying a list of sites you've visited recently and frequently. See Figure 1-5.

Figure 1-5   New tab open

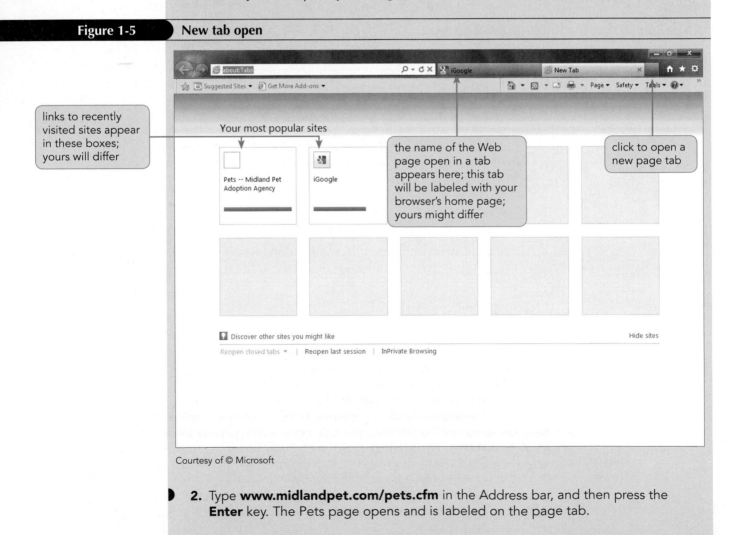

links to recently visited sites appear in these boxes; yours will differ

Your most popular sites

Pets -- Midland Pet Adoption Agency

iGoogle

the name of the Web page open in a tab appears here; this tab will be labeled with your browser's home page; yours might differ

click to open a new page tab

Discover other sites you might like   Hide sites

Reopen closed tabs ▾ | Reopen last session | InPrivate Browsing

Courtesy of © Microsoft

2. Type **www.midlandpet.com/pets.cfm** in the Address bar, and then press the **Enter** key. The Pets page opens and is labeled on the page tab.

3. On the Pets page, right-click the **Home** link, and then click **Open in new tab** on the shortcut menu. A third tab appears on the tab row labeled "Midland Pet Adoption Agency." To display this page in the browser window, you need to click the new tab.

4. Click the **Midland Pet Adoption Agency** tab on the tab row on the Navigation bar. The home page is displayed in the browser window.

5. Press and hold the **Ctrl** key, click the **Training Programs link**, and then release the Ctrl key. The Training -- Midland Pet Adoption Agency page opens in a new tab.

6. Click the **Training -- Midland Pet Adoption Agency** tab. The tab for the training programs is displayed, as shown in Figure 1-6. Notice that the page tabs become smaller as you open additional tabs, and the text identifying the Web pages displayed on the tab becomes truncated.

TIP

To see the entire title and URL of a Web page in a ScreenTip, point to its page tab.

Figure 1-6	Internet Explorer with four tabs open

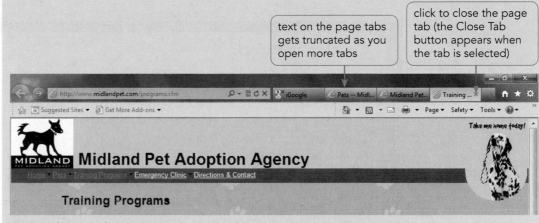

text on the page tabs gets truncated as you open more tabs

click to close the page tab (the Close Tab button appears when the tab is selected)

Courtesy of © Microsoft; © Cengage Learning

7. Point to the **Pets -- Midland Pet Adoption Agency** tab, and then click the **Close Tab** button that appears. The tab closes.

8. On the Training -- Midland Pet Adoption Agency tab, click the **Close Tab** button. The tab closes and the home page for the Midland Pet Adoption Agency site reappears in the browser window.

9. Click the **Close Tab** button on the tab for your browser's home page. The Midland Pet Adoption Agency home page is the only open tab in the browser window.

You like the format of the Midland Pet Adoption Agency's home page, so you want to make sure that you can go back to that page later if you need to review its contents. You can write down the URL so you can refer to it later, but Internet Explorer makes it easier to return to a previously visited Web page using the Favorites Center.

Using the Favorites Center

The Favorites Center lets you store and organize a list of Web pages that you have visited so you can return to them easily. The View favorites, feeds, and history button located next to the Home button at the right end of the Navigation bar opens the Favorites Center. The Favorites Center has three tabs: Favorites, Feeds, and History. The Favorites tab allows you to create a **favorite**, which is a stored shortcut containing the URL of a Web page. You create, organize, and access your stored favorites on the Favorites tab. The Feeds tab is used to store and organize **RSS feeds**, which provide content published by a Web site that is updated often. The History tab records your browsing activity by organizing and storing the URLs of the Web sites you have visited by date, site, most visited, order visited today, or search history.

Creating and Organizing Favorites

As you use the Web to find information, you can create favorites so you can easily return to sites of interest. You might very quickly find yourself creating so many favorites that it is difficult to find a specific favorite. When you start accumulating favorites, it is helpful to keep them organized so that you can quickly locate the site you need. On the Favorites tab, you can add, delete, and organize favorites into folders that best suit your needs and working style. You can also add favorites that you want to access very frequently to the Favorites bar, which is a toolbar that appears below the Address bar on which you create buttons to access favorites. Keep in mind that the favorites and folders you create are available only on the computer on which you are working.

REFERENCE

Creating a Favorite

- Open the Web page you want to save as a favorite.
- Click the View favorites, feed, and history button on the Navigation bar to open the Favorites Center, and then click the Add to favorites button to open the Add a Favorite dialog box (or right-click a blank area of the Web page, and then click Add to favorites on the shortcut menu).
- If necessary, type a title for the Web page in the Name box.
- If necessary, click the Create in arrow and click a folder in which to store the favorite.
- To create a new folder in which to store the favorite, click the New folder button to open the Create a Folder dialog box. Type the name of the new folder in the Folder Name box, and then click the Create button to close the Create a Folder dialog box.
- Click the Add button in the Add a Favorite dialog box.

or

- Open the Web page you want to save as a favorite.
- Click the View favorites, feed, and history button on the Navigation bar to open the Favorites Center, click the Add to favorites button arrow, and then click Add to Favorites bar (or click the Add to Favorites bar button on the Favorites bar).

You will save the URL for the Midland Pet Adoption Agency Web page as a favorite, and create a Pet Adoption Agencies folder in which to store this favorite.

To create a favorite and a folder to store a link to the agency's home page:

▶ 1. With the Midland Pet Adoption Agency home page open, click the **View favorites, feeds, and history** button on the Navigation bar to open the Favorites Center.

▶ 2. If necessary, click the **Favorites** tab to display a list of Favorites on your computer. See Figure 1-7.

Figure 1-7	Favorites Center

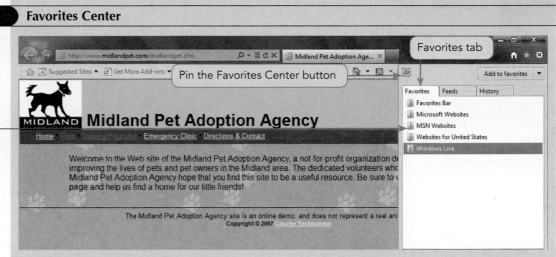

click a folder icon to open the folder and display the favorites stored in it; your list of folders and favorites might differ

Courtesy of © Microsoft; © Cengage Learning

The Favorites Center opens on the right side of the browser window, overlapping the Web page displayed. When you are working in the Favorites Center, you might prefer to dock it on the left side of the browser window using the Pin the Favorites Center button in the upper-left corner of the Favorites Center so that it doesn't obstruct the Web pages you are viewing.

3. Click the **Pin the Favorites Center** button in the upper-left corner of the Favorites Center. The Favorites Center remains open, and appears along the left side of the browser window; the Midland Pet Adoption Agency home page is fully visible as well.

4. In the Favorites Center, click the **Add to favorites** button. The Add a Favorite dialog box opens.

5. If the text selected in the Name box is not "Midland Pet Adoption Agency" (without the quotation marks), type **Midland Pet Adoption Agency**. You want to store the Midland Pet Adoption Agency favorite in a new folder.

6. Click the **New folder** button. The Create a Folder dialog box opens. The Create in box indicates the new folder will be stored as a subfolder within the Favorites folder.

7. Type **Pet Adoption Agencies** in the Folder Name box, and then click the **Create** button. The Create a Folder dialog box closes, the Pet Adoption Agencies folder is added to the Favorites tab, and you return to the Add a Favorite dialog box.

8. Click the **Add** button to create the favorite and close the dialog box. The favorite is saved in the Pet Adoption Agencies folder on the Favorites tab. You can test the favorite by opening it from the Favorites Center.

9. On the Midland Pet Adoption Agency home page, click the **Emergency Clinic** link to open that page in your browser.

10. In the Favorites Center, click the **Pet Adoption Agencies** folder to open it, as shown in Figure 1-8.

Figure 1-8   **Favorites Center with new folder and favorite**

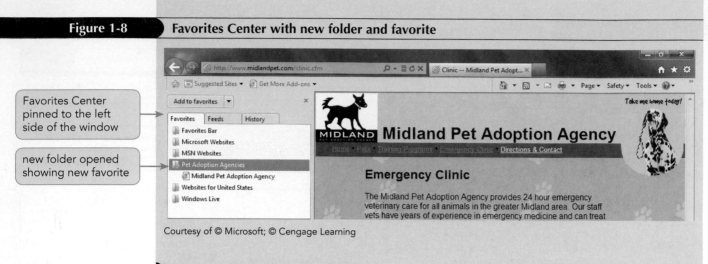

Favorites Center pinned to the left side of the window

new folder opened showing new favorite

Courtesy of © Microsoft; © Cengage Learning

▶ **11.** Click **Midland Pet Adoption Agency**. The Midland Pet Adoption Agency home page opens in the browser.

In the previous set of steps, you created a favorite and a folder in which to store it. You can also create folders and move existing favorites into these folders on the Favorites tab of the Favorites Center. You can reorganize the favorites and folders stored in the Favorites Center at any point, such as by creating new folders and rearranging favorites and folders within folders.

You saved the Midland Pet Adoption Agency's URL as a favorite, which you stored in a new folder named Pet Adoption Agencies in the Favorites Center. Because Trinity might want you to collect information about adoption agencies in different states as you conduct your research, you will organize the information about adoption agencies by state. The Midland Pet Adoption Agency is located in Minnesota, so you will put information about the Midland Pet Adoption Agency in a separate folder named MN (the two-letter abbreviation for Minnesota) within the Pet Adoption Agencies folder. As you collect information about other agencies, you will add folders for the states in which they are located, too.

To move the Midland Pet Adoption Agency favorite into a new folder:

▶ **1.** In the Favorites Center, right-click the **Pet Adoption Agencies** folder, and then click **Create new folder** on the shortcut menu. A new folder appears in the Favorites Center, with the default folder name "New folder" selected.

▶ **2.** Type **MN** as the folder name, and then press the **Enter** key to rename the folder. Now that you have created a folder, you can move your favorite for the Midland Pet Adoption Agency Web page into the new folder.

▶ **3.** If necessary, click the **Pet Adoption Agencies** folder to open it, and then click and drag the **Midland Pet Adoption Agency** favorite to the new MN folder, as shown in Figure 1-9.

Figure 1-9   **Favorite being moved to a new folder**

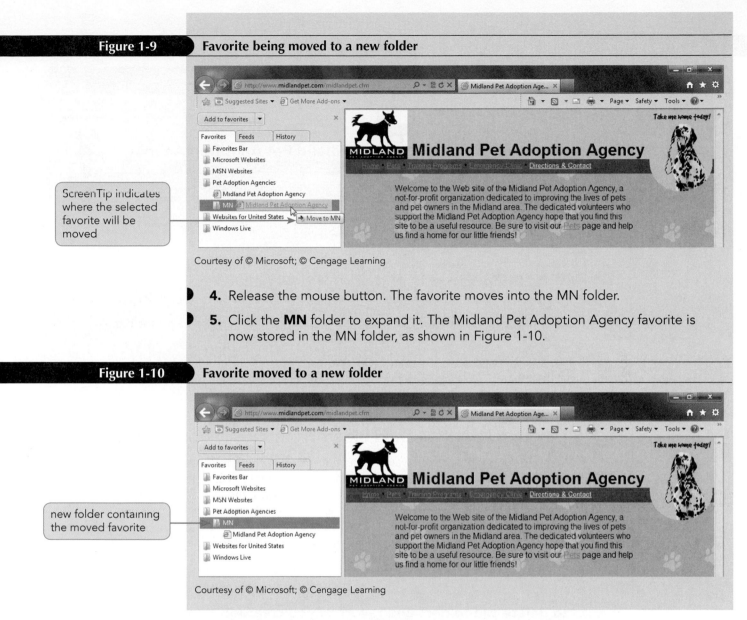

ScreenTip indicates where the selected favorite will be moved

Courtesy of © Microsoft; © Cengage Learning

4. Release the mouse button. The favorite moves into the MN folder.

5. Click the **MN** folder to expand it. The Midland Pet Adoption Agency favorite is now stored in the MN folder, as shown in Figure 1-10.

Figure 1-10   **Favorite moved to a new folder**

new folder containing the moved favorite

Courtesy of © Microsoft; © Cengage Learning

You realize that you will need to go to the Midland Pet Adoption Agency home page frequently. Although it's easily available from the Favorites Center, it would be even faster to access that page from the Favorites bar.

You'll add the Midland Pet Adoption Agency's URL as a link on the Favorites bar.

To add the Midland Pet Adoption Agency home page to the Favorites bar:

1. Click the **Add to Favorites** bar button on the Favorites bar. A button appears on the Favorites bar labeled with the Web page's title, as shown in Figure 1-11.

Trouble? If the Favorites bar doesn't appear on your screen, right-click the blank area to the right of the page tabs, and then click Favorites bar on the shortcut menu.

Figure 1-11

Figure 1-11	Favorite added to the Favorites bar

click to add a favorite to the Favorites bar

new favorite on the Favorites bar

Courtesy of © Microsoft; © Cengage Learning

▶ **2.** Click the **Back** button on the Navigation bar to return to the Emergency Clinic page.

▶ **3.** Point to the **Midland Pet Adoption Agency** button on the Favorites bar. A ScreenTip displays the full title of the Web page and its URL.

▶ **4.** Click the **Midland Pet Adoption Agency** button on the Favorites bar. The Midland Pet Adoption Agency home page opens in the browser.

Deleting Favorites and Folders from the Favorites Center

Creating favorites is a great way to keep track of sites you know you want to visit on a regular basis. However, sometimes you no longer want to visit a site, such as when you saved favorites related to a specific project. Other times, the URL for a site has changed or the site no longer exists. In all these instances, you'll want to delete the favorites and the folders in which they are stored. You can delete a specific favorite, or you can delete a folder in the Favorites Center. When you delete a folder, the folder and all of its contents are moved to the Recycle Bin.

To delete the folders and favorites you created:

▶ **1.** In the Favorites Center, right-click the **Midland Pet Adoption Agency** favorite in the MN folder, and then click **Delete** on the shortcut menu. The favorite is deleted.

▶ **2.** In the Favorites Center, right-click the **Pet Adoption Agencies** folder, and then click **Delete** on the shortcut menu. The Delete Folder dialog box opens so you can confirm that you want to move the folder to the Recycle Bin.

▶ **3.** Click the **Yes** button. The folder and all of its contents are deleted from the Favorites Center.

▶ **4.** Click the **Close the Favorites Center** button on the Favorite Center's title bar to close the Favorites Center.

▶ **5.** On the Favorites bar, right-click the **Midland Pet Adoption Agency** link, and then click **Delete** on the shortcut menu. The favorite is deleted from the Favorites Bar.

Navigating Web Pages Using the History List

Creating favorites is a great way to keep track of sites you know you want to visit on a regular basis. Another way to return to a site that you have visited recently is with the history list. The history list, which you open by clicking the History tab in the Favorites Center, is useful when you know you visited a site recently, but you did not create a favorite and you cannot recall the URL of the site. From the History tab, you can view a list of the sites that were visited on that computer during the last three weeks. You can display the history of visited sites organized by date, by site, by sites most visited, or by the order visited on a single day. You can also use the History tab to search for a specific site. To return to a specific Web page, just click its link in the history list.

Not every site that you visit as you research pet adoption sites for Danville Animal Shelter will warrant being saved as a favorite. The history list will be helpful if you want to show Trinity the breadth of sites you visited during your research. You will view the history list next.

To view the history list for this session:

TIP

If you are using a computer in a computer lab or a public computer, the history list will include sites visited by anyone who has used the computer, not just you.

1. Click the **View favorites, feeds, and history** button on the Navigation bar, and then click the **History** tab in the Favorites Center. The pages that you have visited are grouped by date of visit, so the last icon in the list is labeled "Today" and includes Web sites you visited today. The other icons are labeled with the names of days of the week (Monday, Tuesday, and so on) if Internet Explorer has been used regularly. If not, the icons will be labeled with week names (Last Week, Two Weeks Ago, and so on).

2. Click the **Today** icon to open a list of folders for the Web sites you visited today. Clicking a folder opens a list of the links to each page on that site that you visited today in the order in which you visited them.

TIP

You can see the full URL of any item in the history list by pointing to that item.

3. Click the **midlandpet (www.midlandpet.com)** folder. See Figure 1-12. Each page you visited on the Midland Pet Adoption Agency site is stored in this folder in the order you visited it. Notice the home page for the site appears in the list more than once because you navigated back to that page from the other pages on the site. To return to a particular page, click that page's entry in the list.

| Figure 1-12 | History tab in the Favorites Center |

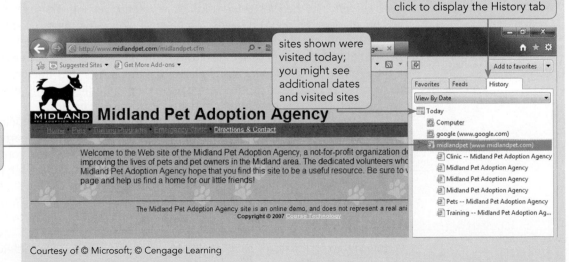

Courtesy of © Microsoft; © Cengage Learning

> **4.** Click the **Training -- Midland Pet Adoption Agency** link to navigate to that page. The Favorites Center closes and the Training Programs page for the Midland Pet Adoption Agency appears in the browser window.

Erasing Your Browsing History

In some situations, such as when you are finishing a work session in a school computer lab or on any public computer, you might want to remove the list of Web sites that you visited from the history list of the computer on which you had been working. Erasing your browsing history helps protect your personal information and guard your privacy when working on a shared computer. You can delete your browsing history in Internet Explorer by clicking the Tools button on the Navigation bar or Command bar, and then clicking Internet options to open the Internet Options dialog box. In the Browsing history section of the General tab, click the Delete button to open the Delete Browsing History dialog box. Click the History check box to select it (unless it is already selected). If any other check boxes are selected, click each of them to clear the selections. After ensuring that only the History box is checked, click the Delete button to erase the entire browsing history stored on the computer.

Managing Cookies

All Web browser users should know about the use of cookies. A **cookie** is a small text file that a Web server saves on the hard drive of the computer that is running the Web browser software. A cookie is used to store information about your visit to a specific Web site, such as your login name and password, which pages you viewed, and your shopping cart information if you purchased something from the Web site. By storing this information on your computer, the Web server can retrieve the information when you return to that site, enabling it to perform functions such as automatic login, which makes it easier to sign in to Web pages you have visited before. However, the user often is unaware that cookie files are being written to the computer's hard drive.

When the site you are visiting places a cookie on your computer, it is called a **first-party cookie**. However, many cookies are written by companies that sell advertising on Web pages. The advertising elements of the Web page are delivered by the advertisers' Web servers, not the Web server of the site you are visiting. These cookies record which ads have appeared on Web pages you have viewed. Advertisers use these cookies to determine which ads they will deliver the next time you open a Web page. This can be beneficial because it prevents sites from showing you the same ads over and over again. On the other hand, many people believe that this sort of user tracking is an offensive invasion of privacy. Cookies that are placed by companies other than the company whose Web site you are visiting are called **third-party cookies**.

Most Web browsers, including Internet Explorer, allow you to block cookies from your computer or to specify general categories of cookies (such as first-party or third-party) to block. In Internet Explorer, you can specify privacy settings that control the writing of cookie files to your computer's hard drive. You can specify which types of cookies to block or you can block particular types of cookies from specific sites. These options are available on the Privacy tab in the Internet Options dialog box. You will learn more about the different types of cookies, how they work, and how best to deal with them in Tutorial 6.

Internet Explorer stores each cookie in a separate file. You can delete the cookies from your computer at any time or whenever you exit Internet Explorer. To delete all of the cookies stored on your computer, click the Tools button on the Navigation bar or the

Command bar and then click Internet options to open the Internet Options dialog box. On the General tab, click the Delete button in the Browsing history section to open the Delete Browsing History dialog box. In this dialog box, you click the Cookies check box to select it (unless it is already selected). Clear any other check boxes for items you do not want to delete, and then click the Delete button.

Because some cookies benefit users, you might not want to delete all of the cookies on your computer. For example, if you regularly visit a site that requires you to log in, the Web server can store your login information in a cookie on your computer so you do not have to type your user name each time you visit the site. You should always consider carefully whether the advantages of cookies outweigh the disadvantages for you before you delete all of your Internet Explorer cookies.

Trinity wants you to check the privacy settings related to cookies in Internet Explorer on your computer.

To view privacy settings for cookies in Internet Explorer:

1. Click the **Tools** button on the Navigation bar, and then click **Internet options**. The Internet Options dialog box opens.

2. Click the **Privacy** tab. See Figure 1-13.

Figure 1-13   **Privacy tab in the Internet Options dialog box**

selected privacy setting (yours might differ)

drag the slider to select a different privacy setting

description of the selected privacy setting

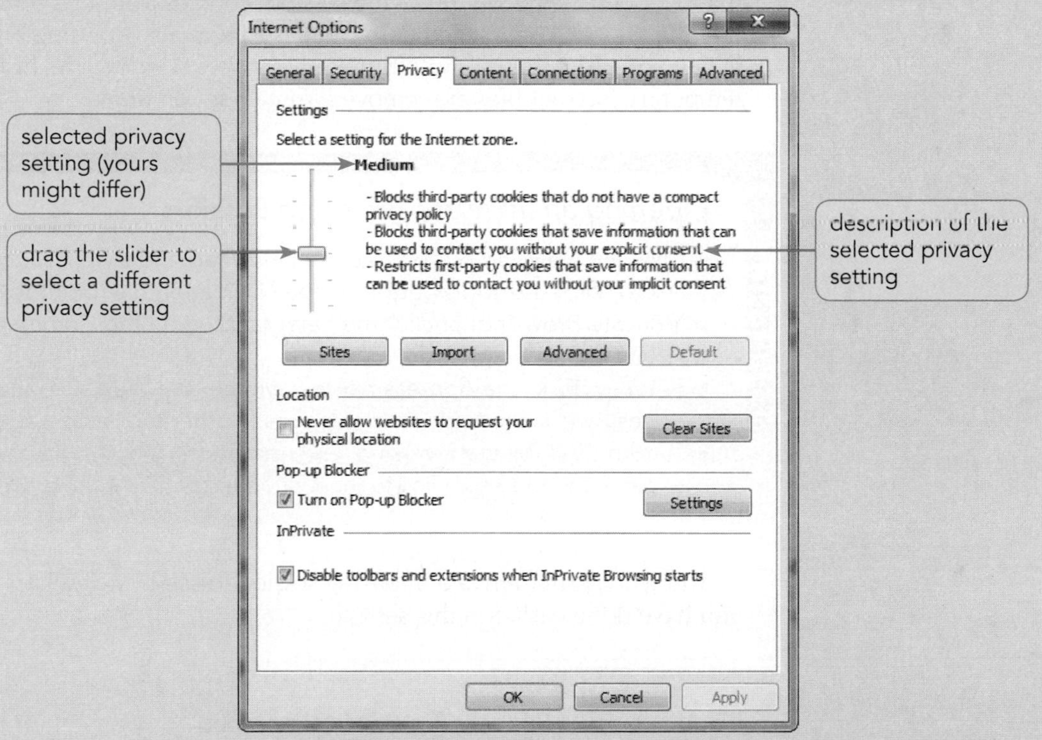

Courtesy of © Microsoft

3. Click and drag the slider control in the Settings section to examine the various settings available that control placement of first-party and third-party cookies on your computer.

4. Click the **Cancel button** to close the Internet Options dialog box without saving any changes to the privacy settings.

Private Web Browsing

As you have learned, Internet Explorer stores a considerable amount of information about your Web browsing activity. It stores a list of all the Web pages you have viewed in the history list, and it stores cookies that can contain information about your logins and passwords. It even stores information about which ads have been displayed on the Web pages you have viewed.

Internet Explorer also stores copies of all or part of the Web pages you visit on whatever computer you are using. If you do not wish to have this information stored, you can use Internet Explorer in InPrivate Browsing mode. In **InPrivate Browsing mode**, Internet Explorer does not store your browsing history, cookies, or copies of the Web pages you visit. In other words, there is no record in Internet Explorer of what sites you visited and what you looked at. When you are using a computer other than your own (such as a friend's computer or a computer at work, school, or another public location), InPrivate Browsing mode can help protect your privacy and security.

To start InPrivate Browsing, you can click the New Tab button to open a new tab, and then click the InPrivate Browsing link. You can also start an InPrivate Browsing session by clicking the Safety button on the Command bar or by clicking the Tools button on the Navigation bar, pointing to Safety, and then clicking InPrivate Browsing, which then opens a new browser window with the "InPrivate is turned on" page displayed in the browser window, the InPrivate label on the page tab, and the InPrivate indicator to the left of the Address bar.

As you visit Web pages in the InPrivate Browsing browser window or in any tabs in that window, the history list of the session, cookies from that session, and temporary Internet files will be tracked only while the InPrivate Browsing browser window is open. When you close the InPrivate Browsing browser window, the history list, cookies, and temporary Internet files are removed from your computer.

REFERENCE

Opening an InPrivate Browsing Session

- Click the New Tab button to open a new tab and then click the InPrivate Browsing link (or click the Tools button on the Navigation bar, point to Safety, and then click InPrivate Browsing; or click the Safety button on the Command bar, and then click InPrivate Browsing).
- Enter a URL in the Address bar to navigate to a Web site, and navigate to other Web pages by clicking links or open pages in other tabs as usual.
- To turn off InPrivate Browsing, click the Close button on the Internet Explorer title bar to close the browser window and all open tabs.

You will try an InPrivate Browsing session to see how it differs from the Web browsing you have done earlier in this session.

To start an InPrivate Browsing session:

1. Click the **Safety** button on the Command bar, and then click **InPrivate Browsing**. A new browser window opens, displaying a Web page with the message "InPrivate is turned on." The Address bar has the blue InPrivate indicator next to it, and the text "about:InPrivate" appears selected in the Address bar. See Figure 1-14.

Figure 1-14 **InPrivate Browsing mode**

indicates that Internet Explorer is in InPrivate Browsing mode

description of InPrivate Browsing mode

InPrivate is turned on

When InPrivate Browsing is turned on, you will see this indicator

InPrivate Browsing helps prevent Internet Explorer from storing data about your browsing session. This includes cookies, temporary Internet files, history, and other data. Toolbars and extensions are disabled by default. See Help for more information.

To turn off InPrivate Browsing, close this browser window.

Learn more about InPrivate Browsing | Read the Internet Explorer privacy statement online

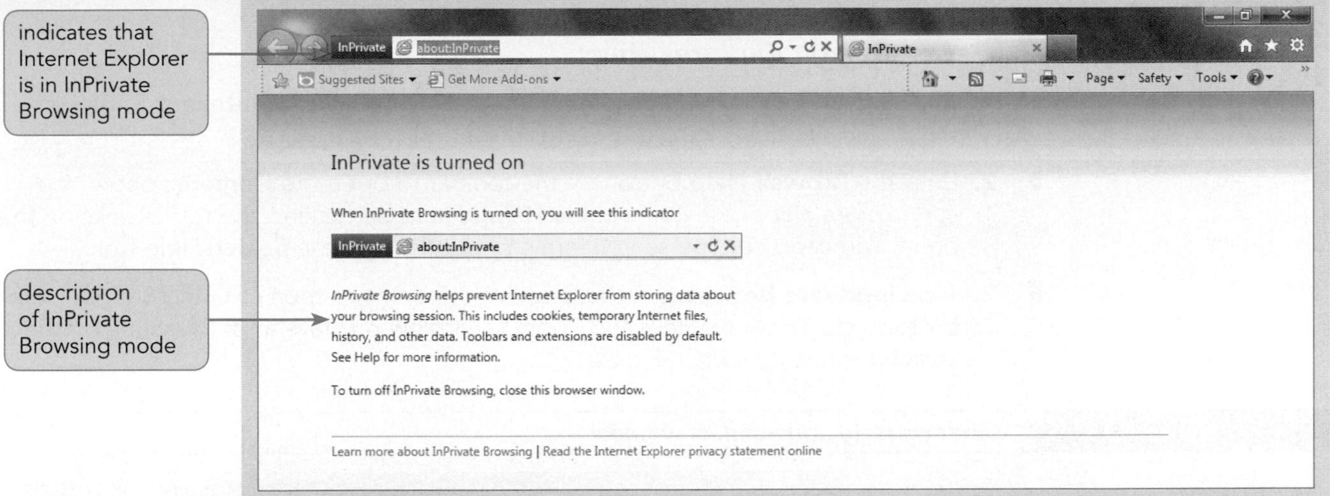

Courtesy of © Microsoft

2. Type **www.midlandpet.com** in the Address bar, and then press the Enter key.

3. Click any link on the Web page to visit another part of the Midland Pet Adoption Agency Web site, and then click other links to visit several other pages on the site.

4. Click the **Close** button on the Internet Explorer title bar to close the browser window and end the InPrivate Browsing session. You return to the browser window displaying the Midland Pet Adoption Agency Training page.

If you examine the browser's history listing, you will see that it includes no record of the Web pages you just visited. Although the browser does not record the pages you have visited (or other information, such as cookies), the network server that connects the computer to the Internet might have software that does. Therefore, it is best not to rely on InPrivate Browsing mode to keep private the Web pages you visit while using a computer at work or another public location.

Getting Help in Internet Explorer

Internet Explorer has an online Help system that includes information about how to use the browser and how it is different from previous versions of the browser. It also provides tips for exploring the Internet.

REFERENCE

Using Internet Explorer Help

- Click the Help button on the Command bar, and then click Internet Explorer Help (or press the F1 key) to open the Windows Help and Support window.
- Click the Browse Help button on the toolbar in the Windows Help and Support window.
- Click a link to access information on a specific Help topic or type a search term or query in the Search Help box, and then click the Search Help button.
- Click the Close button on the Windows Help and Support window.

Trinity wants you to learn more about InPrivate Browsing. You will use Internet Explorer Help to find more information about this feature.

To use Internet Explorer Help:

1. Click the **Help** button on the Command bar, and then click **Internet Explorer Help**. The Windows Help and Support window opens.

2. Click the **Browse Help** button on the toolbar to open the Contents page. You can explore any of the items in the Help system by clicking the topics links on this page. You can also type search terms or queries into the Search Help box.

3. Type **inprivate browsing** in the Search Help box and then click the **Search Help** button. The Windows Help and Support window displays a list of results for the search term, as shown in Figure 1-15.

Figure 1-15   Windows Help and Support window

type a search term or question here

Browse Help button opens the Contents page

click a link to display that Help topic

search results

27 results for **inprivate browsing**

1. What is InPrivate Browsing?
2. InPrivate: frequently asked questions
3. Tabs, Accelerators, and InPrivate Browsing: recommended links
4. Protect your privacy using Internet Explorer 9
5. Open tabs you've previously closed
6. How to delete your browsing history in Internet Explorer 9
7. Tabbed browsing: frequently asked questions
8. Internet Explorer at a glance
9. Online privacy and security: frequently asked questions
10. Suggested Sites: frequently asked questions
11. Delete webpage history
12. Internet Explorer keyboard shortcuts
13. Security and privacy features in Internet Explorer
14. How to use the New Tab page in Internet Explorer 9
15. Internet Explorer 9 keyboard shortcuts

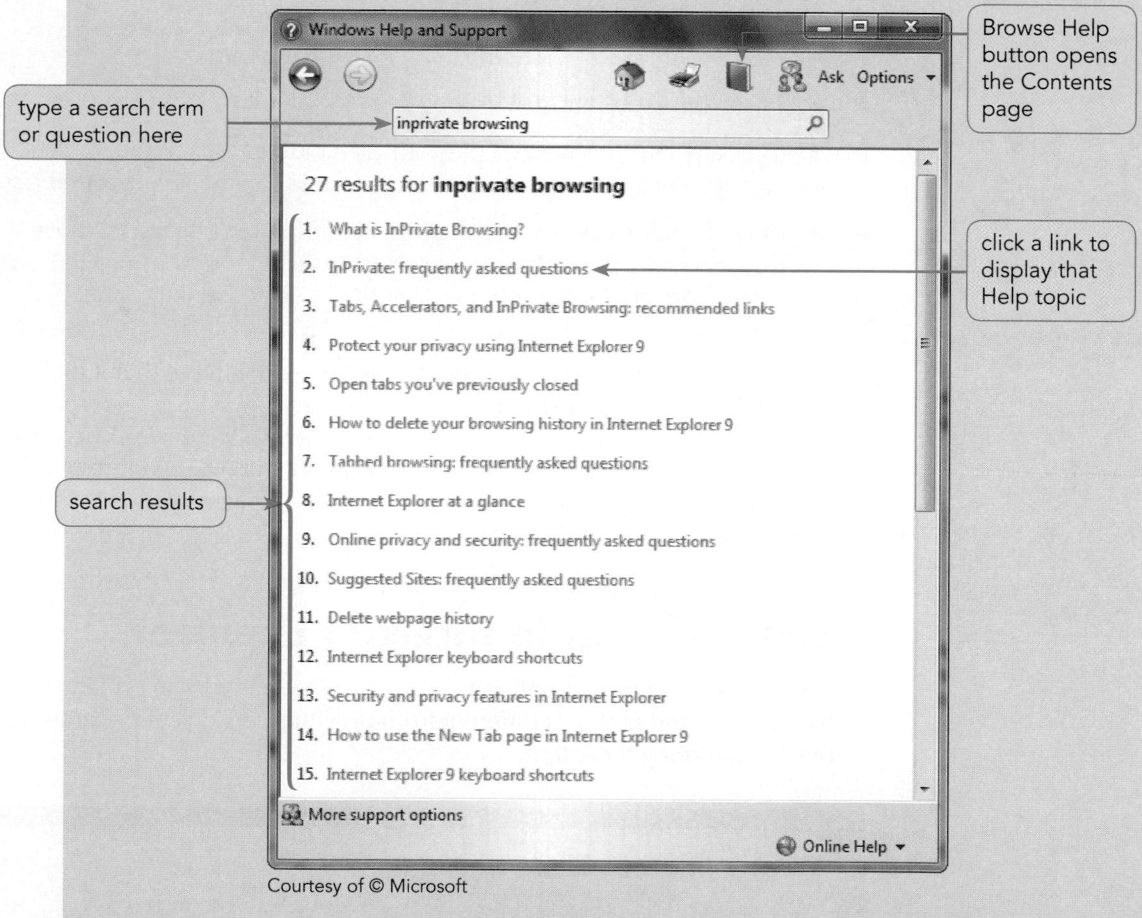

Courtesy of © Microsoft

4. Click the **InPrivate: frequently asked questions** link to open a page of frequently asked questions about InPrivate Browsing.

5. Click the **What is InPrivate Browsing?** link, and read the paragraph that appears under the link.

6. When you are finished, click the **Close** button on the Windows Help and Support window title bar.

Saving Web Page Content

At times you will want to refer to the information that you have found on a Web page without having to return to the site. In Internet Explorer, you can save entire Web pages, particular graphics, or selected portions of Web page text.

Saving an Entire Web Page

When you save the entire Web page, you use the Save Webpage dialog box, which is similar to the Save As dialog box in other programs. To open the Save Webpage dialog box, click the Tools button on the Navigation bar, point to File, and then click Save as. You can also click the Page button on the Command bar, and then click Save as to open the Save Webpage dialog box.

Internet Explorer by default saves the complete Web page, including the graphic page elements along with the Web page's text and the HTML markup codes. You can select a different format from the Save as type list in the Save Webpage dialog box. The Webpage, HTML only format saves the Web page's text along with the HTML markup codes. The Text File format saves the Web page's text without the HTML markup codes. The Web Archive, single file format saves the Web page in a proprietary archive format (the .mht format) that can be read by Internet Explorer Web browsers, but not necessarily other Web browsers. Avoiding the Internet Explorer proprietary format will ensure that anyone using another Web browser can read the page you saved.

You will save the Midland Pet Adoption Agency home page to show to Trinity. This Web site will provide Trinity an example of a well-designed site with appropriate text and graphics.

To save the Midland Pet Adoption Agency home page:

1. Return to the Midland Pet Adoption Agency home page.

2. Click the **Page** button on the Command bar, and then click **Save as**. The Save Webpage dialog box opens.

3. Navigate to and select the **Tutorial.01\Tutorial** folder included with your Data Files. This is the location where you will save the Web page.

   Trouble? If you don't have the starting Data Files, you need to get them before you can proceed. Your instructor will either give you the Data Files or ask you to obtain them from a specified location (such as a network drive). In either case, make a backup copy of the Data Files before you start so that you will have the original files available in case you need to start over. If you have any questions about the Data Files, see your instructor or technical support person for assistance.

4. Type **Midland Pet Home Page IE** in the File name box.

5. Click the **Save as type** arrow, and then click **Webpage, complete (*.htm, *html)** to select this format if it is not already selected.

6. Click the **Save** button. The Save Webpage dialog box closes. The Web page for the Midland Pet Adoption Agency's home page is saved in the location you specified.

Saving an Image from a Web Page

Most Web pages include graphics or pictures to provide interest, illustrate a point, or present information. You can save a graphic or picture instead of the entire Web page.

REFERENCE

Saving an Image from a Web Page

- Right-click the image on the Web page that you want to save, and then click Save picture as on the shortcut menu to open the Save Picture dialog box.
- Navigate to the location in which you want to save the image, and change the default filename, if necessary.
- Click the Save button.

The Directions & Contact Web page also includes a street map that shows the location of the Midland Pet Adoption Agency. You will save this map to show Trinity as well.

To save the street map image:

1. Click the **Directions & Contact** link to open the Web page that contains the address and phone number for the Midland Pet Adoption Agency.

2. On the Directions & Contact page, scroll the page as needed to display the map.

3. Right-click the **map**, and then click **Save picture as** on the shortcut menu to open the Save Picture dialog box.

4. Navigate to and select the **Tutorial.01\Tutorial** folder included with your Data Files. This is the location where you will save the map graphic.

5. Type **Midland Pet Map IE** as the filename, and then click the **Save** button to save the graphic.

Understanding Copyright for Web Page Content

A **copyright** is the legal right of the author or other owner of an original work to control the reproduction, distribution, and sale of that work. A copyright comes into existence as soon as the work is placed into a tangible form, such as a printed copy, an electronic file, or a Web page. Copyright laws can place significant restrictions on the way that you can use information or images that you copy from another entity's Web site. Because of the way a Web browser works, it copies the HTML code as well as the graphics and media files to your computer before it can display them in the browser. Just because copies of these files are stored temporarily on your computer does not mean that you have the right to use them in any way other than having your computer display them in the browser window.

The United States and most other countries have copyright laws that govern the use of photocopies, audio or video recordings, and other reproductions of authors' original work. The copyright exists even if the work does not contain a copyright notice. If you do not know whether material that you find on the Web is copyrighted, the safest course of action is to assume that it is.

U.S. copyright law has a **fair use** provision that allows a limited amount of copyrighted information to be used for purposes such as news reporting, research, and scholarship. The source of the material used should always be cited. Commercial use of copyrighted material is much more restricted. You should obtain permission from the copyright holder before using anything you copy from a Web page. The copyright holder can require you to pay a fee for permission to use the material from the Web page. The steps in this tutorial are designed so that your use of copyrighted Web pages and elements of those pages falls within the fair use provisions of U.S. copyright law.

Copying Text from a Web Page

You can also copy and paste portions of a Web page to a file or email. This can be helpful when you want to save specific information from a Web page, such as a schedule of events, directions to a location, or information about a place.

Trinity plans to visit the Midland Pet Adoption Agency while she is traveling in Minnesota next week. She wants to contact Midland's director and schedule a meeting. You can copy and paste the agency's address and telephone number from its Web site into a document or an email for Trinity.

To copy and paste text from the Midland Pet Adoption Agency Web site:

1. On the Directions & Contact page, select the address and telephone number for Midland Pet Adoption Agency at the top of the page.

2. Right-click the selected text, and then click **Copy** on the shortcut menu to copy the selected text to the Clipboard, which is a temporary storage area in Windows.

3. Click the **Start** button on the taskbar, point to **All Programs**, click the **Accessories** folder, and then click **WordPad** to start the program and open a new document.

4. On the Home tab on the WordPad Ribbon, click the **Paste** button to paste the text into the WordPad document, as shown in Figure 1-16.

Figure 1-16	**WordPad document with pasted text**

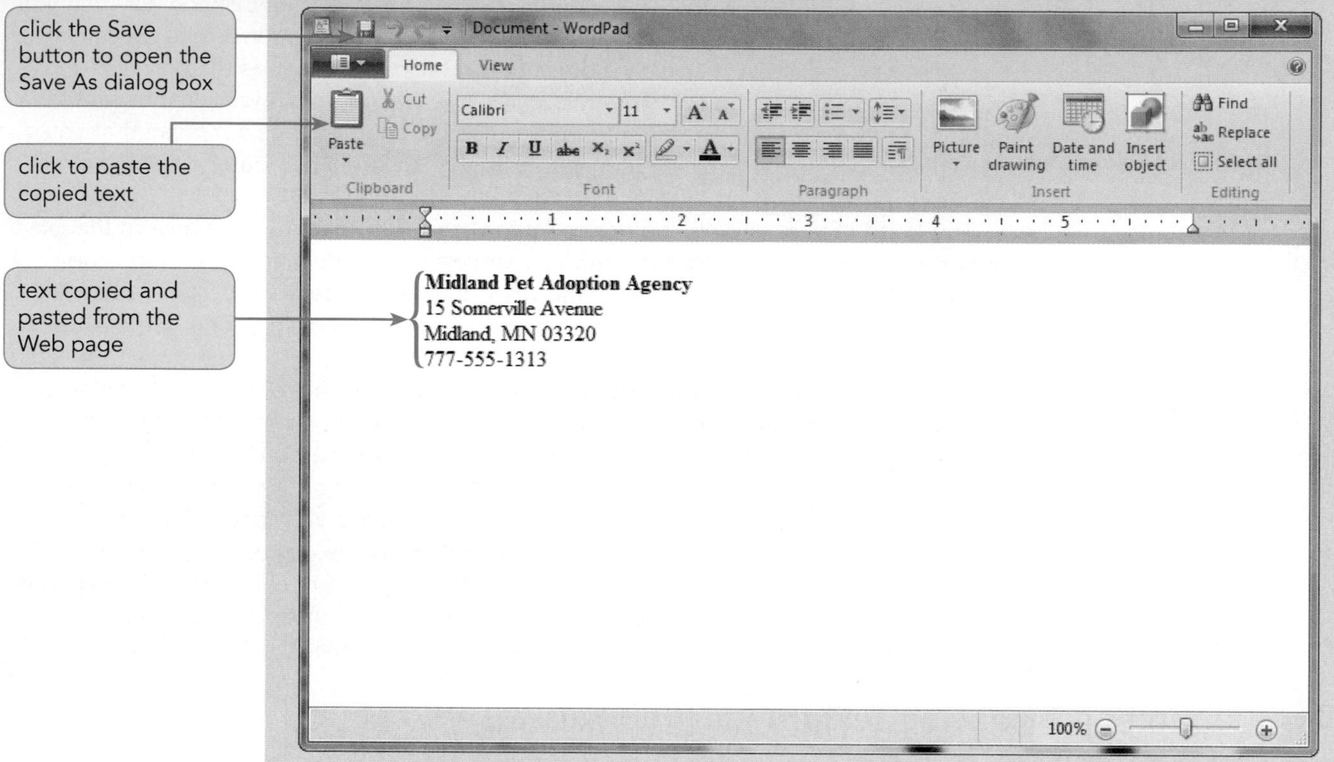

click the Save button to open the Save As dialog box

click to paste the copied text

text copied and pasted from the Web page

Midland Pet Adoption Agency
15 Somerville Avenue
Midland, MN 03320
777-555-1313

Courtesy of © Microsoft

5. Click the **Save** button on the WordPad Quick Access Toolbar to open the Save As dialog box.

6. Navigate to and select the **Tutorial.01\Tutorial** folder included with your Data Files. This is the location where you will save the WordPad document.

7. Click the **Save as type** button, and then click **Rich Text Format (RTF)** if necessary.

8. Type **Midland Pet Contact Info IE** in the File name box, and then click the **Save** button. The address and phone number of the agency are now saved in a text file for future reference.

9. Click the **Close** button on the WordPad title bar to close it.

Printing a Web Page

Sometimes you will want to print a Web page. This might occur when you want to keep a printed page for reference, save a record or receipt of an online purchase, or have a coupon to use at a local store or restaurant. As with other programs, you can send the displayed page directly to the printer by clicking the Print button on the Command bar, or you can select options in the Print dialog box by clicking the Print button arrow on the Command bar and then clicking Print. The Print dialog box includes options for selecting a printer, setting a page range, and specifying the number of copies to print.

You can also use the Page Setup dialog box to change aspects of a Web page printout, including the page size and orientation, margins, and headers and footers that print at the top and bottom of the page, respectively. The default header prints the Web page title in the left section, nothing in the center section, and the page number and the total number of pages in the right section. The default footer prints the URL in the left section, nothing in the center section, and the date in the right section. To open the Page Setup dialog box, click the Print button arrow on the Command bar, and then click Page setup.

Before printing a Web page, you should preview what the printout will look like to ensure that it will print in the best way possible. For example, you want to ensure that extra or unnecessary pages won't print, that the printed page is legible, and that what will print is what you wanted to print. This extra step helps you to save resources, including paper and printer ink. To open the Print Preview window, click the Print button arrow on the Command bar, and then click Print preview. The Print Preview window shows how the current Web page will look on the printed page. It also provides access to common printing options. From the toolbar, you can open the Print dialog box, change the page orientation, open the Page Setup dialog box, toggle headers and footers on or off, change the number of pages in the preview, and adjust the print size. Changing the print size enables you to shrink the Web page to fit better on the page or enlarge the Web page on the printout so it's more legible.

REFERENCE

Printing the Current Web Page

- Click the Print button on the Command bar to print the current Web page with the default print settings.

or

- Click the Print button arrow on the Command bar, and then click Print to open the Print dialog box.
- On the General tab, select the printer you want to use, specify the page range you want to print, and set the number of copies to print.
- Click the Print button.

You will preview a copy of the Midland Pet Adoption Agency home page, and then print it.

To preview and print the Midland Pet Adoption Agency home page:

1. Return to the Midland Pet Adoption Agency home page.

2. Click the **Print button arrow** on the Command bar, and then click **Print preview**. The Print Preview window opens. See Figure 1-17.

Figure 1-17 **Print Preview window**

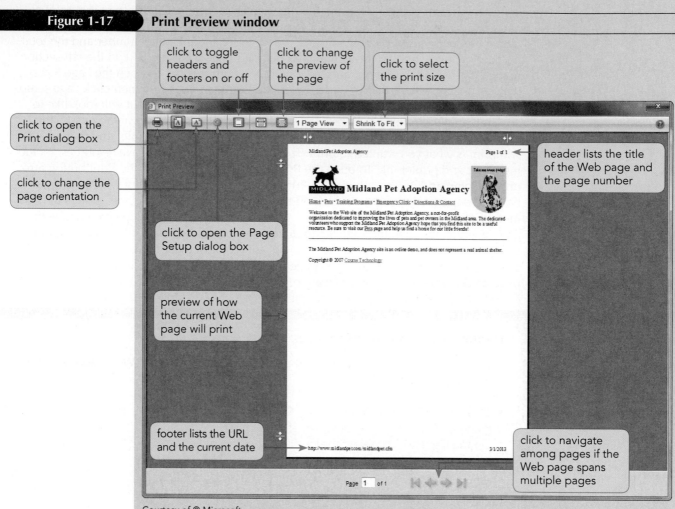

click to toggle headers and footers on or off

click to change the preview of the page

click to select the print size

click to open the Print dialog box

click to change the page orientation

click to open the Page Setup dialog box

preview of how the current Web page will print

footer lists the URL and the current date

header lists the title of the Web page and the page number

click to navigate among pages if the Web page spans multiple pages

Courtesy of © Microsoft

The preview looks fine, so you will print the page.

3. Click the **Close** button on the title bar to close the Print Preview window.

4. Click the **Print button arrow** on the Command bar, and then click **Print** to open the Print dialog box.

5. Make sure that the printer selected in the Select Printer box is the printer you want to use; if not, click the icon of the printer you want to use to change the selection.

6. If necessary, click the **Pages** option button in the Page Range section of the Print dialog box, and then type **1** in the text box to specify that you only want to print the first page. (If the text box already contains a "1" you do not need to change it.)

7. Make sure that the Number of copies box displays **1**.

8. Click the **Print** button to print the Web page and close the Print dialog box.

9. Click the **Close** button on the Internet Explorer title bar to close the Web browser.

You have copies of the Midland Pet Adoption Agency home page and map that will show Trinity how to get to the agency during her trip to Minnesota. Trinity will be able to use her Web browser or other software to open the files and print them.

In this session, you worked with Internet Explorer as you browsed the Midland Pet Adoption Agency Web site. You navigated among pages, worked with favorites, reviewed the history list, saved and copied Web pages, and printed a Web page from the site.

REVIEW

Session 1.1 Quick Check

1. Briefly explain the difference between a network and the Internet.
2. What is a hypertext link?
3. What is a URL?
4. What is a favorite?
5. If you have recently visited a Web site, but cannot recall the URL and didn't save it as a favorite, what feature can you use to return to that site?
6. Briefly explain what a cookie is.
7. What is InPrivate Browsing mode?
8. Can you use an image you save from someone else's Web site on your Web site? Explain your answer.
9. Why should you preview what the printout will look like before printing a Web page?

Note: If your instructor assigned Session 1.2, continue reading. Otherwise, complete the Review Assignments and Case Problems at the end of this tutorial.

SESSION 1.2 VISUAL OVERVIEW

The **Firefox button** opens a menu with options for all the main functions and features in the browser.

Firefox is a **Web browser**, which is software you run on your computer to make it run as a Web client, allowing it to locate and display Web pages.

Page tabs allow you to have multiple Web pages open at once, and to easily navigate among them.

The **Navigation toolbar** is used to open and move among Web pages and search for Web pages.

You type the **Uniform Resource Locator (URL)**, or the address for a Web page, in the Location bar to open that Web page in the browser.

A **Web page** is a document that has been created using **HTML**, a programming language used to format documents containing text and images so they can be viewed in a Web browser.

You use the **Library** to organize and display links to your preferred Web sites and view the History list of recently visited sites.

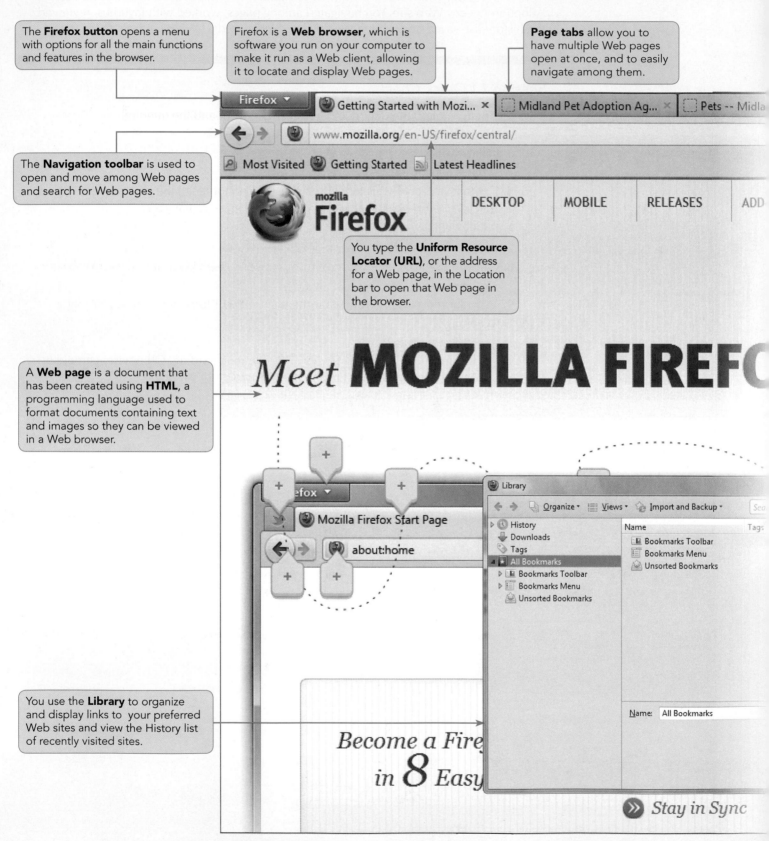

Courtesy of The Mozilla Foundation

MOZILLA FIREFOX

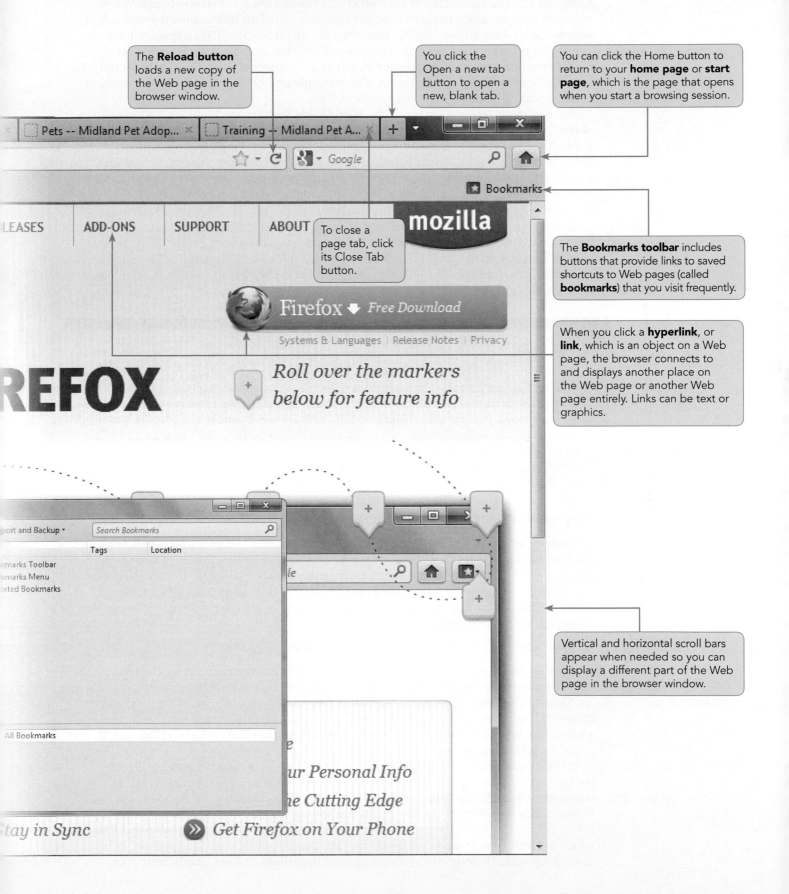

The **Reload button** loads a new copy of the Web page in the browser window.

You click the Open a new tab button to open a new, blank tab.

You can click the Home button to return to your **home page** or **start page**, which is the page that opens when you start a browsing session.

To close a page tab, click its Close Tab button.

The **Bookmarks toolbar** includes buttons that provide links to saved shortcuts to Web pages (called **bookmarks**) that you visit frequently.

When you click a **hyperlink**, or **link**, which is an object on a Web page, the browser connects to and displays another place on the Web page or another Web page entirely. Links can be text or graphics.

Roll over the markers below for feature info

Vertical and horizontal scroll bars appear when needed so you can display a different part of the Web page in the browser window.

The Internet and the Web

Computers can be connected to each other in a configuration called a **network**. When networks are connected to each other, the system is called an **interconnected network** or **internet** (with a lowercase "i"). The **Internet** (with an uppercase "i") is a specific interconnected network that connects computers all over the world using a common set of interconnection standards. Although it began as a computer science project sponsored by the U.S. military, the Internet today allows people and businesses all over the world to communicate with each other in a variety of ways.

The part of the Internet known as the **World Wide Web** (or the **Web**) is a collection of files that reside on computers, called **Web servers**, that are connected to each other through the Internet. Most files on computers, including computers that are connected to the Internet, are private; that is, only the computer's users can access those files. The owners of the computer files that make up the Web have made the files publicly available by placing them on the Web servers. Thus, anyone who has a computer connected to the Internet can obtain access to the files.

When you use an Internet connection to become part of the Web, your computer becomes a **Web client**. A **Web browser** is software that allows your computer to connect to, locate, retrieve, and display Web content. You can read Appendix A to learn more about the history of the Internet and the Web, how they work, and the technologies behind their operation.

INSIGHT

Choosing a Browser

There are a variety of Web browsers available. Some of the most common are Microsoft Internet Explorer, Mozilla Firefox, Google Chrome, Apple Safari, and Opera. You can download and install these browsers for free, enabling you to choose the one you want. All Web browsers have similar features, but some are more robust and others are more streamlined. To help evaluate and decide which Web browser you want to use, you can read reviews, explore the product pages, take tours or demos of the browsers, and download and try them.

Hypertext Markup Language and Hyperlinks

The public files on Web servers are ordinary text files, much like the files created and used by word-processing software. To enable Web browser software to read these files, the text must be formatted according to a generally accepted standard. The standard used on the Web is **Hypertext Markup Language (HTML)**. HTML uses codes, or **tags**, that tell the Web browser software how to display the text contained in the text file. For example, a Web browser reading the following line of text

```
<B>A Review of the Book <I>Wind Instruments</I></B>
```

recognizes the <B> and </B> tags as instructions to display the entire line of text in bold and the <I> and </I> tags as instructions to display the text enclosed by those tags in italics. Different Web clients that connect to this Web server might display the tagged text differently. For example, one Web browser might display text enclosed by bold tags in a blue color instead of displaying the text in bold. A text file that contains HTML tags is called an **HTML document**.

HTML provides a variety of text formatting tags that can be used to indicate headings, paragraphs, bulleted lists, numbered lists, and other text enhancements in an HTML document. (You will learn more about HTML tags in Tutorial 8.) The real power of HTML, however, lies in its anchor tag. The **HTML anchor tag** enables Web designers to link HTML documents to each other. Anchor tags in HTML documents create **hypertext links**, which are instructions that point to other HTML documents or to another section of the same document. Hypertext links also are called **hyperlinks** or **links**. The linked HTML documents can be on the same computer or on different computers. These computers can be anywhere in the world if they are connected to the Internet. When a Web browser displays an HTML document, it is often referred to as a **Web page**.

Starting Mozilla Firefox

Mozilla Firefox is a Web browser currently maintained by the Mozilla Foundation. If you want to use Firefox as your Web browser, you usually need to download and install the software. In this session, you will use the Firefox Web browser to do your work for the Danville Animal Shelter. This introduction assumes that you have Firefox installed on your computer.

To start Firefox:

▶ **1.** Click the **Start** button on the taskbar, point to **All Programs**, and then click **Mozilla Firefox**. After a moment, Firefox opens.

 Trouble? If you cannot find Mozilla Firefox on the All Programs menu, check to see if a Mozilla or Firefox shortcut icon appears on the desktop, and then double-click it. If you do not see the shortcut icon, ask your instructor or technical support person for help. The program might be installed in a different location on the computer you are using.

▶ **2.** If the program window does not fill the screen entirely, click the **Maximize** button on the title bar. Your screen should look similar to the Session 1.2 Visual Overview.

 Trouble? The Session 1.2 Visual Overview shows the Mozilla Firefox Start page, which is the page that Firefox opens the first time the program is started after being installed on a computer. Your computer will almost certainly be configured to open to a different Web page, or no page at all.

 Trouble? The Session 1.2 Visual Overview shows the Mozilla Firefox program window with the Navigation toolbar and Bookmarks toolbar displayed with the new tabs opened on top. Some of these may be hidden on your screen. You will learn how to customize the program window later in this session. In addition, other programs can add icons and toolbars to the Firefox program window. So if you are using a computer that has been used by other people, or your own computer on which other software has been installed, you might see icons and toolbars that are not shown in the figure.

 Trouble? If the Bookmarks toolbar shown in the Session 1.2 Visual Overview is not displayed on your screen, click the Firefox button, point to Options, and then click Bookmarks Toolbar to check this option and display the toolbar.

 Trouble? If you don't see a page tab in the browser window as shown in the Session 1.2 Visual Overview, then your browser is set to hide page tabs when only one Web site is open. Click the Firefox button, point to Options, and then click Options to open the Options dialog box. Click the Tabs icon in the Options dialog box, and then click the Always show the tab bar check box to select it. Click the OK button to close the dialog box.

The very first time Firefox starts, only the Firefox button and the Navigation toolbar are displayed in the program window. The Firefox button provides access to all of the features and functions available in Firefox. The Navigation toolbar contains the Location bar for opening Web pages, the Go back one page and Go forward one page buttons for navigating among previously visited pages, the Search bar for finding specific Web pages, and the Home and Bookmarks buttons to go to your start page or favorite sites. This streamlined version provides more screen space for viewing Web pages.

You can, however, display additional toolbars, including the Bookmarks toolbar, which is shown in the Session 1.2 Visual Overview. You can also customize the toolbars by deleting icons and adding new icons. Firefox allows you to change the toolbar settings because some people like to have many commands available on the screen, while others prefer to have more space available for displaying the Web page. Also, other software programs installed on your computer can place icons on the Firefox toolbars so that you can use these programs from within Firefox. As a result, your Firefox browser window might have different toolbars displayed or the toolbars might contain icons not shown in the Visual Overview.

Customizing the Firefox Window

In Firefox, you can display or hide the menu bar and toolbars as needed. When the menu bar and toolbars are hidden, more of the Web page is displayed in the browser window. The menu bar and most toolbars are hidden by default. To display the menu bar or a toolbar, right-click a blank area of the Navigation toolbar, and then click the corresponding option on the shortcut menu. You can also display or hide the menu bar or a toolbar by clicking the Firefox button, pointing to Options, and then clicking the corresponding option to display or hide the menu bar or a toolbar.

At any point, you can switch to **Full Screen mode**, which temporarily hides the program window—the Firefox button, the Navigation toolbar, and any other toolbars as well as the Windows taskbar—leaving only the Web page visible on your screen. You can switch to Full Screen mode by clicking the Firefox button and selecting Full Screen on the menu. When the window is in Full Screen mode, you can display the hidden toolbars by pointing to the top of the screen. When you move the pointer away from the toolbars, they will become hidden again. To exit Full Screen mode, point to the top of the screen until the toolbars appear, right-click a blank area above the Navigation toolbar, and then click Exit Full Screen Mode on the shortcut menu.

REFERENCE

Hiding and Restoring Toolbars in Firefox

- To switch to Full Screen mode, click the Firefox button, and then click Full Screen (or press the F11 key).
- To temporarily restore the toolbars in Full Screen mode, point to the top of the screen until the toolbars appear.
- To exit Full Screen mode, point to the top of the screen to display the toolbars, right-click a blank area above the Navigation toolbar, and then click Exit Full Screen Mode on the shortcut menu (or press the F11 key).
- To display or hide individual toolbars, click the Firefox button, point to Options, and then click a toolbar name on the menu (or right-click a blank area of the Navigation toolbar, and then click a toolbar name on the shortcut menu). If the toolbar name is already checked, the toolbar will be hidden when you click the name. If the toolbar name is not checked, the toolbar will be displayed when you click the name.

Next, you will customize the Firefox window by displaying and hiding the toolbars. In these tutorials, you will use the Navigation toolbar and the Bookmarks toolbar, so you will leave them displayed.

To display and hide toolbars in Firefox:

1. Click the **Firefox** button, and then point to **Options**. A menu opens, listing the available toolbars. A check mark appears to the left of each toolbar that is displayed.

2. Click **Navigation Toolbar** on the menu to remove the check mark and deselect this option. The Navigation toolbar is hidden.

   Trouble? If the Navigation toolbar appears, it was already hidden. Continue with Step 4.

3. Click the **Firefox** button, point to **Options**, and then click **Navigation Toolbar** to display the toolbar. This on-off, or toggle, function works for all of the toolbars.

4. Click the **Firefox** button, point to **Options**, and then click **Menu Bar** on the menu to display the menu bar.

   Trouble? If the menu bar disappears, it was already displayed. Continue with Step 6.

5. Right-click a blank area of the Navigation toolbar, and then click **Menu Bar** on the shortcut menu to hide the menu bar.

6. If the Bookmarks toolbar is not displayed, click the **Firefox** button, point to **Options**, and then click **Bookmarks Toolbar**. The Bookmarks toolbar appears below the Navigation toolbar. You can temporarily hide the Firefox button and the toolbars.

7. Click the **Firefox** button, and then click **Full Screen**. The Web page fills the entire screen.

   Trouble? If the toolbars do not immediately roll up out of view, move the pointer away from the top of the screen.

8. Point to the top of the screen. The toolbars scroll back down into view.

   Trouble? If the toolbars don't scroll back into view, this feature is not working on your computer. Press the F11 key to exit Full Screen mode and skip Step 9.

9. Right-click a blank area on the Navigation toolbar, and then click **Exit Full Screen Mode** to redisplay the toolbars.

> **TIP**
>
> Another way to switch Full Screen mode on and off is to press the F11 key.

Now that you are familiar with the tools in the browser window, you are ready to navigate to a Web site.

Navigating Web Pages

To identify a particular Web page's exact location on the Internet, Web browsers rely on an address called a Uniform Resource Locator (URL). The URL is the address of a specific Web page. Every Web page has a unique URL. A URL is a four-part addressing scheme that tells the Web browser:

- The protocol to use when transporting the file
- The domain name of the computer on which the file resides
- The path for the folder or directory on the computer in which the file resides
- The name of the file

So in the URL *http:www.nytimes.com/pages/sports/index.htm*, the *http://* is the transfer protocol, which is the set of rules that computers use to move files from one computer to another. The two most common protocols used to transfer files on the Internet are Hypertext Transfer Protocol (HTTP) and File Transfer Protocol (FTP). The second part of the URL, the domain name, is *www.nytimes.com* and this references the location of the computer on which the Web page resides; *www* indicates the computer is connected to the Web, *nytimes* is the name of the Web site, and *.com* identifies the Web site as being a commercial organization. The */pages/sports* portion of the

URL provides the path for the folder in which the Web page file is located, and the last portion of the URL, *index.htm*, is the filename.

Entering a URL in the Location Bar

You can use the Location bar, which is located on the Navigation toolbar, to enter a specific URL and go directly to that Web page. For example, you can enter the complete URL for a Web site, such as http://www.cnn.com, to load that Web page. As you begin to type, a list opens, displaying pages you have previously visited that begin with the letters you are typing; you can select a URL and press the Enter key to return to that Web page. Also, Firefox will try to complete partial URLs that you type in the Location bar. For example, if you type cnn. com, Firefox will convert it to www.cnn.com and load the Web page at that URL.

If you don't see the URL you want in the Location bar list, you can use the Search bar on the Navigation toolbar to find a specific Web site. You enter a partial URL or a search word in the Search bar, and Firefox contacts the search engine selected for your browser. A **search engine** performs a search based on the text you type in a search box—in this case, the Location bar—and displays the search results. You can click any link in the search results to go to that Web page. You will learn more about search engines in Tutorial 3.

INSIGHT

Understanding Home Pages

The term "home page" is used at least three different ways on the Web, and it is sometimes difficult to tell which meaning people intend when they use the term. The first definition of home page indicates the main page that all of the other pages on a particular Web site are organized around and link back to. This home page is the first page that opens when you visit that Web site. The second definition of "home page" is the first page that opens when you start your Web browser. This type of home page might be an HTML document on your own computer. Some people create such home pages and include hyperlinks to Web sites that they frequently visit. If you are using a computer on your school's or employer's network, its Web browser might be configured to open the main page for the school or firm. The third definition of "home page" is the Web page that a particular Web browser loads the first time you use it. This page usually is stored at the Web site of the firm or other organization that created the Web browser software. Home pages that meet the second or third definitions are sometimes called start pages.

Trinity wants you to start your research by examining the Midland Pet Adoption Agency's Web site. She has provided the URL for the home page.

To load the Midland Pet Adoption Agency's home page:

1. Click in the **Location bar** to select the current URL, and then type **www.midlandpet.com**. This is the URL for the Midland Pet Adoption Agency Web site.

   Trouble? The Location bar might display a list of suggested URLs as you type; ignore these suggestions and continue typing.

2. Press the **Enter** key. The home page of the Midland Pet Adoption Agency Web site loads, as shown in Figure 1-18.

| **Figure 1-18** | **Midland Pet Adoption Agency Web page** |

URL

graphic image

hyperlinks are underlined and a different color

Courtesy of The Mozilla Foundation; © Cengage Learning

PROSKILLS

Written Communication: The Importance of Organization in a Web Site

Web sites are written communications media just as printed brochures and newsletters are. When visiting a Web site, you can learn a great deal about how to create a Web site for your organization, just as you can learn to design brochures by reading brochures produced by other organizations. The writing that appears on a Web site's pages must be organized to reflect the organization's communication goals for the site. For example, the Midland Pet Adoption Agency's main page includes links to information that it believes Web site visitors will be seeking, such as:

- Pets available for adoption (including their name and pictures)
- Training programs offered
- The agency's emergency clinic
- Directions to the agency and contact information

The Midland Pet Adoption Agency's Web site is organized so that each of these information sets appears on its own Web page. The links are organized on the home page in order of importance, from left to right. For example, the first link next to the Home page link is the Pets link, which opens a page of information about pets available for adoption. This is the agency's primary mission and is the most important set of information it wants to convey to site visitors.

Another important point in organizing the Web site is that the navigation tools (in this case, the links) should appear in the same place and in the same form on every page. This consistent structure reinforces the site visitors' knowledge that the site is well organized and tells them that they are still on the same Web site. For example, the Home page link appears in the upper-left corner of all the site's pages, providing the visitors a consistent means to return to the site's main page. The use of common color combinations and consistent headers and graphics (for example, the use of the same two graphics at the top of each page, along with the reminder to "Take me home today!") reinforces the primary message of the Web site, which is to encourage visitors to stop by and adopt a pet, and conveys a sense of urgency regarding doing so.

Good written communications are clearly organized around a theme that conveys the message while guiding readers to the most important information in a direct way. You can accomplish this in a Web site by understanding what your site's visitors will be looking for and structuring your site to organize that information and make it easy to find.

Clicking Links

Most Web pages include links to other Web pages. A link might open a Web page that is related to the original Web page, such as the Pets link on the home page, which opens a page listing pets available from the Midland Pet Adoption Agency. A link could also be a link to a company, such as the Course Technology link at the bottom of the home page. Other times, a link could open a Web page with related information or an advertised product or service. The easiest way to move from one Web page to another is to click a link in the open Web page. You'll use links to open the Training Programs and Pets Web pages.

To use links to navigate the Midland Pet Adoption Agency Web site:

1. On the Midland Pet Adoption Agency home page, point to the **Training Programs** link, as shown in Figure 1-19. The pointer changes to the shape of a hand with a pointing index finger, and a ScreenTip listing the URL to which the link points appears in the lower-left corner of the browser window.

Figure 1-19   **Using a hyperlink**

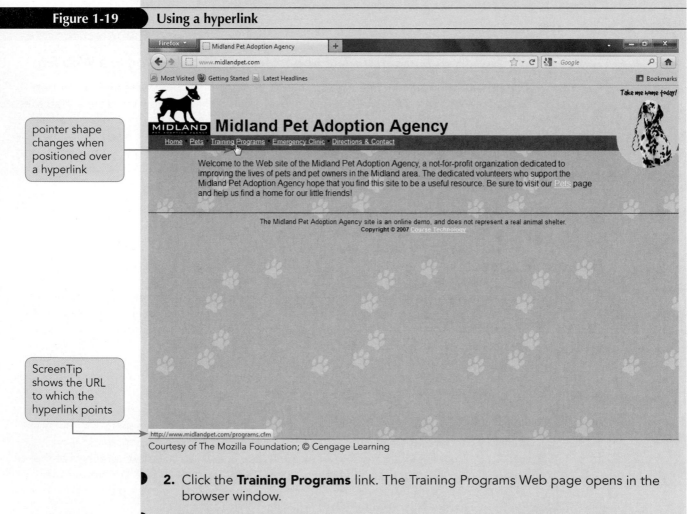

pointer shape changes when positioned over a hyperlink

ScreenTip shows the URL to which the hyperlink points

http://www.midlandpet.com/programs.cfm

Courtesy of The Mozilla Foundation; © Cengage Learning

2. Click the **Training Programs** link. The Training Programs Web page opens in the browser window.

3. On the Training Programs Web page, click the **Pets** link. The Pets page opens in the browser window.

4. On the Pets Web page, click the **Meet Maxie** link. The Web page with information about the cat named Maxie opens in the browser window.

Moving Among Visited Web Pages

The Go back one page and Go forward one page buttons on the Navigation bar let you navigate among the pages you have just visited. After you visit more than one Web page, the arrow in the Go back one page button changes to black, indicating that the button is active and available. Clicking the Go back one page button returns the browser to the previous Web page you visited. You can continue clicking the Go back one page button until you reach the first page you viewed when you started Firefox. Once you click the Go back one page button, the arrow in the Go forward one page button changes to black, and you can click the Go forward one page button to return to later pages you have visited. You can also right-click either button to display a list of the Web pages you have visited during the session and click a specific name to return to that page.

As you move among the pages you visited, you might want to reload, or refresh, a Web page you return to. The Reload current page button on the Navigation toolbar loads a new copy of the Web page that currently appears in the browser window. Firefox stores a copy of every Web page it displays on your computer's hard drive in a Temporary Internet Files folder in the Windows folder. Storing this information increases the speed at which Firefox can display pages as you move back and forth through the Web pages you have visited because the browser can load the pages from a local disk drive instead of reloading them from the remote Web server. When you click the Reload current page button, Firefox contacts the Web server to see if the Web page has changed since it was stored in the Temporary Internet Files folder. If it has changed, Firefox gets the new page from the Web server; otherwise, it loads the copy stored on your computer.

You'll use the Go back one page, Go forward one page, and Reload current page buttons to navigate among the Web pages you visited on the Midland Pet Adoption Agency Web site.

To navigate among visited pages on the Midland Pet Adoption Agency Web site:

1. Right-click the **Go back one page** button on the Navigation toolbar. A shortcut menu listing the pages you visited so far appears, as shown in Figure 1-20. The current page is in bold type. Clicking the button displays the previous page—in this case, the Pets page. Or you can click any page name on the shortcut menu to return directly to that page.

Figure 1-20	Navigating among pages

click to return to a more recently viewed page

click to load a new copy of the current page

click to display the previous page in the browser; right-click to open a list of recently viewed pages; click a name to return to that page

Midland Pet Adoption Agency
Pets -- Midland Pet Adoption Agency
Training -- Midland Pet Adoption Agency
Midland Pet Adoption Agency
Mozilla Firefox Start Page

Courtesy of The Mozilla Foundation; © Cengage Learning

2. Click **Training -- Midland Pet Adoption Agency** to return to the Training Programs page.

3. Click the **Go back one page** button to return to the home page.

4. Click the **Go forward one page** button on the Navigation toolbar. The Training Programs page is redisplayed.

5. Right-click the **Go forward one page** button, and then click **Pets -- Midland Pet Adoption Agency** to return to the Pets page.

6. Click the **Reload current page** button on the Location bar to load a new copy of the Pets page. Because the content on the page hasn't been updated, you won't see any differences on the reloaded page.

Returning to Firefox's Home Page

When you click the Home button on the Navigation toolbar, the browser displays the home (or start) page for your installation of Firefox. You can select one or more pages to display as the default home page. If you select multiple pages, each page opens in a separate tab when you click the Home button. You can set the page or pages you want to use as the default home page in the Options dialog box, which you open by clicking the Firefox button, and then clicking Options.

REFERENCE

Changing the Default Home Page in Firefox

- Click the Firefox button, click Options to open the Options dialog box, and then if necessary click the General icon in the Options dialog box.
- To use the current page, use a bookmarked page, or use the default Mozilla Firefox start page, click the corresponding button in the Startup section. If you have more than one tab open, the Use Current Pages button saves all the open pages as your start page.
- To specify a home page, type the URL of that Web page in the Home Page box. To open multiple home pages on separate tabs, type the URL for each home page separated by commas in the Home Page box.
- Click the OK button.

You will use the Home button to return to your browser's home page, and then you will view the home page settings.

To view the settings for your browser's home page:

1. Click the **Home** button on the Navigation toolbar. The home page for your browser appears in the browser window. This is the same page that opened when you started your browser at the beginning of this session.

2. Click the **Firefox** button, and then click **Options**. The Options dialog box opens.

3. If necessary, click the **General** icon to display the General panel with options for specifying your home page. See Figure 1-21.

TIP

Many organizations set the home page defaults on all of their computers and then lock those settings.

Figure 1-21	Options dialog box

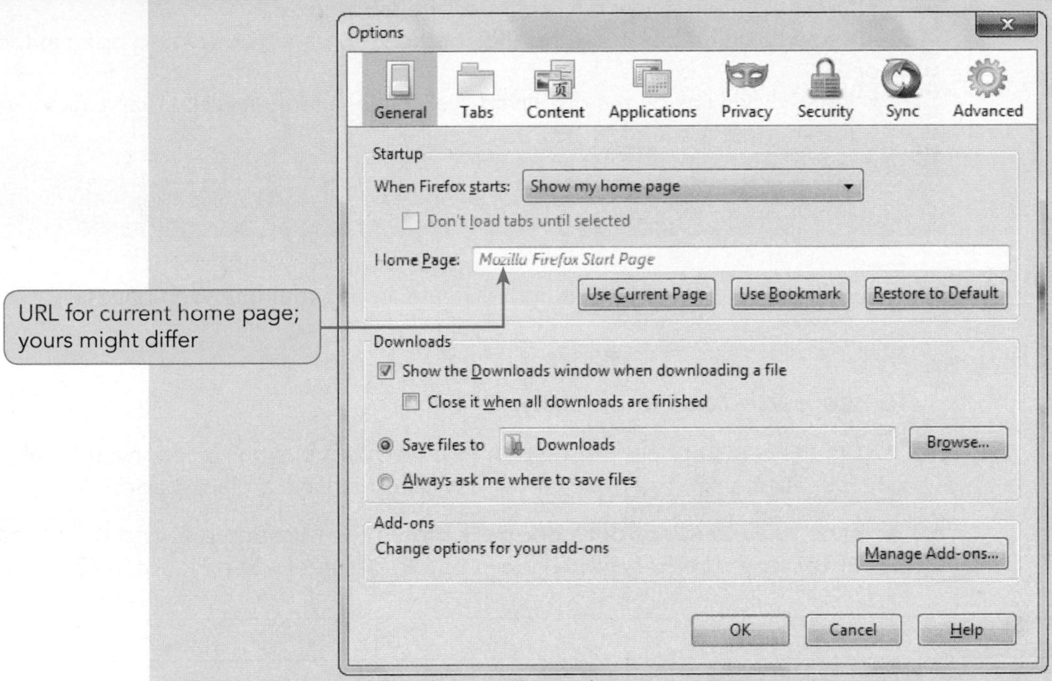

URL for current home page; yours might differ

Courtesy of The Mozilla Foundation

To use the currently loaded Web page as your home page, you would click the Use Current Page button. To use one of your bookmarks as your home page, you would click the Use Bookmark button. To use the default home page that was installed with Firefox, you would click the Restore to Default button. If you want to specify a home page other than the current, bookmarked, or default page, you would type the URL for that page in the Home Page box.

4. Click the **Cancel** button to close the dialog box without making any changes.

Using the Page Tabs

So far, all the Web pages you have visited have been displayed on the same tab. You can open additional page tabs on the tab strip next to the Firefox button, and load different Web pages on each tab instead of opening additional Web pages in separate browser windows. This tabbed browsing technique is especially useful when you need to open many pages or move frequently back and forth among multiple Web pages.

There are several methods for opening a Web page in a new tab. You can click the Open a new tab button on the tab strip, and then open a Web page as usual. You can right-click a link on a Web page, and then click Open Link in New Tab on the shortcut menu. Or, you can press the Ctrl key as you click a link. To close a tab, you click the Close Tab button on that page tab. If you have only one tab open, you must exit Firefox to close that tab. Conversely, if you try to exit Firefox when you have more than one tab open, a dialog box opens, confirming that you want to close all of the open tabs.

REFERENCE

Opening Web Pages in Tabs

- Click the Open a new tab button on the tab strip.
- In the Location bar, enter the URL for the Web page you want to open in the new tab.

or

- Right-click a link on the displayed Web page, and then click Open Link in New Tab on the shortcut menu.

or

- Press the Ctrl key as you click a link on the displayed Web page.

You'll use page tabs to open and navigate among multiple Web pages.

To use page tabs in Firefox:

1. On the tab strip, click the **Open in a new tab** button. A second tab, labeled New Tab, appears in the browser window and displays a blank page.

2. Type **www.midlandpet.com/pets.cfm** in the Location bar, and then press the **Enter key**. The Pets page opens on the page tab. See Figure 1-22.

Figure 1-22 New tab open

Courtesy of The Mozilla Foundation; © Cengage Learning

3. On the Pets page, right-click the **Home** link, and then click **Open Link in New Tab** on the shortcut menu. A third tab appears on the tab row labeled "Midland Pet Adoption Agency." To display this page in the browser window, you need to click the new tab.

4. Click the **Midland Pet Adoption Agency** tab on the tab strip. The home page is displayed in the browser window.

5. Press and hold the **Ctrl** key, click the **Training Programs** link, and then release the Ctrl key. The Training -- Midland Pet Adoption Agency page opens in a new tab.

6. Press and hold the **Ctrl** key, click the **Emergency Clinic** link, and then release the Ctrl key. The Clinic -- Midland Pet Adoption Agency page opens in a new tab.

7. Click the **Training -- Midland Pet Adoption Agency** tab. The tab for the training programs is displayed, as shown in Figure 1-23. The page tabs become smaller as you open additional tabs, and the text identifying the Web pages displayed on the tab becomes truncated.

TIP

To see the entire title of a Web page in a ScreenTip, point to its page tab.

Figure 1-23	Firefox with five tabs open

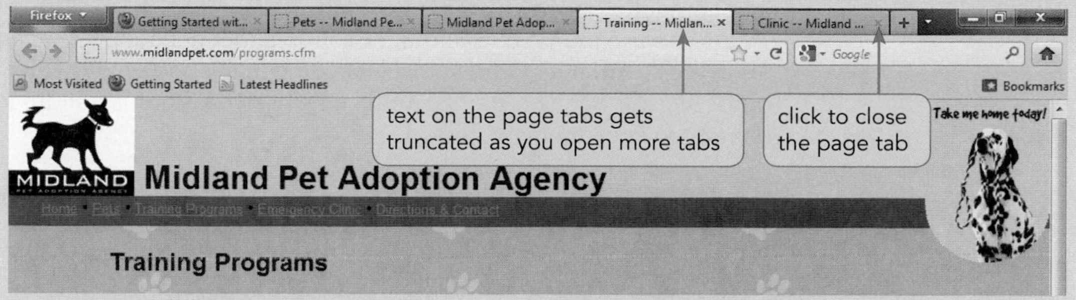

Courtesy of The Mozilla Foundation; © Cengage Learning

8. Point to the **Pets -- Midland Pet Adoption Agency** tab, and then click the **Close Tab** button. The tab closes.

9. On the Clinic -- Midland Pet Adoption Agency tab, click the **Close Tab** button. The tab closes.

10. On the Training -- Midland Pet Adoption Agency tab, click the **Close Tab** button.

11. Click the **Close Tab** button on the tab for your browser's home page. The Midland Pet Adoption Agency home page reappears in the browser window on the only open tab.

You like the format of the Midland Pet Adoption Agency's home page, so you want to make sure that you can go back to that page later if you need to review its contents. You can write down the URL so you can refer to it later, but Firefox makes it easier to return to previously visited Web pages using the Library.

Using the Library

The Library includes tools for managing and organizing a list of Web pages that you have visited so you can return to them easily. You open the Library by clicking the Bookmarks button on the Bookmarks toolbar or Navigation toolbar, and then clicking Show All Bookmarks; or by clicking the Firefox button, pointing to Bookmarks, and then clicking Show All Bookmarks. The Library tracks three items: History, Tags, and Bookmarks. A **bookmark** is a stored shortcut containing the URL of a Web page. A **tag** is a label or keyword you create to help you identify your bookmarks. History records your browsing activity by organizing and storing the URLs of the Web sites you have visited sorted in a variety of ways, including by date, name, visit count, location, and keyword.

Creating and Organizing Bookmarks

As you use the Web to find information, you can create bookmarks so you can easily return to sites of interest. To create a bookmark, you navigate to the page you want to bookmark, and then you click the Bookmark this page button on the Location bar. You might very quickly find yourself creating so many bookmarks that it is difficult to find a specific bookmark. When you start accumulating bookmarks, it is helpful to keep them organized so that you can quickly locate the site you need.

In the Library, you can add, delete, and organize bookmarks into folders that best suit your needs and working style. You can also create descriptive labels, called tags, and assign them to your bookmarks to help organize your bookmarks into categories. A bookmark can have more than one tag, and you can view the bookmarks associated with each tag in the Library. You can also add bookmarks that you want to access very frequently as buttons on the Bookmarks toolbar, which appears below the Navigation toolbar. Keep in mind that the bookmarks and folders you create are available only on the computer on which you are working.

As you use the Web to find information about pet adoption agencies and other sites of interest, you might find yourself creating many bookmarks so you can return easily to these sites. When you start accumulating bookmarks, it is helpful to create folders in the Library to keep them organized.

REFERENCE

Creating a Bookmark

- Open the Web page you want to save as a bookmark.
- Click the Bookmark this page button on the Location bar to bookmark the page.
- Click the Edit this bookmark button on the Location bar to open the Edit This Bookmark window.
- Click the Show all the bookmarks folders button to expand the Edit This Bookmark window.
- Click the Folder button, and then click Bookmarks Toolbar to add the bookmark as a button on the Bookmarks toolbar, or click a folder in which you want to store the bookmark in the Library.
- If you want to store the bookmark in a new folder, click the New Folder button, type a name for the new folder, and then press the Enter key.
- Click in the Tags box, and then type labels that are separated by commas.
- Click the Done button.

You will save the URL for the Midland Pet Adoption Agency Web page as a bookmark, and then create a Pet Adoption Agencies folder in which to store this favorite.

To create a bookmark and folder to store a link to the agency's home page:

1. With the Midland Pet Adoption Agency home page open, click the **Bookmark this page** button on the Location bar. The Bookmark this page button changes from gray to orange, indicating a bookmark for this page has been created in the Library, and the button becomes the Edit this bookmark button.

2. Click the **Edit this bookmark** button on the Location bar. The Edit This Bookmark window, as shown in Figure 1-24, opens with options for removing the bookmark, changing the bookmark name, changing the folder in which the bookmark is stored, and adding tags to the bookmark.

Figure 1-24	Edit This Bookmark window

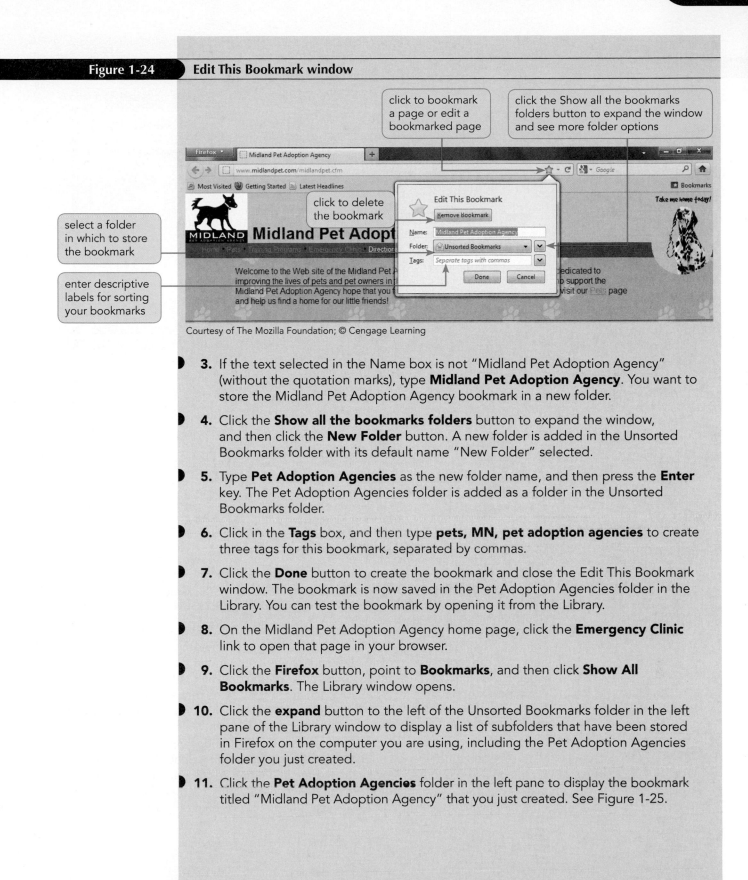

Courtesy of The Mozilla Foundation; © Cengage Learning

3. If the text selected in the Name box is not "Midland Pet Adoption Agency" (without the quotation marks), type **Midland Pet Adoption Agency**. You want to store the Midland Pet Adoption Agency bookmark in a new folder.

4. Click the **Show all the bookmarks folders** button to expand the window, and then click the **New Folder** button. A new folder is added in the Unsorted Bookmarks folder with its default name "New Folder" selected.

5. Type **Pet Adoption Agencies** as the new folder name, and then press the **Enter** key. The Pet Adoption Agencies folder is added as a folder in the Unsorted Bookmarks folder.

6. Click in the **Tags** box, and then type **pets, MN, pet adoption agencies** to create three tags for this bookmark, separated by commas.

7. Click the **Done** button to create the bookmark and close the Edit This Bookmark window. The bookmark is now saved in the Pet Adoption Agencies folder in the Library. You can test the bookmark by opening it from the Library.

8. On the Midland Pet Adoption Agency home page, click the **Emergency Clinic** link to open that page in your browser.

9. Click the **Firefox** button, point to **Bookmarks**, and then click **Show All Bookmarks**. The Library window opens.

10. Click the **expand** button to the left of the Unsorted Bookmarks folder in the left pane of the Library window to display a list of subfolders that have been stored in Firefox on the computer you are using, including the Pet Adoption Agencies folder you just created.

11. Click the **Pet Adoption Agencies** folder in the left pane to display the bookmark titled "Midland Pet Adoption Agency" that you just created. See Figure 1-25.

Figure 1-25   **Library window**

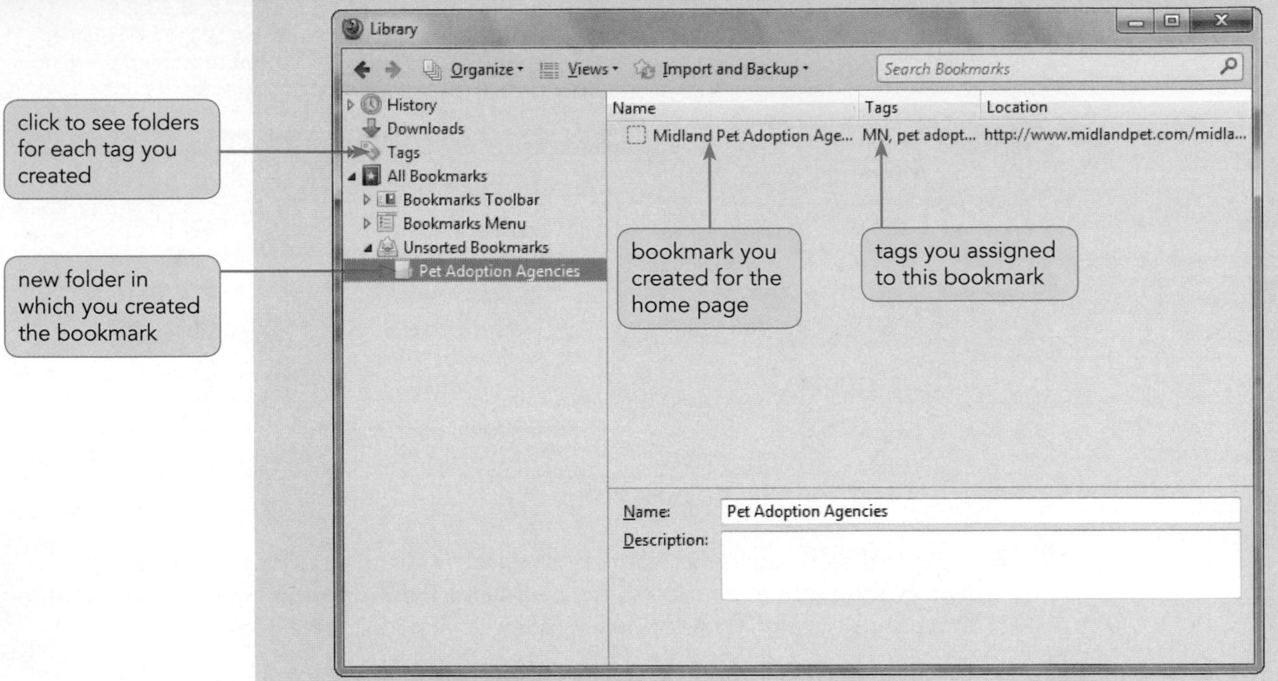

click to see folders for each tag you created

new folder in which you created the bookmark

bookmark you created for the home page

tags you assigned to this bookmark

Courtesy of The Mozilla Foundation

12. Click **Tags** in the left pane to display the tags saved on your computer, including the three tags you just created: MN, pet adoption agencies, and pets. Notice that the tags are in alphabetical order.

13. Double-click the **MN** tag folder in the right pane to display the bookmark you created for the Midland Pet Adoption Agency home page.

14. Click the **pet adoption agencies** tag in the left pane to see that the bookmark also appears in that tag folder. As you see, one bookmark can appear in multiple tag folders, enabling you to sort and access your bookmarks in a wide variety of ways.

In the previous set of steps, you created a bookmark and a folder in which to store it. You can also create folders and move existing bookmarks into these folders in the Library. You can reorganize the favorites and folders stored in the Library at any point by creating new folders and rearranging bookmarks and folders within folders.

You saved the Midland Pet Adoption Agency's URL as a bookmark, which you stored in a new folder named Pet Adoption Agencies in the Library. Because Trinity might want you to collect information about adoption agencies in different states as you conduct your research, you will organize the information about adoption agencies by state. The Midland Pet Adoption Agency is located in Minnesota, so you will put information about the Midland Pet Adoption Agency in a separate folder named MN (the two-letter abbreviation for Minnesota) within the Pet Adoption Agencies folder. As you collect information about other agencies, you will add folders for the states in which they are located, too.

To move the Midland Pet Adoption Agency bookmark into a new folder:

1. In the left pane of the Library, right-click the **Pet Adoption Agencies** folder, and then click **New Folder** on the shortcut menu. The New Folder dialog box opens, with the default name "New Folder" selected in the Name box.

2. Type **MN** in the Name box, and then click the **Add** button. The MN folder appears in the right pane of the Library, as shown in Figure 1-26. Now that you have created a folder, you can move your bookmark for the Midland Pet Adoption Agency Web page into the new folder.

| Figure 1-26 | New folder created for bookmarks |

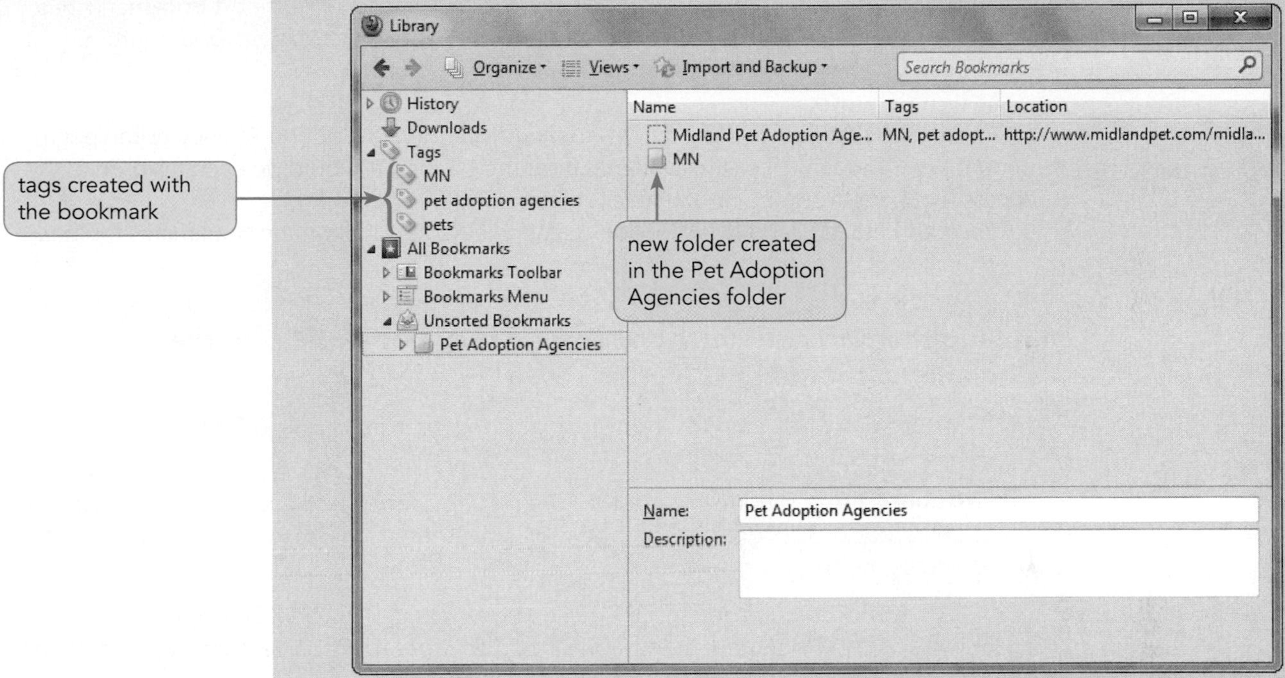

tags created with the bookmark

new folder created in the Pet Adoption Agencies folder

Courtesy of The Mozilla Foundation

3. Click and drag the **Midland Pet Adoption Agency** bookmark in the right pane down to the new MN folder, and then release the mouse button. The Midland Pet Adoption Agency bookmark moves into the MN folder.

4. Click the **Close** button on the Library window title bar to close the Library.

5. Click the **Bookmarks** button on the Bookmarks toolbar, point to **Recently Bookmarked** to see a list of recent bookmarks created on your computer, and then click **Midland Pet Adoption Agency**. The home page opens in the browser window.

INSIGHT

Saving Bookmarks

Once you have a collection of bookmarks, you might want to use them on other computers in different locations. Firefox lets you save your bookmark file to a portable storage device or network disk drive so you can do this. When you save Firefox bookmarks to a device or drive, all of the bookmarks are saved. You cannot save just one bookmark or only selected bookmarks. To save your bookmarks, click the Import and Backup button on the Library window toolbar, and then click Export Bookmarks to HTML to open the Export Bookmarks File dialog box. Navigate to the location where you want to save the bookmark file, type a name for the bookmark file in the File name box, and then click the Save button. To open the bookmark file from your portable storage device on another computer, open the Firefox Library window, click the Import and Backup button on the toolbar, click Import Bookmarks from HTML to open the Import Bookmarks File dialog box, locate and select your bookmarks file, and then click the Open button.

You realize that you will need to go to the Midland Pet Adoption Agency home page frequently. Although it's easily available from the Library, it would be even faster to access that page from the Bookmarks toolbar.

You'll add the Midland Pet Adoption Agency's URL as a link on the Bookmarks toolbar.

To add the Midland Pet Adoption Agency home page to the Bookmarks toolbar:

1. Click the **Edit this bookmark** button on the Location bar. The Edit This Bookmark window opens.

   Trouble? If the Bookmarks toolbar doesn't appear on your screen, right-click the blank area to the right of the page tabs, and then click Bookmarks Toolbar on the shortcut menu.

2. Click the **Folder** button, and then click **Bookmarks Toolbar**. The bookmark moves to the Bookmarks toolbar as a button labeled with the Web page's title, as shown in Figure 1-27.

Figure 1-27   Bookmark added to the Bookmarks toolbar

new bookmark on the Bookmarks toolbar

select to store the bookmark on the Bookmarks toolbar

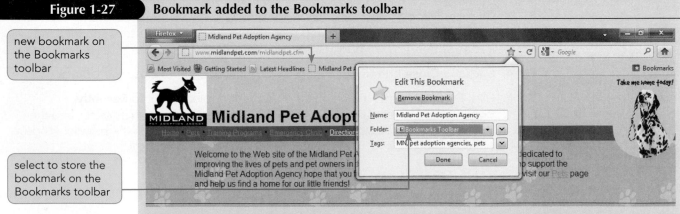

Courtesy of The Mozilla Foundation; © Cengage Learning

3. Click the **Done** button.

4. Click the **Go back one page** button on the Navigation toolbar to return to the Emergency Clinic page.

5. Point to the **Midland Pet Adoption Agency** button on the Bookmarks toolbar. A ScreenTip displays the full title of the Web page and its URL.

6. Click the **Midland Pet Adoption Agency** button on the Bookmarks toolbar. The Midland Pet Adoption Agency home page opens in the browser.

Deleting Bookmarks and Folders from the Library

Creating bookmarks is a great way to keep track of sites you know you want to visit on a regular basis. However, sometimes you no longer want to visit a site, such as when you saved favorites related to a specific project. Other times, the URL for a site has changed or the site no longer exists. In all these instances, you'll want to delete the bookmarks and the folders in which they are stored. You can delete a specific bookmark, or you can delete a folder in the Library. When you delete a folder, the folder and all of its contents are moved to the Recycle Bin.

To delete the bookmark and folders you created:

TIP

You can also right-click a button on the Bookmarks toolbar, and then click Delete on the shortcut menu to remove the bookmark.

1. Click the **Edit this bookmark** button on the Location bar. The Edit This Bookmark window opens.

2. Click the **Remove Bookmark** button. The bookmark is deleted from Firefox, and the button disappears from the Bookmarks toolbar.

3. Click the **Bookmarks** button on the Bookmarks toolbar, and then click **Unsorted Bookmarks**. The Library window opens with the Unsorted Bookmarks folder selected in the left pane.

4. In the left pane, click **Tags**. As you can see, the three tags were also deleted when you deleted the bookmark.

5. In the left pane, click the **Pet Adoption Agencies** folder. The MN folder appears in the right pane.

6. Right-click the **Pet Adoption Agencies** folder in the left pane, and then click **Delete** on the shortcut menu. The folder and all of its contents are deleted from the Library.

7. Click the **Close** button on the Library window title bar to close the Library.

Navigating Web Pages Using the History List

Creating bookmarks is a great way to keep track of sites you know you want to visit on a regular basis. Another way to return to a site that you have visited recently is with the History list. The History list is useful when you know you visited a site recently, but you did not create a favorite and you cannot recall the URL of the site. You can see your recent browsing history by clicking the Firefox button, and then pointing to History to display a list of the last 15 Web pages that you visited on the History menu. You can see your complete History list by clicking the Firefox button and then clicking History to open the History list in the Library. From the History list, you can view a list of the sites that were visited on that computer during the last six months. You can display the history of visited sites organized by date, by site, by sites most visited, or by alphabetical order. You can also use the Search History box to search the History list for a specific site. To return to a specific Web page, just click its link in the History list.

Not every site that you visit as you research pet adoption sites for the Danville Animal Shelter will warrant being saved as a bookmark. The History list will be helpful if you want to show Trinity the breadth of sites you visited during your research. You will view the History list next.

To view the History list for this session:

1. Click the **Firefox** button, and then point to **History**. A list of the last 15 Web pages you viewed appears on the History menu.

TIP

If you are using a computer in a computer lab or a public computer, the History list will include sites visited by anyone who has used the computer, not just you.

2. Click **Show All History**. The Library window opens with History selected in the left pane. The right pane displays folders that contain the browsing history organized by date, with the most recent folder first. Usually, the folders will include Today, Yesterday, Last 7 days, and a list of the most recent five months followed by an Older than 6 months folder. You can change the way pages are organized in the History list by clicking the Views button on the Library window toolbar, pointing to Sort, and then clicking an option. For example, you can list the pages alphabetically by Web page title or by location (which groups all Web pages by the Web server from which they originated).

3. Double-click the **Today** folder in the right pane to open a list of Web sites visited most recently today in the order in which they were visited, including the Midland Pet Adoption Agency Web pages you visited in this session. Notice the home page for the site appears in the list more than once because you navigated back to that page from the other pages on the site. To return to a particular page, click that page's entry in the list.

4. Click **Midland Pet Adoption Agency**. The Web page's name, location, and tag information appear at the bottom of the Library window. See Figure 1-28.

Figure 1-28   **History list in the Library**

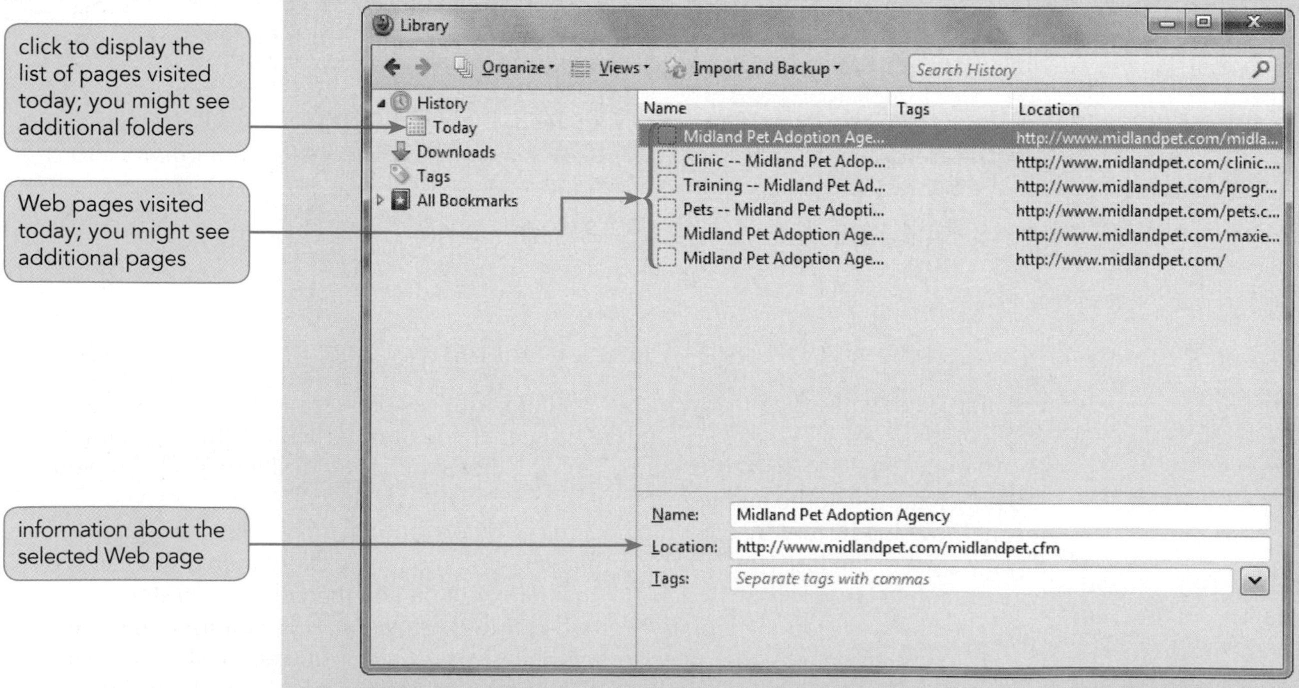

click to display the list of pages visited today; you might see additional folders

Web pages visited today; you might see additional pages

information about the selected Web page

Courtesy of The Mozilla Foundation

> **5.** Double-click **Training -- Midland Pet Adoption Agency** in the History list. The Training -- Midland Pet Adoption Agency page appears in the browser window, and the Library window is minimized.

> **6.** Point to the **Firefox** program button on the Windows taskbar, and then click the **Library** thumbnail to display the Library window.

> **7.** Click the **Close** button on the Library window title bar to close the Library.

INSIGHT

Erasing Your Browsing History

In some situations, such as when you are finishing a work session in a school computer lab or on any public computer, you might want to remove the list of Web sites that you visited from the History list of the computer on which you had been working. Erasing your browsing history helps protect your personal information and guard your privacy when working on a shared computer. You can delete your browsing history in Firefox by clicking the Firefox button, pointing to History, and then clicking Clear Recent History to open the Clear All History dialog box. You then click the Time range to clear arrow and select either a time range of browsing history to clear or Everything to clear the entire History list. If you select Everything, the dialog box will expand to show a list of items that will be deleted. Make sure the Browsing & Download History is the only check box selected in this list. If any other check boxes are selected, click each of them to clear the selections. After ensuring the Browsing & Download History is the only option checked, click the Clear Now button to erase the entire browsing history stored on the computer.

Managing Cookies

All Web browser users should know about the use of cookies. A **cookie** is a small text file that a Web server saves on the hard drive of the computer that is running the Web browser software. A cookie is used to store information about your visit to a specific Web site, such as your login name and password, which pages you viewed, and your shopping cart information. By storing this information on your computer, the Web server can retrieve the information when you return to that site, enabling it to perform functions such as automatic login, which makes it easier to sign in to Web pages you have visited before. However, the user often is unaware that cookie files are being written to the computer's hard drive.

When the site you are visiting places a cookie on your computer, it is called a **first-party cookie**. However, many cookies are written by companies that sell advertising on Web pages. The advertising elements of the Web page are delivered by the advertisers' Web servers, not the Web server of the site you are visiting. These cookies record which ads have appeared on Web pages you have viewed. Advertisers use these cookies to determine which ads they will deliver the next time you open a Web page. This can be beneficial because it prevents sites from showing you the same ads over and over again. On the other hand, many people believe that this sort of user tracking is an offensive invasion of privacy. Cookies that are placed by companies other than the company whose Web site you are visiting are called **third-party cookies**.

Most Web browsers, including Firefox, allow you to block cookies from your computer or to specify general categories of cookies (such as first-party or third-party) to block. In Firefox, you can specify privacy settings that control the writing of cookie files to your computer's hard drive. You can specify which types of cookies to block or you can block particular types of cookies from specific sites. These options are available on the Privacy panel in the Options dialog box. You will learn more about the different types of cookies, how they work, and how best to deal with them in Tutorial 6.

Firefox stores each cookie in a separate file. You can delete the cookies from your computer at any time or whenever you exit Firefox. To delete all of the cookies stored on your computer, click the Firefox button, click Options to open the Options dialog box, and then click the Privacy icon. You then can click the Show Cookies button to open the Cookies dialog box, and then click the Remove All Cookies button.

Because some cookies benefit users, you might not want to delete all of the cookies on your computer. For example, if you regularly visit a site that requires you to log in, the Web server can store your login information in a cookie on your computer so you do not have to type your user name each time you visit the site. You should always consider carefully whether the advantages of cookies outweigh the disadvantages for you before you delete all of your Firefox cookies.

Trinity wants you to view the cookies in Firefox on your computer.

To view cookies in Firefox:

1. Click the **Firefox** button, and then click **Options** to open the Options dialog box.

2. Click the **Privacy** icon to display the Privacy panel with the options for privacy settings.

3. Click the **Firefox will** button, and then click **Use custom settings for history**. Options appear in the History section. See Figure 1-29.

Figure 1-29 **Options dialog box**

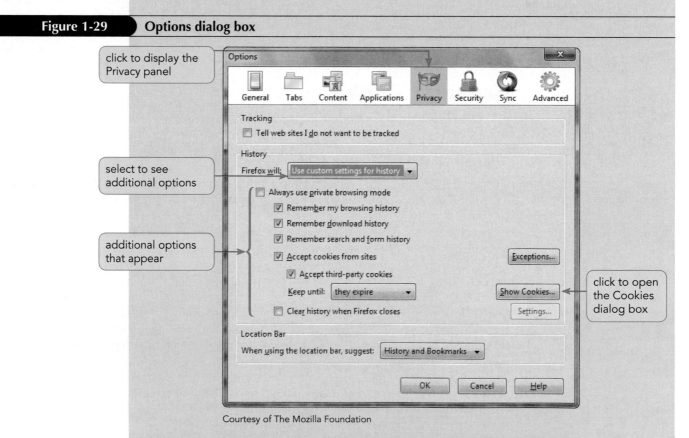

click to display the Privacy panel

select to see additional options

additional options that appear

click to open the Cookies dialog box

Courtesy of The Mozilla Foundation

4. Click the **Show Cookies** button to open the Cookies dialog box.

You will examine the cookies for one of the Web sites that appears in the Cookies dialog box.

5. Click one of the Web site folders listed in the top section of the Cookies dialog box, and then click the arrow icon to the left of the folder.

6. Click one of the cookies placed on your computer by that Web site, and then read the cookie information that is displayed in the bottom panel of the dialog box. An example of a Cookies dialog box with several cookies appears in Figure 1-30. Your list of cookies will be different. Information about the selected cookie appears below the list of cookies.

Figure 1-30   Cookies dialog box

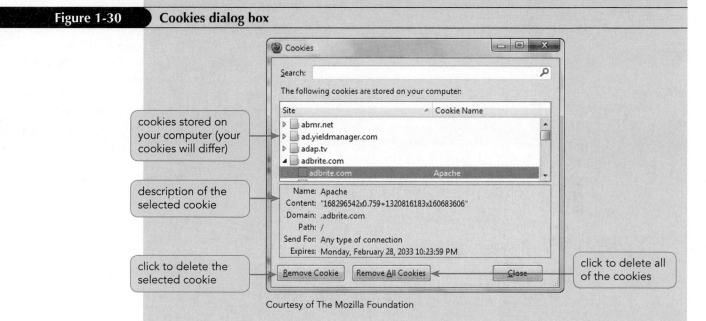

cookies stored on your computer (your cookies will differ)

description of the selected cookie

click to delete the selected cookie

click to delete all of the cookies

Courtesy of The Mozilla Foundation

7. Click the **Close** button to close the Cookies dialog box.

8. Click the **Cancel** button in the Options dialog box to close the Options dialog box without saving any changes.

Private Web Browsing

As you have learned, Firefox stores a considerable amount of information about your Web browsing activity. It stores a list of all the Web pages you have viewed in the History list, and it stores cookies that can contain information about your logins and passwords. It even stores information about which ads have been displayed on the Web pages you have viewed.

Firefox also stores copies of all or part of the Web pages you visit on whatever computer you are using. If you do not wish to have this information stored, you can use Firefox in Private Browsing mode. In **Private Browsing mode**, Firefox does not store your browsing history, cookies, or copies of the Web pages you visit. In other words, there is no record in Firefox of what sites you visited and what you looked at. When you are using a computer other than your own (such as a friend's computer or a computer at work, school, or another public location), Private Browsing mode can help protect your privacy and security.

To start a Private Browsing session, you click the Firefox button, and then click Start Private Browsing. The Private Browsing tab opens and displays a Private Browsing information page to confirm that you are in Private Browsing mode. In addition, the Firefox button changes from orange to purple and remains that way until you end the Private Browsing session. To end a Private Browsing session, you can click the Firefox button and then click Stop Private Browsing to return to the Web page you were viewing before the Private Browsing session, or you can simply close the browser window to exit Firefox.

As you visit Web pages in Private Browsing mode, the history list of the session, cookies from that session, and temporary Internet files will be tracked only during the Private Browsing session. When you end the Private Browsing session, the history list, the cookies, and temporary Internet files are removed from your computer.

Opening a Private Browsing Session

- Click the Firefox button, and then click Start Private Browsing on the menu.
- If the Start Private Browsing dialog box opens, click the Start Private Browsing button.
- Enter a URL in the Location bar to navigate to a Web site, and navigate to other Web pages by clicking links or opening Web pages on other tabs as usual.
- To end a Private Browsing session, click the Firefox button, and then click Stop Private Browsing; or click the Close button on the Firefox title bar to close the browser window and all open tabs.

You will try an InPrivate Browsing session to see how it differs from the Web browsing you have done earlier in this session.

To start a Private Browsing session:

1. Click the **Firefox** button, and then click **Start Private Browsing**. The Start Private Browsing dialog box opens to confirm that you want to switch to Private Browsing mode.

2. Click the **Start Private Browsing** button in the Start Private Browsing dialog box. The Private Browsing page appears in the browser window, and the Firefox button changes to purple. See Figure 1-31.

| Figure 1-31 | Private Browsing mode |

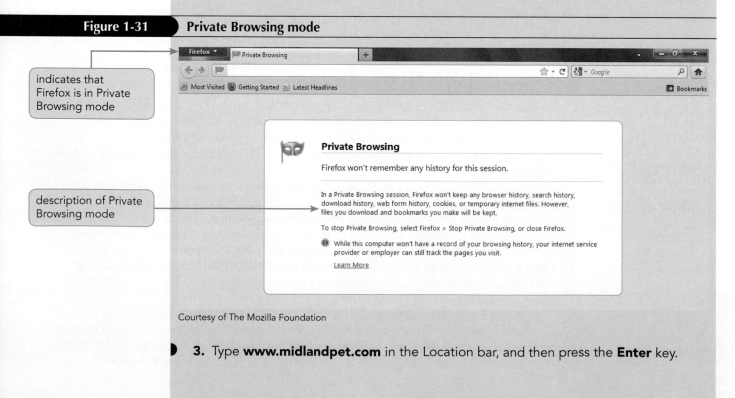

indicates that Firefox is in Private Browsing mode

description of Private Browsing mode

Courtesy of The Mozilla Foundation

3. Type **www.midlandpet.com** in the Location bar, and then press the **Enter** key.

4. Click the **Pets** link on the home page to visit the Pets page, click the **Training Programs** link to visit the Training page, and then click the **Directions & Contact** link to visit the Directions page. Notice that the links don't change color to show that they've been followed.

5. Click the **Firefox** button, and then click **Stop Private Browsing** to end the Private Browsing session. The Firefox button is once again orange, and the Midland Pet Adoption Agency Training page reappears on the only open tab in the browser window.

If you examine the browser's History, you will find that it includes no record of the Web pages you just visited. Although the browser does not record the pages you have visited (or other information, such as cookies), the network server that connects the computer to the Internet might have software that does. Therefore, it is best not to rely on Private Browsing mode to keep private the Web pages you visit while using a computer at work or another public location.

Getting Help in Firefox

Firefox has an online Help system that includes information about how to use the browser, getting started with Firefox, and troubleshooting information. You can also contact volunteers who can help find answers to your specific questions.

REFERENCE

Using Firefox Help

- Click the Firefox button, and then click Help to open the Firefox Support Home Page in a new tab.
- Type a question in the What do you need help with? box, and then click the Search button to display relevant topics or click a link to a Help topic listed on the page.
- Close the browser tab when you are finished.

Trinity wants you to learn more about Private Browsing. You will use Firefox Help to find more information about this feature.

To use Firefox Help:

1. Click the **Firefox** button, point to **Help** to see the different Help options, and then click **Help**. The Firefox Support Home Page opens in a new tab. See Figure 1-32. On this Web page you can enter a search topic in the What do you need help with? box. You also can click the links in the Top Issues section to find out information on current issues Firefox users are having, or you can click a link in the Explore Help Topics section.

Figure 1-32   **Firefox Support Home Page**

type a search term or question here

click a link to display that Help topic

Courtesy of The Mozilla Foundation

2. Under the Privacy & Security heading, click the **Private Browsing** link. The Private Browsing Help page opens with a brief description of Private Browsing and a Table of Contents listing links to related content.

3. Click the **What does Private Browsing not save?** link under the Table of Contents heading, and then read the information on the page that appears.

4. Click other links and read the information provided. When you are finished reading, click the **Close Tab** button on the Private Browsing tab to close this tab and return to the Midland Pet Adoption Agency Training page.

Saving Web Page Content

At times you will want to refer to the information that you have found on a Web page without having to return to the site. In Firefox, you can save entire Web pages, particular graphics, or selected portions of Web page text.

Saving an Entire Web Page

When you save the entire Web page, you use the Save As dialog box, which is similar to the Save As dialog box in other programs. To open the Save As dialog box, click the Firefox button, and then click Save Page As.

Firefox by default saves the complete Web page, including the graphic page elements along with the Web page's text and the HTML markup codes. With the default format—Web Page, complete—Firefox saves each graphic element in its own file stored in a separate folder it creates with the same name as the HTML document. You can select a different format from the Save as type list in the Save As dialog box. The Web Page, HTML only format saves the Web page's text along with the HTML markup codes, but not any of the graphic page elements. When you open that file, the Web page will appear as it was originally formatted, but any graphics will be missing. The Text Files format saves the Web page's text without the HTML markup codes.

When you save to your computer from Firefox, the Downloads window opens to help you keep track of the files. The window shows information about the file, including its name, size, and original location. From the Downloads window, you can open a file or delete the record of that file among other actions.

You will save the Midland Pet Adoption Agency home page to show to Trinity. This Web site will provide Trinity an example of a well-designed site with appropriate text and graphics.

To save the Midland Pet Adoption Agency home page:

▶ **1.** Return to the Midland Pet Adoption Agency home page.

▶ **2.** Click the **Firefox** button, and then click **Save Page As**. The Save As dialog box opens.

▶ **3.** Navigate to and select the **Tutorial.01\Tutorial** folder included with your Data Files. This is the location where you will save the Web page.

   Trouble? If you don't have the starting Data Files, you need to get them before you can proceed. Your instructor will either give you the Data Files or ask you to obtain them from a specified location (such as a network drive). In either case, make a backup copy of the Data Files before you start so that you will have the original files available in case you need to start over. If you have any questions about the Data Files, see your instructor or technical support person for assistance.

▶ **4.** Type **Midland Pet Home Page FF** in the File name box.

▶ **5.** Click the **Save as type** arrow, and then click **Web Page, complete** to select this format, if necessary.

▶ **6.** Click the **Save** button. The Save As dialog box closes. The Web page for the Midland Pet Adoption Agency's home page is saved in the location you specified and appears in the Downloads window.

▶ **7.** Click the **Close** button on the title bar of the Downloads window to close it.

Saving an Image from a Web Page

Most Web pages include graphics or pictures to provide interest, illustrate a point, or present information. You can save a graphic or picture instead of the entire Web page.

REFERENCE

Saving an Image from a Web Page

- Right-click the image on the Web page that you want to save, and then click Save Image As on the shortcut menu to open the Save Image dialog box.
- Navigate to the location in which you want to save the image, and change the default filename, if necessary.
- Click the Save button.

The Directions & Contact Web page also includes a street map that shows the location of the Midland Pet Adoption Agency. You will save this map to show Trinity as well.

To save the street map image:

▶ 1. Click the **Directions & Contact** link to open the Web page that has the address and phone number for the Midland Pet Adoption Agency.

▶ 2. On the Directions & Contact page, scroll the page as needed to display the map.

▶ 3. Right-click the **map**, and then click **Save Image As** on the shortcut menu to open the Save Image dialog box.

▶ 4. Navigate to and select the **Tutorial.01\Tutorial** folder included with your Data Files. This is the location where you will save the map graphic.

▶ 5. Type **Midland Pet Map FF** as the filename, and then click the **Save** button to save the graphic.

▶ 6. Click the **Close** button on the title bar of the Downloads window to close it.

INSIGHT

Understanding Copyright for Web Page Content

A **copyright** is the legal right of the author or other owner of an original work to control the reproduction, distribution, and sale of that work. A copyright comes into existence as soon as the work is placed into a tangible form, such as a printed copy, an electronic file, or a Web page. Copyright laws can place significant restrictions on the way that you can use information or images that you copy from another entity's Web site. Because of the way a Web browser works, it copies the HTML code as well as the graphics and media files to your computer before it can display them in the browser. Just because copies of these files are stored temporarily on your computer does not mean that you have the right to use them in any way other than having your computer display them in the browser window.

The United States and most other countries have copyright laws that govern the use of photocopies, audio or video recordings, and other reproductions of authors' original work. The copyright exists even if the work does not contain a copyright notice. If you do not know whether material that you find on the Web is copyrighted, the safest course of action is to assume that it is.

U.S. copyright law has a **fair use** provision that allows a limited amount of copyrighted information to be used for purposes such as news reporting, research, and scholarship. The source of the material used should always be cited. Commercial use of copyrighted material is much more restricted. You should obtain permission from the copyright holder before using anything you copy from a Web page. The copyright holder can require you to pay a fee for permission to use the material from the Web page. The steps in this tutorial are designed so that your use of copyrighted Web pages and elements of those pages falls within the fair use provisions of U.S. copyright law.

Copying Text from a Web Page

You can also copy and paste portions of a Web page to a file or email. This can be helpful when you want to save specific information from a Web page, such as a schedule of events, directions to a location, or information about a place.

Trinity plans to visit the Midland Pet Adoption Agency while she is traveling in Minnesota next week. She wants to contact Midland's director and schedule a meeting. You can copy and paste the agency's address and telephone number from its Web site into a document or email for Trinity.

To copy and paste text from the Midland Pet Adoption Agency Web site:

▶ **1.** On the Directions & Contact page, select the name, address, and telephone number for Midland Pet Adoption Agency at the top of the page.

▶ **2.** Right-click the selected text, and then click **Copy** on the shortcut menu to copy the selected text to the Clipboard, which is a temporary storage area in Windows.

▶ **3.** Click the **Start** button on the taskbar, point to **All Programs**, click the **Accessories** folder, and then click **WordPad** to start the program and open a new document.

▶ **4.** On the Home tab of the WordPad Ribbon, click the **Paste** button to paste the text into the WordPad document, as shown in Figure 1-33.

| Figure 1-33 | WordPad document with pasted text |

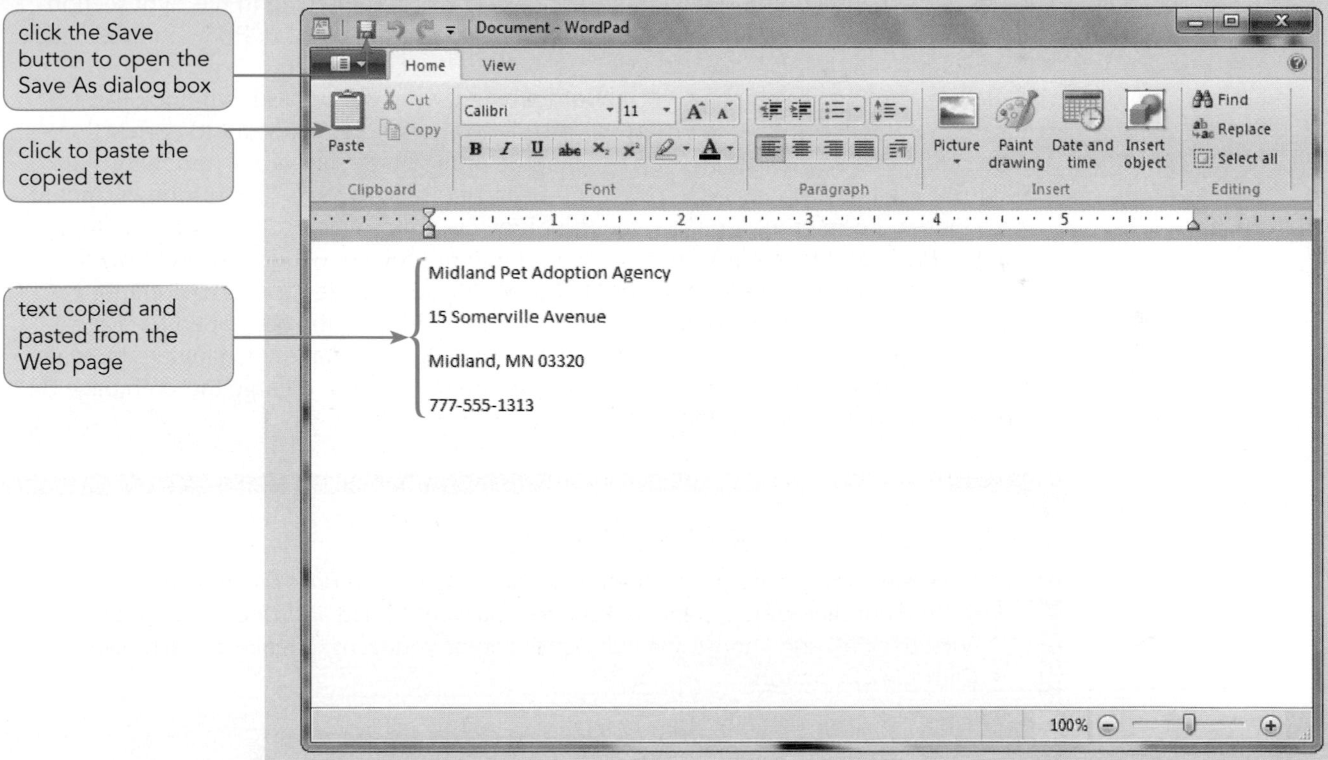

click the Save button to open the Save As dialog box

click to paste the copied text

text copied and pasted from the Web page

Midland Pet Adoption Agency

15 Somerville Avenue

Midland, MN 03320

777-555-1313

Courtesy of © Microsoft

▶ **5.** Click the **Save** button on the WordPad Quick Access Toolbar to open the Save As dialog box.

▶ **6.** Navigate to and select the **Tutorial.01\Tutorial** folder included with your Data Files. This is the location where you will save the WordPad document.

▶ **7.** Click the **Save as type** button, and then click **Rich Text Format (RTF)**.

8. Type **Midland Pet Contact Info FF** in the File name box, and then click the **Save** button. The name, address, and phone number of the agency are now saved in a file for future reference.

9. Click the **Close** button on the WordPad title bar to close it.

Printing a Web Page

TIP

If you encounter a page that is difficult to print, be sure to look on the Web page for a link to a version of the page that is designed to be printed.

Sometimes you will want to print a Web page. This might occur when you want to keep a printed page for reference, save a record or receipt of an online purchase, or have a coupon to use at a local store or restaurant. You access the Print commands by clicking the Firefox button and pointing to Print on the menu to open a submenu of printing options. Clicking Print opens the Print dialog box, which includes options for selecting a printer, setting a page range, and specifying the number of copies to print.

You can also use the Page Setup dialog box to change aspects of a Web page printout, including the page orientation, print size, page background, margins, and headers and footers that print at the top and bottom of the page, respectively. The default header prints the Web page title in the left section, nothing in the center section, and the URL in the right section. The default footer prints the page number and the total number of pages in the left section, nothing in the center section, and the date in the right section. To open the Page Setup dialog box, click the Firefox button, point to Print, and then click Page Setup.

Before printing a Web page, you should preview what the printout will look like to ensure that it will print in the best way possible. For example, you want to ensure that extra or unnecessary pages won't print, that the printed page is legible, and that what will print is what you wanted to print. This extra step helps you to save resources, including paper and printer ink. To open the Print Preview window, click the Firefox button, point to Print, and then click Print Preview. The Print Preview window shows how the current Web page will look on the printed page. It also provides access to common printing options. From the toolbar, you can open the Print dialog box, open the Page Setup dialog box, adjust the scale, and change the page orientation. Changing the scale enables you to shrink the Web page to fit better on the page or enlarge the Web page on the printout so it's more legible.

REFERENCE

Printing the Current Web Page

- Click the Firefox button, and then click Print to open the Print dialog box.
- In the Print dialog box, select the printer you want to use, indicate the pages you want to print, and choose the number of copies you want to make of each page.
- Click the OK button.

You will preview a copy of the Midland Pet Adoption Agency home page, and then print it.

To preview and print the Midland Pet Adoption Agency home page:

▶ **1.** Return to the Midland Pet Adoption Agency home page.

▶ **2.** Click the **Firefox** button, point to **Print**, and then click **Print Preview** on the menu that appears. The Print Preview window opens. See Figure 1-34.

Figure 1-34	Print Preview window

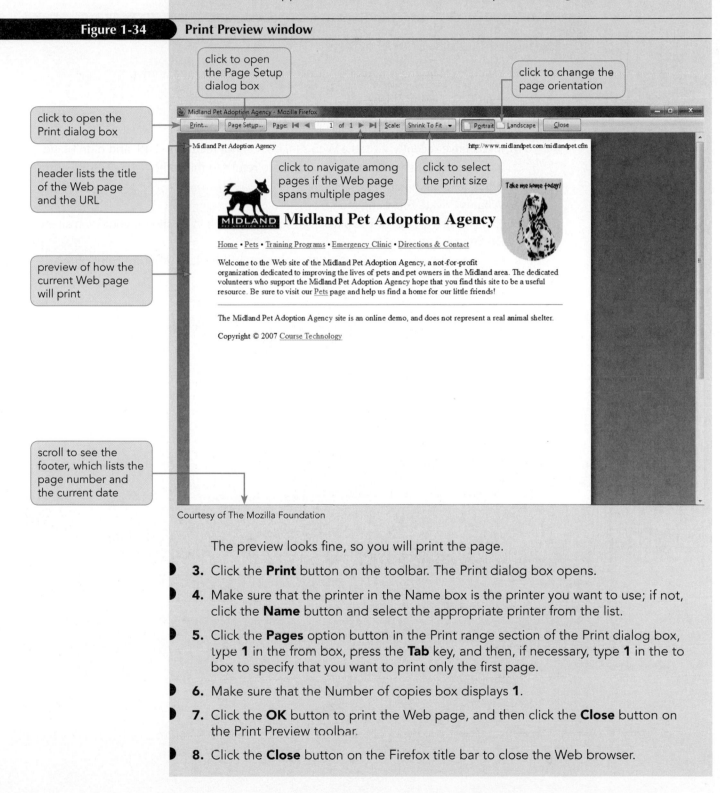

click to open the Page Setup dialog box

click to change the page orientation

click to open the Print dialog box

header lists the title of the Web page and the URL

click to navigate among pages if the Web page spans multiple pages

click to select the print size

preview of how the current Web page will print

scroll to see the footer, which lists the page number and the current date

Courtesy of The Mozilla Foundation

The preview looks fine, so you will print the page.

▶ **3.** Click the **Print** button on the toolbar. The Print dialog box opens.

▶ **4.** Make sure that the printer in the Name box is the printer you want to use; if not, click the **Name** button and select the appropriate printer from the list.

▶ **5.** Click the **Pages** option button in the Print range section of the Print dialog box, type **1** in the from box, press the **Tab** key, and then, if necessary, type **1** in the to box to specify that you want to print only the first page.

▶ **6.** Make sure that the Number of copies box displays **1**.

▶ **7.** Click the **OK** button to print the Web page, and then click the **Close** button on the Print Preview toolbar.

▶ **8.** Click the **Close** button on the Firefox title bar to close the Web browser.

You have copies of the Midland Pet Adoption Agency home page and map that will show Trinity how to get to the agency during her trip to Minnesota. Trinity will be able to use her Web browser or other software to open the files and print them.

In this session, you worked with Firefox as you browsed the Midland Pet Adoption Agency Web site. You navigated among pages, worked with favorites, reviewed the history list, saved and copied Web pages, and printed a Web page from the site.

REVIEW

Session 1.2 Quick Check

1. Briefly explain the difference between a network and the Internet.
2. What is a hypertext link?
3. What is a URL?
4. What is a bookmark?
5. If you have recently visited a Web site, but cannot recall the URL and didn't save it as a favorite, what feature can you use to return to that site?
6. Briefly explain what a cookie is.
7. What is Private Browsing mode?
8. Can you use an image you save from someone else's Web site on your Web site? Explain your answer.
9. Why should you preview what the printout will look like before printing a Web page?

Practice the skills you learned in the tutorial using the same case scenario.

Review Assignments

There are no Data Files needed for the Review Assignments.

Trinity is pleased with the information you gathered so far about the Midland Pet Adoption Agency's Web pages. In fact, she would like you to extend your research to other Web sites. She wants you to examine the Web sites of other charitable organizations that provide animal welfare services to their communities, and choose one site that would be a good example for the Danville Animal Shelter to follow as it updates its own Web site. She asks you to compile some information about the site you choose, including some specific files, by completing the following steps, using either Internet Explorer or Firefox:

1. Start your Web browser, and then enter the URL **www.cengagebrain.com** in your browser's Address or Location bar. On the CengageBrain home page that opens, enter the ISBN number for this book in the Search box at the top of the page, and then click the Find button. (*Hint:* The ISBN for your book can be found above the bar code located in the lower-right corner of the back cover of your book. You can use either the ISBN-13 or ISBN-10 number to locate this book on CengageBrain.) On the Web page for this book, click the Access Now button to open the Book Companion page.

2. Click the Weblinks link under the Book Resources heading, click the Download Now link for Tutorial 1, and then click the Review Assignments link.

3. Click one of the links listed under the Review Assignments heading and explore the Web site. These Web sites belong to organizations that have goals and activities similar to those of the Danville Animal Shelter. The list includes more links than you will need; however, Web sites can change their URLs and the organizations that created them can even close. If a link you have chosen does not lead you to an active site, or if it leads you to a site that you believe is not relevant to this assignment, simply click another link. Explore at least three more Web sites, opening each site on a separate page tab.

4. Choose one of the four sites that you think is well organized and has complete information presented concisely. Save a copy of the home page of your chosen Web site with the filename **Pet Home Page** to the Tutorial.01\Review folder included with your Data Files in the HTML only format.

5. Create a favorite (if you are using Internet Explorer) or a bookmark (if you are using Firefox) for the Web page of your chosen site, and accept the default name for the favorite or bookmark. Store it in a new folder in the Favorites Center or Firefox Library named **Pet Home Page**.

6. Using the links on the pages of your chosen site, navigate the site until you find a page that contains the organization's address and contact information (telephone number, email address, or similar information). Preview and print the Web page.

7. Navigate to a page that contains a photograph of a pet, and then save the photograph with the filename **Pet Picture** in the Tutorial.01\Review folder.

8. Navigate to a page that includes a statement about the site's copyright or restrictions on use of its content. (*Hint:* You can search a Web page using either Internet Explorer or Firefox for specific text, such as "copyright" or "content," by pressing the Ctrl + F keys to open the Find bar, typing the search text in the Find box that appears, and then clicking the Next button.) Copy and paste that text into a WordPad document and save it with the filename **Pet Web Site Copyright Page** in the Tutorial.01\Review folder.

9. Use your browser's Help system to find information on how cookies are tracked and managed in the browser. In a brief report to your instructor, summarize the Help information you find. Make sure your report identifies the title of the Help page you found, the definition of a cookie, the steps to view cookies if available, and the steps for deleting cookies.

10. Turn on InPrivate Browsing in Internet Explorer or start Private Browsing in Firefox. Repeat Steps 1 and 2 to access the Weblinks for the Review Assignments, and then click a link to another Web site you have not viewed. Click at least four links to explore the Web site and/or other sites it links to. When you are done, end the private browsing session.

11. View the history list to confirm that the Web pages you explored in the previous steps have not been recorded. Close the Internet Explorer Favorites Center or the Firefox Library when you are done.

12. If you are working in a computer lab or on a public computer, delete the folder and the favorite or bookmark you created in Step 5, and then close your Web browser.

Navigate to Web pages using tabbed browsing, collect favorites or bookmarks, and store them in appropriate folders.

APPLY

Case Problem 1

There are no Data Files needed for this Case Problem.

South High School Evening Program You are the assistant to Angela Dixon, who is the new director of South High School's evening program for adult learners. The program offers lessons for students who are not native speakers of English in its English as a Second Language (ESL) course. It also offers a math refresher course for adults who need help brushing up on their high school math skills as they apply for better jobs or return to college after being out of high school for several years. Angela wants to add books to the school's library that will provide resources for students in these two courses, and she asks you to help her find suitable titles at Amazon.com. Complete the following steps using either Internet Explorer or Firefox:

1. Start your Web browser, and then enter the URL **www.cengagebrain.com** in your browser's Address or Location bar. On the CengageBrain home page that opens, enter the ISBN number for this book in the Search box at the top of the page, and then click the Find button. (*Hint:* The ISBN for your book can be found above the bar code located in the lower-right corner of the back cover of your book. You can use either the ISBN-13 or ISBN-10 number to locate this book on CengageBrain.) On the Web page for this book, click the Access Now button to open the Book Companion page.

2. Click the Weblinks link under the Book Resources heading, click the Download Now link for Tutorial 1, and then click the Case Problem 1 link.

3. Click one of the links under the Case Problem 1 heading to open the home page of a Web site for a bookseller.

4. Click the Search arrow, and then click Books or All Books. In the Search box, type **ESL books**, and then click the Go or Search button to open a list of links to books that could be useful to students in South High's ESL course.

5. Locate an ESL book that you believe would be useful for Angela, and then right-click the book's title and open the book's page on a new tab. Repeat this for two more books.

6. Create a folder titled **ESL Book Recommendations** in the Internet Explorer Favorites Center or in the Firefox Library in which you will store favorites or bookmarks to pages that Angela can examine as she reviews books for the library's collection.

7. Create shortcuts (as favorites if you are using Internet Explorer; as bookmarks if you are using Firefox) for the three books you have found, and place these in the ESL Book Recommendations folder you created in the previous step.

8. In the search box at the top of the page, type **high school math**, and then click the Go button to open a list of links to books that could be useful for students in South High's math refresher course.

9. Locate a math book that you believe would be useful for Angela, and then right-click the book's title to open the book's page on a new tab. Repeat this for two more books.

10. Create a folder titled **Math Book Recommendations** in the Internet Explorer Favorites Center or in the Firefox Library in which you will store favorites or bookmarks to pages that Angela can examine as she reviews books for the library's collection.

11. Create shortcuts (as favorites if you are using Internet Explorer; as bookmarks if you are using Firefox) for the three books you have found, and place these in the Math Book Recommendations folder you created in the previous step.

⊕ **EXPLORE** 12. In the Internet Explorer Favorites Center, expand the two folders you created so the favorites stored within them are displayed; or in the Firefox Library, click one of the two folders you created so the bookmarks stored within them are displayed. Press the Print Screen key to make a copy of the Web page, start WordPad, and then click the Paste button in the Clipboard group on the Home tab. If your instructor requests it, print a copy of the WordPad document.

13. Delete all of the folders and favorites or bookmarks you created in this Case Problem, and then close your Web browser.

Research competitors' Web sites to identify features to include in or omit from a new Web site design.

R E S E A R C H

Case Problem 2

There are no Data Files needed for this Case Problem.

Central Tools Central Tools is a company that sells woodworking tools to hobbyists, carpenters, and cabinetmakers in the South Valley metropolitan area. Most hardware stores sell a variety of hammers, saws, chisels, and other woodworking tools, but Central Tools focuses on the special needs of skilled woodworkers. These tools are of high quality, can be hard to find, and are expensive. Central Tools has developed an excellent reputation over the years throughout South Valley for its tool selection and fair prices. It also brings in famous woodworkers from time to time who conduct seminars on the latest techniques and traditional woodworking skills. Hal Porter, the owner of Central Tools, is thinking about selling tools online and has asked you to gather information about Web sites that would be Central Tools' competition on the Web. Complete the following steps using either Internet Explorer or Firefox:

1. Start your Web browser, and then enter the URL **www.cengagebrain.com** in your browser's Address or Location bar. On the CengageBrain home page that opens, enter the ISBN number for this book in the Search box at the top of the page, and then click the Find button. (*Hint:* The ISBN for your book can be found above the bar code located in the lower-right corner of the back cover of your book. You can use either the ISBN-13 or ISBN-10 number to locate this book on CengageBrain.) On the Web page for this book, click the Access Now button to open the Book Companion page.

2. Click the Weblinks link under the Book Resources heading, click the Download Now link for Tutorial 1, and then click the Case Problem 2 link.

3. Click the links listed under the Case Problem 2 heading and explore the Web sites of Central Tools' potential online competitors. Choose one of the listed sites that you believe would be a good example for Hal to follow as he takes his business online, and then save a copy of the site's home page as **Competitor Home Page** in the Tutorial.01\Case 2 folder included with your Data Files in the HTML only format. Perform the remaining steps for the Web site you have chosen.

4. Create a folder in the Internet Explorer Favorites Center or in the Firefox Library window named **Product Page Examples** in which you will store favorites or bookmarks to pages that Hal can examine.

⊕ **EXPLORE**

5. Navigate the pages of your chosen site to find Web pages that include the following four types of woodworking tools: chisels, clamps, drills, and saws. Pick four pages, one for each type of tool, that you believe would be a good example for Hal. Create favorites in Internet Explorer or bookmarks in Firefox for each page, named **Chisels**, **Clamps**, **Drills**, and **Saws**, respectively. Store the four shortcuts in the folder you created in the preceding step.

⊕ **EXPLORE**

6. Write a report that answers the following specific questions about each Web site you have chosen:

   a. Does the site's home page include contact information or an easy-to-identify link to a page that contains contact information? What contact information is included?

   b. List three things about the site that you would recommend including in the Central Tools Web site.

   c. List three things about the site that you believe Hal should avoid when designing the Central Tools Web site.

   d. Does the site include links to videos about the products for sale?

   e. Does the site include information about how to use the tools or provide ideas for woodworking projects (including plans or drawings) that site visitors could build?

   f. Provide one example of how the Web site provides focus in its presentation.

   g. Provide one example of how the Web site is well organized.

7. Delete the folder and favorites or bookmarks you created in this Case Problem, and then close your Web browser.

Read Web pages to learn more about cookies and the risks they pose, and compare cookies' risks to their benefits.

RESEARCH

Case Problem 3

There are no Data Files needed for this Case Problem.

Nestor Analytics   Nestor Analytics is a financial market research firm in New York City. You have just started an internship working for Sally Nestor, the firm's director. Sally recently read an article that discussed potential security risks posed by Web servers that place cookie files on computers running Web browser software. She is concerned about this issue and asks you to research it for her. Sally explains to you that all employees of Nestor Analytics have laptop computers that they use to work from the office, their homes, and client locations. The firm's research analysts have powerful desktop computers at Nestor headquarters that store sensitive financial information about the firm's clients and details of their confidential trading strategies. All of these computers are connected to the Internet and run Web browser software. Sally is interested in learning more about any possible security issues that might arise from cookie files. She asks you to collect more information for her review by completing the following steps using either Internet Explorer or Firefox:

1. Start your Web browser, and then enter the URL **www.cengagebrain.com** in your browser's Address or Location bar. On the CengageBrain home page that opens, enter the ISBN number for this book in the Search box at the top of the page, and then click the Find button. (*Hint:* The ISBN for your book can be found above the bar code located in the lower-right corner of the back cover of your book. You can use either the ISBN-13 or ISBN-10 number to locate this book on CengageBrain.) On the Web page for this book, click the Access Now button to open the Book Companion page.

2. Click the Weblinks link under the Book Resources heading, click the Download Now link for Tutorial 1, and then click the Case Problem 3 link.

⊕ **EXPLORE**   3. Click the links listed under the Case Problem 3 heading and explore the Web sites to which they lead. These sites provide information about Web cookies that Sally might find helpful. As you read information on these sites, remember the distinction between first-party cookies and third-party cookies that you learned about in this tutorial.

4. Create favorites or bookmarks to any Web pages that you believe Sally should read in a folder titled **Nestor Analytics Cookie Research**.

5. Create a report to Sally that summarizes what you learned from your research. Make sure your report does the following:

   a. Name and briefly describe two risks that cookie files might pose to Nestor Analytics.

   b. Briefly describe the benefits that Nestor Analytics employees gain by allowing Web servers to write cookies to their computers.

   c. Provide a general assessment of the level of risk posed to Nestor Analytics by cookie files, rating the risk high, medium, or low. Briefly state the reasons for your assessment.

   d. Include the URLs for the Web pages you referenced during your research. (*Hint:* Select the URL in the Address bar or Location bar, and then copy and paste it as usual.)

6. Delete the folder and favorites or bookmarks you created in this Case Problem, and then close your Web browser.

Research and compare the features of the two leading Web browsers.

RESEARCH

Case Problem 4

There are no Data Files needed for this Case Problem.

Briar Lake Assisted Living Center   Nancy Francis is the events coordinator at Briar Lake Assisted Living Center. Recently, the center received a donation of five laptops and Nancy plans to make these available to residents. She knows that many of the residents are either new to computers or haven't used them recently, so she is considering offering small group workshops on basic computer skills. She wants to set these computers up with the necessary software for residents to be able to send and receive email, write letters, and browse the Internet. To help Nancy decide which browser software to install on the computers, you will research and compare the features of the two most prevalent browsers: Internet Explorer and Firefox. Complete the following steps:

1. Start your Web browser, and then enter the URL **www.cengagebrain.com** in your browser's Address or Location bar. On the CengageBrain home page that opens, enter the ISBN number for this book in the Search box at the top of the page, and then click the Find button. (*Hint:* The ISBN for your book can be found above the bar code located in the lower-right corner of the back cover of your book. You can use either the ISBN-13 or ISBN-10 number to locate this book on CengageBrain.) On the Web page for this book, click the Access Now button to open the Book Companion page.

2. Click the Weblinks link under the Book Resources heading, click the Download Now link for Tutorial 1, and then click the Case Problem 4 link.

3. If you completed Session 1.1 of this tutorial using Internet Explorer, then click the Firefox link under the Browsers heading to open the Firefox product page. If you completed Session 1.2 using Firefox, then click the Internet Explorer link under the Browsers heading to open the Internet Explorer product page.

4. Use the link on the browser's product page to familiarize yourself with the features and tools the browser offers. In your research, try to find answers to the following:

   a. How are the tools and commands accessed in the browser?

   b. Can you customize the browser window in any way?

   c. Is there a way to keep track of your browsing activity, and if so, how?

d. Are there any privacy tools, and if so, how easy are they to manage?

e. Is there a search feature?

5. In a report, compare the information you found in Step 4 to your experience and knowledge of the Web browser you used in this tutorial. Be sure to compare and contrast the main features of the browsers. Identify features that might exist in one browser but not the other. If similar features exist in both browsers, assess whether you think one browser is easier or more difficult to use in that way. Conclude your report with a recommendation for Nancy as to which browser you think might work best for the residents at Briar Lake Assisted Living Center.

6. Close your browser.

Identify other Web browsers that are available and describe their features.

RESEARCH

Case Problem 5

There are no Data Files needed for this Case Problem.

West Shore Community Center   Alex Jacoby is the youth coordinator at West Shore Community Center. Children come to the community center to play basketball, swim, learn crafts, and enjoy other activities. They can also use the community center's computer lab to complete school work and get help with assignments. Alex wants to update the Web browsers on the computers, and realizes that he can choose from a variety of browsers. To help Alex decide which browser or browsers to install, you will research and compare the features of two browsers. Complete the following steps:

1. Start your Web browser, and then enter the URL **www.cengagebrain.com** in your browser's Address or Location bar. On the CengageBrain home page that opens, enter the ISBN number for this book in the Search box at the top of the page, and then click the Find button. (*Hint:* The ISBN for your book can be found above the bar code located in the lower-right corner of the back cover of your book. You can use either the ISBN-13 or ISBN-10 number to locate this book on CengageBrain.) On the Web page for this book, click the Access Now button to open the Book Companion page.

2. Click the Weblinks link under the Book Resources heading, click the Download Now link for Tutorial 1, and then click the Case Problem 5 link.

3. Click one of the links under the Case Problem 5 heading to open the product page for a Web browser.

4. Use the links and videos on the browser's product page to familiarize yourself with the features and tools the browser offers. In your research, try to find answers to the following:

a. What features are available in the browser?

b. How are the tools and commands accessed in the browser?

c. Can you customize the browser window in any way?

d. Is there a way to keep track of your browsing activity, and if so, how?

e. Are there any privacy tools, and if so, how easy are they to manage?

f. Is there a search feature?

5. Repeat Steps 3 and 4 for a second browser.

6. In a report, compare and contrast the main features of the two browsers. Identify features that might exist in one browser but not the other. If similar features exist in both browsers, assess whether you think one browser is easier or more difficult to use in that way. Conclude your report with a recommendation for Alex as to which browser you think might work best at West Shore Community Center.

7. Close your browser.

INTERNET

OBJECTIVES

Session 2.1
- Learn how email works
- Understand basic email features and functions
- Learn about viruses, antivirus software, and spam

Session 2.2
- Create a Windows Live Hotmail email account
- Configure and use Windows Live Hotmail to send, receive, and print email messages
- Create and maintain contacts, and use them to address messages
- Explore Windows Live Web-based services

Basic Communication on the Internet: Email

Using Email and Sharing Files

Case | *Kikukawa Air*

Since 2001, Sharon and Don Kikukawa have operated a small hot air balloon service in Albuquerque, New Mexico. At first, Kikukawa Air employed only Sharon, who managed the office, reservations, and the company's financial records, and her husband Don, who served as pilot for the couple's brightly colored hot air balloon. After many successful years in business, Sharon and Don expanded their business to include longer scenic tours of the beautiful New Mexico mountains, special trips that feature meals or several balloons flying larger parties of clients to a specific destination, and participation in hot air balloon festivals and races. As a result of their expansion, Kikukawa Air now has 11 hot air balloons, 14 pilots, and a growing office staff of 10 people who coordinate reservations and accommodations for their clients.

Although most employees already use email to communicate with each other and with clients and vendors, they are not all using the same email provider. In addition, employees are currently having problems sending and receiving messages on their mobile devices while working across the state of New Mexico. Sharon believes that Kikukawa Air could benefit from the company's employees using the same email provider. This will make it easier to manage the accounts and troubleshoot connection problems on the mobile devices, and will streamline the company's operations.

Sharon asks you to investigate a solution for her employees to use Web-based email accounts to exchange email messages, and to share business documents and other files on their computers and mobile devices.

STARTING DATA FILES

Tutorial	Review	Cases	
Timeline.pdf	KAir.gif	Bales.jpg	Paper.jpg
		Chance.jpg	Rocky.jpg
		Maple.jpg	Scout.jpg

SESSION 2.1 VISUAL OVERVIEW

Protocols are the rules that determine how message packets move over the Internet. **SMTP (Simple Mail Transfer Protocol)** handles a user's outgoing mail and determines the paths an outgoing email message takes on the Internet.

mail server

Windows Live™ Hotmail

network

G✉ail

The sender uses an email program on a computer or other device or a Web browser to enter the recipient's email address, compose the email message, attach optional files, and send the message.

The sender's local network sends the message to the sender's mail server.

Messages are sent to a **mail server**, which is a hardware and software system that determines from the recipient's address one of several electronic routes on which to send the message.

HOW EMAIL WORKS

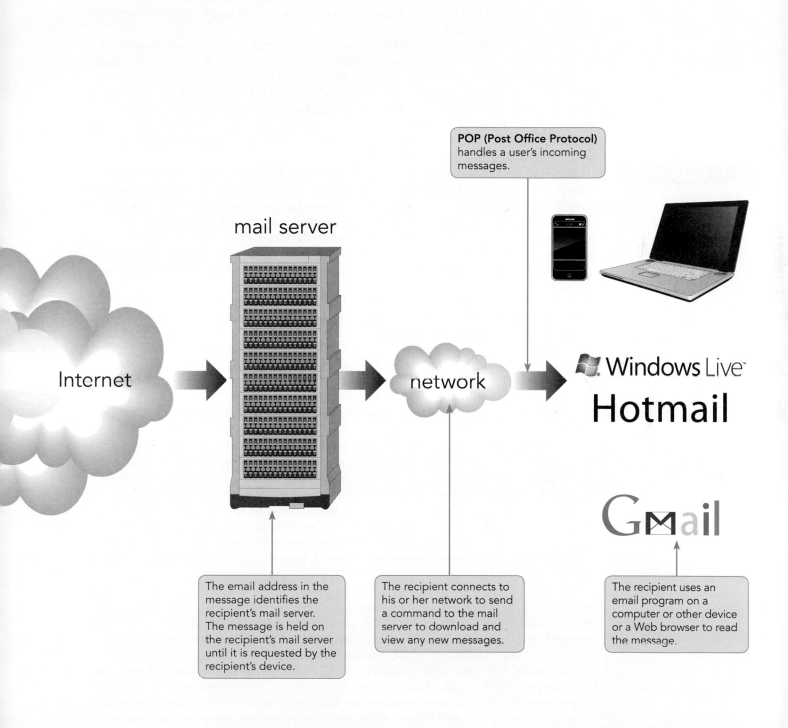

POP (Post Office Protocol) handles a user's incoming messages.

mail server

Internet

network

Windows Live™
Hotmail

G☒ail

The email address in the message identifies the recipient's mail server. The message is held on the recipient's mail server until it is requested by the recipient's device.

The recipient connects to his or her network to send a command to the mail server to download and view any new messages.

The recipient uses an email program on a computer or other device or a Web browser to read the message.

What Is Email and How Does It Work?

Electronic mail, or **email**, is a form of communication in which electronic messages are created and transferred between two or more devices connected to a network. Email is one of the most popular forms of business communication, and for many people it is their primary use of the Internet. As shown in the Visual Overview for Session 2.1, email travels to its destination across the network to the recipient's account on a mail server. For many personal and business reasons, people rely on email as an indispensable form of written communication.

Similar to how Web pages and files move across networks, email messages also use protocols that send and receive them on networks. The two most common protocols for sending and receiving email messages are POP and SMTP, which are both described in the Session 2.1 Visual Overview. Two additional protocols, IMAP and MIME, also handle email messages. **IMAP (Internet Message Access Protocol)** retrieves mail messages from a remote server or messages stored on a large local network. **MIME (Multipurpose Internet Mail Extensions)** specifies how to encode nontext data, such as graphics and sound, so it can travel over the Internet.

When an email message arrives at its destination mail server, the mail server's software handles the details of distributing the message locally, in the same way that a mailroom worker opens a mailbag and places letters and packages into individual mail slots. To check for new email messages, you use a program stored on your Internet device—which might be a computer, cell phone, or other device, such as a tablet—to request the mail server to deliver any stored mail to your device. The software that requests mail delivery from the mail server to an Internet device is known as **mail client software**, or an **email program**.

An **email address** uniquely identifies an individual or organization that is connected to the Internet. To route an email message to an individual, you must identify that person by his or her account name, or **user name**, and also by the name of the mail server that manages email sent to the domain. The two parts of an email address—the user name and the domain name—are separated by an "at" sign (@). Sharon Kikukawa, for example, selected the user name "Sharon" for her email account. Kikukawa Air purchased the domain name "KikukawaAir.com" to use both as its Internet address (URL) and in the email addresses for Kikukawa Air employees. Therefore, Sharon's email address is Sharon@KikukawaAir.com.

A user name usually identifies one person's email account on a mail server. When you are given an email address from an organization, such as your school or an employer, the organization might have standards for assigning user names. Some organizations set standards so user names consist of a person's first initial followed by up to seven characters of the person's last name. Other organizations assign user names that contain a person's first and last names separated by an underscore character (for example, Sharon_Kikukawa). When you are given the opportunity to select your own user name, you might use a nickname or some other name to identify yourself. On a mail server, all user names must be unique.

The domain name is the second part of an email address. The domain name specifies the name of the server to which the mail is to be delivered on the Internet, just like the domain name identifies the name of the computer on which a Web site resides. Domain names contain periods, which are usually pronounced "dot," to divide the domain name. The most specific part of the domain name appears first in the address, followed by the top-level domain name. Kikukawa Air's Web site address, KikukawaAir.com (and pronounced "Kikukawa Air dot com"), contains only two names separated by a period. The *com* in the domain name indicates that this company falls into the large, general class of commercial organizations. *KikukawaAir* indicates the domain name associated with the IP address for KikukawaAir.com.

Most email addresses aren't case-sensitive; the addresses sharon@kikukawaair.com and Sharon@KikukawaAir.com are the same. It is important for you to type a recipient's address carefully; if you omit or mistype even one character, your message could be undeliverable or sent to the wrong recipient. When a message cannot be delivered, the receiving mail server might send the message back to you and indicate that the addressee is unknown. Sometimes mail that cannot be delivered is deleted on the receiving mail server without notifying the sender.

Managing More than One Email Address

Keep in mind that an email account that was assigned to you by your school or employer is subject to the rules of use that the organization has established. Some schools and most employers have policies that dictate the permitted use of their equipment and email accounts. You should not use your employer's email address for personal correspondence unless your employer specifies that your personal use of the email account and your workplace computer is acceptable. In some cases, an employer might terminate employees who abuse the company's resources for personal use. In many cases, email is subject to monitoring by the organization, so messages you send with your organization-sponsored account are not guaranteed to be private.

For this reason, many people have more than one email address to manage their correspondence. It is very common for people to have a primary email address that they use for personal or business correspondence, and a secondary email address that they use for online subscriptions, online purchases, and mailing lists. If you are careful about how you distribute your primary email address, you might reduce the amount of unsolicited mail that you receive. When your secondary email address starts getting a lot of unwanted messages, you can discard it and create a new one. If you keep track of who has your secondary email address, it will be easy to update your contacts if you need to change your secondary email address.

Common Features of an Email Message

An email message consists of three parts: the message header, the message body, and an optional signature. The **message header** contains information about the message, and the **message body** contains the actual message content. A **signature** might appear at the bottom of an email message and contain standard information about the sender, which the recipient can use to contact the sender in a variety of ways.

Figure 2-1 shows a message that Don Kikukawa wrote to Jack Clancy, Margaret Durring, his pilots, and Sharon about an upcoming hot air balloon festival using an email program called Windows Live Mail, which you can download for free from the Windows Live Web site. The message contains an attached file named MealPlan.docx. Don created this file using Microsoft Word, saved it, and then attached it to the message. The primary features of this message are described in the next sections.

Figure 2-1   **Common features of an email message**

To line contains the message's primary recipient(s)

Bcc line contains recipient(s) receiving a blind courtesy copy of the message

Subject line contains the message topic

message body

signature

Cc line contains recipient(s) receiving a courtesy copy of the message

attachment filename and size

message header

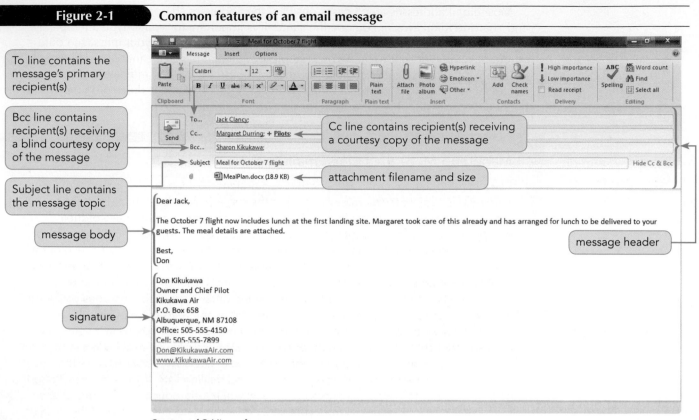

Courtesy of © Microsoft

To, Cc, and Bcc

You type the recipient's full email address in the **To line** of a message header. You can send the same message to multiple recipients by typing a comma or semicolon between the recipients' email addresses in the To line. If you have saved a recipient's email address in your address book—the feature of an email program that stores information about the people you exchange email with—the email program might display the address using the person's name, as shown in Figure 2-1, instead of the recipient's actual email address. The number of addresses you can type in the To line or in the other parts of the message header that require an address is not limited, but some mail servers will reject messages with too many recipients (usually 50 or more) as a way of controlling unsolicited mail. In Figure 2-1, Don used the To line to address his message to one recipient, Jack Clancy, whose email address was already stored in Don's address book.

You can use the optional **courtesy copy (Cc)** and **blind courtesy copy (Bcc)** lines to send mail to people who should be aware of the email message, but are not the message's main recipients. When an email message is delivered, every recipient (including Bcc recipients) can see the addresses of other recipients listed in the To and Cc lines. Because Bcc addresses are excluded from messages sent to addresses in the To and Cc lines, neither the primary recipients (in the To line) nor the Cc recipients can view the list of Bcc recipients. Bcc recipients are unaware of other Bcc recipients, as well. For example, if you send a thank-you message to a salesperson for performing a task especially well, you might consider sending a blind courtesy copy to that person's supervisor. That way, the supervisor knows a customer is happy and that the praise was unsolicited. In Figure 2-1, Don sent a courtesy copy of his email message to Margaret Durring and a blind courtesy copy to Sharon Kikukawa.

Sometimes an email address is not one person's address, but rather a special address called a **category** (also called a **group** in some email programs). In a category, a single email address can represent several or many individual email addresses. For example,

Don created a group named "Pilots" that includes the email addresses of the pilots who work for him so he can quickly address a new message to all pilots by typing the "Pilots" group name, instead of entering each pilot's email address individually. In Figure 2-1, Don included the Pilots group in the Cc line of the email message, so each member of the Pilots group will receive a copy of the message.

From

The **From line** of an email message includes the sender's name, the sender's email address, or both. Most email programs automatically insert the sender's name and email address in the From line of all outgoing messages. You usually do not see the From line in messages that you are composing, but you can see it in messages that you receive. Figure 2-1 does not show a From line because this is a message that Don is composing.

Subject

The content of the **Subject line** is very important. Often the recipient will scan an abbreviated display of incoming messages, looking for the most interesting or important message based on the content in the Subject line. If the Subject line is blank, then the recipient might not read the associated message immediately or at all. Including an appropriate subject in your message helps the reader determine its content and importance. For example, a Subject line such as "Just checking" is less informative and less interesting than "Urgent: New staff meeting time." The email message shown in Figure 2-1, for example, contains the subject "Meal for October 7 flight" and thus indicates that the message concerns food for an upcoming trip.

Attachments

You can send only text messages using SMTP, the protocol that handles outgoing email. When you need to send a more complex document, such as a Word document, an Excel workbook, a picture, or a PDF file, you send it along as an attachment. An **attachment** provides a simple and convenient way of sending files to one or more people. An attachment is encoded so that it can be carried safely over the Internet, to "tag along" with the message. Frequently, the attached file is the most important part of the email message, and the message body contains only a brief statement, such as "Here's the file that you requested."

Don's email message (see Figure 2-1) contains an attached file, whose filename and size in kilobytes appear in the message header. (A **kilobyte (KB)** is approximately 1,000 characters.) You can attach more than one file to an email message; if you include multiple recipients in the To, Cc, and Bcc lines of the message header, each recipient will receive the message and the attached file(s). However, keep in mind that an email message with many attachments quickly becomes very large in size, and it will take longer for the recipients to download the message. In addition, some Internet service providers (ISPs) place limits on the size of messages that they will accept; in some cases, an email message with file attachments larger than 10 megabytes in size might be rejected and returned to the sender.

Email programs differ in how they handle and display attachments. Some email programs identify an attached file with an icon that represents a program associated with the attachment's file type. In addition to an icon, some programs also display an attached file's size and filename. Other email programs display an attached file in a preview window when they recognize the attached file's format, and can start a program on the user's device to open the file. Double-clicking an attached file usually opens the file using a program on the user's device that is associated with the file type of the attachment. For example, if a workbook is attached to an email message, double-clicking the icon for the workbook attachment might start a spreadsheet program and open the workbook.

> **TIP**
> Before sending a message with a large attachment, ask the recipient for the best way to send it.

> **TIP**
> Before opening an attachment, be sure to scan it for viruses and other threats. You will learn more about detecting threats in this tutorial.

Similarly, a Word document opens in the Word program window when you double-click the icon representing the attached document, as long as you have the Word program, or a program that can open Word documents, installed on your device.

Viewing an attachment by double-clicking it lets you open a read-only copy of the file, but it does not save the file on your device. (A **read-only** file is one that you can view but that you cannot change.) To save an attached file on your device, you need to perform a series of steps to save the file in a specific location, such as on a hard drive. Some programs refer to the process of saving an email attachment as **detaching** the file. When you detach a file, you must indicate where to save it. You won't always need to detach an email attachment; if you simply keep the email message, you also keep a copy of the attachment for future use. You will learn how to attach and detach files later in this tutorial.

Message Body and Signature Files

Most often, people use email to write short, quick messages. However, email messages can be much longer. An email message is often less formal than a business letter that you might write, but it's still important to follow the rules of formal letter writing when composing an email message. You should begin your messages with a salutation, such as "Dear Jack," use proper spelling and grammar, and close your correspondence with a signature. After typing the content of your message—even a short message—you should check your spelling and grammar. You can sign a message by typing your name and other information at the end of each message you send, or you can create a signature file.

If you are using email for business communication, a **signature file** usually contains your name, your title, and your company's name. Signature files might also contain a mailing address, telephone numbers, a Web site address, and a company's logo. If you are using email for personal communication, signatures can be more informal. Informal signatures can include nicknames and graphics or quotations that express a more casual style found in correspondence between friends and acquaintances.

You can set your email account to insert a signature automatically into every message you send so you don't have to type its contents. You can modify your signature easily or choose not to include it in selected messages. You can usually create multiple signature files so you can choose which one to include when sending a message.

When you create a signature, don't overdo it: It is best to limit a signature to a few lines that identify ways to contact you. Figure 2-2 shows two examples of signatures. The first signature, which Don might use in his business correspondence to Kikukawa Air employees and friends, is informal. Don uses the second, more formal signature for all other business correspondence to identify his name, title, and contact information to make it easy for people to reach him.

Figure 2-2   **Sample signatures**

Courtesy of © Microsoft

Internet Etiquette (Netiquette)

Netiquette, a term coined from the phrase "Internet etiquette," is the set of commonly accepted rules that represent proper behavior on a network. Just as there are rules of proper conduct on networks that are owned or operated by schools and organizations, the Internet has its own set of acceptable rules. Unlike business networks on which administrators and webmasters set guidelines for acceptable use, and moderators are authorized to restrict usage of that network by users who don't follow those rules, the Internet is self-policing. Email has its own set of rules, which have evolved over time and will continue to evolve as it gains new users.

Because it sometimes takes so little time and effort to compose an email message, you might be tempted to take some shortcuts in your writing, such as omitting the salutation and using acronyms for commonly used phrases, such as the ones shown in Figure 2-3. These shortcuts are fine for informal messages that you might send to your friends and family members, but they are not acceptable in business communication.

Figure 2-3   Commonly used acronyms

Acronym	Meaning
atm	At the moment
b/c	Because
btw	By the way
iac	In any case
iae	In any event
imho	In my humble opinion
imo	In my opinion
iow	In other words
jk	Just kidding
thx	Thanks

© Cengage Learning

An email message is a business document, just like a memo or letter, and you should treat it with the same level of formality. Sending a message containing spelling and grammatical errors to a colleague or a potential employer is a poor reflection on you and your work. Many employers seeking to fill open positions automatically disregard email messages that do not contain a subject line or information in the message body describing the contents of the attachment and the applicant's intention to apply for the position. In addition, some employers will not seriously consider applications that are sent with email messages that contain typos or demonstrate poor communication skills.

Because email can be an impersonal form of communication, some writers use emoticons to express emotion. An **emoticon** is a group of keyboard characters that when viewed together represent a human expression. For example, a smiley :-) looks like a smiling face when you turn your head to the left. Some writers use emoticons to show their readers a form of electronic body language. Figure 2-4 shows some commonly used emoticons that are used in email messages. The user can create these emoticons by using either typed characters or a feature of the email program that inserts an emoticon's picture equivalent. Just like acronyms, emoticons are appropriate in informal correspondence but not in business correspondence.

TIP

Some email programs let you insert emoticons as pictures instead of typing keyboard combinations.

Figure 2-4   Commonly used emoticons

some email programs include a button that lets you insert emoticons as pictures

Commonly used emoticons in email messages

:-) or :) means 😊, a smile
;-) or ;) means 😉, a winking smile
:'(means 😢, a crying face
:-(or :(means 😞, a sad face
:-o or :o means 😮, a surprised face
:-p or :p means 😛, a tongue sticking out
:-D or :D means 😁, a big-grinned smile
^o) means 😏, a sarcastic smile
:-\ means 😒, an annoyed face

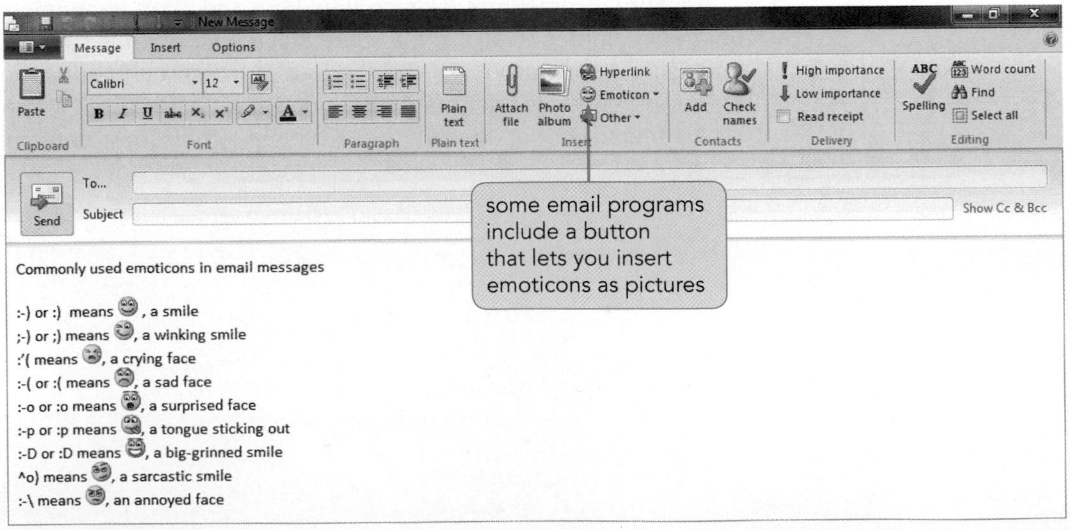

Courtesy of © Microsoft

You can learn more about netiquette by following the links in the Netiquette section of the Weblinks page for Tutorial 2.

PROSKILLS

Written Communication: Generally Accepted Rules for Email Messages

When composing email messages, keep the following generally accepted rules in mind, especially for business correspondence:

- Avoid writing your messages in ALL CAPITAL LETTERS BECAUSE IT LOOKS LIKE YOU ARE SHOUTING.
- Keep your messages simple, short, and focused on their topics.
- Don't use the "Reply All" feature when only the sender needs to know your response.
- Don't assume that everyone you know likes to receive jokes or family pictures. Check with the recipients first.
- When sending messages to a large group, use the Bcc field for the recipients' email addresses to protect their privacy and to prevent them from receiving additional responses from people who use the "Reply All" feature to respond.
- Include a descriptive subject in the Subject line and a signature, so the recipient knows the content of your message and how to get in touch with you.
- Use a spell checker, read your message, and correct any spelling or grammatical errors before sending it.
- Don't overuse formatting and graphics, which can make your email message difficult to read. The fonts you select on your device might not be available on the recipient's device and therefore the message might not display as you intended.
- Email is not private; don't divulge private or sensitive information in an email message. It's very easy for the recipient to forward your message to everyone he or she knows, even if it's by accident.
- Use caution when attempting sarcasm or humor in your messages, as the recipient might not appreciate the attempt at humor and might actually misunderstand your intentions. Without the sender's body language and tone of voice, some written statements are subject to misinterpretation.
- Use common courtesy, politeness, and respect in all of your written correspondence.
- When specifying a user name for your email address, select something that is appropriate for both professional and personal correspondence, and that clearly identifies you to recipients.

Email Programs

Different software companies that produce Web browsers might also produce companion email programs that you can use to manage your email. For example, when you install Microsoft Internet Explorer for Windows XP, the Outlook Express email program is also installed. Windows Vista and Windows 7 users might choose to install Windows Live Mail, and Mozilla Firefox users might choose to install the companion Thunderbird email program to manage their email messages. You can use these types of email programs to manage messages that are routed through a domain that sends email messages using the POP protocol. Messages that are routed through a domain in this way are called **POP messages** or **POP3 messages** because of the protocol used to send them. You might also have multiple email programs installed on your computer; in this case, the choice of which email program to use is up to you.

Before you can use an email program to send and receive your email messages, you must configure it to work with your email accounts. Before you decide which email program to use, you should be familiar with the different ones available. The Email Clients section of the Weblinks page for Tutorial 2 includes links to some popular email programs, some of which are free. You can explore these links to learn more about these programs and their features.

TIP

In Session 2.2, you will learn how to configure and use Windows Live Hotmail.

Common Features of Email Programs

Although there are many different ways to send and receive email messages, most email programs have common features for managing mail. Fortunately, once you learn the process for sending, receiving, and managing email with one program, it's easy to use another program to accomplish the same tasks.

Sending Messages

After you finish addressing and composing a message, it might not be sent to the mail server immediately, depending on how the email program or service is configured. A message can be **queued**, or temporarily held with other messages, and then sent when you either exit the program, connect to your ISP or network, or check to see if you have received any new email. Most email programs and services include a "Drafts" folder in which you can store email messages that you are composing but that you aren't ready to send yet. These messages are saved until you finish and send them.

Receiving and Storing Messages

When your mail server receives messages for your account, those messages are held on the mail server until you ask the server to retrieve your messages. Most email programs allow you to save delivered mail in any of several standard or custom mailboxes or folders on your Internet device. Once the mail is delivered to your device, one of two things can happen to it on the server: Either the server's copy of your mail is deleted, or it is preserved and marked as delivered or read. Marking mail as delivered or read is the server's way of distinguishing new mail from mail that you have read. For example, when Don receives mail on the Kikukawa Air mail server, he might decide to save his accumulated mail on the server—even after he reads it—so he can access the messages again from another device. On the other hand, Don might want to delete old mail to save space on the mail server. Both methods have advantages.

Saving old mail on the server lets you access your mail from any device that can connect to your mail server. However, if you automatically delete mail after reading it, you don't have to worry about storing and organizing messages that you don't need, which requires less effort. Some ISPs and email providers impose limits on the amount of data you can store, so you must occasionally delete mail from your mailbox to avoid interruption of service. In some cases, once you exceed your storage space limit, you cannot receive any additional messages until you delete existing messages from the server, or the service deletes your messages without warning to free up space in your mailbox.

Printing a Message

Reading mail on a computer or other device is fine, but there are times when you will need to print some of your messages. Most email programs let you print a message you are composing or that you have received. The Print command usually appears on the File menu or as a Print button on the toolbar.

Organizing Messages

Most email programs let you create folders in which to store related messages in your mailbox. You can create new folders when needed, rename existing folders, or delete folders and their contents when you no longer need them. You can move mail from the incoming folder to any other folder to file it. Some programs let you define and use a **filter** or rule to move incoming mail into a specific folder, or to delete it automatically based on the content of the message. Filters are especially useful for moving messages from certain senders into designated folders, and for moving **junk mail** (or **spam**), which

TIP

Filters aren't perfect. When using filters to move messages to specific folders or to the trash, it's a good idea to check your folders occasionally to make sure that your incoming messages are downloaded to the correct folder.

is unsolicited mail usually advertising or selling an item or service, to a trash folder. If your email program does not provide filters, you can filter the messages manually by reading them and moving them to the appropriate folders.

Forwarding a Message

You can forward messages that you receive to additional recipients. When you **forward** a message to another recipient, a copy of the original message is sent to the new recipient you specify without the original sender's knowledge. You might forward a misdirected message to another recipient, or forward a message to someone who was not included in the original message routing list.

When you forward a message, your email address and name appear automatically in the From line; most email programs amend the Subject line with the text "Fw," "Fwd," or something similar to indicate that the message has been forwarded. You simply add the new recipient's address to the To line and send the message. Depending on your email program and the preferences you set for forwarding messages, a forwarded message might be sent as an attached file or as quoted text. A **quoted message** is a copy of the sender's original message with your inserted comments. A special mark (a > symbol or a solid vertical line) sometimes precedes each line of the quoted message. Figure 2-5 shows a quoted message; the quoted message appears at the bottom of the message, and the "Fw:" text in the Subject line indicates a forwarded message.

| Figure 2-5 | Sample forwarded message |

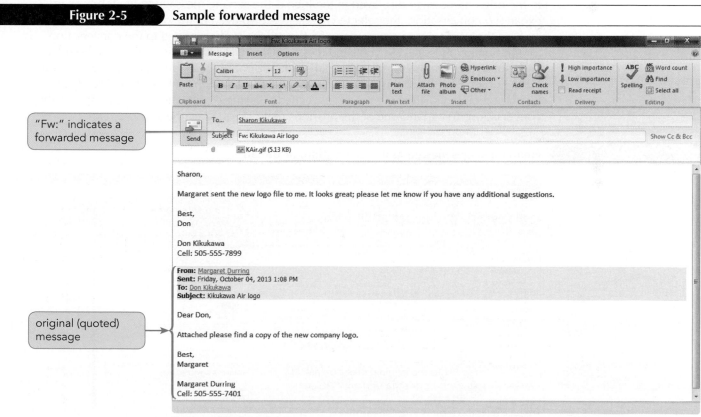

"Fw:" indicates a forwarded message

original (quoted) message

Courtesy of © Microsoft

Replying to a Message

Replying to a message sends a response to a message you have received. Most email programs provide two options for replying to a message: You can reply to only the original sender using the Reply option, or you can reply to the original sender and all other To and Cc recipients of the original message by using the Reply All option. When you **reply** to a message that you received, the email program creates a new message and automatically addresses it either to the original sender (when you select the Reply option), or to the original sender and all of the original To and Cc recipients of the message (when you select the Reply All option). Most email programs will add "Re:" to the beginning of the original subject text in the header and copy the contents of the original message and place it in the message body of the reply. Like forwarded messages, a special mark might appear at the beginning of each line to indicate the content of the original message. When you are responding to more than one question, you might type your responses below the original questions so the recipient can better understand the context of your responses. When you respond to a message that was sent to several people, make sure that you select the correct option when replying.

Some email programs display replies to messages as conversations, or **threads**. When you receive an email message as part of a conversation, it appears in your Inbox on a single line, instead of as stacked individual messages on separate lines. In Figure 2-6, the first message in Don's Inbox appears as a collapsed conversation, with a small arrow indicating that there are additional messages with the same subject line linked to the original message displayed in the Inbox. The second message in the Inbox is an expanded conversation; the selected message is displayed in the preview pane. If you reply to the original message as part of a thread, the reply is added to the conversation for the original message. As you send messages back and forth with the original sender, each subsequent reply from the original sender or from you is added to the conversation for the original message. Instead of needing to find and open multiple messages from different recipients, all of the messages related to a single original message appear in the conversation. To expand one of the previous replies, you click the sender's name.

Figure 2-6	Email messages viewed as a conversation, or thread

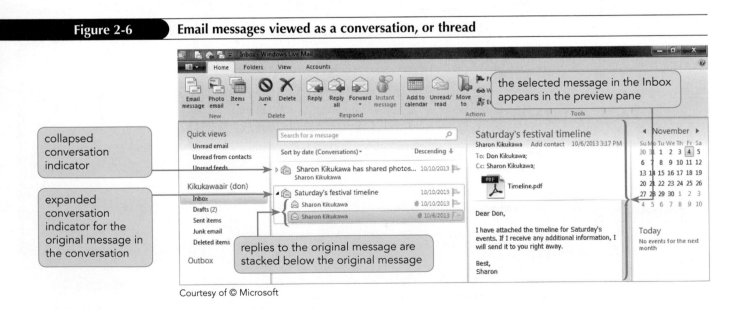

Courtesy of © Microsoft

Deleting a Message

Deleting a message is usually a two-step process. First, you temporarily delete a message by placing it in a "trash" folder or by marking it for deletion. Then you permanently delete the trash or marked messages by emptying the trash folder or indicating to the email program to delete the messages. It is a good idea to delete mail you no longer need because it takes up a lot of space on the drive or server on which your email messages are stored.

Managing Your Contacts

You use a **contact list** to save email addresses and other optional contact information about the people and organizations with which you communicate. The features of a contact list vary by email program. Usually, you can organize information about individuals and groups. Each entry in the contact list can contain an individual's full email address (or a group email address to represent several individual addresses), full name, and complete contact information. In addition, most email programs allow you to include notes for each contact. You can assign a unique nickname to each entry so it is easier to address your email messages. A **nickname** might be "Mom" for your mother or "Maintenance Department" to represent all the employees working in a certain part of an organization. Figure 2-7 shows the contact for Sharon Kikukawa in Don Kikukawa's address book. Notice that there are other options for storing a contact's personal, work, and other information.

Figure 2-7 **Sharon's contact in Don's address book**

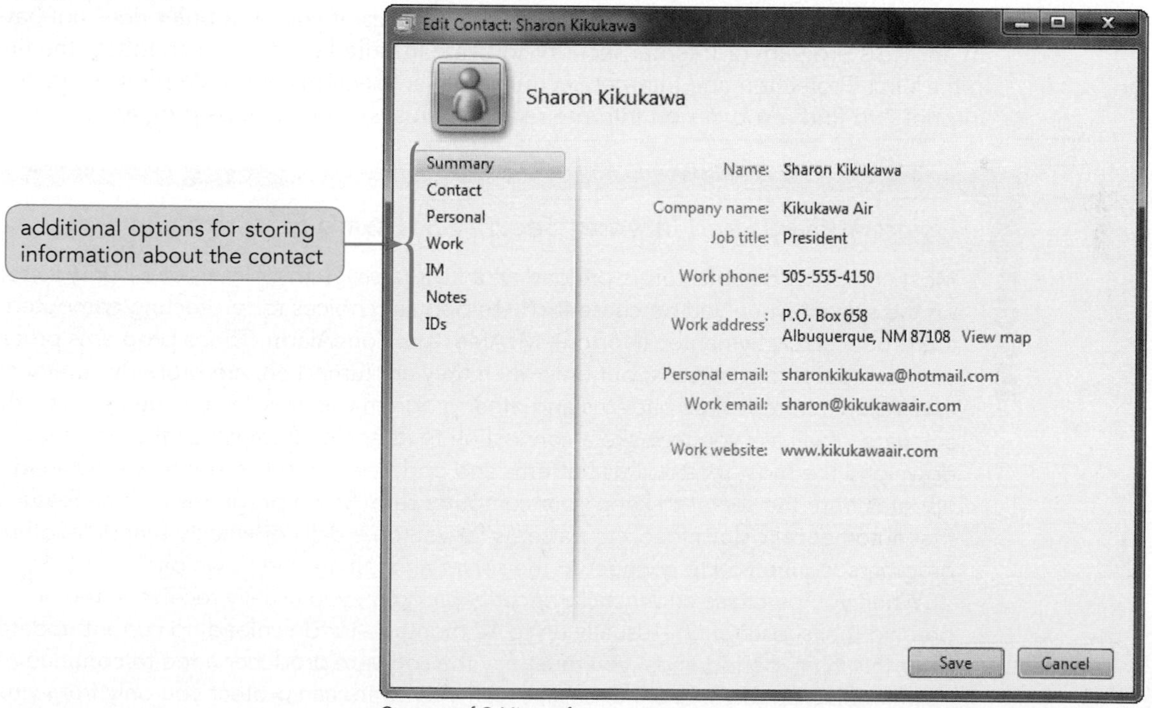

additional options for storing information about the contact

Courtesy of © Microsoft

After saving entries in the contact list, you can refer to them at any point while you are composing, replying to, or forwarding a message. You can review your contact list and sort the entries in many ways.

Protecting Your Computer from Viruses

Email attachments, just like any other computer files, can contain malicious programs called **viruses** that can harm your computer and its files. Some users send attachments containing viruses without realizing that they are doing so; other users send viruses on purpose to infect as many computers as possible. If you receive an email message from a sender that you don't recognize and the message contains an attached file, you should not open that file until you are sure that it doesn't contain a virus.

People create viruses by coding programs that hide by attaching themselves to other programs on a computer. Some viruses simply display an annoying or silly message on your screen and then go away, whereas others can cause real harm by reformatting your hard drive, changing the file extensions and their associations, or sending a copy of the virus to everyone in your email program's contact list. You must know how to detect and eradicate viruses if you plan to download anything, including data, programs, instant messages, or email attachments, from any Internet server.

Software that detects and eliminates viruses is called an **antivirus program**. The category of software that detects viruses and other common security threats on the Internet is called **Internet security software**. This software usually includes tools that eradicate specific Internet threats, including viruses. Internet security software and antivirus programs start automatically when you start the computer, regularly scan the files on your computer and the files being downloaded to your computer, and compare them to a signature that known viruses carry. A **virus signature** (also called a **virus pattern** or a **virus definition**) is a sequence (string) of characters that is always present in a particular virus.

An antivirus program can scan a single file or folder or your entire computer to search for infected files. When the antivirus program finds a virus signature, it might delete the file containing the virus or quarantine it and ask you how to proceed. Most antivirus programs can clean infected files by removing the virus. If your computer does not have an antivirus program or Internet security software installed on it, you can follow the links in the Virus Protection and Internet Security Software sections of the Weblinks page for Tutorial 2 to find resources on Internet security, viruses, and antivirus programs.

TIP

An antivirus program might be part of an Internet security suite that includes other programs that scan files for additional security threats and perform other tasks, such as blocking unwanted pop-up ads.

INSIGHT

Using Antivirus and Internet Security Software Effectively

Most computer manufacturers preload an antivirus program or Internet security suite on the system when you purchase it. Three popular choices for protecting computers are produced by Symantec (Norton), McAfee, and ZoneAlarm. These programs protect your computer from viruses, but only when they are turned on, are properly configured, and include current virus patterns and other program updates. When you first start the software, it will ask you to make a connection to its server, from which the program will download the most recent virus patterns and updates. You must regularly download updates from the server to keep your computer safe. Some programs include features that automatically download the patterns for you on a daily or weekly schedule; other programs require you to connect to the server and initiate the download.

When you purchase and install a security program, you usually receive a free or prepaid trial subscription—usually up to 12 months—for downloading current updates. After this initial period ends, you must pay the software producer a fee to continue downloading updates. In either case, security software can protect you only from viruses and other security threats that it recognizes. If you install a program to protect your computer and do not regularly download updates, your computer won't be protected from dozens of new threats that develop each month. In addition, if your software isn't turned on or set to scan downloaded files, it cannot protect your computer.

And, finally, keep in mind that you usually have to open or execute a file to run any virus it contains. By regularly scanning your computer for viruses, downloading regular updates, configuring the program to work automatically, and scanning all downloaded files, you can protect your computer from viruses and other threats.

Dealing with Unsolicited Messages

Spam, also known as **unsolicited commercial email (UCE)** or junk mail, includes unwanted solicitations, advertisements, or chain letters sent to an email address. For most Internet users, spam represents waste in terms of the time it takes to download, manage, and delete. Besides wasting people's time and their computers' disk space, spam can consume large amounts of network capacity. If one person sends a useless email message to hundreds of thousands of people, that unsolicited message consumes Internet resources for a few moments that would otherwise be available to users with legitimate communication needs.

Although spam has always been an annoyance, companies are increasingly finding it to be a major problem. In addition to consuming bandwidth on company networks and space on mail servers, spam distracts employees who are trying to do their jobs and requires them to spend time deleting unwanted messages. In addition, a considerable number of spam messages include content that is offensive or misleading to its recipients. According to the Messaging Anti-Abuse Working Group (MAAWG), approximately 88% to 91% of all email messages sent every day are spam. In real numbers, this is billions of email messages a day.

One way to reduce spam in your Inbox is to control the exposure of your email address in places where spammers look for them. Spammers use software robots to search the Internet for character strings that include the "@" character that appears in every email address. These robots search Web pages, discussion groups, and other online sources that might contain email addresses. If you don't provide your email address to these sources, you reduce the risk of a spammer getting it.

Some individuals use multiple email addresses to reduce spam. They use one address for display on a Web site, another to register for access to Web sites, another for shopping accounts, and so on. If a spammer starts using one of these addresses, the individual can stop using it and switch to another. Many Web hosting services include a large number of email addresses—often up to 10,000—as part of their service, so this is a good solution for people or small businesses with their own Web sites.

These strategies focus on limiting a spammer's access to, or use of, an email address. Other approaches use one or more techniques that filter email messages based on their contents. Many corporate organizations fight spam aggressively by blocking it on the mail server and preventing it from being downloaded to individual user accounts. Individual users can also set filters that analyze the content in their incoming messages, and move spam messages to a trash folder or other folder when they are downloaded. From the perspective of a corporation, ISP, or other organization, it is more effective and less costly to eliminate spam before it reaches users. The problem with this approach, however, is that it is difficult for a filter to accurately differentiate "real" messages from spam. In many cases, legitimate messages are prevented from reaching the recipient when a spam filter misdirects the message.

Because spam continues to be a serious problem for all email users and providers, an increasing number of approaches have been devised or proposed to combat it. Figure 2-8 shows the home page from the Spam site, sponsored by the Federal Trade Commission, which gives advice to consumers and businesses about combating spam.

Figure 2-8   **Federal Trade Commission Spam page**

United States Federal Trade Commission, www.ftc.gov

Many U.S. jurisdictions have passed laws that provide penalties for sending spam. In January 2004, the U.S. CAN-SPAM Act (the law's name is an acronym for "Controlling the Assault of Non-Solicited Pornography and Marketing") went into effect. The CAN-SPAM Act was the first U.S. federal government effort to legislate controls on spam. It regulates all email messages sent for the primary purpose of advertising or promoting a commercial product or service, including messages that promote the content displayed at a Web site.

The law's main provisions are that unsolicited email messages must identify the sender, contain an accurate message subject and a notice that the message is an advertisement or solicitation, make it possible for the recipient to "opt out" of future mailings within 10 days of receipt of the request, include the sender's physical postal address, and prohibit the sender from selling or transferring an email address with an opt-out request to any other entity. Each violation of a provision of the law is subject to a fine of up to $16,000. Additional fines are assessed for those who violate one of these provisions and also harvest email addresses from Web sites, send messages to randomly generated addresses, use automated tools to register for email accounts that are subsequently used to send spam, and relay email messages through a computer or network without the permission of the computer's or network's owner.

To learn more about preventing spam, follow the links in the Fighting Spam section of the Weblinks page for Tutorial 2.

Now that you understand some basic information about email, you are ready to start using Windows Live Hotmail, which you will do in Session 2.2.

Session 2.1 Quick Check

REVIEW

1. The rules that determine how the Internet handles packets flowing on it are called _____.
2. What are the three parts of an email message?
3. True or False. On receipt, Bcc recipients of an email message are aware of other Bcc recipients who received the same email message.
4. Can you send a Word document with an email message? If so, how?
5. What are the two parts of an email address, and what information do they provide?
6. Why is it important to delete email messages that you no longer need?
7. What are two strategies for controlling the receipt of spam?

SESSION 2.2 VISUAL OVERVIEW

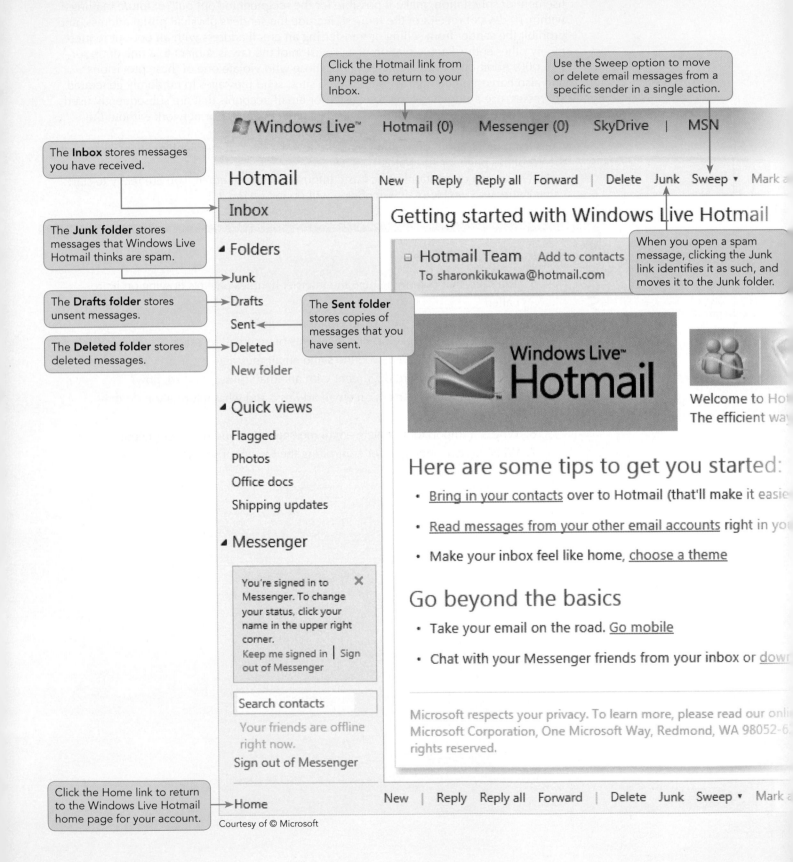

Click the Hotmail link from any page to return to your Inbox.

Use the Sweep option to move or delete email messages from a specific sender in a single action.

The **Inbox** stores messages you have received.

The **Junk folder** stores messages that Windows Live Hotmail thinks are spam.

The **Drafts folder** stores unsent messages.

The **Deleted folder** stores deleted messages.

The **Sent folder** stores copies of messages that you have sent.

When you open a spam message, clicking the Junk link identifies it as such, and moves it to the Junk folder.

Click the Home link to return to the Windows Live Hotmail home page for your account.

Windows Live™   Hotmail (0)   Messenger (0)   SkyDrive | MSN

Hotmail   New | Reply Reply all Forward | Delete Junk Sweep ▾ Mark a

Inbox

Getting started with Windows Live Hotmail

▲ Folders

Junk

Drafts

Sent

Deleted

New folder

▲ Quick views

Flagged

Photos

Office docs

Shipping updates

▲ Messenger

☐ Hotmail Team   Add to contacts
To sharonkikukawa@hotmail.com

Windows Live™ Hotmail

Welcome to Ho
The efficient wa

Here are some tips to get you started:

- Bring in your contacts over to Hotmail (that'll make it easie
- Read messages from your other email accounts right in you
- Make your inbox feel like home, choose a theme

Go beyond the basics

- Take your email on the road. Go mobile
- Chat with your Messenger friends from your inbox or down

You're signed in to Messenger. To change your status, click your name in the upper right corner.
Keep me signed in | Sign out of Messenger

☒

Search contacts

Your friends are offline right now.

Sign out of Messenger

Home

Microsoft respects your privacy. To learn more, please read our onli
Microsoft Corporation, One Microsoft Way, Redmond, WA 98052-6
rights reserved.

New | Reply Reply all Forward | Delete Junk Sweep ▾ Mark a

Courtesy of © Microsoft

MESSAGE IN HOTMAIL

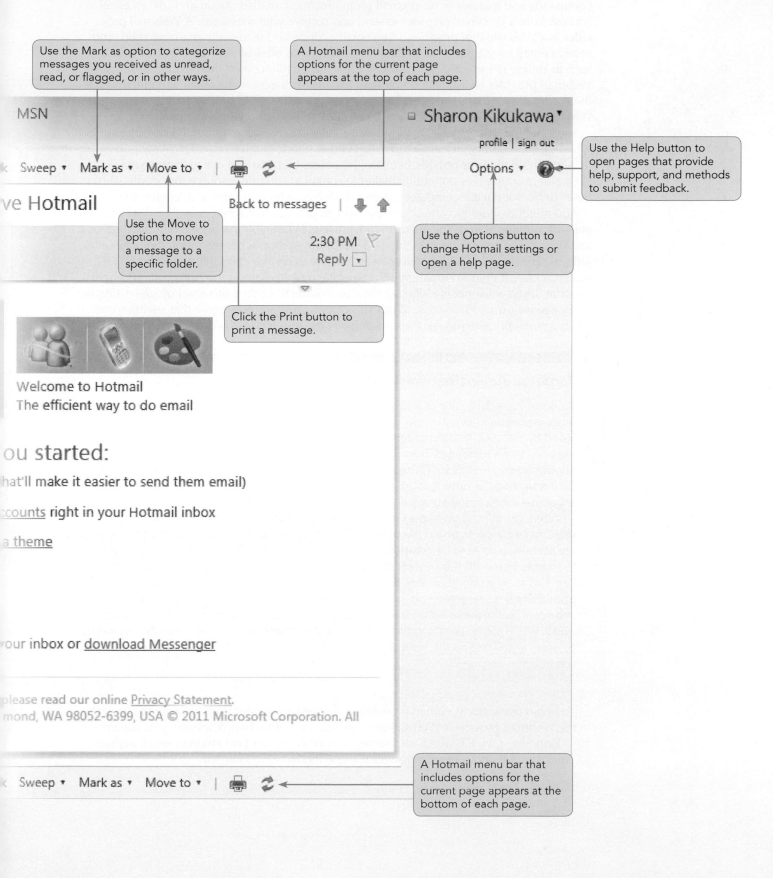

Use the Mark as option to categorize messages you received as unread, read, or flagged, or in other ways.

A Hotmail menu bar that includes options for the current page appears at the top of each page.

Use the Help button to open pages that provide help, support, and methods to submit feedback.

MSN

Sharon Kikukawa ▾

profile | sign out

Sweep ▾   Mark as ▾   Move to ▾ | 🖨   ⇄

Options ▾   ❓

ve Hotmail   Back to messages | ⬇   ⬆

Use the Move to option to move a message to a specific folder.

2:30 PM   ⚑
Reply ▾

Use the Options button to change Hotmail settings or open a help page.

Click the Print button to print a message.

Welcome to Hotmail
The efficient way to do email

ou started:

hat'll make it easier to send them email)

ccounts right in your Hotmail inbox

a theme

our inbox or download Messenger

please read our online Privacy Statement.
mond, WA 98052-6399, USA © 2011 Microsoft Corporation. All

Sweep ▾   Mark as ▾   Move to ▾ | 🖨   ⇄

A Hotmail menu bar that includes options for the current page appears at the bottom of each page.

Webmail Providers

In Session 2.1, you learned about the basic features of an email message, and the basic commands and features in most email programs. You can also obtain and use an email address from a Webmail provider to send and receive your messages. A **Webmail provider** is a Web site that provides a free email address and features to manage, send, and receive email messages. Most Webmail providers also offer other Web-based services, such as online file sharing, to registered users. An email account that you have with a Webmail provider is also called **Webmail** because you access the email account through the Webmail provider's Web site. Two popular examples of Webmail providers are Windows Live Hotmail, which you'll use in this session, and Google's Gmail.

Most people who use Webmail providers have Internet access from their employer, school, public library, home provider, or cellular phone service provider. Many public and school libraries provide free Internet access that you can use to access your Webmail account. This portability makes Webmail a valuable resource for people who travel or do not have a computer or other device on which to send and receive email.

You might wonder how these companies can provide free services such as Webmail—after all, nothing is free. The answer is advertising. When you use a Webmail provider or any Web-based service, you might see advertising, such as a banner ad on the page or links to services sponsored by businesses that pay to display their information on your screen, or insert their information into the email messages you send from your Webmail account. Users must decide whether they are willing to endure this level of advertising in exchange for using the service. Most users of these free services agree that seeing some ads is a small price to pay for the convenience the free services provide.

INSIGHT

Targeted Advertisements in Webmail

Webmail providers, such as Microsoft and Google, are largely supported by adding advertisements to email messages based on message content and other information provided by the user. Ads are added to the user's messages based on predefined keywords included in the messages. For example, when your email message includes a discussion about meeting friends for Chinese food later, ads for local Chinese restaurants—based on the zip code or other geographical information you provided when you created your account—might automatically appear in your message window.

Although there is no human intervention to produce these advertisements, some users have concerns about the privacy of the email messages they receive because they are scanned and read by computers. Some people do not like the idea of seeing advertisements based on the content of the messages they send and receive because they see it as an invasion of privacy. Gmail has made efforts to ensure that its advertising appears only as targeted text ads. This strategy is different from those of other Webmail providers that include untargeted advertising in the form of banners and pop-up windows, which some users find to be more invasive. Just like any other free service, it is up to users to determine the level of advertising they are willing to endure in exchange for the free service provided.

To begin using any Webmail provider, you need to use your Web browser to connect to the Webmail provider's Web site and create an account. In this session, you will create a Windows Live ID, which also serves as your Windows Live Hotmail email address, so you can send and receive messages using Windows Live Hotmail.

Creating a Windows Live ID

The steps in this session assume that you have a Web browser and can connect to the Internet. Before you can use Windows Live Hotmail, you need to create a Windows Live ID. If you have an existing Hotmail email address, you can use it as your Windows Live ID and skip the following steps, which ask you to create a Windows Live ID.

TIP

Detailed directions for accessing the Weblinks for this book are printed on the inside front cover of this book.

To create a Windows Live ID:

1. Start your Web browser, go to **www.cengagebrain.com**, open the Tutorial 2 Weblinks page, click the **Session 2.2** link, and then click the **Windows Live** link to open the Windows Live Sign In page, which will look similar to Figure 2-9.

Figure 2-9   Windows Live Sign In page

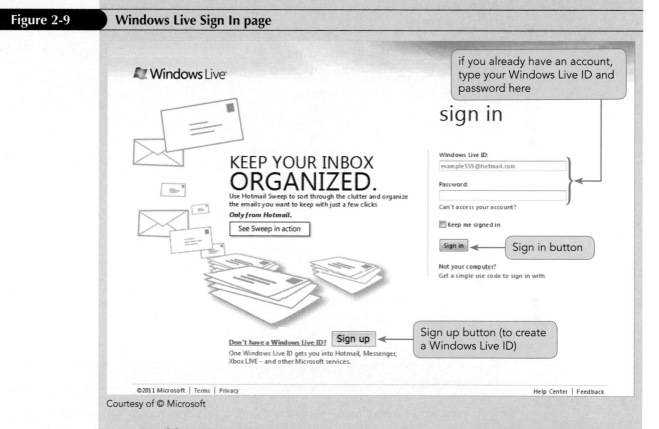

Courtesy of © Microsoft

Trouble? The Windows Live Sign In page and other Windows Live Hotmail pages might change over time. Check the Weblinks page for Tutorial 2 for notes about any differences you might encounter.

Trouble? If you already have a Windows Live ID, Windows Live Hotmail address, Messenger account, or Xbox LIVE account, use the "sign in" section to enter your user name and password, click the Sign in button, and then skip this set of steps.

2. Click the **Sign up** button. (If you do not see a Sign up button, Windows Live may have redesigned the Web site. Examine the page carefully until you find the button or tab that lets you create a Windows Live ID or Hotmail account.)

The Create your Hotmail account page shown in Figure 2-10 opens.

Figure 2-10   **Create your Hotmail account page**

Windows Live™   Sign in

Create your Hotmail account
This is your Windows Live ID—it gets you into other services like Messenger and SkyDrive.
All information is required.

If you use **Hotmail**, **Messenger**, or **Xbox**
LIVE, you already have a Windows Live ID.
Sign in

Hotmail address: [   ] @ [hotmail.com ▾]   This Hotmail address is also your
                                                       Windows Live ID. You can use it to
Create a password: [   ]   sign in to other Windows Live sites
                                                       and services.
                   6-character minimum; case sensitive

Retype password: [   ]

Mobile phone: [United States (+1)   ▾]

              [(425) 555-0100   ]

Alternate email address: [   ]

              Or choose a security question for password
              reset

First name: [   ]

Last name: [   ]

Country/region: [United States   ▾]

ZIP code: [   ]

Gender: ◉ Male ◉ Female

Birth date: [Month ▾] [Day ▾] [Year ▾]

Enter the characters you see
New | Audio | Help

cntactu **Hickman**

[   ]

☑ Send me email with promotional offers
   and survey invitations from Windows Live,
   Bing, and MSN. (You can unsubscribe at
   any time.)

Clicking **I accept** means that you agree to the Microsoft service agreement and privacy statement.

[I accept]

© 2011 Microsoft   Terms   Privacy   About our ads   Advertise   Developers   Help Center   Feedback   English

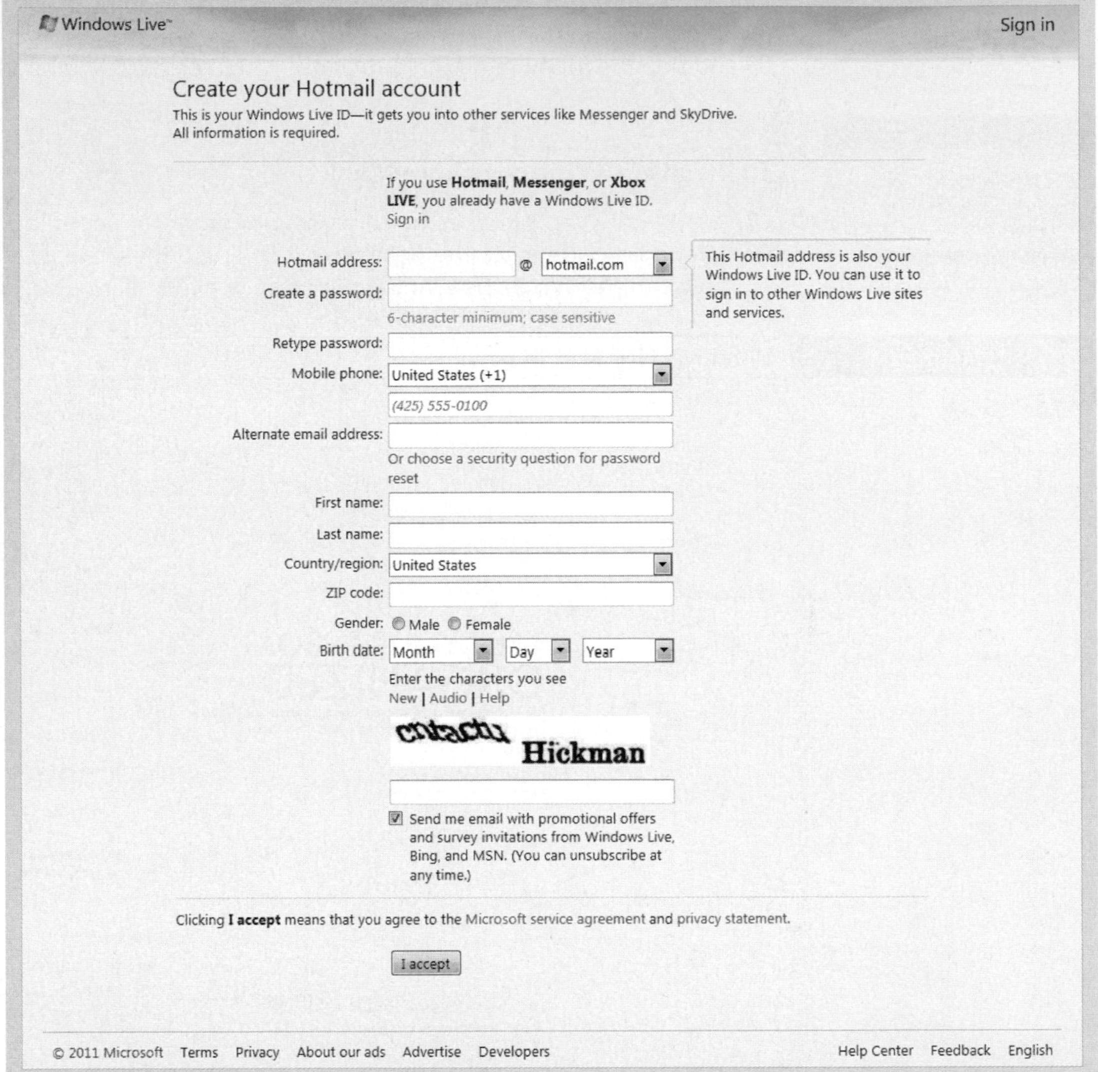

Courtesy of © Microsoft

Trouble? The Create your Hotmail account page might change over time. If your page looks different, follow the on-screen instructions to create a Windows Live ID.

The first step in creating a Hotmail account is to create a **Windows Live ID** (Windows Live also calls this a sign-in name or a user name), which you will also use as your Windows Live Hotmail email address. A Windows Live ID can contain letters, numbers, or underscore characters (_), but it cannot contain any spaces. After creating a Windows Live ID, you must create a password containing letters and/or numbers, but no spaces. You type your password twice to ensure that you entered it correctly. Finally, to help remember your password in the event that you forget it, you enter a question and its secret answer so Windows Live can verify your identity in the future, as necessary.

3. Click in the **Hotmail address** box, and then type a user name, which you will use as your Windows Live ID and your Windows Live Hotmail address. Your user name must be unique. You can try typing your first and last names, separated by an underscore character, followed by your birth date or year of birth, such as sharon_kikukawa0616. A Windows Live ID can contain only letters, numbers, periods, hyphens, and underscores.

4. If necessary, click the **arrow** on the box to the right of the Hotmail address box, and then click **hotmail.com**. (If the menu closes, click the arrow on the box to open the menu again.)

5. Click in the **Create a password** box, and then type a password with at least six characters. The most effective passwords are ones that are not easily guessed and contain letters and numbers. As you type your password, dots or asterisks appear in the Create a password box to protect your password from being seen by other users. In addition, the Password strength indicator analyzes the password you typed to identify its strength. A weak password is one that contains only letters, such as "pencil." A stronger password includes letters and numbers, such as "pencil87." The strongest password is one that does not form a word and that includes mixed-case letters, numbers, and special characters, such as "p2nc1L%."

6. Press the **Tab** key to move to the Retype password box, and then type your password again. Make sure to type the same password you typed in Step 5.

7. Click in the **Alternate email address** box. If you have an existing email address, enter it in the Alternate email address box. This is the email address that Windows Live will use to send you your password in case you forget it.

    Trouble? If you don't have another email address, click the Or choose a security question for password reset link below the Alternate email address box, click the Question arrow that appears, select a question that you know the answer to, click in the Secret answer box, and then type the answer (using a minimum of five characters) to your question.

Now that you have entered a Windows Live ID and a password, you need to provide your account information.

To enter your account information:

1. Click in the **First name** box, type your first name, press the **Tab** key to move to the Last name box, and then type your last name. Your first and last names will appear in all email messages that you send.

2. If necessary, click the **Country/region** arrow, and then click the country or region where you live.

3. If necessary, click in the **ZIP code** (or **Postal Code**) box, and then type your zip code or postal code. Windows Live will use this information to provide you with additional services, such as local weather forecasts, that you might request in the future.

4. Click the appropriate option button in the Gender section to indicate your gender.

5. Click in the **Birth date Month** box, click your birth month in the list, click in the **Birth date Day** box, click your birth day from the list, click in the **Birth date Year** box, and then click the four-digit year of your birth.

The last part of creating a Windows Live ID is to verify that you are a person and not an automated program, and also to read and accept the agreements that govern the use of a Windows Live ID account.

To finish creating a Windows Live ID:

1. Scroll down the page as necessary so you see characters in a box. Many Web sites use a collection of characters, called a **CAPTCHA** and shown in Figure 2-11, as a way of verifying that a person is using the form to create an account instead of a computer. Created by professors at Carnegie Mellon University, CAPTCHA stands for "Completely Automated Public Turing test to tell Computers and Humans Apart."

Figure 2-11 Required character entry to prevent abuse

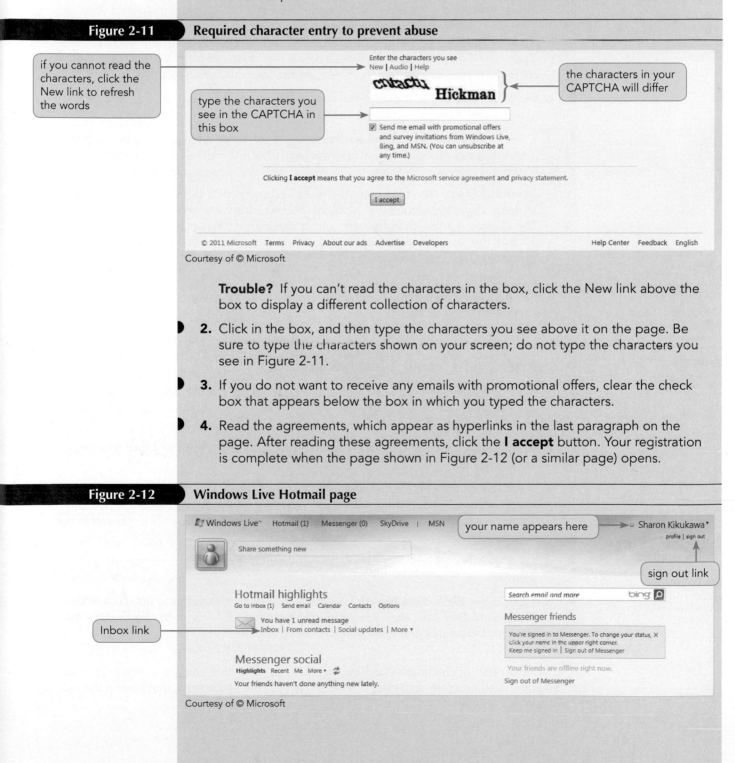

if you cannot read the characters, click the New link to refresh the words

type the characters you see in the CAPTCHA in this box

the characters in your CAPTCHA will differ

Courtesy of © Microsoft

Trouble? If you can't read the characters in the box, click the New link above the box to display a different collection of characters.

2. Click in the box, and then type the characters you see above it on the page. Be sure to type the characters shown on your screen; do not type the characters you see in Figure 2-11.

3. If you do not want to receive any emails with promotional offers, clear the check box that appears below the box in which you typed the characters.

4. Read the agreements, which appear as hyperlinks in the last paragraph on the page. After reading these agreements, click the **I accept** button. Your registration is complete when the page shown in Figure 2-12 (or a similar page) opens.

Figure 2-12 Windows Live Hotmail page

your name appears here

sign out link

Inbox link

Courtesy of © Microsoft

Trouble? Windows Live might redesign its Web site, in which case your screen might not match the one shown in Figure 2-12.

Trouble? After clicking the I accept button, a page similar to the one shown in Figure 2-13 will appear if the user name you selected is already in use. Select the text in the Hotmail address box, type a new user name, repeat Steps 1 and 2, and then click the I accept button until you find a valid user name and see the page shown in Figure 2-12.

| **Figure 2-13** | **Message that appears when a user name is taken** |

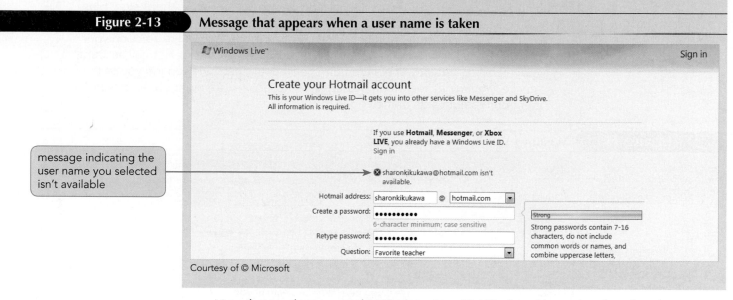

message indicating the user name you selected isn't available

Courtesy of © Microsoft

Now that you have created a Windows Live ID, Windows Live opens the Inbox for your Windows Live Hotmail address. So that you can practice signing in to your Windows Live account, you'll sign out. Signing out closes your account and logs you out of the system. You should always sign out of your account when you have finished working so that other users cannot access your email or send messages using your email address.

To sign out of your account:

 1. In the upper-right corner of the page and below your name, click the **sign out** link. The MSN home page (or another page) appears in your browser.

 2. Return to the Weblinks page for Tutorial 2, and then click the **Windows Live** link. The Windows Live Sign In page opens.

Accessing Your Windows Live Account

Depending on your browser configuration, you might see your Windows Live Hotmail address in the Windows Live ID box on the Windows Live Sign In page. If you see your Windows Live Hotmail address, you can enter your password and then click the Sign in button to sign in to your Windows Live account. If you will be accessing your Windows Live account from your own computer, you might decide to click the Keep me signed in check box to select this option, so you won't need to enter your login information in the future. This option presents a security risk because other users with access to your computer can sign in to your account when they open the Windows Live Sign In page.

If you are having problems logging in to your account, you can enter your Windows Live ID and then click the Can't access your account? link to identify the problem you're having. The site will provide a method to correct the problem, which might involve asking you to answer the question you specified when you created your account, or sending information or instructions for resetting your password to your alternate email address, if you specified one.

Next, you'll sign in to your Windows Live account and open your Inbox.

To sign in to your Windows Live account:

1. If necessary, enter your Hotmail email address (your user name, the @ sign, plus hotmail.com) in the Windows Live ID box, type your password in the Password box, click the **Sign in** button, and then, if necessary, click the **Inbox** link to open your Hotmail Inbox, as shown in Figure 2-14. If you just created your Hotmail account, you might see one new message from the Hotmail Team, welcoming you to the service. (You might see other messages, as well.) You also might see an advertisement on the right side of the page.

| Figure 2-14 | Windows Live Hotmail Inbox |

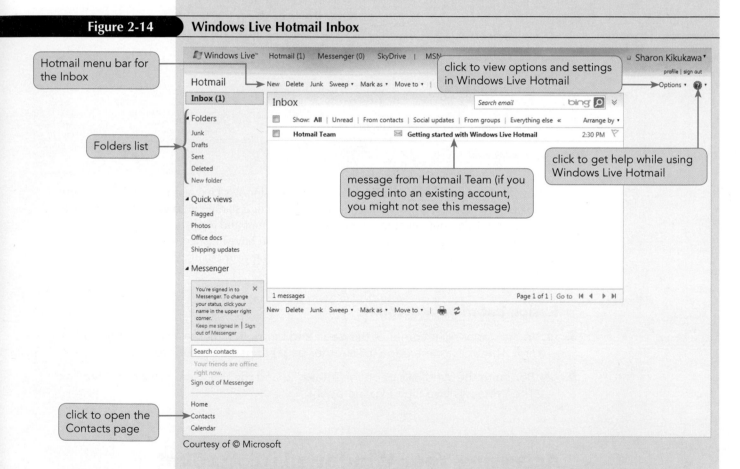

Courtesy of © Microsoft

Trouble? If you receive a message that your Windows Live ID or password is not found, clear the Windows Live ID and Password boxes, and then reenter your information. If you are still having problems, click the Can't access your account? link and follow the on-screen instructions. If you are still having problems, ask your instructor or technical support person for help.

Figure 2-14 displays the Home, Contacts, and Calendar links in the lower-left corner of the page. Clicking the Home link opens the home page that you see when you log in to your Windows Live Hotmail account. Clicking the Contacts link opens the **Contacts page**, which contains options for managing information about your contacts. Clicking the Calendar link opens the **Calendar page**, which contains options for organizing your scheduled appointments and daily calendar using **Windows Live Calendar**, another Windows Live service.

2. In the Inbox, click the subject for the message you received from the Hotmail Team (or any other message in your Inbox) to open the message. Depending on your browser's security settings, you might see advertisements when you view your email messages. See Figure 2-15.

Figure 2-15	Message from Hotmail Team

Courtesy of © Microsoft

Trouble? Your message might look different from the one shown in Figure 2-15. This difference causes no problems.

Now that you have created a Windows Live ID and a Hotmail email address, you are ready to send a message to Don.

Sending a Message Using Windows Live Hotmail

To send a message in Windows Live Hotmail, click the New link on the Hotmail menu bar, which opens the New Message page. The New Message page contains the message header and a place to type your message.

REFERENCE

Sending a Message Using Windows Live Hotmail

- On the Hotmail menu bar, click the New link to open the New Message page.
- In the To box in the message header, type the recipient's email address. To send the message to more than one recipient, use commas or semicolons to separate multiple email addresses.
- If you need to address the message to Cc and Bcc recipients, click the Show Cc & Bcc link on the right side of the message header, and then type the email address of any Cc or Bcc recipients in the appropriate boxes. Use commas or semicolons to separate multiple email addresses.
- If necessary, click the Attachments link in the message header, browse to and select the file to attach, and then click the Open button.
- Click in the message body, and then type your message.
- Check your message for spelling and grammatical errors.
- Click the Send link on the Hotmail menu bar.

When you use Windows Live Hotmail to send a message with an attached file to Don, you will also send a courtesy copy of the message to your own email address to simulate receiving a message.

To create a message with an attachment:

1. On the Hotmail menu bar, click the **New** link. The New Message page opens, and the insertion point appears in the To box in the message header. See Figure 2-16.

   Trouble? If you don't have the starting Data Files, you need to get them before you can proceed. Your instructor will either give you the Data Files or ask you to obtain them from a specified location (such as a network drive). In either case, make a backup copy of the Data Files before you start so that you will have the original files available in case you need to start over. If you have any questions about the Data Files, see your instructor or technical support person for assistance.

Figure 2-16	Creating a new message

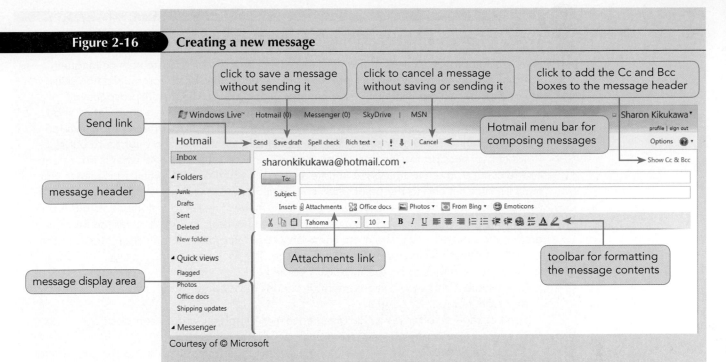

Courtesy of © Microsoft

Trouble? Your screen might l ook slightly different, depending on your computer's operating system, the browser you are using, and future changes to the site. These differences should not affect how Windows Live Hotmail functions.

2. In the To box, type **Don@KikukawaAir.com**.

   Trouble? Make sure that you use the address Don@KikukawaAir.com or its lowercase equivalent, don@kikukawaair.com. If you type an email address incorrectly, your message will be returned as undeliverable.

3. In the upper-right corner of the message header, click the **Show Cc & Bcc** link to add the Cc and Bcc boxes to the message header.

4. Click in the **Cc** box, and then type your full email address. When you send this message, you and Don will both receive it.

   Trouble? If you make a typing mistake on a previous line, use the arrow keys or click the insertion point to return to a previous line so you can correct your mistake. If the arrow keys do not move the insertion point backward or forward in the message header, press Shift + Tab or the Tab key to move backward or forward, respectively.

5. Click in the **Subject** box, and then type **Saturday's festival timeline**.

6. Click the **Attachments** link below the Subject box. The Open dialog box opens.

7. Navigate to the Tutorial.02\Tutorial folder provided with your Data Files, click **Timeline**, and then click the **Open** button. The message header now displays the attached file's name.

TIP

As you begin typing your email address, Windows Live Hotmail might open a menu with your complete email address in it. Pressing the Enter key adds the full email address to the Cc box and closes the menu.

PROSKILLS

Written Communication: Guidelines for Business Correspondence

Nearly all employees have some writing responsibility to communicate with colleagues, customers, and clients. Many corporate recruiters report that basic communication skills are one of the key items they assess when evaluating job candidates. A prospective employee's first contact with a company is often written and includes a cover letter and a résumé, sometimes submitted as an email message. A person's written communication skills are often a strong indicator of the type of employee that person might turn out to be.

Most busi ness professionals are busy and will only take time to read what is important and relevant to them at that point in time, especially when reading email. This means you must be succinct and to the point when composing email messages. When it comes to written precision, there are a few basic principles that will make your documents more polished. Because email messages are usually short and written quickly, it is easy to introduce grammatical mistakes that are more commonly found in oral communication, because the writer is "talking" while composing the message. The following guidelines will help you revise your messages to be grammatically correct:

- Avoid subject and verb disagreement. Pronouns must agree with the words they refer to in person, number, or gender.
- Don't change verb tenses within a sentence, paragraph, or written composition.
- Be sure to rewrite any run-on, incomplete, or unclear sentences.

Remember that the placement of commas, periods, apostrophes, and other punctuation marks can affect how the reader interprets your message. Before sending a message, verify that your punctuation is correct in the following situations:

- Use apostrophes to show possession ("The group's decision is to promote Gretchen.") or to indicate a contraction ("It's the best restaurant in town.").
- Do not use an apostrophe for plural nouns (DVDs, CDs), to reference a time period or numbers (the 1980s, "She is in her 20s."), or with possessive pronouns (yours, ours, hers, its).
- Use a colon to introduce a list of items or an explanation ("Campers should bring the following items: flashlight, sleeping bag, insect repellent, and water bottle."), in business letter salutations ("Dear Mrs. Robinson:"), and to maximize the impact of a word or phrase that follows ("There is only one word to describe the event: magnificent.").
- Use a comma to indicate a brief pause in a sentence, or to join or separate sentence parts. Use a comma before "and" in a list or series ("Steven, Hannah, and Annie went to the beach."), between two or more adjectives that describe a noun ("Please bring a new, unused gift for the toy drive."), to separate an introductory phrase or word ("However, the team won."), to separate clauses that won't change the meaning of a sentence if they are omitted ("The airport, which is located 30 miles south of town, has off-site parking."), between names and titles or degrees (John F. Kennedy, Jr. or Susan Marino, Ph.D.), and inside a quotation mark in a sentence ("I'll be there soon," replied Juan.).
- Use a period in certain abbreviations (J.D., Jr., Mrs.) or to end a sentence. If a sentence ends with an abbreviation that ends in a period, no additional period is needed. When a sentence ends with a quote, the period goes inside the quotation mark.
- Use a semicolon to join independent, closely related thoughts ("My favorite activity is reading; I read at least three books a week.").

You can learn more about business correspondence by following the links in the Business Writing section on the Weblinks page for Tutorial 2.

Next, you will type, proofread, and send a brief message to Don.

To type, proofread, and send the message:

1. Click in the message display area, type **Dear Don,** (including the comma), and then press the **Enter** key twice to insert a blank line.

2. In the message display area, type **I have attached the timeline for Saturday's events. If I receive any additional information, I will send it to you right away.**

3. Press the **Enter** key twice, type **Best,** (including the comma), press the **Enter** key, and then type your first name to sign your message. See Figure 2-17.

| Figure 2-17 | Completed message |

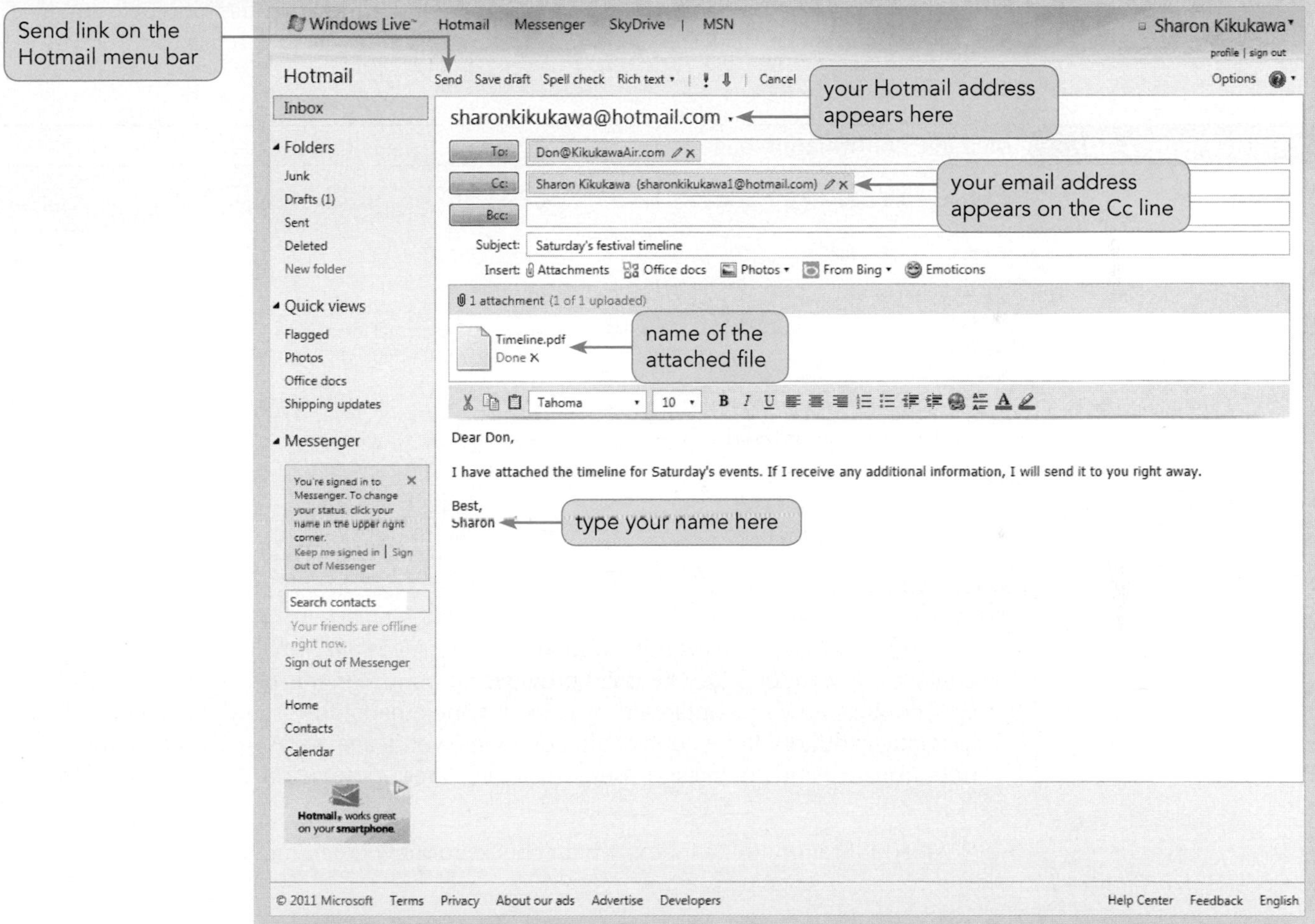

Send link on the Hotmail menu bar

Courtesy of © Microsoft

Before sending your message, you can click the Spell check link on the Hotmail menu bar to check the message for spelling errors. Misspelled words and words not in the dictionary (such as proper names) will appear with a red, wavy underline. When you right-click one of these words, you have the choice of selecting a word from a menu, ignoring the word, or adding it to the dictionary. If you don't see the correct word in the menu, you can correct the misspelled word directly.

4. Click the **Spell check** link on the Hotmail menu bar, review your message for typing or grammatical errors, and, if necessary, correct any errors.

TIP

Even when you use the spell checker to find spelling errors, it is still important to proofread your message and make any necessary corrections before sending it.

Trouble? If you are using Firefox, a dialog box might open and tell you that the browser is checking the spelling automatically. Click the OK button, and then check the message for spelling errors by looking for words with red, wavy lines under them. Make any necessary corrections, and then continue with Step 5.

Trouble? Google Chrome doesn't include a Spell check link. Check your message for spelling and grammatical errors, and then continue with Step 5.

5. Click the **Send** link on the Hotmail menu bar to send the message. A message confirmation page opens and shows that your message has been sent. See Figure 2-18.

Trouble? If you see a yellow message bar asking you to enter characters to stop spammers, click the "enter characters before sending your message" link on the yellow message bar, enter the characters shown on the Help us fight junk email page that opens, click the Continue button, and then close the tab to return to your message. Repeat Step 5 to send the message.

Figure 2-18	Message confirmation page

Courtesy of © Microsoft

If the email addresses you include in your messages are not already saved in your contact list, Windows Live Hotmail provides an option on this page for you to add new contacts to your contact list by selecting the email address and clicking the Add to contacts button. If the contact already exists, you'll see an "Already a contact" note. You will add contacts to your contact list later, so no action is necessary now.

Next, you'll return to the Inbox, which checks for new email messages.

Receiving and Opening a Message

When you receive new email messages, messages that you have not opened are displayed in the Inbox with closed envelope icons, and messages that you have opened are displayed with open envelope icons. You will check for new mail next.

To check for new mail:

1. Click the **Return to inbox** link. The Saturday's festival timeline message appears in the Inbox.

   Trouble? If you don't see the message, click the Inbox link on the left side of the page. It might take a few seconds for the message to arrive.

   Because you haven't read this message yet, it appears in bold in the message list. After you read the message, it will appear in a normal font. To read a message, you click its sender or subject.

2. Click the **Saturday's festival timeline** subject in the message. The message opens and displays the message header and content. See Figure 2-19.

Figure 2-19	Message received

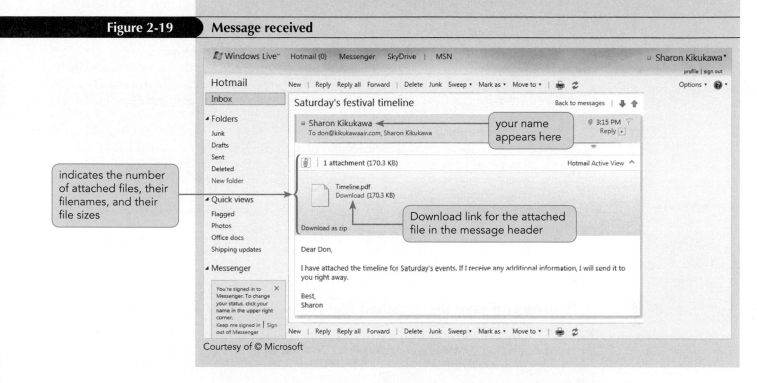

Courtesy of © Microsoft

Viewing and Saving an Attached File

If a message includes an attachment, the attachment information appears in the message header. When you receive a message with one or more attachments, you can open the attachment or save it.

Viewing and Saving an Attached File in Windows Live Hotmail

- In the Inbox, click the message that contains the attachment.
- To open the file using a program on your computer, click the attached file's Download link in the message header, and then click the Open button on the message bar in Internet Explorer. If you are using Firefox, click the Open with option button, choose the program to use to open the file, and then click the OK button. If you are using Chrome, click the Keep button on the message bar at the bottom of the screen, and then click the Timeline.pdf button to open the file.
- To save the file using Internet Explorer, click the attached file's Download link in the message header, click the Save button arrow on the message bar, click Save as to open the Save As dialog box, browse to the drive and folder where you want to save the attached file, click the Save button, and then click the Close button on the message bar.
- To save the file using Firefox, click the attached file's Download link in the message header, click the Save File option button in the dialog box that opens, and then click the OK button. Depending on your browser's settings, you might also need to specify the location in which to save the file; otherwise, the file will be saved automatically in the Downloads folder. Click the Close button if necessary to close the Downloads window.
- To save the file using Chrome, click the attached file's Download link in the message header, click the Show all downloads link on the right side of the message bar at the bottom of the screen, click the Show in folder link for the attachment that you want to save, and then move the file in the Downloads folder to the folder in which you want to save it.

You want to make sure that your attached file was sent properly, so you decide to open it. Then you will save the file.

To view and save the attached file:

1. Click the **Download** link in the message header. The message bar opens at the bottom of the browser window and asks if you want to open or save the file, or cancel the operation.

   Trouble? If you are using Firefox, the dialog box that opens is named Opening Timeline.pdf. Click the Open with option button in the Opening Timeline.pdf dialog box, click the OK button, and then continue with Step 3.

   Trouble? If you are using Chrome, click the Keep button on the message bar at the bottom of the screen, click the Timeline.pdf button, and then continue with Step 3.

2. Click the **Open** button. Adobe Reader or another program on your computer starts and opens the attached file. If necessary, maximize the program window that opens.

3. Review the page, and then click the **Close** button on the program window's title bar to close the program window that opened the attachment. Now that you have viewed the attachment, you can save it.

   Trouble? If a Downloads dialog box is open, click the Close button on its title bar to close it.

4. Click the **Download** link in the Attachment section, click the **Save button arrow** on the message bar at the bottom of the browser window to open a menu, click **Save as**, navigate to the **Tutorial.02\Tutorial** folder provided with your Data Files, click the **Save** button, and then click the **Yes** button to replace the existing file with the same name.

   Trouble? If you are using Firefox, the Opening Timeline.pdf dialog box opens. Click the Save File option button, and then click the OK button. Depending on your browser settings, you might need to specify a location in which to save the file. In this case, browse to and select the Tutorial.02\Tutorial folder, click the Save button, click the Yes button to overwrite the existing file with the same name, and then skip Step 5. If you don't need to specify a file location, click the Close button on the Downloads dialog box to close it.

5. If you are using Internet Explorer, click the **Close** button on the message bar at the bottom of the window to close it.

When you receive a message with an attached file, you can view and save the attachment for as long as you store the message. When you delete the message, you delete the file attached to the message. When you detach a file from an email message and save it on a disk or drive, it is just like any other file that you save. Be sure to save any important attachments soon after receiving them so you do not inadvertently delete the messages containing them.

Replying to and Forwarding Messages

Replying to and forwarding messages are common tasks for email users. You can forward any message you receive to one or more email addresses. Similarly, you can respond to the sender of a message quickly and efficiently by replying to a message.

Replying to an Email Message

To reply to a message, click the Reply link on the Hotmail menu bar to reply only to the sender, or click the Reply all link on the Hotmail menu bar to reply to the sender and other people who received the original message (all email addresses listed in the To and Cc boxes). Windows Live Hotmail opens a reply message page and places the original sender's address in the To box; other email addresses that received the original message appear in the To and Cc boxes as appropriate. You can leave the Subject box as is or modify it. Most programs, including Windows Live Hotmail, copy the original message and place it in the reply window. Figure 2-20 shows a reply to a message.

Figure 2-20   **Replying to a message**

click the Send link on the Hotmail menu bar to send the reply

"RE" indicates a reply

recipient's reply

sender's original message

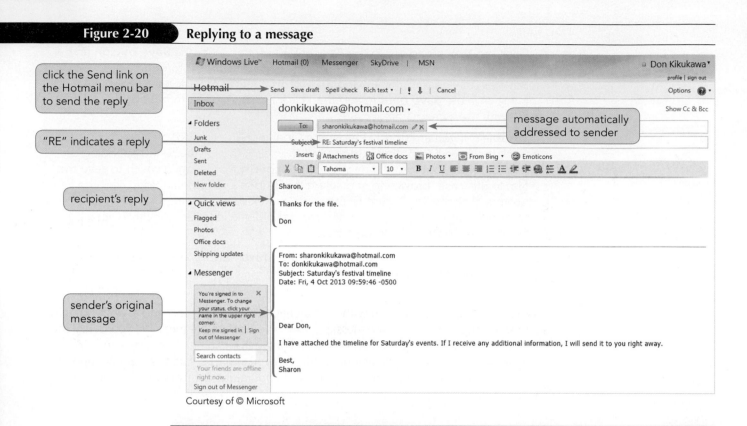

Courtesy of © Microsoft

REFERENCE

Replying to a Message Using Windows Live Hotmail

- Open the message you want to reply to.
- Click the Reply link on the Hotmail menu bar to reply to the sender, or click the Reply all link on the Hotmail menu bar to reply to the sender and other To and Cc recipients of the original message.
- Type other recipients' email addresses in the message header as needed.
- Change the text in the Subject box if necessary.
- Edit the message body as necessary.
- Click the Send link on the Hotmail menu bar.

Forwarding an Email Message

When you forward a message, you are sending a copy of the message, including any attachments, to one or more recipients who were not included in the original message. (If you do not want to forward the original sender's attached file to the new recipients, click the Close button next to the name of the attached file in the message header to remove it from the message.) To forward an existing mail message to another user, open the message you want to forward, and then click the Forward link on the Hotmail menu bar. A Forward message page opens, in which you can type the address of the recipient in the To box. If you want to forward the message to several people, type their addresses, separated by commas, in the To box (or Cc or Bcc boxes). Windows Live Hotmail includes the original message in the message display area and adds a blank line above it so you can add an optional message to provide context for the recipient. Figure 2-21 shows a forwarded copy of a message.

Figure 2-21   Forwarding a message

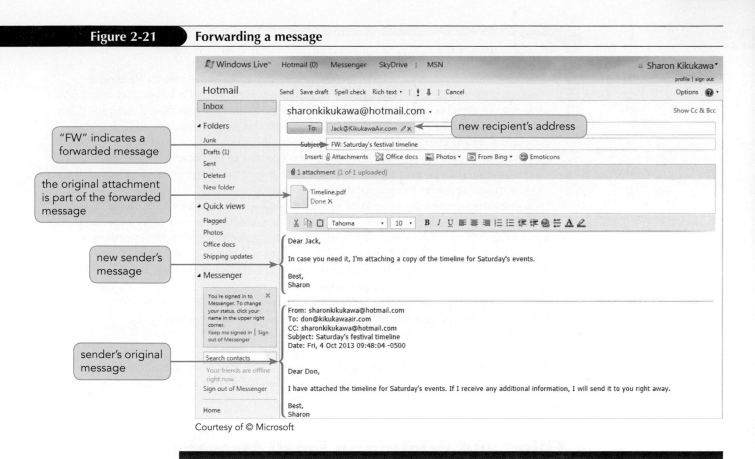

"FW" indicates a forwarded message

the original attachment is part of the forwarded message

new sender's message

sender's original message

new recipient's address

Courtesy of © Microsoft

REFERENCE

Forwarding an Email Message Using Windows Live Hotmail

- Open the message that you want to forward.
- Click the Forward link on the Hotmail menu bar.
- Click the To box, and then type one or more email addresses, separated by commas. Add Cc and Bcc email addresses as necessary.
- Click the blank line above the quoted message, and then type an optional message to add context for the recipient(s).
- Click the Send link on the Hotmail menu bar.

INSIGHT

Forwarding Messages Appropriately

When forwarding a message to a new recipient, and especially when forwarding a message that was forwarded originally to you, keep in mind that a forwarded message includes the email addresses of all the message's previous recipients and senders. When you need to forward a message to a new recipient and it's not important for the new recipient to know who sent you the original message, you can use the Copy and Paste commands in your email program to paste the content of the forwarded message into a new message, thus protecting the privacy of the message's original recipients and making the message easier to read for its new recipients.

Some people routinely send information about Internet viruses and hoaxes, or about emotional or charitable causes, such as cancer research, to everyone they know in an attempt to "spread the word." Often, these messages contain incorrect information. Before being alarmed by information about viruses or hoaxes, contributing to any charity that you learn about in this way, or forwarding the message to other users, be sure to check one of the many reputable Internet resources for more information. The Email Hoaxes and Rumors section of the Weblinks page for Tutorial 2 contains links to sites that contain information about viruses, hoaxes, and fraudulent schemes.

Occasionally, Don receives messages he wants to keep for later reference. In Windows Live Hotmail, you can file email messages so you can refer to them later or print them as needed.

Filing and Printing an Email Message

You can use the Windows Live Hotmail folders to file your email messages by category. When you file a message, you move it from the Inbox to a folder. You will file your message in a new folder named "Festivals" for safekeeping.

To create the new folder:

1. Click the **Inbox** link, and then click the **New folder** link in the Folders list on the left side of the page. The New folder page opens, and the insertion point appears in the Folder name box. See Figure 2-22.

| Figure 2-22 | Creating a new folder |

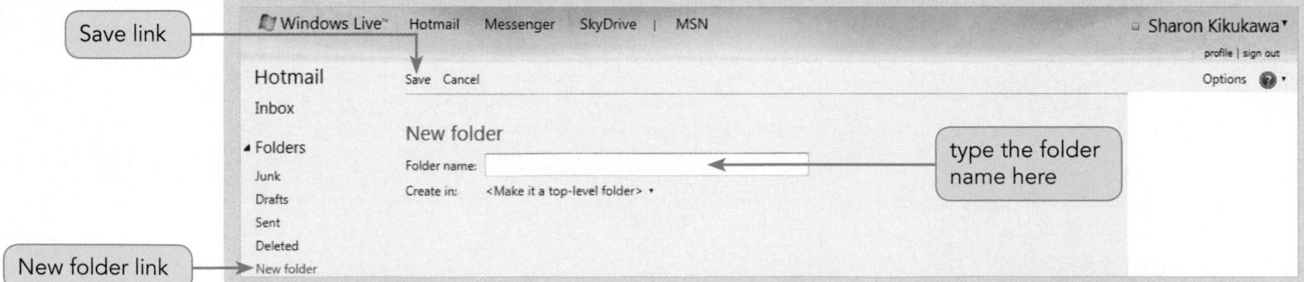

Courtesy of © Microsoft

2. With the insertion point in the Folder name box, type **Festivals**.

3. Click the **Save** link on the Hotmail menu bar. The page changes to show the list of folders and details about the folders' contents. The Festivals folder appears in the list of folders.

After you create a folder, you can transfer messages to it. Besides transferring messages from the Inbox, you can select messages in any other folder and then transfer them to a different folder. You will move the Saturday's festival timeline message from the Inbox to the newly created Festivals folder.

To file a message in the Festivals folder:

1. Click the **Inbox** link.

2. Click the **check box** to the left of the Saturday's festival timeline message to add a check mark to it.

3. Click the **Move to** link on the Hotmail menu bar to open a list of folders, and then click **Festivals** in the list. The message is transferred to the Festivals folder.

4. Click the **Festivals** link in the Folders list on the left side of the page. The message appears in the **Festivals** folder.

You might want to print certain messages for future reference. You can print a message at any time—when you receive it, before you send it, or after you file it. You will print the Saturday's festival timeline message next.

To print the email message:

1. Click the subject for the **Saturday's festival timeline** message to open it.

2. Click the **Print** button on the Hotmail menu bar. A new window opens and displays a "printer-friendly" version of the message, and the Print dialog box opens.

3. If necessary, select your printer in the list, and then click the **Print** button (or the **OK** button). The message is printed.

4. Close the window with the printer-friendly version of the message, and then click the **Inbox** link.

TIP

A "printer-friendly" version of a message excludes ads and other content on the page, such as links.

When you no longer need a message, you can delete it.

Deleting a Message and a Folder

When you don't need a message any longer, you can delete it by opening the message or selecting the message in the Inbox, and then clicking the Delete link on the Hotmail menu bar. You can delete a folder by selecting it and then clicking the Delete link on the Hotmail menu bar. When you delete a message or folder, you are simply moving it to the Deleted folder. The default setting for Windows Live Hotmail accounts is for the system to delete all messages in the Deleted folder periodically. However, if you want to remove items permanently, you can delete them from the Deleted folder.

REFERENCE

Deleting a Message in Windows Live Hotmail

- Open the folder that contains the message you want to delete.
- Click the check box to the left of the message you want to delete to add a check mark to it, and then click the Delete link on the Hotmail menu bar.
- To delete items permanently, click the Deleted link in the Folders list on the left side of the page, click the Delete link or the Empty link on the Hotmail menu bar, and then, if necessary, click the OK button.

Now you will delete the Saturday's festival timeline message.

To delete the message:

1. Click the **Festivals** link in the Folders list on the left side of the page.

2. Click the **check box** that appears to the left of the Saturday's festival timeline message to add a check mark to it and select the message.

3. Click the **Delete** link on the Hotmail menu bar. The message is deleted from the Festivals folder and is moved to the Deleted folder.

4. Click the **Deleted** link in the Folders list on the left side of the page. The Saturday's festival timeline message appears in the folder.

5. Click the **check box** to the left of the Saturday's festival timeline message to add a check mark to it, and then click the **Delete** link on the Hotmail menu bar. The message is permanently deleted from your Windows Live Hotmail account.

You will delete the Festivals folder using the Manage folders link.

REFERENCE

Deleting a Windows Live Hotmail Folder

- Point to Folders on the left side of the page to display the More actions for folders button, click the More actions for folders button to open a menu of options, and then click Manage folders to open a page showing the folders for your account and the details of each folder's contents.
- Click the check box to the left of the folder you want to delete.
- Click the Delete link on the Hotmail menu bar.
- Click the OK button.

Windows Live Hotmail won't let you delete the default system folders, but you can delete folders that you created. You'll delete the Festivals folder next.

To delete the Festivals folder:

1. Point to the **Folders** link on the left side of the page to display the More actions for folders button to the right of the word "Folders."

▶ 2. Click the **More actions for folders** button to open a menu of options, and then click **Manage folders**. A page opens and displays the folders in your Windows Live Hotmail account, along with the number of messages in each folder and their combined file sizes.

▶ 3. Click the **check box** to the left of the **Festivals** folder to select it.

▶ 4. Click the **Delete** link on the Hotmail menu bar. A dialog box opens and warns that deleting the folder also deletes any messages stored in the folder.

▶ 5. Click the **OK** button. The Festivals folder is deleted.

▶ 6. Click the **Inbox** link.

Maintaining Your Contact List

As you use email to communicate with business associates and friends, you might want to save their contact information in your contact list to make it easier to enter addresses into the header of your email messages.

Adding a Contact to the Contact List

You can open your contact list by clicking the Contacts link on the left side of the page. To create a new contact, click the New link on the Hotmail menu bar, and then enter the contact's information in the appropriate boxes.

Adding a Contact to the Contact List

- Click the Contacts link to open the All contacts page.
- Click the New link on the Hotmail menu bar to open the New contact page.
- Enter the contact's information in the appropriate boxes on the New contact page.
- Click the Save link on the Hotmail menu bar.

Now you can add contacts to your contact list. You begin by adding Jack Clancy's contact information.

To add a contact to your contact list:

▶ 1. On the left side of the page, click the **Contacts** link (you might need to scroll down the page to see this link). The All contacts page opens.

▶ 2. Click the **New** link on the Hotmail menu bar. The New contact page opens and displays boxes for entering a contact's first name, last name, nickname, personal email address, Windows Live ID, and other information.

▶ 3. Click in the **First name** box, and then type **Jack**.

▶ 4. Press the **Tab** key to move the insertion point to the Last name box, and then type **Clancy** in the Last name box.

5. Scroll down the page to the Work info section, click in the **Work email** box, and then type **Jack@KikukawaAir.com**. See Figure 2-23.

Figure 2-23	Adding a contact to the contact list

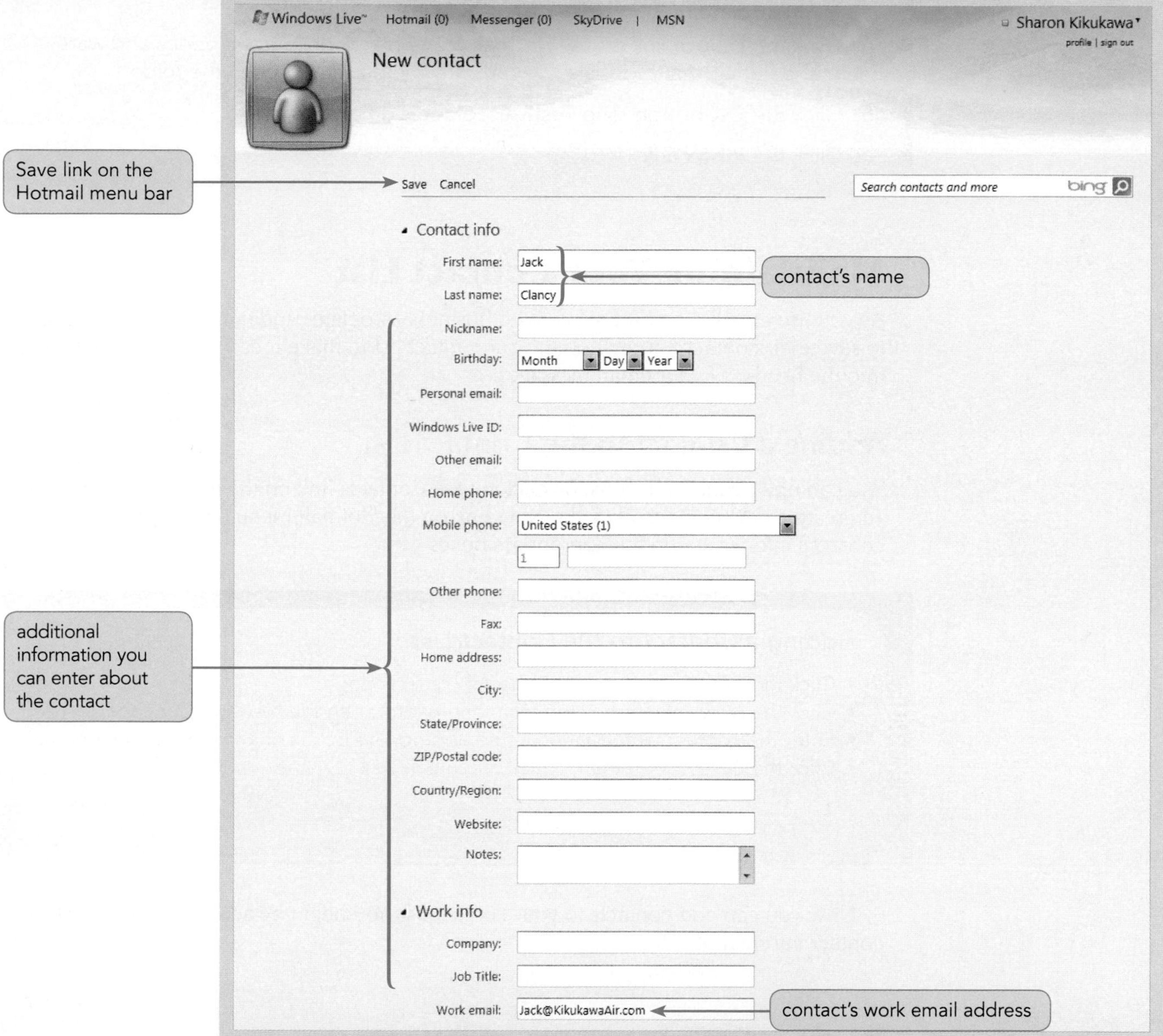

Courtesy of © Microsoft

6. Scroll down and then click the **Save** button at the bottom of the New contact page. Jack's name and email address are stored in your contact list.

7. Repeat Steps 2 through 6 to create contacts for the following Kikukawa Air employees:

First name	Last name	Work email
Don	**Kikukawa**	**Don@KikukawaAir.com**
Margaret	**Durring**	**Margaret@KikukawaAir.com**

8. On the lower-left side of the page, click the **Inbox** link.

Now that you have stored the names and email addresses for Jack, Don, and Margaret in your contact list, you can click the To, Cc, or Bcc button that appears to the left of a To, Cc, or Bcc box in a new message, and then click one of their names in the contact list to enter that person's email address in the message header.

Creating a Category

You can create a group of contacts, called a category or distribution list, and use the category to address messages to a group of recipients. For example, Sharon frequently sends messages to Jack, Don, and Margaret as a group because they work as a team when participating in hot air balloon festivals and racing events. You will create a category in your contact list so you can type one nickname for the group of email addresses, instead of having to type each address separately.

REFERENCE

Creating a Category in the Contact List

- Click the Contacts link on the left side of the page to open the All contacts page.
- Click the Categories link on the Hotmail menu bar, and then click New category to open the New category page.
- Type a name for the category in the Name box.
- Click in the Members box, and then type the names of existing contacts to add to the category or the email addresses of contacts who are not in your contact list.
- Click the Save link on the Hotmail menu bar.

You'll create a category next.

To create a category in your contact list:

1. If necessary, scroll down the page, and then click the **Contacts** link to open the All contacts page.

2. Click the **Categories** link on the Hotmail menu bar to open a menu of options, and then click **New category**. The New category page opens. The insertion point appears in the Name box.

3. In the Name box, type **Race Team**.

4. Click in the **Members** box, and then type **Jack**. As you type Jack's first name, his name appears in a box that opens. Press the **Enter** key to add Jack's name to the category.

5. With the insertion point in the Members box, type **Don**. When Don's name appears in the box, press the **Enter** key to add Don's name to the category.

6. With the insertion point in the Members box, type **Margaret**. When Margaret's name appears in the box, press the **Enter** key to add Margaret's name to the category. The category contains three contacts. See Figure 2-24.

TIP

To remove a contact from the category, click the Close button on the contact name.

Figure 2-24 **Category added to contact list**

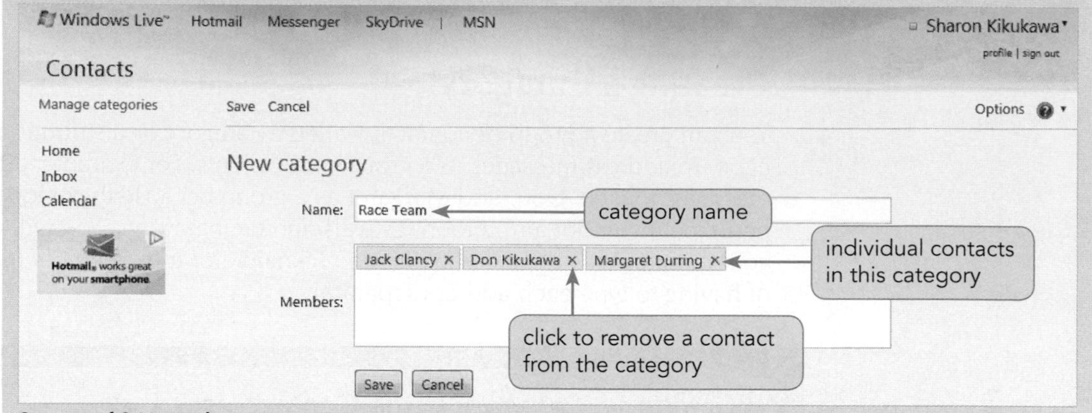

Courtesy of © Microsoft

7. Click the **Save** link on the Hotmail menu bar to save the category.

Now, you will test the category by creating a new message.

To address a message to a category:

1. Click the **Inbox** link, which appears on the left side of the page, and then click the **New** link on the Hotmail menu bar to open the New message page.

2. Click the **To** button to the left of the To box. A pop-up window opens and displays your individual contacts on the People tab. To see the Race Team category, you need to display the Categories tab.

3. Click the **Categories** tab. The Race Team category appears in the list. The notation "3 people" indicates the number of individual contacts stored in the category.

4. Click the **check box** to the left of the Race Team category to add a check mark to it. The Race Team category name is added to the To box. The pop-up window stays open until you close it, so you can add additional recipients to the message if necessary.

5. Click the **Close** link on the pop-up window to close it. The Race Team category appears in the To box.

6. Click the **Show Cc & Bcc** link to add the Cc and Bcc boxes to the message header.

7. Click the **Cc** button in the message header, click the **People** tab, click the **check box** for your email address, and then click the **Close** link. Your email address is added to the Cc box. See Figure 2-25.

TIP

Clicking the plus sign to the left of a category in the To box displays the individual email addresses in the category so you can delete a recipient or confirm the recipients by name.

Figure 2-25   **Using the contact list to address a message**

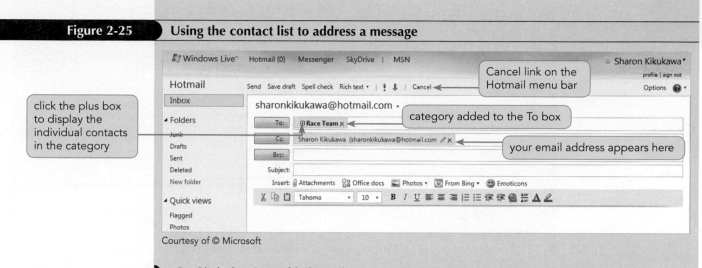

Courtesy of © Microsoft

▶ **8.** Click the **Cancel** link on the Hotmail menu bar to cancel the message, and then click the **OK** button in the message box asking you to confirm that you want to discard the message. You return to the Inbox.

When you need to modify a category's contacts, you can do so by clicking the Contacts link on the left side of the page, clicking the Manage categories link on the left side of the page, and then clicking the category's name on the Manage categories page to add or remove individual contacts in the category, or edit the category name. To delete the category (but not the individual contacts), select the check box for the category on the Manage categories page, click the Delete link on the Hotmail menu bar, and then click the OK button. Deleting a category does not delete the individual contacts it stores; it only deletes the category.

Using SkyDrive to Share Files

In this session, you learned how to use email to send and receive messages with files attached to them. When you need to send multiple files or large files to other users, it is often impractical to attach them to an email message because your mail server or the recipient's mail server might reject the message due to the number or size of its attachments. In other cases, you might need to collaborate on a document, workbook, or other file with multiple users, or simply share the content of a document with multiple users. In these situations, you can use another Windows Live service, called **SkyDrive**, to post your files to a server and then use your Windows Live Hotmail account to share access to these files with users that you specify.

Sharon might want to post pictures of balloon races or tours using her Windows Live account, so she asks you to explore the options for posting photos on SkyDrive.

To view the SkyDrive options for sharing photos:

▶ **1.** At the top of the page, click the **SkyDrive** link. The SkyDrive page opens.

▶ **2.** Point to the **SkyDrive** link at the top of the page to open a menu. See Figure 2-26. The menu includes options for sharing existing files and photos with other users. You can also use the "New" links to create a new Word document, Excel workbook, PowerPoint presentation, or OneNote notebook and store it in your SkyDrive account.

Figure 2-26   **SkyDrive menu**

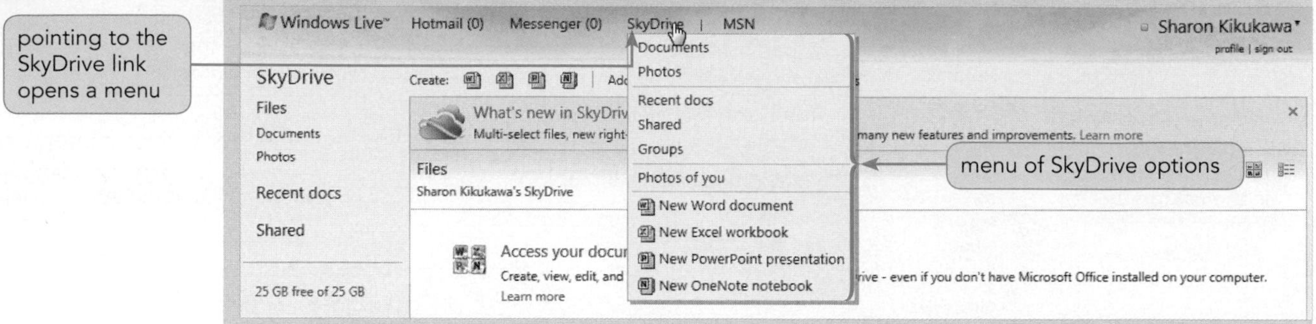

pointing to the SkyDrive link opens a menu

menu of SkyDrive options

Courtesy of © Microsoft

3. On the menu, click **Photos** to display the Photos page for SkyDrive.

4. Click the **New folder** link on the SkyDrive menu bar to create a new photo album folder. You can assign a name to the album and change the settings to control how to share the album. The default folder (album) name is selected.

5. Type **My photos** and then press the **Enter** key. The folder name is updated.

6. Click the **My photos** folder to select it, and then click the **Add files** link on the SkyDrive menu bar. A window opens and includes a link to add files to the folder. Clicking the "select them from your computer" link opens the Open dialog box, where you can browse to and select one or more photos to upload. (You will not upload any photos at this time.)

7. Click the **Close** button on the Add files window to close it.

8. On the right side of the page, click the **Share folder** link to display the options for sharing your photos. Notice that you can choose to restrict access to your photos by sharing them only with people you specify using their email addresses. You can also choose to restrict who can edit your photos or require people to log in before viewing your photos.

9. Click the **Close** button to close the Share box.

10. Click the **SkyDrive** link near the top of the page to return to the SkyDrive page.

Sharon might also like to use SkyDrive to create and post files, such as Word documents and Excel workbooks, to make it easy for employees to access and collaborate on their work. She asks you to explore the feature that lets you create a file next.

To view the SkyDrive options for creating a file:

1. At the top of the page, point to the **SkyDrive** link. The SkyDrive menu opens.

2. On the menu, click **New Excel workbook**. The New Microsoft Excel workbook window opens.

3. Click the **Create** button to accept the default filename, Book1, for the file. The Microsoft Excel Web App window opens the Book1 workbook that you created. Notice that the Excel Web App includes a Ribbon with features similar to what is available in the full Microsoft Excel program. These features let you create and edit a worksheet. See Figure 2-27.

Figure 2-27   **Microsoft Excel Web App window**

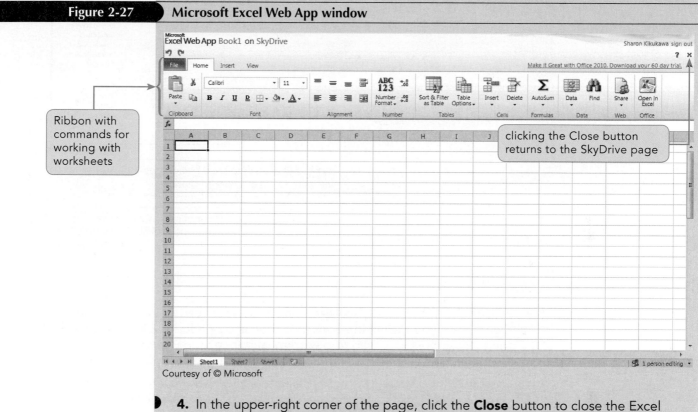

Ribbon with commands for working with worksheets

clicking the Close button returns to the SkyDrive page

Courtesy of © Microsoft

4. In the upper-right corner of the page, click the **Close** button to close the Excel Web App window and to return to the SkyDrive page. The Book1 workbook appears on the Files page for your SkyDrive account.

5. If necessary, click your name in the Last modified by column for the Book1 file to open the details pane for the Book1 workbook on the right side of the screen. See Figure 2-28. The details pane includes options for working with the selected file. Notice that you can rename or delete the file, or click the Share link in the Sharing section to change the settings for who can access the file.

Figure 2-28	SkyDrive Files page for Sharon

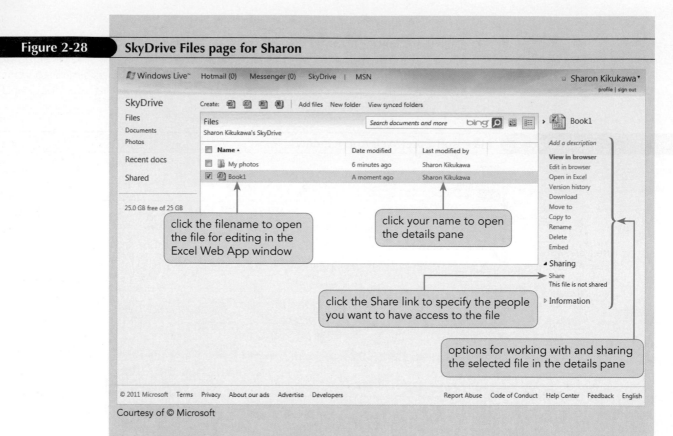

Courtesy of © Microsoft

Trouble? If you see the Excel Web App window instead of the page shown in Figure 2-28, you clicked the Book1 filename and opened it. Click the Close button to close the Excel Web App window, and then repeat Step 5, making sure to click your name in the Last modified by column and not the filename.

Trouble? If the Sharing section is collapsed, click the arrow to the left of the word "Sharing" to expand the section so you can see its options.

After uploading a file to SkyDrive, you can add comments to it, rename it, or move it into a folder that you create. As with most file-sharing sites, part of the user and terms of service agreements that you must accept when creating a Windows Live account prohibit you from uploading copyrighted material to the Windows Live site without authorization from the copyright's owner. SkyDrive also puts other restrictions on file uploads; for example, you cannot upload a file that is larger than 100 megabytes or a file that has the same name as a file that you already uploaded to SkyDrive. For more information about SkyDrive and other file-sharing services, you can follow the links in the File Sharing section of the Weblinks page for Tutorial 2.

Signing Out of Your Windows Live Account

You are finished evaluating Windows Live, so you need to sign out of your Windows Live account and close your browser. It is important that you sign out before closing the browser to ensure the security of your email and to prevent unauthorized access. If you do not sign in to your Windows Live Hotmail account within a specified time period after creating it, Microsoft might deactivate your email address or delete it.

To sign out of Windows Live and close your browser:

▶ **1.** Click the **sign out** link below your name near the upper-right corner of the page. The MSN.com home page (or another Web page) opens.

▶ **2.** Click the **Close** button on the browser's title bar to close your browser.

In this session, you learned how to use Windows Live Hotmail to create, send, receive, and manage email messages. You also learned how to create and use the contact list to manage information about contacts. Finally, you learned about using SkyDrive to share photos and other files.

REVIEW

Session 2.2 Quick Check

1. What information is required when you create a Windows Live account?
2. True or False. When using a computer in a public library to access your Windows Live Hotmail account, you should sign out of your account when you are finished viewing your messages to protect your privacy.
3. When you receive a message with an attachment in Windows Live Hotmail, what two options are available for the attached file?
4. When you delete a Hotmail message, can you recover it? Why or why not?
5. What information can you store about a person in the contact list?
6. What are three types of files you can create using Windows Live SkyDrive?

Practice the skills you learned in the tutorial using the same case scenario.

PRACTICE

Review Assignments

Data File needed for the Review Assignments: KAir.gif

Now that you have learned how to use Windows Live Hotmail to manage your email messages, Sharon asks you to submit a review of your experience using the Webmail provider and a recommendation about whether Kikukawa Air should continue using it. Sharon also wants to see how graphics are sent over the Internet, so she asks you to send her the Kikukawa Air logo to simulate how it appears when sent by Kikukawa Air employees.

1. Start your Web browser, go to **www.cengagebrain.com**, open the Tutorial 2 Weblinks page, and then click the Review Assignments link. Click the Windows Live link.

2. Sign in to your Windows Live Hotmail account.

3. Add your instructor's full name and email address and Sharon Kikukawa's full name and email address (Sharon@KikukawaAir.com) to your contact list.

4. Create a category named **Classmates** using the full names and email addresses of three of your classmates.

5. Create a new message. Address the message to Sharon and to your instructor. Add your email address to the message header so you will receive a courtesy copy of the message, and so the members of the Classmates category will receive a blind courtesy copy of the message. Use the subject **Hotmail review** for the message.

6. In the message body, type three or more sentences describing your overall impressions about Windows Live Hotmail. Be sure to evaluate the program's features, ease of use, and other important considerations that you determine.

7. In the message body, press the Enter key twice, and then type your full name and email address on separate lines.

8. Attach the **KAir.gif** file, which is saved in the Tutorial.02\Review folder included with your Data Files, to the message.

9. Check the spelling of your message before you send it, and correct any mistakes. Proofread your message and verify that you have created it correctly, and then send the message.

10. Wait a few seconds, check for new messages, and then review the message you sent to Sharon and your instructor.

11. Forward the message and the attached file to your instructor. In the message body, describe the appearance of the file you attached to the message and explain your findings in terms of attaching a graphic to a message. Send the message.

12. Create a new folder named **Reviews**, and then file the Hotmail review message in the Reviews folder.

13. Sign out of your Windows Live Hotmail account.

Apply the skills you learned to send an email message with attached files.

APPLY

Case Problem 1

Data Files needed for this Case Problem: Bales.jpg and Paper.jpg

Greenfield County Recycling   Greenfield County boasts a 98% compliance rate in the county's extensive recycling program from residential, business, and government customers. Separate facilities process all types of paper, glass, cans, plastics, household goods and appliances, and yard waste. The county just opened its eighth paper facility and needs you to send some pictures to the media liaison and to two managers in the county's technology office for an upcoming press release. Complete the following steps:

1. Start your Web browser, go to **www.cengagebrain.com**, open the Tutorial 2 Weblinks page, and then click the Case Problem 1 link. Click the Windows Live link.

2. Sign in to your Windows Live Hotmail account.

3. Create individual contacts using the full name and email address of your instructor and two classmates.

4. Create a category named **Managers** using the two classmates you added in Step 3.

5. Create a new message addressed to your instructor. Add the Managers category to the message header so its members will receive a courtesy copy of the message. Add your email address to the message header so you will receive a blind courtesy copy of the message. Use the subject **Facility pictures**.

6. In the message display area, type a short note telling the recipients that you are attaching two pictures of the new recycling facility, and ask them to respond to you when they receive your message. Sign your message with your first and last names.

7. Attach to the message the files named **Bales.jpg** and **Paper.jpg**, which are saved in the Tutorial.02\Cases folder included with your Data Files.

8. Send the message, wait a few seconds, and then check your Inbox for new messages.

9. Create a new folder named **Paper Facility**, and then file the message you received in the Paper Facility folder.

10. Sign out of your Windows Live Hotmail account.

Case Problem 2

Use Windows Live Hotmail to learn how to manage unsolicited messages.

RESEARCH

There are no Data Files needed for this Case Problem.

Estancia Ridge Estate   Bridget Estancia owns and operates the Estancia Ridge Estate, a small, private, family-owned olive grove specializing in locally grown olives that are pressed into olive oil on the premises. Bridget manages the gardens, the historic estate where she also lives, tours of the home and grove, and a gift shop. Olive oil sales are Bridget's largest income item, but she has seen a rise in tourism over the past year at her unique estate. Because of this rise in tourism, Bridget is advertising in local tourism publications and other publications that might attract people to visit the estate. As part of the advertisements, she includes the estate's phone number, its Web site address, and her email address. Although she receives many email messages from interested tourists, she has also started to receive many unsolicited messages as her email address is added to different mailing lists, some of which distribute information that she does not want to receive. Bridget asks you to research how she can use Windows Live Hotmail to manage the messages she receives by blocking senders from whom she does not want to receive messages, deleting junk mail, and filtering messages into categories or different views so she receives fewer messages in her Inbox. Complete the following steps:

1. Start your Web browser, go to **www.cengagebrain.com**, open the Tutorial 2 Weblinks page, and then click the Case Problem 2 link. Click the Windows Live link.

2. Sign in to your Windows Live Hotmail account, and then open your Inbox.

3. Click the Options button in the upper-right corner of the page, and then click More options to open the Hotmail Options page. The Hotmail Options page displays general help topics for Windows Live Hotmail.

4. Click the links on the page that deal with topics such as preventing junk email, using filters, and setting safe and blocked senders. Review the information you find to learn more about the tools Bridget can use to reduce or prevent junk email messages. If you would like to do so, set one or more options for your account, and then click the Save button. If you do not make any changes, click the Cancel button to return to the previous page without making any changes, or click the Options or Hotmail link on the left side of the page to return to the Hotmail Options page.

5. On the Hotmail Options page, click a link that lets you create rules for sorting new messages, and then examine the page that opens. Review the options on the page and consider how Bridget could use a rule to limit or reduce messages she receives from specific senders. If you would like to do so, set one or more options for your account, and then click the Save button. If you do not make any changes, click the Options or Hotmail link on the left side of the page to return to the Hotmail Options page.

6. Click the Hotmail link near the top of the page. Create a new message addressed to your instructor. Add your email address to the message header so you will receive a courtesy copy of the message. Use the subject **Filter and junk mail options**.

EXPLORE
7. In the message display area, explain how Bridget can use Windows Live Hotmail to manage the mail she receives better in two or three paragraphs. Use information from the Hotmail Options page in your response, and cite specific features and steps for your recommendations. Sign your message with your first and last names.

8. Send the message to your instructor.

9. Sign out of your Windows Live Hotmail account.

Use Windows Live Hotmail to learn how to create a signature for your outgoing email messages.

CREATE

Case Problem 3

There are no Data Files needed for this Case Problem.

Trinity Cablevision   You have just been hired as an installation contractor for Trinity Cablevision, which provides digital cable television, digital phone service, and high-speed Internet services to residential and business customers. Because you are a contractor, you will need to use your Windows Live Hotmail account for your business correspondence. To identify yourself to email recipients, you decide to create a signature for your outgoing messages that identifies your name, city, email address, and contractor license number. Complete the following steps:

1. Start your Web browser, go to **www.cengagebrain.com**, open the Tutorial 2 Weblinks page, and then click the Case Problem 3 link. Click the Windows Live link.

2. Sign in to your Windows Live Hotmail account.

3. Click the Options button in the upper-right corner of the page, and then click More options to open the Hotmail Options page. The Hotmail Options page displays general help topics for Windows Live Hotmail.

4. Locate and click a link on the page that deals with creating a signature (or a signature file).

EXPLORE
5. Use the page that opens to create a signature with your first and last names on the first line, your city and state on the second line, and your email address on the third line. On the fourth line, type **Contractor number** and any six-digit number. When you are finished, click the Save button.

6. Click the link to return to the Inbox.

7. Create an individual contact using the full name and email address of your instructor.

8. Create a new message addressed to your instructor. Add your email address to the message header so you will receive a courtesy copy of the message. Use the subject **Contractor cable services**.

EXPLORE
9. Use the toolbar to change your name in your signature for the current message to a blue, bold font.

10. Send the message, wait a few seconds, and then check for new messages.

EXPLORE
11. Create a second message, address it to your instructor, and add your email address to the message header so you will receive a courtesy copy of the message. At the top of the message, explain the steps you need to take to send a message that does not

include your signature. Delete your signature from the message, sign the message with your first and last names, and then send the message.

12. Sign out of your Windows Live Hotmail account.

Use SkyDrive to create a photo album.

CHALLENGE

Case Problem 4

Data Files needed for this Case Problem: Chance.jpg, Maple.jpg, Rocky.jpg, and Scout.jpg

Rescue Me Canine   Amy Brask works as a volunteer for Rescue Me Canine, an agency that places healthy puppies and dogs that have been picked up by animal control officers with people who agree to care for these pets either as foster or adoptive families. Amy receives many email messages from local vets and community leaders who refer potential foster and adoptive families to her. Amy had been sending pictures of dogs to prospective families, but she would rather post them in one place. She decides to investigate using a SkyDrive photo album to see if this might make distributing photos of pets easier and more efficient.

1. Start your Web browser, go to **www.cengagebrain.com**, open the Tutorial 2 Weblinks page, and then click the Case Problem 4 link. Click the Windows Live link.

2. Sign in to your Windows Live account.

3. Create individual contacts using the full name and email address of your instructor and two classmates.

4. Open the SkyDrive page, point to the SkyDrive link at the top of the page to open a menu of options, and then click the Photos option.

✦ **EXPLORE**   5. Near the top of the page, click the New folder link on the SkyDrive menu bar to create a new folder (album) named **Dogs**, press the Enter key, and then click the Dogs folder. Click the Add files link on the SkyDrive menu bar; click the link to select photos from your computer; browse to and select the Tutorial.02\Cases folder with your Data Files; press and hold the Ctrl key; click the files **Chance.jpg**, **Maple.jpg**, **Rocky. jpg**, and **Scout.jpg**; release the Ctrl key; and then click the Open button. Four files are uploaded to the album. (*Note:* Depending on your Internet connection speed, it might take a minute or longer to upload the files.)

✦ **EXPLORE**   6. After the files have been uploaded, click the Share folder link in the Sharing section on the right side of the page. In the To box, type the names of the recipients you created in Step 3, and then type your own email address in the To box. (Be sure to press the Enter key after typing an address to add it to the To box.) Click the Share button.

7. Click the Hotmail link at the top of the page and check for new messages. Examine the message that you sent to yourself, use the option in the message to view the photos in the album you created, and then examine the page that displays your photos and its features as you review the photos you posted.

8. Sign out of your Windows Live Hotmail account.

Expand the skills you learned in this tutorial to create a document using the tools available in SkyDrive.

CHALLENGE

Case Problem 5

There are no Data Files needed for this Case Problem.

Mangietti's Pizza Garden   Mangietti's Pizza Garden serves pizza and other Italian specialties. Its claim to fame is its coal-fired pizza oven and homemade, hand-tossed pizza dough. Customers are asked for their email addresses when they pay their bills so Mangietti's can send them coupons and follow-up surveys. You are working on an advertisement for the local newspaper and want to use actual customer comments in the ad, so you decide to gather these comments using a survey that you will send to customers with an email message that includes a 10% discount off their next meal. Because you need to coordinate the survey's questions with the owner and a few other staff members, you decide to post it on SkyDrive so the group can collaborate on the document before it is finalized and sent to customers. Complete the following steps:

1. Start your Web browser, go to **www.cengagebrain.com**, open the Tutorial 2 Weblinks page, and then click the Case Problem 5 link. Click the Windows Live link.

2. Sign in to your Windows Live Hotmail account.

3. Create individual contacts using the full name and email address of your instructor and two classmates. Then create a category named **Ad Survey Group** and add these three contacts to the group.

4. On the SkyDrive page, point to the SkyDrive link at the top of the page to open a menu, and then click the New Word document option.

5. In the Name box, type **Customer Survey** as the name of the document to create, and then click the Create button. The Word Web App window opens a blank document. The Ribbon contains options that let you work with documents, similar to how you work with documents in the Microsoft Word program.

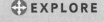 **EXPLORE**

6. Use Figure 2-29 and the options on the Ribbon to create the content and formatting in the document.

Figure 2-29   **Content for SkyDrive document**

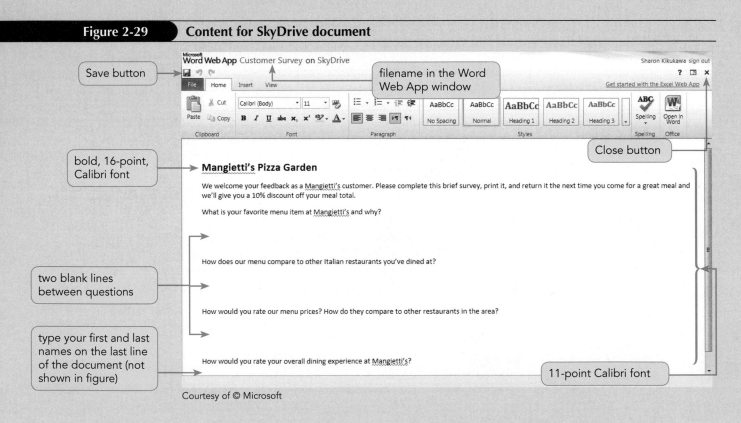

Courtesy of © Microsoft

7. At the bottom of the document, type your first and last names.

8. When you are finished, click the Save button above the File tab on the Ribbon. Then click the Close button in the upper-right corner of the page, below the sign out link, to close the Word Web App window. The Customer Survey document appears in your list of files in SkyDrive.

9. If necessary, click your name in the Last modified by column for the Customer Survey document to open the details pane for the document you created. If necessary, expand the Sharing section.

⊕ EXPLORE   10. In the details pane, click the Share link in the Sharing section to open the Share window for the document. In the To box, enter the Ad Survey Group category you created in Step 3, type your own email address, and then click the Share button to send a notification to your instructor and the two classmates you entered in Step 3 that your document is finished, along with a link to view it.

11. Check your Hotmail account for the message you sent to yourself, and then use it to open the document you shared.

12. Close the Word Web App window, and then sign out of your Windows Live Hotmail account.

TUTORIAL 3

Searching the Web

Using Search Engines and Directories Effectively

OBJECTIVES

Session 3.1
- Determine whether a research question is specific or exploratory
- Formulate an effective Web search strategy to answer research questions
- Use Web search tools including search engines, Web directories, metasearch engines, and Web bibliographies effectively

Session 3.2
- Apply Boolean logic and filtering techniques to improve your Web searches
- Perform complex searches in search engines
- Use advanced search options in Web search engines
- Assess the validity and quality of Web research resources

Case | *International Executive Reports*

International Executive Reports (IER) is a company that publishes a variety of weekly newsletters, monthly reports, and annual reviews of major trends in economic conditions and management developments. IER's clients are top-level managers and other people who serve on the governing boards of large companies and not-for-profit organizations. IER publications are mailed or emailed to subscribers. The subscription rates range from $300 to $900 per year.

The IER writing staff provides content for all of its publications. In some cases, content that is developed for one publication is edited and used in other publications. Anne Hill, the managing director for content at IER, has recruited an excellent staff of editors, writers, and researchers who work together to create a wide variety of content. Anne has hired you to fill an intern position on the research staff. Your job will involve conducting online research and fact-checking for two of the staff writers, Dave Burton and Ranjit Singh. Dave is an international business specialist, and Ranjit is an economist who writes about current economic trends.

STARTING DATA FILES

There are no starting Data Files needed for this tutorial.

SESSION 3.1 VISUAL OVERVIEW

A search engine includes a database of URLs and keywords, and several types of software for processing requests and returning results.

Search Engine

The search engine's Web formatting software converts the results of a database query to a Web page, which it sends to the user's Web browser.

Web page formatting software

Search expression query processing software

The user formulates a question into a search expression, enters it into the search engine's Web page, and then the user reads the search results returned by the search engine.

The search engine's search expression query software converts the user's search expression into a database-readable query.

HOW A SEARCH ENGINE WORKS

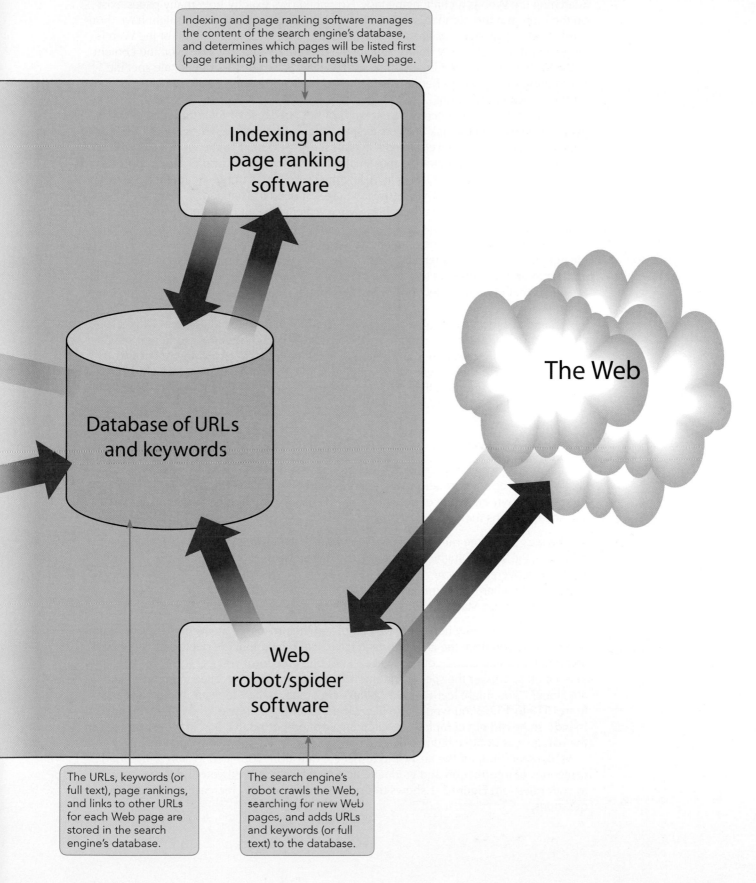

Indexing and page ranking software manages the content of the search engine's database, and determines which pages will be listed first (page ranking) in the search results Web page.

Indexing and page ranking software

Database of URLs and keywords

The Web

Web robot/spider software

The URLs, keywords (or full text), page rankings, and links to other URLs for each Web page are stored in the search engine's database.

The search engine's robot crawls the Web, searching for new Web pages, and adds URLs and keywords (or full text) to the database.

Types of Search Questions

Searching the Web is a challenging task. No one knows exactly how many pages exist on the Web, but the number is now in the billions. Each of these pages might have thousands of words, images, or links to downloadable files. Thus, the content of the Web is far greater than that of any library. Unlike the content of a library, however, the content of the Web is not indexed in any standardized way. So to successfully locate specific information for Dave and Ranjit, you will need to develop appropriate search strategies for their research questions.

Dave and Ranjit will need different kinds of help because of their different writing goals. Dave will need quick answers to specific questions. Dave writes about business opportunities and developments in almost every country in the world. His writing requires background research on most major businesses and industries. To support Dave, you need to be able to "get the facts" using the Web. For example, he might need to know the population of Bolivia or the languages spoken in Thailand.

Ranjit writes longer, more thought-provoking pieces about broad economic and business issues. The Web is a good place to find unusual and interesting views on the economy and general business practices. Ranjit needs you to use the Web as a source for locating information on interesting concepts and new angles on old ideas, rather than as a place to find fast answers to specific questions. For example, he might need you to find Web sites that contain collections of research papers that discuss the causes of the Great Depression.

You can use the Web to obtain answers to both of these question types—Dave's specific questions and Ranjit's exploratory questions—but each requires a different search strategy. A **specific question** is a question that you can phrase easily and one for which you will recognize the answer when you find it. In contrast, an **exploratory question** is an open-ended question that can be harder to phrase; it is also difficult to determine when you find a good answer.

Finding Answers to Specific Questions

The characteristics of a specific question are that the question can be answered with a single fact or set of information, and that the search for the answer involves a process of narrowing down the range of potential answers you examine in each step. Examples of specific questions include:

- Who was the prime minister of the United Kingdom during World War II?
- What is the second-highest mountain peak in the world?
- Who discovered radium?
- What is the chemical formula for table salt?
- In what year did Magellan circumnavigate the globe?

You will always know when you have completed the process of answering a specific question because you have the answer or you have determined that the question *cannot* be answered. In some cases, your answer will not be in the form you expected. For example, in a search to answer the specific question "In what year did Magellan circumnavigate the globe?," you might learn that Magellan's circumnavigation took almost three years, from 1519 to 1522. You would also likely learn that Magellan was killed in the Philippine Islands, so he did not complete the circumnavigation personally; and that the purpose of the voyage was not to circumnavigate the globe, but to find a trading route to Asia.

When searching for the answer to a specific question, you need to start with broad categories of information and gradually narrow the search until you find the answer to your question. Figure 3-1 shows this process of sequential, increasingly focused questions.

Figure 3-1   **Specific research question search process**

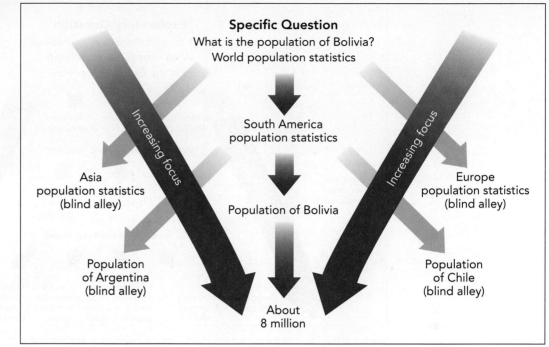

© Cengage Learning

As you narrow your search, you might find that you are heading in the wrong direction or down a blind alley. In that case, you need to get back on track by moving back inside the funnel defined by the two large red arrows shown in Figure 3-1. You can keep searching for increasingly narrow elements of information until you find the exact answer to your question. In the example shown, you might first find sources of population statistics for the entire world, and then narrow your search to the specific continent (South America) and the specific country (Bolivia).

Finding Answers to Exploratory Questions

An exploratory question cannot be answered with a single fact or set of information. Examples of exploratory research questions include:

- What workplace conditions increase the risk of cancer?
- What is the best way to measure intelligence?
- Why did the Japanese maintain an isolationist policy in the 17th and 18th centuries?
- What are the safest and most effective ways to lose weight?
- How did jazz evolve as an American musical form?

An exploratory search starts with general questions that lead to other, less general questions. The answers to the questions at each level should lead you to more information about the topic in which you are interested. This information then leads you to more questions. Figure 3-2 shows how this questioning process leads to a broadening scope as you gather information pertinent to the exploratory question.

Figure 3-2 Exploratory research question search process

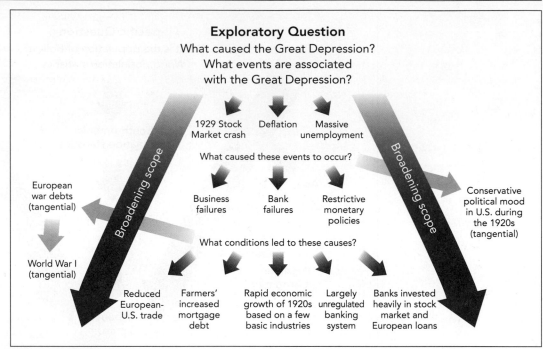

© Cengage Learning

In Figure 3-2, you can see that a search for causes of the Great Depression resulted in five distinct facts or sets of information. Further research would tell you that the relative importance and validity of each of these causes is still debated by economists today. As you expand an exploratory search, you might find yourself collecting tangential (secondary or nonessential) information that is somewhat related to your topic but does not help answer your exploratory question.

Determining Useful Information

The boundary between useful and tangential information can be difficult to identify for exploratory search questions. Sometimes, what appears to be tangential information at first can later turn out to be useful information that leads you to expand your exploratory search in a fruitful direction. Do not be too quick to classify information as tangential. Remember, an exploratory search involves examining an increasingly wider range of information and identifying new insights in that information as you continue to search.

INSIGHT

Formulating Effective Web Search Strategies

Once you have established the type of question you need to answer, you can implement an effective search strategy for finding the information you need.

If your question is specific, the first step in your search strategy is to formulate and state your question. Next, you select the appropriate tool or tools to use in your search and translate your question into a search query that will work with your chosen search tool. (Web search tools will be discussed in the next section.) You then run the query and evaluate your results to determine whether they provide a specific answer to your question. If your results do not answer your question, you can continue the search by deciding whether a different search tool might produce useful results using your original question. If you do not believe a different search tool will help, you can revise and narrow your question and repeat the process.

If your question is exploratory, you begin your search strategy by formulating and stating questions that will yield information related to the area of your inquiry. Then you select appropriate search tools and translate each of your questions into search queries that will work in each search tool. After running the queries, you review your results and determine whether the information you have gathered is related to your question and whether you have collected sufficient information to answer your question. If not, you can formulate and state additional questions and repeat the process until you do have sufficient information to answer your original question.

Note that the first four steps are quite similar for both specific and exploratory questions, but the determination of when your search process is completed is different for the two types of questions. Figure 3-3 illustrates the search strategies for both types of questions so you can compare the processes used for each.

Figure 3-3   **Effective Web search strategies**

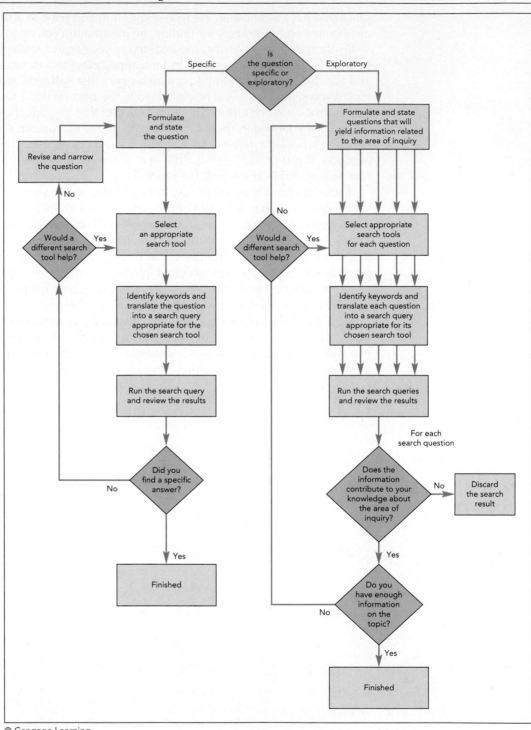

© Cengage Learning

Problem Solving: Repeating the Search Process

What happens if you conduct a Web search and you do not find an answer to your question? You can repeat the search process as many times as necessary until you obtain either the specific answer you seek or a satisfactory range of information regarding your exploratory topic. Sometimes, you might find that the nature of your original question is different than you had originally thought. You also might find that you need to reformulate, or more clearly state, your question. As you restate your question, think of synonyms for each word. Unfortunately, many words in the English language have multiple meanings. For example, the word "mogul" can mean an influential businessperson, an Indian person of Mongolian or Persian descent, or a small bump in a ski run. If you use a word in your search that is common and has many meanings, you can be buried in irrelevant information or be led down many blind alleys. Identifying unique phrases that relate to your topic or question is a helpful way to avoid some of these problems. For example, if you are searching for sites that discuss ways to ski safely over a mogul, you could include the word "skiing" or "slope" in your search expression to reduce the chances of obtaining results that link to Web pages about Indian people or business magnatesds.

An important part of any search is evaluating the quality of the search results you obtain. You will learn how to assess the validity and reliability of Web pages you find during your searches in the next session.

Web Search Tools

To implement any Web search strategy, you will use one or more Web search tools. **Web search tools** include four broad categories of sites: search engines, directories, metasearch engines, and other Web resources such as Web bibliographies. The Additional Information section of the Tutorial 3 Weblinks page at www.cengagebrain.com includes links to many of these Web search tools.

In this section, you will learn how to use each type of search tool.

Understanding Search Engines

A Web **search engine** is a Web site (or part of a Web site) that finds other Web pages that match a word or phrase you enter into the search engine's search page. This word or phrase is called a **search expression** or a **query**. A search expression or query might also include instructions that tell the search engine how to search; you will learn how to formulate search expressions that include additional search instructions later in this tutorial. The basic search page for Bing, a popular search engine site, is shown in Figure 3-4.

Figure 3-4   **Bing basic search page**

A basic search page includes a text box for entering a search expression and a command button to begin the search. The basic search page for Google, one of the most popular search engines, appears in Figure 3-5.

Figure 3-5   **Google basic search page**

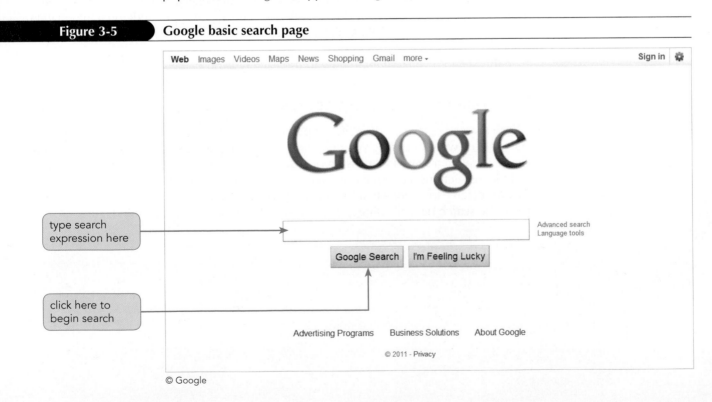

When a user enters a search query into a search engine, the search engine does not search the Web to find a match; it searches only its *own* database of information about Web pages that it has collected, indexed, and stored. A search engine's database includes the URL of the Web page (recall from Tutorial 1 that a Web page's URL, or Uniform Resource Locator, is its Web address). The Session 3.1 Visual Overview shows how a search engine works. Most search engines use Web robots to build their databases of links to Web pages. A **Web robot**, also called a **bot** or a **spider**, is a program that automatically searches the Web to find new Web sites and update information about old Web sites that are already in the database. One of a Web robot's more important tasks is to delete information in the database when a Web site no longer exists. The main advantage of using an automated searching tool is that it can examine far more Web sites than an army of people ever could. However, the Web changes every day, and even the best search engine sites cannot keep their databases completely updated.

People who create Web pages want their sites to be found by people who are interested in the content of those pages. Therefore, many search engines allow Web page creators to submit the URLs of their pages to the databases of search engines. This gives search engines another way to add Web pages to their databases. Most companies that operate search engines screen Web page submissions to prevent a Web page creator from submitting a large number of duplicate or similar Web pages. When the search engine receives a submission, it sends its Web robot out to visit the submitted URL and collect data about the site.

INSIGHT

Varying Results from Search Engines

If you enter the same search expression into different search engines, you will often get different results because each search engine has collected a different set of information in its database, and each search engine uses different procedures to search its database. Some search engines do not collect their own information to build their databases. These search engines buy the right to use the database of another search engine. However, because each search engine uses different procedures to retrieve information from its database, a search engine that uses another search engine's database can still yield different results even though it uses the same database.

After you enter your search query into the search page, the search engine returns a series of **results pages**. These are Web pages that list hyperlinks to the Web pages in the search engine's database that contain text that matches your search expression. An example of a search results page (for a search on the word "car") from the Google search engine appears in Figure 3-6.

Figure 3-6   Google search results for the search term "car"

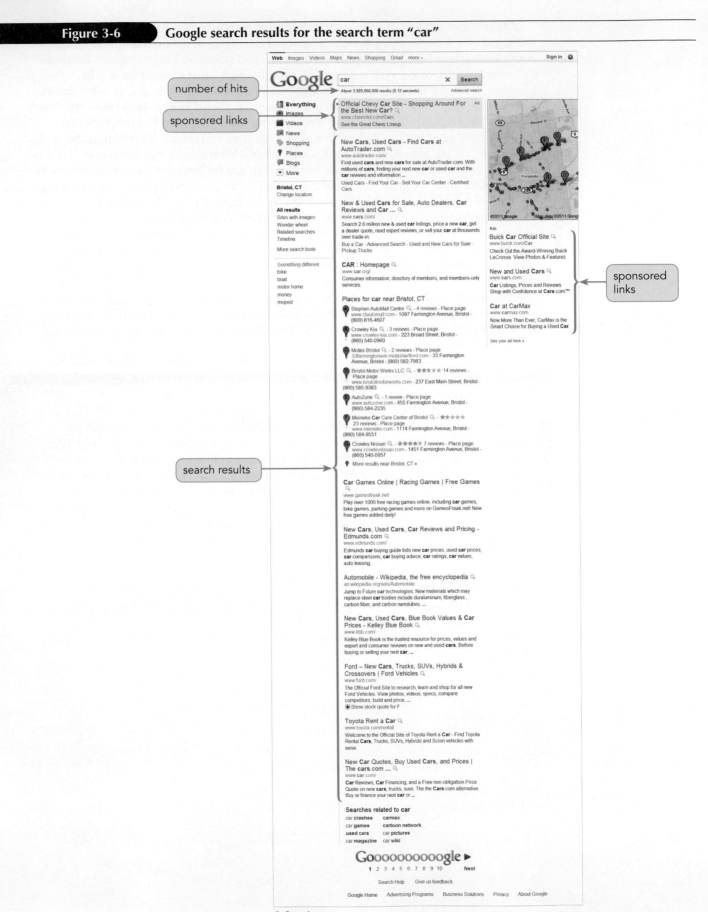

Most search engines report the number of hits they find on the results page. A **hit** is a Web page that is indexed in the search engine's database, and that contains text that matches a specific search expression. When you click hyperlinks on a search engine results page, you might find that some of the Web pages no longer exist. A hyperlink to a Web page that no longer exists or has been moved to another URL is called a **dead link**. Web pages or Web sites that have a number of dead links are said to suffer from **link rot**.

The organizations that operate search engines often sell advertising space on the search engine Web page and on the results pages. An increasing number of search engine operators also sell paid placement rights on results pages. A **paid placement** is the right to have a link to your Web site appear on the search results page when a user enters a specific search term. For example, Toyota might want to purchase the right to have its site listed on the search results page whenever a user enters the search term "car." When you enter a search expression that includes the word "car," the search engine creates a results page that will have a link to Toyota's Web site at or near the top of the results page. Most, but not all, search engines label these paid placement links as "sponsored," and they are usually called **sponsored links**. Figure 3-6 shows sponsored links to advertisers that have paid for placement on this page. If the advertising appears in a box on the page (usually at the top, but sometimes along the side or at the bottom of the page), it is usually called a **banner ad**. Banner ads usually include pictures and other graphic elements in addition to the text of the ad.

Search engines use the revenue from sponsored links and banner ads to generate profit after covering the costs of maintaining the computer hardware and software required to search the Web, and the costs to create and search the database. The only price users pay for access to these useful search tools is being exposed to banner ads on the search results pages and having to scroll through a few sponsored links at the top of results pages.

Your first research assignment is to find the amount of average rainfall in Belize for Dave. This search question is a specific question, not an exploratory question, because you are looking for a fact and you will know when you have found that fact. You can use the process shown earlier in Figure 3-3 as follows:

- Formulate and state the question. In this case, the question can be formulated as "What is the average rainfall amount in Belize?"
- Because the question is very specific, you decide that a basic search engine would be a good tool to use.
- To translate the question into a search query, you can use the keywords "Belize," "annual," and "rainfall" from your question to create an appropriate search query. These terms should appear on any Web page that includes the answer to the question. The term "Belize" should be especially useful in narrowing the search to relevant Web pages.
- When you obtain the results, review and evaluate them, and then decide whether they provide an acceptable answer to your question.
- If the results do not answer the question to your satisfaction, you can redefine or reformulate the question so it is more specific, and then conduct a second search using a different tool, question, or search expression until you find the fact you seek.

To find the average annual rainfall in Belize:

▶ 1. Start your Web browser, go to **www.cengagebrain.com**, open the Tutorial 3 Weblinks page, and then click the **Session 3.1** link.

▶ 2. Click a link to one of the search engines in the Basic Search Engines section to open that search engine's Web site.

▶ 3. Type **Belize annual rainfall** in the search box.

▶ 4. Click the appropriate button to start the search. The search results appear on a new page. This page should indicate that there are hundreds, perhaps even thousands, of Web pages that might contain the answer to your question.

▶ 5. Scroll down the results page and examine your search results. Click some of the links until you find a page or several pages that provide annual rainfall information for Belize. If you do not find any useful links on the first page of search results, click the link to view more search results pages (usually located at the bottom of the first results page).

▶ 6. Click your browser's **Back** button to return to the results page. You should find that Belize has several climate zones and that the annual rainfall ranges from 60 to 160 inches.

When you formulated and stated your question, you probably expected that you would find one rainfall amount that would be representative of the entire country; but that is not the case. Web searches often disclose information that helps you adjust the assumptions you made when you formulated the original research question.

Because you are fact-checking for a story that IER will publish, you will confirm what you have found by searching again using a different search engine.

To conduct the same search to confirm your results:

▶ 1. Return to the Tutorial 3 Weblinks page, and then click a link to another of the search engines in the Basic Search Engines section.

▶ 2. Type **Belize annual rainfall** in the search box.

▶ 3. Click the appropriate button to start the search. You will most likely see a completely different set of links on your search results page.

▶ 4. Scroll down the results page and examine your search results, and then click some of the links until you find a page that provides the average annual rainfall for Belize.

▶ 5. Return to the Tutorial 3 Weblinks page. Once again, you should find that Belize has several climate zones and that the annual rainfall ranges from 60 to 160 inches, confirming the information you found in your first search. If this was not the case, you can conduct additional searches to determine the reason your answers are not consistent.

You might notice your second search returned a different set of links because each search engine includes different Web pages in its database, and because different search engines use different rules to evaluate search expressions. Some search engines will return hits for pages that include *any* of the words in the search expression. Other search engines return hits only for pages that include *all* of the words in the search expression. You might also have noticed that many of the links on the results pages led to Web sites that have no information about Belize rainfall at all. This is why most researchers routinely use at least two search engines; answers that are difficult to find using one search engine are often easy to find with another.

The best way to determine how a specific search engine interprets search expressions is to read the Help pages on the search engine Web site. As you become an experienced Web searcher, you will find that you use two or three particular search engines for most of your work. Read the Help pages on those Web sites regularly because search engines do change the way they interpret search expressions from time to time. You should also get in the habit of checking other search engines occasionally because new search engines are launched and old search engines often make changes to stay competitive.

Understanding Search Engine Databases

Search engine databases store different collections of information about the pages that exist on the Web at any given time. Many search engine robots do not search all of the Web pages at a particular site. Further, each search engine database uses its own approach to index the information it has collected from the Web. Some search engine robots collect information only from a Web page's title, description, keywords, or HTML tags; others read only a certain number of words from each Web page. Figure 3-7 shows the first few lines of HTML from a Web page that contains information about developments in climate change research.

Figure 3-7	Meta tags in a Web page

```
<head>

<title>
Current Developments in Climate Change Research
</title>

<meta name="description" content="Current news and
reports about climate change research.">

<meta name="keywords" content="climate change, global
warming, greenhouse gas, GHG, emissions, CO2, carbon
dioxide, ozone layer, fossil fuels">

</head>
```

© Cengage Learning

The description and keywords tags are examples of HTML meta tags. A **meta tag** is HTML code that a Web page creator places in the page header for the specific purpose of informing Web robots about the content of the page. Meta tags do not cause any text to appear on the page when a Web browser loads it; rather, they exist solely for the use of search engine robots.

The information contained in meta tags can become an important part of a search engine's database. For example, the "keywords" meta tag shown in Figure 3-7 includes the phrase "climate change." These keywords could be a very important phrase in a search engine's database because the two individual words "climate" and "change" are common terms that often are used in search expressions that have nothing to do with climate change research. A search engine that includes the full phrase "climate change" in its database will greatly increase the chances that a user interested in that topic will find this particular page.

Some search engines store the entire content of every Web page they index; but most search engines store only parts of Web pages. Search engines that store a Web page's full content are called **full text indexing** engines. If you use a search engine that is not full text indexing, and the terms you use in your search expression are not in the part of the Web page that the search engine stores in its database, the search engine will not return a hit for that page. Many search engines, even those that claim to be full text indexed search engines, omit common words such as "and," "the," "it," and "by" from their databases. These common words are called **stop words**. For example, if you enter a search expression of "Law and Order" (without the quotes) while looking for pages related to the television show of that name, a search engine that omits stop words will return a large number of irrelevant links because it will search on the two words "law" and "order." Most search engines will include stop words if you include them as part of a phrase enclosed in quotes. You can find out how a particular search engine handles stop words by examining the search engine Web site's Help pages; many search engines include information about their search engines, robots, and databases on their Help or About pages.

Search Engine Features

Page ranking is one technique that search engines use to find Web pages that might be relevant to a specific search expression. **Page ranking** is a way of grading Web pages by the number of other Web pages that link to them. The URLs of Web pages with high rankings are presented first on the search results page. A page that has more Web pages linking into it (these connections are called **inbound links**) is given a higher ranking than a page that has fewer pages linking into it. In complex page ranking schemes, the value of each link varies with the linking page's rank.

For example, a Web page with many inbound links might have a lower ranking than another Web page that has fewer inbound links if the second page's inbound links are from Web pages that, in turn, have a large number of inbound links themselves. As you can imagine, calculating page ranks can be complex; but the rankings can effectively identify pages that are likely to meet the needs of users. Although Google was the first search engine to use page ranking, and continues to lead in the development of highly sophisticated page ranking algorithms, most other search engines now use page ranking and are constantly working to refine the effectiveness of their algorithms.

Most search engines automatically use **stemming** to search for variants of keywords. For example, if you search using the keywords "Canada travel guide," most search engines will return hits that include the keywords "Canadian" and "Canada" along with pages containing variants of the words "travel" and "guide." Figure 3-8 shows how a search engine can use stemming to create multiple combinations of these terms and their variants to expand the results it will return for this query.

Figure 3-8   **How a search engine uses stemming to expand its results**

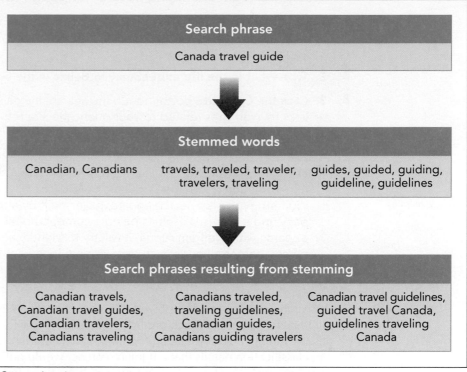

© Cengage Learning

Another feature that some search engines have attempted to include in their pages is natural language querying. A **natural language query interface** allows users to enter a question exactly as they would ask a person that question. For example, using a natural language query, you might phrase the Belize rainfall search as "How much rain does Belize get each year?" You could ask the same question in various ways. The search engine analyzes the question using knowledge it has been given about the grammatical structure of questions, and then uses that knowledge to convert the natural language question into a search query. This procedure of converting a natural language question into a search expression is called **parsing**.

Although no major search engine has yet been able to make a truly successful natural language query interface, the mathematical software company Wolfram has a Web site that offers a natural language interface to a database of collected facts. This site, Wolfram Alpha, lets users ask questions in natural language that relate to the facts in its database. You will use Wolfram Alpha to find out what the life expectancy is for people living in Belize.

To use the Wolfram Alpha natural language interface:

1. Return to the Tutorial 3 Weblinks page, and then in the Basic Search Engines section, click the **Wolfram Alpha** link to open the Wolfram Alpha search engine page.

2. Type **what is the life expectancy in Belize** in the box near the top of the page.

3. Click the **Compute** button to run the search. Instead of a results page listing links to Web sites related to your query, the site returns an actual answer to the question.

4. Examine the results and notice that, in addition to returning the answer as a value in years for the life expectancy in Belize, the site returns a good bit of information about the population of Belize and its characteristics. Although Wolfram Alpha is a search engine, it was built by a mathematics software company and advertises itself as being a computational engine, too. When you run a search with Wolfram Alpha, it will try to identify additional calculations that a person entering your search expression might want to perform. It performs those calculations and reports their results along with the search results.

Search engines provide a powerful tool for executing keyword searches of the Web, but they do have their limitations. Most search engine URL databases are built by computers running programs that perform the search automatically, so they can miss important classification details that a human searcher would notice instantly. For example, if a search engine's robot found a Web page with the title "Test Data: Do Not Use," it would probably not recognize the text as a warning and would include content from the page in the search engine database. If a person were to read such a warning in a Web page title, that person would know not to include the page's contents. However, with billions of Web pages on the Internet today, it is impossible to have people screen every Web page.

Using Directories and Hybrid Search Engine Directories

Web directories use a completely different approach from search engines to build useful indexes of information on the Web. A **Web directory** is a listing of hyperlinks to Web pages that is organized into hierarchical categories. The difference between a search engine and a Web directory is that the Web pages included in a Web directory are selected and organized into categories before visitors use the directory. In a search engine, the database is searched in response to a visitor's query, and results pages are created in response to each specific search.

Most Web directories have human editors who decide which Web pages will be included in the directory and how they will be organized; however, some Web directories use computers to perform these tasks. Web directory editors, who are knowledgeable experts in one or more subject areas and skilled in various classification techniques, review candidate Web pages for inclusion in the directory. When these experts decide that a Web page is worth listing in the directory, they determine the appropriate category in which to store the hyperlink to that page.

The main weakness of a directory is that users must know which category is likely to yield the information they desire. If users begin searching in the wrong category, they might follow many hyperlinks before they realize that the information they seek is not in that category. Some directories overcome this limitation by including hyperlinks in category levels that link to lower levels in other categories.

TIP

Most Web directories allow a Web page to be indexed in several different categories.

One of the oldest and most respected directories on the Web is Yahoo! Directory. David Filo and Jerry Yang, two Stanford University doctoral students who wanted a way to keep track of interesting sites they found on the Web, started Yahoo! Directory in 1994. Yahoo! Directory currently lists hundreds of thousands of Web pages in its categories—a sizable collection, but only a small portion of the billions of pages on the Web. Although Yahoo! Directory does use some automated programs for checking and classifying its entries, it relies on human experts to do much of the selection and classification work. The Yahoo! Directory home page appears in Figure 3-9.

Figure 3-9   Yahoo! Web directory home page

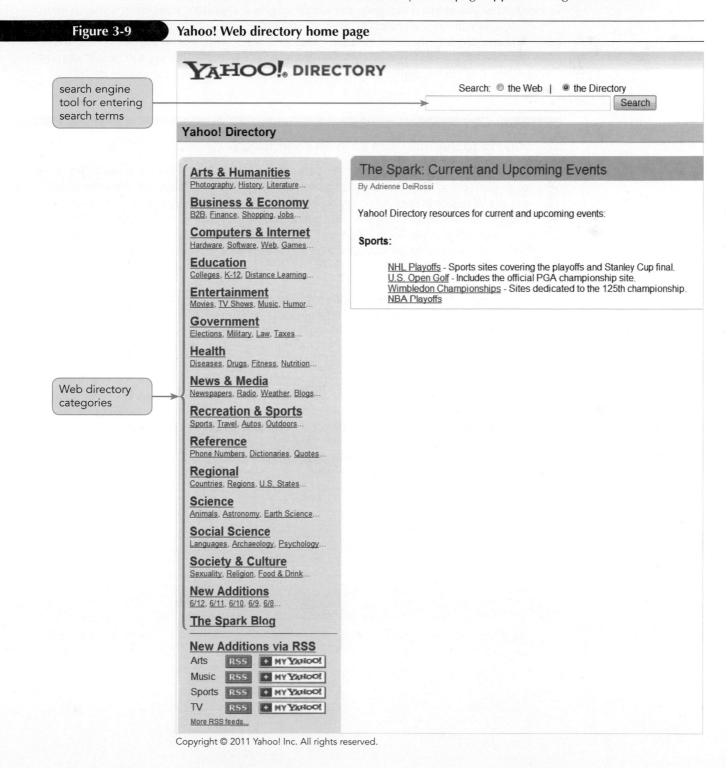

The search tool that appears near the top of the page is a search engine within Yahoo! Directory. You can enter search terms into this tool, and Yahoo! Directory will search its listings to find a match. This combination of search engine and directory is sometimes called a **hybrid search engine directory**; however, most directories today include a search engine function, so many people simply call these sites Web directories. No matter what it is called, the combination of search engine and directory provides a powerful and effective tool for searching the Web. Using a hybrid search engine directory can help you identify which category in the directory is likely to contain the information you need. After you select a category, the search engine is useful for narrowing a search even further; you can enter a search expression and limit the search to that category.

Yahoo! Directory includes 16 main categories, each with several subcategories. These are not the only subcategories; they are just a sample of those that are the largest or most used. You can click a main category hyperlink to see all of the subcategories under that category.

INSIGHT

Paying to Submit URLs to Web Directories

Many Web directories, including Yahoo! Directory, allow businesses that have Web sites to pay a fee and submit their URLs to the directory editors so they can consider including the Web site in their directory. In most cases, the fee does not guarantee that the site will be included in the directory, but it does ensure that the editors know that the site exists. A new site on the Web that does not use a paid submission can wait months before a directory editor notices it and considers including it in a directory.

The Open Directory Project is different from most other Web directories because the editors volunteer their time to create the directory's entries. The home page for the Open Directory Project is shown in Figure 3-10. The Open Directory Project uses the services of more than 40,000 volunteer editors who maintain listings in their individual areas of interest. The Open Directory Project offers the information in its Web directory to other Web directories and search engines at no charge. Many of the major Web directory, search engine, and metasearch engine sites regularly download and store the Open Directory Project's information in their databases. For example, AltaVista, Dogpile, and Google all include Open Directory Project information in their databases.

| Figure 3-10 | Open Directory Project home page |

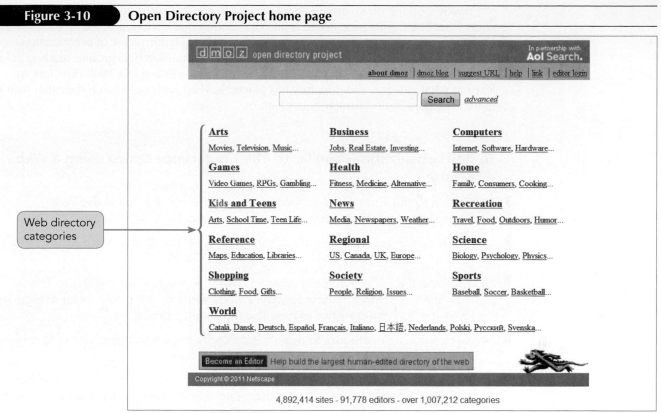

Web directory categories

Copyright © 2011 Netscape

Another Web directory, About.com, hires people with expertise in specific subject areas to create and manage its Web directory entries in those areas. Although both Yahoo! and Bing use subject matter experts this way, About.com takes the idea one step further and identifies its experts. Each About.com expert, called a Guide, hosts a page with hyperlinks to related Web pages, moderates discussion areas, and provides an online newsletter. This creates a community of interested persons from around the world that can participate in maintaining the Web directory.

Dave is working on an article about current trends in corporate governance. He knows that The Conference Board is an organization that conducts research on business issues related to governance. Dave would like you to give him a list of organizations similar to The Conference Board so he can do more extensive background reading before he writes the article. You will try to find The Conference Board in a Web directory to learn in what category the directory has placed it. Then, you can search the other listings in that category to find similar organizations.

To find organizations similar to The Conference Board using a Web directory:

▶ **1.** Return to the Tutorial 3 Weblinks page, and then click a link in the Web Directories section to open a Web directory site.

▶ **2.** In the search box near the top of the page, type **The Conference Board**, and then click the appropriate button to start the search.

▶ **3.** Examine the page that loads in your browser. In the text for the link to The Conference Board, the directory will include a link to the category (or categories) in which that directory has placed The Conference Board.

▶ **4.** Click a link to a category to open the category page and identify links to organizations' Web pages that might be helpful for Dave.

▶ **5.** If you do not find links that might be helpful to Dave, you can search another category if one is listed. You can also search similar categories or try a different Web directory. Figure 3-11 shows the category in which The Conference Board is included in the Yahoo! Directory (Organizations within Business and Economy). This category includes links to several organizations' Web sites that could be helpful to Dave.

| **Figure 3-11** | **Yahoo! Web directory search results page** |

YAHOO! DIRECTORY

◦ Web | ● Directory | ◦ Category   [Search]

Business Organizations   Email this page   Suggest a Site   Advanced Search

Directory > Business and Economy > **Organizations**

category →

CATEGORIES (What's This?)

Top Categories

- **By Region** (10623)

Additional Categories

- **African American@**
- **Christian@**
- **Consumer Economy@**
- **Economic Development@**
- **Education@**
- **Finance and Investment@**

- **Islamic@**
- **Lesbian, Gay and Bisexual@**
- **Professional** (134)
- **Small Business@**
- **Trade Associations** (190)
- **U.S. Hispanic@**

SITE LISTINGS By Popularity | Alphabetical   (What's This?)   Sites **1 - 14** of 14

- **Better Business Bureau (BBB)** (21)
  Provides reports on businesses and charities to help consumers and donors make informed decisions, helps resolve consumer complaints, and promotes ethics in business. Browse a list of regional bureaus.
  dir.yahoo.com/.../Organizations/Better_Business_Bureau__BBB_

- **Service Corps Of Retired Executives (SCORE)**
  Nonprofit association dedicated to entrepreneur education and the formation, growth, and success of small businesses nationwide.
  www.score.org

- **U.S. Chamber of Commerce**
  Federation of businesses, chambers of commerce, American chambers overseas, and trade and professional associations.
  www.uschamber.com

link to The Conference Board Web site →

- **Conference Board, The**
  Nonprofit business membership and research organization for senior executives internationally; produces the Consumer Confidence Index, and Leading Economic Indicators.
  www.conference-board.org

- **World Chamber of Commerce Directory**
  Features a directory of U.S. and international chambers of commerce, tourism boards, and economic development agencies.
  www.chamberofcommerce.com

- **Indus Entrepreneurs (TiE)**
  Global network of entrepreneurs and professionals, established to support entrepreneurship.
  www.tie.org

- **Fabless Semiconductor Association**
  Stimulates technology and foundry capacity by communicating the future needs of the fabless semiconductor segment, and provides interactive forums for the benefit of its members.
  www.fsa.org

- **Business Committee for the Arts**
  Works across the United States to help businesses establish alliances with the arts that meet business objectives.
  www.bcainc.org

- **Business Council for International Understanding**
  International business and trade association that facilitates dialogue between the American business community and U.S. and foreign government leaders.
  www.bciu.org

Now that you have seen how to use a search engine and a hybrid search engine directory, you are ready to use an even more powerful combination of Web research tools: the metasearch engine.

Using Metasearch Engines

You have already seen how the differences in how search engines work cause the various search engines to return significantly different results for the same search expression. As stated previously, to perform a complete search for a particular question, you might need to use several individual search engines. A **metasearch engine** is a tool that combines the power of multiple search engines. Some metasearch tools also include directories.

Using a metasearch engine lets you search several engines at the same time, so you need not conduct the same search multiple times. Metasearch engines do not have their own databases of Web information; instead, a metasearch engine transmits your search expression to several search engines. These search engines run the search expression against their databases of Web page information and return results to the metasearch engine. The metasearch engine then reports consolidated results from all of the search engines it queried.

Dogpile was one of the first metasearch engines on the Web. Dogpile forwards search queries to a number of major search engines and Web directories. The specific search engines and directories that Dogpile uses change from time to time because newer and better search tools become available and older tools disappear. Each item on the search results page is labeled to indicate the search engine or Web directory that found it. When more than one source provides the same result, that entry is labeled with all of the sources. Figure 3-12 shows the Dogpile metasearch engine home page.

| Figure 3-12 | Dogpile metasearch home page |

Courtesy of Copyright 2011 InfoSpace, Inc. All rights reserved.

You want to learn how to use metasearch engines so that you can access information faster. You decide to test a metasearch engine using Dave's Belize rainfall question.

To use a metasearch engine:

▶ **1.** Return to the Tutorial 3 Weblinks page, and then click a link in the Metasearch Engines section to open the Web site.

▶ **2.** Type **Belize annual rainfall** in the search box, and then click the appropriate button to start the search.

▶ **3.** Examine and evaluate your search results. If you did not find the information you were seeking, repeat your search using a different metasearch engine.

As with the other search tools, you will notice that the various metasearch engines can return differing results.

Using Web Bibliographies

In addition to search engines, Web directories, and metasearch engines, the Web includes **Web bibliographies**, another category of search tools. As their name suggests, Web bibliographies are similar to print bibliographies; but instead of listing books or journal articles, they contain lists of hyperlinks to Web pages. Just as some bibliographies are annotated, many of these resources include summaries or reviews of Web pages. Web bibliographies are also called **resource lists**, **subject guides**, **clearinghouses**, and **virtual libraries**. Sometimes they are called Web directories, which can be somewhat confusing. Web bibliographies are usually more focused on specific subjects than Web directories, and Web bibliographies usually do not include a tool for searching within their categories.

Web bibliographies can be very useful when you want to obtain a broad overview or a basic understanding of a complex subject area. Using a search engine to locate broad information on a complex subject is likely to turn up a narrow list of references that are too detailed and that assume a great deal of prior knowledge. For example, using a search engine or directory to find information about quantum physics will probably give you many results that link to technical papers and Web pages devoted to current research issues in quantum physics. However, your search probably will yield very few Web pages that provide an introduction to the topic, and those few pages will be hard to find in the large number of Web pages that deal with advanced details of the subject. In contrast, a Web bibliography search results page can offer hyperlinks to information regarding a particular subject that is presented at various levels. Many of these resources include annotations and reviews of the sites they list. This information can help you identify Web pages that fit your level of knowledge or interest.

Some Web bibliographies, such as Awesome Library and the Librarian's Internet Index, are general references. Most are more focused, such as Martindale's The Reference Desk, which emphasizes science-related links. Some Web bibliographies, such as the Internet Scout Archive, are no longer actively updated, but they are maintained on the Web as useful information resources.

Many Web bibliographies are created by librarians at university and public libraries. You can find Web bibliographies on specific subjects by entering a search term along with the words "subject guide" into a search engine. The results of an example search on the words "Native American subject guide" conducted in the Google search engine appear in Figure 3-13.

Figure 3-13   **Results of a search on "Native American subject guide"**

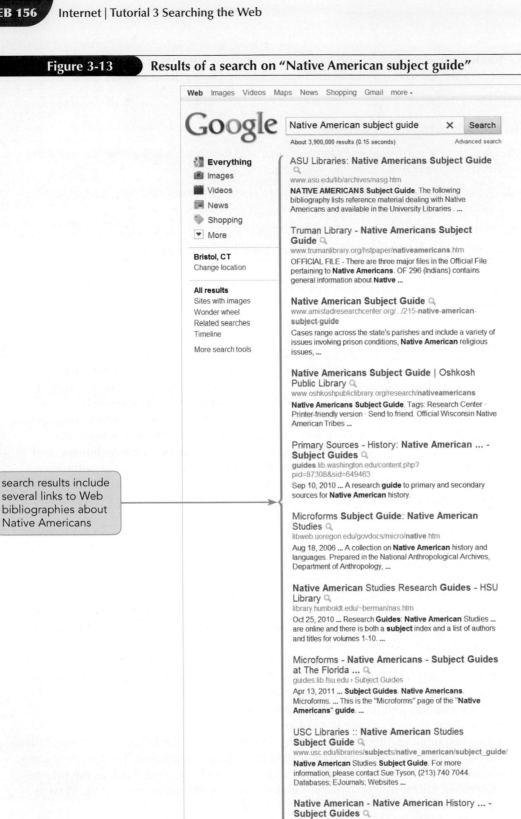

search results include several links to Web bibliographies about Native Americans

TIP

If you regularly conduct research in a specific field, it can be helpful to ask other researchers who work in the field if they know of useful Web bibliographies that specialize in relevant subjects.

Another way to find Web bibliographies is to use a Web directory site. Many Web directories include links to subject-specific Web bibliographies within the category listings for those subjects. For example, the Yahoo! Web directory includes a link titled "Web Directories" within its Social Science category. This link leads to a list of Web bibliographies on the subject of social science. It also has similar links in many of the social science subcategories, such as Economics. Other Web directories include similar links.

Ranjit is planning a series of articles on the business and economic effects of current trends in biotechnology, including information about the potential effects of genetic engineering research. You need to find some Web sites that Ranjit can use to learn more about biotechnology trends in general and genetic engineering research in particular. An exploratory search will locate the required information, and you can use a Web bibliography site for your research. Biotechnology is a branch of the biological sciences, so you will use the three category terms "biotechnology," "genetic engineering," and "biology" as your search terms.

To use a Web bibliography to conduct an exploratory search:

1. Return to the Tutorial 3 Weblinks page, choose one of the sites in the Web Bibliographies section, and then click a link in the Web Bibliographies section to open a Web bibliography's Web site. The home page for most Web bibliography sites provides a search box and a list of subject categories you can choose from to narrow your search.

2. Use the search tool in the Web bibliography you chose to find links to general information about biotechnology, genetic engineering, or biology. Follow those links to gather information relative to your search.

3. Examine your search results and determine whether you have gathered sufficient useful information to provide to Ranjit. If you have not, repeat the search using a different Web bibliography.

4. Close your browser.

You have completed your research for Dave and Ranjit using various search tools to obtain different results. In the next session, you will learn how to structure your search queries to achieve more precise results using Boolean logic and filtering techniques.

Session 3.1 Quick Check

REVIEW

1. What are the key characteristics of an exploratory search question?
2. True or False. The Web is indexed in a standardized way, as is a library's collection of books.
3. The part of a search engine site that is a program that automatically searches the Web to find new Web sites is called a(n) _____.
4. A search engine that uses page ranking will list a Web page near the top of search results pages if the page has many _____.
5. True or False. Most search engines index all Web page contents in their databases.
6. Name one advantage and one disadvantage of using a Web directory instead of a Web search engine to locate information.
7. How does a hybrid search engine directory overcome the disadvantages of using either a search engine or a directory alone?
8. How does a metasearch engine process the search expression you enter into it?
9. How can you find Web bibliographies about a specific subject area?

SESSION 3.2 VISUAL OVERVIEW

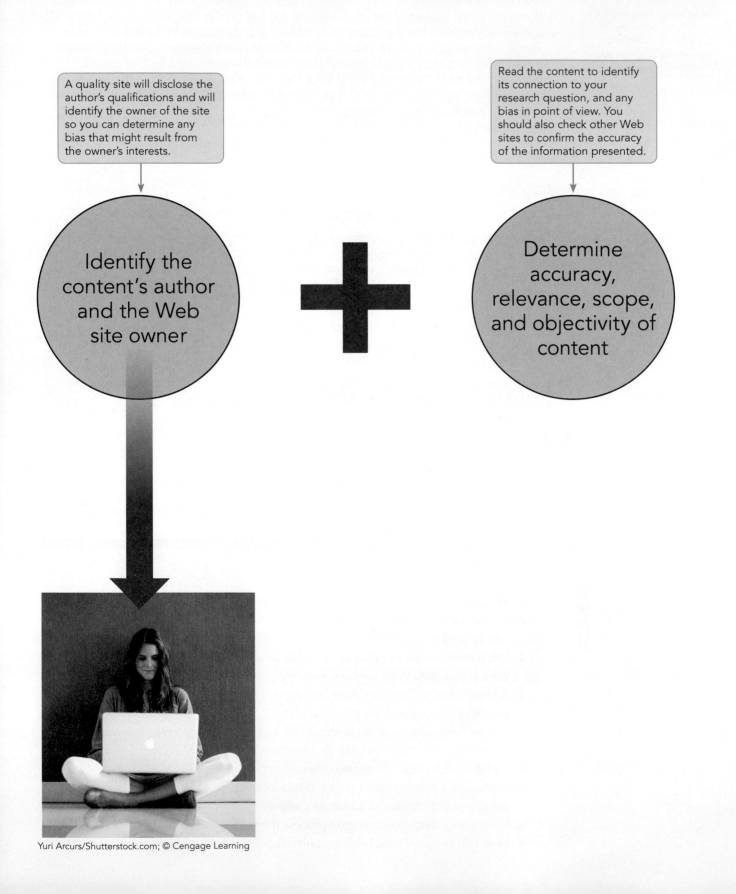

A quality site will disclose the author's qualifications and will identify the owner of the site so you can determine any bias that might result from the owner's interests.

Read the content to identify its connection to your research question, and any bias in point of view. You should also check other Web sites to confirm the accuracy of the information presented.

Identify the content's author and the Web site owner

+

Determine accuracy, relevance, scope, and objectivity of content

Yuri Arcurs/Shutterstock.com; © Cengage Learning

EVALUATING WEB SITES

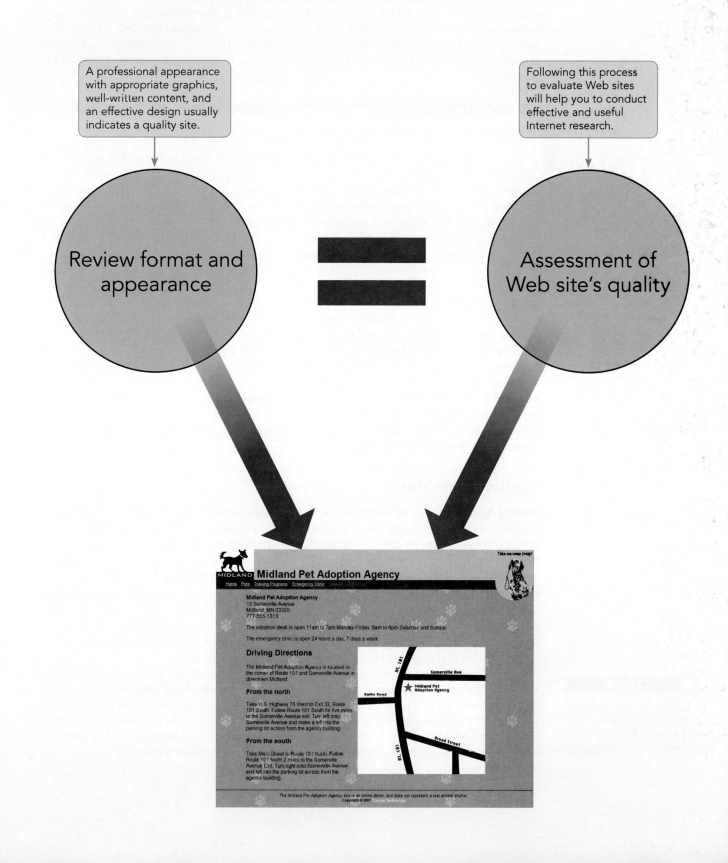

A professional appearance with appropriate graphics, well-written content, and an effective design usually indicates a quality site.

Following this process to evaluate Web sites will help you to conduct effective and useful Internet research.

Review format and appearance

=

Assessment of Web site's quality

Midland Pet Adoption Agency

Home Pets Training Programs Emergency Clinic

Midland Pet Adoption Agency
15 Somerville Avenue
Midland, MN 03326
777-555-1313

The adoption desk is open 11am to 7pm Monday-Friday, 8am to 6pm Saturday and Sunday.

The emergency clinic is open 24 hours a day, 7 days a week.

Driving Directions

The Midland Pet Adoption Agency is located on the corner of Route 101 and Somerville Avenue in downtown Midland.

From the north

Take U.S. Highway 76 West to Exit 32, Route 101 South. Follow Route 101 South for five miles to the Somerville Avenue exit. Turn left onto Somerville Avenue and make a left into the parking lot across from the agency building.

From the south

Take Main Street to Route 101 North. Follow Route 101 North 2 miles to the Somerville Avenue Exit. Turn right onto Somerville Avenue and left into the parking lot across from the agency building.

The Midland Pet Adoption Agency site is an online demo, and does not represent a real animal shelter.
Copyright © 2007

Using Logical Operators and Filtering Techniques in Complex Searches

The most important factor in obtaining good results from a search engine, a metasearch engine, or a search tool within a hybrid search engine directory is careful selection of the search terms you use. When the object of your search is straightforward, you can usually choose one or two words that will work well. More complex search questions require more complex queries, which you can use along with Boolean logic, search expression operators, wildcard operators, or filtering techniques, to broaden or narrow your search expression.

Searching Library Databases

The Boolean operators and filtering techniques you will learn to use in this session can also be helpful when you are doing searches in library databases. These databases, which can be very expensive to purchase, provide much information that cannot be found on the Internet and are often available at school libraries, company libraries, or your local public libraries. Each database has its own implementation of Boolean operators and filtering tools, but the principles you learn here will help you in formulating your searches of these library databases.

When you enter a single word into a Web search tool, it searches for matches to that word. When you enter a search expression that includes more than one word, the search tool makes assumptions about the words that you enter. You learned in Session 3.1 that some search engines assume that you want to match *any* of the keywords in your search expression, whereas other search engines assume that you want to match *all* of the keywords. These alternative assumptions can result in dramatic differences in the number and quality of hits returned. Some search engines are designed to offer both options because users might want to match all of the keywords in one search and any of the keywords in a different search. One way of implementing these options is to use logical operators in the search expression.

Logical Operators

Logical operators specify the relationship between the elements they join, just as the plus sign in arithmetic specifies the mathematical relationship between the two elements it joins. The most commonly used logical operators in complex Web searching are **Boolean operators**, named for George Boole, a nineteenth-century British mathematician who developed a system of logic called **Boolean algebra**. Boolean algebra allows two values, usually *true* and *false*. Although Boole did his work a hundred years before computers became commonplace, his algebra is still useful to computer engineers and programmers. Unlike the algebra you might have learned in your math classes, Boolean algebra does not use numbers or arithmetic operators. Instead, Boolean algebra uses words and logical relationships.

Three basic Boolean operators—AND, OR, and NOT—are recognized by most search engines. You can use these operators in many search engines by simply including them with search terms. For example, the search expression "exports AND France" returns hits for pages that contain both the words "exports" and "France." The expression "exports OR France" returns hits for pages that contain either word, and "exports NOT France" returns hits for pages that contain the word "export" but not the word "France."

Some search engines recognize variants of the Boolean operators, such as "must include" and "must exclude" operators. For example, a search engine that uses the plus sign to indicate "must include" and the minus sign to indicate "must exclude" would respond to the expression "exports + France - Japan" with hits that include pages with the words "exports" and "France" but only if those pages did not also include the word "Japan."

Figure 3-14 shows several ways to use Boolean operators in more complex search expressions that contain the words "exports," "France," and "Japan." The figure shows the matches that a search engine will return if it interprets the Boolean operators correctly. Figure 3-14 also describes information-gathering tasks in which you might use these expressions.

| Figure 3-14 | Using Boolean operators in search expressions |

Search Expression	Search Returns Pages that Include	Use to Find Information About
exports AND France AND Japan	All of the three search terms	Exports from France to Japan or from Japan to France
exports OR France OR Japan	Any of the three search terms	Exports from anywhere, including France and Japan, and all kinds of information about France and Japan
exports NOT France NOT Japan	Exports, but not if the page also includes France or Japan	Exports to and from any countries other than France or Japan
exports AND France NOT Japan	Exports and France, but not Japan	Exports from France to anywhere but Japan or to France from anywhere but Japan

© Cengage Learning

Other Search Expression Operators

When you are creating a search query that combines three or more search terms with Boolean operators, the complexity of the query can make it hard to construct properly. One way to simplify the process is to use precedence operators along with the Boolean operators. A **precedence operator**, also called an **inclusion operator** or a **grouping operator**, establishes specific grouping levels within a complex expression and is usually indicated by the parentheses symbols. You might have used precedence operators (parentheses) in your math or algebra classes in a similar manner to group mathematical expressions. Logical precedence operators work the same way. They establish grouping levels within which the Boolean operators function.

For example, the Boolean search expression "red AND green OR blue" would return results that include red and green along with all results that include blue. Using precedence operators could change the outcome of that search. For example, the expression "red AND (green OR blue)" would return any results that include red and either green or blue. Figure 3-15 shows several ways to use precedence operators with Boolean operators in search expressions.

Search Expression	Search Returns Pages that Include	Use to Find Information About
Exports AND (France OR Japan)	Exports and either France or Japan	Exports from or to either France or Japan
Exports OR (France AND Japan)	Exports or both France and Japan	Exports from anywhere, including France and Japan, and all kinds of other information about both France and Japan
Exports AND (France NOT Japan)	Exports and France, but not if the page also includes Japan	Exports to and from France, except those going to or from Japan
(Exports OR Imports) AND (France NOT Japan)	Either exports or imports, along with France, but not if the page also includes Japan	Exports and imports to and from France, except those to or from Japan

© Cengage Learning

Some search engines use double quotation marks to indicate precedence grouping; however, most search engines use double quotation marks to indicate search terms that must be matched exactly as they appear within the double quotation marks. Using an exact match search phrase can be particularly useful because most search engines ignore stop words by default. You can force most search engines to include a stop word (that they would, by default, otherwise ignore) in a search expression by enclosing it in double quotation marks (or by including it in an exact search phrase that is enclosed in double quotation marks). This technique can be especially helpful when searching a specific topic that includes several stop words. For example, if you were searching for information about J.D. Salinger's novel, *The Catcher in the Rye*, and used those words in your search expression, most search engines would ignore the three stop words included in the title and would search for pages containing "Catcher" and "Rye" only. By using the double quotes to force the search engine to include the stop words, "The Catcher in the Rye," you would be more likely to see search results in which you were interested.

Another useful search expression operator is the location operator. A **location operator**, or **proximity operator**, lets you search for terms that appear close to each other in the text of a Web page. The most common location operator offered in Web search engines is the NEAR operator. If you are interested in French exports, you might want to find only Web pages in which the terms "exports" and "France" are close to each other; for example, "exports NEAR France." Unfortunately, each search engine that implements this operator uses its own definition of "NEAR." One search engine might define NEAR to mean "within 10 words," whereas another search engine might define NEAR to mean "within 20 words." To use the NEAR operator effectively, you must read the search engine's Help pages to determine its definition of NEAR.

Wildcard Characters

Some search engines support the use of a wildcard character in their search expressions. A **wildcard character** allows you to omit part of a search term. The search engines that include this function most commonly use the asterisk (*) as the wildcard character. For example, the search expression "export*" would return pages containing the terms "exports," "exporter," "exporters," and "exporting" in many search engines.

As you learned earlier in this tutorial, many search engines automatically use stemming to search for additional word endings. Using the search term "import" in one of those search engines is exactly the same as using a wildcard character at the end of the search term ("import*") in a search engine that supports wildcard characters. However, a search engine that uses wildcard characters is more flexible than one that uses simple stemming because the wildcard character can be inserted in the middle or at the beginning of the search term, as well as at the end. For example, the expression "wom*n" would return pages containing both "woman" and "women."

Search Filters

Many search engines allow you to restrict your search by using search filters. A **search filter** eliminates Web pages from search results. The filter criteria can include such Web page attributes as language, date, domain, host, or page component (URL, hyperlink, image tag, or title tag). For example, many search engines provide a way to search for the term "exports" in Web page titles and ignore pages in which the term appears in other parts of the page.

Performing Complex Searches

Most search engines implement many of the operators and filtering techniques you have learned about in this session. The way in which various search engines apply these techniques can differ; some search engines provide separate advanced search pages for these techniques, while others allow you to use advanced techniques such as Boolean operators on their simple search pages. When formulating a strategy for a complex search, it is important for you to understand the operators and filtering options available in the search engine you are using, so you can use these tools most effectively to formulate and run your search query.

This section describes how to conduct complex searches in several specific search engines. The steps are correct as this book is printed, but the Web changes constantly. When you perform these steps, the screens you see might look different and you might need to modify the steps. If you encounter difficulties, ask your instructor for assistance or read the Help pages on the search engine site. If major changes occur, the Tutorial 3 Weblinks page at www.cengagebrain.com will be updated to indicate how to make the searches work.

Using Exalead to Perform a Boolean Search

Ranjit is writing about the role that trade agreements play in limiting the flow of agricultural commodities between countries. His current project concerns the German economy. Your job is to find some Web page references that might provide useful background information. Ranjit is especially interested in learning more about the German perspective on trade issues.

This is an exploratory question. You can use the Boolean search capabilities of the Exalead search engine to conduct a complex search for Web pages. Exalead is a search engine that allows the use of several Boolean and precedence operators.

To create an effective search expression, you must identify search terms that might lead you to appropriate Web pages. Some terms you might use for the search are "Germany," "trade," "treaty," and "agriculture." You want to locate a reasonable number of hyperlinks to Web pages, but you do not want to search through thousands of URLs, so you will combine the search terms using Boolean logic to increase the chances that the search engine will return only useful sites. You want your search results to include only Web pages that have the words "Germany" and "trade," along with either of the words "treaty" or "agriculture." Figure 3-16 shows how to use the Boolean operators AND and OR, combined with parentheses as precedence operators, to formulate an appropriate search query.

Figure 3-16   **Combining the Boolean AND and OR with precedence operators**

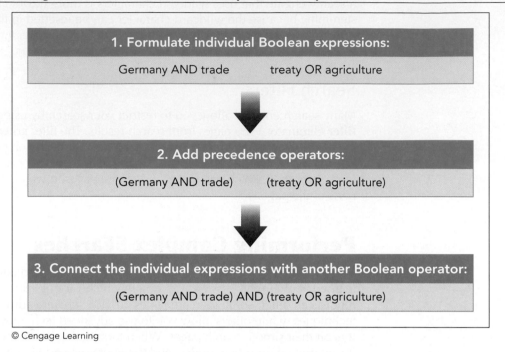

1. Formulate individual Boolean expressions:

Germany AND trade   treaty OR agriculture

2. Add precedence operators:

(Germany AND trade)   (treaty OR agriculture)

3. Connect the individual expressions with another Boolean operator:

(Germany AND trade) AND (treaty OR agriculture)

© Cengage Learning

To perform a Boolean search using Exalead:

1. Start your Web browser, open the Tutorial 3 Weblinks page at www.cengagebrain.com, click the **Session 3.2** link, and then click the **Exalead** link.

2. Click the **Web** link on the Exalead home page, if necessary.

3. Type **(Germany AND trade) AND (treaty OR agriculture)** into the search box.

4. Click the **Search** button to start the search. The results page includes a number of useful links that meet the search criteria along with links to search results that contain related terms. The results page also provides links to search results categorized by file type and Web site type.

Filtered Search in Google

Dave is writing an item about Finland and would like to interview a professor he once met who taught graduate business students there. He does not remember the professor's name or the name of the university at which the professor teaches, but he does remember that the professor taught business subjects at a university in Finland. Dave is confident that he would recognize the university's name if he saw it again. He asks if you can search the Web to find the names of some Finnish universities.

You will use the Google search engine for this task. To create a useful search expression, you must identify search terms that might lead you to appropriate Web pages. In this case, you will include "Finland" as a search term. Also, Dave told you that graduate schools of business in Europe are often called Schools of Economics, so you will include the exact phrase "School of Economics" in your search. The country code for Finland is ".fi," so you will limit the search to Web pages in this top-level domain using the Google filter options. Because Dave reads English only, you also will filter the search to return pages that are in English.

To perform a filtered search using Google Advanced Search:

1. Return to the Tutorial 3 Weblinks page, and then click the **Google Advanced Search** link.

2. Click in the **Find web pages that have all these words** box at the top of the page, and then type **Finland**.

3. Click in the **Find web pages that have this exact wording or phrase** box, and then type **School of Economics**.

4. Click the **Language** arrow, and then click **English**.

5. Click in the **Search within a site or domain** box, and then type **.fi**. Figure 3-17 shows the Google Advanced Search page with the search expressions entered and the filters set.

Figure 3-17	Google Advanced Search page

search expression entered by Google as you type in other fields

language filter

top-level domain filter

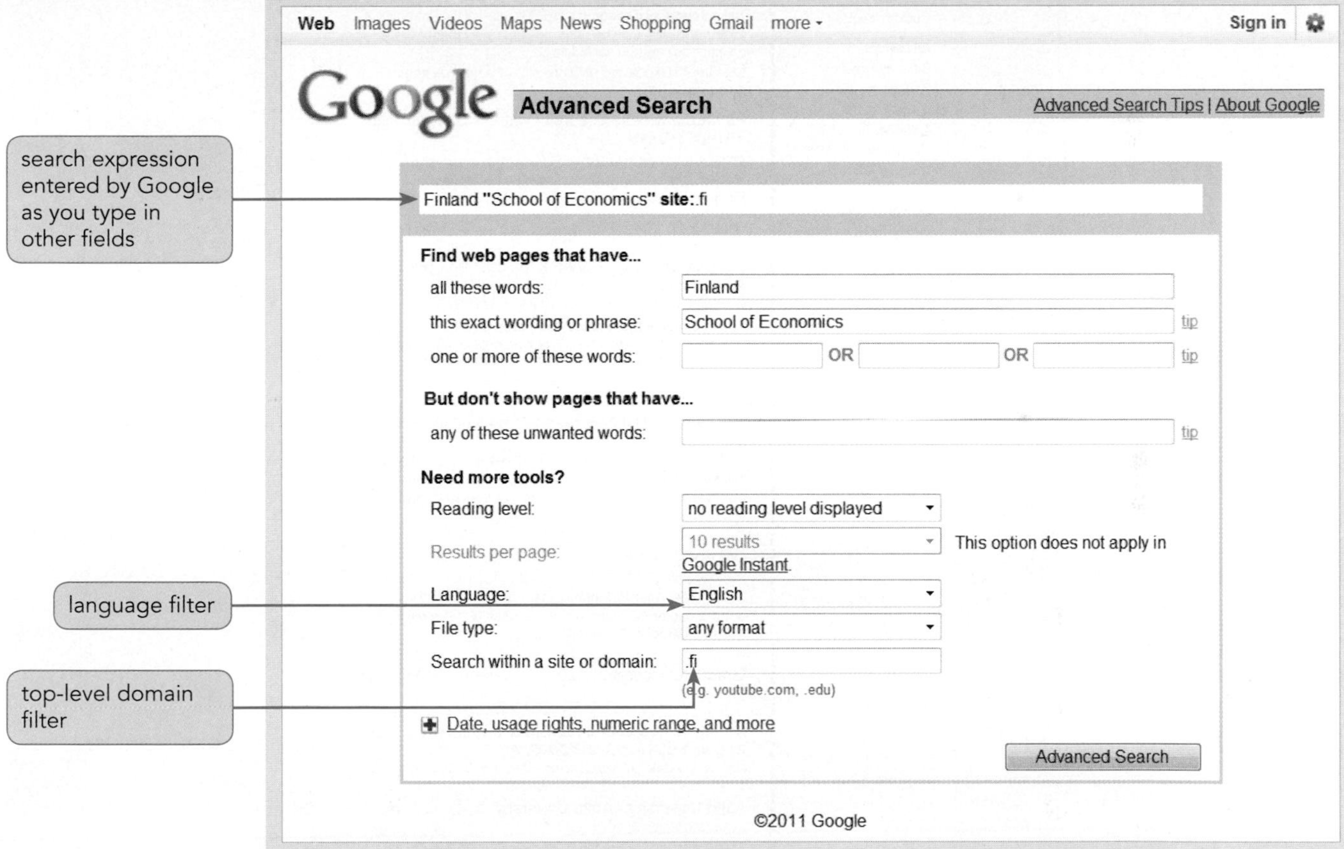

© Google

6. Click the **Advanced Search** button to start the search. The top portion of the search results page appears in Figure 3-18 and includes a number of links to Finnish universities.

Figure 3-18   **Google Advanced Search results page**

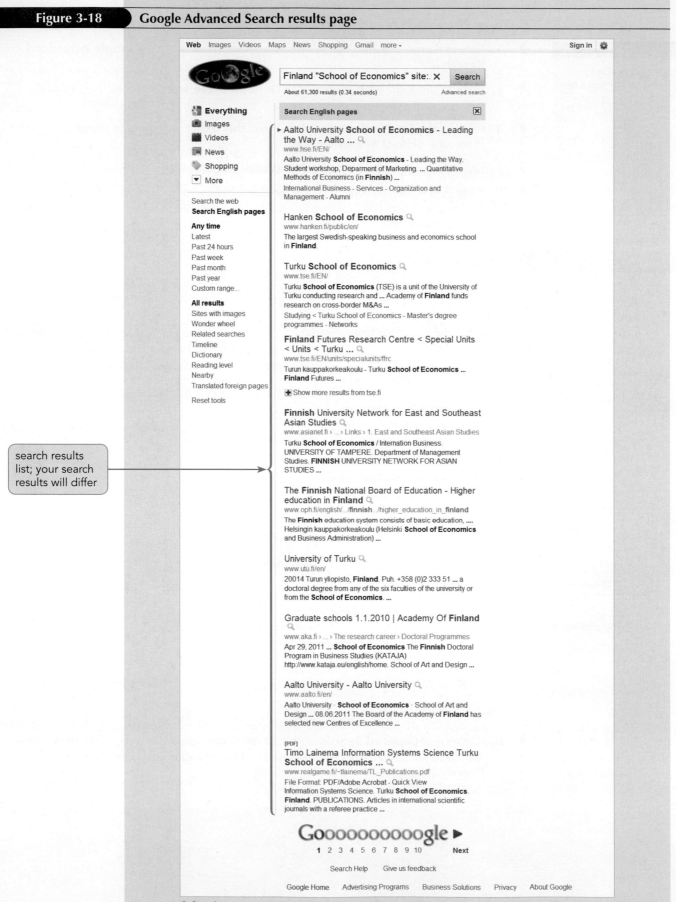

search results list; your search results will differ

© Google

7. Examine your search results and determine which of the hyperlinks in the search results lead to Finnish universities. Remember that you might need to examine several pages of search results to find exactly what you need.

Using Search Engines with Clustering Features

You have seen how Boolean operators and filters can help target the search to return pages that will more likely meet your needs. However, these pages might still number in the tens of thousands (or even millions). Scrolling through hundreds of results pages looking for useful resources is not very efficient. Some search engines group their search results into clusters. The clustering of results is similar to a filtering effect; however, the filtering is done automatically by the search engine after it runs the search. Another difference is that none of the search results are discarded; they are simply sorted into multiple categories, or clusters. Clustering can be especially effective when a word in the search expression has multiple meanings. For example, the word "java" can mean the name of an island, the name of a programming language, or a slang term for coffee. Clustered results place each of these meanings in separate categories.

Search engines that include a clustering feature use one of two strategies to implement clustering. One approach is to create categories as the search engine database is built. Each Web page that is stored in the database is placed into one or more categories. A second approach creates the categories after the search expression is run against the database. The search engine constructs the categories on the fly and uses information about all the words in the search expression (and their relations to each other and keywords in the Web pages selected). For example, the Yippy search engine collects search results into clusters and runs the clustering algorithms as the search results are returned. That is, instead of classifying Web pages into categories in its database, it creates the categories dynamically after it processes the search expression. Yippy defines its clusters using artificial intelligence. The clustering is done in real time for each search and depends on the search expression and the clustering algorithm, which is continually revised.

Ranjit is writing about fast-food franchises in various developing countries. He needs information on this industry's experience in Indonesia. You can run this search using a search engine with a clustering feature such as Yippy. As you know, to create a useful search expression, you must identify search terms that might lead you to appropriate Web pages. Some terms you might use include "Indonesia," "fast food," and "franchise." You are not interested in Web pages that contain the individual terms "fast" and "food," so you will use double quotation marks to specify the phrase "fast food." The Yippy search engine uses its clustering feature as a substitute for Boolean logic, so you will enter a simple expression and let it filter your results into searchable categories.

To obtain clustered search results using Yippy:

1. Return to the Tutorial 3 Weblinks page, and then click the **Yippy** link in the Search Engines with Clustering Features section.

2. Click in the Search box if necessary, and then type **Indonesia "fast food" franchise**. Make sure that you type the quotation marks so that you find the phrase "fast food" instead of the individual terms "fast" and "food."

3. Click the **Search** button to start the search. Figure 3-19 shows the search results page, which includes links to a number of promising Web pages.

Figure 3-19	Yippy search results page

search expression

search results collected into clusters of related hyperlinks

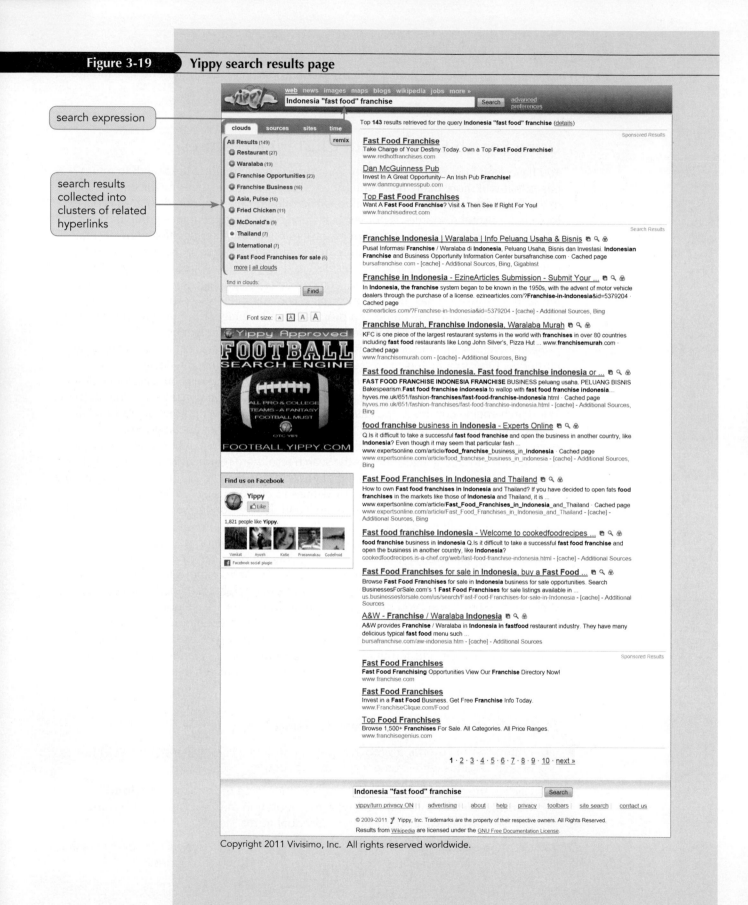

Copyright 2011 Vivisimo, Inc. All rights reserved worldwide.

On the left side of the page, you will see a heading, "clouds," which is the term this search engine uses for its clusters. You can click the plus sign to the left of a cloud heading to open any cluster that looks like it is related to your search topic.

▶ **4.** Click the plus sign next to one of the cloud headings and examine its sub-categories that open. Notice the list of links on the page changes to pages contained in that category.

Exploring the Deep Web

Many different companies and organizations are working on ways to make searching the Web easier and more successful for the increasing numbers of people who use the Web. One weakness of most current search engines and Web directories is that they only search static Web pages. A **static Web page** is an HTML file that exists on a Web server computer. The robots used by search engines to build their databases can find and examine these files.

An increasing number of Web sites do not store information as HTML files. Instead, they store information in a database; and when a user submits a query using the search tools on the site, the site's Web server searches the database and generates a Web page on the fly that includes information from the database. These generated Web pages are called **dynamic Web pages**. For example, if you visit Amazon.com and search for books about birds, the Amazon.com Web server queries a database that contains information about books and generates a dynamic Web page that includes that information. This Web page is not stored permanently on the Web server and cannot be found or examined by search engine robots. Much of the information stored in these databases can only be accessed by users who have a login and password to the Web site that generates dynamic pages from the database.

Several researchers have explored the difficulties that search engine robots face when trying to include information contained in the databases that some Web sites use to generate their dynamic pages. Some researchers call this information the **deep Web**; other researchers use the terms **hidden Web** and **invisible Web**. Many of these researchers are working at universities and research institutes. One team working at the University of Utah has created an experimental Web site that allows visitors to search the deep Web. The home page of this site, called DeepPeep, is shown in Figure 3-20.

Figure 3-20 DeepPeep home page

Courtesy of the National Science Foundation and the University of Utah

Evaluating Web Research Resources

One of the most important issues in conducting research on the Web is assessing the validity and quality of the information provided on the Internet. Because the Web has made publishing information so easy and inexpensive, virtually anybody can create a Web page on almost any subject. Research published in scientific or literary journals is subjected to peer review. Similarly, books and research monographs are often reviewed by peers or edited by experts in the appropriate subject area. However, information on the Web is seldom subjected to the review and editing processes that have become a standard practice in print publishing.

When you search the Web for entertainment or general information, you most likely will not suffer significant ramifications from gathering inaccurate or unreliable information. When you are searching the Web for an answer to a serious research question, however, the risks of obtaining and relying on inaccurate or unreliable information can be significant.

You can reduce your risks by evaluating carefully the quality of any Web resource on which you plan to rely for information related to an important judgment or decision. To develop an opinion about the quality of the resource, you can evaluate four elements of any Web page: the Web page's authorship, ownership, content, and appearance. The Session 3.2 Visual Overview summarizes the process for effectively evaluating Web pages.

Authorship, Expertise, and Objectivity

The first step in evaluating a Web research resource is to determine who authored the page. If you cannot easily find authorship information on a Web site, you should question the validity of the information included on the site. A Web site that does not identify its author has very little credibility as a research resource. Any Web page that presents empirical research results, logical arguments, theories, or other information that purports to be the result of a research process should identify the author *and* present the author's background information and credentials so you can evaluate the author's expertise. The information on the site should be sufficient to establish the author's professional qualifications.

You can also check secondary sources for corroborating information. For example, if the author of a Web page indicates that he or she is a member of a university faculty, you can find the university's Web site and confirm that the author is listed as a faculty member. The Web site should also provide author contact information, such as a street address, email address, or telephone number, so that you can contact the author or consult information directories to verify the addresses or telephone numbers. This allows you to determine that the author is an actual person, and is the person depicted as the author of the Web site content.

You also should consider whether the qualifications presented by the author pertain to the material that appears on the Web site. For example, the author of a Web site concerned with gene-splicing technology might list a Ph.D. degree as a credential. However, if the author's Ph.D. is in history, it would not suggest sufficient expertise to support the credibility of the gene-splicing technology Web site. If you cannot determine the specific areas of the author's educational background from the Web site itself, you can look for other examples of the author's work on the Web. By searching for the author's name and terms related to the subject area, you should be able to find other sites that include the author's work. The fact that a Web site author has written extensively on a subject can provide some evidence—although not necessarily conclusive evidence—that the author has expertise in the field.

In addition to identifying the author's identity and qualifications, author information should include details about the author's affiliations—either as an employee, owner, or consultant—with organizations that might have an interest in the research results or other information included in the Web site. Information about the author's affiliations will help you determine the level of independence and objectivity that the author has with respect to the topics presented on the Web site. For example, research results supporting the contention that cigarette smoke is not harmful presented in a site authored by a researcher with excellent scientific credentials might be less compelling if you learn that the researcher is the chief scientist at a major tobacco company. By reading the page content carefully, you might be able to identify a potential bias in the author.

Web Site Ownership and Objectivity

The author of a Web page is seldom the owner of the Web site. In some cases, it can be difficult to determine who owns a specific Web site. Most Web sites include information about ownership on their About pages; however, some sites do not. In some cases, the owner might be an organization with an intentionally misleading name.

You can make a rough assessment of what type of entity a Web site's owner is by examining the domain identifier in the URL. If the site claims affiliation with an educational institution, the domain should be .edu. A not-for-profit organization would most likely have the .org domain, and a government unit or agency would have the .gov domain. These are not hard-and-fast rules, however. For example, some perfectly legitimate not-for-profit organizations have URLs with a .com domain.

Once you have determined who or what entity owns the Web site, you can assess whether they are likely to have a bias regarding the content of the site. A for-profit company, for example, would be unlikely to provide unbiased evaluations of products or services provided by their competitors.

Accuracy, Relevance, Scope, and Objectivity of Content

When evaluating the actual content on the Web page, you want to assess its accuracy, its relevance to your research question, the depth of the topic's coverage, and the objectivity of the material's presentation.

When considering accuracy, you might first determine the timeliness of the content. If the material was not published recently, the information might no longer be accurate. Check the Web page for a clearly stated publication date or updated date. You can also search other Web sites to confirm that factual information presented is similar to factual information presented on these other sites. However, this does not guarantee that the information is correct because it is possible for a number of sites to have incorrect information.

The relevance of a site's content to your research question can be more difficult to judge; after all, people often search the Web to learn about topics with which they are not familiar. However, some characteristics of the content on a Web page can help you determine whether that content will help you answer your research question.

You can read the content with a critical eye and evaluate whether the included topics are relevant to your research question. You might be able to evaluate the scope of the site by determining whether important topics or considerations are omitted from the sites content. You can do this by comparing the content to what you find on other Web pages devoted to the topic. Comparisons to other Web pages can help you assess the depth of treatment the author gives to the subject.

Finally, to ensure you are getting complete information on your topic, you will want to confirm the Web page content's objectivity—in other words, whether it acknowledges its own bias. Some Web pages present a balance of viewpoints, but many are created for the specific purpose of supporting a particular position. This is especially true if the issue is contentious. The best Web sites with information on contentious issues always make clear which side they are taking in the argument and show respect for the position taken by the other side.

Form and Appearance

A Web site that is a legitimate source of accurate information usually presents its information in a professional form that helps convey its validity. Many Web pages that contain low-quality or incorrect information are poorly designed and not well edited. For example, a Web page devoted to an analysis of Shakespeare's plays that contains spelling errors is likely to be a low-quality resource. Loud colors, graphics that serve no purpose, and flashing text are all Web page design elements that often indicate that the Web page is a low-quality resource. However, these indicators are not infallible. The Web does contain pages full of misinformation and outright lies that are nicely laid out, include professionally produced graphics, and have grammatically correct and properly spelled text.

Evaluating the Quality of a Web Page

Now that you understand the principles of assessing Web page quality, you will apply these principles as you analyze a Web page.

REFERENCE

Evaluating a Web Page

- Open the Web page in your Web browser.
- Identify the author, if possible. If you can identify the author, evaluate his or her credentials and objectivity.
- Examine the content of the Web site for accuracy, relevance, scope, and objectivity.
- Evaluate the site's form and appearance to determine quality and appropriateness.
- Draw a conclusion about the site's overall quality.

Anne Hill has been doing research for IER on how companies can appeal to children on the Web by promoting products while not taking advantage of the children who visit their sites. Anne would like you to evaluate the quality of a Web page titled "Children's Websites" that she has found.

To evaluate the quality of the Children's Websites Web page:

1. Return to the Tutorial 3 Weblinks page, and then click the **Children's Websites** link in the Evaluating Web Research Resources section.

   The browser loads the Web page that appears in Figure 3-21. To evaluate the page, examine the content of the Web page, read the text, examine the titles and headings, and consider the page's appearance.

Figure 3-21 Children's Websites Web page

Web site owner's name →

date of publication

author's name

useit.com → Alertbox → Sept. 2010 Websites for Kids   Search

Jakob Nielsen's Alertbox, September 13, 2010:

Children's Websites: Usability Issues in Designing for Kids

Summary:
New research with users aged 3–12 shows that older kids have gained substantial Web proficiency since our last studies, while younger kids still face many problems. Designing for children requires distinct usability approaches, including targeting content narrowly for different ages of kids.

Millions of children use the Internet, and millions more are coming online each year. Many websites specifically target children with educational or entertainment content, and mainstream websites often have specific "kids' corner" sections — either as a public service or to build brand loyalty from an early age.

Despite this growth in users and services, little is known about how children actually use websites or how to design sites that will be easy for them to use. Website design for kids is **typically based purely on folklore** about how kids supposedly behave — or, at best, on insights gleaned when designers observe their own children, who hardly represent average kids, typical Internet skills, or common knowledge about the Web.

To **separate design myths from usability facts**, we turn to empirical user research: observations of a broad range of children as they use a wide variety of websites.

This research covers **users aged 3–12 years**. (Guidelines for sites targeting 13- to 17-year-olds are available in a report from our separate research with teenagers.)

User Studies

We conducted **two separate rounds of usability studies**, testing a total of 90 children (41 girls and 49 boys):

- Study 1 (9 years ago). In this study, we tested **27 sites with 55 children**, aged 6–11. We conducted about a third of the study in Israel, and the rest in the United States.
- Study 2 (new research). In this study, we tested **29 sites with 35 children**, aged 3–12 years. All of these user sessions were in the U.S.

In Study 1, we conducted sessions in participants' homes, at schools, and in a usability lab. All of Study 2 sessions were run in a lab. We tested some users in friendship pairs, and other individually. Pair sessions worked best for 6- to 8-year-old users. In contrast, for children younger than 6 or older than 8, individual sessions were just as good (and are obviously cheaper, as we had to recruit only one user per session).

Although it can be difficult for shy or very young kids, we encouraged users to think out loud while they were using the sites. We told the children that **they were the experts**, and that we wanted them to teach us how kids use and think about websites. We then explained that, in order for us to learn, they had to explain what they were thinking at all times.

Finally, it's important to **retain a consistent user experience** rather than bounce users among pages targeting different age groups. In particular, by understanding what attracts children's attention, you can "bury" the links to service content for parents in places that kids are unlikely to click. Text-only footers worked well for this purpose.

Advice for Parents and Educators

We conducted this research in order to generate usability guidelines for companies, government agencies, and major non-profit organizations that want to design websites for children. Even so, some of our findings have personal **implications for parents, teachers, and others** who want to help individual children succeed on the Internet:

- The main predictor of children's ability to use websites is **their amount of prior experience**. We also found that kids as young as 3 can use websites, as long as they're designed according to the guidelines for this very young audience. Together, these two findings lead to the advice to start your children on the Internet at an early age (while also setting limits; too much computer time isn't good for kids).
- Campaigns to sensitize children to **the Internet's potential dangers** and to teach them to be wary of submitting personal information are meeting with success. Keep up this good work.
- On a more negative note, kids still don't understand the Web's commercial nature and **lack the skills needed to identify advertising** and treat it differently than real content. We need much stronger efforts to teach children about these facts of new media.

Learn More

Our 275-page report with 130 design guidelines for designing websites for children is available for download.

Other Alertbox columns (complete list)
Sign up for newsletter that will notify you of new Alertboxes

You can see that the author of the page is Jakob Nielsen and that the page has a clear, simple design. You note that the grammar and spelling are correct and the content is neither inflammatory nor overly argumentative, although it does reflect a strong specific viewpoint on the issue. The date on which the page was published is clearly stated at the top of the page. You note that this page appears to be part of a Web publication called "Alertbox" by looking at the page's URL and by noting the link at the top of the page.

2. Click the **Alertbox** link near the top of the Web page to learn more about the Web publication.

   You see that the full title of the publication is "Alertbox: Current Issues in Web Usability" and that it is written by Dr. Jakob Nielsen, a principal of the Nielsen Norman Group. You can also see that the site offers a free email newsletter, and that it has a clearly stated privacy policy that governs the use of any email addresses submitted. Although some sites state policies that they do not follow, the existence of a clearly stated policy is a good indicator of a high-quality site.

3. Click the **Jakob Nielsen** link that appears under the publication title near the top of the page to open a biography page on which you can learn more about Dr. Nielsen.

4. Click your browser's **Back** button to return to the Alertbox page, and then click the **Nielsen Norman Group** link to open the Nielsen Norman Group information page. Reviewing the information on these pages helps you to evaluate the quality of the Children's Websites page.

5. Close your Web browser.

The information you examined should lead you to conclude that the Children's Websites page is of high quality. Dr. Nielsen and his organization are both well respected In the field of Web site usability research. If you would like to do an additional exploration regarding this topic, you could use your favorite search engine to conduct searches on combinations of terms such as "Nielsen" and "Web usability."

Evaluating Wikipedia Resources

Wikipedia is a Web site that hosts a community-edited set of online encyclopedias in more than a dozen different languages. The concept behind Wikipedia is similar to that behind the Open Directory Project you learned about in Session 3.1. Instead of hiring experts to review and edit entries, which is what all print encyclopedias do, Wikipedia relies on contributions from anyone for its entries. Those entries then can be edited by anyone who reads them and thinks they should be changed in some way. The idea is that with enough people reading, editing, and re-editing the entries, the information on the site will evolve to a higher degree of accuracy.

Some of the articles on Wikipedia are well written, authoritatively referenced, and show the benefit of the multiple reviews by qualified volunteer editors. Other articles, especially those about subjects that are not of interest to a large number of readers, are written by authors of questionable qualifications and have not been edited at all. Although unsourced material can be challenged and ultimately removed, this does not occur unless someone who is interested in the topic takes the time and effort to challenge the material. A large number of Wikipedia articles include a dated disclaimer stating that they need additional citations or verification. In many cases, the disclaimer is several years old. Figure 3-22 shows parts of the Wikipedia article on internal rate of return, a topic in corporate finance.

Figure 3-22   **Wikipedia article on internal rate of return**

disclaimer noting the need for additional citations

references and links to related research resources on the topic

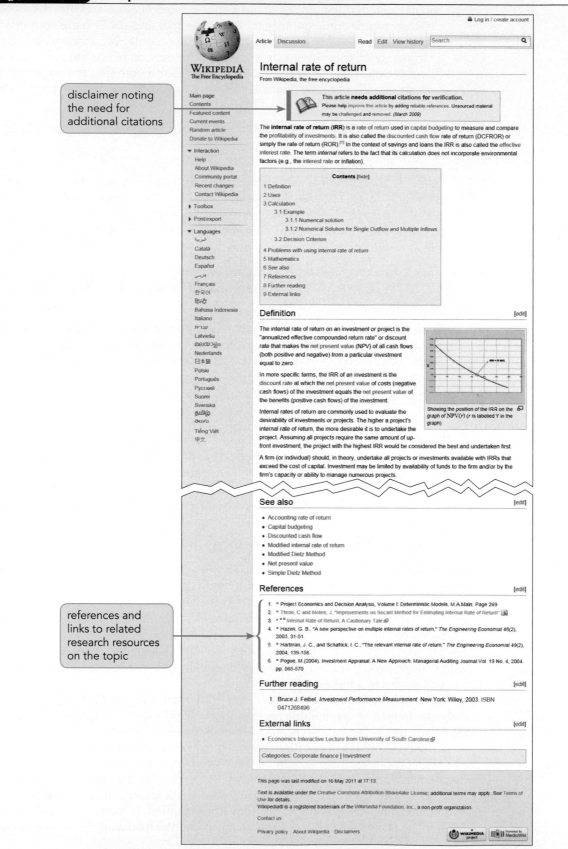

As you can see, the article includes a disclaimer at the top noting that it needs additional citations. The article does provide a few citations (near the bottom of the page) and includes a reference for readers who want to learn more about the topic. However, most people who wanted to learn how to compute the internal rate of return in a specific context would find this article hard to read and incomplete.

The end result of Wikipedia's open nature is that it contains a great deal of useful information, and much of that information is valid. However, Wikipedia's content is only as good as its contributors; and consequently, some of the information on the site is inaccurate, incomplete, or biased.

One of the most important tools you can use to assess the quality of information on the Web is the author's identity. On Wikipedia, contributors may post and edit articles anonymously, in which case the author is identified only by the IP address of his or her connection to the Internet. Even when the author or editor of an article chooses to be identified, it is through a Wikipedia account name and the biographical information included on the user page is entered by the account holder. That information can be limited or incorrect if the account holder so chooses.

PROSKILLS

Written Communication: Using Wikipedia in Web Research

Some researchers have found Wikipedia to be a useful tool for doing preliminary background reading when they are investigating a subject that is new to them. They find that Wikipedia can often give them a general introduction to the subject that they can use to search intelligently for authoritative materials relevant to their information search. However, few researchers would rely on Wikipedia as their sole source of information on a topic, even if the article were well-referenced, written by a credible author, and subjected to multiple edits. Few teachers or employers would accept a research project that referenced Wikipedia as a primary source. In fact, it is always a good idea to check with your instructor for guidance before using online resources, such as Wikipedia, in your research.

In this session, you have learned the process for evaluating Web results when researching the Web. The determination of Web site quality is not an exact science; but with practice, you can develop your skills in this area.

REVIEW

Session 3.2 Quick Check

1. The three basic Boolean operators are _____, _____, and _____.
2. Write a search expression using Boolean and precedence operators that returns Web pages containing information about wild mustang horses in Wyoming, but not information about the Ford Mustang automobile.
3. True or False. The NEAR location operator always returns phrases that contain all keywords within 10 words of each other in a search expression.
4. True or False. In most search engines, the wildcard character is a * symbol.
5. Name three kinds of filters you can include in a Google search run from its Advanced Search page.
6. What function do parentheses serve in an advanced or Boolean search expression?
7. Why is the deep Web so difficult to search?
8. List three factors to consider when evaluating the quality of a Web site.

Practice the skills you learned in the tutorial using the same case scenario.

PRACTICE

Review Assignments

There are no Data Files needed for the Review Assignments.

Anne, Dave, and Ranjit are keeping you busy at IER. You have noticed that Dave and Ranjit frequently need information about the economy and economic forecasts. Your internship will be over soon, so you would like to leave them with links to some resources that they might find useful after you leave. To create the links, complete the following steps:

1. Start your Web browser, go to www.cengagebrain.com, open the Tutorial 3 Weblinks page, and then click the Review Assignments link. The Review Assignments section of the Tutorial 3 page contains links organized under three headings: Search Engines, Web Directories, and Metasearch Engines.

2. Choose at least one search tool from each category and conduct searches using combinations of the search terms "economy," "economics," "forecasts," "conditions," and "outlook."

3. Expand or narrow your search using each tool until you find five Web sites that you believe are good Web research resources that Anne, Dave, and Ranjit should include in their bookmarks or favorites lists to help them locate information about international business stories.

4. For each Web site, record the URL and write a paragraph that explains why you believe the site would be useful to an international business news writer. Identify each site as a guide, directory, or other resource.

5. Evaluate the quality of each Web site. Write a paragraph for each site rating the site's quality as low, medium, or high, and explain the reasons for your rating.

6. When you are finished, close your Web browser.

Apply the skills you learned in this tutorial to choose a search tool and use it to find geographic information.

APPLY

Case Problem 1

There are no Data Files needed for this Case Problem.

Midland University Earth Sciences Institute You are an intern at the Midland University Earth Sciences Institute. The Institute conducts research on the primary effects of earthquakes on land stability, soil composition, and water redirection, as well as secondary effects such as changes in plant and animal life. When an earthquake strikes, the Institute sends a team of geologists, soil chemists, biologists, botanists, and civil engineers to the site to examine the damage to structures, land formations, and rivers. An earthquake can occur without warning nearly anywhere, so the Institute needs quick access to information on local conditions in various parts of the world, including temperature, money exchange rates, demographics, and local customs. In early July, you receive a call that an earthquake has occurred in northern Chile. To obtain information about local midwinter conditions there, complete the following steps:

1. Start your Web browser, go to www.cengagebrain.com, open the Tutorial 3 Weblinks page, and then click the Case Problem 1 link. The Case Problem 1 section contains links to lists of search engines, directories, and metasearch engines.

2. Choose one of the search tools you learned about in this tutorial to conduct searches for information on local conditions in northern Chile. When searching for information on weather conditions, be sure to obtain information about conditions during the month of July. (*Hint:* You might need to conduct preliminary searches to identify terms that you can use to limit your searches to northern Chile.)

3. Prepare a short report that includes the daily temperature range, average rainfall, current exchange rate for U.S. dollars to Chilean pesos, and any information you can obtain about the characteristics of the local population.

4. When you are finished, close your Web browser.

Apply the skills you learned in this tutorial to find information about companies that sell a specific product.

APPLY

Case Problem 2

There are no Data Files needed for this Case Problem.

Lightning Electrical Generators, Inc.   You work as a marketing manager for Lightning Electrical Generators, Inc. John Delaney, the firm's president, has asked you to investigate new markets for the company. One market to consider is the uninterruptible power supply (UPS) business. A UPS unit supplies continuing power to a single computer or to an entire computer system if the regular source of power fails. Most UPS units provide power only long enough for an orderly shutdown of the computer. John wants you to study the market for UPS units in the United States. He wants to know which firms make and sell UPS products. He would also like to know the power ratings and prices of individual units. To provide John with the information he needs, complete the following steps:

1. Start your Web browser, go to www.cengagebrain.com, open the Tutorial 3 Weblinks page, and then click the Case Problem 2 link. The Case Problem 2 section contains links to lists of search engines, directories, and metasearch engines.

2. Use one of the search tools to conduct searches for information about specific UPS products for John. You should design your searches to find the manufacturers' names and information about the products that they offer. (*Hint:* Try searching on the full term, "uninterruptible power supply," in addition to the acronym, "UPS.")

3. Prepare a short report that includes the information you have gathered for at least five UPS products, including the manufacturer's name, model number, product features, and suggested price.

4. When you are finished, close your Web browser.

Apply the skills you learned in this tutorial to find and evaluate the quality of specific Web page content.

APPLY

Case Problem 3

There are no Data Files needed for this Case Problem.

Eastern College English Department   You are a research assistant in the Eastern College English Department. The department head, Professor Garnell, has an interest in Shakespeare. She has spent years researching whether William Shakespeare actually wrote the plays and poems attributed to him. Some scholars, including Professor Garnell, believe that most of Shakespeare's works were written by Christopher Marlowe. Professor Garnell wants to include links on the department Web page to other researchers who agree with her, but she is concerned that many Web pages that discuss this matter are not reputable. Professor Garnell wants to include links to high-quality sites only. To gather the URLs, complete the following steps:

1. Start your Web browser, go to www.cengagebrain.com, open the Tutorial 3 Weblinks page, and then click the Case Problem 3 link. The Case Problem 3 section contains links to lists of search engines, directories, and metasearch engines.

2. Use one of the search tools to find Web sites that contain information about the Shakespeare-Marlowe controversy.

3. Use the procedures outlined in this tutorial to evaluate the quality of the sites you found in the previous step. (*Hint:* Most useful sites will have some connection to a university or research library.)

4. Choose at least five Web sites that Professor Garnell might want to include on her Web page. For each Web site, record the URL and write at least one paragraph in which you describe the evidence you have gathered about the site's quality.

5. When you are finished, close your Web browser.

Research the Web to find specific information, and then evaluate the information.

RESEARCH

Case Problem 4

There are no Data Files needed for this Case Problem.

Glenwood Employment Agency   You work as a staff assistant at the Glenwood Employment Agency. Eric Steinberg, the agency's owner, wants you to locate Web resources for finding open positions in your geographic area. Eric would like this information to gauge whether his own efforts are keeping pace with those of the competition. He wants to monitor a few good pages but does not want to conduct exhaustive searches of the Web every week. To help Eric find current employment information, complete the following steps:

1. Start your Web browser, go to www.cengagebrain.com, open the Tutorial 3 Weblinks page, and then click the Case Problem 4 link. The Case Problem 4 section contains links to lists of search engines, directories, and metasearch engines.

2. Use one of the search tools to find Web sites containing information about job openings in your geographic area. (*Hint:* You can use search expressions that include Boolean and precedence operators to limit your searches.)

3. Prepare a list of at least five URLs of pages that you believe would be good candidates for Eric's monitoring program.

4. For each URL that you find, write a paragraph that explains why you selected it, and then identify any particular strengths or weaknesses of the Web site based on Eric's intended use.

5. When you are finished, close your Web browser.

Create a report that evaluates the effectiveness of a search tool you chose to find specific information.

CREATE

Case Problem 5

There are no Data Files needed for this Case Problem.

Lynda's Fine Foods   For many years, Lynda Rice has operated a small store that sells specialty foods, such as pickles and mustard, and related gift items. Lynda is thinking about selling her products on the Web because they are small, inexpensive to ship relative to their product prices, and easy to package. She believes that people who buy her products might appreciate the convenience of ordering over the Web. Lynda would like to find some specialty food store sites on the Web to learn about possible competitors and to obtain some ideas that she might use when she creates her own Web site. To research selling specialty food items on the Web, complete the following steps:

1. Start your Web browser, go to www.cengagebrain.com, open the Tutorial 3 Weblinks page, and then click the Case Problem 5 link. The Case Problem 5 section contains links to lists of search engines, directories, and metasearch engines.

2. Use one of the search engines to find Web sites that offer gift items such as pickles or mustard. You can use search expressions that include Boolean and precedence operators to limit your searches.

3. Repeat your search using one of the Web directory tools.

4. Compare the results you obtained using a search engine and using a Web directory. Explain in a report of about 100 words which search tool was more effective for this type of search. Your instructor might ask you to prepare a presentation to your class in which you summarize your conclusions.

5. When you are finished, close your Web browser.

TUTORIAL **4**

OBJECTIVES

Session 4.1
- Find current news
- Get up-to-date weather information
- Obtain maps and destination information
- Locate people and businesses
- Purchase items online

Session 4.2
- Understand copyrights, fair use, public domain, and plagiarism
- Learn how to cite Web resources
- Find library and text resources on the Web
- Locate multimedia elements on the Web, including images, audio, and video

Information Resources on the Web

Finding Specific Information Online

Case | *Cosby Promotions*

Marti Cosby is the president of Cosby Promotions—a growing booking agency that handles promotion and concert contract negotiations for musicians and bands. Cosby Promotions works with a wide variety of music acts, including bands that play pop, Latin, heavy metal, techno, industrial, and urban styles of music. Marti wants to use Web searching techniques to help Cosby Promotions' staff stay current on entertainment news and trends that might affect the agency's clients.

The agency does not currently handle many country music acts, but Marti wants to expand its country music business during the next few years. To this end, she is planning a trip to Nashville, Tennessee, home of the Grand Ole Opry. In this tutorial, you will use the Internet to find information for Marti as she prepares for her trip to Nashville, where she will visit a new venue, meet with new clients, and learn more about the country music genre.

STARTING DATA FILES

There are no starting Data Files needed for this tutorial.

SESSION 4.1 VISUAL OVERVIEW

The Internet is a great source for locating maps and driving directions. Popular map sites are Bing Maps, Google Maps, and MapQuest.

A number of Web sites provide weather information and forecasts. Popular weather Web sites are AccuWeather and The Weather Channel.

To do before my trip to Nashville:
- Find campgrounds and motels around Nashville
- Locate an address and phone number for Uncle Joe in Tennessee
- Check the weather for the week of 8/1
- Map the route from here to Nashville
- Research things to do in Nashville

TYPES OF INFORMATION ON THE INTERNET

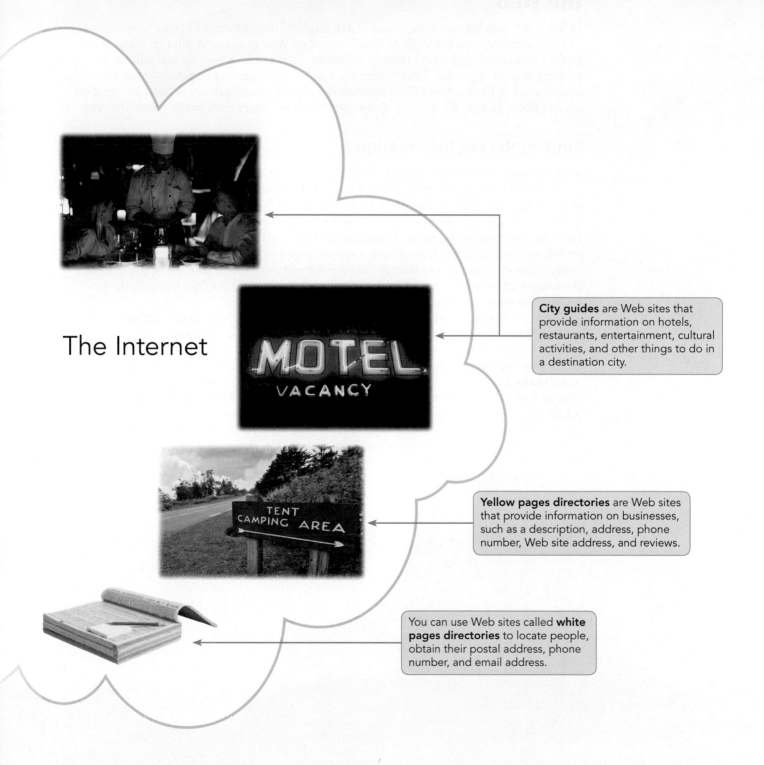

The Internet

City guides are Web sites that provide information on hotels, restaurants, entertainment, cultural activities, and other things to do in a destination city.

Yellow pages directories are Web sites that provide information on businesses, such as a description, address, phone number, Web site address, and reviews.

You can use Web sites called **white pages directories** to locate people, obtain their postal address, phone number, and email address.

Finding Current and Specific Information on the Web

In Tutorial 3, you learned how to use search engines, directories, and other resources to find information on the Web. In many instances, your goal was to find facts about a topic. Often, these facts don't change over time. Sometimes, however, you will need to find the most up-to-date information on a particular subject or event. For example, Marti's work at Cosby Promotions involves finding the most recent news and information about clients, potential sponsors, performance venues, and trends in the music industry.

Finding Recent Information

When you are searching for recent news, you could go directly to the Web sites of local and national newspapers, magazines, television stations, and radio stations. But the news sources you choose to visit might not have articles on the information you want. Instead of this hit-or-miss approach, you can conduct a search to determine which sources have the information you want. Before conducting a search, you should consider which search tool would be the best option: a search engine or a directory. Search engines usually include more recent listings because the editorial review process of many Web directories takes time to complete. In addition, a Web directory might not include listings for the topic you want to find.

Most search engines enable you to search for Web sites that have been modified recently. This feature is usually included as a filter option on the sites' advanced search pages. The filtering options for selecting recently modified Web pages will be different on the various search engines. For example, the Google Advanced Search page allows a search to be filtered based on when the page was last updated, as shown in Figure 4-1. You choose from among the most recent 24 hours, week, month, or year. Exalead includes an advanced search option so you can specify a particular date and search before or after that date, or you can include two date arguments in an Exalead search expression and search for Web pages modified after one date but before another date.

Figure 4-1   Date filter options on the Google Advanced Search page

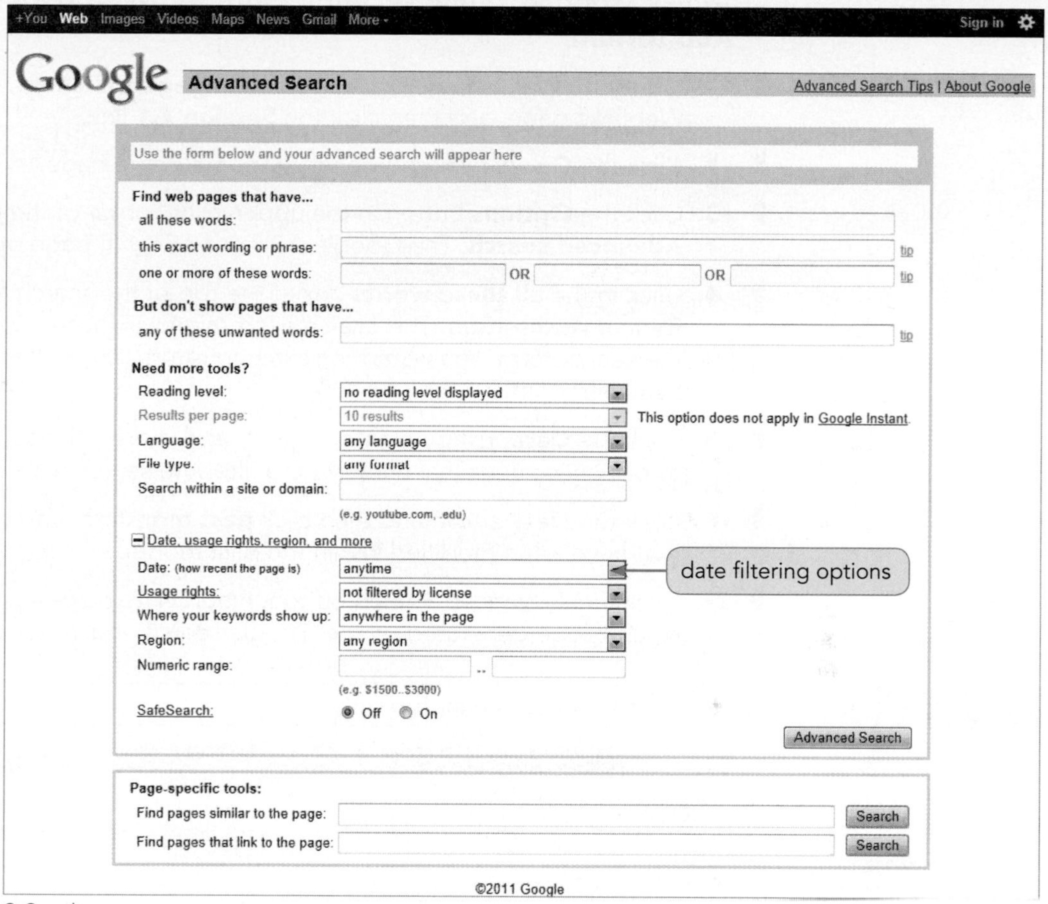

© Google

How Search Engines Filter Results by Date

Search engines can perform date-filtered searches because when Web servers send a Web page to a browser (or a search engine's Web robot), they include a header that contains information about the Web page, such as the date it was last modified. Search engines then store this information in their databases and use it to create date-filtered results.

Marti wants to book several of her newest clients to play at Ryman Auditorium in Nashville, Tennessee, and she needs to find current information about the auditorium to help her prepare for an upcoming meeting with the venue's manager. Although Web directories will collect many useful sites that include the name "Ryman Auditorium" in their databases, a search engine would provide more recent listings. In this case, you will use Google to search for information on Ryman Auditorium from the past month.

To use Google to find recently modified Web pages about Ryman Auditorium:

1. Start your Web browser, go to **www.cengagebrain.com**, open the Tutorial 4 Weblinks page, and then click the **Session 4.1** link.

2. Click the **Google** link to open the Google home page.

3. Click the **Options** button in the upper-right corner of the page, and then click **Advanced search**. The Google Advanced Search page opens.

4. Click in the **all these words** box at the top of the search form, and then type **Ryman Auditorium**. This search expression will locate Web pages that include the search term. You want the search to return pages that have been modified in the last month.

5. Click the **Date, usage rights, region, and more** link near the bottom of the page to display options that allow you to filter the search results.

6. Click the **Date** arrow, and then click **past month** to limit your search to pages that have been modified within the past month.

7. Click the **Advanced Search** button. Figure 4-2 shows a part of the date-filtered results page generated by the Google search engine for this query.

Figure 4-2	Google date-filtered search results

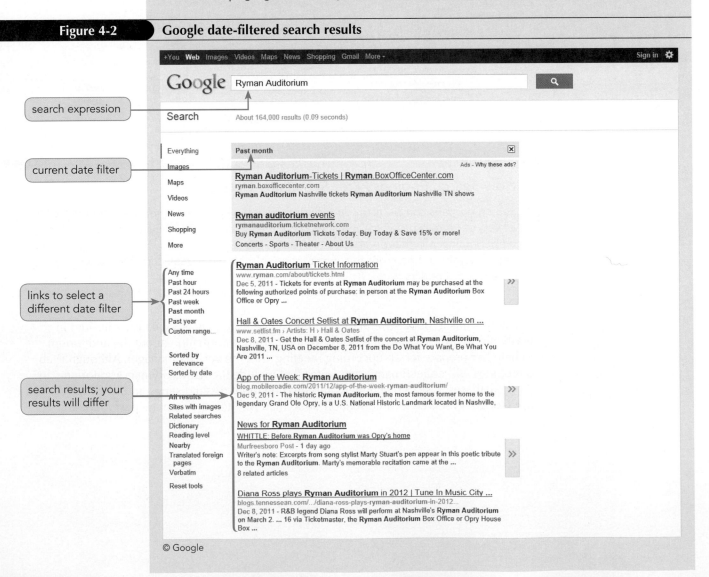

© Google

Search engines' date filtering capabilities are only as good as the information they collect. These databases store the date each Web page was last modified. A page gets a new modification date no matter how large or small the change is. So, even if most of the content on the page did not change, the modification date would still be updated. Because of this, a date-filtered search doesn't always provide the results you want. Another good way to find recent information about companies, people, or events is to look for current news about them.

Getting Current News

TIP

In many instances, you can search the site's archives for older articles.

The Web has a variety of sources for current news stories. Some news outlets are available only online. Others are available both online and offline. Traditional news outlets—including print and broadcast media—often post news stories on the Web in addition to their usual distribution in newspapers and magazines or on the radio and television. These Web sites include search features so you can search the site for specific news stories. Also, search engines and Web directories include links to these types of sources.

PROSKILLS

Written Communication: Evaluating Sources of Information

On the Internet and the Web, information is now disseminated rapidly and extensively, and updated frequently. The quantity of information available is astounding in part because of the low investment required, and in part because of the new sources of information that are easily available. This means that you as the reader need to evaluate the material you are reading.

The cost of publishing on the Web is very low. A Web-based publication can be financially successful with few advertisers, no subscribers, and relatively few readers. As a result, online publications can focus on the specialized, narrow interests of relatively small audiences. Online-only publications such as Slate, Salon.com, and The Huffington Post have become established parts of the media industry.

The low cost of Web publishing also means that anyone with the interest and the financial means can use the Web to promote his or her views—commonly in the form of a Web log (also called a Weblog or blog). A **blog** is a written commentary on current events, personal experiences, or anything else an individual wants to expound upon. Blogs are usually written by a single person (called the blogger) who wants to express a particular point of view. Some blogs allow readers to add comments or reactions to the blogger's statements, which may be edited or deleted by the blogger. Although blogs exist on a wide variety of topics, many blogs focus on political, religious, or other issues about which people have strong opinions. Because the blog owner writes the main content and decides which comments posted by readers will be included in the blog, the content and direction of the blog are controlled by its owner. (You will learn more about blogs in Tutorial 5.)

An alternative form of interactive online writing is the wiki. A **wiki** is a Web site that is designed to allow multiple users to contribute content and edit existing content. "Wiki" is a Hawaiian word that means "fast," and wikis are set up to allow many different users to add and edit content quickly and easily. Most wikis are focused on facts or collaborative work. Wikipedia, the online encyclopedia that you learned about in Tutorial 3, is probably the most famous wiki in the world. A wiki that has received a lot of attention in recent years is WikiLeaks, which provides a way for anonymous sources to leak information to its journalists, including secret government information.

You must also determine whether the content is opinion or fact. And, if you see the same information repeatedly at several sites, you need to determine the original source of that information. For example, various sites could reprint information from the same source, making it seem that the information is being corroborated by multiple sources when in actuality it is all from one source. With the wide variety of information available on the Web, you must be diligent in evaluating the accuracy of the information you are reading.

TIP

In Tutorial 5, you will learn how to subscribe to news feeds from specific sources so you can obtain information from them automatically.

One of the simplest ways to find a wide selection of current news reports is to use a news aggregation Web site. A **news aggregation Web site** collects and displays content from a variety of online news sources, including wire services, print media, broadcast outlets, and even blogs, and displays it in one place. You can then quickly access news stories on a topic from multiple sources.

One example of a news aggregation Web site is Yahoo!, which provides links to different topical sites on its home page. The News link opens the Yahoo! News site, shown in Figure 4-3, with access to the latest news and headlines—both in print and broadcast. You can access the day's top stories, latest news, and stories published by a particular news outlet. The page also features links to different aspects of the news—such as World, Business, Entertainment, Sports, Tech, and Politics—that include corresponding types of news stories. Other news aggregation Web sites include Bing News, Google News, Drudge Report, The Huffington Post, and NewsNow. Keep in mind that news aggregation Web sites, like any other media, may show a bias toward certain points of view.

Figure 4-3   **Yahoo! News home page**

Courtesy of Yahoo! Inc. © 2011 by Yahoo! Inc. YAHOO! and the YAHOO! logo are trademarks of Yahoo! Inc.

You will use a news aggregation Web site to locate current news stories about Ryman Auditorium that might not have appeared in the results of your search of recently modified Web pages.

To find recent news stories on the Web that mention Ryman Auditorium:

1. Return to the Weblinks page for Tutorial 4, locate the heading News Aggregation Web Site in the Session 4.1 section, and then click the **Yahoo!** link to open the search engine Web site.

2. Click the **News** link to open Yahoo! News, the news aggregation Web site.

3. Scroll down to locate the News Search box, type **Ryman Auditorium** in the News Search box, and then click the **News Search** button. The search results show the current headlines along with the source where they were published, as well as the date and time they were published. Figure 4-4 shows a part of the results page generated by Yahoo! News for this search.

| Figure 4-4 | Yahoo! News search results page |

Courtesy of Yahoo! Inc. © 2011 by Yahoo! Inc. YAHOO! and the YAHOO! logo are trademarks of Yahoo! Inc.

4. Click the **Options** link next to the search box at the top of the page, and then click **Advanced Search**. The Advanced News Search page opens with options for narrowing your search. See Figure 4-5.

Figure 4-5	Yahoo! Advanced News Search page

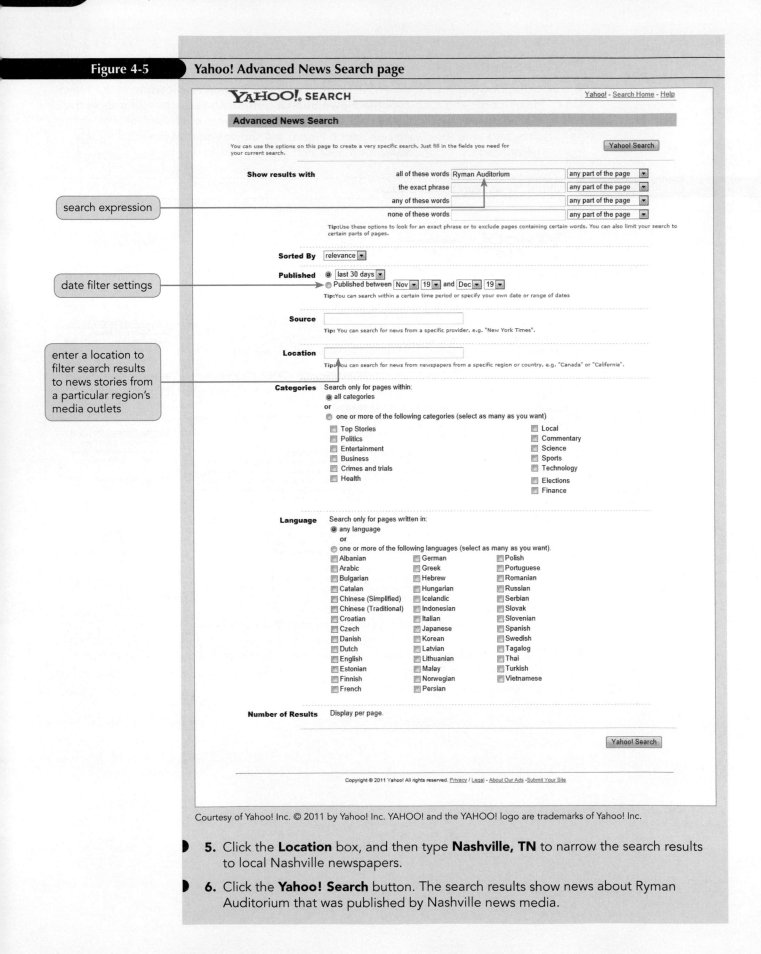

search expression

date filter settings

enter a location to filter search results to news stories from a particular region's media outlets

5. Click the **Location** box, and then type **Nashville, TN** to narrow the search results to local Nashville newspapers.

6. Click the **Yahoo! Search** button. The search results show news about Ryman Auditorium that was published by Nashville news media.

To visit additional news aggregation Web sites, you can use the links in the News Aggregation Web Sites section of the Additional Information section of the Weblinks page for Tutorial 4.

INSIGHT

Understanding How News Gets Distributed Electronically

The content for news outlets comes from wire services, newspapers, and broadcast networks. A **wire service** (also called a press agency or news service) is an organization that hires reporters to gather and write news stories, which it then distributes to newspapers, magazines, broadcasters, Web sites, and other organizations that pay a fee to the wire service.

Although there are hundreds of wire services around the world, most news comes from the four largest wire services: United Press International (UPI) and the Associated Press (AP) in the United States, Thomson Reuters in Great Britain, and Agence France-Presse (AFP) in France. In addition to selling stories to print, broadcast, and online news outlets around the world, these major wire services all publish current news stories on their own Web sites.

Likewise, print, broadcast, and online news outlets hire reporters to write news stories, which might also be distributed or sold to affiliates or other news outlets. Major newspapers, such as *The New York Times*, *Washington Post*, and the *Los Angeles Times*, have Web sites that include current news and many other features from their print editions. All of the major U.S. broadcast networks, including ABC, CBS, CNN, FOX, MSNBC, NBC, and NPR, have Web sites that carry news features. Broadcasters in other countries, such as the BBC in Great Britain, also provide news reports on their Web pages. Local radio and television stations often have their own Web sites where they offer selected news, sports, and weather information for their local market areas.

Because many newspapers, magazines, broadcasters, and news aggregation sites obtain stories from the major wire services and from each other, you often find the same news stories in your search results. Sometimes one news source will edit a story to shorten it or add information that appeals to its local audience. In many cases, different news outlets will just republish the original story without changes. Keep in mind that finding the same story published in multiple places doesn't mean that it is accurate or current. Be sure to evaluate the content as you learned in Tutorial 3 for accuracy and currency.

Finding Up-to-Date Weather Information

Many people consult a weather forecast daily because they want to know the weather conditions before dressing and venturing out for the day. When planning a vacation, they can review weather patterns for their intended destination. Before packing for a trip, they can obtain detailed weather information to guide their clothing choices. Some people enjoy seeing the weather conditions for family and friends who live elsewhere. Many also want to follow current weather conditions when there is a major storm—whether snow, wind, rain, hurricane, etc. These weather forecasts, conditions, and other information are available on the Web.

A number of companies, such as AccuWeather, The Weather Channel, National Oceanic and Atmospheric Administration's National Weather Service, and Weather Underground, provide weather conditions and forecasts on their Web sites. These Web sites also offer a wealth of other features and information, including live radar, graphs,

10-day forecasts, trip planners, severe weather reports, satellite views, desktop weather apps, and video forecasts for different areas. Many sites let you enter your zip code so the page always opens with weather for your area. You can also install a gadget on your desktop or an app on your smartphone to display the current weather conditions for your area.

Some weather sites sell their information to other companies that then include it on their Web sites. So you might see an AccuWeather forecast or weather map on many other Web sites, such as Yahoo! or your local newspaper's site. These same weather sites are also available as a gadget for your Windows desktop or an app for your smartphone.

Local television and radio stations offer weather information on their Web sites. Some of these sites purchase weather information from other outlets such as AccuWeather or The Weather Channel, but larger stations usually employ their own meteorologists and have their own weather prediction equipment. These local weather forecasts can be more accurate and detailed than those provided by the major weather Web sites for your area.

Marti plans to travel to Nashville later in the week to meet with some country music artists whom she hopes to sign as clients for the agency. You will check the weather for the Nashville area.

To find weather information for the Nashville area:

▶ **1.** Return to the Weblinks page for Tutorial 4, and then click one of the links under the Weather Information Web Sites heading in the Session 4.1 section. The weather site opens in your browser. You can search for the weather forecast for a specific location by entering the city and state or a zip code.

▶ **2.** In the search box, type **Nashville, TN** and then click the **Go, Search, Find Weather**, or similar button. The local Nashville forecast appears on the page. Depending on the site you chose, there might be links to the extended local forecast, radar, satellite, and videos or webcams. Figure 4-6 shows the Nashville Weather Forecast and Conditions on The Weather Channel's Web site.

Figure 4-6   **The Weather Channel local forecast page for Nashville**

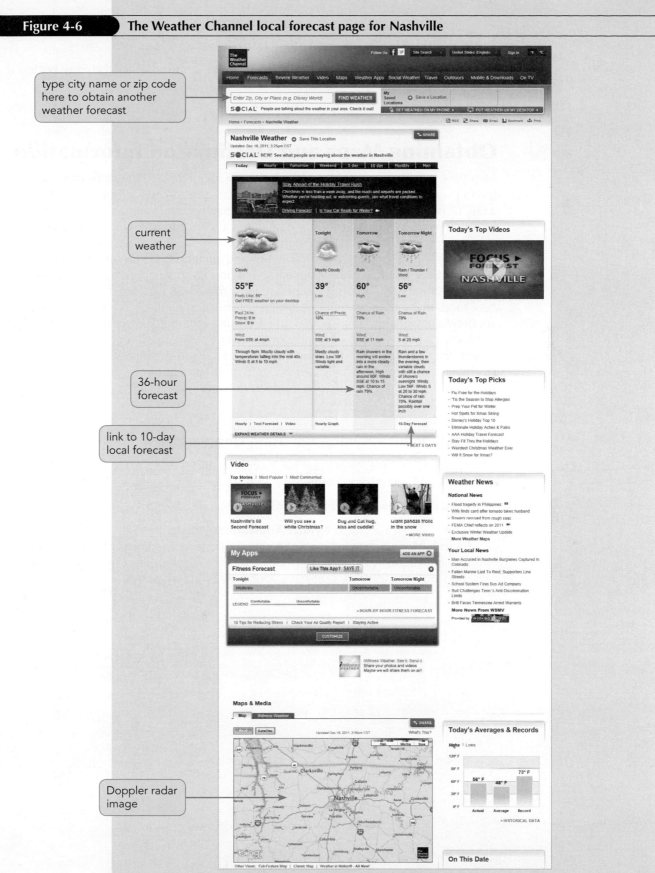

type city name or zip code here to obtain another weather forecast

current weather

36-hour forecast

link to 10-day local forecast

Doppler radar image

▶ **3.** Click a link to see an extended forecast for Nashville.

▶ **4.** If available, play the video of the Nashville weather forecast.

▶ **5.** Click a link to see a satellite map of Nashville, and then click the **Play** button if necessary.

Obtaining Maps and Destination Information

Map sites provide an abundance of information about places. The maps can show a broad overview of a region or state, and they can be zoomed to display detailed maps of a city or neighborhood. You can get directions to a specific location, observe current traffic and weather conditions, look at a satellite view instead of a street map, and in some cases see photos of the location. You can find businesses in the area, including restaurants, hotels, and shops; see what activities and attractions are around; identify services such as banks, libraries, and pharmacies; and find information such as gas prices and parking. Although the information provided by these sites is not perfect (for example, new roads and detours caused by current construction work often are not included), they are helpful travel aids. Some commonly used sites include Google Maps and MapQuest.

Nashville has been a central location for country music performers for many years. In fact, the Grand Ole Opry, a long-running country music radio show, is based in Nashville. Marti wants to include a stop at Ryman Auditorium, which is the home of the Grand Ole Opry. You will use a map site to determine the location of Ryman Auditorium.

To locate Ryman Auditorium using Google Maps:

▶ **1.** Return to the Weblinks page for Tutorial 4, and then click the **Google** link under the Map Site heading in the Session 4.1 section to open the Google home page.

▶ **2.** Click the **Maps** link to open the Google Maps search page.

▶ **3.** In the Search box, type **Ryman Auditorium, Nashville, TN**, and then click the **Search Maps** button. A map of Nashville appears marked with the location of Ryman Auditorium. Figure 4-7 shows the map that appears in Google Maps. The map includes tools for adjusting your view of the map.

Figure 4-7	Ryman Auditorium area map in Google Maps

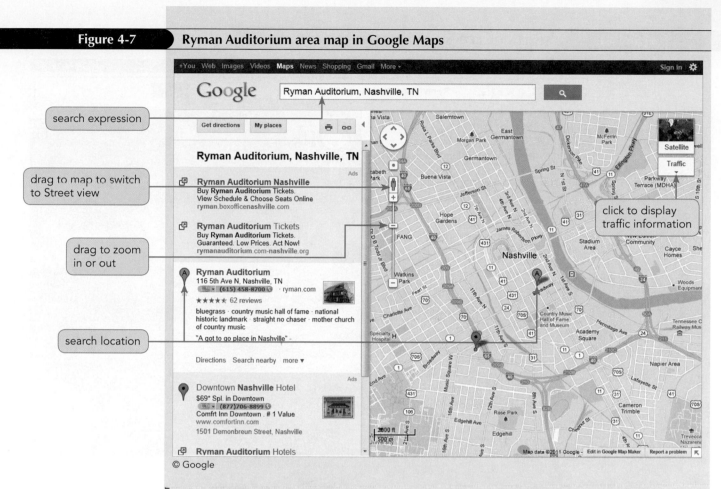

search expression

drag to map to switch to Street view

drag to zoom in or out

search location

click to display traffic information

© Google

4. Click the **Zoom In** button three times, or until you can clearly see that Ryman Auditorium is located on 5th Avenue North. The Google Maps Web site offers views other than Map view, including Street view, which is a group of photos of the location and surrounding area.

5. Drag the **yellow person** icon at the top of the Zoom bar onto the map to display blue lines, and then release the mouse button when the green pointer under the person icon is pointing to the location of Ryman Auditorium on the map. As you drag the person icon to the location, a ScreenTip appears over the person icon's head giving the address of Ryman Auditorium. A photo of the street view of Ryman Auditorium appears in place of the map. Figure 4-8 shows the photo that appears in Google Maps.

Figure 4-8 **Street view of Ryman Auditorium on Google Maps**

click to exit Street view

picture of Ryman Auditorium (you might see a different picture)

Map view of the current picture

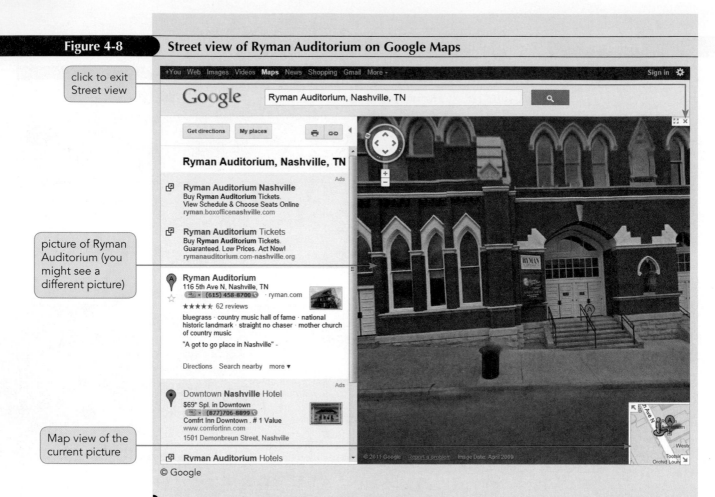

© Google

6. In Google Maps, click the **Exit street view** button in the upper-right corner of the street view photo to return to Map view.

7. Point to the **Satellite** button to open a menu of options for additional information you can display for this location, such as Traffic, Photos, Weather, and Webcams.

8. Click **Traffic** on the menu. Depending on the current traffic conditions, red, yellow, and green lines appear on the map indicating the current traffic status around Ryman Auditorium.

9. Click the **Ryman Auditorium** link next to the letter "A" in the pane to the left of the map. A Web page appears showing a photograph of the auditorium, its address, its phone number, links to printed directions, links to reviews, a description of the venue, and a list of upcoming events.

To visit additional map sites, you can use the links in the Map Sites section of the Additional Information section of the Weblinks page for Tutorial 4.

Although map sites often provide basic listings and information about lodging, restaurants, attractions, and entertainment opportunities for a particular location, you can often find more detailed information and reviews using travel guide sites. These sites include descriptive and comprehensive information about a location, reviews of hotels and restaurants, trip ideas, travel deals, and calendars of events, as well as discussions, photos, and blogs. People often use these sites to plan a trip from selecting a destination to learning about the history and attractions, finding hotels and restaurants, and making flight and hotel reservations. Some common travel guide sites are Fodor's Travel Guides, Frommer's Travel Guides, Let's Go Travel, Lonely Planet Travel Guides and Travel Information, and TripAdvisor.

To further help Marti prepare for her Nashville trip, you want to find some general historical information about Nashville, locate a restaurant for dinner, and get information on a hotel.

To obtain information about Nashville restaurants and entertainment:

1. Return to the Weblinks page for Tutorial 4, and then click a link under the Travel Guides Web Sites heading in the Session 4.1 section.

2. In the search box, type **Nashville, TN**, and then click the search or go button. The search results show a list of links related to Nashville.

3. Click the **Nashville travel guide** link (the specific wording of this link will change depending on the site you use). A variety of information is available about Nashville. Figure 4-9 shows Frommer's Guide to Nashville.

| Figure 4-9 | Frommer's Guide to Nashville |

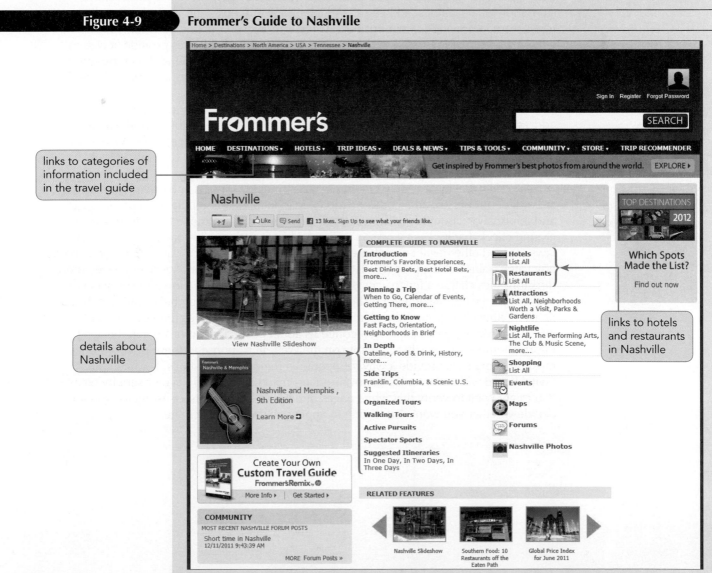

links to categories of information included in the travel guide

details about Nashville

links to hotels and restaurants in Nashville

> **4.** If there is an overview or introduction to Nashville, read the information provided.

> **5.** Locate and click a link that provides a list of Nashville restaurants, and then find a restaurant to recommend to Marti.

> **6.** Locate and click a link that provides a list of Nashville hotels, and then find a top-rated hotel where Marti can stay during her visit.

Marti should have enough information now to solidify her travel plans for her business trip to Nashville. To visit additional Travel Guide sites, you can use the links in the Travel Guides section of the Additional Information section of the Weblinks page for Tutorial 4.

Finding People and Businesses

Online directory Web sites include listings of businesses and people, much like the printed telephone books that were used for decades to find phone numbers and contact information as well as businesses and services. Traditionally, white pages directories store individuals' names, addresses, and telephone numbers, and yellow pages directories store information about businesses. Today, however, the line between yellow and white pages directories is blurred. Most big name online directories provide access to both people and business contact information. Some common online directories are Superpages.com, Yellowbook, YP.com – Yellow Pages, Switchboard, Internet Address Finder, White Pages, and Yahoo! People Search.

When looking for a person, you can search for an individual by name, by postal address, by email address, or by phone number (called a reverse lookup). In some cases, you can find the contact information for people at both home and at work. When looking for a business, you can search for a specific business by name or you can look at businesses in a specific category for a geographic area.

Some sites provide a variety of other features, including maps and driving directions, reviews of businesses, area code and zip code lookup, name popularity, a person's age, and information about his or her relatives. Some provide a resource to perform a background check that looks at a person's criminal history, address history, personal assets, lawsuits, and other legal entanglements. Another resource might be available to find property value, sales history, property details, and neighborhood information. However, most directory sites charge a fee to access this level of detailed information about a person.

Some Web sites make unpublished and unlisted telephone numbers available for public use. Other sites group individual listings by categories, such as religious or political affiliation. Many people expressed concerns about privacy violations when this type of information became easily accessible on the Web. In response to these privacy concerns, most directory sites provide a way for people to remove their listings. For example, Switchboard will accept a list removal request made on its Web page or sent by email. You might want to verify that white pages directories have a correct listing for you and decide whether you want your listing to appear on a white pages site.

TIP

Many online white pages and yellow pages directories are also available as mobile apps for smartphones.

These online directories compile information in several ways. Individuals and businesses can submit new entries as well as update or correct existing entries. Directory sites can also collect information from publicly available sources, published telephone directories, and the Web, such as data provided when signing up for a social network like Facebook. Directory sites also purchase information from third-party sources, such as personal information individuals provided to a business or provided when filling out a form to enter a contest or start a subscription. Businesses then share this information with online directories. All of this information is indexed by the directory so that it can be quickly accessed during a search.

INSIGHT

How Directories Fund Their Services

Business directories provide ads and listings that appear in response to relevant search queries on search engines such as Google or Yahoo!. The ads can be static advertisements like you would see in a print directory, or interactive multimedia ads that include sound and video. And many directory sites provide sponsored results to searches, which means that businesses pay a fee to have their contact information and ads placed higher in the search results. The business pays a fee each time its advertisement is clicked.

Marti is planning to develop reciprocal relationships with local booking agencies in Nashville. She wants to make some initial contacts during this trip and asks you to search the Web to find a list of booking agencies in Nashville. You can use an online directory to find music agencies located in Nashville.

To search online directories for a music agency:

1. Return to the Weblinks page for Tutorial 4, locate the Online Directories heading in the Session 4.1 section, and then click the link to one of the sites listed to open its home page.

2. Click the appropriate link to search for a person (the exact link will vary, but could be labeled People Search, Find People, or Find a Person). Figure 4-10 shows the Find People tab at Superpages.com. Before looking for a music agency, use the site to find your own listing.

Figure 4-10   **Superpages.com Find People**

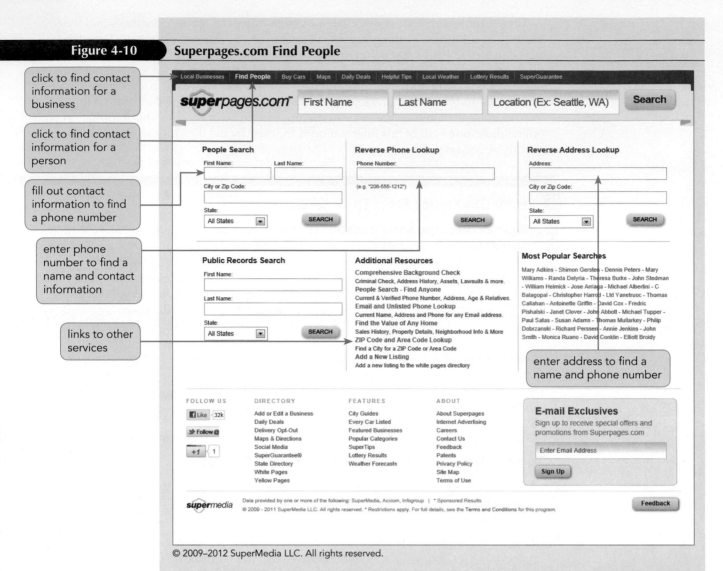

click to find contact information for a business

click to find contact information for a person

fill out contact information to find a phone number

enter phone number to find a name and contact information

links to other services

enter address to find a name and phone number

© 2009–2012 SuperMedia LLC. All rights reserved.

3. In the corresponding boxes, enter your first name, last name, city and state, or your zip code, and then click the **Search** or **Find** button. Examine your listing that appears.

   Trouble? If you do not find your listing, your telephone number might be listed under another person's name, such as a parent or roommate. Repeat Step 3 using that person's name to find your listing. If you still cannot find a listing for yourself, try searching for a friend's listing or a relative's listing, or try your search in a different directory.

4. Click the appropriate link to search for a business (the exact link will vary, but could be labeled Local Businesses, Find a Business, or Business).

TIP

You also can type Music Agent, Nashville TN in the search box to return results for music agents in that city.

5. In the corresponding boxes, enter **Music Agents** as the category of the business you want to find and **Nashville, TN** as the location, and then click the **Find** or **Search** button. The results page shows information about music booking agencies in Nashville. This search can be challenging because no single category description is universally used by companies that book performing musicians. Figure 4-11 shows the results page for a search using the term "Music Agents" on the Superpages.com site.

Figure 4-11	Superpages.com search results page

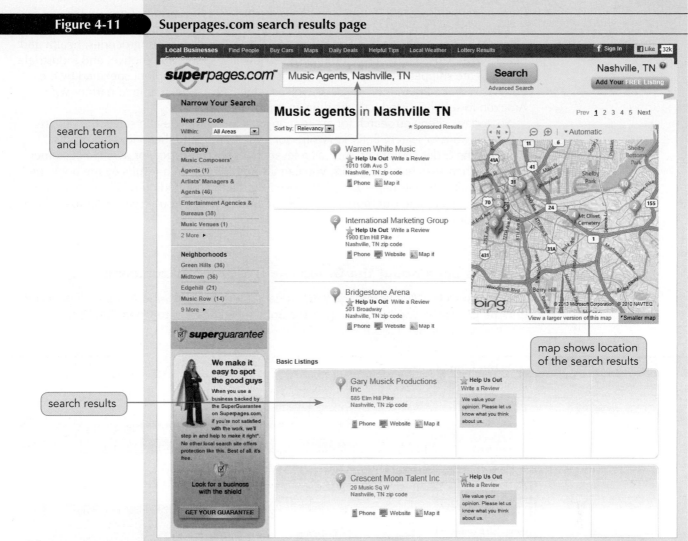

Trouble? If your search doesn't yield any results, try again using business catego-ries such as agent, artist, recording artist, or booking agent. If you still don't find any appropriate results, return to the Weblinks for Session 4.1 and try using a dif-ferent directory site.

Finding Products and Services Online

Many items are available for purchase on the Web: food, clothing, books, computers, software, games, music, specialty items, office supplies. Pretty much anything you can think of is available. Retailers—big and small as well as international, national, and local—have a presence on the Web. Some retailers have both a physical location and a Web site; others such as Amazon.com are online only without a storefront/brick-and-mortar store. In addition, individuals have flocked to the Web to sell their products and services. **E-commerce**, or electronic commerce, refers to the process of developing, mar-keting, selling, delivering, servicing, and paying for products and services online. You'll learn more about e-commerce in Tutorial 9.

TIP

Retail business that occurs online is also sometimes called e-tail.

Perhaps the most prevalent e-commerce site is Amazon.com. Amazon.com was founded by Jeff Bezos in 1995 to sell books on the Web. Since then, Amazon has expanded to sell a wide variety of products and services in the categories of books, movies, music, games, electronics and computers, home, garden, tools, groceries, health and beauty, toys, kids and babies, clothing, shoes, jewelry, sports, automotive, and industrial. All items are shipped directly to the purchaser or to another recipient specified by the purchaser. Since 2000, individuals as well as retailers have been able to partner with Amazon to sell their products, creating an online marketplace.

So, today, when you search for an item on Amazon.com, you can select the department you want to search, enter keywords for your search, and then view the results sorted in the order you prefer, such as relevance, popularity, price, or average customer review. When searching for books, you can also filter the search results by the book format you want, such as paperback, hardcover, Kindle e-reader edition, HTML, or audio.

Marti wants to find out more about the Grand Ole Opry. You'll search Amazon for a suitable book.

To find a book about the Grand Ole Opry on Amazon.com:

1. Return to the Weblinks page for Tutorial 4, and then click the **Amazon** link under the Online Shopping heading in the Session 4.1 section to open that Web site's home page. See Figure 4-12.

Figure 4-12	Amazon home page

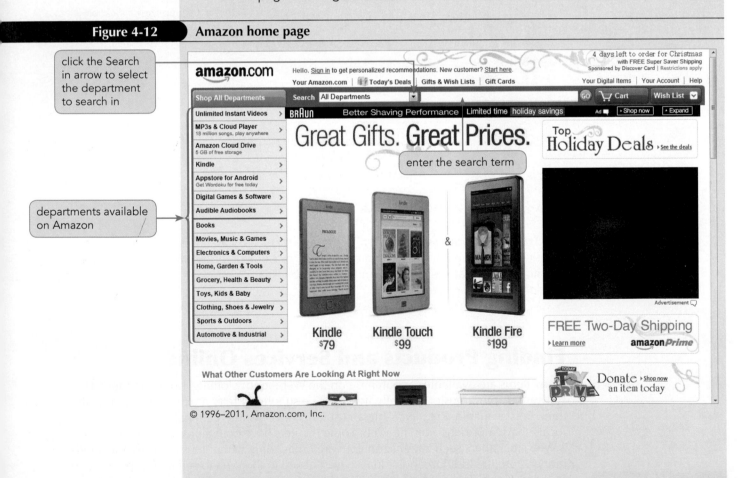

click the Search in arrow to select the department to search in

departments available on Amazon

enter the search term

© 1996–2011, Amazon.com, Inc.

▶ **2.** At the top of the page, click the **Search in** arrow, and then click **Books**. Your search will be limited to books rather than all departments.

▶ **3.** Type **Grand Ole Opry** in the Search for box, and then click the **Go** button. The results show books about the Grand Ole Opry sorted by relevance.

▶ **4.** At the top of the page, click the **Kindle Edition** link to filter the books to only those that are available for the Kindle e-reader.

▶ **5.** Click the **Sort by** arrow, and then click **Popularity**. The books are reordered to show the most popular title first.

▶ **6.** Scroll through the items to get a sense of which books are available and how much they cost.

Individuals can also sell items on the Web using sites such as eBay and craigslist. eBay identifies itself as the world's online marketplace where buyers and sellers come together to trade almost anything. Pierre Omidyar founded the auction site in 1995 as AuctionWeb, creating a marketplace for individuals to exchange goods. The site's name was changed to eBay in 1997. Today, eBay boasts more than 97 million users around the world. It has sites throughout the globe and has acquired or launched a variety of businesses, including PayPal (a global online payment company), Shopping. com (an online comparison shopping site), Half.com (a marketplace for used books, movies, music, and games), Rent.com (a listing site for rental housing in the United States), Milo.com (a product search company), brands4friends (an online shopping club for fashion and lifestyle), and eBay Classifieds (a listing site for classified advertisements). In 2011, it launched Fashion Outlet, the first virtual outlet mall in the United States.

You can find a variety of items on eBay, ranging from autographs to toys to antiques to books. Individuals place items for sale, choosing either to create an auction listing and accept only bids for the item, or to allow people to purchase the item right away for a set amount. For the online auction, the seller sets the minimum bid and the length of the auction; then, at the end of the allotted time, the highest bid wins. For a Buy It Now listing, the first person willing to pay the indicated price gets the item. Payment for an item is made through PayPal, which is a global online payment company people can use to send or receive secure payments without sharing their personal financial information. Anyone can view the items up for auction, but you must register with eBay to post or bid on an item.

Another popular site where individuals can buy and sell items is craigslist. In 1995, Craig Newmark started sending emails to friends about events in the San Francisco Bay Area. The following year, he changed his email distribution list into a Web-based service that included additional categories. In 2000, craigslist started expanding to other cities in the United States.

Today, craigslist is a network of more than 700 local sites in 70 countries that features free online classified advertisements with sections devoted to jobs, housing, personals, for sale, services, community, gigs, resumes, and discussion forums. See Figure 4-13. To buy or sell an item, a seller posts an ad following the site's guidelines, and buyers contact the seller to arrange the purchase, payment, and delivery of that item.

Figure 4-13 craigslist Nashville home page

© 2010 Craigslist

Marti is considering creating a contest to promote her country music clients, and she wants to find an autograph of a country music star that she can use as the prize. You'll see what is available on eBay.

To search for an autograph of a country musician on eBay:

1. Return to the Weblinks page for Tutorial 4, and then click the **eBay** link under the Online Shopping heading in the Session 4.1 section to open that Web site's home page. See Figure 4-14.

| Figure 4-14 | eBay home page |

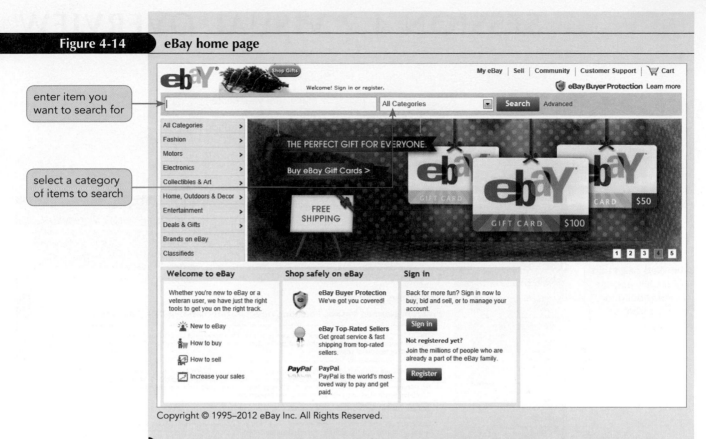

enter item you
want to search for

select a category
of items to search

2. Type **country music autographs** in the Search box, and then click the Search button. The results show all of the autographs available.

3. Scroll through the items to get a sense of which autographs are available and how much the cost to purchase them could be. Notice that you can see how many bids were made for the item, the minimum bid accepted, whether you can buy the item immediately, and how much time is left in the auction.

4. Return to the Weblinks page for Tutorial 4.

In the next session, you will learn about multimedia resources on the Web and the copyright issues that arise when you use them.

REVIEW

Session 4.1 Quick Check

1. How can you find Web pages that contain news published during the past week?
2. What is a news aggregation Web site?
3. What types of information are provided on weather sites?
4. What types of information are provided on map sites?
5. What types of information are provided on travel guide sites?
6. What kind of Web site would you use to find contact information for people or businesses?
7. True or False. Some Web sites make unpublished and unlisted telephone numbers available for public use.
8. _____ refers to the process of developing, marketing, selling, delivering, servicing, and paying for products and services online.

SESSION 4.2 VISUAL OVERVIEW

Note the Web site URL in the address or location bar.

The Web site title is usually located prominently on the page.

Make sure you locate and note the name of the publisher or institution that maintains the Web site on which the page is stored.

The Web page title will usually appear directly above the main content of the page.

The author of this Web page is Norman Paskin.

The date the Web page was published is often found at the bottom of the Web page. Also remember to document the date you access the Web page because its content might be changed or updated when someone else views the page at a later date.

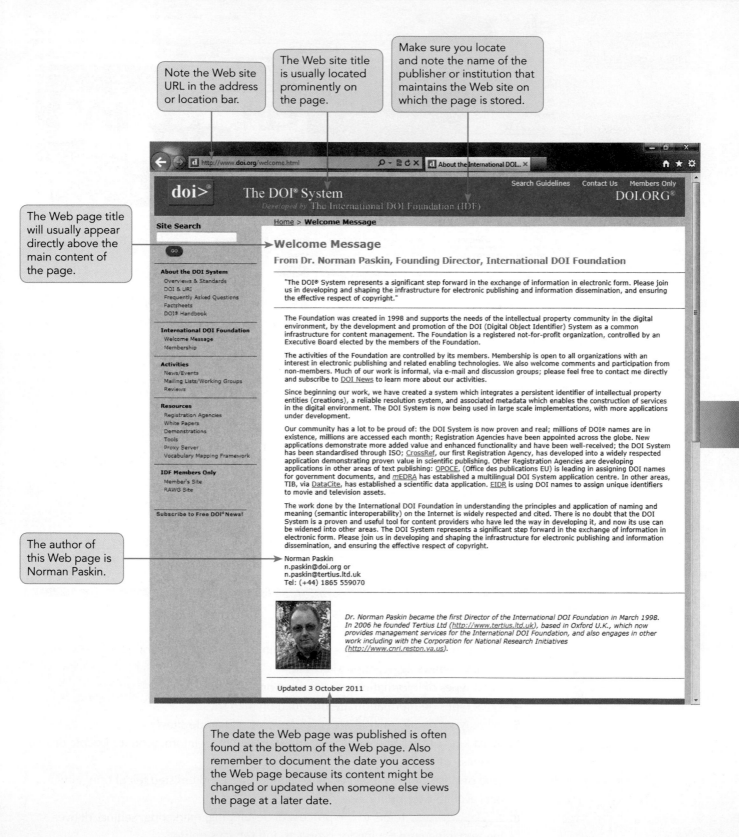

WEB PAGE CITATION GUIDELINES

When citing the author, use the Last Name, First Initial, Middle Initial format.

The year the page was published appears in parentheses; use (n.d.) if the page is not dated.

The Web page title is not in quotes or italic and is followed by a period.

The Web site title is in italic and is followed by a period.

APA Citation

Paskin, N. (2011). Welcome message. In *The DOI system*. Retrieved April 21, 2014, from http://www.doi.org

The date you viewed the page is presented in Month, Day, Year format.

Include the DOI if available or the URL of the home page; if it extends over two or more lines, break the lines after a forward slash.

Don't use ending punctuation that readers might think is part of the URL or DOI.

When citing the author, use the Last Name, First Name, Middle Name or Initial format.

The Web page title is in quotes if part of a larger work and is in italic if independent.

The Web site title is in italic and followed by a period.

The medium of publication appears after the date.

MLA Citation

Paskin, Norman. "Welcome Message." *The DOI System*. The International DOI Foundation, 3 October 2011. Web. 21 April 2014. <http://www.doi.org/welcome.html/>.

The date you viewed the page is presented in Day, Month, Year format.

The Web site owner or publisher is not in italic and is followed by a comma; use N.p. if not available.

Include the URL within brackets only if the reader cannot locate the source without it.

If the URL extends over two or more lines, break the lines after a forward slash.

Understanding Copyright

Many Web page elements and other items you find online are a form of **intellectual property**, which includes all creations of the human mind, such as original ideas and creative works presented in a form that can be shared or that others can recreate, emulate, or manufacture. On a Web page, intellectual property includes the images, videos, and text on the page, as well as the design of the page itself. Intellectual property as a tangible expression of an idea is protected just like other tangible forms of property, such as houses, and cars. Each country has its own rules and laws governing intellectual property rights and protection. In the United States, intellectual property is protected through patents, trademarks, trade secrets, and copyrights.

As you learned in Tutorial 1, a copyright is literally the right of a person to make copies of his or her work. Copyrights are granted by a government to the author or creator of an original work who creates a tangible expression of that work or creation. Creations that can be copyrighted include virtually all forms of artistic or intellectual expression, such as books, music, artwork, audio and video recordings, architectural drawings, choreographic works, product packaging, and computer software. The tangible form of the work can be words, numbers, notes, sounds, pictures, and so forth. Copyright protection exists whether the work is published or unpublished.

A collection of facts can be copyrighted, but only if the collection is arranged, coordinated, or selected in a way that causes the resulting work to rise to the level of an original work. For example, the Yahoo! Directory is a collection of links to URLs. These URLs existed before Yahoo! selected and arranged them into the form of its directory. However, most intellectual property experts would argue that the selection and arrangement of the links into categories probably makes the directory copyrightable.

The copyright is in effect for the length of time specified in the copyright law and gives the author or creator the exclusive right to reproduce, adapt, distribute, publicly perform, publicly display, or sell the work. In the United States, under the 1976 Copyright Act, works created after 1977 are protected for the life of the author (or the last surviving author in the case of a "joint work" with multiple authors) plus another 70 years. Works made for hire and anonymous or pseudonymous works are protected for 95 years from the date of publication or 120 years from the date of creation, whichever is earlier. The copyright holder can transfer, license, sell, donate, or leave the copyright to his or her heirs. Works created before 1978 are protected under the 1909 Copyright Act and have more complex and variable terms of copyright.

Determining Fair Use

U.S. copyright law allows people to use portions of copyrighted works without obtaining permission from the copyright holder if that use is a fair use. Section 107 of the 1976 Copyright Act lists criticism, comment, news reporting, teaching, scholarship, and research as examples of uses that may be eligible for fair use. However, the circumstances surrounding a particular use determine whether that use is considered fair. Keep in mind that the legal definition of fair use is intentionally broad and can be difficult to interpret. As a result, many disputes about whether a use is fair have landed in court. Courts generally consider the following four factors when determining fair use:

1. The purpose and character of the new work. This factor considers such issues as whether the use adds something new to the body of knowledge and arts or just reproduces the work, and whether the use is commercial or for nonprofit educational purposes.
2. The nature of the copyrighted work. In general, more creative works have stronger protection than factual works. Keep in mind that an unpublished work has the same copyright protections for fair use as a published work.

3. The amount and substantiality of the portion used in relation to the copyrighted work as a whole; in other words, how much of the copyrighted work was used. The less work that is used, the more likely it falls under fair use. However, using even a small amount of the work can be copyright infringement if it is the heart of the work. This is especially true with musical compositions. The use of even a small portion of a copyrighted song can be an infringing use.

4. The effect of the use on the potential market, or value, of the copyrighted work. For example, does the use of the copyrighted material hurt the market for the original work, and does it impair or limit the ability of the copyright owner to earn income or otherwise benefit from the work?

Again, no hard-and-fast rule determines fair use. If you are unsure whether your use is indeed fair use, the safest course of action is to contact the copyright owner and ask for permission to use the work.

One area where fair use disputes are prevalent is videos being posted on YouTube. Consider that any one video can include both original and copyrighted material. A video that includes even a small clip from a movie or television show or part of a song written or performed by someone else can constitute copyright infringement. This means that the copyright owner can sue the person who created and posted the video.

To learn more about fair use, you can use the links in the Fair Use section of the Additional Information section of the Weblinks page for Tutorial 4.

Works in the Public Domain

Once the term of the copyright has expired, the work moves into the **public domain**, which means that anyone is free to copy the work without requesting permission from the last copyright holder. Older literary works, such as *A Tale of Two Cities* by Charles Dickens that was published in 1859, are in the public domain and may be reproduced freely. Songs or musical works published earlier than 1922, such as the Star Spangled Banner written by Francis Scott Key in 1814, are also in the public domain in the United States, although sound recordings are not in the public domain.

A copyright can protect a particular expression of a creative work in addition to the work itself. For example, a Mozart symphony is in the public domain because it was written hundreds of years ago and is no longer protected by Austrian copyright law. But Mozart's creative work was writing the notes of the symphony down on paper in a particular form. If the Cleveland Orchestra makes an audio recording of that public domain Mozart symphony, its performance is a separate work that can be copyrighted by the Cleveland Orchestra and protected under current copyright laws.

Authors or creators can place their work into the public domain voluntarily at any time. For example, some Web sites provide graphics files that visitors can use free of charge. You can include public domain content on a Web page, in a paper, or in any other form of creative expression. However, you should still acknowledge the source of the public domain material and not represent the work as your own, which is plagiarism.

TIP

Web sites that offer free files for noncommercial use often carry a restriction against selling or redistributing those files.

The Digital Millennium Copyright Act

When Congress passed the 1976 Copyright Act, personal computers, the Internet and Web, email, digital photos, and other electronic content did not exist. However, with these newer technologies and media came new copyright concerns and issues.

In 1998, Congress passed the Digital Millennium Copyright Act (DMCA) to help protect copyright owners from online infringement or piracy. The DMCA addresses the following common issues: circumvention of copyright protection systems, fair use in a digital environment, and online service provider liability. The DMCA prohibits individuals from bypassing technologies that the copyright holders have added to their works to prevent others from using them even if that use would be considered a fair use. However, since 2010, the Librarian of Congress has said that accessing a small portion for educational uses by college professors and students would no longer be prohibited. Finally, the DMCA protects online service providers that act as "mere conduits" to provide transitory digital communications or that host third-party material on their servers and networks such as YouTube. As long as the service providers respond to copyright owners' claims, take down the material, and cancel accounts of repeat offenders, they are protected from some copyright infringement liability.

One Nashville country music band that Marti wants to sign has the same name as a band in another part of the country. You will find out whether it is possible to copyright the name of a band.

To find information about copyrights:

1. Start your Web browser, go to **www.cengagebrain.com**, open the Tutorial 4 Weblinks page, click the **Session 4.2** link, and then click the **United States Copyright Office** link to open the U.S. Copyright Office home page. The Copyright Office Web site provides basic information on copyright laws and the application of the law. At this site you can also register a work for copyright and record a copyright document. See Figure 4-15.

Figure 4-15 **U.S. Copyright Office home page**

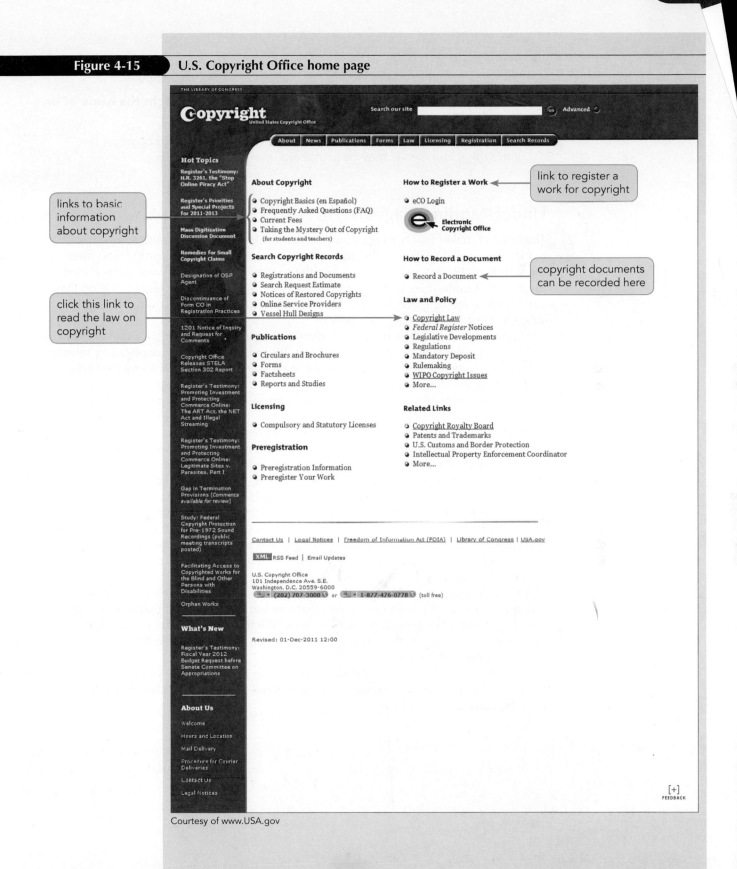

Courtesy of www.USA.gov

> **2.** In the About Copyright section, click the **Frequently Asked Questions (FAQ)** link. The Frequently Asked Questions about Copyright page opens.

> **3.** Read some of the questions, and then click the **Can I copyright the name of my band?** link in the What Does Copyright Protect? section.

> **4.** Read the answer to find out that names are not protected by copyright law, although some names may be protected under trademark law.

Understanding Plagiarism

The Internet makes it very easy to copy someone else's work. If you use someone else's work, whether the work is in the public domain or protected by copyright, you must cite the source of the material. Failure to cite the source of material that you use is called **plagiarism**. Claiming someone else's work as your own is a serious legal violation that can lead to a failing grade, being expelled from school, being fired from a job, or being subjected to a hefty fine or prosecution.

Plagiarism can be as simple as including a sentence or two from someone else's work without using quotation marks or attribution. It can be as blatant as duplicating substantial parts of someone else's work and claiming it as your own. It can be more subtle, such as paraphrasing someone else's content without the proper citation of the source. Another form of plagiarism is when students purchase essays, term papers, and even theses or dissertations from commercial services and then pass them off as their own.

To combat the growing issue of plagiarism, academic instructors, researchers, publishers, and others have turned to Web resources. A number of plagiarism checker sites are available for free or for a fee to detect plagiarism in written content. These sites compare the submitted work against archived student papers; publications including articles in journals, periodicals, and newspapers; books; databases; and Web page content. These sites can check for exact duplication or a paraphrase of someone else's work.

For example, Turnitin is a Web site that checks a submitted paper against 14 billion Web pages, 150 million student papers, and millions of articles from leading library databases and publications, and then determines how much of the paper is unoriginal. Figure 4-16 shows the home page for Turnitin.

To ensure that you don't unintentionally plagiarize someone else's work, be sure to properly reference the sources of works that you use. Keep in mind that just including a source citation is not enough if you plan to use the finished product commercially. You must also obtain the copyright holder's permission if you want to use the work in a way that falls outside of fair use.

To learn more about sites that check your writing for plagiarism, you can use the links in the Plagiarism Checkers section of the Additional Information section of the Weblinks page for Tutorial 4.

Figure 4-16   Turnitin home page

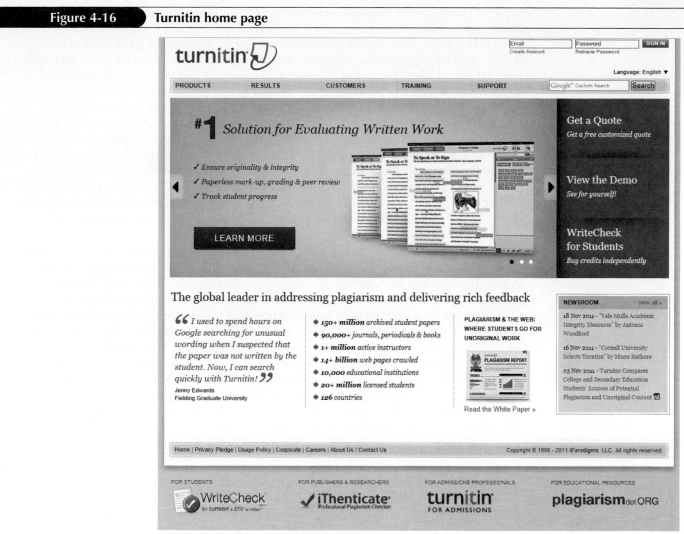

Citing Web Resources

To avoid charges of plagiarism, all works you reference in a report or paper—whether they are protected by copyright, in the public domain, or considered fair use—need to be documented. This gives proper credit to the original authors as well as provides readers with the information they need to find and review the works you used.

However, documentation can become a challenge when you are referencing a Web page. Because the Web is a dynamic medium that changes constantly, the content of any given page can change in an instant. Also, its URL can change or disappear from day to day. Unlike published books and journals, which have a physical existence, a Web page exists only in an HTML document on a Web server computer. If the file's name or location changes, or if the Web server is disconnected from the Internet, the page is no longer accessible.

To address this issue, digital intellectual content such as online journals, articles, reports, and white papers are assigned a unique alphanumeric string of characters, called a **digital object identifier (DOI)**, to identify that content and provide a persistent link to its location (or locations) as long as the content exists somewhere on the Internet.

All DOI numbers begin with *10.* followed by a prefix of a unique combination of four or more digits, then a slash, and finally a suffix that is any alphanumeric combination that identifies the publisher. The International DOI Foundation issues prefixes to DOI Registration Agencies, such as CrossRef.org, which then assign them to publishers and others. The publisher assigns the suffix using a unique identifier such as the book's ISBN. The DOI usually appears near the copyright notice. Unlike a URL, a DOI does not change when the content moves to a new location. If the content exists in multiple forms on the Web—for example, in one location as an Adobe PDF file and in another as a Microsoft Word file—all forms will have the same DOI.

For academic research, the two most widely followed standards for citations are those of the American Psychological Association (APA) and the Modern Language Association (MLA). The APA and MLA formats for Web page citations are similar. Both include the information shown in the Visual Overview for Session 4.2, which shows both APA and MLA citations for a specific Web page and how that information is obtained from the Web page. Figure 4-17 shows examples of other Web page citations that conform to the APA citation style. Be aware, however, that both the APA and MLA standards change from time to time. Consult these organizations' Web sites as well as the APA and MLA style guides for the latest rules and updates to these styles before using them. Also, always check to see if your instructor or editor (for work you are submitting for publication) has established other guidelines.

Figure 4-17	APA Web page citations

Web page with a title and an author, undated

Norman, D. (n.d.). Welcome to jnd.org. In *Don Norman's jnd website*. Retrieved April 21, 2014, from http://www.jnd.org

Web page with a title and authors, dated

Koeppel, D. (2011, August 19). The future of light is the LED. In *Wired*. Retrieved April 23, 2014, from http://www.wired.com/magazine/2011/08/ff_lightbulbs

Web page with a title but no author, undated

Pew Environment Group. (n.d.). In *The PEW Charitable Trusts*. Retrieved April 23, 2014, from http://www.pewenvironment.org

Web page with no title and no author, undated

United States Postal Service [Home page]. (n.d.). Retrieved April 23, 2014, from http://www.usps.com

© Cengage Learning

INSIGHT

Formatting URL Line Breaks

One difficulty of including long URLs or DOIs is typesetting them in printed documents. However, if you must include one and it does not fit on one line, you should break the URL or DOI only after a slash that occurs in the address. Also, you should not add a hyphen at the line break because a reader might mistakenly type the hyphen as part of the URL.

To learn more about format styles for citing sources, use the links in the Citation Formats section of the Additional Information section of the Weblinks page for Tutorial 4.

Accessing Text-Based Resources Online

Over the past decades, many reference materials that were once available only in print have become available electronically, and in many cases on the Web. Before that, anyone wanting to learn more about a topic had to go to a library to perform research using print resources. For example, encyclopedias were one of the first types of resources made available in electronic format; cross-references to other topics were made into hyperlinks, glossary definitions were changed to pop-up windows, and the entire encyclopedia became searchable by keyword. Unlike the print editions, digital versions could include audio and video clips. One of the earliest and most popular digital encyclopedias was Microsoft Encarta, which was available starting in 1993 on CD-ROMs. Dictionaries, thesauri, and almanacs soon followed. As access to the Web became more widespread, these sources were placed online.

Today, libraries offer content (books, periodicals, journals, and so forth) in a wide variety of formats. With the huge number of books being published every year, libraries don't have enough shelf space to store print versions of every resource. As a result, libraries are buying fewer printed books and offering more content electronically. Publishers are encouraging this trend by making digital content cheaper and easier to access. Consequently, an increasing number of books are available as e-books, which are electronic versions of books that are read on electronic readers (also called e-readers) such as the Kindle and the iPad as well as computers, tablets, and smartphones.

In addition, libraries can subscribe to huge databases that offer a wealth of information, which individuals cannot usually afford. For example, Dow Jones Factiva is a comprehensive global news and business information and research tool that provides access to top media outlets, trade and consumer publications, and business Web sites along with in-depth company, executive, and industry profiles; expert analysis; market data; and detailed reports. ProQuest Dialog is a combination of online research tools that provides online-based information services in subject areas such as business, science, engineering, finance, and law, in a format designed to meet the specific needs of a wide range of users, including information professionals and end users at business, professional, scientific, academic, and government organizations in more than 100 countries.

Likewise, other print resources—such as periodicals, scholarly journals, and government resources—have become available on the Web. This has helped these resources to remain current and easily accessible to their audiences. In addition, it means that these resources are now available day and night, regardless of whether the business or library in which they are housed is open.

Online References

TIP

In many instances, virtual libraries and online reference sites overlap and/or link to one another.

The Web contains many online references, including dictionaries, thesauri, encyclopedias, atlases, almanacs, quotations, grammar checkers, rhyming dictionaries, and language-translation sites to name just a few. These online references range in quality from very low to very high, so be sure to consider the results for accuracy. Some online reference resources require a subscription fee, but many free online reference tools also exist. Some common free online reference sites include Dictionary.com, Thesaurus.com, Merriam-Webster Online dictionary and thesaurus, World Sites Atlas, Enclopedia.com, Britannica Online Encyclopedia, BrainyQuote, and The Quotations Page. To learn more about online references, use the links in the Online References section of the Additional Information section of the Weblinks page for Tutorial 4.

The Web also includes sites that offer full-text copies of works that are no longer protected by copyright. Two well-known full-text sites are the Project Gutenberg and Bartleby.com Web sites. These volunteer efforts have collected the contributions of many people throughout the world who have spent enormous amounts of time entering or converting printed text into electronic form. The Project Gutenberg site currently offers more than 36,000 free e-books and is supported by donations. The Bartleby.com site, which is named for the main character in Herman Melville's famous short story "Bartleby the Scrivener," was converted into a privately held corporate site in 1999. Since then, it has used advertising to generate revenue to support its operations. The Bartleby.com home page is shown in Figure 4-18.

| Figure 4-18 | **Bartleby.com home page** |

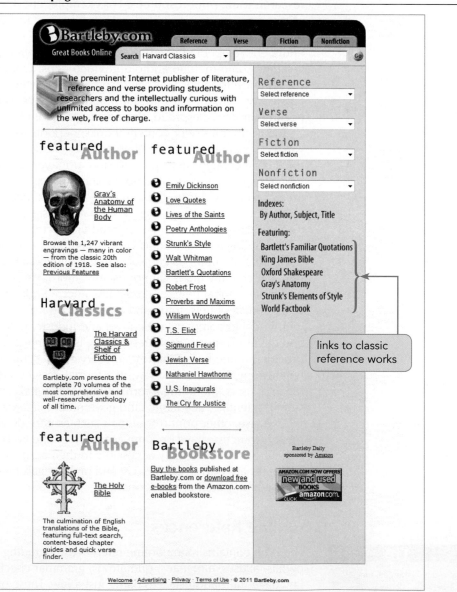

© 2011 Bartelby.com

The Web itself has become the subject of archivists' attention. The Internet Archive's Wayback Machine provides researchers with a series of snapshots of Web pages as they were at various points in the history of the Web. The site has archived more than 150 billion Web pages since 1996. The Internet Archive site also stores text, moving image, audio, and other files that have been contributed to the site. The wide array of information at the Internet Archive site makes it a valuable resource for a variety of research projects. The Internet Archive home page is shown in Figure 4-19.

Figure 4-19 **Internet Archive home page**

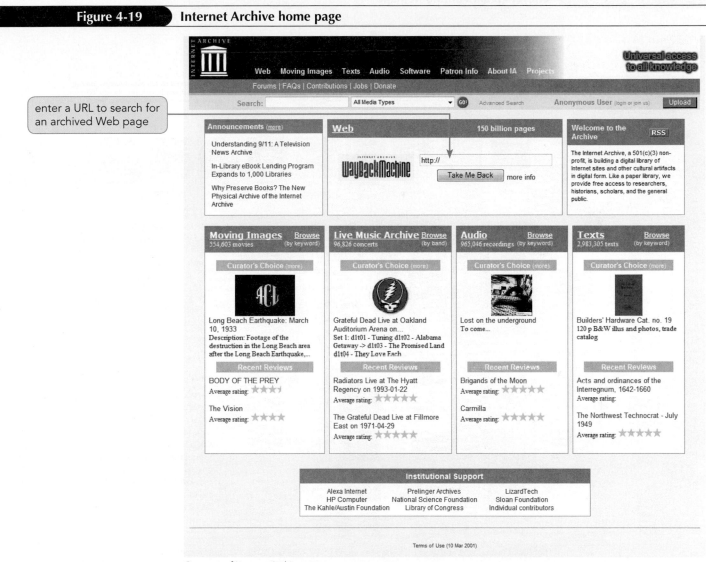

Courtesy of Internet Archive.com

The Weblinks page for Tutorial 4 includes links to Web sites that offer electronic texts and archives in the Additional Information section under the Electronic Texts and Archives heading.

Before her trip to Nashville, Marti wants to find more information about country music. You'll search an online encyclopedia to learn more about this type of music.

To search an online encyclopedia for information about country music:

1. Return to the Tutorial 4 Weblinks page for Session 4.2, and then in the Encyclopedias section, click one of the encyclopedia links to open the home page. Figure 4-20 shows the Encyclopedia.com home page.

Figure 4-20 **Encyclopedia.com home page**

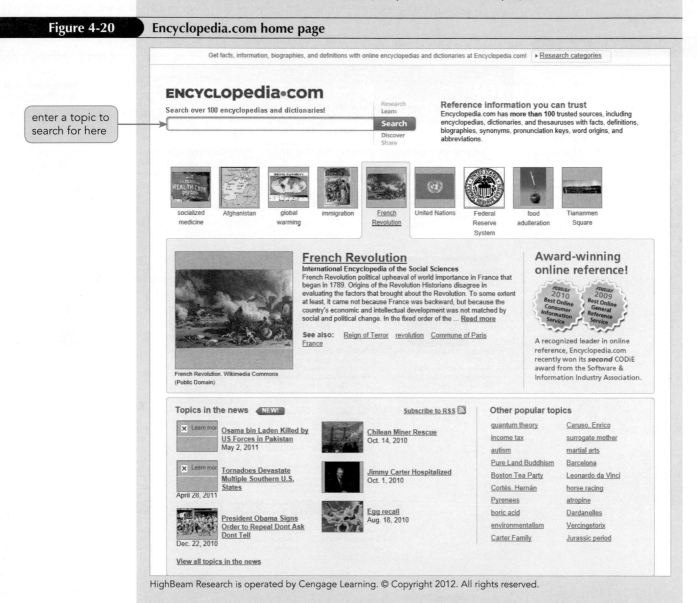

enter a topic to search for here

HighBeam Research is operated by Cengage Learning. © Copyright 2012. All rights reserved.

2. Type **country music** in the search box, and then click the appropriate button to start the search. A list of topics related to your search term appears.

3. Click a link that is most related to the keywords "country music" or "country and western music" to display an entry with information about country music along with links to related topics.

4. Read the information, and when you are finished, return to the Weblinks page for Tutorial 4.

Periodical Databases

Periodicals—magazines, journals, and other articles—related to almost any industry, field, or topic abound. Originally periodicals were available only in printed format at libraries, but now thousands of periodicals are available on the Web. If you know what periodical you want to search, you could go directly to its Web site. If you are more interested in articles related to a particular topic, then you can use a periodical database to locate them. For example, MagPortal.com is a search engine and directory for finding online magazine articles. It has indexed articles from hundreds of magazines. You can browse the indexed articles by topic or you can search for articles based on a keyword you supply.

Marti wants to find current information about digital music and how it is affecting the music industry. You will see what information you can find using MagPortal.com.

To find information about digital music in magazine articles:

1. On the Weblinks page for Session 4.2 in the Periodical Database section, click the **MagPortal.com** link to open the MagPortal.com home page. On MagPortal you can search articles by quality of match, date, publication, or category.

2. In the Search for Magazine Articles box, type **digital music rights** in the Search box, and then click the **Search** button. As shown in Figure 4-21, the Search Results box lists articles related to your search expression. Each result shows the name of the magazine, the publication date, the article's author in the left column, and the article's title followed by a brief description in the right column and two icons. The My Articles icon lets you mark articles you find interesting so you can find them later. The Similar Articles icon opens a list of articles that are similar to the original article.

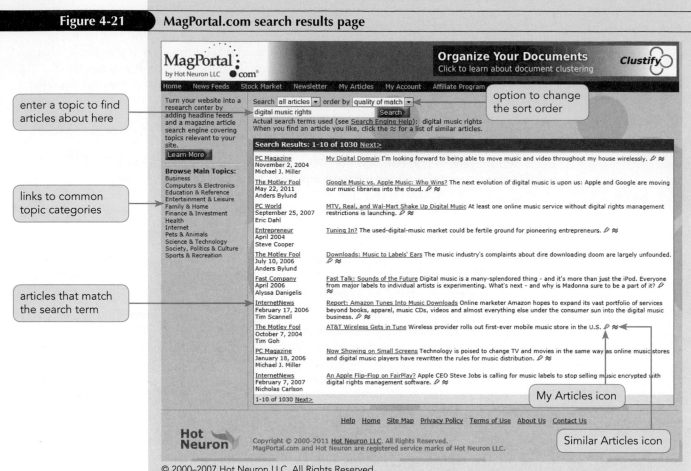

Figure 4-21   MagPortal.com search results page

3. Review the list of articles in the search results, and then click the **Similar Articles** icon next to one that you find interesting. A list of similar articles appears.

4. Return to the Weblinks page for Tutorial 4.

Online and Virtual Libraries

Most libraries now provide online access to their collections and services. You can search the library catalog and reserve books or place books on hold. You can access articles from newspapers and magazines, and search databases to which the library subscribes. You can also access general reference resources, including encyclopedias, almanacs, dictionaries, thesauri, language dictionaries, quotations, time and calendar information, world facts, population, and statistics. Many libraries also provide access to Web-based books and videos, as well as make available e-books, e-journals, and digital audiobooks for download to use on a computer, an e-reader such as a Kindle or an iPad, or a mobile device.

Another way to access library information is through a **virtual library**, which is a Web site that provides online access to library information services. Some virtual libraries are also portal sites that link to a variety of library and reference sites on the Web. A **portal site** is a Web site that you use as a gateway or entry to other sites on the Web. The portal site can be general and provide access to a wide variety of Web sites, or it can be specialized and provide access to related sites.

One virtual library, ipl2, describes itself as a global information community that offers a collaborative research forum, and supports and enhances library services by providing authoritative collections, information assistance, and instruction for the public. From its Web site, you can access resources by subject, newspapers and magazines, featured collections on specific topics that were created by ipl2 contributors, references, and topical resources specifically for kids and teens. Another free virtual library resource is LibrarySpot.com. It includes many of the same materials you would find in a public or school library. You can access reference materials, electronic texts, and other library Web sites from one central Web page. Unlike a brick-and-mortar library, these libraries are open 24 hours a day and seven days a week.

Marti has never visited Tennessee before and she wants to learn more about that state before she travels there. You'll explore a virtual library and see what you can find.

To find information about Tennessee using a virtual library:

▶ **1.** In the Virtual Libraries section of the Tutorial 4 Weblinks page, click the **LibrarySpot** link to open the home page for this virtual library. See Figure 4-22.

| Figure 4-22 | LibrarySpot home page |

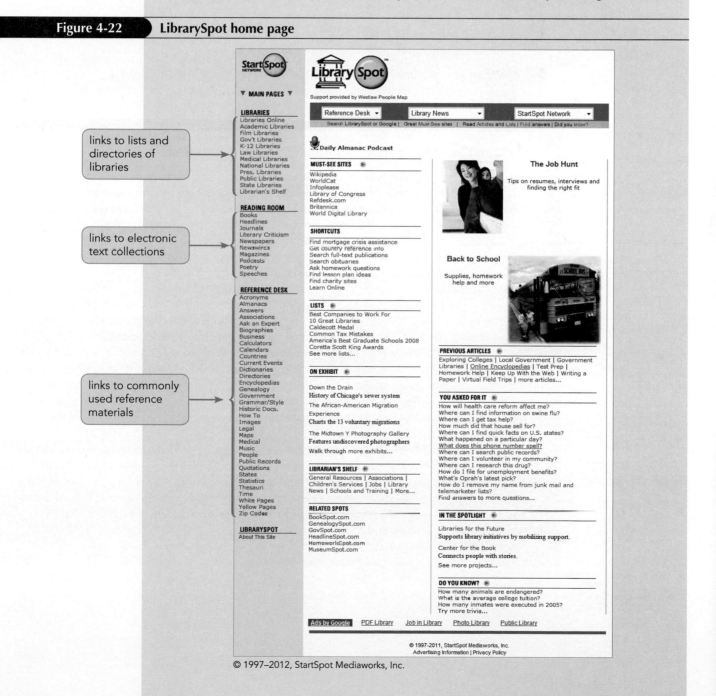

links to lists and directories of libraries

links to electronic text collections

links to commonly used reference materials

2. On the LibrarySpot home page, click the **States** link listed under the Reference Desk heading to open the State Information page, and then click the **TN** state on the map. A page listing links to information about the state of Tennessee opens.

3. Click some of the links to find facts about Tennessee that might be of interest to Marti.

4. Return to the Tutorial 4 Weblinks page, and then click the **ipl2** link under the Virtual Libraries heading. The home page for ipl2, another virtual library, opens. On ipl2, you can search for a topic by entering a search term or phrase in the search box, or you can browse the site, which is organized by subject, newspapers and magazines, special collections, and information for kids and teens.

5. On the ipl2 home page, click in the **search** box, type **Tennessee**, and then click the **Search ipl2** button. A Web page listing links to information about Tennessee displays.

6. Scroll the list of links and select one that looks appropriate for Marti's needs. Read the information on the page that opens.

7. When you are finished, return to the Weblinks page for Tutorial 4.

PROSKILLS

Written Communication: Summarizing Research Results

Research is the first step toward conveying information and facts in a written report. When you summarize your research results, how you organize the information and write the report is just as important as the quality of the research that you have done. If you do an excellent job gathering the facts, be sure to deliver a report that is clear and easy to understand. This ensures that your audience benefits from your hard work and gets the information they need. A lack of clarity can introduce noise into the communication and prevent readers from getting the message you intend to convey.

As you research a topic, be sure to take accurate notes about what you learn. Remember to include complete information about your sources so you can cite them as needed in your report. After you finish your research, you should organize your notes into a logical order so that you can present the information clearly and logically.

As you begin writing, make sure it's apparent why you are writing in the first place. Are you writing to inform, to entertain, or to express your opinion? When writing a factual report, your opinions are not relevant and should not be included. Next, determine the appropriate writing style: formal or informal. If you are writing for a professor or supervisor, you usually use a more formal tone than you would in a casual email to a colleague, friend, or family member.

When you have finished your report, be sure to read it carefully, keeping the recipient's viewpoint in mind. Make sure your points are clear and are presented in a logical order. Also, check your spelling and grammar, and correct any errors that you find. However, do not rely only on spelling and grammar checkers because they do not always find all errors. You might find it helpful to read what you have written out loud to determine whether your intended message and tone are coming through clearly. As a final step, you could ask a friend or colleague to read your final report and provide feedback.

Government Sites

The United States government collects and creates a wide variety of information and provides many services—from laws, tax codes, and Supreme Court rulings, to data on the census, the environment and energy, commerce, jobs, education, public safety, science and technology, travel and transportation, health and nutrition, and voting and elections.

Much of this information is available on the Web. You can go to local, state, and federal government agency sites to locate specific information, such the U.S. Census Bureau, the U.S. Government Printing Office, NASA, and the U.S. Library of Congress. For example, the U.S. Library of Congress Web site includes links to a huge array of research resources, ranging from the THOMAS legislative information site to the Library of Congress archives. The home page for the THOMAS section of the Library of Congress Web site is shown in Figure 4-23. The THOMAS Web site is a serious research tool that provides access to the full text of bills that are before the U.S. Congress, the *Congressional Record*, and Congressional Committee Reports. News reporters, investigative journalists, and civic-minded citizens all use this site to find detailed information about how the U.S. government operates.

| Figure 4-23 | U.S. Library of Congress THOMAS home page |

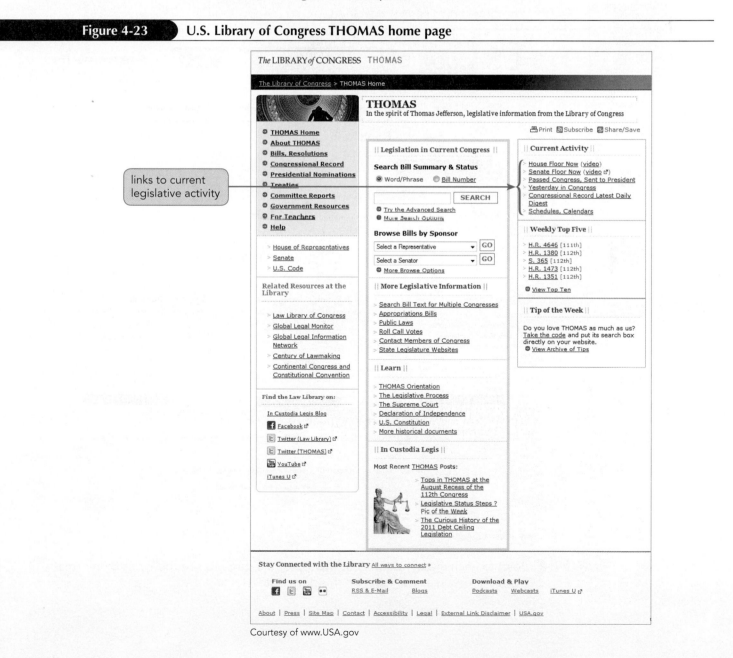

Courtesy of www.USA.gov

You can also use a portal site to access any government-related information from a central place. USA.gov is the official Web portal for the U.S. government. It provides access to all official U.S. government services and information in one place so you can easily find all U.S. government information that has been posted on the Internet.

To learn more about government sites and portals, use the links in the Government Sites section of the Additional Information section of the Weblinks page for Tutorial 4.

Marti wants to know more about the demographic statistics for Nashville. You will use the USA.gov Web portal to track down this data.

To find demographic information about Nashville:

1. In the Government Portal section of the Tutorial 4 Weblinks page, click the **USA.gov** link to open the USA.gov home page. See Figure 4-24.

Figure 4-24	USA.gov home page

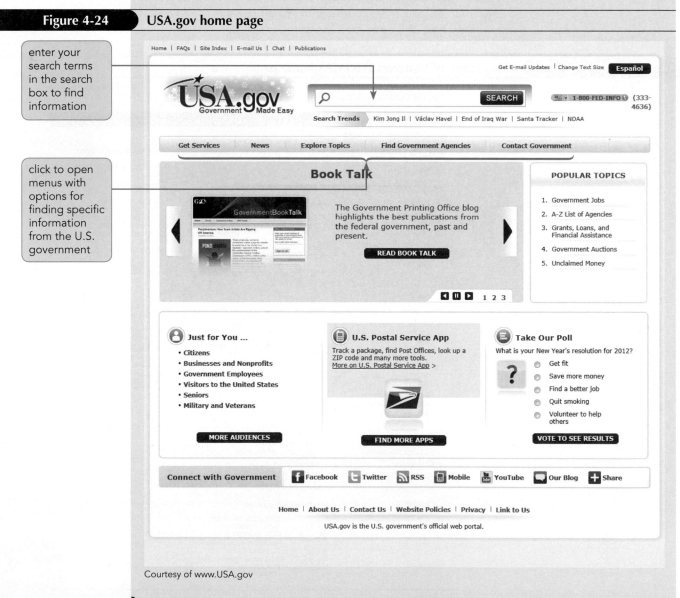

enter your search terms in the search box to find information

click to open menus with options for finding specific information from the U.S. government

Courtesy of www.USA.gov

2. Point to each menu option near the top of the page to see the types of information and resources available on this portal site.

3. Type **Nashville demographics** in the search box, and then click the Search button. The search results show relevant Web pages. See Figure 4-25.

| Figure 4-25 | Search results |

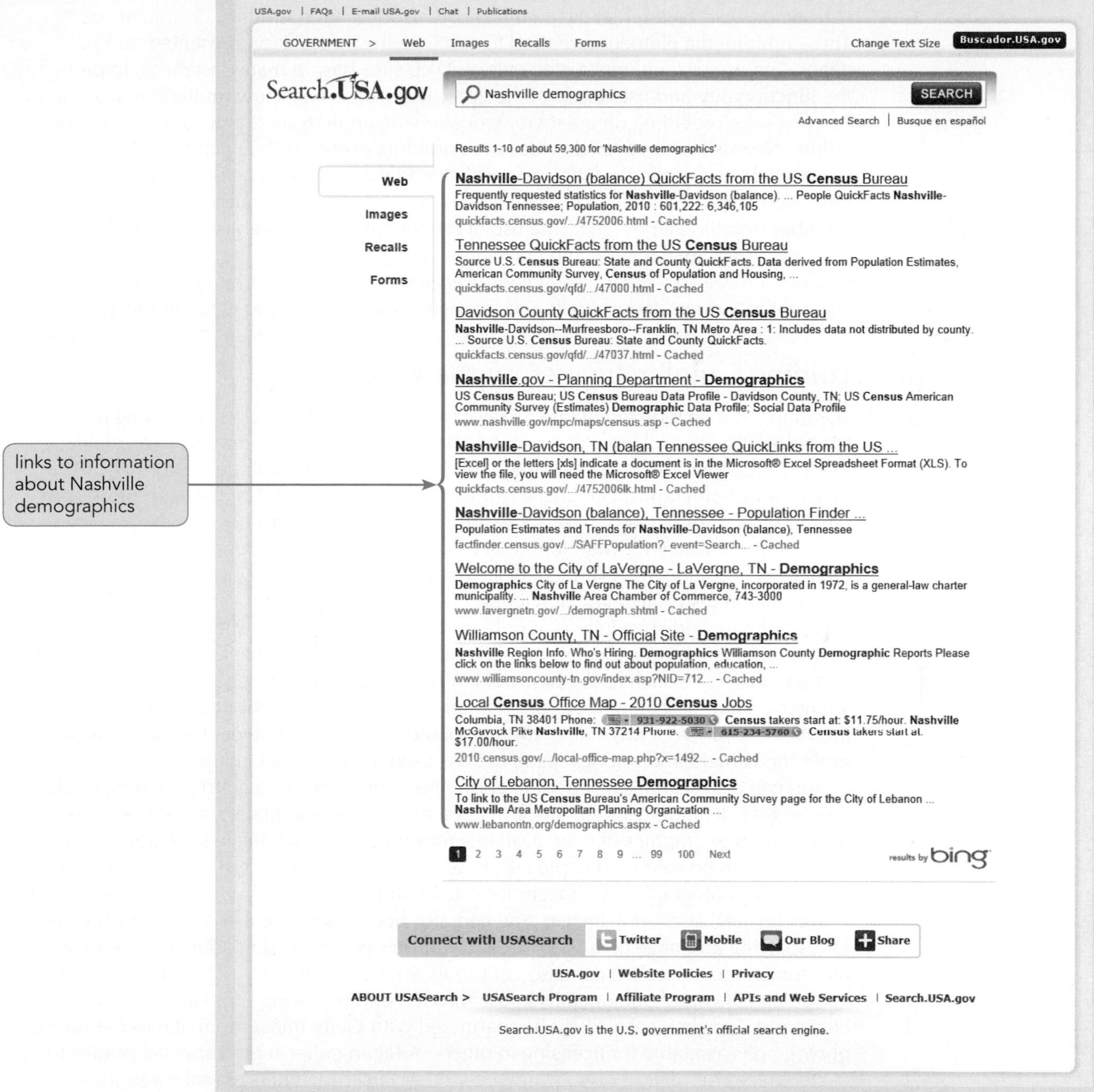

links to information about Nashville demographics

Courtesy of www.USA.gov

4. Click a link to a Web page that provides census data for Nashville, and then find the population data for the city.

5. Return to the Weblinks page for Tutorial 4.

In addition to the vast text-based material on the Internet, you can find graphics such as clip art, animations, and photos, as well as audio and video clips.

Multimedia on the Web

Most Web pages include a variety of multimedia elements. **Multimedia** is anything you can see or hear, including text, pictures, audio/sound, videos, films, or animations. These multimedia elements are used to enhance the information presented on Web pages. The use of multimedia elements on Web sites has, in many instances, improved the functionality and usefulness of the Web. Retail sites can show multiple images of an item for sale, providing different views or showing an item such as a shirt in different colors. News sites can provide videos of unfolding events as they happen. Music sites can include audio clips to let customers listen to parts of songs before they buy them. Do-it-yourself help sites can provide videos that show demonstrations, such as a master plumber installing a new sink. The use of multimedia on the Web is limited only by the Web designer's imagination and creativity.

The Web is also a great resource for users seeking specific multimedia such as graphics, photos, videos, and music to use for their own purposes and entertainment.

Finding Graphic Images on the Web

"Graphic" is a generic term that can refer to a variety of still images, including photographs, clip art, and line drawings. An abundance of graphic images are available in electronic form on the Web. These are commonly in one of three file formats: JPEG images for photographs, GIF images for line drawings, and PNG images for more complex graphics. You'll learn more about these file formats in Tutorial 8.

There are a variety of ways to find graphic images on the Web. You can use a search engine such as Google or Bing to locate images related to your search term. You can filter the search results to show only images, and then further refine the filter to show only images of a certain size; full-color or black-and-white images; a specific type of image such as a face, a photo, clip art, or a line drawing; as well as images posted during a certain time frame such as the past week. When you click an image in the search results, a larger version of that image appears along with information about the image, including the Web site where it originated, the size of the image, the file type, the date, and sometimes the camera and settings specifications used to create that image.

You can also search stock photography sites, which are devoted to providing stock images for sale and licensing. **Stock images** are professional photographs, line drawings, and other graphics that are available for purchase. Stock images are immediately available, can be sold to multiple customers, and are usually affordable. Companies that offer stock photographs and images for sale include Shutterstock, Bigstock, iStockphoto, Corbis Images, and Getty Images. You can also license specific uses of the images, such as displaying an image on a Web page. Some sites permit downloading of at least some files for personal use. You can also contribute your own photos and images to the sites.

You can also find photographs to use through photo-sharing sites such as Yahoo! Flickr and Google Picasa. Flickr has partnered with Getty Images to make its members' photographs available for licensing to others. You can either submit specific photos to Getty Images for review, or you can allow other Flickr members to make a request to license any of your images. Getty Images reviews requests and handles the permissions, releases, and pricing details. You'll learn more about Flickr and photo-sharing sites in Tutorial 5.

To learn more about finding images, use the links in the Stock Images and Photo Sharing Sites section of the Additional Information section of the Weblinks page for Tutorial 4.

Marti wants to find some photos of Nashville bands to use in promotional literature about her agency's latest venture into signing country music artists.

To find images of Nashville bands:

1. In the Image Search Engines section of the Tutorial 4 Weblinks page, click a link to open the home page for a search engine.

2. Click the **Images** link to open the images search page.

3. Type **Nashville TN bands** in the search box, and then click the search button. The search results appear on the results page. The search results page shows thumbnails of images of bands with a connection to Nashville. Depending on the image search engine you used, you might see links to filter the search results by size, color, type, and so forth.

4. Click a thumbnail image on the results page. A Web page opens, showing a larger version of the image you selected. Again, depending on the image search engine you used, you might see a description of the image, detailed information about the image such as file size and type, and a note about any copyright restrictions. Figure 4-26 shows the enlarged image on the Google Images page.

Figure 4-26	Google Images details

information about the selected image

© Google; Photo courtesy of http://www.concertblast.com

Finding Audio Files on the Web

In addition to images, you can find audio files on the Web. The term "audio" refers to sounds of any type: instrumental music, songs with vocals, speeches, audio books, sound effects such as a creaky door or a barking dog, and so forth. Audio searches are most commonly conducted to find music and books. Other popular searches include special effects and sounds that might be used on a Web site.

Audio files are available in a variety of formats. Most music is now available in the MP3 file format. MP3 (MPEG Audio Layer 3) files can hold information about the music they store, such as the title, the artist's name, and even a photo of the album cover. Other sounds might be in WAV, MIDI, or AU formats, which are described in Figure 4-27.

Figure 4-27   **Audio file formats**

Format File	Extension	Description
MP3 (MPEG Audio Layer 3)	.mp3	The audio portion of the MPEG file format; most popular for music and audio books.
WAV (Wave)	.wav	Jointly developed by Microsoft and IBM; stores digital audio and can be played on any Windows computer that supports sound; can be recorded at different quality levels, which results in different size files (higher quality means a larger file).
MIDI (Musical Instrument Digital Interface)	.midi or .mid	The standard adopted by the music industry for controlling devices that create and read musical information; much smaller than WAV files.
AU (audio UNIX) format	.au	The original audio format because much of the Internet was originally constructed on computers running the UNIX operating system; stores sound at various quality levels, creating files that are approximately the same size as WAV files recorded at similar quality levels.

© Cengage Learning

Music CDs are recorded in the WAV format at a very high-quality level. A standard CD has a capacity of about 650 MB and can hold about 74 minutes of high-quality stereo music. Files in the MP3 format are somewhat lower in quality than WAV format files, but they are 90% smaller. This means that a CD that holds 15 popular songs in high-quality WAV format (about 40 megabytes per song) could instead hold 150 popular songs in MP3 format (about 4 megabytes per song).

The MIDI format records information about each element of the sound—including its pitch, length, and volume—in a digital format. Most keyboard synthesizers and other electronic instruments use MIDI so that music recorded on one instrument can be played on other instruments. MIDI files can also be played on computers that have a MIDI interface or MIDI software. It is much easier to edit music recorded in the MIDI format than music recorded in the WAV format because the individual characteristics of the sound can be manipulated with precision. MIDI files are much smaller than WAV files and are used when storage space is at a premium. Many mobile phone ringtones, for example, are in the MIDI format.

Although very few new audio files are created in the AU format today, this format still appears on the Web and most Web browsers can read it. The AU format can store sound at various quality levels, and the resulting files are approximately the same size as WAV files recorded at similar quality levels.

INSIGHT

Downloading Plug-Ins

Unlike graphic files, audio and video files appear on the Web in many different formats. In order for your Web browser to play these different formats, you might need to install additional software extensions. These software extensions, or **plug-ins**, are usually available as free downloads. The companies that offer media players as free downloads earn their profits by selling encoding software to developers who want to include audio and video files in that format on their Web sites. Each company that creates a format has an incentive to promote its use, so a variety of audio and video formats are used on the Web today. You will learn more about plug-ins in Tutorial 8.

You can find audio on the Web in a variety of places. A growing number of recording artists and bands sell and distribute their music on their own Web sites. Many online stores, such as Amazon.com, also sell digitized music. These sites have obtained the legal right to distribute the musical works they offer for sale. Some of these sites charge a download fee per song, whereas others charge a monthly fee that allows subscribers to download as many songs as they wish. There are also digital music subscription services such as Rhapsody, Pandora, and Rara Music that you can subscribe to and create custom playlists from millions of songs that are available on the service. Sometimes referred to as Internet radio stations, you can listen to the music on most connected devices, including computers, smartphones, and tablets.

Digital audio books are also popular download items. Like music, you can purchase audio books directly from publishers, from etailers such as Amazon.com, or on sites devoted to audio books, such as LibriVox, Audible, and Audiobooks.com. Some books are in the public domain and have been recorded so that people can listen to them for free. Others are still protected by copyright and must be purchased or used as part of a subscription service. Some libraries also offer digital audio books for checkout just like printed books in their catalog.

To learn more about digital audio books, use the links in the Digital Audio Books Sites section of the Additional Information section of the Weblinks page for Tutorial 4.

Some sites that sell downloadable music place restrictions on the number of copies you can make of each song. A few of these sites restrict you from converting downloaded song files into other formats, or they restrict the types of devices on which you are permitted to play the song. The restrictions are implemented in the files themselves, using systems of encoding called **digital rights management (DRM)**. Because different online music vendors use different DRM systems, their files might not be compatible with each other. Because of these differing DRM systems and because you can incur legal liability by using or copying downloaded files (even those you have purchased) in ways that the vendor prohibits, you should always check the site carefully for details about file formats and copying restrictions before you buy songs or sign up for a subscription.

Marti wants to listen to some classic country music before meeting with potential clients in Nashville. You will find songs by Johnny Cash that can be purchased and downloaded.

TIP

Make sure that the files from a particular site are compatible with your portable music player before you sign up for a download subscription.

To search for country music songs to purchase online:

1. Return to the Weblinks page for Tutorial 4, and then click a link under the Online Music Stores heading in the Session 4.2 section to open that Web site's home page. Figure 4-28 shows the eMusic home page.

Figure 4-28   eMusic home page

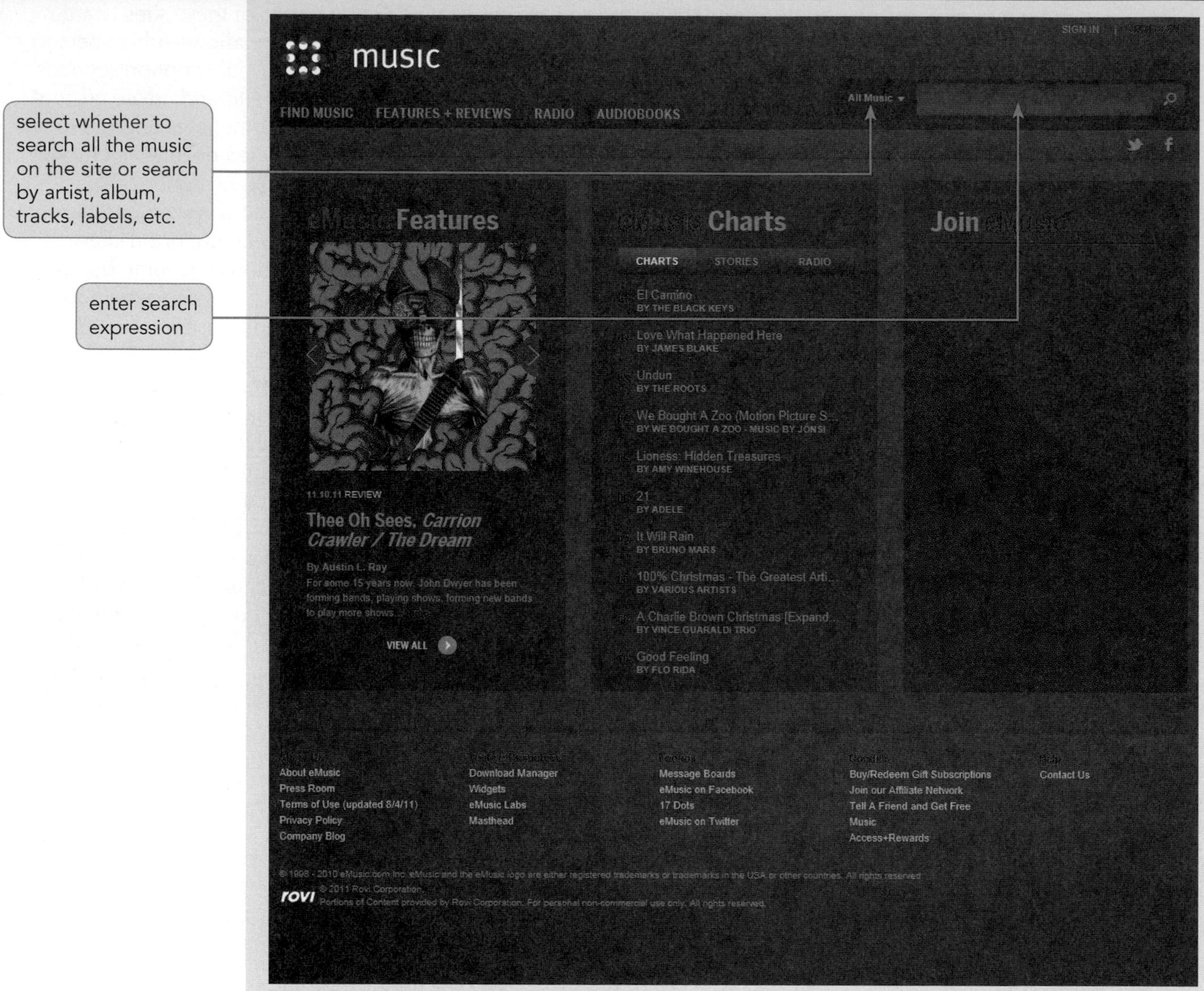

select whether to search all the music on the site or search by artist, album, tracks, labels, etc.

enter search expression

© 1998–2010 eMusic.com Inc. All Rights Reserved.

2. In the search box, type **Johnny Cash** and then click the **Search** button (or something similar) to display the results.

   Trouble? Some online music stores require you to sign up for a trial membership before you can search for music. Many of these trial memberships are free. If you do not want to sign up for a membership, try another music store.

3. Click one of the songs or albums to see more information about that item, if necessary.

4. Make sure your speakers are turned on or your headphones are connected and the sound is unmuted, and then click a song to play a preview of the song.

INSIGHT

Storing Multimedia Files in the Cloud

Image, music, and audio books are more commonly being stored in the cloud. The **cloud** is a group of technologies and services that provide computing over the Internet so people can interact with programs and data using any device that can access the Internet, including computers, tablets, and smartphones. People are using cloud computing to share software and networking resources. More sites are providing cloud storage in which you can save and access files. This allows users to store their files remotely and access them from any device with the appropriate software and Internet access. For example, in 2011 Apple launched iCloud, which provides subscribers with space to store digital content, including music, photos, books, and documents. It also keeps changing content such as email, calendars, and contacts up to date on all your devices running iCloud. So you can use your iPhone, iPad, iPod touch, and computer to access the same files and information.

Finding Video Files

The term **video** refers to content that has a progression of visual images and can include audio as well. Video clips are commonly included in a variety of different types of Web sites, including news sites to show events that have occurred, retail sites to demonstrate how a product works, broadcasting sites to play television shows, and music sites to show bands performing their songs.

High-quality audio files and video files of any significant length can be very large, especially if the files are in a digital format. Therefore, all online video is compressed to make it faster to download or play. Although a video file can be completely downloaded and then played, streaming transmission lets users watch the video file in real time.

In a **streaming transmission**, the Web server sends the first part of the file to a Web browser or a media player program such as RealPlayer or Windows Media Player, which uncompresses and then plays the file. While the first part of the file plays, the server is sending the next segment of the file. Streaming transmission allows you to access large audio or video files in less time than the download-then-play procedure because the streamed file begins playing before it finishes downloading. RealNetworks, Inc. pioneered streaming technology. Video files on the Web are available in a variety of formats, including Flash, MPEG, AVI, and 3GP formats. Figure 4-29 describes some of the more common formats.

Figure 4-29   Video file formats

Format File	File Extension	Description
RealAudio RealVideo	.ra .rv	The original formats for streaming audio and video files, developed by RealNetworks.
WMV (Windows Media Video)	.wmv	A streaming video format developed by Microsoft to compete with RealVideo.
Flash Video	.flv	A common streaming video format; requires the Adobe Flash Player plug-in to play Flash video files. Flash files can include video, high-resolution moving graphics, and graphic elements that interact with the user's mouse movements.
Moving Picture Experts Group (MPEG)	.mp2, .mpe, .mpeg, .mpv2, .mpg, .3gp, .mpg4	A series of standards for compressed file formats created by the International Organization for Standardization. The file extension identifies the version of the MPEG standard with which the file was encoded.
AVI (Audio Video Interleaved)	.avi	An older video file format created by Microsoft.
QuickTime	.mov	An older video file format created by Apple; usually requires a plug-in to play the files.

© Cengage Learning

You can find videos on the Web in a variety of ways. Some sites are devoted to video distribution, such as YouTube and Hulu. You will learn more about video-sharing sites such as YouTube, which allows users to upload video files that they have created and view videos that others have created, in Tutorial 5. Other sites provide stock videos, including Shutterstock Footage, iStock Video, and Thought Equity Motion. You can also use a search engine, such as Google Videos and Bing Videos, to find video files on the Web.

Because Marti will be visiting Ryman Auditorium when she travels to Nashville, she wants to see a video that features the auditorium.

To search for videos about Ryman Auditorium:

1. Return to the Weblinks for Session 4.2, click a link in the Video Search Engines section to open the search engine's home page, and then click the **Video**, **Videos**, or **Footage** link at the top of the page.

2. Type **Ryman Auditorium** in the search box, and then click the search button. Videos that feature Ryman Auditorium appear on the search results page. Depending on the search engine you are using, filters might appear so you can narrow the search results to show videos of a specific duration, from a certain time frame, of a specific quality, and from a specific source. Figure 4-30 shows the search results and filter options for videos on Google Videos.

Figure 4-30 | **Google Videos search results**

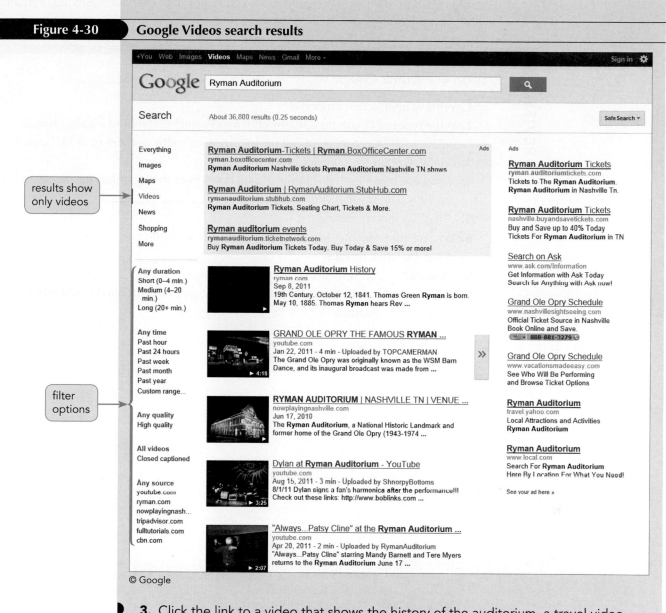

results show only videos

filter options

© Google

3. Click the link to a video that shows the history of the auditorium, a travel video that features the auditorium, or a performance that was recorded at the auditorium, and then watch the video.

    Trouble? If you cannot hear the audio portion of the video, you might need to turn on the computer's speakers or unmute the sound.

    Trouble? If the video doesn't play, you might need to install a plug-in to play that video format. Return to the search results and select a different video.

4. Close your Web browser.

Marti is now up to date on copyright issues and information about Nashville, Ryman Auditorium, and country music. She's ready for her trip to Nashville.

Session 4.2 Quick Check

1. What is intellectual property?
2. What types of books do Bartleby.com and Project Gutenberg legally provide online in their entirety without paying royalties to the authors of those books?
3. Briefly explain the concept of fair use.
4. If you use material that is in the public domain or that qualifies for fair use without citing the source, you might be guilty of _____.
5. What is a virtual library?
6. What kinds of elements can a multimedia file include?
7. What are stock images?
8. Most music is now available in what file format?
9. _____ transmission begins to play an audio or video file before it finishes downloading.

Practice the skills you learned in the tutorial using the same case scenario.

PRACTICE

Review Assignments

There are no Data Files needed for the Review Assignments.

Marti is preparing to visit a new techno band in Chicago, Illinois, that she would like to sign. While in Chicago, she wants to visit several clubs that feature blues artists. You'll find information for Marti's upcoming trip and then write a report summarizing your findings. You'll need to include citation information for each site you visit. Complete the following steps:

1. Start your Web browser, go to **www.cengagebrain.com**, open the Tutorial 4 Weblinks page, and then click the Review Assignments link.

2. Use one or more of the links in the News Search Engines section of the Weblinks page to find an article in a Chicago-area newspaper from the past month that discusses a local blues band or an area blues club that features live music. Summarize the article in a short report to your instructor and include a citation to the article in the report.

3. Return to the Tutorial 4 Weblinks page to obtain a local weather forecast for the Chicago area for the coming week using one of the links in the Weather Sites section for the Review Assignments (or consult your favorite weather sites). Record the upcoming forecast and the citation information in your report.

4. The techno band is renting practice space in a warehouse near the corner of West 35th Street and South Morgan Street in Chicago's South Side. Return to the Tutorial 4 Weblinks page, and then use one of the links in the Map Sites section for the Review Assignments to find a map that shows the location. View a street-level map and switch between map view and aerial, satellite, or street view of the location. In your report, describe what you learned and record the citation information for the Web pages you visited.

5. Return to the Tutorial 4 Weblinks page, and use one of the links in the Travel Guides Web Sites section for the Review Assignments to locate three restaurants in the Chicago area that you would recommend to Marti for entertaining clients. Include this information in your report along with the appropriate citation information.

6. Return to the Tutorial 4 Weblinks page, and use one of the Travel Guide sites listed in the Travel Guides Web Sites section for the Review Assignments to locate at least two blues clubs that Marti can visit while she is in Chicago. Describe these clubs in your report along with the citation information for the Web pages you visited.

7. Return to the Tutorial 4 Weblinks page, and use one of the links listed in the Online Directories section for the Review Assignments to find the address of the House of Blues. Record the information in your report along with a citation to the Web page where you found the information.

8. Return to the Tutorial 4 Weblinks page, and use one of the links listed in the Online Shopping section for the Review Assignments to locate blues memorabilia that Marti can purchase. Include a description of a memorabilia item you find and its cost in your report, along with the citation information for the Web pages you visited.

9. Return to the Tutorial 4 Weblinks page, and use one of the links in the Encyclopedias section for the Review Assignments to find out the history of blues music. Include a brief summary of what you learned in your report along with citations of the Web pages you visited.

10. Return to the Tutorial 4 Weblinks page, and use one of the links in the Online Music Stores section for the Review Assignments to find recordings of blues music. Listen to the previews of three songs. In your report, list the songs you listened to and your opinion of them. Include citations for the Web pages you visited.

11. Return to the Tutorial 4 Weblinks page, and use a link in the Video Search Engines section for the Review Assignments to find video clips of blues musicians playing their songs. View two videos. List the videos you watched along with your opinion of the performances in your report. Include citations for the Web pages you visited.

12. Close your Web browser.

Apply the skills you learned in this tutorial to prepare for a business trip.

APPLY

Case Problem 1

There are no Data Files needed for this Case Problem.

Davenport Trenchers, Inc. You are a sales representative for Davenport Trenchers, Inc., a company located in Davenport, Iowa. The company sells trenchers, which are machines used for digging small trenches in the ground that hold water lines, drainage pipe, and electrical conduit. Davenport's customers include builders, landscape contractors, and stores that rent the trenchers to other businesses and individuals for short-term use. You have been promoted to manage the company's office in St. Louis, Missouri, and are planning your first sales trip there. Because you will drive to St. Louis, you need information about the best route as well as a map of St. Louis. Because you hope to generate new customers on this trip, you need to identify sales prospects in the area. Complete the following steps:

1. Start your Web browser, go to **www.cengagebrain.com**, open the Tutorial 4 Weblinks page, and then click the Case Problem 1 link.

2. Use one of the Web sites provided in the Map Sites section to obtain driving directions from Davenport, Iowa (your starting address) to St. Louis, Missouri (your destination address). Record the information in a report along with a citation for the Web page you used to obtain the directions.

3. To identify sales prospects in the St. Louis area, return to the Tutorial 4 Weblinks page, and use one or more of the directories listed in the Online Directories section for Case Problem 1 to search for builders, landscape contractors, and equipment rental stores in the St. Louis area that sell concrete. The results pages for your searches should include contact information for a number of companies that would be good prospects. In a report to your instructor, document at least three sales prospects. Include a citation for the Web pages that provided the information.

4. Return to the Tutorial 4 Weblinks page and use the link in the Government Site section for Case Problem 1 to explore QuickFacts from the U.S. Census Bureau to find out the latest population of St. Louis. Record this information in your report along with a citation for the Web page where you found this information.

5. Return to the Tutorial 4 Weblinks page. Using one of the links in the Stock Images Sites section for Case Problem 1, find an image of a trencher that might be good to use in your sales material. Document the image you found along with the site where you found it.

6. Return to the Tutorial 4 Weblinks page. Using one of the links in the Video Search Engines section for Case Problem 1, find footage that shows a trencher in action. Again, document the video and the Web page where you found it.

7. Close your Web browser.

Find MIDI files and copyright restrictions on downloaded music files.

RESEARCH

Case Problem 2

There are no Data Files needed for this Case Problem.

Midland Elementary School Music Classes You are a third-grade language skills teacher at Midland Elementary School. The school has closed its music program because of budget cuts. However, you believe that it is important to expose your students to the music of the great composers, such as Beethoven and Mozart. You do not have a budget for buying CDs, but you do have a computer with an Internet connection in the classroom as well as a small electronic piano that can play audio files in MIDI format. You want to find music files to play on the computer and the electronic piano, but you need to make sure that any use of these files complies with U.S. copyright law. Some musical instruments, particularly pianos, sound realistic when synthesized in MIDI format. You would, therefore, like to find some music in this format to begin your collection for the class. Complete the following steps:

1. Start your Web browser, go to **www.cengagebrain.com**, open the Tutorial 4 Weblinks page, and then click the Case Problem 2 link.

2. Use one of the links in the Search Engines section to locate resources for elementary music teachers that you can use to prepare your class lessons. In preparation for writing a report to your instructor, document the sites you visited and identify the sites that you think will be helpful.

3. Return to the Tutorial 4 Weblinks page. Click one or more of the links provided in the MIDI Files Sites section for Case Problem 2 to find sources of MIDI files of classical music that you could play on the classroom computer or piano. Read the Web pages you find that include downloadable MIDI files, and then evaluate their terms and conditions of use. In particular, look for copyright statements and any restrictions on the use of downloaded files. (*Hint*: The copyright restrictions might not be listed on the page from which you download the files, so be sure to look for links to pages with titles such as Terms of Use on the site's home page.) Are there any copyright issues with playing these recordings directly from the Web? Document your findings to include in the report to your instructor.

4. Return to the Tutorial 4 Weblinks page. Use the links in the Copyrights section for Case Problem 2 to learn more about U.S. copyright law, fair use, and public domain as they relate to music. Record your findings to include in the report to your instructor.

5. Return to the Tutorial 4 Weblinks page and use the links in the Digital Audio Books Sites section for Case Problem 2 to find at least one audio book that would be suitable for teaching your students about Beethoven, Mozart, or your favorite classical composer. Note the titles and authors of the books you find along with the URLs of the pages where you found those books to include in your report.

6. Write a short report to your instructor that summarizes your findings. In your report, describe any copyright restrictions that you find and evaluate whether your use of the files in the classroom would infringe on the files' copyright. Be sure to include citations to the Web pages you visited.

7. Close your Web browser.

Case Problem 3

Find current information about mine safety issues and related government legislation.

CREATE

There are no Data Files needed for this Case Problem.

Hamilton Mining   Headquartered in Wheeling, West Virginia, Hamilton Mining operates six deep shaft coal mines in the state. The company has an excellent safety record and spends a considerable amount of money every year promoting safety in its mines. The company is aware that mining accidents can focus the public's attention on mining safety issues, and can lead to criticism of companies that operate mines. Because a mining accident can happen at any time, Hamilton Mining maintains a public relations plan that it can implement immediately when an accident occurs in the industry. You are an intern in the office of Joan Caruso, a public relations consultant who does work for Hamilton Mining. Joan has asked you to help her with some background research as she creates a proposal for integrating a mine safety Web site into Hamilton Mining's public relations program. You need to research Hamilton Mining's competitors, and then evaluate each competitor's safety information. Joan also asks you to find out whether any bills are pending in the U.S. Congress that will affect mine safety regulations because any public relations campaign must consider the impact of pending legislation. Complete the following steps:

1. Start your Web browser, go to **www.cengagebrain.com**, open the Tutorial 4 Weblinks page, and then click the Case Problem 3 link.

2. Use the links in the News Search Engines section to find at least three current (within the past three or four months) news reports about mine safety, mining accidents, or the coal mining industry in general. In a report to your instructor, summarize the major issues identified in these reports. Be sure to include citations for each article you used in your research.

3. Use your favorite search engine to find a mining company in the United States, visit its Web site, and then review the safety information provided on its Web site. Summarize this information for your instructor. Again, include a citation for the Web site you visited.

4. Return to the Tutorial 4 Weblinks page, and then click the Library of Congress THOMAS link in the Government Site section for Case Problem 3. Search the site using the phrase **mine safety**. Read one of the bills listed and prepare a one-paragraph summary for your instructor of the bill's likely effects on the mining industry. Include citations for the Web pages you visited.

5. Close your Web browser.

Case Problem 4

Create a report that summarizes current arguments for or against prison privatization.

CHALLENGE

There are no Data Files needed for this Case Problem.

Johnson for Senate Campaign   You work for the campaign team of Vivianne Johnson, who is running for a seat in the state senate. One issue that promises to play a prominent role in the upcoming election campaign is privatization of the state prison system. It is important for Vivianne to establish a clear position on the issue early in the campaign, and she has asked you to prepare a briefing for her. Vivianne has no particular preference on the issue and she wants you to obtain a balanced set of arguments for each side so she can assess the political risks associated with taking each position. Complete the following steps:

1. Start your Web browser, go to **www.cengagebrain.com**, open the Tutorial 4 Weblinks page, and then click the Case Problem 4 link.

2. Choose one or more of the search engines listed to conduct a search for **privatization prisons**.

3. Examine your search results for authoritative sites that include positions on the issue. (*Hint*: You might need to follow a number of results page hyperlinks to find suitable Web pages.)

4. Find at least one Web page that states a clear position in favor of privatization, and at least one Web page that states a clear position against privatization.

5. Write a report that summarizes the arguments for each position using the content of the Web pages you visited. Include full citations for the Web pages.

6. Close your Web browser.

*Find images
for a menu
and determine
the copyright
limitations on
their use.*

CHALLENGE

Case Problem 5

There are no Data Files needed for this Case Problem.

Europa River Cruises   You have just started a summer internship in Bonn, Germany,
working for Europa River Cruises. Europa operates luxury cruises on the Danube, the
Rhine, and other major rivers in Europe. You have been assigned to work for Dieter
Welker, the manager of restaurant operations on all of the company's cruise ships. The
Europa line is famous for its fine dining and features the cuisine of different countries
each night. The menus and table settings are illustrated with graphics and photos that
represent the country whose food is being featured that night. Dieter is supervising a
redesign of the menus and table settings for each night. He wants you to help the design
team by gathering art and photos from the Web that the team might use in the illustration
of the menus or design of the table settings. Complete the following steps:

1. Start your Web browser, go to **www.cengagebrain.com**, open the Tutorial 4 Weblinks
   page, and then click the Case Problem 5 link.
2. Click one of the links in the Image Search Engines section and use it to conduct a
   search for images or photos that represent France, Italy, Spain, Germany, Portugal,
   and Ireland.
3. Return to the Tutorial 4 Weblinks page, and repeat the search using another search
   engine.
4. Examine the search results for images or photos that would be suitable to use in the
   menu redesign assignment. Find two images or photos for each country (a total of 12).
5. When you find a suitable image, examine the Web site on which you found it to
   determine what copyright or other restrictions exist for using that image. (*Hint*: You
   need to look for restrictions that could prevent the team from using the images or
   photos in print; these restrictions might be different from restrictions on online use.)
6. Prepare a report that includes a brief description of each image or photo, its source,
   the URL of the site where you found it, and a summary of the restrictions on Europa's
   use of the image in printed materials. If the Web site does not include any description of restrictions, state your opinion (based on what you have learned in this tutorial) regarding what restrictions might exist on Europa's use of the image.
7. Close your Web browser.

User-Generated Content on the Internet

Evaluating Different Methods of Internet Communication

Session 5.1
- Understand push and pull communication
- Learn about Web 2.0
- Examine email-based communication
- Understand Really Simple Syndication (RSS) feeds
- Explore the technology used in podcasting
- Use a mashup site

Session 5.2
- Explore different methods of chat communication
- Examine online social and business networks
- Learn about photo- and video-sharing sites
- Learn about blogs and microblogs
- Explore ways to protect your online privacy, identity, and reputation

Case | *Shilling Social Media*

A few years ago, Kay Shilling lost her corporate job as a marketing executive when her company implemented a workforce reduction strategy. Kay contacted dozens of potential employers for months, only to discover that jobs in her field were scarce. After many disappointments, Kay began helping small businesses in her community get started with their Internet marketing, including building and maintaining Facebook pages and Twitter accounts. Kay realized that her extensive experience in marketing and social networking gave her a perfect skill set for starting a new business, which she has incorporated using the business name Shilling Social Media. Her business will offer her professional services to help new and existing small to medium-sized businesses create, maintain, and manage the online "social" side of their marketing efforts.

Kay already has the basis for the business in her home: a dedicated home office, a new laptop computer, and a smartphone, along with many references from local businesses that she has already helped. She will begin by reviewing the Internet and its many forms of communication, keeping a watchful eye on any new technologies and communication methods that she can use in running own business, or that might be appropriate for her clients' needs.

STARTING DATA FILES

There are no starting Data Files needed for this tutorial.

SESSION 5.1 VISUAL OVERVIEW

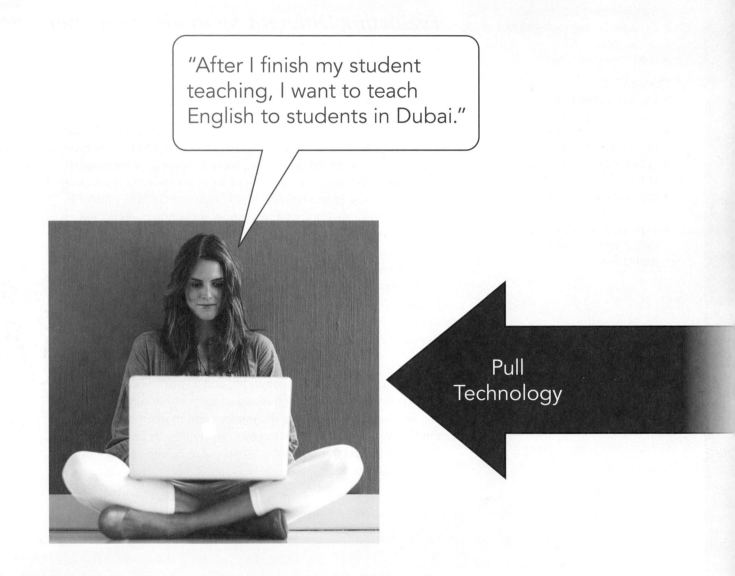

"After I finish my student teaching, I want to teach English to students in Dubai."

Pull Technology

PULL TECHNOLOGIES

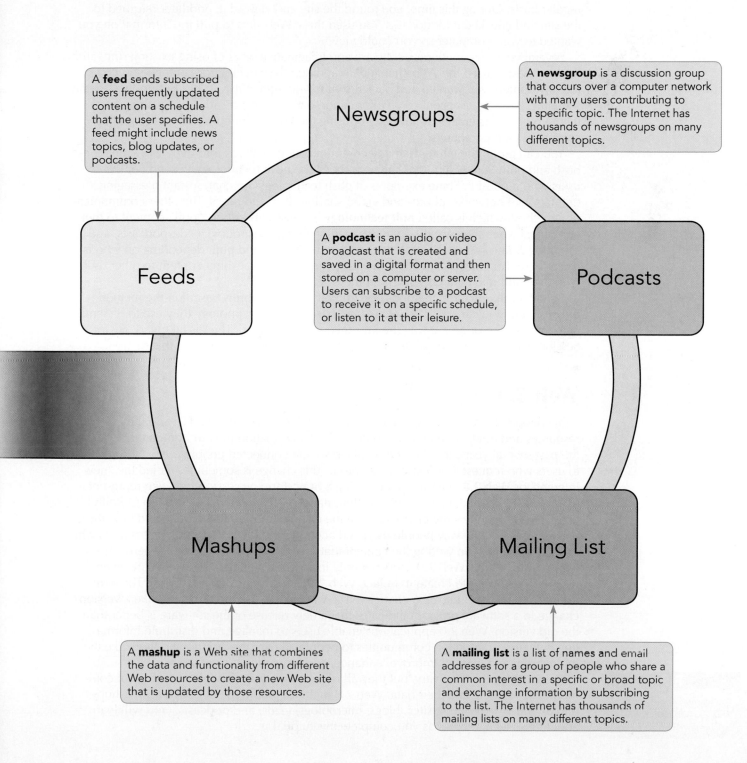

A **feed** sends subscribed users frequently updated content on a schedule that the user specifies. A feed might include news topics, blog updates, or podcasts.

Newsgroups

A **newsgroup** is a discussion group that occurs over a computer network with many users contributing to a specific topic. The Internet has thousands of newsgroups on many different topics.

Feeds

A **podcast** is an audio or video broadcast that is created and saved in a digital format and then stored on a computer or server. Users can subscribe to a podcast to receive it on a specific schedule, or listen to it at their leisure.

Podcasts

Mashups

Mailing List

A **mashup** is a Web site that combines the data and functionality from different Web resources to create a new Web site that is updated by those resources.

A **mailing list** is a list of names and email addresses for a group of people who share a common interest in a specific or broad topic and exchange information by subscribing to the list. The Internet has thousands of mailing lists on many different topics.

Push and Pull Communication

Until a few years ago, users would search the Internet for information and use links to visit a Web page or multiple Web sites to gather information. In this scenario, the Web was a resource—much like a library on a school campus—that required action on your part to get information from it. You found the sites, reviewed them, and perhaps even used your Web browser to create bookmarks so you could revisit those sites. These Web sites were mostly static, with updates being posted by the Web site's developer on a regular basis. During this time, you found the site and viewed it, and later returned to the site and checked it for updates. You used these Web sites to pull the information you wanted to your computer so you could view it.

Several years ago, with new software and imaginative ways of using existing software, the way people used the Web changed. In addition to searching for content, you could identify content you wanted and have it *sent* to you, either at your request or on a certain schedule. As more users put more information on the Web, this idea of "pushing" content to other users created a new way of using the Web for people who were "pulling" content to their computers.

You can group the Internet's many communication methods into two basic categories: push and pull. Some communication methods use **push technology** to send content to users who request it. Some examples of push technology are chat, instant messaging, online social networks, photo- and video-sharing sites, and blogs. The other communication method, which is called **pull technology** because subscribers "pull" content to their computers when they want it, includes mailing lists, newsgroups, feeds, podcasts, and mashups. Some communication methods are both push and pull, depending on who is using them. For example, the person who writes a blog is pushing content to other users, who then pull it to their computers so they can read it.

Some communication methods don't fit into neat categories based on the method they use, but you can still categorize them based on the technology they use to disseminate information or on the way the information is combined. The Visual Overview for Session 5.1 describes the pull technologies that you will learn about in this session.

Web 2.0

Some people think of pulling content as the "old" Internet—you had to find the resources and establish how you would pull the information to your computer. Over the past several years, the Web has evolved so that connected people *push* information to users who request it or just wander into it. This change is sometimes called the "new Internet" or **Web 2.0**, a term coined during a brainstorming session between representatives of O'Reilly Media and MediaLive International. During the session, Tim O'Reilly and Dale Dougherty were characterizing the changes in Web technology and how these changes affected the way people used and accessed the Web. Web 2.0 creates users who actively participate in writing the content that they are viewing—hence the term "user-generated content." Web 2.0 users not only interact with content; they also are given new and easy ways to create it. In fact, Web 2.0 isn't a "new" Internet at all. The term itself is intended to indicate a change in the way people use the Web, just like a version change in a software program indicates that a new release of the software is better than the old version. Web 2.0 applications enable users to manage and distribute information gathered from online communities to people all over the world, who then take the information and work to improve, enhance, and forward it to new users.

Web 2.0 applications vary, but they all rely in some way on the interactions of communities of people and their data. Web 2.0 includes online social networks, mashups, photo- and video-sharing sites, blogs, microblogs, feeds, and podcasts. (You will learn about these technologies as you complete this tutorial.)

TIP

You learned about another Web 2.0 application, wikis, in Tutorial 4.

Two decades ago, virtual communities were an essential part of the online experience for people using the Internet. Although these virtual communities continue to thrive, Web 2.0 has expanded the overall number and types of virtual communities and has increased their numbers dramatically. A virtual community, now more commonly called an **online social network**, provides a way for people to discuss issues and share information using the Internet or cellular networks. People who share common interests—such as the high school or college they attended, the sports they watch or participate in, their religious preferences, their careers or jobs, or even the types of diets they follow—use social networks to connect to other people with similar characteristics and interests.

Kay wants to explore the different types of Internet communication so she can share new ideas with her clients as they build their Internet-based business communications. She knows that almost all of her clients will rely on some kind of email communication with their customers, so she decides to investigate some of the Internet's email-based communication methods first.

Email-Based Communication

In Tutorial 2, you learned how to use email to communicate with other people. You can also use email-based communication to access and share other information stored on the Web. For example, you might use email-based communication to gather ideas, conduct research, or contact other people who share your interests.

One way of sharing information is to join, or **subscribe** to, a mailing list. These mailing lists are not like the ones you created in Tutorial 2, in which you grouped related individuals in your email program's address book for convenience; nor are they like the email messages that you might request and receive from Web sites to learn more about a special promotion or a new product. A mailing list uses a **list server** to send subscribers messages from other list members. Once popular for exchanging ideas on many subjects, mailing lists today are used primarily to share information about very specific subjects, such as software testing and product development. Each person who wants to join a mailing list is responsible for subscribing to the list by sending an email message to the list's administrative address or by using a Web site to request to be added to the list. A mailing list might be moderated, in which case an individual or group called the **list moderator** monitors messages sent to the list and discards inappropriate content; this type of list is called a **moderated list**. A mailing list that does not have a list moderator is called an **unmoderated list**. When a mailing list has a list administrator who oversees the list's members, the list is called a **closed list**. When anyone can subscribe to a mailing list, it is called an **open list**.

> **TIP**
>
> A list server runs email list software to manage the functions of a mailing list.

Another email-based communication is the **Usenet News Service**, or **Usenet**, which was founded in 1979 at Duke University as a way of collecting information and storing it by topic category. Usenet was one of the first large, distributed information databases in the world. A **distributed database** is stored in multiple physical locations, with portions of the database replicated in different locations. The original Usenet News Service was devoted to transmitting computing news and facilitating discussions among employees of university computing departments on topics such as operating systems and programming languages. The topic categories on Usenet originally were called newsgroups or forums. Many people still use these terms when they refer to Usenet categories, but another popular term is **Internet discussion group**. Most of these newsgroups are available to the general public; however, some newsgroups are limited to users at a specific site or to those affiliated with a particular organization.

Newsgroups are similar to mailing lists in that they accept messages from users and make them generally available to other users. However, newsgroups do not use a list server to forward copies of submitted messages to subscribers. The server that stores a newsgroup is called a **news server**; the collection of news servers connected to the

Internet make up Usenet. Organizations that operate news servers include most ISPs, universities, large businesses, government units, and other entities connected to the Internet. A newsgroup stores items on a server as **articles** or postings that are sorted by topic. Users pull the content they need to their computers in the form of articles posted to the newsgroup. Users can simply read these articles, or they can optionally reply to them.

When the Usenet News Service began operating in 1979, the only way to read or post articles to newsgroups was to install and run a software program, called a **newsreader**, that could manage and display the articles. Later, email programs included features that managed the articles. Now, you can easily search and read newsgroup articles by using a Web site that archives articles, such as the Google Groups directory. Google Groups stores millions of newsgroup articles dating from 1981 in its database. Figure 5-1 shows the Google Groups home page.

Figure 5-1	Google Groups home page

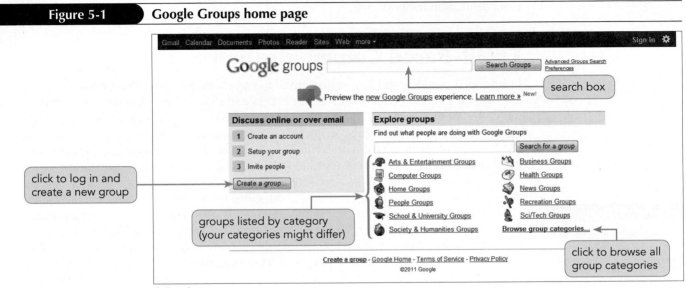

© Google

You can search the Google Groups directory by typing keywords in the search box, or you can click the general group categories to open a list of subcategories, which often lead to additional subcategories. As you drill down through the categories, you'll find a page with the individual groups. The summary for each group includes a hyperlinked group name, a brief summary paragraph with the group's focus and content, and often a note about the number of members in the group and the number of messages per month the group generates. To read the messages in a specific group, click the group's hyperlink.

Keep in mind that most groups are unmoderated; as a result, many groups contain a large number of off-topic threads, including messages that contain advertisements for unrelated products and services and messages about other topics. Unfortunately, many postings are potentially offensive to some readers. In an unmoderated list, there is no moderator to handle the disposition of objectionable material, so you must assume that job yourself.

Protecting Your Online Privacy

Joining a mailing list or newsgroup often requires you to identify yourself on a registration page before the site accepts your membership. You should consider carefully whether to provide detailed personal information when you register because most current laws do not require a Web site administrator to maintain the confidentiality of your information. In addition, your email address or your user name at the site might reveal some part or all of your entire identity. In a mailing list, messages that you send to the list are forwarded by the list server to everyone who has subscribed to the list. In some cases, your identity includes your name, location, email address, and other details about you. To protect your privacy, you should consider deleting your signature from email messages you post to a mailing list and using a Web-based email account (such as Yahoo! or Windows Live Hotmail) that does not include your name when you register for different sites. This way, you protect your "real" email address and your privacy.

Getting Information from RSS Feeds

Usenet is just one example of a feed (also commonly called a **newsfeed** or a **Web feed**) that uses pull technology to deliver changing content to users. This changing content might be from a blog, a Web site, or a news organization. The format that is used to syndicate (distribute) published content from one site to another is called **RSS**, an acronym for **Really Simple Syndication**; another format is **Atom**. Both RSS and Atom make it possible for computers to share updates. Feeds are similar to newsgroups in that they let you subscribe to content that you want to receive on your device. However, feeds differ from newsgroups because of the way that content is delivered to subscribers. Newsgroup postings are delivered via email messages, whereas feeds are delivered through a program that includes a summary and a link to the published or actual content, depending on how you choose to receive it.

Feeds are also used by organizations and individuals that create and maintain blogs, and on social networking sites as a way to publish content and alert subscribers to changes in the content.

As you learned in Tutorial 4, to receive feed content, you can install a program called an aggregator on your device. An aggregator is similar to an email program in that it requests content from feeds to which you have subscribed and displays that content in a format similar to an email message. Most Web browsers, email programs, and social networking sites have built-in aggregators that let you subscribe to, view, and remove feeds. Most Web sites that syndicate content also include built-in aggregators that you can use to search for, subscribe to, and view syndicated content using any Web browser.

To subscribe to a feed with content that you would like to view, you can use a feed directory to find a source. However, a more common method is to use the tools provided on the Web site that includes the feed. Web sites that include feeds will display a small, orange RSS or Atom icon that you can click to subscribe to the feed. Sometimes the link to subscribe to feeds is a text link with the letters "RSS" to indicate the file format of the syndicated content. Figure 5-2 shows a page from MedlinePlus, a site that includes feeds. In Internet Explorer, the Feeds button on the Command bar changes color from gray to orange when the site includes syndicated content. Clicking the arrow on the orange Feeds button opens a menu that identifies the feeds on the page by name; clicking a feed name opens a new page that displays the feed's content.

TIP

When only *part* of a Web page is coded to syndicate content, such as a sports score or a weather update, you can subscribe to it using a Web Slice (Internet Explorer) or a Webchunk (Firefox).

| **Figure 5-2** | **MedlinePlus page showing syndicated content in Internet Explorer** |

> click the arrow on the orange Feeds button to view the names of feeds available from the Web site

> after subscribing to a feed, click the Favorites button to access the feed on the Feeds tab

Courtesy of © Microsoft; Courtesy of U.S. National Library of Medicine, National Institutes of Health

TIP

In Firefox, feeds are called Live Bookmarks.

Figure 5-3 shows the same page from MedlinePlus in Firefox. Clicking the Bookmarks button on the Bookmarks Toolbar shows that the Subscribe to This Page button is orange, which indicates that the currently displayed page contains one or more feeds. When more than one feed is available from a site, pointing to the Subscribe to This Page option opens a submenu with the names of the available feeds; clicking a feed name in the submenu opens a new page with options for subscribing to the feed.

| **Figure 5-3** | **MedlinePlus page showing syndicated content in Firefox** |

Courtesy of The Mozilla Foundation; Courtesy of U.S. National Library of Medicine, National Institutes of Health

Kay has used feeds in the past and has liked the convenience of viewing timely articles on various topics. She wants to search for feeds that might be of interest to self-employed individuals, so she decides to use a search engine to investigate this type of content.

To search for Web sites that include feeds:

1. Start your Web browser, go to **www.cengagebrain.com**, open the Tutorial 5 Weblinks page, click the **Session 5.1** link, and then click one of the links in the Search Engines section.

2. In the site's search box, type **self employment guide**, and then run the search.

3. Examine the search results and look for Web sites that include links to sites that might interest Kay, such as those dealing with general self-employment issues and home-based business guides.

4. Click one of the links to open the Web site, and then examine the page to determine if it contains any feeds. You'll know that a site contains one or more feeds when the Feeds button on the Command bar in Internet Explorer or on the Bookmarks menu in Firefox is orange in color.

Trouble? If the site you opened doesn't include any feeds, return to your search results and select another Web site until you find one that contains a feed.

5. If you are using Internet Explorer, click the **Feeds** button arrow on the Command bar, click the name of a feed of interest to view the feed's articles, and then click a link to an article that might interest Kay and scan the content. Figure 5-4 shows the feeds for the NPR News page.

Figure 5-4	NPR News feeds page in Internet Explorer

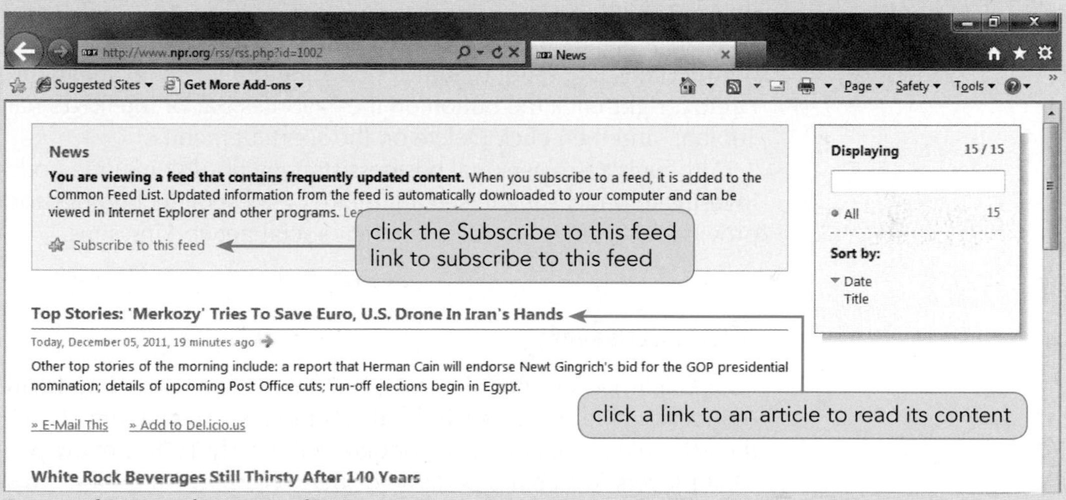

Courtesy of © Microsoft; Courtesy of NPR

6. If you are using Firefox, click the **Bookmarks** button on the Bookmarks Toolbar, click the **Subscribe to This Page** option on the Bookmarks menu, and then, if necessary, click the name of a feed of interest to view the feed's articles. Figure 5-5 shows the feeds for the NPR News page.

Figure 5-5	NPR News feeds page in Firefox

Courtesy of The Mozilla Foundation; Courtesy of NPR

> **Trouble?** If the Bookmarks button is hidden, click the Firefox button on the title bar, and then point to Bookmarks on the menu.
>
> ▸ **7.** Review one or more articles to see if they contain content that might interest Kay, who is self-employed. (Do not subscribe to any feeds at this time.)
>
> ▸ **8.** Return to the Weblinks page for Session 5.1.

Depending on how you subscribe to a feed and the device you are using to view the feed's content, the feed's content might be displayed in different ways. With an aggregator, you might see summaries of the feed's content, similar to how you receive email messages, with links to the full articles. Clicking the link opens a page in a Web browser. Feeds are added using default settings that indicate the frequency with which to download new content from the source. You can change the feed's update schedule by changing its properties.

To cancel a feed, you just delete it. In Internet Explorer, right-click the feed's name on the Feeds tab in the Favorites Center, and then click Delete on the shortcut menu. In Firefox, right-click the button on the Favorites Bar or the feed's name on the Bookmarks Toolbar, and then click Delete on the shortcut menu.

Although Kay's personal business strategy doesn't include podcasts, she decides to investigate podcasting to see if it might be a useful technology for clients who want to provide recordings or videos on their social networking sites.

Podcasting

As you learned in Tutorial 4, MP3 is a compressed digital audio file format that greatly reduces the file size of an audio file without sacrificing the clarity of its content. When the MP3 file format became popular in the early 1990s, many people began purchasing MP3 players, which are portable devices that play MP3 files. Now, most cell phones and many other types of devices can play audio and video files.

At the same time that these types of devices became affordable and readily accessible, people who knew how to make different types of technology work on these devices found new uses for them. In the early 2000s, a group of programmers created the technical specifications necessary to encode audio recordings in feeds. Soon after, they worked toward the goal of being able to synchronize and encode audio files in feeds, which led to the development of podcasting in 2004. **Podcasting** lets a user subscribe to an audio or video feed, and then listen to it or watch it at the user's convenience on a compatible device, which might include the user's computer, or a mobile device such as an iPod or a cell phone.

Podcasting's original use was to make it easy for people to create and broadcast their own radio shows, but many other uses soon followed. Podcasts are used by the media to store and disseminate interviews with politicians and professors on specific subjects; by colleges and universities to record lectures for distance learning classes; and by movie studios to promote new movie releases. Some podcasts have different names that further identify the type of content they contain, such as a Godcast to denote a religious broadcast, a vidcast to identify a video feed, or a learncast to identify content that is educational in nature, such as a podcast produced by a university or other educational institution.

Although you can play a podcast using a media player, such as Windows Media Player or Apple's QuickTime, you will need to use software to subscribe to a podcast. This software, called a **podcatcher**, manages the schedule for downloading files to your device. When you connect your device to the Internet, the podcatcher will automatically download subscribed podcasts to your device so you can play them later.

TIP

The word "podcast" is a combination of the words "iPod" and "broadcasting," but you can play a podcast on any device with a media player.

TIP

Many instructors record their lectures and make them available as podcasts for students who miss class.

Figure 5-6 shows the Podcasts page for iTunes, which contains podcasts in many different categories. The user can click a category to examine its available podcasts on this page. For example, clicking the Action Sports category opens a list of podcasts related to sports; clicking a link to one of the sports podcasts begins playing it. To subscribe to the podcast using iTunes, click the Subscribe button to add the podcast's feed to your iTunes Library, which in turn downloads the podcast's file and transfers it to your device.

Figure 5-6	Podcasts page for iTunes

podcasts grouped by categories

Kay wants to review some sites that organize podcasts by category so she can get a sense of the type of information a podcast might include and its format. One of her clients, a small hospital, is considering including interviews with doctors, who will discuss basic medical conditions, on its social networking site. Kay might advise the hospital to produce podcasts to push content to patients, so she will examine podcasting next.

To explore podcast directories:

1. On the Weblinks page for Session 5.1, click one of the links in the Podcast Directories section. Figure 5-7 shows the Podcast Directory page for LearnOutLoud.com, a site that stores audio and video podcasts on hundreds of subjects that are geared toward personal and professional education and development. You can search for podcasts by using the search box or by navigating the different podcast categories.

Figure 5-7 **LearnOutLoud.com Podcast Directory page**

Search box

links to podcast
categories

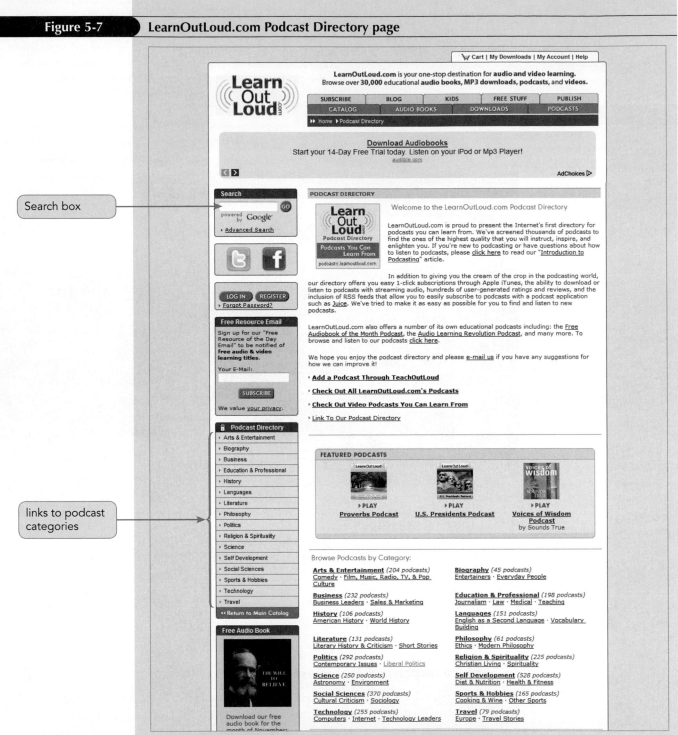

2. Use the links to categories (such as Science & Medical or Education and Professional) on the site you selected, or type keywords (such as **medical** or **physician**) in the site's search box, to explore the different categories of medical podcasts. As you are reviewing the podcasts, also note the dates of the broadcasts. You will probably notice that the broadcast dates are very recent, with some occurring on the day of or within a few days of completing this step. Because the podcasts are recent, the information they contain is current. Some sites provide archives of past podcasts that become a source for online research.

> **3.** If the site allows you to do so, click a podcast link to play the file. If your computer can play the podcast, it will start in a new window. Listen to the podcast for a few minutes to get a sense of the content it provides, and then close the window playing the podcast.
>
> **Trouble?** If the file does not start playing, close the window that opened and skip Step 3. You need a plug-in, such as QuickTime or Windows Media Player, to play a podcast, and you need speakers to hear it.
>
> **4.** Return to the Weblinks page for Session 5.1, and then click another link in the Podcast Directories section. Explore the site to search for podcasts that might interest Kay's client.
>
> **5.** When you are finished exploring the site, return to the Weblinks page for Session 5.1.

Podcasts might be an interesting way for the physicians at the hospital to push general health information to their patients. Kay also represents a group of local real estate agents, who might be interested in another technology in which the content of two or more Web sites is combined into a single site. She decides to review this type of site next.

Mashups

When your computer runs a certain operating system, such as Windows 7, and you install software programs on that computer, the operating system and the software programs communicate with each other to handle specific tasks such as displaying content on the screen or printing. A software program uses an **application programming interface (API)** to communicate with an operating system or some other program.

An API is written by a programmer or developer with a specific goal in mind, such as displaying content on a screen or accessing a file system. When programs are developed for a specific operating system, developers might reference an API used by the operating system to print a document or display it on the screen, instead of writing the content themselves. APIs reduce the amount of coding for third-party software programs and ensure that the programs work together well.

The developers of most operating systems write new APIs and make them available to third-party developers by request. This relationship between developers wasn't always easy because the operating system developers often didn't give third-party developers what they needed to run their own programs. In addition, sometimes the APIs from one developer were not made available to other developers, and vice versa, so data was not shared between companies.

Instead of keeping data to itself, a company such as eBay or Amazon.com writes an API and makes it available to *any* developer who wants to use it—usually for free. When APIs are shared in this way, the term **Web services** describes the process of organizations communicating through a network to share data without needing extensive knowledge of each other's systems. As more companies make their APIs available, developers can use them to enhance their own sites by combining content from two or more sites. Amazon.com was the first to make APIs available to other developers, who in turn used them to link to and integrate their content with the Amazon.com Web site.

When Web content is combined in this way, the new Web site is called a mashup. In a mashup, a developer combines the services from two (or more) different sites using APIs to create a completely new site that uses features from each site. Some examples of mashups are sites that combine the "25 best companies to work for" feature from *Fortune Magazine* with an API from Google Maps that produces a map with locations of the companies; or a list of apartments available on craigslist for rent in a specific city that uses an API from Yahoo! to plot the apartments on a map with details about the apartments, such as the square footage, the number of bedrooms, and the monthly rent.

Figure 5-8 shows a site that combines an interactive map of the Las Vegas Strip from the Google Maps API with several APIs from social networking sites that provide user comments and user-posted photos and videos, along with pricing information from the individual hotels in the area, such as Caesars Palace. The resulting Web site combines all of this data for the user to make it very easy to find a hotel to stay at while visiting Las Vegas.

Figure 5-8   Vegas Hotel Hunt page for Caesars Palace

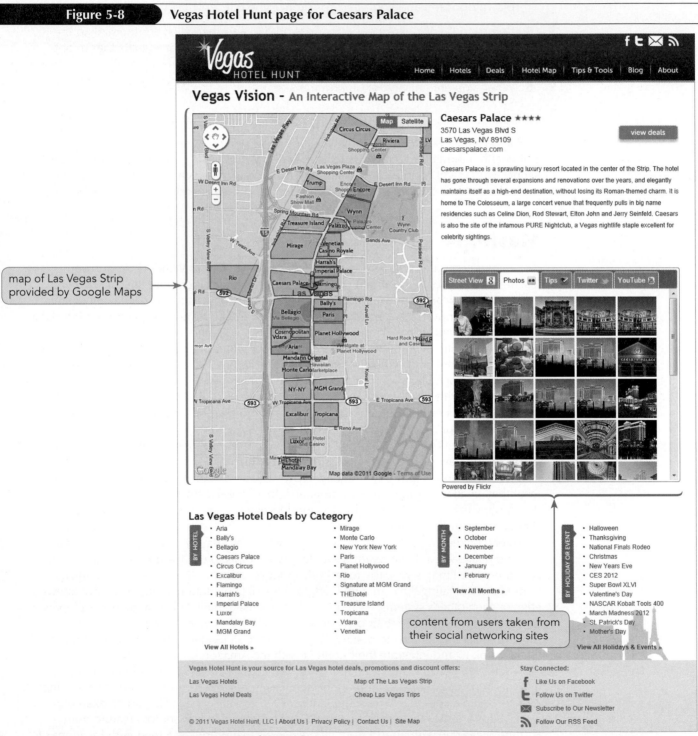

map of Las Vegas Strip provided by Google Maps

content from users taken from their social networking sites

© 2011 Vegas Hotel Hunt, LLC

Kay realizes that a mashup might be very useful for her real estate client, so she decides to review a mashup site next to see how it works. She is going to Boston next week for a conference, so she decides to use a mashup site to calculate the cost of taking a taxi from the conference center to the airport.

To view a mashup site:

1. In the Mashups section of the Weblinks page for Session 5.1, click the **TaxiWiz** link to open the TaxiWiz home page. This site lets you calculate the cost and distance of taking a cab from one location to another in different cities. The first thing you need to do is identify the city you are visiting. You'll use Boston, MA, as the city, and calculate the estimated fare to take a taxi from the Prudential Center to Logan Airport.

2. Click the **Select City** arrow, and then click **Boston** in the list. This sets Boston as the city and adds common starting points and destinations to the menus on the site to make it easy for users to use the site.

Trouble? The TaxiWiz site might change over time, in which case you might use different tools to select your starting point and destination. If the site changes, use the Taxi Tips tab or link to review the current instructions, and then run the requested search as identified in the steps.

Trouble? If the TaxiWiz site is no longer available, return to the Weblinks page for Session 5.1 and click a link in the Mashups section to visit another site. Use the tools on the site you select to explore the features of a mashup site and skip to Step 7.

3. Click the **Starting point** arrow, and then click **Prudential Center** in the list.

4. Click the **Destination** arrow, and then click **Logan Airport** in the list.

5. Click the **Go!** button to submit your request. Figure 5-9 shows the page from TaxiWiz with the results of your search. This page uses Google APIs to combine a page displaying a map of Boston, MA, and the estimated route and fare for taking a taxi from the Prudential Center to Logan Airport after entering these locations into the site's form. The site generates a page that shows a map of Boston with an overlay of the route the taxi might take to arrive at the entered destination from the entered starting point, and an estimate of the fare the user might incur for the service. In addition, Google's AdSense API displays links to services that might interest the user, such as links to limo services in different cities.

| Figure 5-9 | TaxiWiz estimated fare page for Boston, MA |

city (Boston), starting location (Prudential Center), and destination (Logan Airport)

estimated fare for taking a taxi from the Prudential Center to Logan Airport; yours might differ

ads with links to related services; yours might differ

map provided by Google Maps shows the starting location, destination, and route

© Google

> **6.** Return to the Weblinks page for Session 5.1, and then click another link in the Mashups section and explore the Web site. Try to determine the resources the site combines, use the site to explore its features, and try to determine the intended consumer use of the site.

> **7.** Return to the Weblinks page for Session 5.1.

You might wonder how a mashup is profitable to its developer. The developer usually includes additional APIs on the mashup site that link to Google AdSense or other content that generates revenue through customized advertising on the site, similar to the ads displayed on the right side of the TaxiWiz page in Figure 5-9. The mashup's developer most likely has an agreement with Google AdSense or another API provider to display this advertising and to share the income generated by users who click the links to these ads.

Because mashups rely on Web site data that already exists and APIs that are created by other companies, developers with the necessary programming background find mashups to be relatively easy to create and maintain, and profitable for the efforts needed to create them. For this reason, mashups constitute one of the fastest growing segments of Web sites on the Internet.

Kay wonders where she can get more information about APIs that she can use to generate new content that might be useful to her clients. Some Web sites list APIs by category, and include descriptions of the APIs and links to sites that use them. Because all of her clients rely on social networks, Kay wants to examine the APIs available for integrating social networking.

To view APIs available on the Web:

> **1.** In the Session 5.1 section of the Weblinks page for Tutorial 5, click the **ProgrammableWeb.com** link. Figure 5-10 shows the home page, which contains a variety of information about API resources. The site also provides a directory of available APIs that you can search by API category or by using keywords.

Figure 5-10 **ProgrammableWeb.com home page**

Mashups link

API Directory link

search box lets you search for APIs using keywords

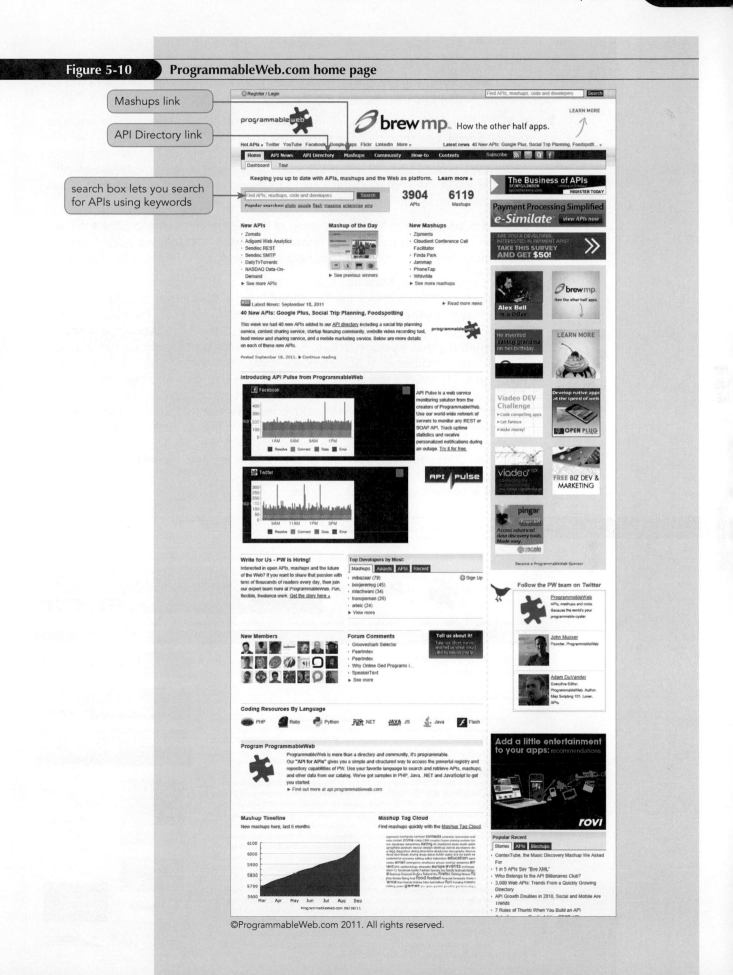

2. Near the top of the page, point to or click the **API Directory** link, and then click the **APIs By Category** link or the **By Category** link. The Web Services Directory page displays options for filtering the directory to find specific APIs.

3. In the Hide Filters section, click the **Category** arrow, scroll down the menu and click **Social**, and then click the **Filter This List** button. The filter displays APIs for the Social category. These APIs are used by developers to integrate the services from social networks with other Web sites. For example, you might use an API that displays the contacts from a social network with an API that displays a map so a user can locate a contact geographically.

4. Scroll down the page and review some of the APIs and their descriptions in the Social category. Because this list is updated daily as new APIs are added by the contributing sites, the list changes frequently. Next you will search for mashup sites.

5. Point to or click the **Mashups** link near the top of the page, and then click the **Mashup Tag Cloud** link or the **Tag Cloud** link. As developers add APIs to the site, they code them with keywords, called tags, that identify their use in a way that categorizes them. When used in the context of APIs or Web sites, a **tag** is something that a person uses to categorize a Web site, photo, post, video, or almost any other form of Web content based on the information it contains. Figure 5-11 shows a **tag cloud**, with all the tags that describe the different APIs or mashups uploaded to this site shown in an alphabetical list and a cloud arrangement. Larger words in the cloud indicate more APIs and mashups in that category. Pointing at a word in the tag cloud displays a ScreenTip that indicates the number of APIs and mashups associated with the tag. This feature gives you an idea of the relative popularity of each API or mashup category, and lets you search for all the related APIs and mashups quickly by clicking the tag that identifies the content you are searching for.

Figure 5-11   **ProgrammableWeb.com tag cloud**

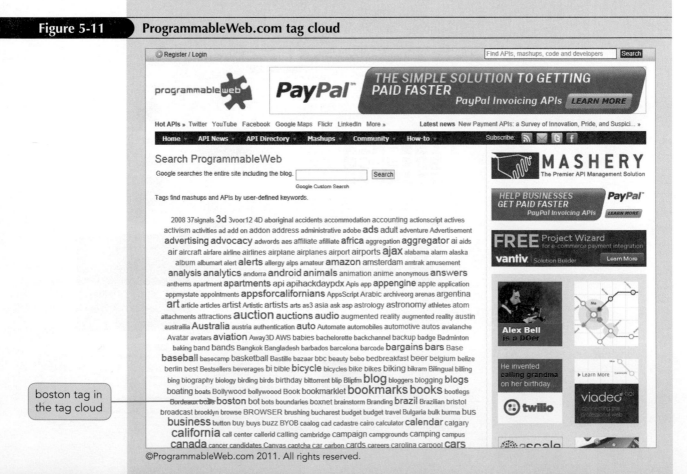

6. Point to the word **boston** in the cloud. A ScreenTip appears showing how many APIs and mashups are coded with this tag.

7. Click the **boston** tag to open a page listing other APIs and mashups that use the boston tag to describe their functionality. Scroll down the page, noticing the various sites. For example, you might see sites that find the best parking or restaurants in the city of Boston.

8. Find a site that interests you, and then click the site's name. A page opens and describes the site's content, identifies the APIs it uses and the tags that describe it, and lists the date the site was created, its author, and a link to the actual site.

9. Return to the Weblinks page for Session 5.1.

PROSKILLS

Problem Solving: How to Ensure Effective Collaboration with a Virtual Team

Many push and pull technologies make it possible for members of a virtual team to be physically separated but able to work as if everyone is in the same room. Some of the technologies you learned about in Session 5.1, and the technologies you will learn about in Session 5.2, are used by virtual teams to collaborate on projects such as market research, product development, advertising and marketing campaigns, and sales presentations.

Virtual teams often must work rapidly to accomplish tasks, so identifying which technologies team members should use to collaborate on projects is critical. For example, when collaborating on a PowerPoint presentation, the team leader must determine the best method for team members to share the file. For example, will they use email to exchange copies of the file, or will they use another method? Will routine communication and updates be conducted by email or using another method? How will team members handle urgent communication? The decision to use one technology over another has many considerations, such as ensuring that the technology is cost effective, private, and available to everyone on the team, and that all team members are proficient at using it. The leader may change as well, depending on the stage of work the team is completing, so the method of communication must be one in which the person leading the group can take it over quickly and easily.

To ensure that your virtual team is successful, decide which communication technologies the team will use to keep the flow of information moving smoothly, and then reevaluate your choices periodically to verify that the technology is complementing and enhancing the work of the team.

In the next session, you will learn about push technologies.

REVIEW

Session 5.1 Quick Check

1. Describe push technology and pull technology, and provide examples of each.
2. What are three examples of Web 2.0 applications?
3. What term is given to a series of postings on a particular newsgroup or mailing list topic?
4. When viewing a Web page in Internet Explorer and Firefox, how can you determine that the page contains one or more feeds?
5. What is a podcatcher and what does it do?
6. What is a mashup?
7. What information is provided in a tag cloud?

SESSION 5.2 VISUAL OVERVIEW

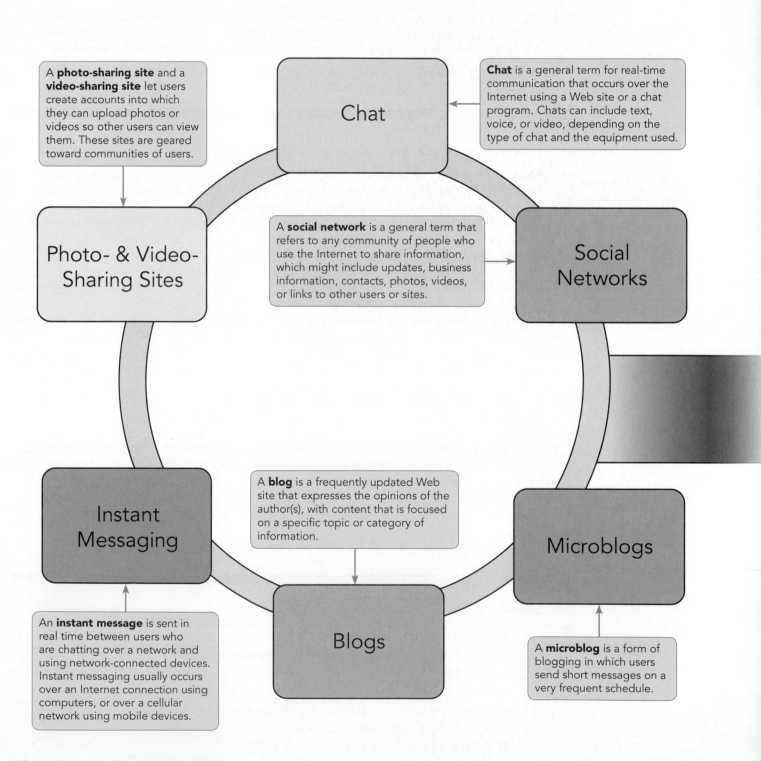

A **photo-sharing site** and a **video-sharing site** let users create accounts into which they can upload photos or videos so other users can view them. These sites are geared toward communities of users.

Chat is a general term for real-time communication that occurs over the Internet using a Web site or a chat program. Chats can include text, voice, or video, depending on the type of chat and the equipment used.

Chat

Photo- & Video-Sharing Sites

A **social network** is a general term that refers to any community of people who use the Internet to share information, which might include updates, business information, contacts, photos, videos, or links to other users or sites.

Social Networks

Instant Messaging

A **blog** is a frequently updated Web site that expresses the opinions of the author(s), with content that is focused on a specific topic or category of information.

Microblogs

An **instant message** is sent in real time between users who are chatting over a network and using network-connected devices. Instant messaging usually occurs over an Internet connection using computers, or over a cellular network using mobile devices.

Blogs

A **microblog** is a form of blogging in which users send short messages on a very frequent schedule.

PUSH TECHNOLOGIES

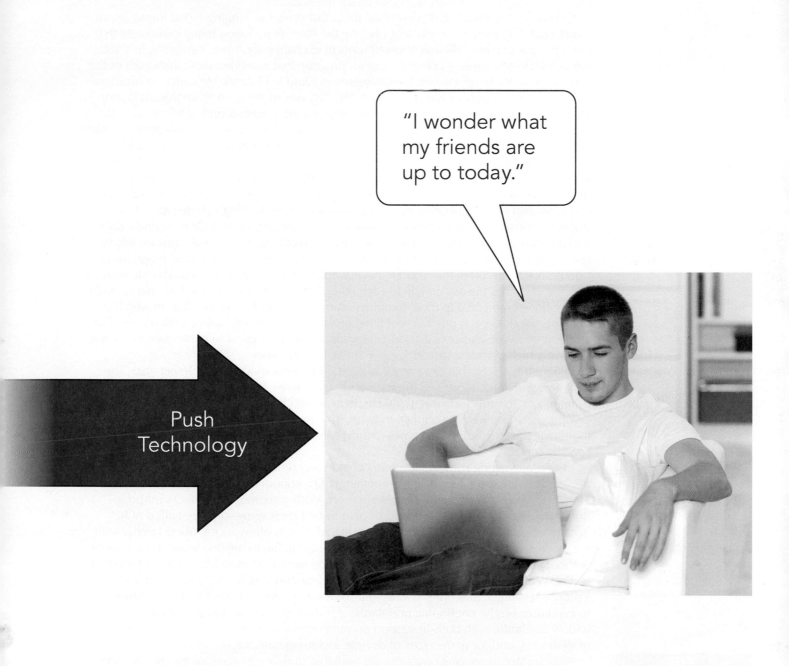

Internet Chat Communication

Until now, you have learned about Internet communication methods that let users pull information to their devices when they want it. You can also use the Internet to push information to users. Some of these communication methods are older and being used less frequently as new technologies take their places, but their history is important to understanding the evolution of more current methods.

Originally, the term "chat" described the act of users exchanging typed messages, or a **text chat**. The early networks that became the Internet included many computers that ran a program called **Talk** that allowed users to exchange short text messages. In 1988, Jarkko Oikarinen wrote a communications program that extended the capabilities of the Talk program for his employer, the University of Oulu in Finland. He called his multiuser program **Internet Relay Chat (IRC)**. By 1991, IRC was running on more than 100 servers throughout the world. IRC became popular among scientists and academicians for conducting informal discussions about experiments and theories with colleagues at other universities and research institutes. IRC is still widely used today around the world.

In addition to text-only chats, people in the 1990s used their Web browsers to visit a virtual **chat room**, where they could send text-only messages to other users in the room or just read the messages without contributing to the discussion. (The practice of reading messages and not contributing to the discussion is called **lurking**.) These types of sites still exist; today, however, chats can involve exchanging pictures, videos, sounds, data, and programs using a variety of technologies and methods. Some chat software lets you give control of your computer to another user so that person can use your programs or troubleshoot a problem that you are having. You can also use chat to collaborate with another user on a file as you talk to each other. Users with a sound card, speakers, and a microphone connected to their computers can participate in a **voice chat**, in which participants speak to each other in real time, much like they would using a telephone. The addition of a Web camera (also called a webcam) enables users to participate in a **video chat**, in which participants can see and speak to each other.

Different types of chat programs can be used to participate in an Internet chat. The chat program you choose and the type of chat you have (text, voice, or video) depend primarily on the software and hardware that you and other users have installed on your computers, your Internet connection types, and the conversation you plan to have (public or private). Some chat types require specific chat software and a connection to a specific server.

Instant messaging software lets users chat in real time using an Internet-connected device. The first instant messaging program, **ICQ** (pronounced "I seek you"), started in 1996 and still has millions of worldwide users. Within six months of ICQ's introduction, America Online (AOL) created its own instant messaging software called AOL Instant Messenger (AIM). AOL originally created AIM to allow its members to chat with each other, but subsequently made the software available to anyone (even those people without AOL accounts) for use on the Web. Soon Microsoft introduced MSN Messenger (called Windows Live Messenger in Windows Vista and Windows 7), Yahoo! introduced Yahoo! Messenger, and other portals and software vendors released their own products to capitalize on the continuing popularity of instant messaging. Instant messaging is now widely available, with built-in support on many social networking sites and other types of Web sites, and for many types of devices including computers and cell phones.

Most instant messaging programs are available in different versions for specific operating systems and devices, so you should select the correct version for the device on which you will use it. After starting the software, you sign in using your user name and password. Then you use the software to create or install a list of contacts.

Kay mostly communicates with her clients using email messages and phone calls, but some of her clients prefer to use instant messages to contact her. She decides to explore some popular instant messaging software programs next so she can communicate better with her clients. In addition, she is interested in learning how to integrate existing instant messaging software with social networks.

TIP

Some people use the term "IM'ing" when using instant messaging. "IM" is also used as a verb, as in "to IM a friend."

TIP

Some instant messaging software programs refer to online contacts as "buddies" or "friends."

To learn more about instant messaging software:

1. Start your Web browser, go to **www.cengagebrain.com**, open the Tutorial 5 Weblinks page, click the **Session 5.2** link, and then click a link in the Instant Messaging section.

2. Follow some of the links on the site's home page to learn more about its services. Try to determine if the service includes video and voice chat features, or if it is just text-based chat. Make sure to look for information that Kay needs, such as how to get started and on which types of devices the software works, and if it is accessible through social networking sites. Figure 5-12 shows the Windows Live Messenger home page, which includes links to other pages that describe some of the features that Kay wants to learn more about.

Figure 5-12   **Messenger home page**

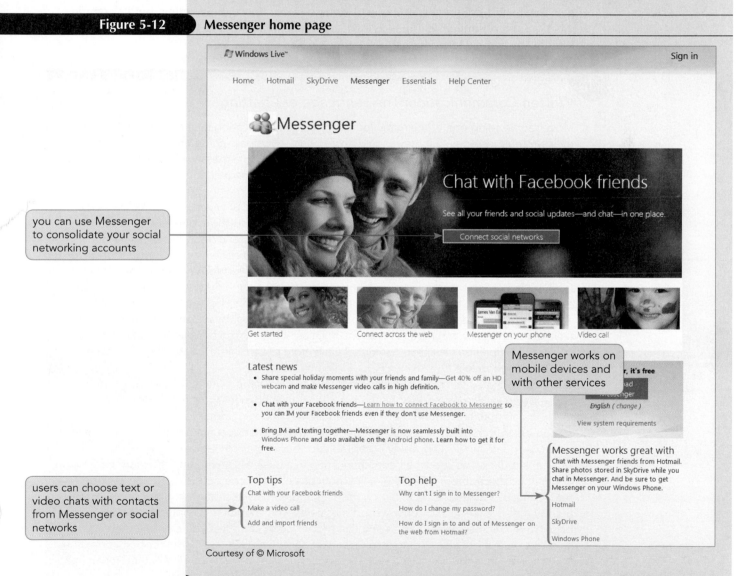

you can use Messenger to consolidate your social networking accounts

Messenger works on mobile devices and with other services

users can choose text or video chats with contacts from Messenger or social networks

Courtesy of © Microsoft

3. When you are finished exploring the first Web site, return to the Weblinks page for Session 5.2, and then click another link in the Instant Messaging section.

4. Follow some of the links on the site's home page to learn more about the program you selected. If you see links to videos and other interactive demos that describe the features and you have the required software to view them, click the links and watch the demos. Make sure to look for information that Kay needs, such as how to get started, on what types of devices the software runs, and options for accessing feeds from other social networking accounts.

5. When you are finished exploring the Web site, return to the Weblinks page for Session 5.2.

Another type of instant message, called a **text message**, occurs over a cellular network between users who are connected to the network using cell phones or other mobile devices. Text messaging uses different technology than instant messaging, but its communication is very similar. Text messaging lets users send and receive very short messages (usually 140 characters or less) in real time.

PROSKILLS

Written Communication: The Language of Chatting

Most people using one of the many forms of chat communication take certain shortcuts in their written messages that they should avoid using in business communication. For a conversation between friends or family members, responding to a message with only the letter "K" might indicate the sender's acknowledgement of a message that is requesting a certain action, and agreeing to complete the assigned task. This typing shortcut is fast, which is how most written chat conversations occur. Because of the speed at which chat participants react to each other's messages, it's not unusual to take other written shortcuts—such as not using capital letters, complete sentences, or proper grammar—to send your messages faster.

How you express your messages during a chat might also convey your emotional involvement in the message, as well. Messages written in all capital letters have a common interpretation of indicating that the sender is shouting or screaming the message for emphasis. Chat participants often use the same emoticons that email users find helpful to display humor and emotions in their messages. In addition, chat participants might use common acronyms as a typing shortcut for common expressions, such as "bbl" for "be back later," "c u" for "see you (later)," "lol" for "laughing out loud," "jam" for "just a minute," and "ttfn" for "ta-ta for now" (or "goodbye").

Because chat, instant messaging, email, and texting are convenient, cost effective, and widely available methods of communication, most business professionals use these methods on their cell phones and other mobile devices to communicate with clients and customers. Although the previously mentioned typing shortcuts are acceptable between friends and family, they are *never* acceptable for business communication.

The language you use when communicating in a business environment should be understandable without the use of any emoticons or other characters that express your true feelings, and should be clearly written. In addition, even though you are using a technology that is intended to convey short messages, your business communications should be written in complete sentences and use proper grammar. After you create a message, be sure to review it before sending it to make sure that a spell checker or other text correction feature didn't change any of the words in your message in a way that alters their meanings.

Voice over Internet Protocol

Some instant messaging programs include support for voice communications, using software that lets users engage in voice conversations using their software and the required equipment for engaging in a voice chat. Another option for voice calls is **VoIP**, which is an acronym for **Voice over Internet Protocol**. VoIP is frequently used as a cost-effective alternative to the traditional "landline" telephone service provided by residential and commercial phone companies. Because VoIP providers rely on the Internet as their network instead of the physical communications structure required by landlines, VoIP eliminates monthly service fees and taxes and usually includes long-distance and international calling for free or for a nominal charge. Most VoIP providers, such as the Skype service shown in Figure 5-13, include calling features that you expect from landlines, such as caller ID, call forwarding, call waiting, and voice mail services. If your landline is already provided by your cable provider, you might already be using VoIP for your telephone service.

| Figure 5-13 | Skype home page |

©2011 Skype Limited

For business customers, VoIP is a way to reduce costs by routing voice conversations over existing Internet networks while at the same time providing other business services such as faxing, conference calls, and Web conferencing.

The primary disadvantage of VoIP is its limitations in identifying a caller's physical location for emergency services (911) operators because VoIP uses an IP address instead of a physical location such as a person's home address to identify a call's origin. VoIP providers use Enhanced 911 service to transmit all 911 calls from their subscribers to the appropriate emergency services provider, along with the caller's telephone number and the physical address provided by the subscriber upon initiation of the VoIP service. This process is slower than what you might expect from making an emergency call from a traditional landline.

Kay knows that in addition to using a Web browser and other types of devices for chatting, she can also chat with friends from other social networks, such as Facebook.

Online Social Networks

In the past, social networks connected people with specific common interests. For example, one of the first social networks on the Internet, Classmates.com, started in 1995 as a way to connect people from specific graduating classes at high schools and colleges, and in the military.

Another early online social network, craigslist, which was created in 1995 by Craig Newmark, started as an information resource for San Francisco area residents. This online community has expanded to include information for most major cities in the United States and in countries around the world. The company started as a not-for-profit organization but was incorporated as a for-profit company in 1999. According to the site's fact sheet, craigslist retains its .org domain as a way to symbolize the relatively noncommercial nature of the service and its noncorporate culture. This mission is evident in the site's very basic design and function.

The craigslist Web site was an early pioneer, and it is still operated as a community service. Most of the revenue earned by craigslist comes from the 1 million job postings it features each month at a cost of $25 to $75 each, depending on the city in which the ad is placed, and brokered apartment listings in New York City. According to craigslist, more than 50 million people visit more than 700 craigslist sites in countries around the world each month.

Connecting with Friends

Another early pioneer of Web 2.0, Friendster, was launched by Jonathan Abrams in 2003 and was an immediate sensation on the Web. In the same year, Google saw the advertising potential for the online social network and offered Abrams a $30 million buyout, which Abrams turned down in favor of obtaining venture capital from another source.

Members used Friendster to post profiles with information about themselves and, at their option, to upload their photos and videos. They could use the Friendster site to ask friends who were already members to link to their profiles so they could interact with each other by chatting and sharing pictures and other information. Members could invite their nonmember friends to become Friendster members, which is one reason the site grew so rapidly at first. At one point, Friendster had more than 120 million users; but as other social networking sites came online and provided new and more interactive features, Friendster's popularity rapidly declined. By 2011, Friendster's membership was fewer than 1 million members and it had moved its headquarters to Asia, where most of those members were located. In addition, Friendster discontinued its social networking features and changed its focus to a social gaming site.

Other social networking sites that use the same technology as Friendster have been enormously successful. Facebook, which began in 2004 as a closed network for college students and later was expanded to include high school students, was founded by Mark

---

TIP

In 2011, Google launched its own social network, Google+, which is integrated with users' Gmail accounts and other Google services, as a competitor to Facebook.

Zuckerberg, then a student at Harvard University. After gaining new members at a rate three times faster than its competitors, the Facebook network was opened to anyone age 13 and older with an email address.

Many social networks operate in niche markets, such as networks for people speaking specific languages or living in specific geographic areas; people with certain hobbies and other interests; people of the same religious preference; and people who share other common characteristics, much like you would find in traditional peer groups. Most of these sites provide a directory that lists members' locations and interests. On some sites, a member can offer to communicate with any other member, but the communication does not occur until the intended recipient approves the contact (usually after reviewing the sender's directory information). By gradually building up a set of connections, members can develop contacts within a community. Some of these social networking sites have proven track records for re-creating (on a much larger scale) the essence of the original Internet communities.

Advertising Revenues from Social Networks

Most, if not all, social networking sites rely heavily on advertising to generate the revenue they need to operate. Successful social networks have not only catered to members' needs, but also have had an open mind with regard to advertising and creativity. In 2003, Myspace, capitalizing on its large membership of people ages 16 to 34 years old, allowed Procter & Gamble to create a profile for singer/actress Hilary Duff that included logos and links to free downloads of three of her pop songs. The profile and links were surrounded by a marketing pitch for Procter & Gamble's Secret Sparkle deodorant to a large number of people in the product's target market. In addition to personal connections and profiles, many corporations now use social networks as a way of connecting with consumers by harvesting data in user profiles and displaying relevant advertising, garnering product feedback, and offering coupons and other incentives for purchasing their products and services.

Expanding on promoting products for the first time using social networks, in 2005, the band Arctic Monkeys made history when its first single was released without an album and climbed to number one on the charts in the United Kingdom. Instead of gathering momentum from an album release or a tour, the band used its Myspace profile to "release" and publicize the single. The band used Myspace to successfully connect with its audience by capitalizing on the social network's popularity, something that had never been done before.

Facebook is a particularly attractive site for advertisers because of its large number of active users—800 million and counting—and more than 50% of its users check their Facebook pages daily. Now the largest social network in the world, Facebook has become an essential communication tool for individuals and a valuable marketing tool for corporations: Even something as commonplace as a brand of toilet paper has a Facebook page. Political candidates, grassroots campaigns, television programs, and millions of businesses have Facebook pages that are an integral part of their marketing efforts. Figure 5-14 shows the Help page for Facebook; notice how many help topics relate to business use of this social network.

TIP

Some industry analysts have estimated Facebook's annual revenues to be in excess of $1 billion, mostly from advertising.

Figure 5-14   Facebook Help Center page

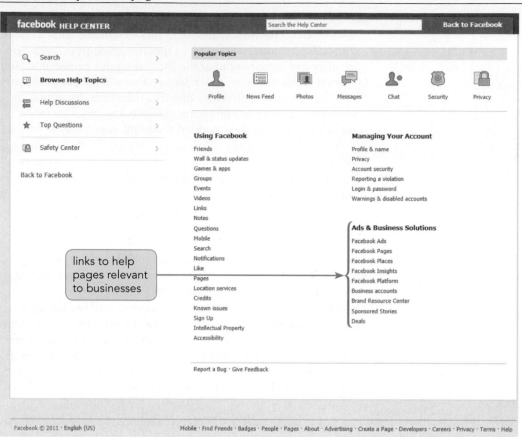

Facebook ©2011

In 2011, Facebook was still a privately held company despite purchase offers from Yahoo! and Google. Founder and CEO Mark Zuckerberg, who owns the largest share of Facebook, has stated that the company will remain private to fulfill its mission statement of providing new technologies and innovative ways to connect people in natural ways. However, in early 2012, there was speculation in the business community that Facebook would become a publicly traded company at some point in the future. The Facebook sign up page includes the slogan, "It's free and always will be." Because of the enormous success of Facebook's social network and advertising models, becoming a publicly traded company most likely will not change the way the Facebook site operates.

Online Business Networks

LinkedIn, a social network started in 2003 for business professionals, has more than 135 million individual members who use the site to make connections to other professionals and companies around the world, and to build an online résumé. More than 2 million companies around the world use the site to connect with professionals, professional networks, and other companies as a recruiting and marketing tool. LinkedIn is just one of many sites that focus primarily on professional networking, but it is the largest. Other business network sites, such as Ryze (for "rise up," with 500,000 members) and Sermo (a site restricted to credentialed U.S. physicians that has more than 120,000 members), are smaller but still connect business professionals. Users of these sites are usually seeking jobs, searching for potential business partners, recruiting workers, joining professional networks, exchanging ideas, and engaging in other business development and career activities.

Users of online business networks are not looking to build social connections to users like those on Facebook. Online business networks are used by people and organizations that are looking for specific business solutions, such as a company recruiting employees with specific skills, a vendor hoping to place its product in a particular retail outlet, or an organization searching for a consultant who can provide assistance on a specific topic. Online business networks tend to use categories that reflect these specific interests and try to make it easy for businesspeople to find the connections they need as quickly and efficiently as possible. Figure 5-15 shows the "What is LinkedIn?" page, which illustrates the ways that the LinkedIn site connects its users.

| Figure 5-15 | What is LinkedIn? page |

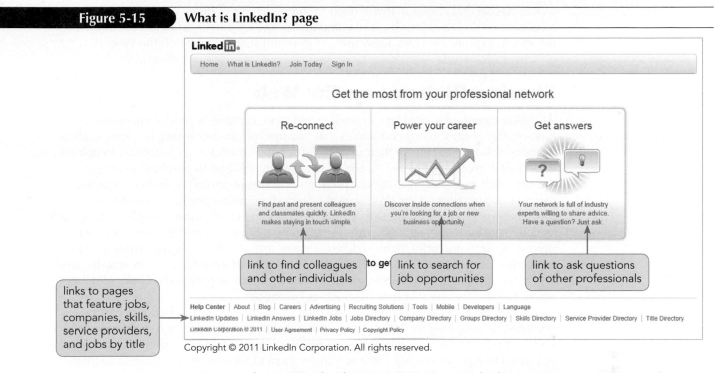

Copyright © 2011 LinkedIn Corporation. All rights reserved.

As part of promoting her business, Kay uses a LinkedIn account to connect to colleagues and clients. She hasn't explored the part of the LinkedIn site that lets users ask and answer questions, so she decides to view those pages next.

To learn more about LinkedIn:

1. On the Weblinks page for Session 5.2, click the **What is LinkedIn? page** link under the Business Networks heading. The page shown in Figure 5-15 opens.

2. In the Get answers box, click the **Just ask** link. The LinkedIn Answers page opens. Professionals can use this page to ask questions, which are mostly related to specific business needs and industries. The Browse section on the right side of the page lists questions by topic, such as "Hiring and Human Resources."

   Trouble? If LinkedIn redesigns its site and you cannot find the page described in Steps 1 and 2, click the LinkedIn Answers link at the bottom of the home page to open the LinkedIn Answers page. If this page is no longer available or requires a login, explore the parts of the LinkedIn site that are available without logging in.

> **3.** Scroll down the page and examine some of the questions posed by users. Notice that many of the questions are written in languages other than English, a fact that reflects the worldwide use of the LinkedIn site.

> **4.** On the right side of the page, click a link to a category that might interest Kay and explore some of the questions posed by users.

> **5.** Return to the Weblinks page for Tutorial 5.

Kay has several clients that will need to share pictures of items such as homes for sale, custom-designed jewelry, and company-sponsored events on their Web sites. She decides to explore sites that allow users to post and share pictures on the Web.

Sharing Pictures on the Web

As digital cameras became less expensive and more capable of producing extremely high-quality photos, many companies that provided photo-processing services, such as drugstores, began to change their offerings. They started allowing consumers to upload their digital images to a Web site and print photographs, and to purchase items sold by the site (such as coffee cups, mouse pads, and t-shirts) imprinted with those images. Eventually, new sites on the Web started offering these same services plus enhanced tools that made it easy for users to upload pictures and create more complex items, such as calendars and Web galleries. These sites, such as Shutterfly and Snapfish, let users upload pictures and print them in different ways, and also let users share their pictures with other users. Some sites, such as Flickr, have evolved even further and now let users tag images by category or person and share these photos as part of the Flickr social network or with other social networks, such as Facebook.

These sites, generally called photo-sharing sites, enable users to become part of a community by uploading their images from a digital camera or from a mobile device, and then posting them for other users to see. In many of these sites, users can add photos uploaded to a photo-sharing site and transfer them to their Facebook page or to their blog to share them with their existing networks of friends. Many of these sites let users post photos for free, up to a certain online storage limit. In this case, the site might be supported by advertisements that target users based on the content of the photographs they upload; other sites impose fees for all users.

Sharing photos on the Web can be done privately or publicly, depending on your goal. Almost every site includes features that let you post photos and restrict who can view them by sending invitations to view your gallery through email messages to authorized users. Other sites let you post your photos and make them available to any user.

Kay decides to explore the Flickr site next so that she will be prepared to discuss the functionality of a photo-sharing site with clients that will share different types of photos with their customers.

To learn more about sharing photos on the Web:

> **1.** In the Photo-Sharing Sites section of the Tutorial 5 Weblinks page, lick the **Flickr** link to open the site's home page, which is shown in Figure 5-16 (your page might differ).

Figure 5-16   Flickr home page

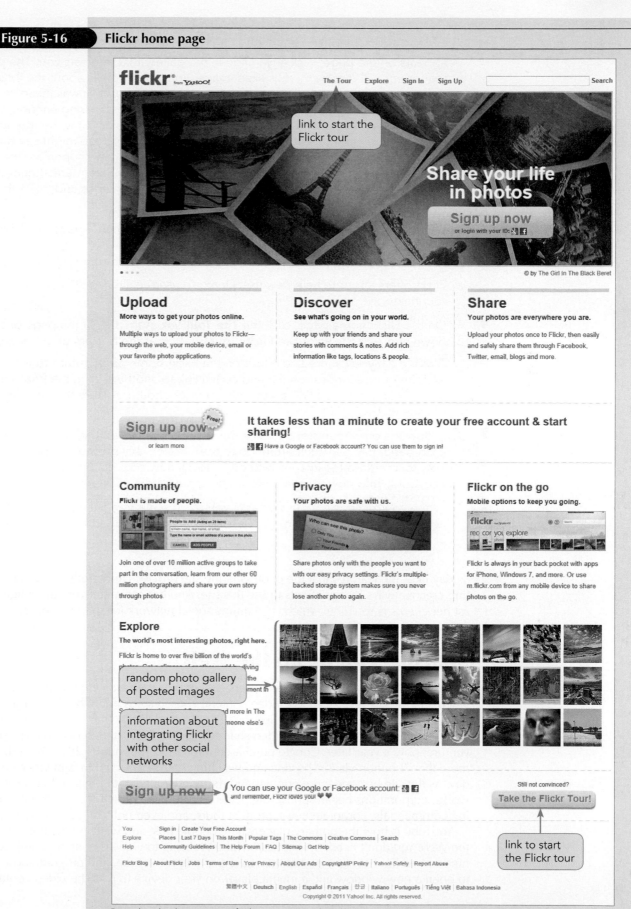

2. Scroll down the page and examine its contents. Notice the photo gallery that appears on the page; click any image in the gallery that interests you. The page that opens will display the full-sized image along with details about the image, such as the photographer's name, where and when the photo was taken, and a caption describing the image. If the image has been posted long enough, you might see feedback about the image from other Flickr users; it is this interaction with other users that creates a social network. In addition, you might see tags that assign categories to the photo. Clicking one of these tags will open another page of photos related to that category. As users find images that interest them, they can create connections to the photographers of those images and make them part of their social network.

3. Click your browser's **Back** button to return to the Flickr home page, and then click another picture in the gallery and explore the page that opens to learn more about the photograph. When you have finished, return to the Flickr home page.

Flickr offers a tour to help new users learn to use the site. You'll explore this tour next.

4. On the Flickr home page, click the **The Tour** link at the top of the page or scroll down and click the **Take the Flickr Tour!** button at the bottom of the page.

Trouble? If you cannot find a tour on the Flickr home page, return to the Weblinks page for Session 5.2 and click a link to another site in the Photo-Sharing Sites section until you find a site with a tour or another feature that explains how the site works.

5. Follow the on-screen steps to take the tour, being sure to read the content on each page. Pay particular attention to the site's privacy settings for photographs; how to integrate the images with other social networks, such as Twitter and Facebook; and how to create blogs and groups from your photos.

6. When you reach the page that asks you to create a free account and log in, return to the Weblinks page for Session 5.2. (Do not log in or create an account at this time.)

Kay likes the features that the photo-sharing site provides and predicts that she might find creative ways for her clients to use this site. Another social network that might interest her clients is YouTube, which is an online social network for sharing videos.

Sharing Videos on the Web

Similar to photo-sharing sites, where users post photos to share with other users, a video-sharing site lets users post video content. These videos might be short clips shot from someone's cell phone, or professionally produced movie trailers, news segments, or interviews. The most popular video-sharing site, YouTube, started in 2005 as a private venture; only a year later, Google purchased it for $1.65 billion. By 2011, YouTube had more than 2 billion visitors posting and watching hundreds of millions of videos each day. As the site became more popular and more integrated with other online social networks, corporations began sponsoring pages and uploading their own material, including commercials, corporate news, product tours, and even political ads and rallies.

YouTube is now the primary place where people post and watch video content on the Web. You don't need to visit the YouTube Web site to view its content; many companies embed links to content that they have posted on YouTube, and program those links to open a new window and a media player on your device to play the video content directly from their Web page. For example, Figure 5-17 shows a video playing on the MindTap About Us page. This video, produced by Cengage Learning, includes an explanation of the company's philosophy and innovations in textbook publishing. Cengage Learning also posted this video to its accounts on other social networking sites, including Twitter, Facebook, and YouTube, and included links to these sites on the page so visitors can easily view MindTap content on these other sites.

Figure 5-17   Video playing on the MindTap About Us page

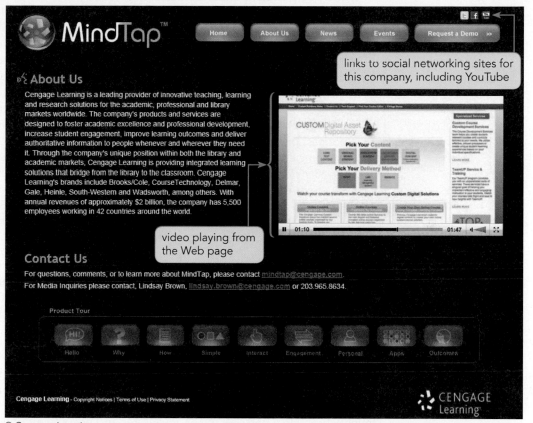

© Cengage Learning

Although YouTube is the most popular and active video-sharing site on the Internet, most other portals, such as Yahoo! and Bing, also include dedicated sites where users can post and share videos. In some cases, you'll find the same video posted on multiple sites, and also on the owner's site. For example, the video that appears in Figure 5-17 also appears on YouTube.

When YouTube first started, it was immediately popular with people who were already participating in well-established social networks. Word of mouth traveled quickly, and users began uploading and sharing video content on YouTube. The site didn't really need to advertise itself: Its innovative approach became a social network of its own, and the people using YouTube were quick and eager to pass it on. YouTube now has strategic partnerships with many major television and cable networks and music labels to broadcast their content. In addition to these partnerships, YouTube relies heavily on display ad placement, brand channels (advertising focused on a specific brand), and contests to generate revenue.

INSIGHT

Effectively Searching Video-Sharing Sites

Aside from users posting videos of their pets doing tricks or something funny, amateur athletic events, world events, or other human interest stories, YouTube and other sites that let users post video content are also a repository for millions of commercially uploaded segments, such as professional sporting events, movie trailers, unaired alternate endings for television shows, news broadcast segments, commercials, and seminars by corporations and individuals. The videos you'll find on these sites range from low-quality videos shot with a cell phone camera to commercial-quality, high definition, professionally produced segments.

Depending on your reason for visiting a video-sharing site, you might find something that makes you laugh, or find videos to supplement or begin a research project or to increase your knowledge about a specific topic. Most video-sharing sites let users tag content, which makes it easy to find video content related to research projects or specific subjects. In addition, these sites include search tools that let you search for video content with keywords or by browsing categories, much like you would search for a podcast or blog.

When viewing content on a video-sharing site, you need to use the same skills you learned in Tutorial 3 to properly investigate the site's source and creator so you can evaluate its credibility. Most video-sharing sites include categories that let users add their videos to channels, some of which include titles such as "Science & Technology" or "Politics and Current Events." Depending on the source of these videos, they might contain information that you can deem reliable.

You can visit the Web sites for YouTube and other video-sharing sites by using the links in the Video-Sharing Sites section of the Weblinks page for Tutorial 5.

Blogs

As you learned in Tutorial 4, a blog is a Web site that is published to express the blogger's opinions about a particular topic. The blog's author, usually a person or a specific organization, often invites the blog's readers to add comments to the blog entries. A blog might chronicle a person's life or adventures and become an online personal journal, or it might function as a forum to communicate political, religious, or other opinions of groups of people. Some blogs function much like news organizations by disseminating information about a specific story or from a specific organization. A blog might contain only text and comments, but it usually includes photographs, links, videos, and other content, and lets readers integrate the blog content they are viewing into their own social networks by clicking buttons for Facebook, email, and other social networks.

Figure 5-18 shows a page from the official blog of the Federal Communications Commission, an agency that regulates interstate and international radio, television, wire, satellite, and cable communication in the United States. Notice that the blog includes tools that the blog's reader can use to repost the blog's content on other social networks. Clicking the Facebook share link, for example, lets a reader log in to a Facebook account and post the blog's content on the reader's Facebook page, thus sharing the content with other communities.

Figure 5-18   **Official FCC Blog page**

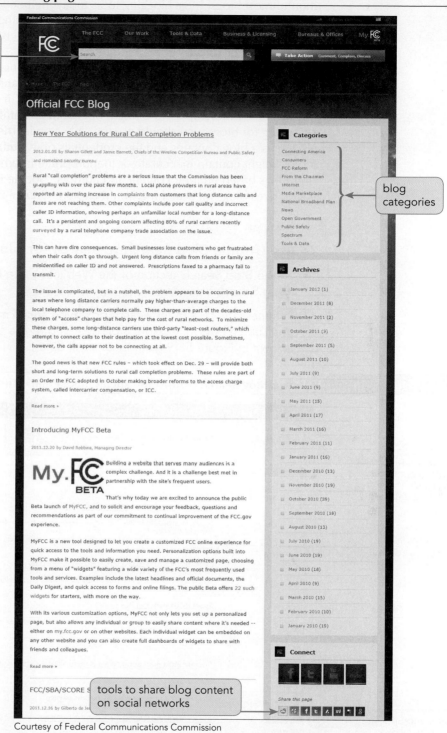

use this box to search the blog using keywords

blog categories

tools to share blog content on social networks

Courtesy of Federal Communications Commission

Many blogs are published using free blogging tools available from sites such as Blogger, WordPress, and Windows Live Writer to publish content to the author's own Web site or to a subdomain on the host's Web site. These blogging tools often include templates that format the blog's content and provide the blog's overall design, create a form to post comments, create a **widget** of tools to post the content on other sites, and provide code snippets to create hyperlinks and embed photos in the postings. As postings are added to the blog, they appear at the top of the comments section, with older postings appearing below the newer ones. This chronological method of posting is common to most blogs. Most blogging tools today include features that let the blog's author update the blog's content from a mobile device, making it possible for the blog's content to be updated constantly. You can use the links in the Blogs section on the Weblinks page for Tutorial 5 to visit different blogging sites.

Because anyone can write a blog, there are millions of them on the Internet. Some are from reporters working for well-known news organizations such as *The New York Times*, CNN, ZDNet, Reuters, and local newspapers in many U.S. markets. Other blogs are written by individuals who might not claim any affiliation to an organization. When searching for blogs, you should use the skills you learned in Tutorial 3 to evaluate the resources a blog contains and the credentials of its authors. Just like any other Web site, a blog might contain inaccurate or inappropriate information. Fortunately, it is easy to find blogs based on their content and authors. Google Blog Search is one resource that categorizes blogs for searching. You'll explore Google Blog Search next.

To use Google Blog Search to search for blogs:

1. In the Blog Search section of the Weblinks page for Session 5.2, click the **Google Blog Search** link.

2. If necessary, click in the search box, type **social media marketing**, and then click the search button. Google Blog Search opens a search page, similar to the one shown in Figure 5-19 (your results will differ).

Figure 5-19	Google Blog Search results for "social media marketing"

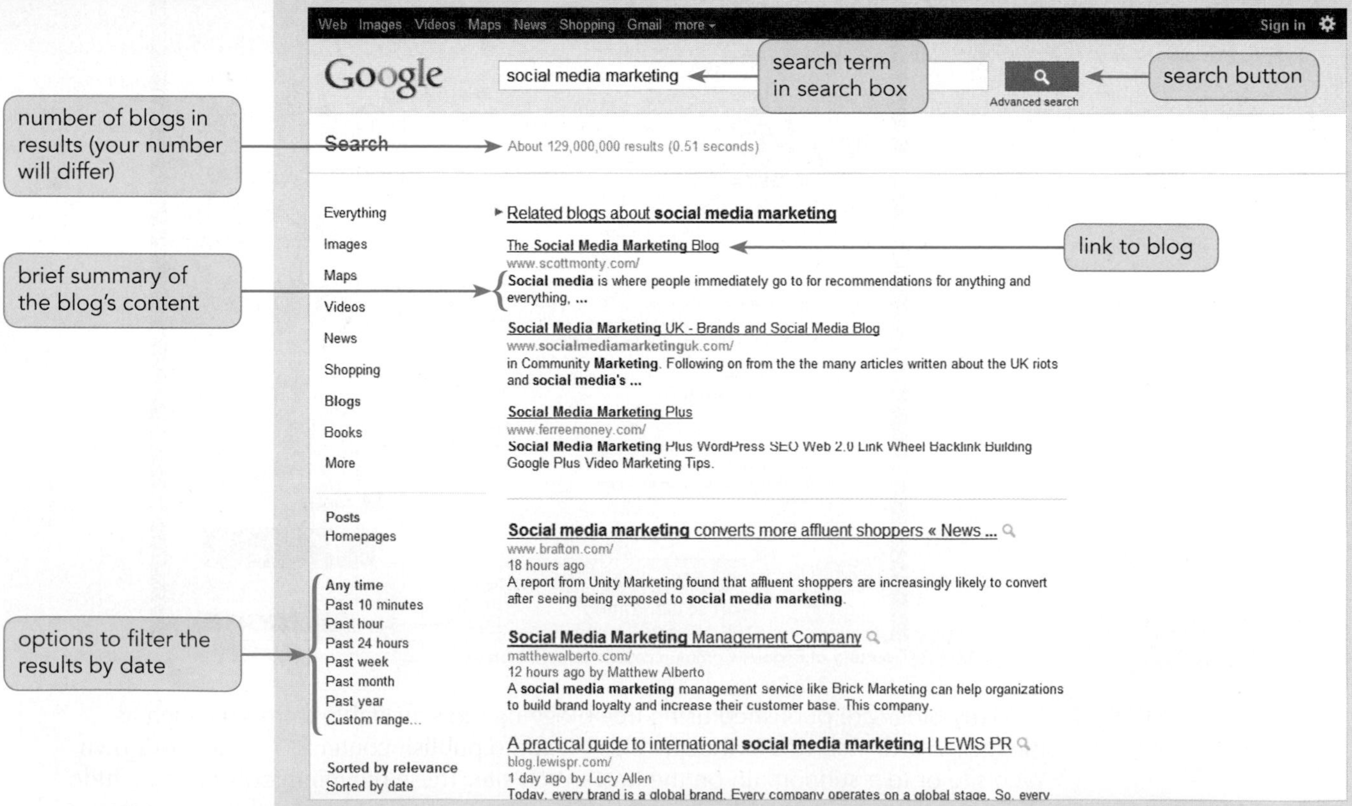

© Google

The Google Blog Search shown in Figure 5-19 returned links to millions of post-ings related to the search text, "social media marketing." Each blog posting includes a link to the blog's source and to the complete posting, a brief summary of the posting, and a link to the site. You can use the feature on the left side of the page to fine-tune your search to a specific time period, such as "Past 10 min-utes," or a custom date that you specify after clicking the "Custom range" link.

  3. Explore some of the links to the listed blogs that contain relevant information to the search topic. Then use the evaluation skills you learned in Tutorial 3 to exam-ine the information listed about the site and its author(s) to get a sense of the site's credentials with regard to whether this site produces expert, documented content on social media marketing research and trends, or is more geared toward expressing individual opinions.

  4. Close your browser.

Microblogs

The popularity of using blogs to create an online personal journal, combined with the proliferation of Internet-connected devices, resulted in a new type of blog called a microblog. A microblog is a form of blogging that sends short messages—usually 140 characters or less—on a very frequent schedule. Whereas a blogger might spend hours updating his or her blog daily, weekly, or monthly with long posts that include text, photos, and links, a microblogger might update his or her content hourly or even more frequently using just a few words or a single sentence. The content of a microblog differs from that of a traditional blog in that it answers the question, "What are you doing?" A microblogger might send one sentence or a few words to describe what's going on in his or her life at that exact moment, whereas a blogger might take several hours to describe a vacation or express an opinion.

Microblog postings are sometimes called **tweets**, and the act of microblogging is sometimes called **tweeting**; both terms are references to the popular microblog Web site, Twitter. The Twitter page for CengageBrain, a companion site for this textbook's publisher, is shown in Figure 5-20.

Figure 5-20 **Twitter page for CengageBrain**

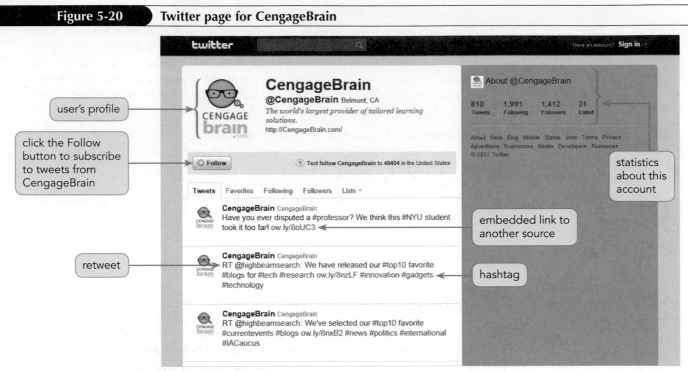

© Cengage Learning

To post content using a microblog such as Twitter, you need to create an account. To read the content of someone else's microblog, you choose the option to follow that person's or organization's account. In microblogging, the term **follower** identifies a person or an organization who is receiving your updates. You don't need to create an account to view someone else's postings; you can simply go to the microblog's Web site and find his or her page of postings and read it. However, if you already have an account, you can become a follower, in which case the updates appear in your microblog account as soon as they are posted by other users. You might receive content through your account on the microblog Web page, or via instant or text messages on a wireless device.

Because many people use cell phones to post and receive content on their microblogs, and messages are usually limited to fewer than 140 characters, many microbloggers use the same text message acronyms that you find in instant messages. Just like in a blog, as you post content, it might be read by your friends or by people you don't know. It is this act of following people on a microblog that makes it social.

Postings on a microblog site, such as the Twitter site shown in Figure 5-20, show up as individual messages. The person or organization that posted the message appears in bold; in Figure 5-20, the postings are all by the user named "CengageBrain." The postings are all very short, concise messages. Some of the postings include an embedded link to a photo or video; these links are shown in red and, when clicked, load the photo or other embedded content on the user's device. Notice that the link name is just a generated link and not a URL to a site or photo.

In addition, users include user-defined keywords called **hashtags** to create topical categories that link to other messages with the same hashtags. For example, in Figure 5-20, the hashtags #professor, #technology, and #currentevents in the first, second, and third messages indicate that the author is linking messages to other messages on the Twitter network related to these categories. Clicking a hashtag provides a listing of all other messages that include the same hashtag to link together the messages and their authors. You will also find hashtags related to people's moods (such as #bummedout to indicate a letdown or #soexcited for something exciting happening) or their location (such as #Boston). Because users can create new hashtags based on any single keyword or combination of keywords (which contain more than one word, without spaces), millions of them appear in messages on the network. As users include messages with hashtags, their messages become linked together. This linking of messages and their followers, in addition to the messages themselves, creates the social network of the microblog.

Similar to the evolution of blogs, microblogs have gained popularity beyond the online personal journal and are now widely used for a variety of purposes. Many organizations, including well-known retailers and educational institutions, now use microblogs to communicate with customers, students, and other types of followers. Many actors and politicians have Twitter accounts and use them to communicate with their followers; Twitter provides a way to interact with fans and voter bases. Some microblogs, such as Yammer, are used by companies and other organizations to provide a private social network for employees to use to communicate about work-related business by restricting followers to people with valid email addresses from the organization. Other microblogs let you create private groups that also might be suitable for business communication.

TIP

A **retweet** happens when a user forwards a message to another user.

Social Media: You Can't Always "Take It Back"

Although social media sites can have a very positive impact on the way their users interact with the world, they can also have a very real and very negative impact on individual users. According to Merriam-Webster Online, one definition of a scandal is the "loss of or damage to reputation caused by actual or apparent violation of morality or propriety." For centuries, individuals, groups, and organizations have been victims of scandals of all types. In the 21st century, however, the visibility of scandals has increased dramatically due to the speed at which information travels over social networks and the Internet. In the past several years, social media have quickly communicated scandals, sometimes within minutes of their occurrences. For example, consider the following news stories from 2011:

- After a major earthquake and a tsunami caused billions of dollars of damage and resulted in the deaths of thousands of people in Japan, comedian Gilbert Gottfried used his Twitter account to make jokes about the disaster. A sponsor who used Gottfried's voice in its advertising campaign terminated his contract after the incident.
- Both Congressman Christopher Lee and Congressman Anthony Weiner resigned from the House of Representatives after admitting to sending inappropriate photographs over the Internet.

Other lapses in judgment occur every day by users of social networks, but they aren't as well publicized and immediately forwarded to thousands or millions of users in an instant. News organizations regularly report about instances in which employees disparage their employers or coworkers on their personal Facebook pages, or students breach university rules and attest to their indiscretions with photographs posted on their Twitter accounts. For some people, the end result of these incidents is being fired or expelled.

The immediacy of social networks can provide important details about unfolding events, such as crises. But this immediate communication should be treated with the same respect that is found in other forums that are not electronic. Before you post something on a social network, you should consider the following:

- Evaluate who can access your comments. Even if you change your account settings to share your posts only with friends that you designate, your friends might forward your posts to other users. If you intend for your posts to be private, the only way to ensure privacy is to not post them at all.
- Consider your state of mind when posting comments. A good rule is to avoid posting comments when you are upset or angry, and to make sure that you confirm your facts. Attempts at jokes might be misinterpreted or misunderstood, especially when the reader has no way to gauge the seriousness of your comments. A comment that you posted in jest might seem real to another person.
- Don't say something online that you wouldn't say in person. The isolation of typing comments makes some people bolder and causes them to say something that they might later regret. Before submitting or sending content, consider whether you would say the same thing in exactly the same way in front of a large group of people in an auditorium. If you wouldn't, then you shouldn't say it online, either.

The most important consideration when using social media is to remember that it is very difficult to take comments back because comments you post appear in all of your friend's feeds. If you do find yourself in a situation in which you made a mistake, be quick to delete the offensive comment and to apologize to the parties involved.

You can use the links in the Microblogs section on the Weblinks page for Tutorial 5 to visit the Web sites for different microblogging sites.

Protecting Your Privacy and Identity on Social Networks

Social and business networks can be powerful tools for keeping in touch with friends and family, communicating with business associates, or locating people around the world who share your hobbies and interests. However, the very nature of these open networks can result in problems for users who are not careful about how they use them. When creating a profile on an online social network, consider the following:

- There is a strong likelihood that many people in the world share your same name and maybe even some common life details. When you contact someone as a "friend" through the network, you might not be contacting the correct person—you might just be contacting someone with the same name. Likewise, you could be contacting someone who is pretending to be someone else.

- Some sites have restricted areas or prohibit use for underage users; but with millions of users, it's likely that some of them will be able to access restricted content simply by falsifying their age. Parents need to be especially diligent to monitor the use of online social networking by minors to protect their privacy and the material they view while online. In response to this and other problems associated with minors using social networking sites, some school districts in the United States have blocked access to Facebook, Twitter, and other online social networks on their school computers in an attempt to protect children from inappropriate content and Internet predators. Many corporations and large organizations, such as the Department of Defense, also block their computers from accessing online social networks. Many do so for the sake of "security," but some admit that the blocks occur because employees waste too much time at work visiting these sites.

- **Cyberbullying**—using Internet communication such as email, text and instant messages, blogs, microblogs, or social networks to harass, threaten, or intimidate someone—is a problem usually associated with children but can involve adults as well. Most online social networks have codes of conduct that establish penalties for this type of behavior, which should be reported immediately. In addition, the site's Help section usually outlines the steps you can take to prevent cyberbullies from contacting you again and to report them to the network's administration.

- Because the nature of an online social network requires you to provide real information about yourself—your name, hometown, education, birth date, picture, and other personal information—and because this information you provide, by design, is made public, you might be putting yourself at risk for identity theft and other privacy problems. Most sites include tools that let you hide parts of your profile from other users until you give them permission to access your complete profile. Be sure to read the site's privacy policy and change the default security settings as necessary to protect your privacy in a way that makes you feel comfortable and secure when using the site. However, keep in mind that the contacts you have on these social networks have access to your information, and so do all of their contacts. A member with 20 contacts might feel comfortable sharing personal information with those 20 contacts, but must be mindful of the fact that each of those 20 contacts can share your information with their contacts—some of whom are strangers to you.

Protecting Your Reputation

In addition to protecting your privacy and identity, it's important to protect your reputation and control the information that you make available to the public. The information you post on a social network is public—and it is often archived even after you delete it. Many employers check Twitter, Facebook, and other online social networks for information that you have posted about yourself. Applicants with exemplary résumés are often passed over for interviews when their Twitter accounts or Facebook pages show them acting in ways that are inappropriate for a corporate culture.

Schools are especially careful to monitor online sites; most parents would demand action from school districts if they find that their child's teacher is participating in inappropriate online behavior, even if that behavior is on his or her "own time." Some universities have policies that prevent student athletes from creating profiles on Facebook and other sites. Although the reasons for these bans vary, one stated reason is to protect the privacy of athletes, some of whom travel significantly as part of their involvement in a student athletic program. Another stated reason is to protect the reputation of the school; some universities view student athletes as "ambassadors" of the university, and having athletes involved in inappropriate behavior documented on their online profiles could result in an embarrassment to the school and other athletes.

Another issue related to privacy is the use of your online profile by people in positions of authority. On several college campuses across the United States, students' online profiles provided proof that they violated the code of conduct agreements that they signed when they became tenants of student housing. In one case, students at North Carolina State University took pictures of themselves in a dorm room while consuming alcohol. One of the students posted pictures of the party on his Facebook page. When a university official found the pictures, they became proof of the violation to the student housing contract and proof of the students' underage drinking. In similar cases on other college campuses, the students were suspended. At some schools, students regarded this lurking by university officials on online sites as an invasion of privacy. Other schools have updated their codes of conduct to specifically authorize the monitoring of students' online profiles as a legal way of taking action against a student when inappropriate or illegal behavior is proven with information students post on their profiles.

Unfortunately, sometimes the online content that is posted about a specific person or a business might not be true, resulting in damage to his or her online reputation, or the information might be true and cause problems with job applications or required background screenings for different reasons. When the information posted is not true, you might need to employ the services of a reputation management firm to help remove it. These types of businesses are becoming more prevalent on the Internet as a way to help people and organizations monitor their online reputation and, when necessary, work to clear any offensive or negative content from online social networks, blogs, and other sites. ReputationDefender, a product of one such company that specializes in online reputation management, is shown in Figure 5-21. You can explore this site and other online reputation management firms by clicking the links in the Monitoring Your Online Reputation section of the Weblinks page for Tutorial 5.

Figure 5-21   ReputationDefender product page

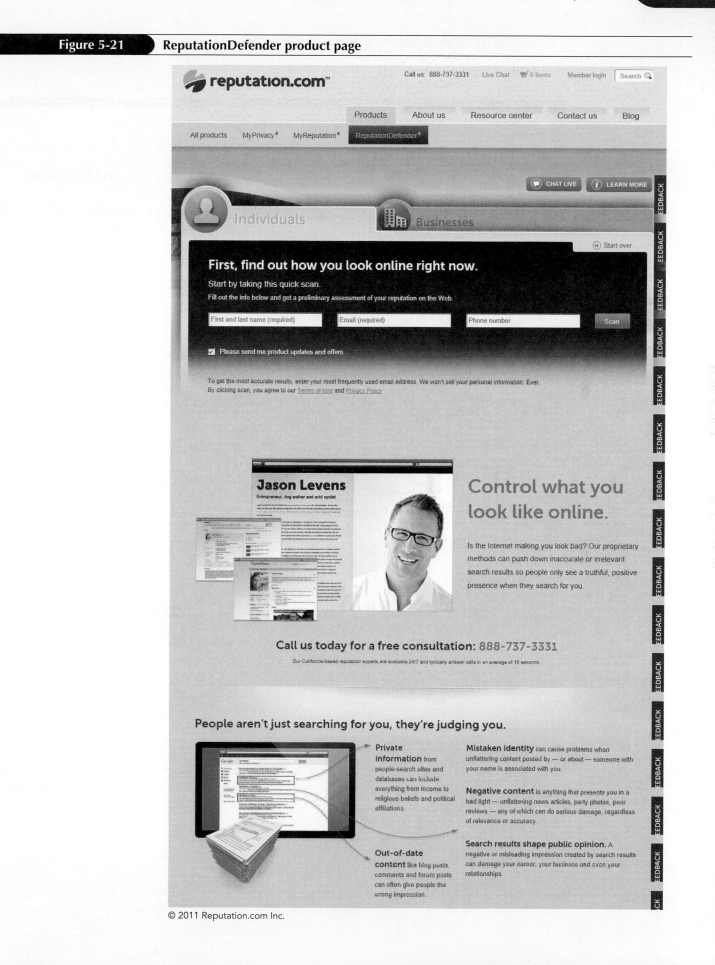

Kay is confident that she can use the information she found while exploring the different push technologies to enhance the communication strategies of her own new business and of her new clients.

Session 5.2 Quick Check

REVIEW

1. What is lurking?
2. What is VoIP? What is the primary advantage and primary disadvantage of using VoIP for residential telephone service?
3. How do most social networks earn the necessary income to run their sites?
4. What feature of a photo-sharing site makes it social?
5. What is a hashtag? How and where is it used?
6. What is cyberbullying?

Practice the skills you learned in the tutorial using the same case scenario.

PRACTICE

Review Assignments

There are no Data Files needed for the Review Assignments.

Shilling Social Media has just been hired by the local school district's board of trustees to help identify how the district can use social media to improve communication with students and parents. The district has a Web site and in the past has relied on it to communicate information about important school events, school board elections, and other important district information. Last year, several natural disasters occurred during the school day and required immediate communication with parents, which exposed the district's lack of planning to facilitate an emergency communication method with parents. To address this problem and enhance overall communication with students and parents, the district wants to explore using social networks. Kay Shilling knows that electronic communication with minors adds a layer of complexity to any marketing campaign, so she needs to research the acceptable use guidelines and other rules of the sites the district plans to use to make sure that the district operates within established legal and site guidelines. Complete the following steps:

1. Start your Web browser, go to **www.cengagebrain.com**, open the Tutorial 5 Weblinks page, and then click the Review Assignments link.

2. Click a link in the Chat & Instant Messaging section, and then explore the site to learn about its features, paying particular attention to the district's communication needs. Determine if this site might be a good way to communicate with parents in general and during emergencies. Explore the site's terms of use (or terms of service) and privacy policies to determine if there are any limits on minors under the age of 18 or another specific age using the site. In a report, note your findings about this site in the first paragraph.

3. Return to the Weblinks page for the Review Assignments, and then choose another link in the Chat & Instant Messaging section. Repeat Step 2 to evaluate this site, and then add your findings to the second paragraph of your report.

4. Return to the Weblinks page for the Review Assignments, and then explore at least two of the sites in the Photo- & Video-Sharing Sites section. Repeat Step 2 to evaluate the site, and then add your findings to the next two paragraphs of your report.

5. Return to the Weblinks page for the Review Assignments, and then explore at least two of the sites in the Social Networks section. Repeat Step 2 to evaluate the site, and then add your findings to the next two paragraphs of your report.

6. Close your browser.

7. In the final paragraphs of your report, evaluate the information you found by answering the following questions and supporting your answers with details from the sites that you visited:

   a. Which of the communication tools that you evaluated would best fulfill the district's goal of enhancing general communication with parents? Which of the communication tools that you evaluated would best fulfill the district's goal of providing a method of communicating with parents in an emergency? Why did you make these choices?

   b. If any of the sites have policies restricting the use of the site by minors, would you still recommend that the district use the site to communicate? Why or why not?

   c. Do any of the sites that you are recommending have features that will make it easy for the district to integrate its different communication strategies with other online sites? What are these features and which sites do they integrate with?

d. For the communication tools that you recommended in Step 7a, what kind of opportunities does the district have if it chooses these tools? For example, how could the district use a photo-sharing site or a microblog?

e. Based on your research and with regard to communication with minors, are there any networks or sites that the district should not use? Why or why not?

APPLY

Learn more about using tags to categorize images at photo-sharing sites.

Case Problem 1

There are no Data Files needed for this Case Problem.

Biology II   Before Bruce Hill became a high school biology teacher, he studied and worked as a botanist who collected, analyzed, and studied the life cycle of plants. Consequently, botany is his favorite unit to teach to his high school class. A project he assigns asks his students to collect 30 samples of indigenous wildflowers and prepare a notebook that includes the plant sample, photographs of the plant in its wild state, the plant's common and scientific names, and details about the plant's habitat, growing cycle, and other pertinent information. Over the years, Bruce has amassed a large, personal collection of wildflowers and frequently uses his pictures to help students identify their own samples. During class last week, one of his students suggested that he create an account for the class on a Web site so the students could upload their photos and contribute to his collection. Bruce thinks that this is a great idea and decides to explore using a photo-sharing site on the Internet to collect the photos. Because of his interest in botany, he is also interested in connecting to other teachers who might be assigning similar projects, so he can expand his plant collection beyond the geographic area of his school. Complete the following steps:

1. Start your Web browser, go to **www.cengagebrain.com**, open the Tutorial 5 Weblinks page, and then click the Case Problem 1 link.

2. Click one of the links to a photo-sharing site and use the site to learn more about tagging photos. A good starting point is to search the site's Help feature for the word "tag" or to examine the frequently asked questions page. As you are reviewing the information you find, note the site's suggestions for tagging content. After you are finished, use the site to examine photos with tags related to botany, such as specific wildflower or plant names. If you need help determining your search text, use a search engine to find the names of flowers and plants, and then return to the photo-sharing site to enter those names and search for them.

3. After searching the site, review the site's community guidelines, its terms of use, or a similarly named page to make sure that the site is appropriate for high school sophomores who are at least 15 years old.

4. Return to the Weblinks page for Case Problem 1, and then click another site in the Case Problem 1 section. Repeat Steps 2 and 3 for the second site.

5. Close your browser.

⊕ EXPLORE

6. In a report containing two to four paragraphs, answer the following questions:

a. Can the photo-sharing sites you visited support the use that Mr. Hill proposes, as explained in the introductory paragraph at the beginning of this case problem? Why or why not?

b. Do either of the sites you visited have restrictions that might limit the use of the site by high school sophomores? If so, what are these restrictions?

c. Which site do you think would be better for Mr. Hill to use? Why?

d. Do you think that Mr. Hill's intention of connecting with other high school biology teachers through his photos is possible? Why or why not?

Investigate online business networks to learn more about their career-building features.

RESEARCH

Case Problem 2

There are no Data Files needed for this Case Problem.

Garrett Cordero, RN, BSN, CNP   After working for several years as a Registered Nurse, Garrett Cordero studied at Northern Arizona University to complete his master's degree in nursing. He recently finished his training and completed the licensing requirements to become a Certified Nurse Practitioner (CNP), with a specialty in pediatrics. As a pediatric CNP, Garrett will work under a physician's supervision to provide routine medical care for children under the age of 18. He worked with the university's career services department before he graduated and secured a job working for a physician in Scottsdale, Arizona. Garrett will be relocating to Scottsdale in a few weeks, and he is interested in connecting with other CNPs in the area to start building a network of friends and colleagues who can help him with his transition to his new job and his new community. He asks you to help him establish these connections. Complete the following steps:

1. Start your Web browser, go to **www.cengagebrain.com**, open the Tutorial 5 Weblinks page, and then click the Case Problem 2 link.

⊕EXPLORE

2. Click one of the links to a professional network and explore the site to determine if the site provides specific social groups for recent college graduates in the nursing field. As you explore the site, evaluate the other resources the site offers and its ease of use. In addition, be on the lookout for links that might interest Garrett, such as relocation services, career advice, general advice for nursing professionals, or forums that let users ask questions or seek advice about nursing.

⊕EXPLORE

3. Return to the Weblinks page for Case Problem 2, and then evaluate the resources at another site.

4. In a report containing two to four paragraphs, describe your experiences at the sites and the quality of information they provide. In your report, recommend two features at the sites for Garrett to use to prepare for his new career, and explain your choices. In addition, evaluate the overall effectiveness of the sites in terms of their career-building features.

5. Close your browser.

Find and evaluate the privacy policies at several social networking sites.

RESEARCH

Case Problem 3

There are no Data Files needed for this Case Problem.

Lakeside Police Department   Detectives at the Lakeside Police Department, which patrols an area outside of Chicago, Illinois, have received several calls in the past month from victims of identity theft. In each case, the detectives traced the initiation of the theft back to the user's social networking page. As part of the department's community education division, detectives want to offer a course in protecting users' privacy and identity on social networking sites. Because the detectives have busy caseloads, they have asked for your help in researching some precautions users can take. As part of your research, they also would like you to visit a few sites and examine their privacy controls. Complete the following steps:

1. Start your Web browser, go to **www.cengagebrain.com**, open the Tutorial 5 Weblinks page, and then click the Case Problem 3 link.

2. Several of the Case Problem 3 links are to video content posted on YouTube. If your computer can play these videos, watch at least two of them and take notes about the steps the reporter or the person being interviewed suggests for protecting a user's identity on a social networking site, such as Facebook. (*Note:* If you cannot play these videos, skip this step.)

⊕ **EXPLORE**

3. Return to the Weblinks page for Case Problem 3, and then choose one of the non-video links. Search the site's home page for a link that will lead to information about the site's rules of conduct. (You should not need to log in or create an account to carry out this research.) Look for links titled "Terms of Service," "Code of Conduct," "Rules and Etiquette," "Terms of Use," or a similarly named link. You might also consult the provider's Help menu or a link to a Help system. If you cannot find any rules at the site you choose, return to the Weblinks page for Case Problem 3 and choose another site to use in your search. As you review the site's rules of conduct, search for information about the acceptable rules of use, age limits of participants, language guidelines, banned topics of conversation, and other items that would be of interest in protecting a person's privacy and identity. If you could watch the videos in Step 2, use the background information you found in the videos to help guide your exploration of the site. Be sure to evaluate the resources the site provides for reporting unacceptable behavior and the site's commitment to enforcing its rules.

4. After finding the rules at the first site you selected, return to the Weblinks page for Case Problem 3 and choose another site. Search this site for its rules of conduct.

5. After finding the rules at the second site you selected, return to the Weblinks page for Case Problem 3 and choose another site. Search this site for its rules of conduct.

⊕ **EXPLORE**

6. In a report containing four to six paragraphs, summarize your findings about what kinds of problems can result from having information posted on an online social network, and the methods the sites recommend to prevent these problems. In your opinion, does the burden of protecting an individual's online privacy and preventing identity theft fall on the individual using the network, the network itself, or both? What kinds of problems can be prevented by following the site's recommendations? Support your recommendations with facts you found at the sites you visited.

7. Close your browser.

Examine mashups to determine how they combine sources and generate revenue.

CHALLENGE

Case Problem 4

There are no Data Files needed for this Case Problem.

Evaluating Mashup Content and Ad Placement   In this tutorial, you learned about the technology that combines content from two or more Web sites to create a mashup. Because the technology that combines mashups is relatively simple and inexpensive or free, new mashups are added to the Web every day. Some mashups are created as public services, others are created for profit. In this Case Problem, you will review two mashup sites and evaluate the content that they contain, the origin of that content, and the advertising included on the site. Complete the following steps:

1. Start your Web browser, go to **www.cengagebrain.com**, open the Tutorial 5 Weblinks page, and then click the Case Problem 4 link. Click one of the sites in the list.

2. Evaluate the content on the site to determine where the data comes from. Your evaluation of the source data can come from information posted on the site or from your analysis of the content.

3. Note whether the site includes advertising and try to determine its source. How do the ads relate to the content you are viewing on the site? Do you see any ads that are relevant to the city or town in which your computer is connected? If so, how do you think that these ads were generated? If the site doesn't include ads, does it include another feature that might generate revenue?

4. Return to the Weblinks page for Case Problem 4, and then choose another site. Use the information provided in Steps 2 and 3 to evaluate the data and ads featured on the second site.

✛ **EXPLORE**   5. In a report containing two to four paragraphs, describe the content you evaluated in Step 2 and answer the questions in Step 3 for each Web site. How do the two sites you selected compare in terms of the information provided, their ease of use, and the advertising they feature? Use information on the sites to support your responses.

6. Close your browser.

Evaluate the resources at news organizations and compare them to directory content.

CHALLENGE

Case Problem 5

There are no Data Files needed for this Case Problem.

Evaluating Syndicated Information Resources   In this tutorial, you used directories to find information about blogs and podcasts. Almost all major newspapers and news organizations use blogs, podcasts, and feeds to provide information, in addition to their published editions and Web sites. When you are researching a specific topic, these news organizations can provide you with a broad range of information written by objective journalists, and opinions written by outside contributors and content experts. To see what information is available on the Web, you'll choose a search topic that interests you and then evaluate the information you find. Complete the following steps:

1. Start your Web browser, go to **www.cengagebrain.com**, open the Tutorial 5 Weblinks page, and then click the Case Problem 5 link.

✛ **EXPLORE**   2. Click a link to a feed, podcast, or blog resource. Review the site's content and find a category of information that interests you. For example, you might choose to explore health, sports, science, or Internet topics. Do not subscribe to anything, but use the links to the content to see the articles and postings available for a category. For example, clicking a health category might open a page with articles or postings about health topics. Review the material that you find and evaluate it to see if it fulfills your information needs. Click the individual links to open the postings so you can read them directly. If the content is not what you need, return to the categorical listing and choose another topic until you find one that you like.

✛ **EXPLORE**   3. Use the Web pages where the content is posted to evaluate the source of the postings. For several articles, note the author and the date the content was published, and then read a few paragraphs of each article to get a sense of whether the content expresses the author's opinion or contains objective reporting.

✛ **EXPLORE**   4. Return to the Weblinks page for Case Problem 5, and then click a link in the Blogs, Feeds, or Podcast Search section. Use the search feature of the site you selected to search for the same topic using the category you selected in Step 2. Use the links on the search results page to review a few of the sources.

✛ **EXPLORE**   5. In a report containing two to four paragraphs, discuss the content you viewed and evaluate the quality of the information at the news organization using the search directory. What is your impression of the content you viewed at the news organization? What is your impression of the same content you viewed using the blog, feeds, or podcast search directory? In your opinion, which option provides better information? Why?

6. Close your browser.

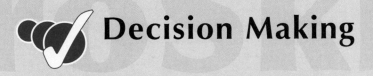

Decision Making

Evaluating Search Results

Decision making is the process of identifying, evaluating, and selecting a course of action in a specific situation or when solving a problem. The steps involved for making good decisions include the following:

1. Obtaining relevant information
2. Identifying possible courses of actions or solutions
3. Selecting the best course of action
4. Developing and implementing an action plan
5. Monitoring the result, verifying the accuracy of the decision, and taking corrective action, if needed

The Internet can be a valuable resource during the decision-making process.

Step 1: Obtaining Relevant Information

Before evaluating a potential course of action for a given situation or problem, you must gather the data and other information you need to make a decision. This data might be information that you obtain from people, reports, or other sources, such as blogs, podcasts, newsgroups, and news feeds. All of these resources can help you to understand the problem you are seeking to understand and solve.

Step 2: Identifying Possible Courses of Action or Solutions

After collecting information to help you solve a problem, you can identify courses of actions or solutions. Some decisions need to be made quickly, in which case, you must evaluate the information you find in a limited amount of time.

Step 3: Selecting the Best Course of Action

Once you have identified multiple courses of actions or solutions, you need decide on the best one. Sometimes, you might ask questions, such as:

- Which course of action make sense for the long term?
- Which course of action easily implemented, given the resources you have available?
- Are you comfortable with the course of action?

ProSkills

Step 4: Developing and Implementing an Action Plan

Once you have made a decision, you need to decide how to implement the necessary steps to put the decision into effect. You should have a pretty good idea of what the final outcome needs to look like in order to consider all relevant steps.

After making a decision, you can begin implementing a plan. As you complete your work, you can check off the required tasks as you complete them and assess your progress against the overall schedule. If you veer off schedule, you must be able to determine the cause of any problems and decide how to correct them.

Step 5: Monitoring Results and Verifying the Accuracy of the Decision

After implementing your plan, you should verify that your decision was correct and solved the problem you were working on. To assess the effect of the implemented plan, you can collect feedback from any affected parties to help you determine how well your solution worked.

PROSKILLS

Evaluating and Using Search Results in Decision Making

You make decisions every day: Some are as simple as what to eat for breakfast, and others are more complex, such as deciding which route to take from one location to another. Deciding how to get from one place to another can be a surprisingly complex decision in a city like New York. When making a decision, you should gather relevant information and then evaluate it in the context of criteria you have developed for evaluating that information to achieve the best decision outcome.

To decide which route is best, you will need to consider many factors, some of which will depend on the time of day (a taxi might be safer than the subway or walking if you are traveling late at night), how much time you have (are you on vacation and wanting to see the sights or are you late for a business meeting), and how much money you have to spend on this trip. You might also want to consider other factors, such as how many calories you will burn or what the environmental impact of your choice could be.

In Tutorials 1 through 5, you learned how to locate and evaluate information on the Internet. When faced with a problem to solve, the Internet can be a useful tool for gathering information to help you make the best decision. For example, you could use a Web site such as HopStop to find ways to navigate around a large city such as New York. The search results will provide you with many different options. For example, a search for directions in New York City will usually give you options to take the subway, a bus, a taxi, or an hourly car rental. The site will also give you specific directions for riding a bicycle or walking, which are often different in New York because the city has many one-way streets and streets that are closed to vehicular traffic.

ProSkills

When HopStop presents its directions, it will give specific information for each routing option, including:

- Estimated time duration (of the trip overall and for each leg of the trip)
- Walking time (even trips that use a bus or subway require walking to and from the station or bus stop)
- Cost (bus/subway/taxi fare or car rental fee)
- Calories burned (if you are walking)

You can use these factors to make an informed decision about which route and travel method to take, giving consideration to how much money you will spend, how long it will take you to travel, and how good you will feel after getting some exercise.

Note: Please be sure not to include any personal information of a sensitive nature in the documents you create to be submitted to your instructor for this exercise. Later on, you can update the documents with such information for your own personal use.

1. Start your browser, and then use a search engine to find and open the HopStop Web site or another Web site that helps commuters determine the best transportation method to use when navigating New York City.
2. Use the tools on the site to change the location to New York City.
3. Set your starting location as the Crowne Plaza Times Square, which is located at 1605 Broadway Avenue, Midtown, NY 10019.
4. Set your destination as the Metropolitan Museum of Art, which is located at 1000 Fifth Avenue, New York, NY 10028.
5. Compute the transportation route using the Subway/Rail only option, the Walking option, and the Taxi cost/time option. Note the distance travelled and the estimated travel time for each option. For the Taxi cost/time option, note the estimated cab fare.
6. Based on the following information, make a decision about how you would get from the Crowne Plaza Times Square hotel to the Metropolitan Museum of Art. Use the information in this ProSkills exercise and from the HopStop site to support the steps you took to make your decisions for each situation described below:
   a. You need to arrive at the museum in a hurry because you are meeting a friend there and you are running late.
   b. You are on a strict budget while visiting New York City, but it is snowing and very cold outside.
   c. It is a beautiful day and you are not in a hurry to arrive at the museum.
   d. It is late at night, and you are visiting New York City for the first time.

ProSkills

7. In an email message addressed to your instructor, describe each decision you made.

8. Evaluate the site's other options, such as its city guide and maps. Can you determine how this information is created on the site? For example, do you find any evidence of using APIs to create this information? How do you suppose that a site like HopStop earns revenue? Use specific information from the site to support your conclusions and add this content to your email message.

9. Send the email message to your instructor and close your browser.

Internet Security

Managing Common Security Threats

OBJECTIVES

Session 6.1
- Explore basic security concepts and countermeasures
- Study how encryption works
- Learn about phishing and digital watermarking
- Understand denial-of-service attacks and how to prevent them
- Recognize and prevent identity theft
- Explore security concerns for users of social networks

Session 6.2
- Understand security threats to Web clients and how to prevent them
- Investigate the use of programs that detect and remove malware
- Recognize the potential security issues that arise from electronic tracking devices
- Study how a firewall is used to block communication
- Learn how to secure a Web server

Case | *Day-to-Day Business Solutions*

After two decades of practicing law for a large firm in Chicago, Illinois, Fiona Day resigned her job as an attorney in favor of working independently and part-time so she could balance her career and her family's needs better. Because she was no longer with a firm, she lost the services traditionally provided by an assistant. At first, Fiona was able to manage the tasks of a clerical and legal assistant on her own; but soon the daily clerical and research needs of her clients and business overwhelmed her.

From her social network connections to other self-employed individuals and small business professionals, Fiona soon recognized that others in her position want support in completing the same types of routine office tasks. She began to visualize a new strategy for dealing with the need for skilled, on-demand clerical and legal assistance. Fiona has developed a plan and business strategy for her own company, Day-to-Day Business Solutions, which will contract with highly skilled individuals who can support the business needs of both individuals and small businesses. She plans to leverage her existing contacts in the Chicago area by contracting with professionals with whom she has existing relationships to provide needed services to new clients looking for administrative support. She hired a Web site designer to produce a Web site that will describe the business services her company provides, accept résumés from contractors who perform these services, and accept payments from new and existing clients for services. The Web server will also securely store business documents and other work products for clients.

As an attorney, Fiona's first concern is to understand the security issues involved in conducting transactions using a Web site. She wants to protect her clients' data and privacy, and also secure both the information and the integrity of the information the site sends and receives. As part of Fiona's business plan, she wants to ensure that she has effective strategies in place to manage, control, and contain common threats. Fiona will use the Internet to research security issues and protection strategies.

STARTING DATA FILES

There are no starting Data Files needed for this tutorial.

SESSION 6.1 VISUAL OVERVIEW

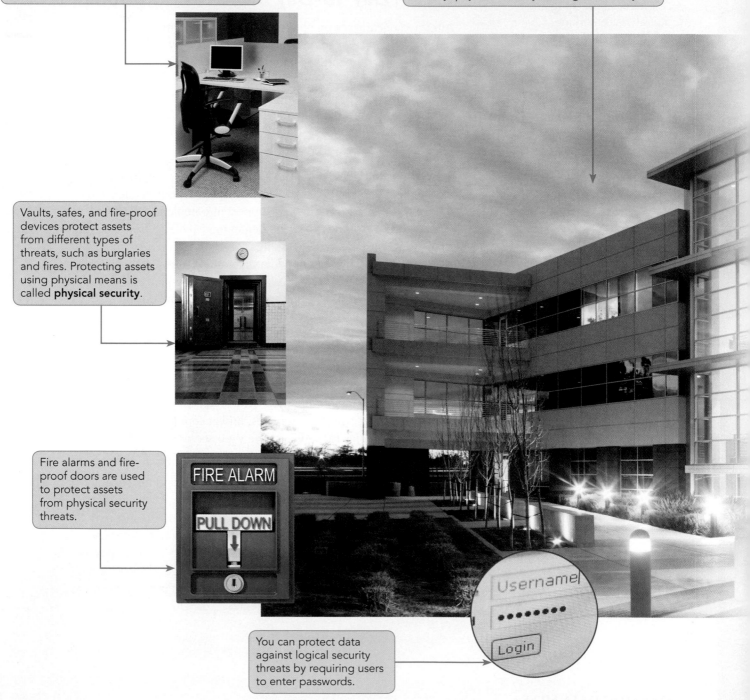

Protecting assets using nonphysical means is called **logical security**. Using logical security techniques to protect data stored on computers is sometimes called **computer security**.

Security is broadly defined as the protection of assets from unauthorized access, use, alteration, or destruction. There are two general types of security: physical security and logical security.

Vaults, safes, and fire-proof devices protect assets from different types of threats, such as burglaries and fires. Protecting assets using physical means is called **physical security**.

Fire alarms and fire-proof doors are used to protect assets from physical security threats.

FIRE ALARM

PULL DOWN

You can protect data against logical security threats by requiring users to enter passwords.

Username

Login

PHYSICAL AND LOGICAL SECURITY

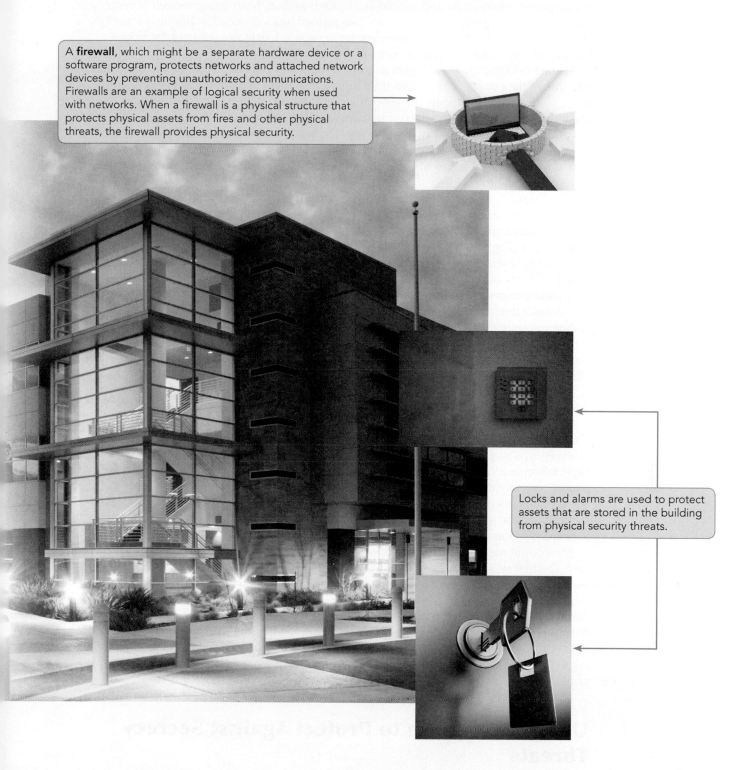

A **firewall**, which might be a separate hardware device or a software program, protects networks and attached network devices by preventing unauthorized communications. Firewalls are an example of logical security when used with networks. When a firewall is a physical structure that protects physical assets from fires and other physical threats, the firewall provides physical security.

Locks and alarms are used to protect assets that are stored in the building from physical security threats.

Security Basics

"Security" is a general term that describes any method that protects physical assets, such as computers and servers, and logical assets, such as data, from unauthorized access, use, alteration, or destruction. There are two general types of security: physical security and logical security. The Visual Overview for Session 6.1 explains some of the devices that provide these two types of security to different assets.

Any act or object that endangers an asset is known as a **threat**. This tutorial will focus on some of the common logical security threats that affect computers and data in a network. Logical security threats are generally classified into three categories: secrecy, integrity, and necessity. Some threats can be classified into more than one category. A **secrecy threat** occurs when data is disclosed to an unauthorized party, an **integrity threat** results in unauthorized data modification, and a **necessity threat** causes data delays (which slow down the transmission of data) or denials (which prevent data from getting to its correct destination).

As technology changes and new threats emerge, individuals and organizations must be diligent and proactive to safeguard their assets from threats that include stolen identities, files, programs, and hard drive space; misdirected, altered, or intercepted email messages; or illegally obtained and used passwords that allow unauthorized access to protected data and services. The strategies for protecting assets from physical and logical security threats are collectively called countermeasures.

A **countermeasure** is a physical or logical procedure that recognizes, reduces, or eliminates a threat. Depending on the value of the asset being protected, the goal of a countermeasure might be to detect, deter, or eliminate a threat. For example, you might set a password for a computer as a way of deterring unauthorized use by people who do not know the password. To detect a threat, a computer might maintain a log of access attempts and store the IP addresses of users as a way of identifying their locations. To detect a threat, a computer might lock out a user who has attempted to log in more than three times as a way of eliminating the threat of unauthorized use.

When protecting an asset, the countermeasure that an individual or organization chooses often depends on the expected types of threats to that asset and its value. For example, you might hang your jacket on a public coat rack in a restaurant with a low expectation of it being stolen. However, if you store your wallet and keys in the jacket's pocket, you might be less likely to hang your jacket on that same public coat rack because the jacket's theft will result in a much greater loss than simply losing the jacket. In this case, you are likely to keep your jacket with you at all times as a countermeasure to prevent its loss.

The countermeasures that individuals and organizations use to protect against threats vary. The best way to safeguard against a threat is to prevent it from occurring in the first place, but not every threat is preventable. In some cases, individuals and organizations must implement different countermeasures to identify, contain, and control threats, or to plan for losses in service or theft by purchasing insurance or installing backup systems. To implement effective countermeasures, you must identify the risk, determine how to protect the affected asset, and calculate the cost of the resources needed to protect the asset. This process of risk management focuses on identifying threats and determining available and affordable countermeasures to protect assets from those threats.

Using Encryption to Protect Against Secrecy Threats

Secrecy threats are the best known of the logical security categories; maintaining the secrecy of communication has been a challenge throughout history. To verify the contents of a private message, the recipient needs proof that the message was not altered or intercepted during transit and was sent by the sender who signed it. The sender needs proof that the message was sent without being altered or intercepted and was delivered to the intended recipient. These standards apply to all forms of messages, including those exchanged on paper, in electronic communication such as email messages, or with a Web server.

The study of ways to secure information is called **cryptography**. Encryption is the most common cryptographic process and the most widely used form of protection for data transmitted on any network, including the Internet. **Encryption** is the process of coding information using an algorithm to produce a string of characters that is unreadable. An **algorithm** is a formula or set of steps that solves a particular problem; some algorithms also use a **key**, which is a fact that the encryption algorithm uses as part of its formula. For example, a simple algorithm that does not use a key would be "reverse the order of the letters" ("time" would become "emit"). An example of an algorithm that uses a key would be "if the key is *x*, reverse the order of the letters" ("time" would become "emit") and "if the key is *y*, use the next letter in the alphabet" ("time" would become "ujnf"). Using a key to process encrypted text so it is readable is called **decryption**. To decrypt text, you use a key to unlock it. Without the key, the program alone cannot reveal the content of the encrypted message. Encrypted information is called **cipher text**, whereas unencrypted information is called **plain text**.

The two basic types of encryption used on networks are private-key encryption and public-key encryption. **Private-key encryption** (also called **symmetric encryption**) uses a **private key**, or **common key**, known by both the sender and receiver, or by the programs that the sender and receiver are using to exchange messages. Figure 6-1 illustrates how private-key encryption works. In this example, the sender writes an email message and uses a menu command in the email program to encrypt the message with a private key, which might be a password. When the recipient receives the email message, his or her email program uses the same private key (password) to decrypt the message. During transit, the message is protected because it is encrypted. Private-key encryption works well in a highly controlled environment in which the sender and receiver both have the private key—the password in this case—or in which the sender's and receiver's email programs both have the same private key installed.

Figure 6-1	Private-key (symmetric) encryption

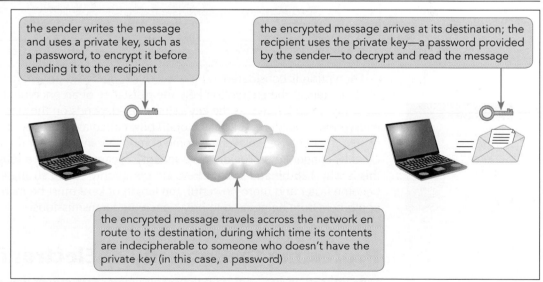

the sender writes the message and uses a private key, such as a password, to encrypt it before sending it to the recipient

the encrypted message arrives at its destination; the recipient uses the private key—a password provided by the sender—to decrypt and read the message

the encrypted message travels accross the network en route to its destination, during which time its contents are indecipherable to someone who doesn't have the private key (in this case, a password)

© Cengage Learning

Public-key encryption, on the other hand, uses two different keys to encrypt messages. When using **public-key encryption** (also called **asymmetric encryption**), these different keys operate as a pair: A **private key** (also referred to as a **secret key**) is known only to one party, and a **public key** is known to everyone. Messages encrypted with a private key must be decrypted with the matching public key, and vice versa.

Figure 6-2 illustrates how public-key encryption works. In this example, the sender encrypts the message with his or her private key, which is known only to the sender. The recipient uses the matching public key to decrypt the message. Because the recipient can only decrypt the message with the sender's matching public key, the recipient can confirm the identity of the sender and read the message by decrypting it with the correct public key. Conversely, the recipient can send a reply to the sender and encrypt it with the same public key. When the sender receives it, only the matching private key will decrypt the message. However, in this case, the sender of a message encrypted with the public key could be anyone with the public key, so the sender's identity cannot be verified by the public key.

Figure 6-2	**Public-key (asymmetric) encryption**

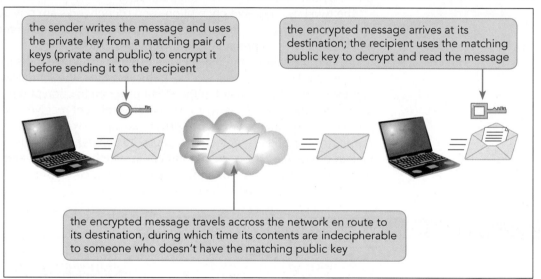

© Cengage Learning

Encryption is considered to be weak or strong based on its algorithm and the number of characters in the encryption key. The resistance of an encrypted message to attack attempts—also k nown as the key's strength—depends on the size of the key used in the encryption procedure. A key size of 40 bits, called a 40-bit key, provides a minimal level of security because the average home computer can decipher (break) the key relatively quickly. Longer keys provide more security because it takes so long to decipher them; this is why 128-bit and 256-bit keys are commonly called **strong keys**. As computers become faster and more powerful, the length of keys must be increased to prevent those computers from being used to break encrypted transmissions.

> **TIP**
>
> A 128-bit key is a number that is 3.4×10^{38} or 3.4 followed by 38 zeroes. It could take billions of years for a computer to break a 128-bit key.

Protecting the Integrity of Electronic Data

Data integrity threats represent the second major category of logical security. Unlike secrecy threats, in which someone simply sees or steals information, integrity threats can change the actions an individual or organization takes by altering the content of a message or transaction. An integrity attack occurs when an unauthorized party alters data during its transfer over a network or while it is stored on a drive or server.

For example, suppose a lawyer uses the Day-to-Day Web site to request a transcript of a legal meeting on a certain date, but an attacker prevents the Day-to-Day Web site from receiving the request and therefore prevents the company from being able to transcribe the meeting. The attacker in this case compromises the integrity of Day-to-Day's reservation data. Alternatively, an attacker could use multiple fictitious names to reserve space with Day-to-Day in an attempt to prevent it from scheduling transcription services on certain dates and times with real clients. In the first case, Day-to-Day cannot fill an order that it never received; in the second case, Day-to-Day loses income that it would have earned if it had received orders for services from legitimate clients. In both cases, the attacker successfully diminishes the reputation and income of Day-to-Day.

Another type of integrity violation occurs when an email message is intercepted and its contents are changed before it is forwarded to its intended destination. In this type of integrity violation, which is called a **man-in-the-middle exploit**, a third party alters the contents of a message in a way that changes the message's original meaning. For Day-to-Day, an attacker could intercept an email message that contains a transcript of a legal meeting and change its content in a way that adversely affects a client.

Phishing Attacks

Another type of integrity threat occurs when you receive an email message that appears to be from someone you know or an established organization that you do business with, such as a bank; but instead, the message is from someone misrepresenting his or her identity in a type of scam known as **spoofing**. The spoofed identity of the sender makes it more likely that you will open the message because the message appears to be from someone you know.

Most individuals have received spoofed email messages from banks, online services, credit card companies, and other businesses indicating that their account data has been lost or must be verified to continue using the service. For many people, a clue to the authenticity of these messages is the fact that they do not have an account with the sender of the message.

However, many individuals *do* have an account with the message's sender. These people read the messages, click a hyperlink to go to a Web site that appears to be the legitimate Web site of the message's sender, and enter the required information into a form. The form illicitly collects the entered data, which usually includes the person's name and address, account number, login information including a password, and often the person's Social Security number or a credit card number.

Because the email message seems genuine and the spoofed site contains the company's correct logos, many people participate in this type of attack without realizing it. Many well-known organizations, including eBay, Citibank, PayPal, and even the Internal Revenue Service, have been spoofed. Some companies become aware of the fraudulent email messages when customers contact them to verify the original message.

This type of attack, called **phishing** because it "fishes" for information, is difficult to prevent because it involves sending email messages that appear to be legitimate but include links to spoofed Web sites instead. Simply receiving the message usually doesn't cause any harm; the recipient must follow the instructions in the message or click its included hyperlinks to actually become a victim of the attack.

The basic structure of a phishing attack is fairly simple. The attacker sends an email message (such as the one shown in Figure 6-3) to a large number of recipients with the goal of finding recipients who have accounts at the targeted Web site (PayPal is the targeted site shown in the figure, but PayPal did not send this message).

Figure 6-3	Spoofed email message used in a phishing attack

the sender's address appears to use the paypal.com domain, which is a legitimate domain for PayPal, but it is actually a spoofed email address

Date: [Date removed] 08:05:42 +0600
From: "Services PayPal" <services@paypal.com>
Subject: PayPal Account sensitive features are access limited!
To: [E-mail addresses removed]

Dear valued **PayPal** member:

PayPal is committed to maintaining a safe environment for its community of buyers and sellers. To protect the security of your account, PayPal employs some of the most advanced security systems in the world and our anti-fraud teams regularly screen the PayPal system for unusual activity.

Recently, our Account Review Team identified some unusual activity in your account. In accordance with PayPal's User Agreement and to ensure that your account has not been compromised, access to your account was limited. Your account access will remain limited until this issue has been resolved. This is a fraud prevention measure meant to ensure that your account is not compromised.

In order to secure your account and quickly restore full access, we may require some specific information from you for the following reason:

the message asks the user to log in, which steals the user's actual login and provides the phisher with access to the user's real account

We would like to ensure that your account was not accessed by an unauthorized third party. Because protecting the security of your account is our primary concern, we have limited access to sensitive PayPal account features. We understand that this may be an inconvenience but please understand that this temporary limitation is for your protection.

Case ID Number: PP-040-187-541

We encourage you to log in and restore full access as soon as possible. Should access to your account remain limited for an extended period of time, it may result in further limitations on the use of your account.

However, failure to restore your records will result in account suspension. Please update your records within 48 hours. Once you have updated your account records, your **PayPal** session will not be interrupted and will continue as normal.

To update your **Paypal** records click on the following link:
https://www.paypal.com/cgi-bin/webscr?cmd=_login-run

Thank you for your prompt attention to this matter. Please understand that this is a security measure meant to help protect you and your account. We apologize for any inconvenience.

Sincerely,
PayPal Account Review Department

PayPal Email ID PP522

hyperlinks in the message appear to open Web pages at the paypal.com domain, but they are actually pages at a spoofed Web site

Accounts Management As outlined in our User Agreement, **PayPal** will periodically send you information about site changes and enhancements.

Visit our Privacy Policy and User Agreement if you have any questions.
http://www.paypal.com/cgi-bin/webscr?cmd=p/gen/ua/policy_privacy-outside

The email message tells the recipient that his or her account has been compromised and asks the recipient to log in to the account and correct the problem. The email message includes a link that appears to connect to the login page of the actual PayPal Web site. However, the link actually connects to a spoofed Web site, which is designed to look like the PayPal Web site. Figure 6-4 shows how to identify spoofed hyperlinks used in a phishing attack. After clicking a spoofed hyperlink, the victim opens a Web page at the spoofed Web site and uses the page to enter his or her login name and password, which the perpetrator captures and then uses to access the victim's account at the *real* Web site. After using the victim's real login information to access the victim's account, the phisher can access personal information, make purchases, or withdraw funds.

Figure 6-4	Examining a spoofed hyperlink used in a phishing attack

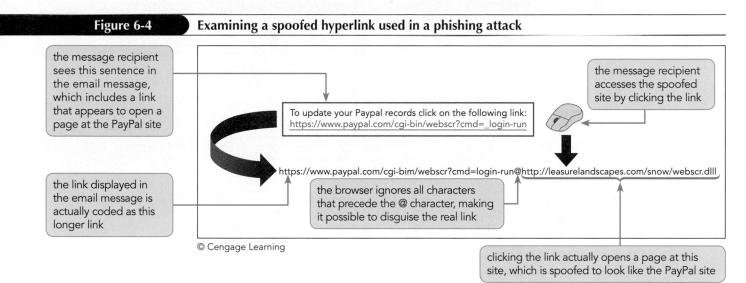

© Cengage Learning

Many email programs alert users when a link in an email message opens a Web page that is coded to a different URL than the one displayed in the message. Phishing attackers use different methods to hide their Web sites' true URLs, including code that creates pop-up windows that look exactly like a browser's address bar. The window is programmed to open very quickly and position itself to precisely cover the browser's address bar. You can learn more about the details of phishing attacks by visiting the Web site for the APWG (Anti-Phishing Working Group), a not-for-profit association focused on eliminating the fraud, crime, and identity theft that result from various types of attacks.

To learn more about phishing attacks:

1. Start your Web browser, go to **www.cengagebrain.com**, open the Tutorial 6 Weblinks page, click the **Session 6.1** link, and then click the **APWG (Anti-Phishing Working Group)** link.

2. On the home page, locate the link to the page that provides consumer advice, and then click the link. Examine the links on the Consumer Advice page and find one that includes information about how to avoid phishing scams. Read the information on the page, and pay particular attention to how to identify a spoofed message and how to prevent a phishing attack from being successful.

3. Return to the Consumer Advice page, and then find and click a link that opens a page with information about what to do if you have already given out your personal information in a phishing attack. Read the information on the page to learn more about the steps you would need to take to recover from giving out your personal information.

4. Return to the Weblinks page for Tutorial 6, and then click the **Microsoft: What is Phishing** link to open the page shown in Figure 6-5.

| Figure 6-5 | What is Phishing page in the Microsoft Safety & Security Center |

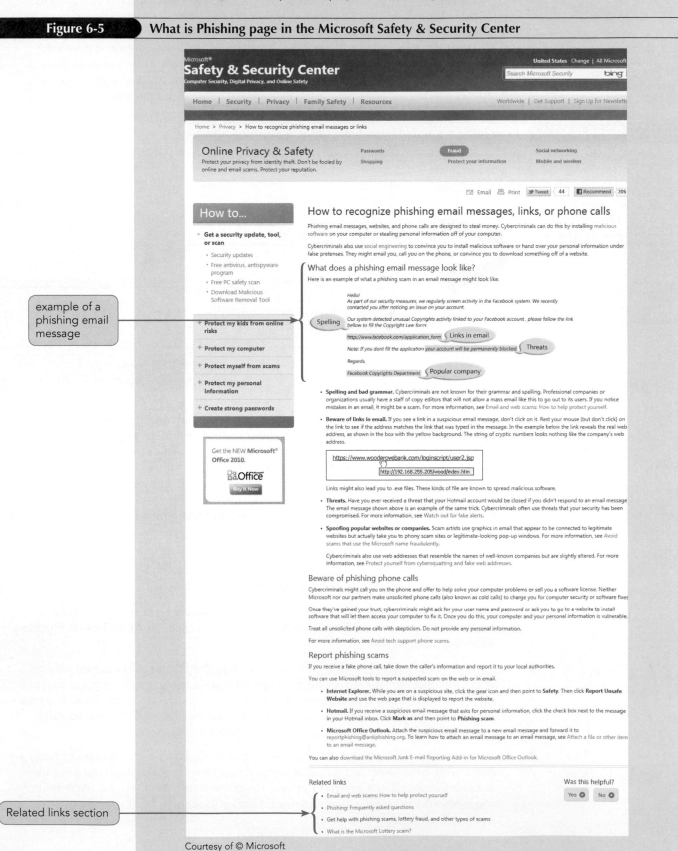

example of a phishing email message

Related links section

Courtesy of © Microsoft

▶ **5.** Read the information provided on the Microsoft site, which discusses common phishing methods, and how to recognize, avoid, and report phishing attacks.

▶ **6.** At the bottom of the What is Phishing page, use the links in the Related links section to learn more about phishing. For example, you might click a link to a page of frequently asked questions (FAQs) or a link to other types of spoofing attacks.

▶ **7.** Read the information on the pages that open from the Related links section to learn more about preventing common phishing attacks. For example, you might read the information about how an email program or Web browser can protect you in a phishing attack.

▶ **8.** Return to the Weblinks page for Tutorial 6.

In addition to protecting the integrity of data, Fiona also needs to understand the methods she can use to protect copyrighted data. One method that she can use to protect copyrighted data is to use a digital watermark.

Protecting Copyrighted Materials Using Digital Watermarks

Protecting copyrighted works from threats is a logical security issue, although the methods used differ from those that protect other types of data. Threats to copyrighted materials result from the relative ease with which existing material can be used without the owner's permission. Actual monetary damage resulting from a copyright infringement is more difficult to measure than damage from secrecy, integrity, or necessity violations, but the harm can be just as great. When material is duplicated or used without consent, the copyright's owner loses the earnings (for example, royalties or related consulting fees) from the material and no longer controls its use by others.

The technology of the Internet facilitates copyright infringement in two ways. First, it is very easy to reproduce an exact copy of anything you find on the Internet, regardless of its copyright restrictions. Second, many people are simply naïve or unaware of copyright restrictions that protect electronic works. Examples of both unwitting and willful Internet copyright violations occur every day.

Although copyright laws were enacted before the creation of the Internet, the Internet itself has complicated the enforcement of copyrights by publishers. Recognizing the unauthorized reprinting of written text is relatively easy; tracing the path of a photograph that has been used on a Web page without authorization is far more difficult.

Some companies that distribute copyrighted art, photographs, and other materials use digital watermarking to help protect their ownership interests in those materials. A **digital watermark** is a digital pattern containing copyright information that is inserted into a digital image, animation, or audio or video file. The watermark is inserted into the file using a software program so that it is invisible and undetectable. To view the digital watermark, a software program unlocks the watermark, retrieving the information it stores.

For example, a photographer might protect a photograph by adding an undetectable digital watermark that includes the photographer's name and contact information, in addition to a copyright notice that is clearly visible on the photograph itself. If the photographer's image is published on a Web server, the photographer could identify the image as his or her own by unlocking the digital watermark stored on the unauthorized copy of the image, even when the visible copyright has been electronically removed.

Fiona wants to learn more about digital watermarks and how to create and use them. She wants to ensure that any files she places on the Day-to-Day Web site, such as audio or video legal depositions or photographs, are appropriately documented and protected.

To learn more about digital watermarks:

1. On the Weblinks page for Tutorial 6, click one of the links in the Digital Watermarks section.

2. Examine the site to learn more about digital watermarking and how it is used to manage and identify a digital file. As you explore the site you chose, look for a frequently asked questions (FAQs) page or other pages that contain information about what type of software is needed to insert the watermark or message, what types of files can use these methods, and what other types of services, such as image tracking, are provided. Figure 6-6 shows a page from the Digital Watermarking Alliance, an international alliance of organizations that provides digital watermarking solutions to content owners, industries, policy makers, and consumers. The links on this page explain how digital watermarks are used to protect all kinds of works.

Figure 6-6   **Digital Watermarking Applications page for the Digital Watermarking Alliance**

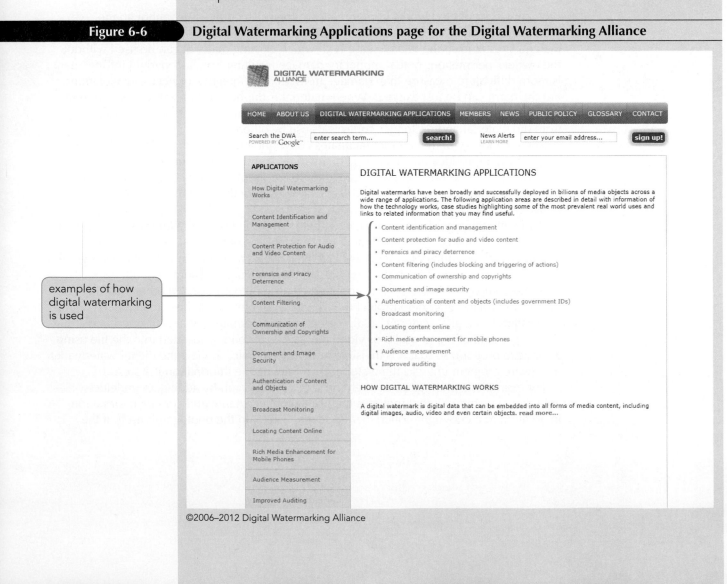

©2006–2012 Digital Watermarking Alliance

3. When you have finished exploring the first site, return to the Weblinks page for Tutorial 6 and select another site in the Digital Watermarks section. Repeat Step 2 to learn more about digital watermarks.

4. When you have finished exploring these sites, return to the Weblinks page for Tutorial 6.

INSIGHT

Hiding Messages Using Steganography

Steganography can also protect digital works. **Steganography** is a process that hides messages within different types of files. Steganography is based on the fact that digital sound, video, image, and animation files contain portions of unused data that can be used to hide messages. Steganography is generally used as a way to covertly conceal messages within different forms of communication, but it can also be used to add copyright information to different types of files.

In addition to protecting personal or business data, you must be alert for other types of security threats that prevent people from accessing a computer or server. These types of attacks, called denial-of-service attacks, are described next.

Preventing Denial-of-Service Attacks

A necessity threat disrupts normal computer processing or denies processing entirely. Programs used in necessity attacks work by reducing a computer's processing speed to intolerably low levels or by completely disabling the computer. The most common necessity attack, called a **denial-of-service (DoS) attack**, occurs when an attacker floods a computer, server, or network with messages with the goal of consuming the network's bandwidth resources and disabling its services and communications. Even if the attack fails to disable the server, computer, or network, the resulting processing delays can render a service unusable or unattractive.

Because a DoS attacker does not need to access an organization's server to attack it, Web sites are particularly vulnerable to DoS attacks. The Web sites for Microsoft, eBay, Amazon.com, and many other companies have been victims of DoS attacks that resulted in service interruptions to their customers.

As you learned earlier in this book, a Web browser loads a Web page by sending a message to a Web server that requests the page. The Web server responds with a message that contains the HTML content of the Web page, along with any image or other files required to display the Web page in the browser. When a Web browser is used in a DoS attack, it sends thousands of page requests per minute to the Web server with the goal of overloading the server. In some cases, each of the page request messages has a false return address, so the Web server consumes processing resources in an attempt to solve the problem. As more page requests arrive at the Web browser, and as the efforts to solve the problem and to process the new requests accumulate, the server becomes overloaded and unavailable to process legitimate requests. Ultimately, the server shuts down.

In a **distributed denial-of-service (DDoS) attack**, the attacker takes control of one or more computers without the owner's permission and uses those computers to launch a DoS attack on other computers, servers, or networks. Most DDoS attacks are launched after the attacking computers are infected with Trojan horse programs. Each Trojan horse program is coded to open and launch a DoS attack at exactly the same date and time.

TIP

DoS attacks can also threaten other types of networks, including cellular, mobile, and wireless networks.

Other computers are hijacked by this type of Trojan horse and, without the knowledge of their owners, are used to help the DDoS attack; such computers are often called **bots** (short for "robots") or **zombies**. Figure 6-7 describes how a client can launch a DoS attack or a DDoS attack on a server.

Figure 6-7	Normal processing, a DoS attack, and a DDoS attack

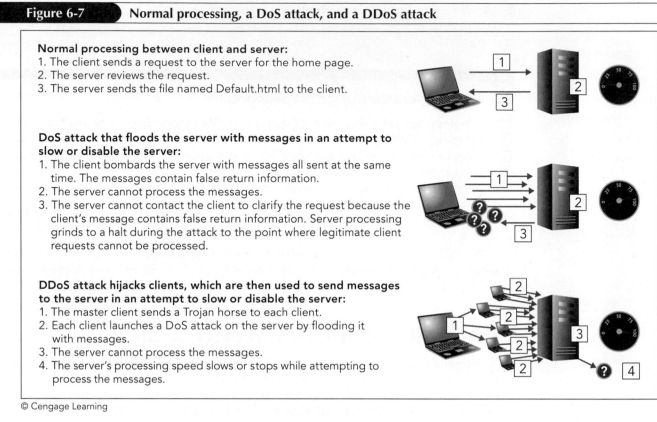

Normal processing between client and server:
1. The client sends a request to the server for the home page.
2. The server reviews the request.
3. The server sends the file named Default.html to the client.

DoS attack that floods the server with messages in an attempt to slow or disable the server:
1. The client bombards the server with messages all sent at the same time. The messages contain false return information.
2. The server cannot process the messages.
3. The server cannot contact the client to clarify the request because the client's message contains false return information. Server processing grinds to a halt during the attack to the point where legitimate client requests cannot be processed.

DDoS attack hijacks clients, which are then used to send messages to the server in an attempt to slow or disable the server:
1. The master client sends a Trojan horse to each client.
2. Each client launches a DoS attack on the server by flooding it with messages.
3. The server cannot process the messages.
4. The server's processing speed slows or stops while attempting to process the messages.

© Cengage Learning

INSIGHT

Recognizing the Symptoms of a DoS or DDoS Attack

Although most DoS attacks are launched to reduce the processing power of or to disable a Web server, it is possible for an individual's personal computer to become a victim of a DoS attack. Some of the first warning signs that a server or computer has been compromised in a DoS attack include the following:

• When a computer is affected, it might take much longer than normal to respond to user requests. Simple actions such as opening a file, downloading email messages, or displaying a particular Web page might happen slowly or the user might receive an error that the request has timed out, which means that the request could not be completed.

• When a server is affected, users will encounter very slow network performance when attempting to download files, access email, or open Web pages. A Web site might not respond at all to user requests or it might display error pages.

• In most cases, the user or server will receive an exceptionally large number of email messages (all spam) at once as the intruder floods the server with requests during the attack.

It is important to note that each of these warning signs can also be the result of other computer and network problems. For example, a computer or server that is slow to respond to user requests might have a virus or be encountering other types of network problems that are unrelated to a DoS threat.

If you believe that your computer is involved in a DoS attack, you should contact your network administrator or ISP immediately to alert them to any unusual activity, and then turn your computer off.

To prevent an attack on your computer or a server that you manage, you must be alert for the warning signs. You can also install different types of hardware and software on your devices and network that will monitor them to detect problems early and prevent attacks. You can use the DoS Attacks section in the Additional Information section of the Weblinks page for Tutorial 6 to explore the different solutions for detecting DoS attacks.

A company can defend its Web server from DoS and DDoS attacks by installing a **denial-of-service filter**, or **DoS filter**, to monitor communication between the Web server and the router that connects it to the Internet. A DoS filter, which can be a separate computer or software running on the Web server, identifies potential attacks by watching for patterns of incoming page requests or for specific repeating elements in the page request messages. The filter can be configured to block messages automatically if they contain similar elements and arrive in rapid sequence. In many cases, DoS attackers try to configure their messages so these filters cannot identify them, but the filter vendors respond by frequently updating their identification criteria. DoS filter functions are often included as part of a network software tool called a **packet sniffer**, which examines the structure of the data elements that flow through a network. Figure 6-8 shows how a DoS filter works to prevent an attack on the server.

| **Figure 6-8** | **Using a DoS filter to prevent DoS and DDoS attacks on the server** |

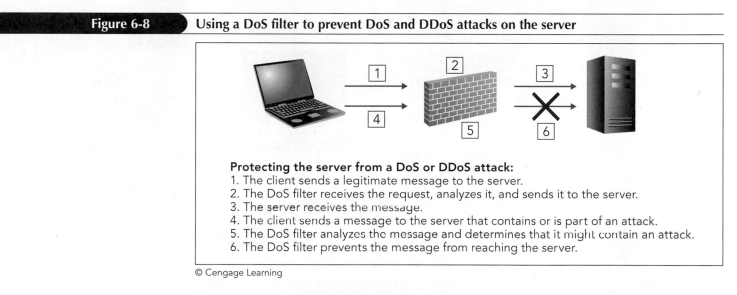

Protecting the server from a DoS or DDoS attack:
1. The client sends a legitimate message to the server.
2. The DoS filter receives the request, analyzes it, and sends it to the server.
3. The server receives the message.
4. The client sends a message to the server that contains or is part of an attack.
5. The DoS filter analyzes the message and determines that it might contain an attack.
6. The DoS filter prevents the message from reaching the server.

© Cengage Learning

Because Fiona will be working with contractors who must provide their confidential personal information, such as their Social Security numbers, to receive payment for their work, she wants to make sure that people who work for her company are protected from becoming victims of identity theft.

Recognizing and Preventing Identity Theft

The amount of personal information that Web sites collect about the page viewing habits, product selections, and demographic information of their visitors can pose a threat to those visitors when this information is collected with the goal of stealing from them. Consumers have become accustomed to providing their credit card and contact information to online vendors, but an increasing amount of personal information is stored on networked computers at banks, credit card issuers, credit reporting agencies, physician's offices, hospitals, and government agencies. As more personal information is stored on these computers, there are more opportunities for theft of that information.

Figure 6-9 identifies some common personal information that can be stolen and used, along with some problems that might result from the theft. When multiple items shown in Figure 6-9 are stolen, a thief can potentially steal a person's entire identity. In this type of crime, called an **identity theft**, a thief can use the victim's personal information to open bank accounts, obtain new credit cards, and purchase items using credit cards, often damaging the victim's credit rating in addition to making transactions for which the victim is responsible. When the victim discovers the identity theft, the thief has already stolen cash and goods. It can take a long time for identity theft victims to clear their credit records of the unpaid charges made by the thief and restore their credit.

Figure 6-9	Common personal information used in thefts

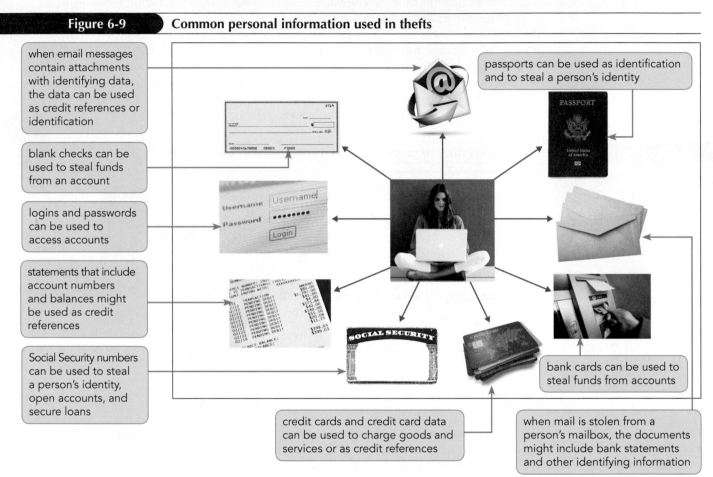

when email messages contain attachments with identifying data, the data can be used as credit references or identification

blank checks can be used to steal funds from an account

logins and passwords can be used to access accounts

statements that include account numbers and balances might be used as credit references

Social Security numbers can be used to steal a person's identity, open accounts, and secure loans

passports can be used as identification and to steal a person's identity

bank cards can be used to steal funds from accounts

credit cards and credit card data can be used to charge goods and services or as credit references

when mail is stolen from a person's mailbox, the documents might include bank statements and other identifying information

© Cengage Learning/Shutterstock.com; iQoncept/Shutterstock.com; JohnKwan/Shutterstock.com; Nicholas Moore/Shutterstock.com; Daboost/Shutterstock.com; Vasily Smirnov/Shutterstock.com; Timothy W. Stone/Shutterstock.com; beboy/Shutterstock.com; Valerie Potapova/Shutterstock.com; Yuri Arcurs/Shutterstock.com

INSIGHT

Protecting Yourself Against Identity Theft

To protect against identity theft, individuals can implement certain habits to reduce the chances of becoming a victim and to make it easier to recover from an identity theft incident. Some important habits include:

- Keeping credit card, bank account, and investment account information (account numbers, passwords, contact telephone numbers, and so on) together in a safe place that is easy to access should an identity theft incident occur.
- Saving credit card and debit card receipts, matching them to monthly statements, and reporting any unauthorized charges to the card issuer immediately. After verifying the charges on the monthly statements, the receipts should be shredded.
- Monitoring expiration dates on credit and debit cards and contacting the issuer if replacement cards do not arrive before the old cards expire.
- Shredding all mail that contains any personal information (such as unsolicited credit card offers) before throwing it into the trash.
- Arranging to have your mail held at the post office or collected by a trusted friend to protect it from theft when you are away from home.
- Only providing your Social Security number to a third party when it is legally required to do so, and never having it printed on your checks.
- Putting a fraud alert on your credit report at all three of the major credit reporting companies (Equifax, Experian, and TransUnion) after suspecting a problem, after a theft, or as a preventive measure. This requires the reporting company to contact you before releasing your credit report to anyone and can help prevent someone else from opening credit accounts in your name.
- Obtaining a free copy of your credit report on a regular basis to monitor your credit history for any problems.
- Purchasing identity theft insurance, which can help pay the expenses required to clear and restore your identity in case of a theft. Some financial institutions offer this insurance for an affordable monthly fee, and some insurance companies offer it as part of a renter's or homeowner's insurance policy. In addition, there are companies that will monitor your credit report and assist with expenses related to identity theft restoration for a monthly or annual fee.

If you believe you are a victim of identity theft, you must act quickly to contact the three credit reporting agencies, every financial institution at which you have an account, and the issuer of every credit card you hold. You can learn more about contacting credit reporting agencies and getting a free annual copy of your credit report by visiting the links in the Contacting Credit Reporting Agencies section of the Weblinks page for Tutorial 6.

You will learn more about identity theft and what you can do to prevent it next.

To learn more about identity theft and how to prevent it:

1. In the Identity Theft section of the Weblinks page for Tutorial 6, click the **Federal Trade Commission Identity Theft site** link. See Figure 6-10.

Figure 6-10 FTC Identity Theft home page

Consumers link

Courtesy of www.USA.gov

2. Near the top of the page, point to or click the **Consumers** link to open a menu, and then click **About Identity Theft** to open the About Identify Theft page.

3. Click the links on this page to learn more about identity theft, including how a thief steals a person's identity and what he or she does with it, how to reduce the risk of becoming an identity theft victim, and what to do if you suspect your identity has been stolen.

4. When you have finished exploring the About Identity Theft page, point to or click the **Consumers** link on the page, and then explore the other pages on this site to learn more about minimizing your risk of identity theft, detecting identity theft, and recovering from an identity theft.

5. After exploring the resources for consumers, point to or click the **Businesses** link and then explore the pages for businesses. These pages include information and resources that businesses such as Day-to-Day can use to assist victims, deal with data breaches, and safeguard information. As you explore these pages, consider what types of safeguards a small business such as Day-to-Day should implement to protect the privacy and safety of its clients' data.

6. Return to the Weblinks page for Tutorial 6, and then click another link in the Identity Theft section. Explore the site you selected to locate additional information about detecting, preventing, and recovering from an identity theft.

7. Return to the Weblinks page for Tutorial 6.

PROSKILLS

Problem-Solving: Recovering from an Identity Theft

Victims of identity theft are often unaware that their accounts or identities have been stolen or compromised, and they usually learn of the theft long after it actually occurred. Some people are careless with their personal property and identifying documents and simply do not realize that their important documents have been lost or stolen.

Regardless of when you discover an identity theft, you should act quickly to prevent further loss. An important organizational tool is to know what you have lost and how to contact the institutions involved. Regardless of what prompted the loss, you should complete the following basic steps as soon as possible:

- Contact financial institutions, credit card companies, and any agencies that issued your identification cards or driver's license and report the loss. Close any affected financial or credit accounts immediately. If you have lost any blank checks, place stop payments on the affected checks.
- Contact all three credit reporting agencies (Experian, TransUnion, and Equifax) and place a fraud alert on your credit report. This will prevent a thief from using your identification to open additional accounts, and it will also alert you to any accounts that have already been illegally opened in your name.
- Contact your local post office to make sure that your mail hasn't been forwarded to another address without your consent. Some thieves immediately change your address to postpone your knowledge of the theft so credit card and other statements are not mailed to you.
- File a police report with local law enforcement to document the theft, and keep a copy of the report.

If you suspect that your entire identity has been stolen, you will also need to contact all of your creditors to report the identity theft. You should change your user name and password on all of your accounts as you report the thefts. As a precaution, do not use the same user name and password at more than one site, and do not reuse any previous user name and password. This will protect your accounts from further loss in case the thief gains access to your user name and password as part of the identity theft.

The Recovering from an Identity Theft section of the Weblinks page for Tutorial 6 includes resources that you can review to learn more about recovering from an identity theft.

Many of Fiona's clients and contractors use social networks for both personal and professional communications. Therefore, she wants to understand the security issues that users face when using these networks, and the countermeasures used to minimize the risk of problems.

Security Concerns for Social Network Users

More than a billion people and businesses around the world use social networks to communicate with friends, family, colleagues, and customers. Most businesses use their individual Web sites to promote and sell their goods and services. Many of these same businesses have created accounts on social networks to provide another way to communicate with and reach their customers. Each day, thousands of users and businesses expand their online presences by creating accounts on the dozens of popular social networks on the Internet. As use of these social networks increases, individuals and businesses must implement appropriate security strategies to protect themselves from different types of problems and threats.

Because Fiona plans to create an account on Facebook, the world's largest social network, and also on LinkedIn, the world's largest social network for business professionals, she wants to review some precautions that will ensure the safety and privacy of her information and her clients' information.

To learn more about social network security issues:

1. In the Social Networks section of the Weblinks page for Tutorial 6, click the **US-CERT: Staying Safe on Social Network Sites** link. See Figure 6-11.

Figure 6-11	US-CERT Staying Safe on Social Network Sites page

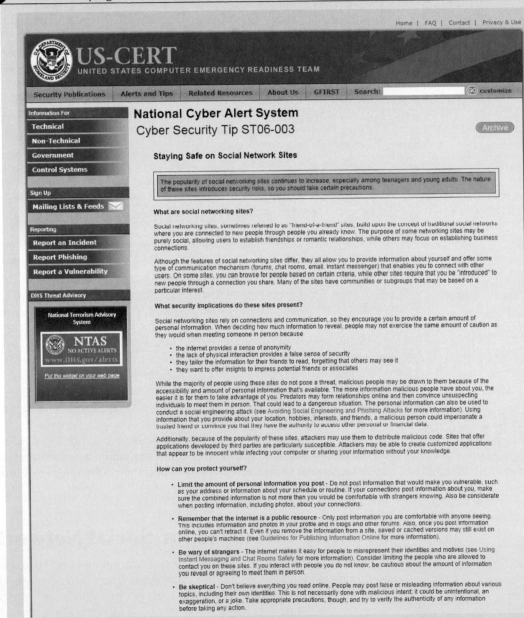

Courtesy of www.USA.gov

2. Read the information, which is provided by the U.S. Department of Homeland Security, about protecting data on a social networking site. Notice that many of the protections listed involve limiting the kind and amount of information a user posts on his or her own page.

3. Return to the Weblinks page for Tutorial 6, and then click the **Facebook Security page** link. Facebook, which has more than 800 million users, regularly updates its security information with information about current threats and countermeasures.

4. Use the links on the left side of the Facebook Security page to read about current threats, taking action, and security tips. As you review the information on each page, be alert for information directed at individuals and businesses. You should notice that there are specific settings to protect the data posted on a social network. In addition, you should find information about what kind of information you should not post and the reasons why sharing certain information might pose a security risk.

5. When you are finished exploring the Facebook Security page, close your browser.

In addition to carefully controlling the information you post on a social networking site and choosing the security settings that offer the most protection, you must also rely on common sense to protect your identity, property, and privacy. Many hoaxes and scams start on social networking sites, such as fake disaster relief funds and assistance programs for people in need. Because you might be viewing these types of pleas for help on your friends' pages, you might be more inclined to trust their genuineness and contribute to them, without realizing that they are not legitimate charities.

With the popularity of sites that allow users to send very short updates of approximately 160 characters or less to their friends, the need to abbreviate links to Web sites has become a necessity. Many Web sites provide a service that lets a user shorten a long URL to include significantly fewer characters. For example, Figure 6-12 shows a long URL for a page at the Cengage Learning Web site and its shortened equivalent, as provided by the TinyURL.com Web site. Clicking the shortened link will open the same Web page at the Cengage Learning Web site without requiring the user to type the full URL.

| **Figure 6-12** | **Creating a shortened URL to link to a Web page** |

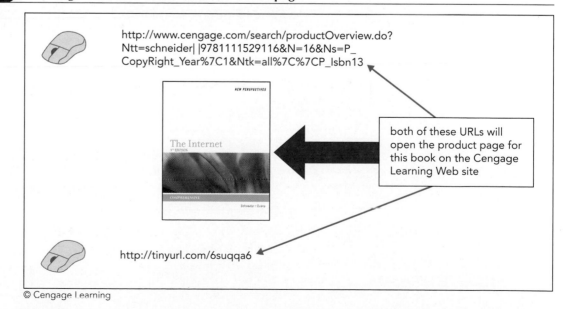

http://www.cengage.com/search/productOverview.do?
Ntt=schneider| |9781111529116&N=16&Ns=P_
CopyRight_Year%7C1&Ntk=all%7C%7CP_Isbn13

both of these URLs will open the product page for this book on the Cengage Learning Web site

http://tinyurl.com/6suqqa6

© Cengage Learning

As you can see, the shortened URL contains significantly fewer characters than the full URL on the Cengage Learning Web site. The shortened URL is easier to include in messages that limit the number of characters per message, or in publications in which a longer URL might be broken across two or more lines. When you can see the full URL in an email message or on someone's social networking site, you can determine that the page is stored on a server with the domain name cengage.com. In addition, the remaining content in the full URL appears to include details that identify a book, such as the author's name and the book's ISBN. If you know that you are receiving a link to the product page for a book, the additional information in the full URL provides evidence that the URL is legitimate.

However, when you see only the shortened URL, you cannot extrapolate the same information found in the full URL. The only information you have is that the URL has been shortened. In this case, clicking the shortened URL in Figure 6-12 opens the book's product page. But in actuality, clicking the shortened URL could open any page or file and lead to a spoofed site, a file that opens and executes a virus, or other problems that could pose a security threat to the user's computer and privacy. Although most shortened URLs are legitimate, it is important to be alert for the potential security problems that they can cause.

Now that Fiona has a better understanding of the main types of online security threats and how they are executed, she can begin her exploration of specific countermeasures. You will learn about specific Web client, communication channel, and Web server threats and countermeasures in Session 6.2.

REVIEW

Session 6.1 Quick Check

1. Define and give one example of physical security and logical security.
2. What is encryption?
3. What is a man-in-the-middle exploit?
4. What is a phishing attack?
5. How can a digital watermark protect a document?
6. What is a denial-of-service attack?
7. What is identity theft?

SESSION 6.2 VISUAL OVERVIEW

Checklist for securing a Web client:

- Prevent ActiveX controls from running by changing the browser's settings
- Install a digital certificate
- Install a program that detects and removes viruses, worms, and Trojan horses
- Install a program that detects and removes malware, adware, and spyware
- Block tracking devices in electronic communications
- Install a firewall

Web Clients

ENHANCING SECURITY

Checklist for securing a Web server:

- Install a server certificate
- User a certificate authority
- Authenticate users
- Require strong passwords for user accounts
- Use an assurance provider

Web Servers

Checklist for securing transactions between a Web client and Web server:

Recognize and verify that your browser has made a secure connection to a Web server when making financial transactions or providing confidential data by using:

- Secure Sockets Layer (SSL)
- Transport Layer Security (TLS)
- Secure Sockets Layer-Extended Validation (SSL-EV)

Browser Protocols

Web Client Security

The Day-to-Day computers and Web server are vulnerable to the types of threats that you learned about in Session 6.1. Fortunately, there are countermeasures that Fiona can implement to protect her computer assets and the data stored on them from harm. In this session, you will learn about security threats and countermeasures for Web clients, the communication channel that connects Web clients to Web servers, and the Web servers themselves. One of the most important Web client security risks arises from the existence of active content.

Active Content: Java, JavaScript, and ActiveX

One of the most dangerous entry points for DoS attacks is from programs that travel with applications to a browser and are executed on the user's computer. These programs, often called **active content**, include Java, JavaScript, and ActiveX components that can run programs on a Web client. Active content components can make Web pages more useful by providing interactive content, such as calculating shipping costs, creating mortgage payment tables, or creating animation. Unfortunately, these components can also be used for malicious purposes.

For example, a **Java applet**, which is a program written in the Java programming language, could execute and consume a computer's resources. Similarly, a **JavaScript program** can pose a threat because it can run without being compiled (that is, translated into computer-readable codes). A cleverly written JavaScript program could examine your computer's programs and email a file from your computer back to a Web server.

ActiveX controls are Microsoft's technology for writing small applications that perform specific actions in Web pages; these controls have access to a computer's file system. For example, a hidden ActiveX control in a Web page could scan a hard drive for specific types of files and print them on any network printer. Similarly, an ActiveX control could reformat a hard drive.

Because ActiveX controls are executed on the client computer, Internet Explorer secures them with a digital signature that confirms each developer's identity. A **digital signature** provides verification of the contents of a file and identifies its author or developer. When a digital signature authenticates an ActiveX control's developer or source, it is called a **signed ActiveX control**. Internet Explorer maintains a list of known developers and examines the digital signature of any ActiveX control before downloading it to the client computer to determine its authenticity. This method protects Internet Explorer users from downloading rogue controls.

ActiveX controls only work in Internet Explorer and other browsers that use the Internet Explorer code base in some way. Thus, Firefox, which does not use any part of the Internet Explorer code base, cannot run a beneficial ActiveX control, nor can it be attacked by a malicious ActiveX control.

Although most Java, JavaScript, and ActiveX controls are beneficial, you can protect your computer from potential attacks that use them by preventing your Web browser from automatically running Java and JavaScript programs.

To strengthen security in Internet Explorer:

1. Start Internet Explorer.

   Trouble? If you are using Firefox, go to the next set of steps. If you are using Chrome, go to the set of steps titled "To strengthen security in Chrome."

2. Click the **Tools** button on the Command bar, and then click **Internet options** on the menu. The Internet Options dialog box opens.

3. Click the **Security** tab to display the browser's security settings. Internet Explorer uses four zones to let the user customize the browser's security settings. The four zones are for the Internet, the local intranet, trusted sites, and restricted sites.

   The Internet zone controls the security settings when viewing Web sites that you haven't previously designated as trusted or restricted sites. The Internet zone's default setting of Medium-high will cause the browser to prompt you before it downloads potentially unsafe content and prevents the browser from download-ing unsigned ActiveX controls. The Local intranet zone has a default security level of Medium-low and controls the security settings for Web sites that are on an intranet to which you are connected. The Trusted sites zone has a default security level of Medium and controls the security settings for Web sites that you have previously designated as being safe. The Restricted sites zone has a default secu-rity level of High and controls the security settings for Web sites that you have previously designated as being potentially unsafe.

4. With the Internet zone selected in the "Select a zone to view or change secu-rity settings" section, click and drag the slider control in the Security level for this zone section to the top position. The security level changes to High, and a description of the selected security level appears with the security setting, as shown in Figure 6-13.

| Figure 6-13 | Changing the security level in Internet Explorer |

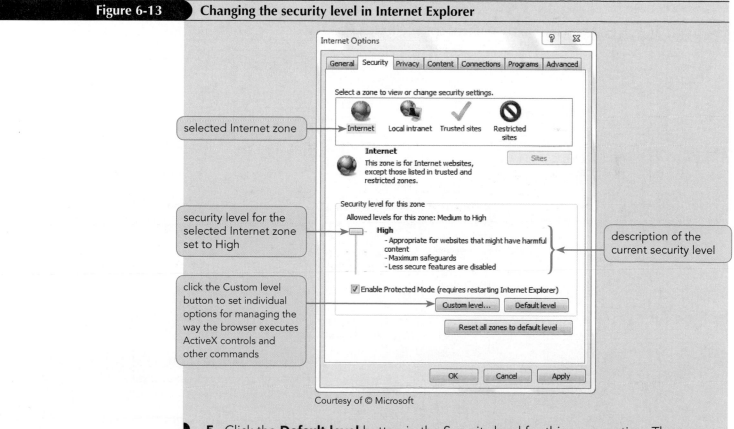

Courtesy of © Microsoft

5. Click the **Default level** button in the Security level for this zone section. The slider control returns to its default setting (Medium-high for the Internet zone).

Trouble? Selecting a higher security level will increase protection for your computer, but it might cause some Web sites that you have visited in the past to stop working properly. Check with your instructor or lab manager before changing any browser's security settings on a school computer.

▶ 6. Click the **Cancel** button to close the dialog box without making any changes.

Firefox includes different settings for increasing its security, as you will see next.

To strengthen security in Firefox:

▶ 1. Start Firefox.

Trouble? If you are using Chrome, go to the next set of steps. If you are using Internet Explorer, skip these steps.

▶ 2. Click the orange **Firefox** button in the top-left corner of the browser window, and then click **Options** to open the Options dialog box.

▶ 3. At the top of the dialog box, click the **Content** icon to display some of the Firefox settings that affect the level of security that the browser provides. See Figure 6-14.

| Figure 6-14 | Viewing the Content options in Firefox |

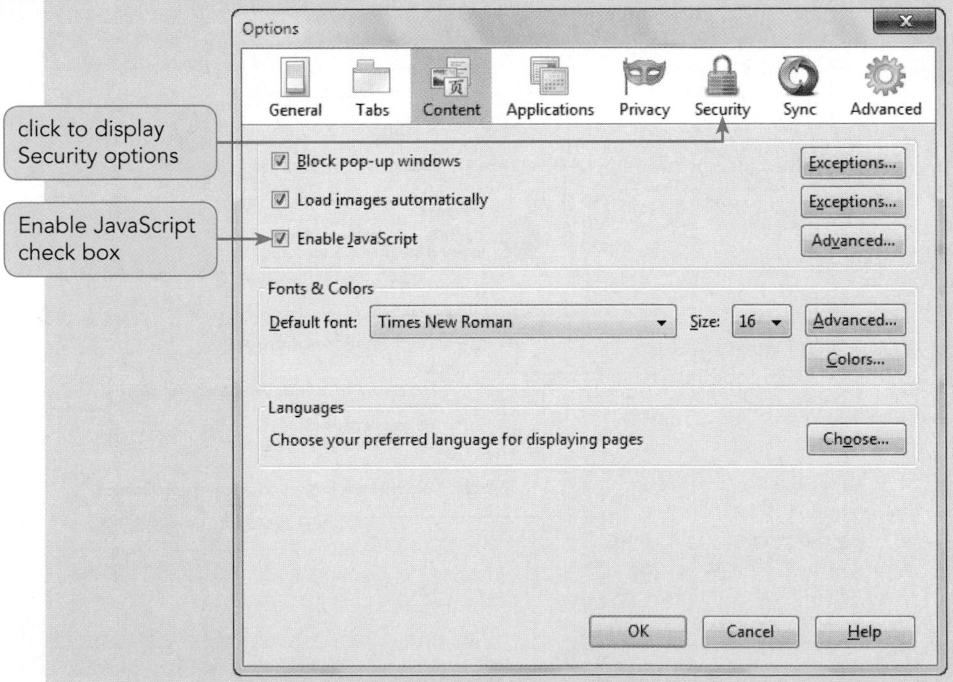

Courtesy of The Mozilla Foundation

Clearing the Enable JavaScript check box will disable JavaScript from running automatically in Firefox.

▶ 4. At the top of the dialog box, click the **Security** icon to display more of the Firefox settings that affect the level of security that the browser provides. See Figure 6-15.

| Figure 6-15 | Viewing the Security options in Firefox |

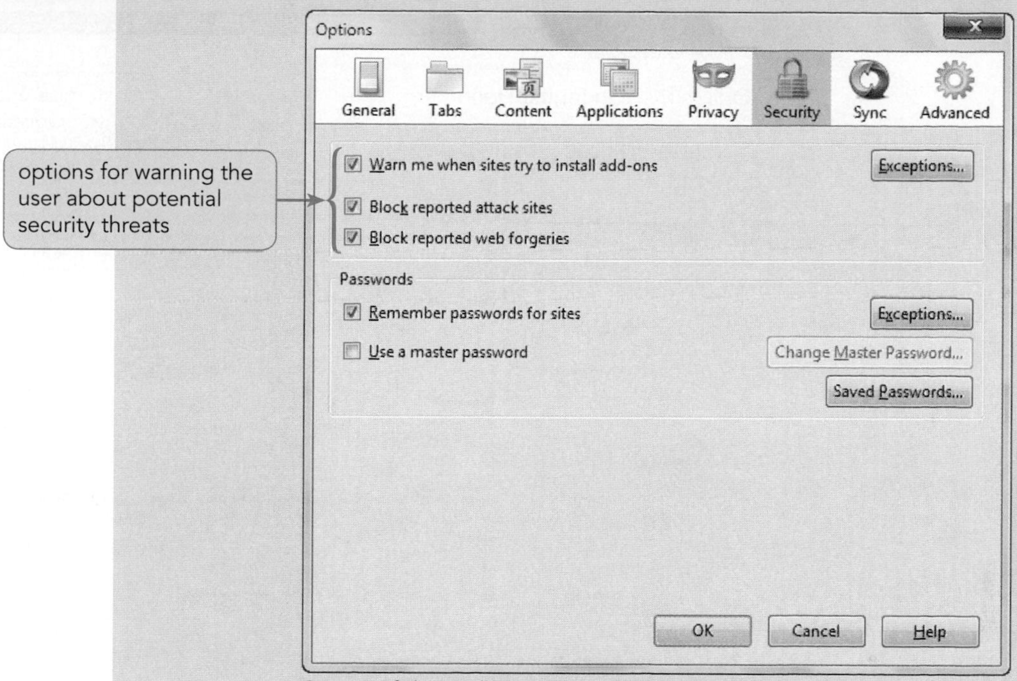

options for warning the user about potential security threats

Courtesy of The Mozilla Foundation

This page contains three options that can prevent various types of attacks from occurring. You can set Firefox to warn you when a site tries to install a program, and you can also block sites that Mozilla has characterized as "attack sites" or "web forgeries" based on reports from users. Enabling these options provides good protection from some types of threats.

Trouble? Selecting a higher security level will increase protection for your computer, but it might cause some Web sites that you have visited in the past to stop working properly. Check with your instructor or lab manager before changing any browser's security settings on a school computer.

▶ **5.** Click the **Cancel** button to close the dialog box without making any changes.

Chrome includes different settings for increasing its security, as you will see next.

To strengthen security in Chrome:

▶ **1.** Start Chrome.

Trouble? If you are not using Chrome, skip these steps.

▶ **2.** Click the **Customize and control Google Chrome** button in the top-right corner of the browser window to open a menu, and then click **Options** to open the Options—Basics page.

▶ **3.** In the Options pane, click **Under the Hood**. The Options—Under the Hood page opens, as shown in Figure 6-16.

Figure 6-16	Viewing the security options in Chrome

privacy options

Options — Under the Hood

chrome://settings/advanced

Options

Search options

Basics

Personal Stuff

Under the Hood

Extensions

Under the Hood

Customize and control Google Chrome button

Privacy

Content settings...   Clear browsing data...

Google Chrome may use web services to improve your browsing experience.
You may optionally disable these services. Learn more

☑ Use a web service to help resolve navigation errors
☑ Use a prediction service to help complete searches and URLs typed in the address bar
☑ Predict network actions to improve page load performance
☑ Enable phishing and malware protection
☐ Automatically send usage statistics and crash reports to Google

Web Content

Font size: Medium ▼   Customize fonts...

Page zoom: 100% ▼

Languages and spell-checker settings...

Network

Google Chrome is using your computer's system proxy settings to connect to the network.

Change proxy settings...

Translate

☑ Offer to translate pages that aren't in a language I read

Downloads

Download location: C:\Users\Public\Downloads   Change...

☐ Ask where to save each file before downloading

© Google

At the top of the Options—Under the Hood page, Chrome includes settings that increase the browser's security.

4. In the Privacy section, click the **Content settings** button to open this page. See Figure 6-17.

Figure 6-17	Viewing the content settings options in Chrome

Options — Content Settings

chrome://settings/content

Options

Search options

Basics

Personal Stuff

Under the Hood

Extensions

Content Settings

Cookies
◉ Allow local data to be set (recommended)
○ Allow local data to be set for the current session only
○ Block sites from setting any data
☐ Block third-party cookies from being set
☐ Clear cookies and other site and plug-in data when I close my browser
Manage exceptions...   All cookies and site data...

Images
◉ Show all images (recommended)
○ Do not show any images
Manage exceptions...

JavaScript options

JavaScript
◉ Allow all sites to run JavaScript (recommended)
○ Do not allow any site to run JavaScript
Manage exceptions...

Handlers
◉ Allow sites to ask to become default handlers for protocols
○ Do not allow any site to handle protocols
Manage handlers...

option for running plug-ins

Plug-ins
◉ Run automatically (recommended)
○ Block all
Manage exceptions...

© Google

On this page, you can choose how to run JavaScript and plug-ins. Disabling these options will strengthen security in Chrome, but you might lose the ability to view content that uses these features at some Web sites.

Trouble? Selecting a higher security level will increase protection for your computer, but it might cause some Web sites that you have visited in the past to stop working properly. Check with your instructor or lab manager before changing any browser's security settings on a school computer.

▶ **5.** Click the **Close** button on the Options - Content Settings tab to close the page without making any changes.

Fiona appreciates the information about active content security threats and how to customize the settings in Internet Explorer, Firefox, and Chrome. The next countermeasure for Web clients is one that detects and removes malicious programs that might be sent with other files to the user's computer.

Detecting and Removing Malware

Malware, a term that means "malicious software," is a category of software that is installed without the user's consent, usually through a hidden program in an email attachment or from a file downloaded from a Web site. Perhaps the biggest threat of malware is that it is designed to be invisible to the user, who might have malicious code running on a device for a long time before suspecting a problem. Viruses, Trojan horses, and worms that attack computers are all examples of malware, and the programs they run are forms of integrity threats.

A virus is a program that replicates itself with the goal of infecting other computers. For a virus to spread from one computer to another, it must be executed so it can infect other files and programs. A **Trojan horse** is a program hidden inside another program. Trojan horse programs claim to be legitimate programs that accomplish some task when, in fact, they cause harm when the user accesses or downloads the program in which they are hidden. Trojan horse programs range from prank programs that display a message and then disappear, to destructive programs that can delete or steal files. Unlike a virus, a Trojan horse does not replicate itself, nor does it affect other files or programs.

Because most Trojan horse programs are hidden, it is possible to infect a computer by executing a file downloaded from a site that offers free software or by opening a file attached to an email message. When you execute the program or open the email attachment, the file secretly launches a separate Trojan horse program, which quietly does its damage. Unfortunately, antivirus software programs and firewalls cannot guarantee that your computer is protected from this type of attack. To protect against this type of threat, you should be careful not to execute a file that you did not request, and you should download files and programs from trusted sources only. Because of the stealth nature of Trojan horse attacks, some people and companies enforce a general policy of not opening any email attachments sent over the Internet.

Another threat is a **worm**, which is a self-replicating and self-executing program that sends copies of itself to other computers over a network. Unlike viruses, a worm can replicate itself on a computer or server, but it cannot attach itself to other files. Many worms arrive as email attachments. When the user opens the attachment, the worm infects the user's computer, and then quickly attempts to send itself to email addresses stored in the address book of the user's email program.

Adware, which is short for "ad-supported software," is a general category of software that includes advertisements to help pay for the program in which they appear. Adware, when installed with the user's consent and knowledge, provides a revenue source for software programs that are offered to users for free. In exchange for their use of the free program, users might see pop-up or other types of advertisements on their computer. This category of adware is not harmful because it does not cause any security threats to the user, who is informed of the ads when installing the program. In addition, the parties responsible for including ads are clearly identified in the programs.

If you use a legitimate adware program, the program's developer tells you that your use of the free software is supported by ads that you will see when you use it, and the developer provides information about how to disable the ads (usually by paying a fee to use a version of the software that does not display ads).

When adware is installed on a computer without the user's knowledge and consent, either by itself or in conjunction with a program that the user did intend to install, it becomes a form of malware called spyware. **Spyware** works much like adware except that the user has no control over or knowledge of the ads and other monitoring features the ads contain. The spyware vendor does not inform the user that the software will include ads. Software that gathers personal information about the user's behaviors (such as which sites the user visits or what search expressions the user enters on a search engine site) or the user's computer (such as what type of software or hardware is installed on the computer) without the knowledge of the user is also a form of spyware.

Internet security software can prevent the spread of viruses, worms, Trojan horses, and other forms of malware by blocking them from being downloaded from the server. Many companies offer different versions of Internet security software that are customized for the needs of individuals, small businesses, and large organizations. An individual or small business might be interested in installing Internet security software on several computers using a single license. A large organization might be interested in software features that let its information technology department update all of the company's computers automatically.

All Internet security software vendors sell their products through Web sites, so you can learn more about the vendors and their products quite easily. Two vendors that provide a full range of products are Norton (from the company named Symantec) and McAfee.

> **TIP**
>
> Internet security programs offer different features. Ensure that the features that are important to you or your business are included in the program you purchase.

To learn more about Norton and McAfee security products:

1. Use your Web browser to go to **www.cengagebrain.com**, open the Tutorial 6 Weblinks page, click the **Tutorial 6** link, and then click the **Session 6.2** link.

2. In the Internet Security Programs section, click the **Norton Products** link. The Norton Products page includes links to information about the company's security products.

3. Locate a product that includes security features, and then click the product link to open a page that includes details about the program. For example, Figure 6-18 shows a product page for the Norton Internet Security program, which protects users from viruses and other security threats.

Figure 6-18	Norton Internet Security product page

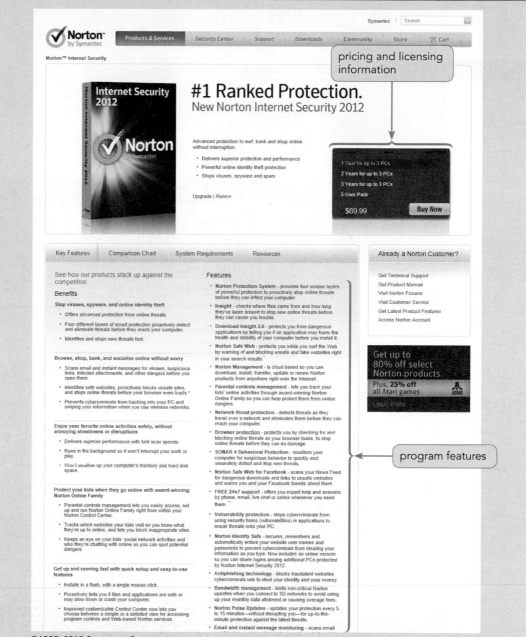

©1995–2012 Symantec Corporation

▶ **4.** Review the key features of the program to get a sense of what kinds of benefits and features it provides to protect the user's computer from virus threats, such as automatically updating the software to prevent new attacks and scanning all downloaded files for viruses. If possible, locate and review information about the cost of the program and the number of computers you can install the program on using a single license.

▶ **5.** When you have finished exploring the antivirus program from Norton, return to the Weblinks page for Tutorial 6.

▶ **6.** In the Internet Security Programs section, click the **McAfee Store** link. The Shop for McAfee Products page includes links to pages that provide information about McAfee security products.

7. Locate a product that includes features for detecting viruses, and then click the product link to open a page that includes details about the program. For example, Figure 6-19 shows a product page for McAfee Total Protection, a program that protects users from different kinds of online and network threats, including viruses.

Figure 6-19   **McAfee Total Protection product page**

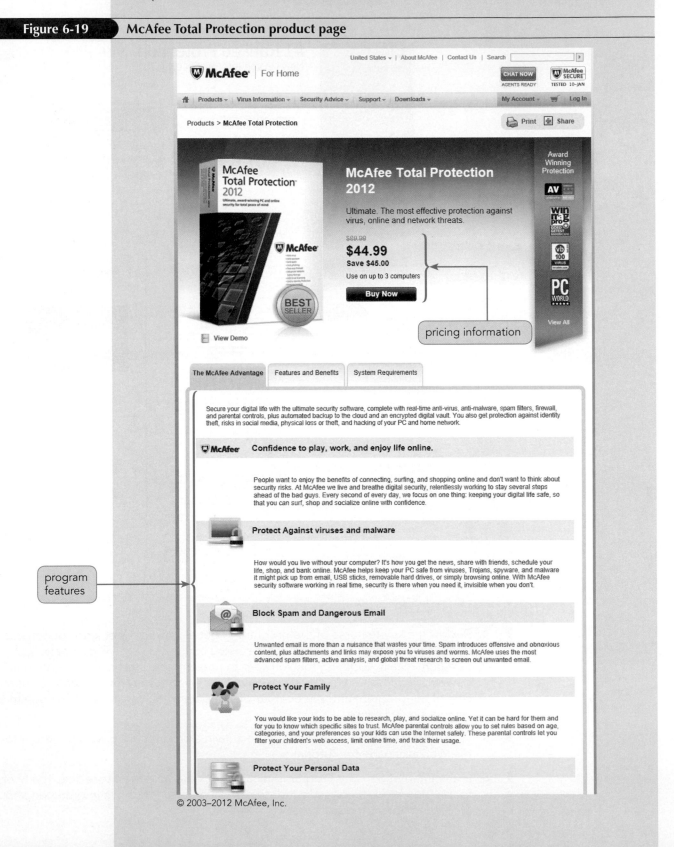

© 2003–2012 McAfee, Inc.

Trouble? If a McAfee chat window opens while you are viewing the product page, click the No Thanks or Close button to close it.

8. Review the key features of the program and get a sense of what kinds of benefits and features it provides to protect the user's computer from virus threats, such as automatically updating the software to prevent new attacks and scanning all downloaded files for viruses. If possible, locate and review information about the cost of the program and the number of computers you can install the program on using a single license.

9. When you have finished exploring the McAfee antivirus product page, return to the Weblinks page for Tutorial 6.

In your research of different security programs, you probably noticed some similarities in their features and benefits. You can use these programs to scan downloaded files, including email attachments, for viruses and other threats. If the program detects a threat, you can set it to alert you to the problem or remove it automatically. Most programs also include options to download updates automatically or on a schedule you set to install program updates as new threats are discovered. In addition, most programs include options to regularly scan your computer to detect and eliminate new threats.

Most Internet security programs include features that detect all forms of malware and prevent it from being downloaded to your computer either by itself or in conjunction with a legitimate program. However, because malware is often hidden in other programs, running an Internet security program might not adequately protect your computer. In this case, you can purchase a separate software program that scans your entire hard drive for malware and includes tools to remove it. If you download many files to your computer, you might want to invest in a separate malware program. Figure 6-20 shows a screen from Lavasoft Ad-Aware Free, a popular program for scanning for adware. This program scans all of the files on the user's computer and detects adware. The limited version, which is free, will eliminate malware threats. Users who want a higher level of protection, such as scanning all downloaded files to the user's computer in real time, can purchase the full version of the software.

Figure 6-20	Results of an Ad-Aware scan

© 2012 Lavasoft. All rights reserved.

PROSKILLS

Problem Solving: Recognizing the Symptoms of a Malware Infection

Even the most diligent computer users occasionally encounter problems on their machines, some of which are the result of a malware infection. Although the following symptoms are not always the result of a malware infection, encountering any one or more of the following problems might indicate a problem. Computer users should be on the lookout for the following symptoms of malware infections:

- Your computer shows an increase in network activity, even though you aren't using the network for your current tasks, indicating the possibility that a hidden program is using your network connection to send data from your computer to a third party.
- If you are using a laptop, you might notice that your battery doesn't last as long as usual, indicating additional processing activity that could be related to a malware infection.
- Your browser's home page suddenly changes to a site that you didn't specify and without your consent, which can result from a Trojan horse or a virus.
- Your antivirus or Internet security program stops working, or is offline, but you didn't make this change. In some cases, you are unable to reactivate these programs, even after restarting your computer. These types of problems are usually the result of a virus.
- You receive alerts from your computer's firewall, antivirus program, or Internet security program indicating the presence of a virus or other problem. These messages might appear to come from your actual firewall, antivirus program, or Internet security program, but the potential exists for them to actually be the result of a malware infection that is designed to look like an actual program alert.
- Pop-up windows appear as you are working, even when you are not using your browser. These windows might contain advertisements or offensive content and are usually a symptom of a virus.
- Clicking a hyperlink in a search engine's results page takes you to a site that you aren't expecting, indicating that the hyperlink has been hijacked by spyware.
- Programs or files are missing from your computer, or you have new programs on the Start menu that you didn't install, potentially indicating a virus.
- Your Windows settings change without your consent. These changes might include the disappearance of the Start button or the mouse pointer, or the appearance of toolbars for programs that you didn't install. The computer might randomly shut down and restart itself. These problems might indicate a Trojan horse.

If you encounter any of these problems, proceed quickly and cautiously to prevent any further security breaches, and immediately run a program that can detect and eliminate any potential malware infections. If you can run the detection program from a drive that you know isn't infected, such as a flash drive, you might get better results. If you have two or more of these problems occurring on a regular basis, and despite your efforts you cannot identify any infection, you might want to bring your computer to a specialist who has experience in detecting and removing malware infections.

You can learn more about malware and the tools that detect and remove it using the links in the Malware Detection section of the Weblinks page for Tutorial 6.

Blocking Tracking Devices in Electronic Communications

In Tutorial 1, you learned that some Web sites use cookies to store data on users' computers to provide information about their site visits, such as which pages they viewed. Most sites that use cookies to enhance the user's experience at a Web site provide information in their privacy policy to let users know that the site uses cookies and what type of data it stores in the cookies it writes to their computers. Although cookies themselves are not harmful, they can pose a security threat. Web sites can collect a great deal of information about customers' preferences, even before they place an order. The most well-known security threat of this type is a Web bug.

A **Web bug** is a small, hidden graphic on a Web page or in an email message that is designed to work in conjunction with a cookie to obtain information about the person viewing the page or email message and to send that information to a third party. The hidden graphic is usually a GIF file with a size of one pixel, which is approximately the same size as the period at the end of this sentence. Because a Web bug is usually created with a GIF file, it is sometimes called a clear GIF or a transparent GIF; it is designed to be hidden on the Web page in which it appears. Figure 6-21 shows a section of an HTML document that creates a Web bug in a Web page.

Figure 6-21	HTML document containing a Web bug

clear GIF file location →

```
<FRAMESET ROWS="*,20" BORDER=0 FRAMEBORDER=0 FRAMESPACING=0>
<!-- Start of Doubleclick Tracking Code: Please do not remove -->
<SCRIPT language="JavaScript">
var axel = Math.random()+"";
var a = axel * 10000000000000;
document.write('<IMG
SRC="http://ad.doubleclick.net/activity;src=585966;type=counter;cat=oran;ord=1;num=' + a + '?"
WIDTH=1 HEIGHT=1 BORDER=0>');
</SCRIPT>
<NOSCRIPT>
<img src='http://127.0.0.1:3388/bug.cgi'>

</NOSCRIPT>
<!-- End of Doubleclick Tracking Code: Please do not remove -->
```

cookie identification number generated for the current user

© Cengage Learning

Notice that the location of the clear GIF shown in Figure 6-21 is a URL for DoubleClick, a division of Google that develops tools for Internet marketing and advertising. When the user loads the Web page that contains this code, the browser downloads the clear GIF file from the DoubleClick server. DoubleClick has a network of thousands of members that provide information to it. The process of downloading the clear GIF file can identify your IP address, the Web site you last visited, and other information about your use of the site in which the clear GIF has been embedded and record it in the cookie file. Figure 6-22 shows part of the Web page that contains the Web bug. Notice that the GIF file is not visible because it is transparent and therefore hidden. You would need to examine the HTML document (shown in Figure 6-21) that is the source file of this Web page to find the Web bug.

Figure 6-22	Web page containing a Web bug

computers   software   electronics   cellular   music   games   video   dvd   books   bags   clearance

© Cengage Learning

clear GIF file location

When you first access a DoubleClick member's Web site, DoubleClick uses a cookie, sometimes called an ad-serving cookie or marketing cookie, to assign you a number and record it. Then, when you visit any DoubleClick member's Web site in the future, DoubleClick reads the cookie it wrote on your hard drive and gets your identification number. As you use your browser to visit different Web sites, DoubleClick can use its cookie to collect information about the sites you visit and sell this information to its members so they can customize their Web sites with advertising tailored to your interests.

For example, if you have been shopping online for a new computer and you notice that suddenly you are seeing a large number of ads for computers on different Web sites, a cookie is likely responsible for the apparent coincidence. A cookie might also cause you to receive email messages that contain ads for computers. Some people see this technology as an invasion of privacy because they might not want computer vendors knowing that they are looking for a new computer, and they might object to receiving email messages from them.

A Web bug is an example of spyware because the clear GIF and its actions are hidden from the user. Spyware is not illegal (unless it is used as part of a criminal activity, such as gathering information to be used in identity theft), but it does create privacy concerns for many Web users. Many people believe that marketing use of spyware is unethical. The programs you install, especially free and limited-use trial versions of programs, might include spyware to track your use of the programs and of the Internet, or they might collect data about you and distribute that data to a third party.

You can prevent Web sites from writing cookies to your computer by changing your browser's settings to prevent cookies from being stored on your computer. However, when you disable cookies, you also will lose some of the positive attributes that cookies can provide. By setting your Internet security program or other program, such as Ad-Aware, to remove cookies on a regular basis, you can eliminate cookies that store user data from your computer.

Blocking Communication Using a Firewall

Like its counterpart in the physical world, which acts as a barrier to keep a fire from spreading from one area of a building to another, the computer version of a firewall is a software program or hardware device that controls access between two networks, such as a local area network and the Internet, or between the Internet and a computer. Firewalls can be used on both Web servers and Web clients. A Web client firewall might be a dedicated hardware device or a program running on a computer.

When a computer is connected to the Internet, it receives traffic from other computers without its user even realizing it. Most of this traffic is harmless; but without protection, an authorized party can gain access to a computer through a port. A **port** on a computer is like a door: It permits traffic to leave and enter a computer. When the port is closed, traffic can't leave or enter the computer. The port might be a hardware interface, such as a port to which you connect a printer, or it might be a virtual port that handles different kinds of information.

Virtual ports use numbers to isolate traffic by type; a computer has more than 65,000 virtual ports for different processes such as HTTP/World Wide Web traffic (port 80), FTP traffic (port 21), SMTP email (port 25), POP3 email (port 110), and SSL (port 443). To connect to the Internet, you must open port 80. If port 80 is not properly protected, an authorized party can use port 80 or other virtual ports to access your computer.

A firewall can control incoming traffic by rejecting it unless you have configured it to accept the traffic. For example, some Web sites include features that let you test the security of your computer by asking the site to run a port scan on your computer. During a **port scan**, one computer tests all or some of the ports of another computer to determine whether its ports are open (traffic is not filtered and the port permits entry through it), closed (the port does not accept traffic, but a cracker could use this port to gain entry to and analyze your computer), or stealth (the port might be open or closed, but permits no entry through it). You can run a port scan by visiting a Web site that offers this service. The Port Scan Sites section of the Weblinks page for Tutorial 6 includes links to such sites.

Most firewalls are installed to prevent traffic from *entering* the network, but firewalls can also prevent data from *leaving* the network. This feature is especially useful for controlling the activities of hidden programs that are designed to compromise the security of a computer. When you install a new program on your computer, a firewall that provides this type of outgoing protection will notify you if the new program tries to access the Internet. You can then adjust the firewall settings to allow the program to access the Internet always, only when you approve such access, or never.

Until the recent increase in the number of users with broadband connections to the Internet, hardware firewalls were used almost exclusively by large organizations because of the number of computers connected to the network and the expense of acquiring, installing, and maintaining the firewall. However, with some firewall software programs available free or at a very low cost, they have become popular with other types of users, including those with home networks or people accessing the Internet using a single computer. One popular personal firewall software program is ZoneAlarm, which offers a free version. Antivirus programs and Internet security suites available from Norton and McAfee also include basic firewalls. Recent versions of the Windows operating system include a basic firewall. You can learn more about using the Windows firewall, along with other firewall resources, by clicking the links listed under the Firewalls heading on the Weblinks page for Tutorial 6.

Because the primary function of a firewall is to block unwanted traffic from reaching the network it protects, each organization that installs a firewall needs to determine what kind of traffic to block and what kind of traffic to permit. For example, Fiona might configure the Day-to-Day firewall to prevent unauthorized access to the network by individuals and computers outside the network, to prevent programs on the client from accessing the network to initiate data transfers, or both.

Now that you have learned about specific security issues for Web client computers, it is time to learn more about security on the communication channel; that is, for information traveling on the Internet itself.

Communication Channel Security

In Session 6.1, you learned how encryption works. Encryption is an important part of securing data that is sent over any network, including the Internet. The first step in securing a communication channel is to verify the identity of the user and the server sending messages.

Authentication is a general term for the process of verifying the identity of a person, computer, or server with a high degree of certainty. Most computer systems implement user identification and authentication with login information in the form of user names (identification) and passwords (authentication). As you learned in Tutorial 2, many Web sites require you to establish a user name and password before you can use the site. To help keep track of their login information for different computers and Web sites, some people use a program called a **password manager**, which stores login information in an encrypted form on their devices. You can learn more about password managers by clicking the links in the Password Managers section of the Weblinks page for Tutorial 6.

Brute Force Attacks

The system that stores and manages user names and passwords must provide security against threats. Most systems store passwords (and sometimes user names) in an encrypted format to protect them. Hackers can run programs that create and enter passwords from a dictionary or a list of commonly used passwords to break into a system. A **brute force attack** occurs when a hacker uses a program to enter character combinations until the system accepts a user name and password, thereby gaining access to the system. (Some systems will send a warning to the computer's operator or lock out a user name when someone makes a predetermined number of unsuccessful attempts to log in to a system.) Depending on the system to which the hacker gained access, the damage can range anywhere from reading a person's email messages to gaining access to accounts at financial institutions. Another example of a brute force attack occurs when a hacker submits combinations of numbers to a Web site that accepts credit card payments until the site accepts one. In this case, the hacker can then purchase goods and services using the card number that he or she has discovered and stolen.

The countermeasure that protects individuals from becoming victims of brute force attacks is to use unique user names and passwords at each Web site that requires a login. In addition, users should develop strong passwords that do not include identifying information about themselves (name or birth date, for example), and use a combination of non-English words, numbers, and characters. Increasing a password's strength makes it more difficult for a brute force attack to obtain the password through trial attempts at guessing it.

Because so many Web sites and other Web services require users to create accounts, a server needs a way to verify a user when he or she forgets his or her login information. User authentication is the process of associating a person and his or her identification with a high level of assurance. In other words, authentication techniques give a high level of confidence that *you* are correctly identified when *you* log in. Authentication countermeasures include using biometrics, such as a retina scan or fingerprint scan, or asking one or more questions to which only the authentic user could know the correct answers.

The combination of a user login plus a password is called **single-factor authentication** because it uses one factor; in this case, something the user knows (a user name and password). **Multifactor authentication** relies on more than one factor. For example, when you use your debit card to make a payment at the grocery store, the bank requires that you enter a PIN (one factor, something you know) and swipe your card through the card reader (a second factor, something you have). A third factor could be something unique to the user (for example, a physical characteristic such as a fingerprint or retinal image).

Banks use multifactor authentication for financial transactions because the risk of loss is significant. Another approach that banks and financial institutions use to add security to online transactions is multiple layers of control. **Multiple layers of control** can be implemented by using more than one authentication method. For example, most online banking sites will require you to answer a challenge question (to which you supplied the answer when you set up your account) in addition to supplying the usual login and password when its Web server detects that you are trying to access your account from a computer that it doesn't associate with your login.

Digital and Server Certificates

Another method that authenticates a user is to install a digital certificate in the program that is being used to send information. A **digital certificate** is an encrypted and password-protected file that contains sufficient information to authenticate and prove a person's or an organization's identity. Usually, a digital certificate contains the following information:

- The certificate holder's name, address, and email address
- A key that "unlocks" the digital certificate, thereby verifying the certificate's authenticity
- The certificate's expiration date or validity period
- Verification from a trusted third party, called a **certificate authority (CA)**, that authenticates the certificate holder's identity and issues the digital certificate

A digital certificate is the electronic equivalent of an identification card. For example, by looking at a person's driver's license, you can verify that person's identity by comparing the height and eye color printed on the license with the person using the driver's license to authenticate his or her identity. You can also compare the picture on the license with the person presenting the license. A digital certificate lets you confirm a person's or an organization's identity using your Web browser or email program.

There are two types of digital certificates, although they basically work in the same way and provide the same information. Individuals can purchase one type called a **digital ID**. Purchasers of digital IDs can use them to identify themselves to other people and to Web sites that are set up to accept digital certificates. Most people who use digital IDs are professionals, such as lawyers and accountants, who use email to send encrypted, confidential data to clients. The other type of digital certificate is used on Web servers and is called a server certificate. A **server certificate** is installed on a Web server to prove the identity of the server to Web clients that connect to it to conduct transactions, such as order processing.

A digital ID is an electronic file that you purchase from a certificate authority and install into a program that uses it, such as an email program or a Web browser. Because a digital certificate is difficult to forge or tamper with, an individual can use one in place of a user name and password at some Web sites. The digital ID authenticates the user and protects data transferred online from being altered or stolen. Some email programs include features that send and receive digital IDs with email messages so recipients can use the digital ID to verify the sender's identity.

A server certificate (sometimes called an SSL Web server certificate) authenticates a Web site so site visitors can be confident that the Web site is genuine and not a spoofed site. A server certificate also ensures that the transfer of data between a user's computer and the server is encrypted so that it is both tamperproof and free from being intercepted. Most Web browsers automatically receive and process server certificates without the user doing anything other than clicking a link or entering a URL to make the connection to the server.

Thawte, one of the first certificate authorities to issue server certificates, provides digital solutions that protect and secure communication and data on the Internet. You can explore the Thawte Web site to learn more about server certificates and how they can benefit Day-to-Day.

To explore the Thawte Web site and learn about server certificates:

1. On the Weblinks page for Session 6.2, click the **Thawte Get Started with SSL** link. See Figure 6-23.

Figure 6-23 **Thawte Get Started with SSL page**

Courtesy of © thawte, Inc. 1995–2012

▶ **2.** Read the information on the page that opens, paying particular attention to the kinds of information a certificate stores, why a company such as Day-to-Day needs a certificate, and the benefits Thawte offers to its clients.

▶ **3.** Continue exploring the site to learn more about purchasing a certificate and how to apply for one.

▶ **4.** When you have finished exploring the Thawte site, return to the Weblinks page for Tutorial 6.

Assurance Providers

An **assurance provider** is a third party that, for a fee paid by a Web site or an individual, will certify that a person or an organization has met some criteria for conducting safe transactions and ensuring privacy before issuing the right to use the assurance provider's seal on a Web site. Web sites can display the logo or seal of the assurance provider for potential customers to examine. Most of these logos are hyperlinks to the assurance provider's site, at which customers can find more information about the nature of the specific assurances given by that provider. Currently, there are four major assurance providers: the Better Business Bureau (BBB), TRUSTe, Norton Secured Seal, and WebTrust.

The Better Business Bureau's BBB Accredited Business Seal (formerly BBBOnLine) certification program grants a Web site the right to use its logo after it has joined the BBB, been in business for at least one year, compiled a satisfactory complaint-handling record, and agreed to follow BBB member guidelines for truthful advertising, prompt response to customer complaints, and binding arbitration of customer disputes. The BBB conducts a site visit during which it verifies the street address, telephone number, and existence of the business. The BBB page for businesses appears in Figure 6-24.

Figure 6-24   BBB Accredited Business Seal for the Web page

© 2008 Council of Better Business Bureaus

The TRUSTe program focuses on privacy issues. To earn the right to display the TRUSTe logo, a Web site must explain and summarize its information-gathering policies in a disclosure statement on the site. The site must adhere to its stated policies and several other guidelines concerning the privacy of communications. TRUSTe enforces its program by various methods, including surprise audits that it and two independent accounting firms conduct.

The Norton Secured Seal (formerly VeriSign) provides a range of services to electronic commerce Web sites, including certification of secure server status and electronic data interchange (EDI) certifications. It is also a partner with the American Institute of Certified Public Accountants (AICPA) in the WebTrust program. The WebTrust program is a comprehensive assurance that requires reviews by a licensed CPA (or Chartered Accountant in Canada) before the site is approved. The review includes examination of Web site performance disclosures, such as delivery times and handling of customer complaints. The site is granted a WebTrust logo only after it satisfies a number of criteria relating to business practices, transaction integrity, and information protection. The WebTrust program requires recertification every 90 days. Links to these assurance providers are included in the Assurance Providers and Rating Services section of the Weblinks page for Tutorial 6.

In addition to confirming the services of an assurance provider, a user can examine the Web browser itself to assess the security of the connection the browser has with the Web server, as you will see next.

Secure Sockets Layer (SSL) and Transport Layer Security (TLS)

Secure Sockets Layer (SSL) was the first widely used protocol for establishing secure, encrypted connections between Web browsers and Web servers on the Internet. SSL was revised several times and is still used today. In 1999, SSL version 3 was improved and reissued by the Internet Engineering Task Force. This improved protocol is called **Transport Layer Security (TLS)**. Both SSL and TLS automatically provide a security "handshake" when a browser and the server to which it is connected want to participate in a secure connection. Most Web sites automatically switch to a secure state and encrypt data when it is necessary to do so, such as when the site requests login or payment information. Web pages secured by SSL or TLS have URLs that begin with *https://* instead of *http://*; the "s" indicates a secure connection. Figure 6-25 shows the Address bar for Internet Explorer with a security icon that indicates that the browser has made a secure connection to the server at cengagebrain.com. Notice that the URL also includes the *https://* indicator.

Figure 6-25	Encryption indicator in Internet Explorer

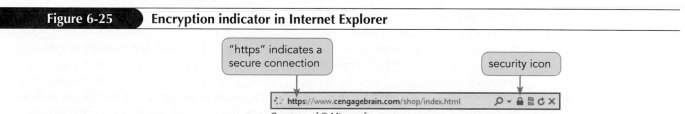

Courtesy of © Microsoft

Figure 6-26 shows the Location bar in Firefox, which displays a Web Site Identity indicator to indicate a secure connection. The URL also displays the *https://* indicator.

| Figure 6-26 | Encryption indicator in Firefox |

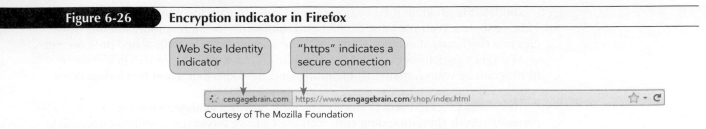

Courtesy of The Mozilla Foundation

Figure 6-27 shows the Address bar in Chrome, which displays a View site information icon to indicate a secure connection. The URL also displays the *https://* indicator.

| Figure 6-27 | Encryption indicator in Chrome |

© Google

Clicking the security icon in Internet Explorer, clicking the Web Site Identity indicator in Firefox, or clicking the View site information icon in Chrome opens a menu that provides details about the site's server certificate. Clicking the View certificates link on this menu in Internet Explorer, clicking the More Information button on this menu in Firefox, or clicking the Certification information link on this menu in Chrome opens a dialog box that displays the certificate's expiration date and identifies the certificate authority that issued it.

SSL and TLS both use a public key to encrypt a private key and send it from the Web server to the browser. Once the browser decrypts the private key, it uses that private key to encrypt information sent to the Web server during the SSL/TLS connection because private-key encryption is faster than public-key encryption. When the user leaves the secure Web site, the browser terminates the SSL/TLS connection and discards these temporary keys, or **session keys**. Session keys exist only during a single connection (session) between a browser and a server.

Although the use of SSL and TLS increased Web users' confidence when using online shopping and banking sites, some certificate authorities were only performing the minimum level of verification of applicants for SSL certificates before issuing them. A growing concern that fraudulent Web sites (including phishing sites) might have obtained SSL certificates led a group of certificate authorities to develop a more stringent set of verification steps. In 2008, this development led to the establishment of stricter criteria and an assurance of a more consistent application of verification procedures. Certificate authorities that followed these more extensive verification procedures were permitted to issue a new type of certificate called **Secure Sockets Layer-Extended Validation (SSL-EV)**.

Before issuing an SSL-EV certificate, a certificate authority must confirm the legal existence of the organization by verifying the organization's registered legal name, registration number, registered address, and physical business address. The certificate authority also must verify the organization's right to use the domain name, and verify that the organization has authorized the request for an SSL-EV certificate. You can tell that you are visiting a Web site that has an SSL-EV certificate by looking at the Address bar for your browser. In Internet Explorer, the background of the Address bar turns green and the verified name of the organization appears to the right of the URL and alternates with the name of the certificate authority, as shown in Figure 6-28.

Figure 6-28 **SSL-EV indicator of a secure site in Internet Explorer**

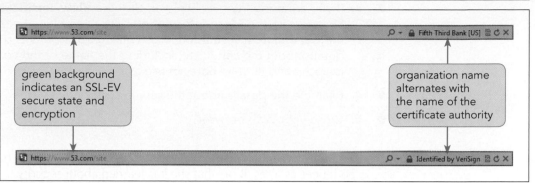

Courtesy of © Microsoft

In Firefox, the site's verified organization name appears in the Location bar to the left of the URL and with a green background, as shown in Figure 6-29.

Figure 6-29 **SSL-EV indicator of a secure site in Firefox**

Courtesy of The Mozilla Foundation

In Chrome, the site's verified organization name appears in the Address bar to the left of the URL and with a green background and the View site information icon, as shown in Figure 6-30.

Figure 6-30 **SSL-EV indicator of a secure site in Chrome**

© Google

You can check the certification status of a Web site using these indicators.

To verify the certification of a Web site:

1. On the Weblinks page for Tutorial 6, click the **Fifth Third Bank** link. After a few moments, your Web browser should display a green background on the Address bar, as shown in Figure 6-28 (in Internet Explorer), Figure 6-29 (in Firefox), and Figure 6-30 (in Chrome).

2. Click the security indicator in the Address bar or Location bar for your browser to open a menu. This menu provides some information about the site, including its identity, and about the secure connection to the server.

▶ **3.** If you are using Internet Explorer, click the **View certificates** link; if you are using Firefox, click the **More Information** button; and if you are using Chrome, click the **Certificate information** link. A dialog box opens and provides additional details about the certificate, including the name of the certificate authority that issued it and its valid dates of use.

▶ **4.** Examine the details about the server certificate, and then close the dialog box.

▶ **5.** Close your Web browser.

Fiona is certain that Day-to-Day employees and clients will have more secure online experiences as a result of what she has learned about security.

REVIEW

Session 6.2 Quick Check

1. What is a digital certificate?
2. A self-replicating and self-executing program that sends copies of itself to other computers over a network is called a(n) _____.
3. Describe malware and name three examples of it.
4. True or False. The category of software called adware is always potentially dangerous to a computer.
5. What is a Web bug and how can it pose a security risk?
6. What is a firewall?
7. How can you tell that a Web page you are viewing with a browser is secure?
8. What is a server certificate?

Practice the skills you learned in the tutorial using the same case scenario.

PRACTICE

Review Assignments

There are no Data Files needed for the Review Assignments.

Fiona is ready to begin purchasing some of the software programs she needs to protect her business computers from the security threats described in this tutorial. You'll help Fiona with this task by reviewing different antivirus and Internet security programs, malware detection and removal programs, firewalls, and password managers. She asks you to provide recommendations on which programs she should consider purchasing and installing. To find this information for Fiona, complete the following steps:

1. Start your Web browser, go to **www.cengagebrain.com**, open the Tutorial 6 Weblinks page, and then click the Review Assignments link.

2. Fiona needs a program that will protect her computers from viruses and other Internet threats, such as phishing email messages, Trojan horses, worms, and spyware. Use the links in the Antivirus and Internet Security section for the Review Assignments to explore the different products offered. Recommend one program as a solution to prevent these types of problems on Fiona's computers.

3. Return to the Weblinks page for the Review Assignments, and then use the links in the Malware, Spyware, and Adware section to review the options for detecting and eradicating these threats on Fiona's computers. Recommend one or more programs for Fiona to use to protect her computers.

4. Return to the Weblinks page for the Review Assignments, and then use the links in the Firewalls section to explore the different firewall solutions. Find a firewall solution for Fiona to use on her business computers, which use the Windows 7 operating system.

5. Return to the Weblinks page for the Review Assignments, and then use the links in the Password Managers section to explore different ways of securely managing user login information. Recommend a solution for Fiona to use on her personal computer for storing and protecting her login data.

6. In an email message addressed to your instructor, identify the programs you are recommending for Fiona to prevent viruses and other Internet security threats; to detect and remove malware, spyware, and adware; to control network communications using a firewall; and to securely store login information. For each program you recommend, list the reasons why you believe it will be a good solution.

7. Send the email message to your instructor and close your browser.

Apply the skills you learned in the tutorial to find more information about transaction security.

APPLY

Case Problem 1

There are no Data Files needed for this Case Problem.

Ski-Town Ski and Snowboarding School   Jon Sagami is the manager of the Ski-Town Ski and Snowboarding School at Arrowhead Mountain in the Colorado Rocky Mountains. The school offers many full-day and half-day classes to teach children and adults how to downhill ski and snowboard. The school also sells lift tickets, equipment (such as freestyle boards, skis, and ski boots), and snow gear (such as snowsuits, insulated gloves, and goggles). Jon wants to expand the school's marketing efforts with a Web site that lets visitors to Arrowhead Mountain learn more about the school and its merchandise, and buy tickets and book time with instructors in advance. Because the Web site will accept online orders, Jon needs to learn more about securing transactions. To help Jon plan the Web site, complete the following steps:

1. Start your Web browser, go to **www.cengagebrain.com**, open the Tutorial 6 Weblinks page, and then click the Case Problem 1 link. Click the Norton Secured Seal (VeriSign) link.

2. Use the information on this site to learn more about the authentication services and security certificates offered to businesses that need to secure their Web servers. Be sure that you understand the different options for purchasing and using SSL certificates and how they work. If possible, locate and use a product selection wizard or other feature on the site to search for product recommendations, and then explore the options listed. Be sure to investigate the seals that Jon can install on his site and what information they convey to potential customers with regard to security and trust.

3. Return to the Weblinks page for Case Problem 1, and then click the TRUSTe link.

4. Use the links on the TRUSTe site to explore the security options for Website Solutions. Use a site feature or explore the links to learn more about options for small businesses. Be sure to understand what the TRUSTe seal does, how it works, and what it means to potential customers with regard to security and trust.

5. Return to the Weblinks page for Case Problem 1, and then click the Thawte link.

6. Use the links on the Thawte site to explore the security options this vendor provides to small businesses with SSL certificates. Be sure to understand what the Thawte Trusted Site Seal does, how it works, and what it means to potential customers with regard to security and trust. If possible, determine which SSL certificate Jon should choose.

7. In an email message addressed to your instructor, recommend a solution to protect the transactions and other data on the company's Web site. Be sure to include specific details from the solution you are recommending, and take into consideration the cost of the service, the level of protection it provides, and the steps required to install it.

8. Close your browser.

Case Problem 2

Expand what you learned about data security by exploring ways to secure email messages.

RESEARCH

There are no Data Files needed for this Case Problem.

Westway Medical Practice   Dr. Cary Grimes owns and operates a small family practice clinic that provides routine and preventive medical care for patients of all ages. Dr. Grimes recently began asking clients for their communication preferences when the office sends them results from routine lab work and other medical tests. Overwhelmingly, his clients would like to receive their results by email instead of through the postal service. Dr. Grimes realizes that the office could save substantial time and money by using email to send patients their results. However, sending results by email is governed by a federal law called HIPAA (which stands for the Health Insurance Portability and Accountability Act of 1996) that requires him to protect the confidentiality of medical data sent electronically to patients. You'll help Dr. Grimes find an electronic solution for sending medical data to patients by completing the following steps:

1. Start your Web browser, go to **www.cengagebrain.com**, open the Tutorial 6 Weblinks page, and then click the Case Problem 2 link. Click the HHS.gov: Health Information Privacy link to open a page at the U.S. Department of Health & Human Services, which is the agency responsible for administering health and human services in the United States.

⊕ EXPLORE   2. Use the links on the page to review the protections available to consumers and to get a sense of the kind of information that must be protected and how it must be protected, paying particular attention to communications about a person's medical records between a medical office and a patient. Use the HHS site to learn more about who must follow the HIPAA laws, again paying particular attention to requirements for a medical office.

⊕ EXPLORE   3. Return to the HHS page and explore the links on the page for "covered entities." Determine whether Westway Medical Practice needs to follow federal laws that protect patient privacy. Explore the links on this page to learn more about how data must be protected. Use the Frequently Asked Questions page to identify questions that might be relevant, such as a specific FAQ addressing the issue of a doctor or other medical provider using email to communicate with a patient.

4. When you are finished reviewing the HHS site, return to the Weblinks page for Case Problem 2. Click one of the links in the Secure Email section.

⊕ EXPLORE

5. Explore the site you selected to determine if it satisfies the HIPAA requirements and provides an encrypted email solution for Dr. Grimes. As you explore the site, pay particular attention to how the service works, its cost, and whether you would consider recommending it for the Westway Medical Practice.

⊕ EXPLORE

6. Return to the Weblinks page, and then click a link to another site in the Secure Email section. Repeat Step 5 to determine if the services provided by the second site might work for Dr. Grimes.

7. In an email message addressed to your instructor, briefly explain why the office can or cannot use email to communicate with patients. If the office can use email to communicate with patients, recommend a service that it can use to protect the data as required by HIPAA. If the office cannot use email to communicate with patients, explain the reasons why and provide specific details for your response.

8. Based on your findings, recommend a course of action for Dr. Grimes. You can base your recommendation on cost, ease of use, federal law, or other considerations that affect your decision.

9. Send the email message to your instructor, and then close your browser.

Expand your skills to recognize and report phishing email messages and spoofed sites.

RESEARCH

Case Problem 3

There are no Data Files needed for this Case Problem.

Anneka Jones   Anneka Jones, a graduate student in geology, is studying overseas for a semester. Because she will live overseas for only six months or less, she continues to bank at the local branch near her university campus. She uses two email accounts, one of which is affiliated with the university she attends, and another that uses a Webmail address. She checks both accounts daily. For the past week, she has been receiving email messages at both of her email accounts telling her that her local bank account and her eBay account have been compromised and she needs to change her user name and password in both places. Both messages appear to be legitimate, but she is suspicious of this communication. She wants to verify the origin of the messages and their content. You'll help Anneka by completing the following steps:

1. Start your Web browser, go to **www.cengagebrain.com**, open the Tutorial 6 Weblinks page, click the Case Problem 3 link, and then click the eBay: Recognizing spoof (fake) eBay websites link.

⊕ EXPLORE

2. Use the resources on the eBay page to identify legitimate email messages from eBay and what steps to take if you believe that you have received fake email messages claiming to be sent from eBay. Use the links on the page to understand eBay's general guidelines for protecting an eBay account, focusing not on the specific details for eBay accounts but rather on the general precautions you can apply to any account that requires a login.

⊕ EXPLORE

3. Return to the Weblinks page for Case Problem 3, and then click the Citibank Online—Security Center link. Explore the resources on this page to learn more about protecting a Citibank account from fraud and other problems.

⊕ **EXPLORE** 4. Return to the Weblinks page for Case Problem 3, click the Regions Fraud Protection link, and explore the resources on this page to learn more about how Regions Bank protects its customers, and how customers can secure their accounts from theft and fraud.

5. Use the information you found to answer the following questions in an email message addressed to your instructor:

a. What advice do these sites give to people who receive email from a bank or other organization that requests confidential information, such as a user name and password or account number?

b. Do these sites encourage people who receive phishing messages to report them? If so, are these reports usually made to the entity being spoofed, to another organization or entity, or both?

c. What are some general indicators that you might find to be common in phishing messages? Be specific in your response, using information you found at the sites you visited.

d. What advice do these sites give to people who believe that they have become victims of a phishing scam?

6. Send the email message to your instructor, and then close your browser.

Explore the use of encrypted online backup services to store data remotely.

CHALLENGE

Case Problem 4

There are no Data Files needed for this Case Problem.

Kristen Zuniga, CPA Kristen Zuniga, a Certified Public Accountant working in a small practice, works out of her home office twice a week and commutes to her main office three times a week. Kristen uses a flash drive to carry copies of tax returns to and from her offices so she can work on them during the busy tax season. However, she is concerned about the security of this method. She wants to investigate a way to store her data remotely and securely so she can access it from any location. You'll investigate online storage services by completing the following steps:

1. Start your Web browser, go to **www.cengagebrain.com**, open the Tutorial 6 Weblinks page, click the Case Problem 4 link, and then click the Carbonite link.

⊕ **EXPLORE** 2. Locate a link on the page that describes the products that Carbonite offers for home and home office users, and then click it. Use the links on the page that opens to learn more about online backups, remote access, and pricing options. Pay particular attention to information regarding the security and accessibility of the files. (*Note:* Do not install any software or subscribe to any services.)

⊕ **EXPLORE** 3. Return to the Weblinks page, and then click another link in the Case Problem 4 section. Use the links on the page to investigate options for home and home office users, and continue your research using the guidelines presented in Step 2. (*Note:* Do not install any software or subscribe to any services.)

⊕ **EXPLORE** 4. Return to the Weblinks page, and then click another link in the Case Problem 4 section. Continue your research about online backups using the guidelines presented in Step 2. (*Note:* Do not install any software or subscribe to any services.)

5. In an email message addressed to your instructor, describe your findings. Should Kristen use an online backup service to secure her files and have the ability to access them from her home office or her main office? Be sure to justify your recommendation using information you found on the Web sites you explored.

6. Send the email message to your instructor and close your browser.

Understand the content of your credit report and request a copy of it from the official site that provides it.

RESEARCH

Case Problem 5

There are no Data Files needed for this Case Problem.

Obtaining and Understanding Your Credit Report   In this tutorial, you learned about different types of security threats to electronic data, and the countermeasures you can use to detect and prevent certain types of attacks. You also learned that despite your best efforts to safeguard your personal information, you can still become a victim of identity theft. In addition to properly protecting your electronic communications and devices, you should also take steps to monitor your credit report for symptoms of online theft and other problems.

Although many companies offer credit-monitoring services and copies of your credit report for a fee, the AnnualCreditReport.com site is the only official site that consumers can use to obtain a free copy of their credit report annually from each of the three major credit reporting agencies (Experian, TransUnion, and Equifax). In this case problem, you will explore the AnnualCreditReport.com site to understand what type of data appears in your credit report. You also will use the site to request a free copy of your credit report by completing the following steps:

1. Start your Web browser, go to **www.cengagebrain.com**, open the Tutorial 6 Weblinks page, and then click the Case Problem 5 link. Click the AnnualCreditReport.com link.

2. Use the feature for your browser to confirm the identity of the Web site that opens and to view its security certificate. Be sure that the page that has opened is encrypted by your browser. In an email message addressed to your instructor, note the name of the assurance provider that issued the site's certificate and its valid dates.

⊕ EXPLORE

3. Click the Frequently Asked Questions link at the top of the page, and then read the responses to the General FAQs listed on the page that opens. In your email message, answer the following questions using the responses provided on the FAQs page:

   a. What information appears in a credit report?

   b. How does this site guarantee the security of your information?

   c. Why would you order your credit report from one agency every four months instead of ordering it from all three agencies at once?

4. Return to the site's home page, and then select your state of residence. (The state you select should be your official state of residence; this might not be the same state where you live while attending school.) (*Note:* You will not be able to request a credit report if you are not a U.S. citizen or if you do not know your Social Security number. If you cannot request your credit report, skip to Step 10.)

5. Click the Request Report button. On the page that opens, enter the requested information. Select the check box that lets you print only the last four digits of your Social Security number on your report. (*Note:* Be sure to protect the confidentiality of your information while entering it so it is not visible to other people in the room or sent over an unencrypted network. If you have any doubts about whether your information is protected, do *not* enter your information and skip to Step 10.)

6. Click the Continue button. On the next page, select one or more of the credit agencies from which to request your report, and then follow the on-screen steps to actually obtain your report(s). For security purposes, you will be asked to confirm some of the information contained in your credit report to provide additional verification of your identity.

7. Review the information provided in your credit report.

8. When you have finished reviewing your credit report, close your browser. (*Note*: Do not leave the browser window that contains your credit report open.)

EXPLORE

9. Without revealing any personal information contained in your credit report, answer the following questions:

   a. Did your credit report contain information that you expected? If so, what is the general nature of this information?

   b. Did your credit report contain any information that you didn't expect? If so, what is the general nature of this information?

   c. Did you find any errors in your credit report? If so, describe the errors in general terms. (Do not provide specific information.)

   d. Did the credit report contain instructions for correcting or disputing information? What is your opinion of the process described for correcting or disputing information?

10. Send the email message to your instructor.

INTERNET

Wireless Networking

Using and Securing Wireless Networks and Devices

OBJECTIVES

Session 7.1
- Explore the history of wireless networks
- Learn about Wi-Fi, MiFi, and wireless mesh networks
- Investigate technologies used in personal area networks
- Learn about wireless wide area networks
- Investigate WiMAX and LTE networks
- Investigate wireless devices and wireless broadband services

Session 7.2
- Investigate security concerns of wireless networks
- Evaluate different wireless encryption methods
- Understand some common security concerns of wireless devices
- Learn about the different types of attacks on wireless devices
- Learn how to protect the data stored on a wireless device

Case | *Mobile Vet Services*

Ruby Wilson began her career as a staff physician at a local veterinary hospital in Dallas, Texas. Many of her clients were senior citizens or disabled individuals, and they often commented that getting to the vet hospital was challenging. Ruby started Mobile Vet Services, a company that uses outfitted recreational vehicles to provide routine pet care, such as immunizations, simple surgical procedures such as biopsies and neutering, lab services and X-ray procedures, and emergency care. Her business employs three veterinarians, two veterinary technicians, and three mobile clinics. In addition, she has an office in Dallas that serves as a base location for staff members and facilities for other services, such as pet boarding, advanced surgical procedures, and long-term care for animals who are ill or recovering from surgery.

One challenge of working in a mobile vet clinic has been maintaining good communication between the main office and mobile staff members. The vets use cell phones to talk to the office, to each other, and to clients. However, because the vets are not using communication methods that let them easily retrieve a lab report or X-ray image, they are forced to drive back to the office to pick up these items throughout the day.

Ruby has hired you as the new office manager. Your first task is to identify ways to improve the clinic's communication, not only among employees, but also between the clinic and its clients. In your previous position as an assistant communications director for a company that sold wireless communication devices, you are already familiar with many ways to expand and enhance mobile communication. You begin your research by examining different ways to improve communication at Mobile Vet Services.

STARTING DATA FILES

There are no starting Data Files needed for this tutorial.

SESSION 7.1 VISUAL OVERVIEW

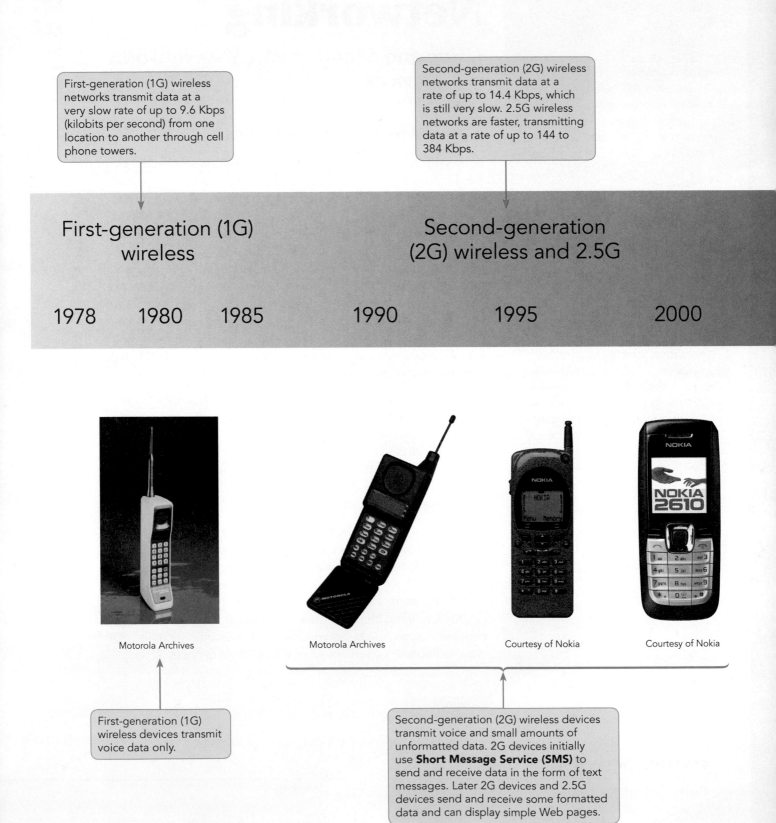

First-generation (1G) wireless networks transmit data at a very slow rate of up to 9.6 Kbps (kilobits per second) from one location to another through cell phone towers.

Second-generation (2G) wireless networks transmit data at a rate of up to 14.4 Kbps, which is still very slow. 2.5G wireless networks are faster, transmitting data at a rate of up to 144 to 384 Kbps.

First-generation (1G) wireless

Second-generation (2G) wireless and 2.5G

| 1978 | 1980 | 1985 | 1990 | 1995 | 2000 |

Motorola Archives

Motorola Archives

Courtesy of Nokia

Courtesy of Nokia

First-generation (1G) wireless devices transmit voice data only.

Second-generation (2G) wireless devices transmit voice and small amounts of unformatted data. 2G devices initially use **Short Message Service (SMS)** to send and receive data in the form of text messages. Later 2G devices and 2.5G devices send and receive some formatted data and can display simple Web pages.

WIRELESS DEVICES TIMELINE

Third-generation (3G) wireless networks transmit data very quickly at rates of up to 2 Mbps (megabits per second), and 3.5G networks transmit data even faster, at rates of up to 10 Mbps.

Fourth-generation (4G) wireless networks transmit data extremely fast at rates of 50 Mbps in 2011, with the goal of transmitting data at a rate of up to 100 Mbps or faster as networks become fully operational.

Third-generation (3G) wireless and 3.5G

Fourth-generation (4G) wireless

Today

2000   2005   2010   2012

Courtesy of Nokia   Courtesy of Research In Motion   iStockphoto.com/ mbbirdy   Courtesy of Verizon   Courtesy of Samsung

Third-generation (3G) wireless devices transmit voice and formatted data. As networks spread geographically, devices roam easily without losing their network connections. Devices can browse the Web, send and receive email, and transfer large files to other users, in addition to SMS and phone calls. Devices also begin to include operating systems, which run programs that expand the device's utility to be more of a personal computer than just a mobile phone.

Fourth-generation (4G) wireless devices transmit voice and formatted data. Because the transfer rate is so fast, devices can easily process multiple tasks simultaneously. All devices include an operating system that lets the devices run applications.

The Evolution of Wireless Networks

When you connect a device such as a computer to an Internet service provider (ISP) using a phone line, cable modem, or DSL modem, you're creating a **wired connection** because the connection between the device and the ISP uses a cable. A **wireless connection** occurs when data, such as a file or a person's voice, is transferred to another location without the use of any wires. As shown in the timeline in the Visual Overview for this session, the first wireless technology was used in 1978, when a voice-only network was started in Chicago and operated on an analog cellular network capable of sending data very slowly by today's standards. These analog cellular networks and the cell phones connected to them were called **first-generation** (**1G**) **wireless** networks.

First-generation cell phones, like the one shown in the Session 7.1 Visual Overview, were some of the first wireless devices to transfer a person's voice. Eventually, cell phone manufacturers found a way to support and send text data over the same connection. Your cell phone probably lets you send and receive very short (up to 160 characters), text-only messages and read them using your phone's display area. This message, called a **text message** because it contains only alphanumeric characters, is a simple message that devices can send to other devices connected to the same or different types of networks. This kind of data transfer occurs over **second-generation** (**2G**) **wireless networks**. The 2G standard transfers data slightly faster than 1G networks, but still much slower than the speed you would experience using a wired device. The 2G wireless data transfer rate is adequate for voice conversations and text messages, but it's extremely slow when you're trying to receive formatted information, such as a Web page. The primary data sent over a 2G network, other than voice conversations, is mostly text messages.

In 1994, carriers created digital networks, or **Personal Communication Service** (**PCS**), on which data was transmitted in bits at a rate of up to 14.4 Kbps. In 1999, the first wireless connections were made to the Internet. At first, the technology was expensive and slow, with poor user interfaces and compatibility problems between mobile devices such as personal digital assistants and cellular phones. A **personal digital assistant** (**PDA**) is a handheld computer that can send and receive wireless telephone and fax calls, act as a personal organizer, perform calculations, store notes, and, in most cases, use a browser to display Web pages. Many PDAs and cell phones perform all of these functions, and they might even have a Global Positioning System (GPS) that displays maps and directions to places around the globe, and a camera and music player.

As cell phone carriers were converting their old analog cellular networks to digital networks (in other words, moving from first-generation to second-generation wireless), PDAs and other handheld computers were growing in popularity for business professionals. Some PDAs and other devices used infrared technology to "beam" information from one source to another without the use of wired connections. This infrared technology initially eliminated the need for wired connections to share data between devices, but its limitations in range increased the need for other wireless methods of transferring data.

In some parts of the United States and the world, 2G wireless networks still provide digital voice services and Short Message Service (SMS). However, most U.S. and worldwide carriers have upgraded their networks to **third-generation** (**3G**) **wireless networks**. The 3G wireless networks offer very fast transfer rates and constant connections. The speed of the 3G network transfer rates enables you to use a wireless device to display Web pages, play MP3 files, watch a video, make and receive phone calls, and send and receive email and text messages. When mobile devices combine the functionality of a cell phone with an operating system that performs these and other functions, they are usually called **smartphones**. Each year, changes and enhancements in technology result in an increasing global market for smartphones. Figure 7-1 shows several popular smartphones, all of which let the user perform many operations, including sending and receiving email messages, making and receiving phone calls, using a browser to access the Internet, playing and recording audio and video files, and using applications to open, edit, and create documents, spreadsheets, PDF files, presentations, and other types of files.

TIP

SMS (more commonly called **text messaging**) is still one of today's most widely used and popular forms of communication methods, with millions of text messages sent each day using wireless devices around the world.

Figure 7-1   **Smartphones: iPhone, Nexus, and BlackBerry**

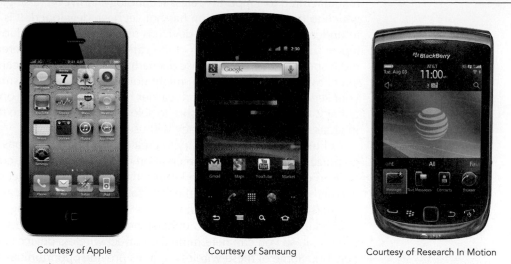

Courtesy of Apple   Courtesy of Samsung   Courtesy of Research In Motion

When establishing nationwide 3G wireless networks in the United States, carriers originally faced two major obstacles. The first was bandwidth. 3G wireless networks must operate in a spectrum where radio frequencies can carry data, and the U.S. government authorizes the use of the spectrum on which 3G wireless networks operate. The second obstacle was cost. Carriers of 3G wireless signals had to purchase licenses to operate 3G wireless networks, and then they had to build cellular transmitters and radio towers to carry the signals. The challenges of converting from 2G to 3G wireless networks were similar to the challenges of converting from analog to digital cellular networks that occurred in the 1990s: The carriers had to invest in technology to make the change. In Europe, the licenses alone have cost carriers more than $95 billion and the cost of building 3G wireless networks has exceeded $125 billion. Much like the early days of cell phones, the technology is only as good as the network and its coverage area. Most U.S. carriers now offer nationwide 3G service, with the exception of limited geographical areas that are mostly rural. These carriers have also successfully established partnerships with the manufacturers of the devices and hardware that operate on their 3G networks.

Between 2G and 3G networks, many carriers transformed and upgraded their existing networks to create **2.5G wireless networks** that deliver faster transfer speeds than the 2G networks. These 2.5G networks allow devices to send files, such as pictures taken with a camera phone, to other users, and to access the Internet. In some areas of the United States where 3G service is unavailable, a device might automatically connect to the 2.5G network. In many cases, the user is unaware of the connection to another network.

The wireless network that followed 3G wireless, which is called a **3.5G wireless network** or **mobile broadband**, provides very fast network connections. By 2009, 3.5G wireless networks existed in the United States, Hong Kong, Singapore, Japan, China, Israel, Argentina, Brazil, Sweden, Norway, and South Korea, and 3.5G networks were being planned and tested in other countries, as well.

In 2010, some carriers created the first, although limited, **fourth-generation wireless networks** (**4G wireless**). 4G technology provides very fast network connection speeds and delivers high-quality audio and video to wireless devices. 4G networks will make it possible for a wireless device to move between the different wireless networks without losing their signals. Because of the tremendous amount of data that 4G wireless networks can send and receive, users can perform multiple tasks on their 4G devices, such as talking on the phone and browsing a Web page simultaneously. Because the devices connected to 4G wireless networks can process many tasks at the same time, this feature is sometimes called **simultaneous support**.

As the number of wireless Internet users continues to increase, more devices will be manufactured to support wireless technology. However, a single network standard on which to transmit information has not yet been developed. It is important for consumers to understand that a wireless device is usually manufactured to work only on a *single* type of network; the networks of the various carriers use different frequencies on the radio spectrum. If you purchase a smartphone for a specific carrier to work on its 3G or 4G network, for example, you might not be able to use that smartphone if you switch your service to another network carrier because your device operates on a different frequency. Consumers must be sure to select the wireless device that will pick up a signal in areas of the world where they will use it.

Cellular was the first industry to create wireless connections that served large geographical areas. Soon after the creation of cellular networks, engineers developed other ways to create wireless networks with different types of devices. Generally, you can classify wireless networking into four categories: wireless local area networking, wireless personal area networking, wireless wide area networking, and metropolitan area networking. It is important to understand each type of network and the technologies used on it, so you can determine the correct wireless devices needed to connect to the network. Some of these wireless options provide opportunities for Mobile Vet Services employees to send and receive important data regardless of the location from which they are conducting business. You will investigate how the different wireless networks and devices can help the Mobile Vet Services employees stay in touch with clients, the main office staff, and each other.

Wireless Local Area Networking

A **wireless local area network** (**WLAN**) is a network on which devices use high-frequency radio waves instead of wires to communicate with a base station, which is connected to the Internet. When most people talk about wireless LANs, they are usually referring to the most common type of wireless network, which is created using the Wi-Fi standard. New computers and all kinds of wireless devices are equipped with **Wi-Fi**, or **wireless fidelity**, which is the trademarked name of the Wi-Fi Alliance that specifies the interface between a wireless client and a base station, or between two wireless clients, to create a **hotspot**, or an area of network coverage. The Wi-Fi Alliance is a not-for-profit organization that certifies interoperability of Wi-Fi products and promotes Wi-Fi as a standard for wireless LANs. Wi-Fi is frequently found in restaurants, stores, and other places where people gather and use wireless devices to access the Internet. Wi-Fi is also used to connect users who are playing electronic games and to connect other types of devices, such as cameras, to the Internet. Many Wi-Fi devices operate in the 2.4 GHz (gigahertz) radio spectrum, which is the same spectrum used by cordless phones, garage door openers, microwave ovens, and other devices. Because this spectrum is unlicensed, it is free. Figure 7-2 compares a traditional wired local area network to a WLAN.

Figure 7-2   **Comparison of wired and wireless local area networks**

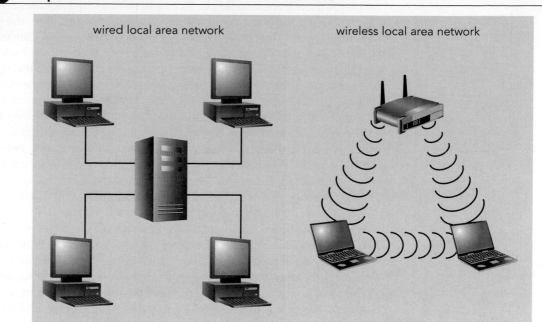

wired local area network   wireless local area network

© Cengage Learning

The Institute of Electrical and Electronics Engineers (IEEE) classifies WLANs using different wireless network standards. Four of the most widely used standards are 802.11a, 802.11b, 802.11g, and 802.11n; for this reason, some people call a wireless LAN an 802.11 network because of the network standard on which Wi-Fi operates. The primary difference between these standards is the radio frequency at which they transmit, the transfer rate of data over the network, and the range at which they operate. The **transfer rate** of data is the speed at which data is transmitted from an access point (or base station) to a wireless device. An **access point** is a hardware device with one or more antennae that permit communication between wired and wireless networks so wireless clients can send and receive data. Generally speaking, the closer the wireless device is to the access point, the faster the transfer rate. The **range** is the physical distance between the access point and the wireless device. Most ranges are averages; the range will vary depending on the physical impediments, such as walls, between the access point and the wireless device. In addition, the transfer rate might be reduced when many devices using the same radio frequency are present in close proximity to the access point.

The term "Wi-Fi" most often refers to the 802.11b standard, which is the one on which most Wi-Fi devices operate. Devices that use the same wireless network standard are compatible with each other. However, the different standards are generally not interoperable; so a device configured for 802.11a is not necessarily compatible with a device configured for 802.11b. A device called a **dual band access point** makes it possible to connect devices configured for different Wi-Fi standards to the same access point, and a **multiple band access point** makes it possible to connect any wireless device to the same access point. However, most businesses will invest in devices created for only one wireless network standard because it is usually less expensive and less technically complicated to do so.

In business settings, Wi-Fi is often used as an alternative in a building or other area in which you might find a traditional wired local area network (LAN); in cases where wiring cannot be installed, wireless networks might be the only way to connect devices to a LAN for Internet access. Wi-Fi is also a popular way to configure wireless devices in homes, especially when rooms in the house where an Internet connection is desired do not have phone or cable outlets. Millions of U.S. households use Wi-Fi to create wireless home networks. As wireless technology becomes more affordable, the number of home wireless networks is expected to increase dramatically worldwide.

New notebook computers and other wireless devices are manufactured with Wi-Fi compatible hardware installed in them and software that locates a Wi-Fi signal and automatically initiates the connection to the wireless network. Because Wi-Fi certified hardware and devices must meet the requirements of the Wi-Fi Alliance for 802.11 wireless standards, any Wi-Fi certified device can connect to any 802.11 certified access point to send and receive signals. A hardware device or a computer running specialized software serves as a central point for wireless clients and provides a connection to the wireless network. These access points already exist in most hotels, airports, convention centers, restaurants, and other public locations across the United States. As long as you are using Wi-Fi certified technology, you can connect to the WLAN when you are within the range of the network and have permission to access it. In most cases, network connections are possible within 200 to 900 feet of the access point, depending on the network standard, surrounding architecture, and other obstacles to the radio waves.

When businesses first started offering Wi-Fi to their customers, many of them charged a fee for its use. Many hotels and retail chains still charge daily fees of up to $15 or more for Wi-Fi connections. However, realizing that Wi-Fi is a way to attract customers and keep them in their businesses, some retailers have changed their Wi-Fi strategies to offer free use instead of paid or limited use. Many hotels now offer free Wi-Fi and access to a business center that includes printers and other electronic devices that guests can use at no charge as a way to increase brand loyalty among frequent travelers. Figure 7-3 shows the Web the page for Holiday Inn Express that describes its services for potential visitors.

Figure 7-3	Holiday Inn Express page describing wireless options for guests

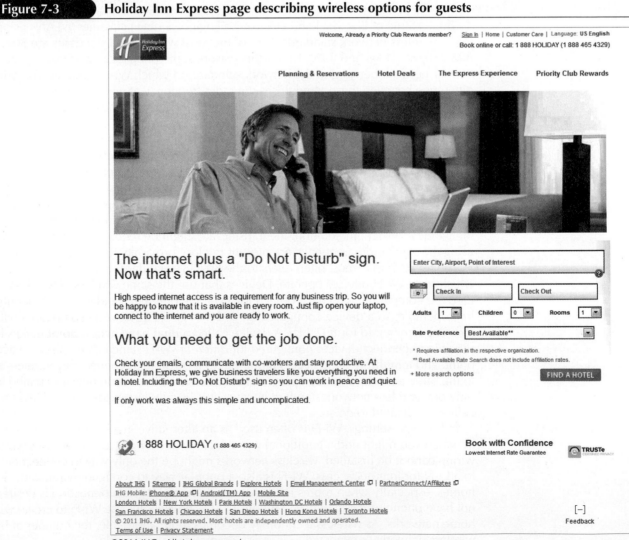

If you position enough access points within the appropriate range of each other, the WLAN can grow to cover an entire office complex or other geographic area. For example, a movement in Seattle in 2001 called for people to put 802.11b access points in their homes and offices, creating a network of access points and an expanded wireless network in the city. You could take your wireless device all over town and still connect to the Internet using the wireless network. But if you traveled outside of Seattle, you would either need to find another access point or use an alternate method to connect to the Internet because you would be out of range of Seattle's wireless network.

In 2004 and 2005, several U.S. cities deployed city-wide Wi-Fi networks in an effort to make affordable Internet connections part of the city's basic services. These city-wide wireless networks are often called **municipal broadband**, **Muni Wi-Fi**, or **Muni-Fi networks** to characterize the wireless network coverage area in terms of a city instead of as a hotspot. However, these networks have faced financing, infrastructure, and management problems. In 2007, Wireless Philadelphia (which became known as Digital Impact Group) was a not-for-profit organization with the goal of creating the nation's largest Wi-Fi network by providing wireless services to individuals and businesses in an area of 135 square miles. Despite support from the community and its leaders, Wireless Philadelphia has struggled to meet its goals, and is now in danger of becoming one of many failed attempts at providing Muni Wi-Fi in an urban area.

Ruby wants more information about how Mobile Vet Services can use wireless devices to communicate. You will investigate a WLAN option for Mobile Vet Services next by searching for information about WLANs using the Web sites of different companies that produce devices that operate on them.

To find information about WLANs:

▶ **1.** Start your Web browser, go to **www.cengagebrain.com**, open the Tutorial 7 Weblinks page, and then click the **Session 7.1** link.

▶ **2.** Find the heading **Wireless LANs** and then click one of the businesses listed to open the site.

Follow the links on the site to learn more about WLAN topics, such as how these networks are configured, the necessary hardware to install them, and other general information that you feel might help you understand the technical requirements, advantages, and disadvantages of using a WLAN for Mobile Vet Services. You do not need to obtain detailed information about the specific hardware that the business sells; your research should focus on general information about WLANs. If the site provides links to demonstrations and your browser can display them, explore these demos to learn more about wireless technology.

Trouble? If you try to view a demonstration and your browser tells you that it is missing a required plug-in, cancel the demo and try another link. Do not download any software or browser plug-ins at this time.

▶ **3.** When you are finished exploring the first business's Web site, return to the Tutorial 7 Weblinks page, and then click a link to another business in the Wireless LANs section. Follow the links on the site to continue your research about WLANs.

▶ **4.** Return to the Weblinks page for Tutorial 7.

Some sites might provide specific information about how to set up a WLAN for Mobile Vet Services. Using Wi-Fi might be a good solution for giving employees some flexibility in where they do their work, either by creating a Wi-Fi network in the main office or by giving them information about where to connect to existing Wi-Fi networks in local businesses.

A different type of WLAN that might interest Ruby is **MiFi**, a small wireless router that a user keeps in a pocket or briefcase and that provides a battery-operated, mobile, personal hotspot for connecting Wi-Fi devices to the Internet. Produced by Novatel and obtaining its broadband signal through a nationwide cellular service, this device creates a mobile Internet connection for Wi-Fi devices. The MiFi device uses a rechargeable battery that operates for several hours before requiring a charge. The hotspot created by MiFi is password protected and can be used to connect as many as five Wi-Fi devices located within 30 feet of the MiFi device to the Internet. When you want to provide other Wi-Fi devices with Internet access through your MiFi hotspot, you simply give the user the password for your MiFi hotspot, which is usually located on the MiFi device. To create a MiFi hotspot, you must first purchase the Novatel device, and then subscribe to a participating broadband service provider. MiFi works anywhere in the United States where the broadband service provider's network is available. Because MiFi doesn't use any wires for its power source or signal, it is an excellent option for mobile Internet connectivity. Figure 7-4 shows the Mobile Broadband page for Verizon Wireless, which includes MiFi as one of its mobile broadband services.

Figure 7-4   **Mobile Broadband page for Verizon Wireless**

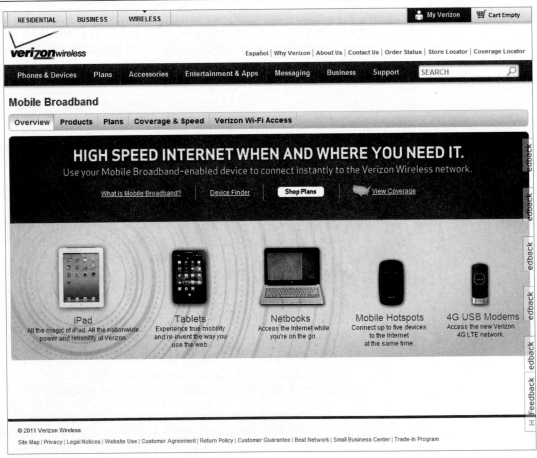

©2011 Verizon

Wireless Mesh Networks

Another type of wireless local area network is a **wireless mesh network**, which is commonly used to extend the reach of Wi-Fi hotspots to an enterprise, such as a university campus, hotel, airport terminal, convention center, sports arena, large office building, or an apartment complex. Unlike a traditional WLAN, in which devices connect through the network to a router that is connected to the Internet, a wireless mesh network is a series of self-configuring wireless nodes (these nodes are usually access points) that communicate with each other to relay communication across the network. The advantage of a wireless mesh network is that as new nodes are installed in the vicinity of the mesh network, they automatically configure themselves to work without the use of cables. Similarly, when a node in the mesh network fails, communication is automatically routed around the failed node with little overall loss to the entire network.

Perhaps the most important feature of a mesh network is that only one of the nodes needs to be wired to the Internet, and then it shares that connection with the other nodes in the network, which automatically determine the best way to transmit data over the entire network. In other words, communication doesn't always go through the router that is connected to the network like it does in a Wi-Fi network—communication goes through the nodes, which transmit data to the next node and act as an access point in the network. This type of wireless network is generally more expensive to create than Wi-Fi hotspots, but it is more effective and efficient at covering large areas with wireless connections because each node is wirelessly connected to the network—not to the router with cables—and each node requires very little power to operate. Figure 7-5 shows an example of a wireless mesh network. Each node might be physically stored on a different floor of an office building or in a different area of an apartment complex to cover the entire geographical area of the structure being connected.

Figure 7-5   **Wireless mesh network configuration**

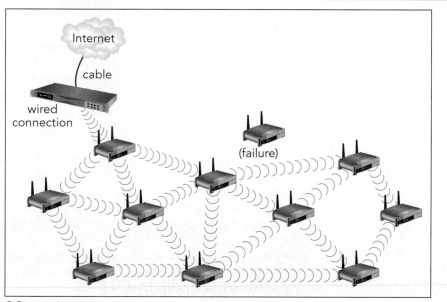

© Cengage Learning

Wireless mesh networks are attractive to organizations trying to provide wireless coverage to a large geographical area. These networks are also frequently found inside buildings, ports, and airport terminals as a method of controlling information from automated services, such as temperature controls, security systems, and fire alarms—all of which use sensors to monitor the operations and status of a large building. In a wireless mesh network, these sensors are linked together through the network and communicate with each other, providing a very reliable and affordable way to monitor the systems in a building or other area.

Ruby wonders if there is a way for staff members to share devices and peripherals without having to install an access point or a wireless mesh network. You will research some options for personal area networks to answer her question.

Personal Area Networking

TIP

Devices that work in a personal area network are sometimes called **PAN devices**.

Personal area networking (PAN) refers to the wireless network that connects personal devices to each other, such as a connection between a smartphone and a wireless headset, or between a notebook computer and a printer. The two major types of personal area networks are infrared and Bluetooth.

Infrared Technology

The **Infrared Data Association** (**IrDA**) is a group dedicated to developing low-cost, high-speed wireless connectivity solutions. Using **infrared** technology, you can wirelessly beam information at up to 4 Mbps from one device to another compatible device using infrared light waves. Infrared provides convenient wireless connections, but there are some limitations. The devices must be compatible and in a direct line of sight with each other for the waves to reach their destinations. In other words, you can't beam information across a room, through a wall, or around a corner. Because infrared uses light waves to carry data, it doesn't interfere with technologies that use radio waves. Originally, this technology was used to provide wireless connections for some computer devices, such as printers. However, now it is used almost exclusively for other types of devices, such as remote controls and cameras, where infrared provides a wireless connection that is not subject to interference from or with other wireless devices.

Bluetooth

The most popular technology in personal area networking, **Bluetooth**, lets you connect compatible devices using radio waves. Named after a 10th century Danish king, Bluetooth provides short-range connections between computers, handheld devices, smartphones, wireless headsets, printers, and other electronic devices. These devices are manufactured with hardware that enables them to receive Bluetooth radio waves. Thousands of Bluetooth-enabled products are on the market, including built-in Bluetooth support in certain Toyota, Mercedes-Benz, BMW, Lexus, Acura, Land Rover, Audi, and Lincoln automobiles. Unlike a WLAN, Bluetooth doesn't need an access point for communication; compatible devices establish their communication with each other automatically. If you want to connect a Bluetooth-enabled device to the Internet, some manufacturers produce Bluetooth access points that function much like their Wi-Fi counterparts in that they connect Bluetooth-enabled devices to a wired network that provides Internet access.

Bluetooth isn't really "owned" by any specific manufacturer or group; according to the official Bluetooth Web site, the goal of the Bluetooth SIG (Special Interest Group) is to "strengthen the Bluetooth brand by empowering SIG members to collaborate and innovate, creating the preferred wireless technology to connect diverse devices." The Bluetooth SIG promoters include Ericsson, Intel, Lenovo, Microsoft, Motorola, Nokia, and Toshiba, along with more than 13,000 associate and adopter member companies; these companies are actively creating new and very creative ways to use Bluetooth technology, and are manufacturing products in the computer, audio, video, medical, personal health, and many other industries to support it. Figure 7-6 shows the home page for the Bluetooth SIG Web site.

Figure 7-6 | **Bluetooth Special Interest Group home page**

© 2011 Bluetooth

Because all Bluetooth-enabled devices must be certified and tested to meet current product specifications, they are compatible with each other regardless of the type of device or manufacturer. Figure 7-7 shows how you might use Bluetooth to create a wireless PAN to connect your electronic devices. When you have visitors to your office, their Bluetooth-enabled devices can also connect to your devices. Because some car models include Bluetooth-enabled phones, you can extend your PAN to include the use of some devices while in your car.

Figure 7-7   **Creating a personal area network using Bluetooth**

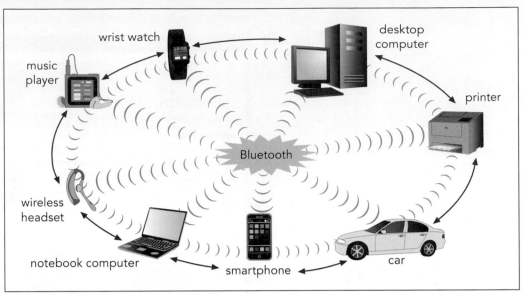

© Cengage Learning

TIP

Most consumer Bluetooth-enabled devices have a range of 30 feet and a data transfer rate of 1 Mbps.

Using Bluetooth technology, you can synchronize and share data among as many as eight Bluetooth-enabled devices within the specified range, usually from 3 to 300 feet, at rates of 1 to 3 Mbps. A collection of devices connected in a personal area network using Bluetooth technology is called a piconet. A **piconet** can connect two to eight devices at a time. However, all devices connected in a piconet must have identical configurations. In a piconet, one device acts as a master during the connection. You can connect piconets with up to eight devices to each other, allowing you to share information between the master devices. You can use Bluetooth-enabled devices to transfer files, listen to music playing on an iPod through a wireless headset, print documents from your office or from another office with a Bluetooth-enabled printer, or use a wireless headset to talk on a smartphone or the integrated phone in your car. Because Bluetooth uses radio waves, the devices must be located within the specified range; but the waves can send data around the corner, down the hall, or from your briefcase, without requiring a direct line of sight. Bluetooth might seem similar to Wi-Fi, but it's not. Figure 7-8 compares wireless network standards to Bluetooth.

Figure 7-8   **Comparing Wi-Fi standards with Bluetooth**

	802.11a	802.11b	802.11g	802.11n	Bluetooth
Used in	Office	Home or office	Home or office	Home or office	Home or office
Range	Up to 100 feet	Up to 200 feet	Up to 200 feet	Up to 900 feet	Up to 300 feet
Connections	64 devices per access point	128 devices per access point	128 devices per access point	128 devices per access point	8 devices per piconet
Radio spectrum	5 GHz	2.4 GHz	2.4 GHz	5 GHz	2.45 GHz
Data transfer rate	Up to 54 Mbps	Up to 11 Mbps	Up to 54 Mbps	Up to 200 Mbps	Up to 3 Mbps

© Cengage Learning

Ruby is interested in knowing more about Bluetooth to synchronize devices and share resources between the mobile vet clinics and the main office. You will research this technology as part of your investigation of wireless networking options.

To find information about Bluetooth:

▶ **1.** In the Session 7.1 section of the Tutorial 7 Weblinks page, find the heading **Bluetooth**.

▶ **2.** Click a link for one of the sites listed, and then follow some of the links on the site to learn more about Bluetooth topics, such as how these networks are configured, what types of devices use Bluetooth technology, and other general information that might help you understand the technical requirements, advantages, and disadvantages of using Bluetooth at Mobile Vet Services. Your research should focus on general information about Bluetooth, not on the specific companies that manufacture Bluetooth-enabled devices. If the site provides links to demonstrations and your browser can display them, explore the demos to learn more about Bluetooth technology.

Trouble? If you try to view a demonstration and your browser tells you that it is missing a required plug-in, cancel the demo and try another link. Do not download any software or browser plug-ins at this time.

▶ **3.** When you are finished exploring the first Web site, return to the Tutorial 7 Weblinks page, and then click another link in the Bluetooth section. Follow the links on the site to continue your research about Bluetooth.

▶ **4.** Return to the Tutorial 7 Weblinks page.

Many manufacturers create products that are certified for Bluetooth applications. Bluetooth will be a technology that Ruby will carefully consider for Mobile Vet Services.

Wireless Wide Area Networking

Many devices have been capable of making wireless Internet connections since 1999, but they were plagued by slow data-transfer speeds, limited interactivity, poor user interfaces, and the limited geographical area of the networks on which they operated.

Devices connecting to a WLAN based on Wi-Fi or to a wireless mesh network must be within the stated boundary of the WLAN. You can use your notebook computer to make a wireless network connection in your office, the conference room, or any other location within the WLAN's range. However, when you're waiting for a plane at the airport or sitting in a hotel room in another state or country, you must use another network to connect to the Internet.

Wireless wide area networking (**WWAN**) makes it possible to access the Internet from anywhere within the boundaries of the WWAN. As its name implies, a WWAN is a wireless network that provides network coverage to a large geographical area. WWANs provide wireless connections to the Internet using 3G and 4G networks created by nationwide cellular phone carriers. To access the Internet using a WWAN, you need an integrated or separate WWAN PC card (also called a mobile broadband card, Aircard, or USB modem) for the device that you want to use and an account with the cellular carrier that operates the network. Once you have a compatible device and an account, you can connect your device to the WWAN and access the Internet from any location where the cellular phone carrier has a signal. For this reason, a WWAN is an excellent option for traveling professionals who need Internet access from many different geographical locations and other areas where Wi-Fi service isn't available. Unlike Wi-Fi connectivity, as you travel, your device will remain connected for as long as the device can receive the cellular phone carrier's signal.

Mobile Wireless Broadband Connections

Most nationwide cellular phone carriers offer consumers wireless Internet service for a daily or monthly rate, and they sell the necessary wireless broadband card or modem. Before purchasing the necessary devices and signing up for wireless Internet service, check the cellular carrier's broadband network coverage maps and make sure that you will be able to pick up the carrier's signal in places where you'll need to connect to the Internet. The coverage area might be identical to where you can get cell phone reception, but this is not always the case, so it's important to check the correct map for wireless service.

Wireless broadband cards and modems are very affordable, but some carriers require a two-year contract for the service when you purchase the device or service. Be sure to understand the contract terms before making a purchase; if you purchase the device or sign up for the service and sign a contract, you might be subject to fines and other fees if you cancel the agreement before the end of the term. With so many broadband options available, you never know when a more affordable option might present itself, so it's a good idea to look for short-term solutions that match your budget.

Ruby might want to consider connecting the mobile clinics using WWAN technologies because this option would make it possible for mobile connections during the workday.

Metropolitan Area Networking

The final networking technology Ruby wants you to explore is metropolitan area networking, the goal of which is to enable wireless networking across broad geographical areas. A **metropolitan area network** (**MAN**) provides wireless broadband Internet service to large geographical areas, usually in hotspots of several square miles each, and connects these hotspots using technology similar to cellular service to create a very large area of network coverage. The two competing standards in this area are WiMAX and LTE, both of which promise to deliver 4G networks around the world.

Worldwide Interoperability for Microwave Access (WiMAX)

Similar to Wi-Fi but operating in a different radio spectrum and using a different network standard, **WiMAX** creates a connected area of network coverage, but in a much larger area than a Wi-Fi hotspot. WiMAX transmitters are usually mounted on the tops of buildings and on existing cellular towers to create network hotspots of up to 10 or more square miles. WiMAX works by connecting a WiMAX tower to an ISP that provides the Internet service. The WiMAX towers are connected to each other via radio signals. WiMAX transmitters, which can be located up to 10 to 30 miles from the towers, send the signal to homes, businesses, and mobile devices that have WiMAX receivers. Subscribers can plug the WiMAX receiver into their existing local area networks to provide high-speed Internet access to all of their connected devices, or use a separate or built-in WiMAX modem to connect a mobile device to the network. Figure 7-9 shows how WiMAX works.

Figure 7-9 **WiMAX network in a metropolitan area**

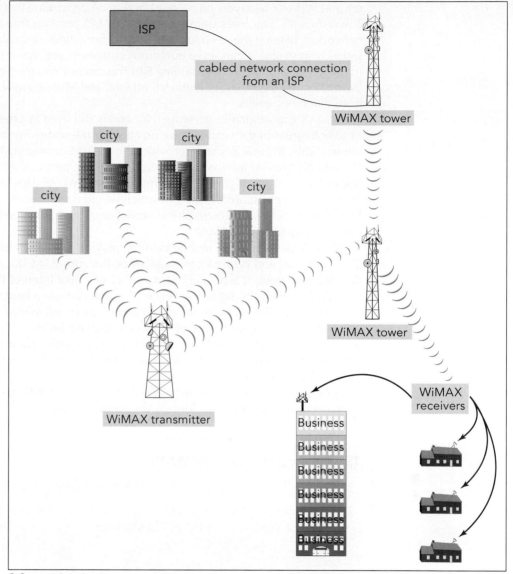

ISP

cabled network connection
from an ISP

WiMAX tower

city city

city

city

WiMAX tower

WiMAX transmitter

WiMAX
receivers

Business
Business
Business
Business
Business
Business

© Cengage Learning

WiMAX uses the 802.16 standards defined by the IEEE for metropolitan area networks, and broadcasts in the 2 to 11 GHz and 10 to 66 GHz radio spectrum. A WiMAX coverage area between the base station and devices varies based on the geography of the area, but most of these hotspots are approximately 10 square miles and operate at speeds of up to 70 Mbps. When multiple WiMAX towers are connected to each other, WiMAX has the potential to solve some of the geographical and speed limitations of wired networks and other wireless networks, including Wi-Fi. For example, the wireless service of many carriers is limited by the coverage area of the network, and Wi-Fi is limited by the number of access points that are connected to each other to form a network. Both of these options provide wireless Internet access, but not at the same speed of a broadband connection such as DSL or a cable modem.

Since 2005, WiMAX has operated in numerous major metropolitan markets, including New York City. In New York City, WiMAX provider Towerstream installed WiMAX towers and WiMAX receivers on rooftops and in office windows of a dense part of the city. Towerstream's customers simply plug the WiMAX receiver into their existing local area network, replacing the need for high-speed phone lines or cables. Because the WiMAX signal is so strong, it can serve numerous customers simultaneously. Since its inception, many major U.S. markets, including San Francisco, Chicago, Seattle, Boston, Dallas-Fort Worth, Tampa Bay, Detroit, Portland, Atlanta, and Miami, are served by WiMAX service from different carriers.

WiMAX was originally developed for and is still used to provide "last mile coverage" to remote areas of the world where no cable or telephone lines exist for wired Internet connections. In New Zealand, provider Broadcast Communications, Ltd., used WiMAX to bring high-speed Internet connections to remote areas where no cable or telephone lines exist for wired high-speed Internet connections. As early as 2005, nearly half of all New Zealand households, many of which would never benefit from high-speed wired broadband because of geographical limitations, had high-speed wireless Internet connections provided by WiMAX.

WiMAX also works for mobile devices, making it possible for users to roam between Wi-Fi hotspots and WiMAX coverage areas. Because WiMAX can support many types of data transmissions, it is also used for VoIP (Voice over Internet Protocol), which converts audio signals to digital packets so that you can use a broadband wired or wireless Internet connection to make local and long-distance telephone calls. Most new desktop and notebook computers and wireless devices have built-in 802.16 cards, as well, which lets them use WiMAX for their Internet service. For older computers and devices, consumers can purchase the required equipment and install it, much like what is available now for Wi-Fi devices.

Ruby wants to learn more about WiMAX so she can anticipate the hardware and other considerations necessary for Mobile Vet Services to use it.

To learn more about WiMAX:

1. On the Weblinks page for Tutorial 7, find the heading **WiMAX**.

2. Click a link for one of the sites listed. Figure 7-10 shows the WiMAX Technology page for Intel, a provider of WiMAX technology in the United States.

| Figure 7-10 | Intel WiMAX Technology page |

© Intel Corporation

3. Follow some of the links on the page to learn more about WiMAX. If the site includes product demonstrations or case studies, use the link provided to run these features. Your research should focus on understanding the current and potential use of WiMAX in a metropolitan area, and on general information about the technology.

   Trouble? If you try to view a demonstration and your browser tells you that it is missing a required plug-in, cancel the demo and try another link. Do not download any software or browser plug-ins at this time.

4. When you are finished exploring the first Web site, return to the Tutorial 7 Weblinks page, and then click another link in the WiMAX section. Follow the links on the site to continue your research about WiMAX.

5. Return to the Tutorial 7 Weblinks page.

   Another technology being used for metropolitan area networking is a competing 4G network standard called LTE.

Long Term Evolution (LTE)

Long Term Evolution (**LTE**) provides 4G wireless broadband connections at very fast speeds to large geographical areas in the United States and in many other areas of the world. Similar to WiMAX, users can connect smartphones and other types of mobile devices to an LTE network for mobile broadband service.

Since 2010, several cellular carriers have built 4G LTE networks for customers with 4G devices in dozens of metropolitan areas. When outside the LTE network's coverage area, these 4G devices automatically connect to the carrier's 3G network for their signals. Some carriers, including AT&T and Verizon Wireless, hope to have nationwide LTE 4G networks in operation by 2013 or 2015. In the meantime, customers with 4G devices should notice faster connections when they are in range of the LTE network.

LTE operates in the radio spectrum from 1.4 MHz to 20 MHz; but most U.S. carriers will operate at 700 MHz, where there is no interference and nationwide availability. LTE has very fast download speeds of up to 100 Mbps and upload speeds of up to 50 Mbps. In some parts of the world, LTE is being used for residential and commercial broadband service; but in the United States, LTE is being developed primarily for mobile devices. Smartphones are being manufactured with embedded modems to connect to the LTE network. For other types of devices, such as notebook computers, users can install a USB device to connect to the network, much like you would use a USB device to connect to a 3G network. In areas where the LTE signal is not as strong, such as indoors, users can connect a device called a femtocell to an existing wired network to improve the performance and signals of their LTE devices. A **femtocell** is a base station that uses minimal power to transmit the LTE signal from a wired connection, such as a cable or DSL modem, to LTE devices within its range to increase their speed.

Ruby wants to learn more about LTE so she can evaluate it for future use. She also wants to get a sense of how WiMAX and LTE markets might develop, and the support various technology manufacturers have for each network.

> **TIP**
>
> A femtocell is also called a Home eNode when used for LTE devices.

To learn more about LTE:

1. On the Weblinks page for Tutorial 7, find the heading **LTE**.

2. Click a link for one of the sites listed. Figure 7-11 shows the 4G LTE page for Verizon Wireless, a carrier that expects two-thirds of its network traffic to be handled by its LTE network by the middle of 2012 and plans to offer nationwide 4G services by the end of 2013.

Figure 7-11	**4G LTE page for Verizon Wireless**

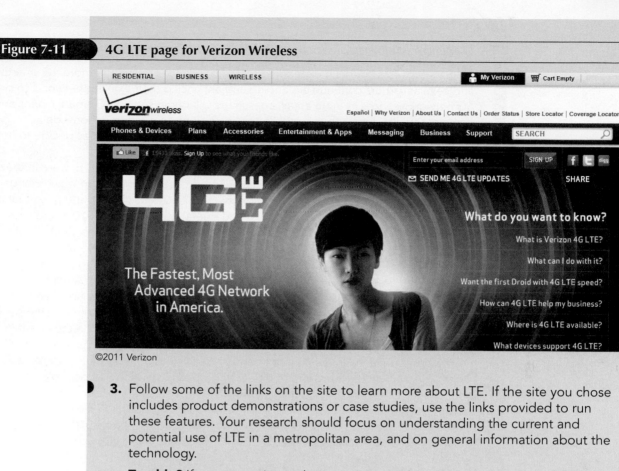

©2011 Verizon

3. Follow some of the links on the site to learn more about LTE. If the site you chose includes product demonstrations or case studies, use the links provided to run these features. Your research should focus on understanding the current and potential use of LTE in a metropolitan area, and on general information about the technology.

   Trouble? If you try to view a demonstration and your browser tells you that it is missing a required plug-in, cancel the demo and try another link. Do not download any software or browser plug-ins at this time.

4. When you are finished exploring the first Web site, return to the Tutorial 7 Weblinks page, and then click another link in the LTE section. Follow the links on the site to continue your research about LTE.

5. Return to the Tutorial 7 Weblinks page.

Decision Making: Choosing a Mobile Broadband Provider

As manufacturers continue expanding their product lines to include more 4G smartphones, and cellular carriers continue expanding and enhancing their existing networks to provide 4G network services in more areas, consumers will begin seeing 4G smartphones and network services across the United States, in addition to existing nationwide 3G services. How and—more importantly—when should consumers and businesses decide to upgrade to this new technology?

In 2011, the two competing 4G network standards, WiMAX and LTE, were in their early stages of development in the United States, but experts disagreed on which standard would be the predominant or prevailing network. WiMAX has an advantage in that it is generally less expensive to implement and operate than LTE. In 2010, more than 120 million customers in many parts of the United States already used WiMAX for their wireless Internet connections. However, LTE has the advantage of two of the nation's largest cellular carriers—AT&T and Verizon Wireless—investing in building LTE networks and providing services starting in 2011 to millions of their LTE customers. As with the upgrades from 2G wireless to 3G wireless, one of the most important factors is how fast these networks are built and how many customers each can attract. It is possible that the network that operates first and fastest, and at the most affordable price, will be the one that attracts the most customers and—for this reason—will become the prevailing choice for 4G.

For individual consumers, it might be wise to delay upgrading their current devices or network service contracts with their cellular carriers for as long as possible so they can choose the service and device that will work the best for them in terms of cost and in the geographic coverage areas in which they require service. Businesses should follow a similar strategy to ensure that the network and devices will address the needs of their users at an affordable cost. By delaying these decisions, individuals and businesses might be able to wait until one network standard becomes the more dominant one, and avoid purchasing devices or service contracts on a smaller or less capable network.

Because all of the vets use wireless devices, you need to know more about the types of tasks that the devices must handle. Ruby tells you her staff is interested in using smartphones for all of their current needs, which includes voice calls, text messaging, Web browsing, sending and receiving large files via email, and taking and sending pictures and video. Because the vets want to download Web pages and transfer large picture and video files taken with their devices, you will need to find an option that has a fast transfer rate and devices that have these desired features. Finally, because the vets travel frequently, the devices they use and the service provider will need to offer connectivity options for the largest possible coverage area without incurring additional costs.

Using Wireless Devices to Access the Internet

Because the vets will rely heavily on their devices, your first priority is to explore device options that use 4G networks to provide Internet connections through a WWAN. Most cellular phone carriers make it easy to select a device that works on a network, and provide other resources such as charts to compare and contrast the different features of the wireless device. Most carriers offer specific products, such as the Droid smartphone, wireless USB modem, and MiFi device shown in Figure 7-12, to work on their wireless networks.

| **Figure 7-12** | **Droid Charge, 4G LTE USB modem, and 4G LTE MiFi device** |

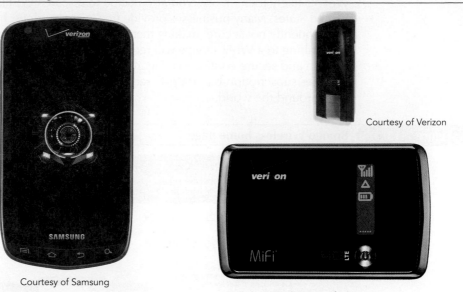

Courtesy of Verizon

Courtesy of Samsung

Courtesy of Verizon

Next, you'll visit the Web sites of some major carriers to explore the costs and functionality of the devices that work on their networks. As you are conducting your research, be sure to consider the ways the staff will use their devices so you can select an appropriate device to meet their needs.

To find information about 4G devices:

1. On the Tutorial 7 Weblinks page, find the heading **Mobile Broadband Devices**.

2. Click a link for one of the sites listed to open its home page.

3. Locate a link that opens a page describing the 4G devices offered by the cellular carrier.

   Trouble? If you are prompted to enter your zip code, enter the zip code for your local or permanent address.

4. Follow some links on the page to learn more about the different 4G devices and their features and functionality. Some sites might provide links to demonstrations; if your browser can display them, explore these demos to learn more about the device's features.

   Trouble? If you try to view a demonstration and your browser tells you that it is missing a required plug-in, cancel the demo and try another link. Do not download any software or browser plug-ins at this time.

5. When you are finished exploring the first Web site, return to the Tutorial 7 Weblinks page, and then click the link to another company in the Mobile Broadband Devices section. Repeat Steps 3 and 4 to continue your research about 4G devices.

6. When you are finished exploring the second site, return to the Tutorial 7 Weblinks page, and then click the link to another company in the Mobile Broadband Devices section. Repeat Steps 3 and 4 to continue your research about 4G devices.

7. Return to the Tutorial 7 Weblinks page.

Because the staff indicated a preference for using their devices in places where Wi-Fi is likely to be in use, you also decide to research Wi-Fi service providers in the United States. Many businesses provide free Wi-Fi services, but these Wi-Fi hotspots are frequently not secure, making them less desirable for business communications. Subscribing to a Wi-Fi service will require a payment for use, but will provide a more reliable and secure connection. Figure 7-13 shows the home page for Boingo, which provides subscription-based Wi-Fi service for its customers in more than 325,000 locations around the world.

Figure 7-13	Boingo Wireless home page

Some networks, such as those found in airports and hotels, let you pay a daily fee to use the network. Other networks require a monthly fee for using the network. Fortunately, there are many plans that would work well for Mobile Vet Services to provide Wi-Fi service that is reliable and secure.

To find information about Wi-Fi subscription services:

▶ **1.** On the Weblinks page for Tutorial 7, find the heading **Wi-Fi Subscription Services**.

▶ **2.** Click a link for one of the sites, and then follow the links on the site to learn more about Wi-Fi subscription services for Mobile Vet Services. Use the site to find information about the type of payment plans and their costs, the coverage area provided, and other details that you will need to learn more about the service. If the site includes information about single-user pricing and corporate pricing, be sure to investigate both options.

   Trouble? If you try to view a demonstration and your browser tells you that it is missing a required plug-in, cancel the demo and try another link. Do not download any software or browser plug-ins at this time.

▶ **3.** When you are finished exploring the first Web site, return to the Tutorial 7 Weblinks page, and then click the link to another business in the Wi-Fi Subscription Services section. Follow the links on the site to continue your research about the provider's products, services, and pricing plans, and the locations it serves.

▶ **4.** Close your browser.

Ruby can discuss the information you found about wireless services, networks, and devices with her staff in their next meeting. You are excited about the possibilities for creating a mobile office to increase the speed at which Mobile Vet Services disseminates and receives information to and from clients and the main office. In the next session, you will examine the different methods for securing wireless networks and wireless devices.

Session 7.1 Quick Check

REVIEW

1. What is the transfer rate of data on a 3G wireless network? What is the transfer rate of data on a 4G wireless network?

2. What is SMS and what is it used for?

3. What is simultaneous support? On which type of network is simultaneous support possible, and why?

4. What is MiFi and how does it work?

5. Name three types of devices that might use Bluetooth to create a personal area network.

6. What is a metropolitan area network and how does it work to provide network services?

7. What is WiMAX? What are its range and maximum data transfer rate?

8. What is LTE? What is its maximum data transfer rate?

SESSION 7.2 VISUAL OVERVIEW

- Attacks that prevent the use of a device
- Attacks that decrease the network's bandwidth

Service Interruptions

Lo-Random/Shutterstock.com

- Garnering login information entered into a wireless device by watching the user enter it on the device
- Stealing or simulating the identity of an access point to gain unauthorized access to its connected users' devices without their knowledge or consent

Interception

Sergey Peterman/Shutterstock.com

- Using logins and other confidential information intercepted from a wireless device to steal property, such as money in a bank account, or to steal data, such as a credit card number used to unlawfully purchase goods
- Theft of the device
- Theft of the data on the device

Theft

Angela Waye /Shutterstock.com

WIRELESS SECURITY CONCERNS

- Forcible access to a wireless device's information or functions, either by illegal entry through a software program or by breaking the password on the device
- Unauthorized access to information being sent over a wireless network

Hacking

antkevyv/Shutterstock.com

- Viruses
- Spyware
- Malware
- Spoofed apps for smartphones

Malicious Files

bofotolux/Shutterstock.com

- Using the GPS information from a wireless device or in a photograph or other file created by the wireless device to locate a person with the intent of harming that user or that user's property

Personal Harm

Login/Shutterstock.com

Security Concerns for Using Wireless Networks

In Session 7.1, you learned about different kinds of wireless networks and the devices you can use to connect to them. The kind of connection you make depends on the type of device you have: A device that was manufactured for a certain cellular network won't necessarily work on another cellular network. The type of connection you make also depends on the network that you are connecting to. Being able to pick up a wireless signal doesn't mean that you can automatically use it to connect to the Internet—nor does it always mean that you *should* connect to a wireless signal that you pick up.

Just like in the wired world of networking, ensuring the security of the data sent over a wireless network presents many challenges. Some of the security challenges are the same between wired and wireless networks; but many of the challenges in protecting a wireless network are complicated by the fact that a wireless network sends its data through the air using radio signals that are subject to interception. Although there are different kinds of threats to wireless networks—and new threats as hackers get better at figuring out how to manipulate the technology and its signals—there are also security threats to individual wireless devices, the most basic of which is theft of the device itself. The Session 7.2 Visual Overview identifies some of the major concerns for wireless connections and wireless devices.

As Ruby considers wireless options for the Mobile Vet Services staff, she needs to understand the various security measures for wireless networks, the threats to the wireless devices, and methods for securing the wireless devices her staff will use to connect and send data using wireless networks.

Methods for Securing Wireless Networks

When setting up a wireless network for a home or small business, you can use one or more techniques to secure the network from different types of attacks and other threats. To protect the data that is transmitted over the wireless network, you can enable specific encryption methods. You also need to protect the network from unauthorized access by limiting the devices that can connect to it. You can set the router and individual devices that connect to the router to protect against unauthorized access.

Wireless Encryption Methods

As you learned in Tutorial 6, encryption is the process of coding information so that it is not readable by devices or people who do not have the secret key used to return the information back to its original, readable state. By default, most wireless networks are unsecured, meaning that any compatible wireless device within range of the network can connect to it. Unfortunately, many home and small business networks are never secured and therefore are vulnerable to various kinds of attacks. There are many wireless encryption methods that provide different levels of protection for wireless networks.

Wired Equivalent Privacy

One of the first methods used to secure wireless networks, **Wired Equivalent Privacy (WEP)**, is a security protocol for wireless LANs (using Wi-Fi) that works by encrypting data sent over the network. When WEP is enabled, it encrypts the data sent over the network with a 64-bit or 128-bit key, sometimes also called a **passphrase**, that is entered by the user. These settings—64-bit key and 128-bit key—are standards used in the electronic commerce industry to represent the security level of the key. The key works because both the wireless router or access point and the device connecting to the wireless network have the same key and use it to encrypt and decrypt messages. The encryption slows down the network somewhat because of the time it takes to encrypt and decrypt the messages. The level of encryption provided by the key depends on the key's length; a 128-bit key is more secure than a 64-bit key because it is longer and contains more characters. A 64-bit key contains 10 hexadecimal characters (the digits 0 through 9 and the letters A though F); a 128-bit key contains 26 hexadecimal characters. Figure 7-14 shows examples of randomly generated 64-bit and 128-bit keys, and a custom 128-bit key based on a user-entered passphrase.

Figure 7-14   **Security keys in hexadecimal characters**

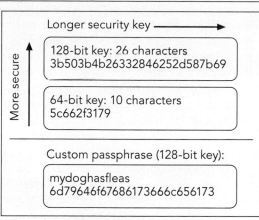

128-bit key: 26 characters
3b503b4b26332846252d587b69

64-bit key: 10 characters
5c662f3179

Custom passphrase (128-bit key):

mydoghasfleas
6d79646f67686173666c656173

© Cengage Learning

Depending on the equipment used and how much time and money a hacker has, it can take time to decipher an intercepted message encrypted with a 64-bit key, and even longer to decipher an intercepted message encrypted with a 128-bit key. Deciphering a key isn't easy, and it requires a substantial amount of computing power and time. But, for a person who has these resources, it is possible to decipher a WEP-encrypted message. For this reason, and because of the actual way that data is encrypted, many computing experts don't recommend WEP because it provides insufficient security for wireless networks.

Another vulnerability of WEP encryption is the fact that the key used to encrypt the data you are sending is sent over the network before the actual data is encrypted, and this same key is used to encrypt every data packet. This means that you send the key over the network with no protection before the data you are sending is encrypted. (If you change the key frequently, you'll provide some additional security to the network.) Although this is a simplified explanation of the problem, it does support the consensus of most experts that using WEP is better than nothing, but it is not ideal for securing a wireless network.

Wi-Fi Protected Access

Wi-Fi Protected Access (**WPA**), another wireless network security protocol, is a standard that was developed by the Wi-Fi Alliance to address some of the inherent weaknesses in WEP. WPA provides better encryption than WEP because WPA uses a preshared key to encrypt data (so the key isn't broadcast before data is encrypted), and individual data packets are encrypted with different keys. This means that a hacker might be able to intercept a data packet, but he won't gain access to the entire message automatically, making the content of the complete message difficult to read. Like WEP, WPA can use a 128-bit key to encrypt data.

Although WPA provides good protection, one drawback is that all devices in the network need to use WPA. Some older devices will still need to use WEP or another protocol to secure data. Some wireless routers and access points let you use a combination of WEP and WPA when your network makes connections to devices that can't manage WPA.

Decision Making: Deciding Which Encryption Method to Use for Wireless Networks

In business settings and in large organizations, networks might carry highly sensitive information such as a person's credit card number or medical history. These businesses must use advanced methods for securing data transmitted over a wireless network.

For home and small business users, however, the choice of which method to use to secure a wireless network is up to the individual user. Unfortunately, many wireless routers are packaged with no security settings enabled on them. This means that users who connect the router and plug it into their DSL or cable modem and then immediately start using the signal that the router transmits are doing so with no encryption or enabled security settings. People in the next room or across the street can also detect your wireless network and use it. They might not do anything to the signal that has negative consequences to you; but at a minimum, they might borrow your Internet connection and use its signal, which slows down the connection speed when you use the network.

It's worth taking the time to read and understand the documentation for a wireless router to make good decisions about how to secure it. You might need to install some software on your computer to access the router so you can change its configurations. If the router and your computer support WPA, you should use this encryption instead of WEP because it is more secure. However, if your computer won't support WPA, using WEP usually provides sufficient protection to keep users from accessing your network's signal.

In addition to adding data encryption to a wireless network, you can use other techniques to secure the network by limiting the devices that can connect to it.

MAC Address Filtering

Every Internet device has a network interface card that it uses to connect to a network. Each manufacturer of network interface cards adds a unique number, called a **Media Access Control address** (or more commonly called a **MAC address**) to identify the device. Another way to protect a wireless network is to designate the devices that you want to allow to connect to the network. Most routers and access points include software that lets you identify the allowable devices using their MAC addresses. If you enable MAC address filtering for a wireless router or access point, then it will only accept connections from the devices with the MAC addresses that you entered. Other wireless devices still might *detect* your wireless network, but they won't be able to connect to it because their MAC addresses are not specified for access. MAC address filtering adds another layer of security to a wireless network because it doesn't allow unknown devices to make connections.

The MAC address for detachable network interface cards, such as ones that you insert into a notebook computer's PC card slot or USB devices, is usually printed on the card or USB device. A MAC address appears in the format 00:00:00:0A:0B:0C, as a combination of digits and letters. When a device contains an internal network interface card, you can see its MAC address by using the Windows Device Manager or the device's settings menu to view the properties for the network interface card.

TIP

Every network interface card has a MAC address; this term refers to the Media Access Control (MAC) address on the device, not to the Macintosh (Mac) computer.

Disabling the SSID Broadcast

When a wireless router or access point sends out its signal, it also broadcasts its **service set identifier** (**SSID**) as a way of identifying the network's name. This feature makes it possible for roaming devices to discover the network and also enables you to log in to the correct network. Most manufacturers of wireless routers and access points use the manufacturer name or the word "default" as the default SSID for the device. When you install a wireless router or access point, you can accept this default name or change it to a name that has up to 32 alphanumeric characters. Most manufacturers strongly recommend that you change the default name as part of its initial configuration. All devices that connect to the wireless network must use the SSID.

INSIGHT

Disabling the SSID in Home Networks

For public wireless networks, sending out the SSID is necessary because it provides information that a wireless device needs in order to connect to the wireless network. However, for home networks, sending out the SSID is not necessary, especially if you already use MAC address filtering to identify the devices that you want to connect to the wireless network. In other words, after you configure your own devices to connect to your wireless network, you don't need to broadcast the SSID any longer because you won't need to roam and find the network—you already know the network's name and its settings, and your wireless devices also know them once they are configured. Disabling the SSID broadcast of a home network makes the network invisible to roaming devices and therefore makes it more difficult for other devices to detect its signal.

If you change the default name of the wireless router or access point, you also prevent unknown users from detecting your network by attempting to randomly connect to a wireless network using a manufacturer name or the word "default" as an SSID. **Wardriving**— driving through a neighborhood with a wireless device with the goal of locating houses and businesses that have wireless networks in order to gain access to them—is a common way for hackers to access unsecured networks. Finding a wireless network that uses "default" or a manufacturer name as its SSID is a good clue to hackers that the wireless network's owner didn't take precautions to secure the wireless network. Used alone and especially with other security precautions, disabling the SSID adds another layer of protection to the network to prevent unknown devices from connecting to it.

You can change the SSID name for your wireless router or access point and disable its signal by logging into the router or access point and changing these settings in the device configuration.

Changing the Default Login

When you install a wireless router or access point for the first time, the device is configured with a default user name and password that is printed in the device's user manual. The default login is provided so you can use your computer to access the device's settings and configure it to work as desired. One of the most serious mistakes that home users make when installing a wireless network is failing to change the default login for the device. By making this mistake, you make it possible for anyone who already knows the manufacturer's generic default login information to access the wireless network. If you haven't implemented any other security for the router, such as changing the default SSID or disabling its broadcast, your wireless network is visible and easy to access using the default login. When you install a wireless network, make it a priority to change the default login and password. Be sure to keep your login in a safe place; after you change it, you won't be able to access the device's configuration page again using the default login.

Ruby realizes that she can purchase a wireless router or access point and start using it right away, but she now understands why it is a good idea to spend some time to learn how to configure it properly. She can use the checklist shown in Figure 7-15 to make it easier for her to configure the wireless network in the office.

Figure 7-15	Security checklist for installing a wireless router or access point

☐ Change the default login and password for the wireless router or access point.

☐ Change the default SSID. Be sure to type the name in the desired case, as the SSID is case sensitive.

☐ Obtain the MAC addresses of the wireless devices that will connect to the wireless network, and then enter their MAC addresses using the configuration for the wireless router or device.

☐ Enable MAC address filtering on the wireless router or access point.

☐ Enable the highest level of security that your wireless devices and wireless router or access point can manage. Be sure to use the most secure key the wireless router or access point offers. If you must use WEP, change the passphrase occasionally.

☐ Make sure that all of your wireless devices can connect to the wireless network with the settings you've implemented.

☐ Disable the SSID for your wireless router or access point.

☐ When not using the wireless network for an extended period of time, such as when leaving on vacation, power it off.

© Cengage Learning

Of course, the safest wireless network is one that is turned off. Most experts recommend disconnecting or powering off your wireless network when you won't be using it for an extended period of time, such as when you leave on vacation.

The methods for securing wireless networks that you have examined so far mostly apply to smaller networks, such as networks for home or small business use, where a small number of devices need to connect to the network. Organizations with many wireless connections from many different devices require an additional resource to protect the networks from the same types of threats common to home and small business users. You'll learn about using software to protect wireless networks next.

Using Software to Protect Wireless Networks

Larger wireless networks with many different devices connecting to them can supply an additional layer of security by running software that prevents unauthorized network use, protects against different kinds of security threats, and monitors the network for other types of problems that might affect the network's reliability and performance. Because the Mobile Vet Services office might install a wireless network and will need to ensure the security of the data transmitted over the network, you'll examine some of these programs next.

To investigate software that protects wireless connections:

1. Start your Web browser, go to **www.cengagebrain.com**, open the Tutorial 7 Weblinks page, and then click the **Session 7.2** link. Find the heading **Wireless Intrusion Software** and click a link to one of the businesses listed to open the site. Figure 7-16 shows the home page for AirTight Networks, a company that provides wireless intrusion software for different types of wireless networks.

Figure 7-16   AirTight Networks home page

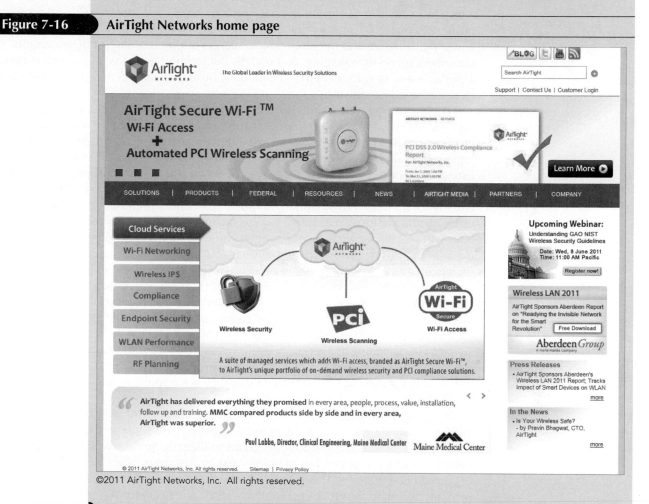

©2011 AirTight Networks, Inc. All rights reserved.

2. Use the links at the site to investigate options for securing wireless connections and detecting intrusions to existing networks. Find out how the software is installed, how it works, and its approximate cost.

3. Return to the Tutorial 7 Weblinks page, and then click a link to another business. Use the guidelines in Step 2 to investigate the products of the second business.

4. When you are finished, close your Web browser.

After ensuring the security of the wireless network, users need to take precautions to secure their individual devices. Some common security threats to wireless devices are described next.

Understanding Security Threats to Wireless Devices

Because wireless technology makes it possible to work in almost any place with a wireless network connection, many people enjoy the freedom of having a mobile office or the convenience of being able to do work outside of the conventional office or home office environment. As you learned in Session 7.1, many businesses offer free Wi-Fi service as a way of attracting and retaining customers. Some customers are irritated when a business offers Wi-Fi service but requires a fee to make connections because so many businesses offer the same service at no charge. Customers expect Wi-Fi service at certain kinds of businesses and in certain areas, such as airport terminals and restaurants, where customers spend time waiting. Fortunately, the technology to install a wireless network is affordable and easy to implement, and many businesses attract and retain customers by installing wireless networks.

Wireless devices of all kinds are subject to many types of attacks, especially when they are used in public places. An **over-the-shoulder attack** occurs when an unauthorized person uses his or her physical proximity to your device to attempt to see your login information, passwords, or other sensitive data while you are working. People who use wireless devices in public places might not question why another person is standing behind them; they might incorrectly assume this person is simply standing in line or waiting for a friend. When working in public places, it's important to be aware of where other people are located in proximity to you and your device, especially if you are using your wireless device to transmit data that you wouldn't want another person to see. For this reason, most security experts advise against activities such as online banking, checking email, and online shopping in public places. Not only are these activities visible to over-the-shoulder attacks, they are also subject to being intercepted.

In an **evil twin attack**, also sometimes called a **café latte attack** because the attack often occurs at coffeehouses, a hacker gathers information about an access point and then uses that information to set up his own computer to use the real access point's signal to impersonate the access point. To other customers, the hacker looks like a customer who is also using the network. As customers use their devices to detect and connect to the network, they are unaware that they are actually connecting to the hacker's computer.

When people use one of the many free public hotspots for wireless Internet connections, the data they send over the network usually is not encrypted or secure. This data is subject to hackers using **sniffer programs** to illegally monitor activity on the wireless network in order to obtain personal information that users might transmit, such as a login or a credit card number. The hacker uses these connections and a sniffer program to read and store the data that the customers send to his system. When customers engage in online banking or online shopping, or log on to Web sites that require passwords, the hacker happily collects this sensitive data. Depending on what data the hacker collects, he might later use the customer's credit card numbers to make online purchases or use login information to access the victim's email account. All of this happens without the customer's or the network owner's knowledge.

A third type of attack, called a **man-in-the-middle attack** (**MITM attack**), occurs when transmissions, such as messages between users, logins, and normal connections with Web servers, that are being sent between two devices are intercepted by a third party. For example, suppose device A is sending a transmission to device B over a wireless network. In a man-in-the-middle attack, a third party—the intruder—uses device C to intercept the transmission. In this case, device C might eavesdrop on the transmission to gain information or alter the transmission in some way. In either case, devices A and B are unaware of the intrusion. Preventing MITM attacks requires users to ensure that their transmissions are encrypted, that they are communicating with known parties and clients, and that they are aware of anything suspicious in the connection that might make them suspect an intruder.

INSIGHT

Using Public Hotspots Safely

To protect your wireless device from different types of attacks, you can refrain from using it in any public place; but there might be times when you are traveling or working outside of your home or office when you need to connect to the Internet. You can take several precautions to protect your wireless device.

First, avoid online banking, online shopping, and visiting Web sites that require you to enter a login or personal information. In other words, don't work in public places if you need to interact with something of value.

What if you must use email or another service that requires a login? Instead of connecting to any free hotspot that your device picks up, establish a connection to a network that provides some kind of login from the access point's owner. Although you might prefer to get your Wi-Fi service for free, your connection is more secure when the hotspot requires an account with an established service provider. You might need to pay for your use of the service, but you're more likely to connect to a wireless network that provides some sort of encryption and security.

Finally, when working in a business facility, such as a convention center, sports arena, or other large building that provides Internet access, or when working in a hotel, opt for a wired Ethernet connection whenever possible. Although your devices are still subject to some basic security threats, connecting to the Internet with a wired connection eliminates the wireless threats to your device.

Just like a personal computer, a wireless device is vulnerable to certain kinds of attacks on the data it stores. Unlike a personal computer, the kinds of attacks are different and they might vary for individual devices. For example, Bluetooth-enabled devices are vulnerable to certain kinds of attacks that do not target non-Bluetooth devices. You'll explore these security issues next.

Security Concerns for Bluetooth-Enabled Devices

Most smartphones and many other devices are enabled with Bluetooth, which lets the user pair devices such as a headset with a smartphone for hands-free use. As you learned in Session 7.1, the usual range for a Bluetooth-enabled device is 10 to 30 feet, and up to 300 feet, depending on the device. This short range and the fact that it is possible to pair Bluetooth-enabled devices without a password make it possible for someone to access your device without your consent or knowledge. Although many smartphone manufacturers have updated their software to prevent some of these types of attacks, having a basic understanding of these security concerns lets you secure your device to prevent these and other types of threats. The most common security problems of Bluetooth devices are bluejacking, bluesnarfing, and bluebugging.

Bluejacking is a term coined from the words "blue" and "ajack." (Ajack is the user name of a person in an Internet forum who claims to have been the first person to bluejack someone else.) The bluejacker sends an anonymous message in the form of a phone contact displayed as a text message to a Bluetooth-enabled device to surprise the owner, express an opinion, or make a social connection. In the first documented bluejacking, Ajack sent a message to the owner of a Nokia phone that said "Buy Ericsson!" to express his preference for Sony Ericsson phones.

Bluejacking, although alarming to some people, is mostly harmless because the victim's device is not breached; it is only sent a message. The message is usually sent by a bluejacker who takes advantage of the victim's unprotected device or is interested in the victim. Bluejacking is temporary: When the bluejacker's device or your device moves out of range, the messages will stop. Because bluejacking uses a feature of the device designed for legitimate purposes, it does not require special software or equipment.

TIP

Some sources state that the word "bluejacking" is coined from the terms "blue" and "hijacking." During a bluejack, the device is not actually hijacked, so this combination of terms is misleading.

A more serious security problem of Bluetooth-enabled devices, **bluesnarfing**, occurs when a hacker with special software can detect the signal from a Bluetooth-enabled device and gain access to its data without the owner's knowledge. The hacker can access data stored on the device, such as the contact list, connect to the Internet, listen in on phone calls, and send email messages from the victim's device. Some hackers wait in crowded areas such as shopping malls and set their device to detect Bluetooth-enabled devices. If the hacker can make a connection to a vulnerable device, he'll use it for as long as it is in range to access data on the device. Since discovering this vulnerability, many manufacturers of Bluetooth-enabled devices have released software updates to prevent the problem—but many owners did not install them. Newer Bluetooth-enabled devices are not subject to bluesnarfing attacks because this vulnerability has been fixed.

The most serious security threat to Bluetooth-enabled devices is **bluebugging**, which occurs when a hacker gains access to the device and its functions without the owner's consent. A bluebugging attack lets the hacker use the device to make phone calls, access data, and use the Internet while the device is in range. Most manufacturers of Bluetooth devices have released updates to fix the security flaw that makes bluebugging possible. Newer Bluetooth-enabled devices are less vulnerable to these attacks.

The two most serious Bluetooth attacks, bluesnarfing and bluebugging, can only occur within the range of the Bluetooth-enabled device and on older devices on which users did not install the software updates necessary to correct these problems. To protect a Bluetooth-enabled device from bluejacking, bluesnarfing, or bluebugging, you can disable the device's Bluetooth feature so that its signal is invisible to other users (also called **undiscoverable mode**). Disabling the device's Bluetooth feature prevents other users from being able to detect the device, which eliminates many types of security issues. A good precaution for users of Bluetooth-enabled devices is to make sure their devices use the latest software and to turn the Bluetooth feature off when working in crowded areas.

Security Risks with Smartphone Applications

One reason many people enjoy having a smartphone is that it has an operating system that can run programs, also called applications or, more commonly, **apps**. As shown in Figure 7-17, an app is installed as a program icon that when activated might display current weather conditions, open a contacts list, start a calculator, download your email, or play music stored on the device or streamed to the device from an Internet site. The predominant operating systems for smartphones are Apple iOS (which runs on the Apple iPhone and also on the Apple iPod Touch and iPad), Windows Mobile, BlackBerry OS, and Google Android. Each operating system runs on many different types of smartphones.

Figure 7-17   **Sample apps on a smartphone**

cobalt88/Shutterstock.com

You download apps for a particular device and operating system by connecting to the online store that sells them, such as the Apple App Store, Windows Marketplace, BlackBerry App World, or Android Market. In these stores, apps are organized by categories such as personal fitness, games, travel, and utilities. In each of these stores, users can download apps for their specific device that are developed by companies or amateur programmers for free or for a fee.

Before an app is made available for download at one of these stores, the app's developer usually must agree to follow the rules stated in the site's acceptable use policy and other requirements before the app is accepted for distribution. For example, the Apple App Store, which includes more than 425,000 downloadable apps for Apple devices, has strict requirements for submitting apps and only distributes an app when the identity of the app's developer can be proven and the app itself does not violate any coding restrictions of the store. As you might expect, not all apps are accepted for distribution.

In some limited cases, an app might contain malware or other security threats that seek to gain access to the user's device, or perform other tasks that might somehow compromise the security of the device or the information it stores. In one documented case, an app was suspended from a store when it was identified as sending the contacts list and other data from the user's device to the developer's server. In other cases, fake apps were released to look like a well-known popular app, but they instead contained malware that provided access to the user's device. In this instance, users thought they downloaded a popular (and safe) app, but instead downloaded an app that contained malware that compromised their devices.

Smartphone users should be especially careful when installing apps that require login information, such as an app that makes a connection to the user's bank account. You should verify the app's origin by confirming that your bank does offer an app and follow the instructions on the bank's Web site to locate and install it. After installing the app, do not set it to save your user name or password on the device in case the device is stolen or lost.

Finally, be cautious about what you install by confirming the source of the download. In general, you can assume a certain level of protection by installing only those apps available through the app store for your device. Some people unlock the operating systems on their devices in order to disable the device so it can run apps from other providers. This practice, called **jailbreaking** when done on an Apple device or **rooting** when done on an Android device, is legal, but not recommended. If you jailbreak or root a device, you will most likely invalidate your device's warranty. In addition, you might disable some of the security features on the device itself, making the device more vulnerable to different types of problems. Although many people feel that jailbreaking or rooting a device makes it more usable, doing so might compromise the security features provided by the device's operating system.

When looking at ways to secure a wireless device, there are some basic precautions that each user must take to secure the actual device and also to secure the connections the device makes.

Methods for Securing Wireless Devices

Almost every wireless device, including smartphones and gaming consoles, has been subject to data breaches in the form of hacking, operating system flaws, or malware. A good way to protect a device is to make sure that the operating system installed on it is always current. Just like for desktop applications, such as the Windows operating system, as new problems are identified, new software updates are pushed to devices to correct these known issues. If you sync your device frequently and set it to download software updates, you can ensure a certain level of protection from known problems. In addition, syncing your device creates a copy of the data it stores on your computer. In the event of a serious device malfunction, theft, or loss, you will be able to use the backup copy of your device to reinstall its data and settings.

Most devices include a usage setting that allows you to track their network activity. If you subscribe to a network plan that limits the amount of data transferred each month, you might use this feature to make sure that you do not exceed your maximum data usage limits. Another reason to check the usage statistics for your device is to look for unauthorized usage. For example, if your device shows several megabytes of data being sent over the network at a time when you were not using it, this information might lead you to suspect that a rogue program has been installed on the device and is using the network connection to send data to a third party. If you suspect this type of activity, turn off your device and take it to your network carrier immediately for further inspection.

TIP

The action of issuing a command to delete everything stored on a wireless device is sometimes called a **remote wipe**. The device must be connected to the network to receive the command.

Be sure to lock your device with a password and set the device to lock immediately or within a minute or two after its use. Locking the device will protect the data on it in the event of loss or theft. Some devices include features or let you install apps that determine the exact location of your device if it is lost or stolen. Some people install apps or enable an additional level of protection on the device to allow them to delete everything on the device when they are certain that they will not recover it. In these cases, if you have been diligently syncing and backing up your device, your data loss should be minimal.

Another precaution that protects a wireless device is to disable the feature that lets the device automatically connect to Wi-Fi networks when it is within range of the network. This feature is sometimes called **autoconnect**, and is similar to the discoverable mode for Bluetooth-enabled devices. When you set your device to prompt you to connect to an in-range network, you prevent an unknown network from connecting to the device without your permission. Keep in mind that free Wi-Fi networks are usually unencrypted, so you should prevent your device from automatically connecting to networks, especially when the data sent over those networks might be vulnerable to interception by an unknown party.

A good practice is to avoid storing login information and passwords used for the apps and other features on your device. For example, if you have a banking app on your device, you'll prevent unauthorized use of your account in the event that you lose your device. If you store your passwords on your device, then anyone who has your device also has access to your bank account, email, or other private information. As shown in Figure 7-18, when you log in to a Web site using a wireless device, you should deselect the option that instructs the device to remember your password—so you must enter the password each time you log in. By entering the password each time, you'll avoid problems with an unauthorized user gaining access to your login information if the device retains the password for future use.

<table>
<tr><td>Figure 7-18</td><td>Login screen set to avoid storing the login password</td></tr>
</table>

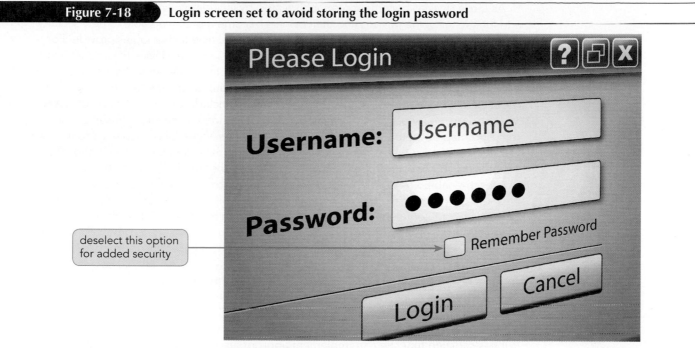

deselect this option for added security

Angela Waye/Shutterstock.com

In addition, you should manage the passwords you use on the device carefully and avoid using the same password for multiple sites. If you know which passwords you have used on the device, you'll be able to change them easily if you need to. If you use different passwords for your various logins, you ensure that your logins are protected in case one account becomes vulnerable.

INSIGHT

New Technologies Bring Heightened Risks

Every day, people around the world use the features and apps on their mobile broadband devices to perform all kinds of tasks, including getting step-by-step directions to a specific location; making and receiving phone calls; taking pictures and videos and sending them to other people via SMS, email, or a social networking site; sending and receiving email messages; updating their social networking pages; and browsing the Internet. As wireless networks continue to increase in size, and the download speeds for mobile broadband devices continue to get faster, mobile Internet users will continue to benefit from the incredible functionality these devices provide.

As these devices become more sophisticated by including new technologies that add functionality, the devices and their owners become more vulnerable to new security and privacy threats that exploit the conveniences these new technologies provide. For example, some of the latest technologies allow you to use your device to conduct financial transactions at retail locations that link your device to your financial accounts, such as a credit card or banking account. In this case, losing your device might make your financial accounts more vulnerable to theft. Many devices include GPS tracking, which users rely on to plan business trips or vacation travel, make hotel reservations, reserve rental cars, and map travel routes. The GPS tracking provides a level of convenience to the user, but this feature also makes it possible for someone to track your location with the intent of threatening you or your property. New technology in the medical and health industry uses Bluetooth-enabled devices to track, manage, and transmit sensitive medical data from a patient with a chronic medical condition directly to his or her physician, which has the potential to put confidential medical data at risk of interception or interruption.

These new technologies require users to be even more vigilant to protect their personal information, their property, and themselves. As more people use mobile devices for routine transactions, they become more vulnerable to the additional risks involved in conducting these transactions. By following the security precautions outlined in this session, they will have a safer and more secure mobile broadband experience.

Ruby is satisfied that she can implement appropriate security precautions on any wireless networks that she installs and uses, and can provide a list of precautions the vets can take to protect their wireless devices and the confidential business and personal data that these devices will store. She will also make sure that Mobile Vet Services staff members who use public hotspots are aware of the precautions you outlined to protect their devices.

REVIEW

Session 7.2 Quick Check

1. What are two types of encryption for wireless networks? Which encryption standard is considered to be more secure? Why?
2. What is a MAC address?
3. Why should you disable the SSID on a wireless network?
4. What is an evil twin attack?
5. What are three kinds of attacks specific to Bluetooth-enabled devices? How can you protect a Bluetooth-enabled device from these attacks?
6. Name one security risk you might encounter from downloading an app to a smartphone.
7. What happens when you jailbreak or root a device? What potential problems are caused by jailbreaking or rooting a device?
8. What is a remote wipe? Why would you execute a remote wipe?

Practice the skills you learned in the tutorial using the same case scenario.

PRACTICE

Review Assignments

There are no Data Files needed for the Review Assignments.

Ruby has decided to implement a wireless network for the main office of Mobile Vet Services. Because the notebook computers Ruby recently purchased include Wi-Fi and broadband network interface cards, she has decided to create a wireless local area network in the main office. Ruby is considering creating accounts with a wireless broadband provider so employees can access the Internet on their wireless devices using both methods. She asks for your help to find Wi-Fi hotspots near the office. She is also curious to see which mobile wireless access plan is better: using a Wi-Fi service or a mobile broadband provider. Finally, based on your findings, Ruby also asks you to draft a mobile device security policy for the office to ensure the safety of the company's confidential data. You conduct your research and summarize its results by completing the following steps:

1. Start your Web browser, go to www.cengagebrain.com, open the Tutorial 7 Weblinks page, and then click the Review Assignments link.

2. Click a link in the Wi-Fi Hotspots section.

3. Use the site to find hotspots in the area of Dallas, Texas or using the zip codes 75201 or 75301. (Depending on the site you choose, you might need to enter the city, state, and zip code to search for hotspots.) Examine the hotspots available in these areas and note the types of businesses that run them. Use the links to two or three Wi-Fi hotspots to learn more about the service provided, including information about the type of network, the security of the network, and the cost of using it.

4. Return to the Tutorial 7 Weblinks page, and then click another link in the Wi-Fi Hotspots section. Use the information provided in Step 3 to learn more about the hotspots you find.

5. Return to the Tutorial 7 Weblinks page, and then click a link in the Wi-Fi Service section. Examine the site to learn more about the hotspots in Dallas to determine the level of coverage in the city. Use the site to investigate how you create an account with the Wi-Fi service provider and the cost of its use. Use the site to learn more about the network's security.

6. Return to the Tutorial 7 Weblinks page, and then click another link in the Wi-Fi Service section. Use the information provided in Step 5 to learn more about creating a Wi-Fi account with this service provider, the cost, the network security, and whether sufficient coverage exists in the city of Dallas.

7. Return to the Tutorial 7 Weblinks page, and then click one of the links in the Mobile Broadband section. Use the links on the page to view a coverage map for the carrier's broadband service. Note whether the carrier provides broadband service in Dallas and the surrounding area. Use the links on the site to find a device that can use the broadband signal, and then print the product page for the device. Be sure to find information about the cost of using the service.

8. In a report addressed to your instructor, identify the following information:

   a. The types of businesses that provide Wi-Fi hotspots in Dallas, the general cost of using them, and information about the level of security they provide.

   b. The Wi-Fi service provider you would recommend that Mobile Vet Services employees use, and why you feel it is the best choice.

   c. The mobile broadband provider you would recommend that the employees use, and why you feel it is the best choice.

d. Should the employees use Wi-Fi hotspots, a Wi-Fi service provider, or a mobile broadband provider for Internet service when they are not in the office? Support your recommendation with information you gathered during your research.

e. Draft a two- to four-paragraph security policy for Mobile Vet Services that outlines the specific steps employees should take to protect their devices and the data transmitted and stored by those devices. Use details from the research you conducted in the steps in this assignment and in the tutorial.

9. Close your browser.

Evaluate competing wireless technologies for 4G wireless networks.

RESEARCH

Case Problem 1

There are no Data Files needed for this Case Problem.

Evaluating Competing 4G Wireless Technologies   Emma Curtis—a lawyer who spends a great deal of her time in the courthouse, and traveling to depose witnesses and meet with clients—tells you that she is interested in signing up for mobile broadband service and purchasing a new smartphone to help her conduct business while she is away from her downtown Chicago office. She downloads a lot of data every day, so she is interested in getting the fastest, most reliable, and most cost-effective connection available in her area. You'll help her evaluate the current or proposed 4G network service in Chicago, Illinois, by completing the following steps:

1. Start your Web browser, go to www.cengagebrain.com, open the Tutorial 7 Weblinks page, and then click the Case Problem 1 link. Choose one of the Web sites provided in the LTE section and click it to open the site's home page.

2. Review the page and find a link or feature that lets you search for the coverage area of the 4G network. Use the city, state, and zip code **Chicago, IL 60601** to determine whether the provider has 4G network coverage in this location. If it does not, return to the Weblinks page for Tutorial 7 and use another link in the LTE section to determine if another carrier provides 4G service for downtown Chicago. If you cannot find 4G (LTE) service for this location, try to determine if this location might be included in the network's planned coverage for the future. (*Note:* If the provider requires a specific street address to determine network coverage, try another provider.)

✦ EXPLORE   3. If you find a carrier that provides 4G (LTE) service for downtown Chicago, evaluate the service by reviewing the page to determine the cost of the service, its data transfer limits, the types of devices the network supports, available roaming options for the device when it is out of the 4G network's range, network security features, and other details that will help you understand the service. Pay particular attention to details that will help you make an informed decision about choosing a service provider. If you cannot find a carrier that provides 4G (LTE) service for downtown Chicago, use the general information on one of the sites to answer the questions in this step.

✦ EXPLORE   4. Return to the Tutorial 7 Weblinks page, and then click a link in the WiMAX section. Repeat Steps 2 and 3 to determine if any of the carriers provide 4G (WiMAX) service for downtown Chicago. If you cannot find any 4G WiMAX providers for this location, use the general information on one of the sites to answer the questions in Step 3.

✦ EXPLORE   5. In a report addressed to Emma, describe your findings for 4G LTE and WiMAX by answering the following questions:

a. Does one 4G technology seem to have a larger network coverage area than another?

   b. Are the costs of subscribing to LTE and WiMAX networks similar or different? Support your answer with specific information from the sites you visited.

   c. Do the networks support the same types of devices? What kinds of devices does each network support? What kinds of features do these devices have?

   d. What kind of security does each network provide?

   e. What is the operating speed for each network?

EXPLORE 6. After answering the questions in Step 5 and providing details to support your answers with information you found as you completed your research, include a final paragraph in your report that indicates which technology you are recommending for Emma. Be sure to support your answers with information you found at each site as you completed your research.

   7. Close your browser.

Explore the way Bluetooth is used in the medical and health industry.

RESEARCH

Case Problem 2

There are no Data Files needed for this Case Problem.

Charlotte Bach, M.D.   Before Charlotte Bach became an endocrinologist, a medical doctor specializing in diseases of the endocrine system, she completed her studies in electrical engineering and worked for a company that developed medical devices. As a doctor with this technological background, Dr. Bach is very interested in using technology to help her diabetic patients monitor their blood sugar levels and control their disease with as little disruption to their daily lives as possible. She asks you to conduct some research to help her identify devices that might be helpful to her patients as they monitor their disease and communicate their test results with her. She is interested in other medical technology, as well. Because she and most of her patients have Bluetooth-enabled devices, she asks you to concentrate your research on Bluetooth technology. Complete the following steps:

   1. Start your Web browser, go to www.cengagebrain.com, open the Tutorial 7 Weblinks page, and then click the Case Problem 2 link.

EXPLORE 2. Click a link to one of the sites provided, and then explore the site to learn more about how Bluetooth is used to enhance medical reporting. Pay particular attention to medical devices used in the treatment and monitoring of diabetes, such as glucose monitors, and the ways patients can use Bluetooth to facilitate communication of their test results with their physicians. Also evaluate other types of devices that would benefit a physician, such as heart monitors and stethoscopes. As you are evaluating these other types of devices, think about how Bluetooth enhances the communication, security, and storage of data.

EXPLORE 3. Return to the Tutorial 7 Weblinks page, and then choose a link to another site. Use the information provided in Step 2 to evaluate the Bluetooth options at the second site. If you feel that you need more information, use the other links for Case Problem 2 to do additional research, as necessary.

EXPLORE 4. After gathering the information from two or more sites, use your favorite search engine to expand your research by searching for other types of Bluetooth-enabled devices available for the medical and health industry. You might choose to explore sites of companies that produce the actual medical and health devices using Bluetooth technology, or sites that focus more on general Bluetooth technology. Find at least one site with new information, and use the site and the information in Step 2 to help you evaluate the Bluetooth options.

⊕ **EXPLORE**

5. In a report, identify the types of medical and health devices you located and explain how their use might enhance Dr. Bach's practice. Which devices do you think she should use to help her diabetic patients? Which other types of Bluetooth-enabled devices would you recommend for Dr. Bach and why? What kind of security do these devices provide? Support your recommendations with specific information you gathered at each site.

6. Close your browser.

Explore the near field communications (NFC) industry.

RESEARCH

Case Problem 3

There are no Data Files needed for this Case Problem.

Expanding Technology in Near Field Communication   Andrew Hernandez, who will begin college in the fall as a finance major, is very interested in new technologies that influence the financial industry. He just returned from a summer trip to India, where he used his smartphone to pay for everything from public transportation fees to restaurant bills. When Andrew leaves for college in the fall, he wants to use his smartphone in a similar way. He decides to research the options for American companies to see if he can replicate the convenience he experienced in India. Complete the following steps:

1. Start your Web browser, go to www.cengagebrain.com, open the Tutorial 7 Weblinks page, and then click the Case Problem 3 link. Click the Google Wallet link.

⊕ **EXPLORE**

2. Use the information at the Google Wallet site and the links to other pages to answer the following questions in a report addressed to your instructor:

   a. What is near field communication (NFC)? How does NFC work?

   b. On which types of devices does NFC work? What hardware is required to conduct NFC transactions, both on the device and by the merchant?

   c. What is the approximate range of NFC transactions?

   d. What security features does NFC provide?

   e. What is the cost of using Google Wallet?

⊕ **EXPLORE**

3. Return to the Tutorial 7 Weblinks page, and then explore the links to NFC resources provided in the Case Problem 3 section. Use the links on these sites to identify and describe at least three additional uses of NFC other than as a payment option at a retail outlet. As you add this information to your report, include the names of the sites you visited.

⊕ **EXPLORE**

4. Conclude your report with a summary paragraph about NFC. Would you feel comfortable using NFC for the purposes you identified in Step 3? Why or why not? What security risks does NFC pose? What solutions exist? Support your conclusions with information you found at the Web sites you visited.

5. Close your browser.

Explore the use of location-based services, and consider some of the security and privacy issues their use presents.

RESEARCH

Case Problem 4

There are no Data Files needed for this Case Problem.

Security and Privacy Issues of Location-Based Services   You just purchased a smart-phone and have used it to map a road trip, reserve a room at a hotel along your route, and find the least expensive gasoline as you traveled. All of these activities have relied on the GPS coordinates of your phone to identify your location so that the information you requested could be processed and customized for your exact location. Although this information has greatly enhanced your trip, you are worried about how this information could be used in ways that might threaten your personal security or the security of your belongings. You decide to research some of the issues involved in location-based services so you can make safe decisions about using this feature. Complete the following steps:

1. Start your Web browser, go to www.cengagebrain.com, open the Tutorial 7 Weblinks page, and then click the Case Problem 4 link.

⊕ **EXPLORE**
2. Click one of the links in the Case Problem 4 section, and then use the search box on the site or browse the site to search for key terms such as geotracking (or geo tracking), location privacy, location-based services, and geotagging. Explore the resources that you find. As you conduct your research, answer the following questions:

   a. What is geotracking? What are some uses of geotracking?

   b. What is geotagging? What are some uses of geotagging?

   c. What is a location-based service? How does it work? What are some examples of location-based services that might be used by emergency responders or law enforcement agencies? What are some examples of location-based services that might be used for unlawful activities? What are some examples of location-based services that might be used to enhance consumers' experiences or for product marketing?

⊕ **EXPLORE**
3. Return to the Tutorial 7 Weblinks page, and then explore another site using the same types of key terms you used at the site you visited in Step 2. If necessary, update your responses to the questions in Step 2 using any new information you find.

⊕ **EXPLORE**
4. Conclude your report by answering the following questions and supporting your conclusions with information you found while conducting your research:

   a. From a privacy standpoint, what are some of the advantages and disadvantages of using location-based services?

   b. Do you feel that governmental agencies—such as the Federal Communications Commission (FCC) and the Federal Trade Commission (FTC), along with Congress and state legislatures—should enact legislation regarding location-based ser-vices, or do you feel that the consumer should have control over their use? Why or why not?

   c. If you own a device that uses location-based services to track your movements, will the research you conducted affect your decision to continue or stop using these services? Why or why not?

5. Close your browser.

Examine the features provided and security issues involved in mobile banking transactions.

RESEARCH

Case Problem 5

There are no Data Files needed for this Case Problem.

Evaluating Mobile Banking Options   Kerrigan McGibbs, a college freshman, is living away from home for the first time while attending school in another state. Just like other college students, she relies on her hometown bank to manage her finances. Her bank just sent her an email message explaining three new services it provides to its customers: a mobile banking app for smartphones, a mobile banking site, and text banking. Kerrigan is curious about these services and decides to investigate them to determine the level of security each option provides to users. Complete the following steps:

1. Start your Web browser, go to www.cengagebrain.com, open the Tutorial 7 Weblinks page, and then click the Case Problem 5 link.

⊕ EXPLORE

2. Use the links in the Mobile Banking Apps section to answer the following questions about mobile banking apps in a report addressed to your instructor:

   a. What features does the mobile banking app provide to customers?

   b. On which kinds of devices does the mobile banking app work?

   c. What kind of security does the mobile banking app provide? Does the bank offer any additional services to ensure secure transactions, such as additional software or login verification? Does the bank guarantee the security of users' transactions? If so, what guarantees does the bank offer?

   d. What types of transactions can users complete?

⊕ EXPLORE

3. Return to the Tutorial 7 Weblinks page, and then use the links in the Mobile Banking Sites section to answer the following questions:

   a. What types of transactions can users complete?

   b. What kind of security does the mobile Web banking site provide? Does the bank offer any additional services to ensure secure transactions, such as additional software or login verification? Does the bank guarantee the security of users' transactions? If so, what guarantees does the bank offer?

⊕ EXPLORE

4. Return to the Tutorial 7 Weblinks page, and then use the links in the Text Banking section to answer the following questions:

   a. What is text banking?

   b. What types of transactions can users complete using text banking?

   c. What kind of security is provided when users perform transactions using text banking? Does the bank guarantee the security of those transactions? If so, what guarantees does the bank offer?

   d. What costs might the customer incur when completing text banking transactions?

⊕ EXPLORE

5. Conclude your report by using the information you found to describe how you would feel about conducting your banking transactions using a mobile banking app for a smartphone, a mobile banking site, and text banking. Do you feel that these methods of communication are sufficiently secure? Why or why not? What security risks exist when using a wireless device to utilize these banking services? How can you protect your data and your device from the other risks that you identify? Be sure to support your answers with information you found as you completed your research.

6. Close your browser.

TUTORIAL **8**

OBJECTIVES

Session 8.1
- Define HTML and understand how it works
- Examine the tools used to create HTML documents
- Create an HTML document
- Use tags, attributes, and anchors
- Add images and links to an HTML document

Session 8.2
- Plan the content for a Web site
- Examine Web site creation and management programs
- Learn about JavaScript, Flash, and Shockwave
- Learn about the different types of images that you can use in a Web page and the programs that create them
- Understand the questions to ask when selecting a Web hosting service
- Understand the issues involved when publishing a Web site
- Learn about search engine submission and search engine optimization

Creating Effective Web Pages

Creating HTML Documents and Understanding Browser Extensions

INTERNET

Case | *Lakeside Police Department*

The Lakeside Police Department employs 18 police officers, six full-time dispatchers, and 10 other full-time employees. The department patrols Lakeside, Illinois, a small suburb outside of Chicago. Officers provide services not found in most major metropolitan areas, such as serving as school crossing guards, being mentors to children attending the local schools, and providing traffic control at city events.

The police chief, Mary Silva, believes that community education programs are an important part of providing effective police patrols and service. Chief Silva's latest community education program is a series of self-defense classes. These classes are directed at specific groups, including children, elderly residents, women, and people with disabilities. Although the crime rate is low in Lakeside, many residents work in Chicago, where the crime rate is higher, and people in these groups are easier targets for assaults.

Chief Silva wants to create a Web site on which to post information about the police department. She needs your help to understand the issues involved in creating and maintaining a Web site. You will create the pages that describe the self-defense program so Chief Silva can add them to the Web site. Chief Silva has asked you to create the pages for the department and then to provide her with the options for creating a Web site so you can publish it on the Web.

STARTING DATA FILES

Tutorial

description.txt
elder_sd.html
lpd_logo.jpg

Review

academy.html
goals.txt
lpd_home.html
lpd_logo.jpg

Cases

invitation.txt
swim.jpg

SESSION 8.1 VISUAL OVERVIEW

The <head> and </head> tags indicate the beginning and end of the head section of the HTML document, respectively. The **head section** includes the tags that contain the page title and other information about the page.

The <html> tag indicates the beginning of an HTML document.

You can include content that you do not want to display in the Web page within the **comment tag** <!-- -->.

The text in the <title> and </title> tags, which are nested in the head section, identifies the title of the Web page.

```
women_sd.html - Notepad                                                    –  □  X
File  Edit  Format  View  Help
<html>
<head>
<!--Women's Self-Defense page
    Content developed by Mary Silva
    Page created by Your Name
    Date
-->
<title>Lakeside Police Department Self-Defense Class for Women</title>
</head>
<body>
<h1 style="text-align: center"><img src="lpd_logo.jpg" alt="Lakeside Police Department logo" /></h1>
<h2 style="text-align: center; color: red">Women's Self-Defense Class</h2>
<p>The Lakeside Police Department is sponsoring a series of self-defense classes for its female, elderly, disabled, and
younger residents. These classes will be taught by Officer Katherine Miller, a veteran police officer since 1992 and a
specialist in preventative services. <i>Officer Miller is offering these classes for free.</i> The first class is for women
ages 14 and older. Women should come comfortably dressed with sneakers. The class lasts approximately two hours. The class is
scheduled for <b>Saturday, September 26, at 2:00 P.M.</b> at the Lakeside Community Center. If you have any questions about
the class, please contact Officer Miller directly at 555-2915.</p>
<ul>
    <li><a href="elder_sd.html">Self-Defense for the Elderly</a></li>
    <li>Safety Class for Children (ages 13 and under)</li>
    <li>Self-Defense for the Disabled</li>
</ul>
</body>
</html>
```

Headings in a Web page are indicated by heading tags. The numbers 1 through 6 in the tag indicate the size of the text to display. For example, the <h1> and </h1> tags create a heading with the largest font size.

The <ul> and </ul> tags create a list. The text in the <li> and </li> tags creates an item in the list.

The </html> tag indicates the end of an HTML document.

The text in the <a> and </a> tags creates a hyperlink. The href attribute identifies the link's target.

The <p> and </p> tags create a paragraph in a Web page.

The <body> tag indicates the beginning of the **body section**, which includes the content of the Web page and the tags needed to format the page content. The body section ends with the </body> tag.

UNDERSTANDING HTML

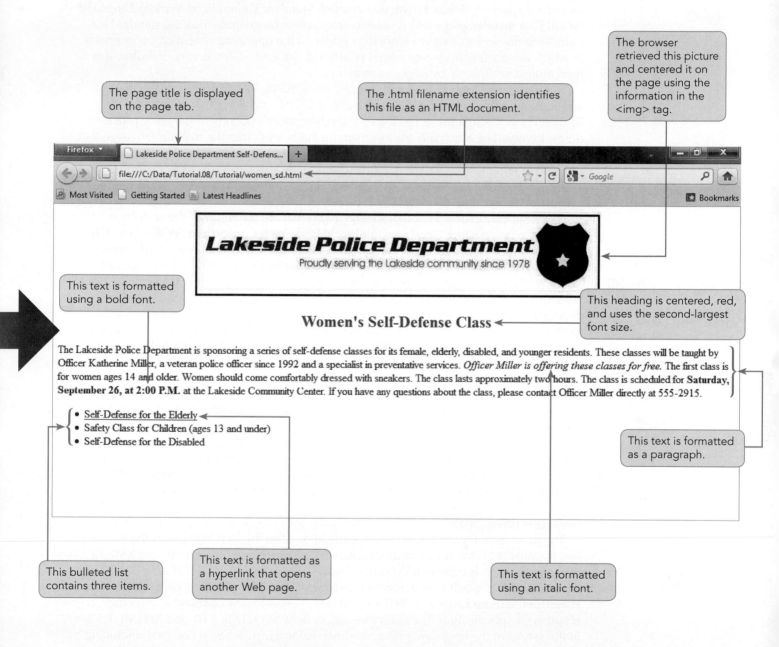

The page title is displayed on the page tab.

The .html filename extension identifies this file as an HTML document.

The browser retrieved this picture and centered it on the page using the information in the <img> tag.

This text is formatted using a bold font.

This heading is centered, red, and uses the second-largest font size.

This text is formatted as a paragraph.

This bulleted list contains three items.

This text is formatted as a hyperlink that opens another Web page.

This text is formatted using an italic font.

Understanding Markup Languages

As you learned in Tutorial 1, Hypertext Markup Language (HTML) is a nonproprietary markup language that a Web browser interprets and uses to display the content as a Web page. The Session 8.1 Visual Overview shows how HTML is used. A **markup language** is a general term that indicates the separation of the formatting of a document and the content of a document. Before HTML was created, **Standard Generalized Markup Language (SGML)**—a **metalanguage** that is used to create other languages—was the standard for formatting documents that were not dependent on the operating system or environment in which the documents were created or viewed. Because SGML is very complex, it is used almost exclusively by large organizations.

The first version of HTML was developed using SGML in 1989 by Tim Berners-Lee and Robert Calliau while they were working at CERN—the European Laboratory for Particle Physics—on a project to improve the laboratory's document-handling procedures. Berners-Lee eventually transformed the initial work into the markup language that is now known as HTML. HTML quickly became the language used to create Web pages because of its simplicity and portability, which made it usable with many operating systems and on different types of computers. The creation of HTML resulted in the World Wide Web as we know it today.

HTML quickly evolved through specifications that are the result of the collective work of the organization known as the **World Wide Web Consortium (W3C)**. The W3C establishes **specifications**, or sets of standards, that identify how a browser interprets the HTML code. In turn, the individuals and companies that create browsers attempt to follow these specifications to ensure that the browsers interpret HTML correctly and consistently. The specifications are voluntary; but because the success of a Web site depends on the browser's ability to follow the specifications, most organizations adhere to them as much as possible. The current specification is HTML 4.01, which is supported by major Web browsers. Since 2004, the W3C has been working on the fifth revision of the HTML specification, called HTML5, which is scheduled to be finalized in 2014. Most Web browsers support the draft version of HTML5 in anticipation of the standard being released.

TIP

You can explore the links in the Additional Information section on the Tutorial 8 Weblinks page to learn more about the existing HTML 4.01 and draft HTML5 specifications.

Another popular markup language is **Extensible Markup Language (XML)**, which was a W3C recommendation that began in 1998 to describe the format and structure of data. XML is used to share data across organizations, especially when data is used on the Internet. Most programs, including Microsoft Office, include features that convert data stored in a proprietary format into XML. Although XML is a markup language, it differs from HTML in that XML uses a set of customizable tags to describe data and its relationship to other tags. HTML uses standardized tags but does not allow this kind of flexibility when describing data.

The most recent markup language specification from the W3C integrates the formatting features of HTML with a stricter syntax that works to combine HTML and XML so that Web content is more readily and easily delivered to all devices that are connected to the Internet. This specification, recommended by the W3C in 2000, is called **Extensible Hypertext Markup Language (XHTML)**. XHTML version 1.1 is compatible with the HTML 4.01 specification. The main differences between HTML 4.01 and XHTML 1.1 are in the syntax of the language. HTML is somewhat forgiving when it comes to including closing tags and supporting older features of earlier HTML specifications. XHTML is not as forgiving; therefore, many Web developers are using the stricter syntax of XHTML in HTML 4.01 documents so that any new applications that support only XHTML specifications will also be able to use the HTML documents.

Figure 8-1 identifies some of the major syntax differences between HTML 4.01 and XHTML 1.1. As a beginning HTML student, it's important to understand some of the differences between the languages that you use to create Web pages as a basis for understanding them. You will learn more about HTML and XHTML syntax as you complete this session.

Figure 8-1	Comparison of HTML and XHTML syntax requirements

HTML	XHTML
No document type declaration is required.	Requires a DOCTYPE declaration at the beginning of the file, such as: `<!DOCTYPE html PUBLIC "-//W3C//DTD XHTML 1.0 transitional//EN" "http://www.w3.org/TR/xhtml1/DTD/ xhtml1-transitional.dtd">`
Tags can be written in uppercase or lowercase letters.	Tags must be written in lowercase letters only.
Attribute values do not need to be enclosed in quotation marks.	Attribute values must be enclosed in quotation marks.
Attributes can be minimized when the attribute name and value are identical, such as `<option selected>` to indicate the status of a selected item in a drop-down list box instead of `<option selected="selected">`.	Attribute minimization is prohibited.
Elements should be closed, although some browsers close elements when the tags are not explicitly included.	All elements must be closed.
One-sided tags are written with the name of the tag only, such as ` ` for a line break.	One-sided tags must be closed by including a space and a forward slash in the tag, such as ` ` for a line break.

© Cengage Learning

HTML specifications that are not included when newer specifications are released or are not included in the XHTML specification are referred to as **deprecated**. In this book, you will use the XHTML syntax as much as possible; deprecated elements are referenced as such but are still covered because some experts agree that the interoperability of the HTML 4.01 and the XHTML 1.1 specifications will result in the continuation of both specifications in the near future.

Understanding Tags and Attributes

A Web page includes different elements, such as headings, paragraphs, and bulleted lists. In an HTML document, these elements are indicated by codes (called tags) that are attached to content. Refer to the Session 8.1 Visual Overview for some examples of the tags you can use in an HTML document and how these tags display content in a Web page.

Because tags must identify all the elements in a Web page, you frequently need to include one or more sets of tags within other tags. Tags that are included within other tags are called **nested tags**. For example, within a set of tags that identify the beginning and end of a paragraph, you might include tags to display certain words in that paragraph using bold or italic. You might also include tags to identify the font size to use for the text in the paragraph.

Tags are either two-sided, such as the paragraph tags that indicate the beginning and end of a paragraph, or one-sided. An example of a one-sided tag is the HTML `<br>` tag (or the XHTML `<br />` tag), which indicates a line break in a Web page. Generally, one-sided tags cause the browser to take a certain action, without regard to turning a formatting feature "on" and "off," like it does for the beginning and end of a paragraph or when applying bold formatting to a word or phrase. As you learn more about HTML and XHTML, you will use tags and learn which tags represent the various elements in a Web page.

Some tags include **attributes** that specify additional information about the content to be formatted by the tag. For example, as described in the Session 8.1 Visual Overview, the <h1> tag is a two-sided tag that creates a large heading in a Web page. The <h1> and </h1> tags can be used to indicate the beginning and end of the heading, respectively. However, you can also include one or more optional attributes in the opening tag to describe the heading's content in other ways, such as indicating the alignment of the heading or the font color of its text. For example, the following tag creates a large heading in a Web page that contains red text and is centered on the page:

```
<h1 style="text-align: center; color: red">Heading 1 Content</h1>
```

When a Web browser interprets this tag, it creates a large heading using the text "Heading 1 Content," centers it on the page, and displays it in a bold, red font color. This syntax conforms to XHTML specifications by using quotation marks to enclose the attribute values.

> **TIP**
>
> All heading tags create bold text.

Some attributes are optional; others are not. You might be familiar with a Web page that contains a form with text boxes into which you might type your first name, last name, and phone number; a group of option buttons so you can select your age group, with options such as 18 to 25 or 26 to 35; or a check box that you click to authorize the site to send information to your email address. An HTML document uses the <input /> tag to create the various inputs on the form, such as the text box or option button. In the <input /> tag, the type attribute is required because it is necessary to specify the type of object to create. For example, setting the type attribute to "radio" creates an option button on the page. (An option button was originally called a radio button, and this is where the attribute gets its name.) If you omit the value for the type attribute, the browser doesn't know what kind of object to create. However, assigning a default value of "yes" or "no" to indicate the status of the object when the browser loads the page is optional; if you omit this attribute, the browser will apply the default option, which creates an unselected object (such as an empty check box). For example, the following tag creates a check box named "list" with the initial value of "yes" (indicating a checked check box):

```
<input type="checkbox" name="list" value="yes" />
```

When a Web browser interprets this tag, it creates a check box that contains a check mark. The name of the check box in the HTML document is "list." This syntax conforms to XHTML specifications by using quotation marks to enclose the attribute values, and a space and a forward slash to close the one-sided tag.

As you work more with HTML, you will learn which attributes you must use with which tags, and which attributes are optional.

Planning an HTML Document

To create a Web page, you can use a text editor, a simple program that includes multiple features for working with Web pages and Web sites, or a program that includes functionality to convert your document to a Web page. An example of a text editor is the Notepad program that is included on computers running the Windows operating system. When you use a text editor to create a Web page, you type the content of the Web page and the tags that you need to format the content. In this case, you must have a thorough understanding of HTML and be able to manage the document structure and enter the tags on your own. The second option is to use a program such as Microsoft Expression Web or Adobe Dreamweaver. These programs provide a graphical user interface (GUI) in which you type the content of your Web page and use toolbar buttons and menus to format it. The program creates all of the necessary tags to format the Web page. The third option is to convert your document to a format that a browser can display, such as when you use the Save As command in Microsoft Word to save your document as a Web page.

No matter which approach you use, it is important to understand some basic HTML before you begin working. You will use Notepad to create the Web page for Chief Silva. Figure 8-2 shows the Web page that she wants you to create.

Figure 8-2	Women's Self-Defense Class Web page

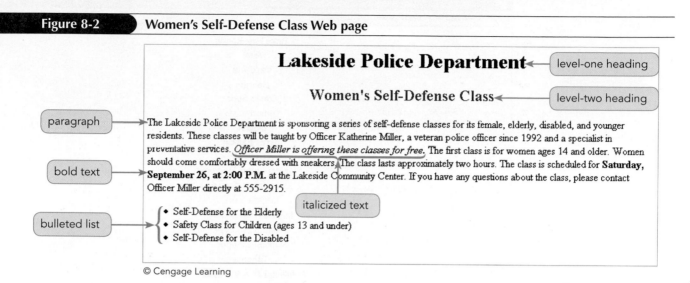

© Cengage Learning

Chief Silva's page includes several elements. The first line of the page contains a heading that is centered and formatted using a larger, bolder font than other text in the page. As you have learned, an HTML document uses tags to format text. The tags that format the headings, such as the document's title, "Lakeside Police Department," are called heading tags, as shown in the Session 8.1 Visual Overview. Because this document's title is a level-one heading, you will code it with the <h1> tag.

The subtitle, "Women's Self-Defense Class," is a level-two heading, so it is coded with an <h2> tag. In addition to using the <h2> tag, you will include attributes to change the font color to red. You can create any one of 16 million colors using HTML tags. However, color is an element that depends on the user's computer and browser to render it correctly. Most computers and operating systems will display the colors in the Web-safe color palette correctly. The **Web-safe color palette** is a collection of 216 colors that all computers render in the same way.

The paragraph below the subtitle is a normal paragraph that uses 12-point Times New Roman font, the default font for Web pages. The fonts displayed in a Web page depend on which fonts are installed on the user's computer. When an operating system is installed on your computer, certain fonts are installed automatically. As you install different programs on your computer, the programs might install new fonts. For example, when you install a Microsoft Office program, you might install new fonts on your computer at the same time. You might also install new fonts by downloading them from Web sites or by installing a font program that you purchased.

In any case, the fonts that are available on *your* computer are not always the same ones that are available on *other* computers. When you create a Web page on your computer, you can use any one of the installed fonts on your computer to change the font in the Web page. A good rule for beginning Web page developers is to use fonts that are considered to be common on all computers. Figure 8-3 identifies the fonts that are commonly installed on all computers that run the Windows operating system. Computers that run other operating systems have equivalent fonts.

TIP

You can learn more about Web-safe colors by exploring the links in the Additional Information section on the Tutorial 8 Weblinks page.

Figure 8-3      Commonly installed Web-safe fonts for the Windows operating system

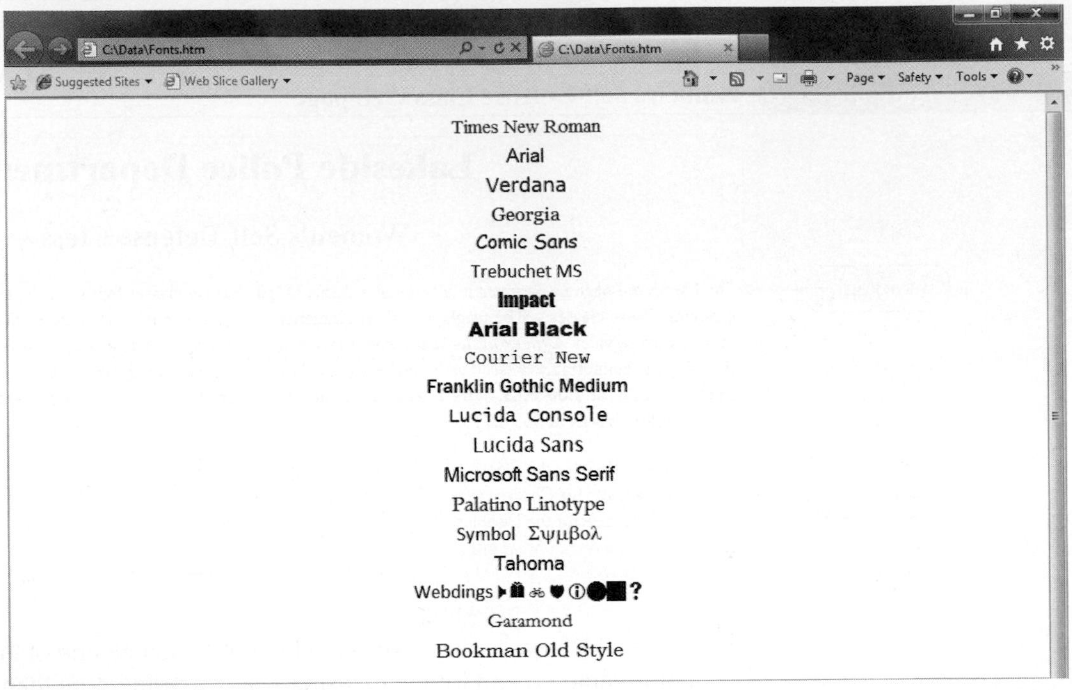

Times New Roman
Arial
Verdana
Georgia
Comic Sans
Trebuchet MS
Impact
Arial Black
Courier New
Franklin Gothic Medium
Lucida Console
Lucida Sans
Microsoft Sans Serif
Palatino Linotype
Symbol Σψμβολ
Tahoma
Webdings ▸ 🕮 ⚗ ♥ ⓘ ●◼ ?
Garamond
Bookman Old Style

Courtesy of © Microsoft

INSIGHT

Using Fonts in a Web Page

If you limit the fonts in your Web pages to the basic fonts shown in Figure 8-3, nearly all of the people who view your Web page will see the exact same fonts when they view the page on their computers. If you use other fonts, some of your page's viewers will see the fonts if they are installed on their computers; users without the fonts will see an equivalent font that the browser substitutes. There are ways to include a wider variety of fonts in a Web page; for example, a Web developer can embed fonts in the Web site so that all users can display the specific font the developer used. However, there are trade-offs when you create a Web page that uses embedded fonts. When pages contain embedded fonts, the files that must be downloaded to each user's computer are much larger. As an HTML beginner, you should use the commonly installed fonts on all computers to ensure that they are displayed correctly when viewed by others.

The paragraph in the Web page that you will create for Chief Silva also includes two nested elements: the italicized sentence and the bold class date and time. Also, the list of items below the paragraph is formatted as a bulleted list. The items in the list in Chief Silva's sketch appear with the default bullet characters for Web pages. After you finish the Web page, Chief Silva will ask you to create other pages and to format the items in this bulleted list as hyperlinks that open the documents describing the self-defense classes for the elderly, children, and the disabled.

Creating an HTML Document

Now that you understand the page that you will create and its elements, you will begin creating it using Notepad, a text editor that is included on computers running the Windows operating system.

TIP

If your computer does not have Notepad, you can use any word-processing program to create an HTML document.

To start Notepad and create the HTML document:

1. Click the **Start** button on the taskbar, click **All Programs**, click **Accessories**, and then click **Notepad**. Notepad starts and opens a new document, titled "Untitled."

   Trouble? If you don't have the starting Data Files for this tutorial, you need to get them before you can proceed. Your instructor will either give you the Data Files or ask you to obtain them from a specified location (such as a network drive). In either case, make a backup copy of the Data Files before you start so that you will have the original files available in case you need to start over. If you have any questions about the Data Files, see your instructor or technical support person for assistance.

2. If necessary, maximize the Notepad program window.

3. Click **File** on the menu bar, click **Save** to open the Save As dialog box, and then navigate to and select the **Tutorial.08\Tutorial** folder included with your Data Files. You will store your HTML document in this location.

4. If necessary, select any text in the **File name** text box, and then type **women_sd.html**.

5. Click the **Save** button. The title bar now displays the filename women_sd.html.

Make sure that you save your HTML documents with the filename extension .html; otherwise, Web browsers will not recognize the file as a Web page.

You created a text file with the .html filename extension; the .html filename extension identifies the file as a Web page. (Sometimes you'll see the .htm filename extension used for a Web page, which is also correct. In this book, you'll use the .html filename extension.)

Decision Making: File Naming Conventions for HTML Documents

When creating a Web site for the first time, following some common file naming conventions as you decide how to name your Web page files will ensure that your Web site is easy to use and manage. Different organizations might use their own in-house standards to ensure a well-organized site. Some common rules for naming files are as follows:

- When saving HTML documents, consider using all lowercase letters in the filenames. Although most Web servers process uppercase and lowercase letters as the same characters, it's a good practice to use lowercase letters in filenames in case you ever move your Web site to a UNIX server. Because UNIX servers process uppercase and lowercase letters as different characters, Web sites hosted on UNIX servers recognize the files named "About.html" and "about.html" as different files.
- Avoid using spaces in filenames. Some Web servers do not support filenames that contain spaces, and some browsers do not correctly convert the space character to its URL-encoded equivalent, %20, resulting in problems when users attempt to access the page.
- A commonly used option for making filenames easier to read is to separate words with underscore characters. For example, use the filename "about_us.html" instead of "about us.html" or "aboutus.html."
- Choose filenames that reflect the file's contents to increase the likelihood of search engines correctly indexing the file, and also to make it easier for developers and users to find files in the site.
- When the organization that operates a site has specific conventions, be sure to understand and follow them. For example, an organization might store all of a site's images in a folder on the server named "images."
- Choose short filenames to make it easier for users to type specific URLs into the browser's address bar, and avoid using abbreviated filenames that are difficult to remember.
- Use the filename index or default (and the appropriate filename extension) for a site's home page, so the Web server sends the correct home page for your site when a user accesses the Web site using only the domain name. For example, when a user types the domain name www.cengage.com in the browser's address bar instead of the domain name and a filename (www.cengage.com/index.html), the server will automatically search for a file named "index" or "default," and then it will display that file in the browser. When the home page is named using a nonstandard filename, such as "cengage_home.html," the Web server will not be able to locate a file named "index" or "default," and the server will display an error page or a directory listing of the Web site's contents instead of the site's home page.

The key to good Web site development is to make sure that you understand and follow any file naming conventions that are required, either by the organization or based on the type of server to which you have decided to publish your Web site.

Creating the HTML Document Structure

In addition to saving the file with the .html filename extension, you must also create the document structure. As shown in the Session 8.1 Visual Overview, every HTML document includes an opening <html> tag to indicate that the file is an HTML document. After this opening tag, you need to define the head and body sections of the HTML document. A good practice is to start your HTML document by creating the head and body sections by typing their opening and closing tags. If you always type your two-sided tags in pairs, you won't make the common mistake of beginners, which is typing the opening tag and then forgetting to type the closing tag.

To create the head and body sections:

▶ **1.** Make sure the insertion point is in the first line of the new document.

▶ **2.** Type the content shown in Figure 8-4 in your HTML document, using lowercase letters for the tags and mixed-case letters for the content. Press the **Enter** key twice at the end of each line to create the blank lines shown in the figure.

Figure 8-4	Basic HTML document structure in Notepad

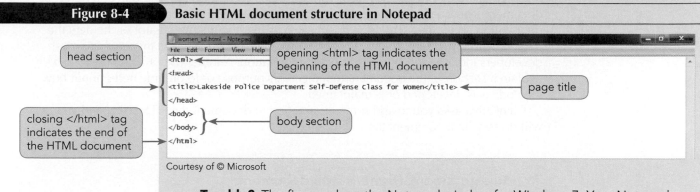

Courtesy of © Microsoft

Trouble? The figures show the Notepad window for Windows 7. Your Notepad window might look slightly different from the ones shown in the figures if you are using an earlier version of Windows, but this difference should not cause any problems.

▶ **3.** Click **File** on the menu bar, and then click **Save**.

Your HTML document has the required head and body sections and a title. Because the browser displays the title on the page tab and also uses it as the default name when you use the browser to save the page as a bookmark or favorite, it is important to use a title that effectively describes the Web page's content.

The blank lines you inserted are not necessary for browsers to interpret the HTML document. In fact, browsers ignore white space in an HTML document, such as the blank spaces between sections. This white space, however, makes your HTML document easier to read.

INSIGHT

Using a Document Type Declaration

In the steps and assignments in this tutorial, you won't include a document type declaration at the beginning of your HTML documents because it is beyond the scope of this book. A **document type declaration (DTD)** is a one-sided tag that tells a browser which syntax version of a markup language your document uses. When you omit the document type declaration in an HTML document, the browser renders the page using something called Quirks mode. In this mode, a browser will render most basic content correctly. If you later decide to take a course on HTML, XHTML, or XML programming, you will learn that you should *always* include the correct DTD in your documents so browsers will render their elements according to the latest standards.

When you create XHTML documents, the DTD is required; in HTML documents it is strongly recommended but optional. You can learn more about DTDs by exploring the Markup Language Resources links in the Additional Information section of the Tutorial 8 Weblinks page.

Adding a Comment to an HTML Document

Some organizations request developers to document their Web pages by identifying the author, purpose, date created or last updated, and other information as required. To add this type of information to an HTML document, you use a comment tag, as shown in the Session 8.1 Visual Overview. Information in a comment tag is visible when you view the HTML document in a text editor, but is not visible when viewing the page in a browser.

Just like other tags, a comment can appear on a single line, or it can span multiple lines separated by line breaks. Also, you can place comments anywhere in an HTML document; you do not need to limit comments to the head section. However, identifying information about the HTML document, such as the document's creator or the date the page was last updated, usually appears in the head section because this is where most developers look for and store this type of information. Another use of a comment is to explain a section of the document to indicate its purpose or to provide notes about how the code was developed or is maintained.

Chief Silva asks you to add some information to document the HTML file, and you will do so with a comment tag.

To add a comment to the HTML document:

1. Click the insertion point at the end of the line that contains the opening <head> tag, and then press the **Enter** key twice.

2. Type the following comment, replacing the text "Your Name" with your first and last names, and replacing the text "Date" with today's date in the format MM/DD/YY. Press the **spacebar** four times to indent the second, third, and fourth lines of code.

```
<!--Women's Self-Defense page
    Content developed by Mary Silva
    Page created by Your Name
    Date
-->
```

3. Save the file.

With the document's structure and documentation in place, you can start adding the document's content.

Inserting and Formatting Headings

TIP

The <h6> and </h6> tags create a heading with the smallest font size.

The first element in Chief Silva's page is a centered heading that uses the largest font size for headings. You'll type the opening tag for the heading, the content of the heading, and then the closing tag for the heading. To create a level-one heading, you use the <h1> tag. To change its alignment to center, you need to add an attribute to the <h1> tag. In HTML, you add the align attribute with the center value (<h1 align="center">), but the center value is deprecated in XHTML. Therefore, to add a code that is compatible with both HTML and XHTML, you will use the style attribute with the text-align: center value (<h1 style="text-align: center">).

To add headings to the HTML document:

1. Click the insertion point after the opening <body> tag, and then press the **Enter** key twice.

2. Type the following line of code:

```
<h1>Lakeside Police Department</h1>
```

This code creates the heading in the Web page. Now you need to add the attribute to center the heading.

3. Change the opening <h1> tag for the heading as follows:

```
<h1 style="text-align: center">
```

4. Press the **End** key, press the **Enter** key twice, and then add the following line of code to the HTML document to create the document subtitle:

```
<h2 style="text-align: center">Women's Self-Defense Class</h2>
```

Now the document includes two headings, both of which will be centered when a browser displays the page. Chief Silva's page shows that the subtitle should use a red font. To make this change, you will add another attribute to the <h2> tag to change the color to red. When using the style attribute, you can separate multiple values with a semicolon.

To change font color:

1. Click the insertion point between the word "center" and the closing quotation mark in the <h2> tag to position the insertion point between the "r" in "center" and the closing quotation mark.

2. Type **; color: red** and then make sure that the opening <h2> tag appears as follows:

```
<h2 style="text-align: center; color: red">
```

Figure 8-5 shows the revised HTML document.

| Figure 8-5 | Headings and comment added to the HTML document |

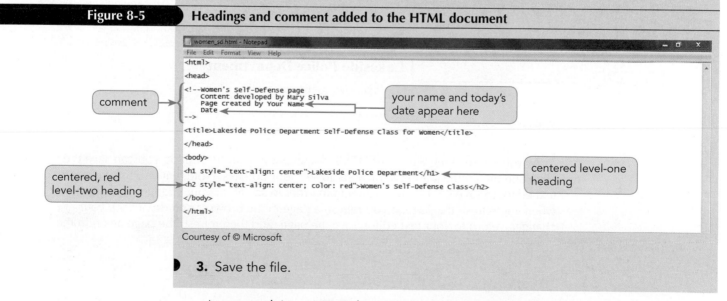

Courtesy of © Microsoft

3. Save the file.

As you work in an HTML document, it is a good idea to check your work periodically in a Web browser to look for problems in your coding and also to make sure that the page you are creating looks correct. You can open your HTML document in any Web browser by using the File menu in the browser.

To view the HTML document in a Web browser:

1. Start your Web browser.

2. If you are using Internet Explorer, click **File** on the menu bar, click **Open**, and then click the **Browse** button in the Open dialog box to open the Windows Internet Explorer dialog box. If you are using Firefox, click **File** on the menu bar, and then click **Open File**. The Open File dialog box opens. If you are using Chrome, click in the address bar, type **file:///** and then the full path to the women_sd.html file with your Data Files (such as file:///C:/Data/Tutorial.08/Tutorial/women_sd.html), press the **Enter** key, and then skip Step 3.

   Trouble? If you do not see the menu bar in Internet Explorer, right-click the Command bar to open the shortcut menu, and then click Menu bar. If you do not see the menu bar in Firefox, right-click a blank area of the title bar to open the shortcut menu, and then click Menu Bar.

3. Open the **Tutorial.08\Tutorial** folder included with your Data Files, and then double-click **women_sd.html**. If you are using Internet Explorer, click the **OK** button in the Open dialog box to open the page.

   Trouble? If you are using Internet Explorer and a dialog box opens and tells you that the browser needs to open a new window, click the OK button.

   Your browser displays the Web page that you created. Notice that the headings are centered, the level-two heading is red, and the page title appears on the page tab. The path to the file appears in the browser's Address or Location bar. The page does not use the http:// protocol because you are opening the page from a disk and not from a Web server. Figure 8-6 shows the page in Internet Explorer.

| Figure 8-6 | **Web page in Internet Explorer** |

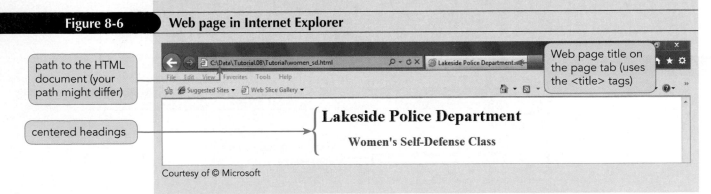

path to the HTML document (your path might differ)

Web page title on the page tab (uses the <title> tags)

centered headings

Lakeside Police Department

Women's Self-Defense Class

Courtesy of © Microsoft

As you are working with your HTML document in your text editor, you can save the page and then refresh it in the browser to see your updates. Note that you must use your text editor to save the HTML document in order to see all of your changes in the browser when you refresh the page. If you refresh a page in the browser and do not see your changes, return to your text editor, save the page, and then refresh the page again in the browser.

Inserting and Formatting a Paragraph

Next, you will continue adding content to the body of the Web page by adding the paragraph that contains the class description. The paragraph you will insert is stored as a text file with your Data Files.

To insert a paragraph in the HTML document:

▶ **1.** Use the taskbar to return to Notepad or your text editor.

▶ **2.** Click the insertion point to the right of the closing </h2> tag, and then press the **Enter** key twice.

▶ **3.** Type **<p>** to enter the opening tag for the paragraph.

▶ **4.** Open Windows Explorer, navigate to the **Tutorial.08\Tutorial** folder included with your Data Files, double-click the **description.txt** file to open the file, select all the text in the document, click **Edit** on the menu bar, and then click **Copy**. The paragraph is copied to the Clipboard.

▶ **5.** Close the window that displays the description.txt file, and then switch to the window that displays the women_sd.html file.

▶ **6.** Click the insertion point to the right of the <p> tag, click **Edit** on the menu bar, and then click **Paste**. The paragraph you copied is inserted in the HTML document.

   Trouble? If you are using Notepad as your text editor and the text does not wrap to the next line in the program window, click Format on the menu bar, and then click Word Wrap to place a check mark next to it.

▶ **7.** Click to the right of the ending period in the paragraph you inserted, and then type **</p>** to enter the closing tag for the paragraph.

   Chief Silva's page shows that the sentence "Officer Miller is offering these classes for free." should be italic, and it shows that the date and time of the class should be bold. To make these changes, you will need to enclose the necessary text in the tags that change text to italic and bold font.

To change font style:

▶ **1.** Click the insertion point to the left of the "O" in the sentence that begins, "Officer Miller is offering..."

▶ **2.** Type the opening tag for italic text, **<i>**.

▶ **3.** Click the insertion point to the right of the period that ends the current sentence, and then type the closing tag for italic text, **</i>**.

▶ **4.** Click the insertion point to the left of the "S" in the word "Saturday," and then type the opening tag for bold text, ****.

▶ **5.** Click the insertion point to the right of the period after the "M" in "P.M." and then type the closing tag for bold text, ****. Figure 8-7 shows the HTML document after making these changes.

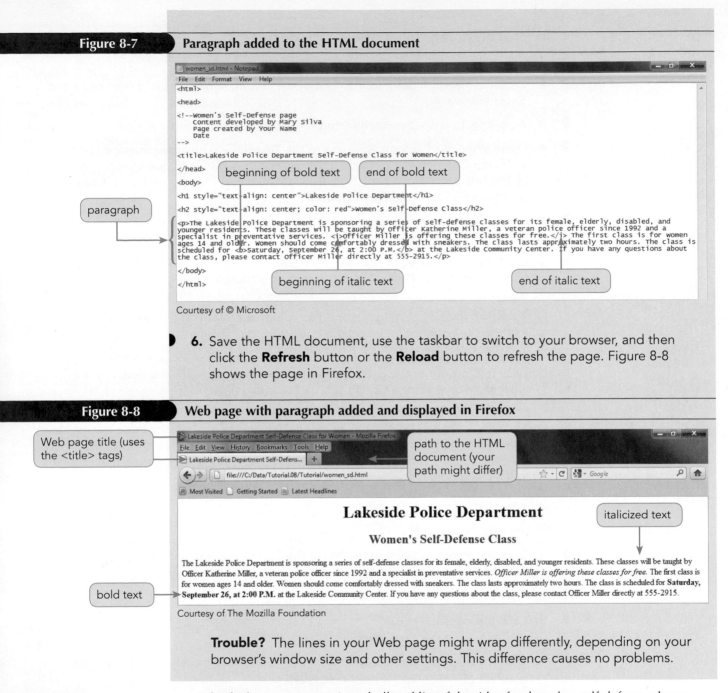

Figure 8-7   **Paragraph added to the HTML document**

Courtesy of © Microsoft

6. Save the HTML document, use the taskbar to switch to your browser, and then click the **Refresh** button or the **Reload** button to refresh the page. Figure 8-8 shows the page in Firefox.

Figure 8-8   **Web page with paragraph added and displayed in Firefox**

Courtesy of The Mozilla Foundation

Trouble? The lines in your Web page might wrap differently, depending on your browser's window size and other settings. This difference causes no problems.

Chief Silva's page contains a bulleted list of the titles for the other self-defense classes that the department will teach. You will add the bulleted list next.

Creating a List

HTML supports three kinds of lists: bulleted, numbered, and definition. A **bulleted list** (also called an **unordered list**) contains a list of items with a bullet character to the left of each item in the list. The default bullet character might be a black dot or a black square, depending on the browser you are using. A **numbered list** (also called an **ordered list**) creates a list of items with sequential numbering for each item. A **definition list** is usually associated with terms and their definitions. For example, you might use a definition list to create a list of terms and then format each term's description as part of the list. Figure 8-9 shows the syntax and an example for each type of list.

Figure 8-9   **HTML supported lists**

List Type	HTML Code	Example

Bulleted	`<ul>`
	  `<li>Item 1</li>`
	  `<li>Item 2</li>`
	`</ul>`
		• Item 1
		• Item 2

Numbered	`<ol>`
	  `<li>Item 1</li>`
	  `<li>Item 2</li>`
	`</ol>`
		1. Item 1
		2. Item 2

Definition	`<dl>`
	  `<dt>Item 1</dt>`
	  `<dd>Definition</dd>`
	  `<dt>Item 2</dt>`
	  `<dd>Definition</dd>`
	`</dl>`
		Item 1
		  Definition
		Item 2
		  Definition

© Cengage Learning

Chief Silva's page uses a bulleted list. You will create this list next.

To create a bulleted list:

1. Switch to your text editor.

2. Click the insertion point to the right of the closing `</p>` tag, and then press the **Enter** key twice.

3. Type the following lines of code to create the bulleted list, pressing the **spacebar** three times at the beginning of each line that begins with the `<li>` tag, so your code is aligned as shown in the figures:

```
<ul>
   <li>Self-Defense for the Elderly</li>
   <li>Safety Class for Children (ages 13 and under)</li>
   <li>Self-Defense for the Disabled</li>
</ul>
```

4. Save the file, and then refresh or reload the Web page in your browser. Figure 8-10 shows the page in Internet Explorer.

Figure 8-10 | **Bulleted list added to the Web page**

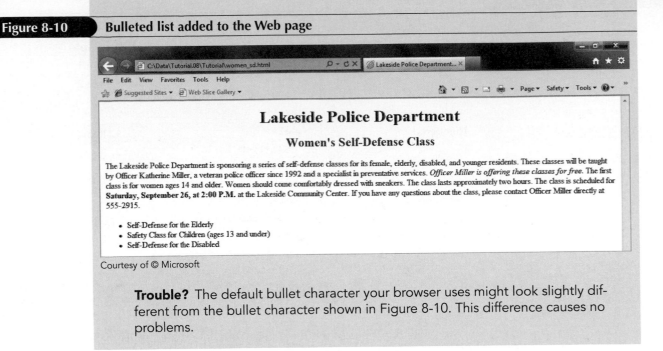

Courtesy of © Microsoft

> **Trouble?** The default bullet character your browser uses might look slightly different from the bullet character shown in Figure 8-10. This difference causes no problems.

Chief Silva is pleased with the appearance of the page. However, she wants the pages for the Lakeside Police Department to include the police department's logo instead of the typed title, "Lakeside Police Department." She asks you to replace the title with the logo.

Using Images in an HTML Document

You have learned that HTML documents are *text* documents. So how do you display an image in a text document? Most Web pages contain some kind of image, such as a photo or a computer-generated image. In HTML, an **image** is any file that contains a picture, such as a photograph, logo, or computer-generated file. To include an image in a Web page, it must be stored as a file. This file might be a digital picture purchased from a company or a digital picture taken with a digital camera. If you have permission to use it, you could also include a scanned copy of an image that exists on paper or a digital version of a clip-art image found at a Web site.

INSIGHT

Using Pictures in Web Pages

Pictures can be saved in a variety of file formats, but some formats are commonly used on the Web because they provide high-quality images with small file sizes and fast download times. The most popular formats for pictures on the Web are JPG (or JPEG), GIF, and PNG. Each of these file formats has advantages and disadvantages. Most people use the JPG format for photographs and complex images because JPG files support up to 16 million colors. Because GIF files are limited to 256 colors, they are a good choice for scanned images, line drawings, and simple graphics. The GIF format is licensed by Unisys, and programs that *create* GIF files must have a license to output files in this format. (You do not need a license, however, to *use* a GIF file in a Web page.) PNG files are similar to GIF files but support up to 16 million colors, and creating PNG files does not require a license. Nearly all Web browsers support JPG, GIF, and PNG files. However, some older versions of browsers do not support PNG files; therefore, the PNG format is not as popular on the Web as the JPG and GIF formats.

To use an image in an HTML document, you must create a reference to the file location where the image is stored. If the image is stored in the same folder as the HTML document, then the browser loads the image from the same folder. If the image is stored anywhere else, the reference to it in the HTML document must include the path to the folder or drive on which the image is stored.

To reference the image in the HTML document, you include the one-sided <img /> tag in the location in which you want to insert the image. When you use the <img /> tag, you must also include the src attribute to define the location (the "source") of the image. You can also use the optional height, width, border, and alt attributes. The height and width attributes describe the image's height and width in pixels; a **pixel** is a single point in an image. The border attribute describes the image's border size (also in pixels). The alt attribute provides alternate text that identifies the image's function or description when it is loaded by a browser that either does not display images or reads Web page content for visually impaired users. Because the alt attribute is required in XHTML, you should always include the alt attribute in your <img /> tag. For example, the code to load the image saved as lpd_logo.jpg into a Web page is as follows:

```
<img src="lpd_logo.jpg" alt="Lakeside Police Department logo" />
```

This code tells the browser that the file lpd_logo.jpg is located in the same folder as the HTML document in which it appears. This type of reference is called a relative path. A **relative path** specifies a file's location *relative* to the location of the current file. If the lpd_logo.jpg file is stored in a folder named "images" on the current drive, then the code to load the image is as follows:

```
<img src="../images/lpd_logo.jpg" alt="Lakeside Police Department
logo" />
```

This reference is also a relative path because the **..** in the file location indicates that the images folder is on the same drive as the current file, but in a different folder. Notice that the slash characters in the path are forward slashes. If the file is stored on a completely different drive from the current file, then the code is as follows:

```
<img src="c:\temp\images\lpd_logo.jpg" alt="Lakeside Police
Department logo" />
```

When the browser interprets this code, it will search drive C on the user's computer for a folder named "temp," and then within the temp folder, it will search for a folder named "images." Within the images folder, it will search for a file named "lpd_logo.jpg" and load it into the Web page. If the user's computer does not have the temp\images folder, or if a file named "lpd_logo.jpg" is not saved in that folder, then the browser will display a broken link to the image or the alternate text specified for the image instead of displaying the image itself. Because this path is the only path in which the browser will search for the file, it is called an absolute path. An **absolute path** specifies a file's location with absolute precision; there is no reference to the current file.

Most Web developers store all of a Web site's images in the same folder as the HTML document or in a folder on the Web site. Usually this folder's name is "images." By storing all of the images in one place, it is easy to create the references to those images using a relative path.

To change the text "Lakeside Police Department" to an image, you need to select the text and replace it with a tag that inserts the image. The file is stored in the Tutorial.08\Tutorial folder included with your Data Files.

To insert the image in the HTML document:

Be careful not to select the opening and closing <h1> tags, or your page will not be displayed correctly.

1. Switch to your text editor, and then select the text **Lakeside Police Department** between the <h1> and </h1> tags.

2. Type the following tag between the <h1> and </h1> tags to insert the image:

   `<img src="lpd_logo.jpg" alt="Lakeside Police Department logo" />`

   The file lpd_logo.jpg is saved in the Tutorial.08\Tutorial folder. Figure 8-11 shows the HTML document.

Figure 8-11	Adding an image to the HTML document

TIP

Type the space and forward slash before typing the tag's closing angle bracket so your code is XHTML compatible.

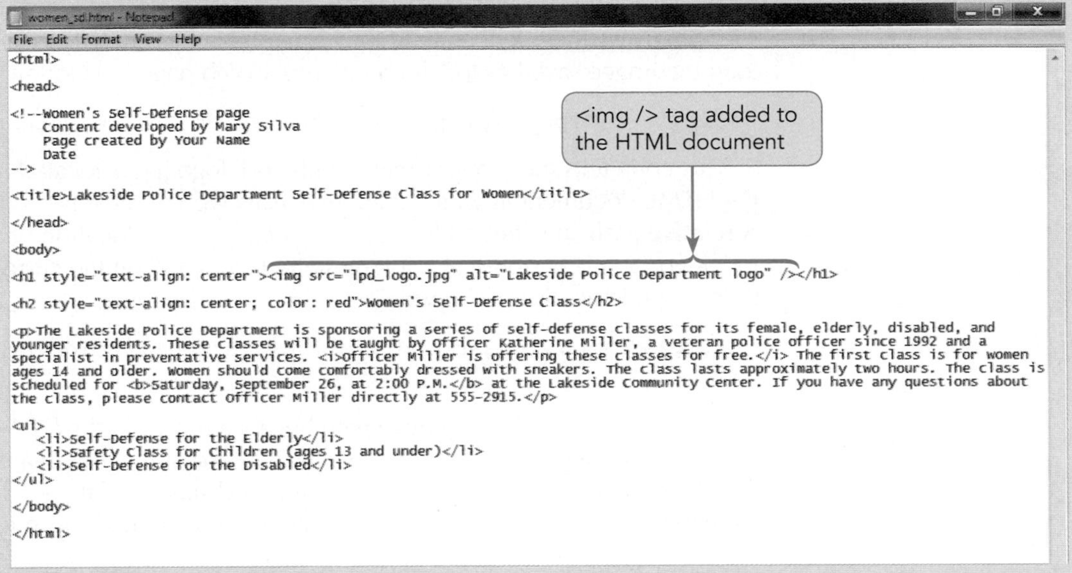

Courtesy of © Microsoft

3. Save the file, switch to your browser, and refresh the page. Figure 8-12 shows the page in Chrome.

Figure 8-12	Image added to the Web page

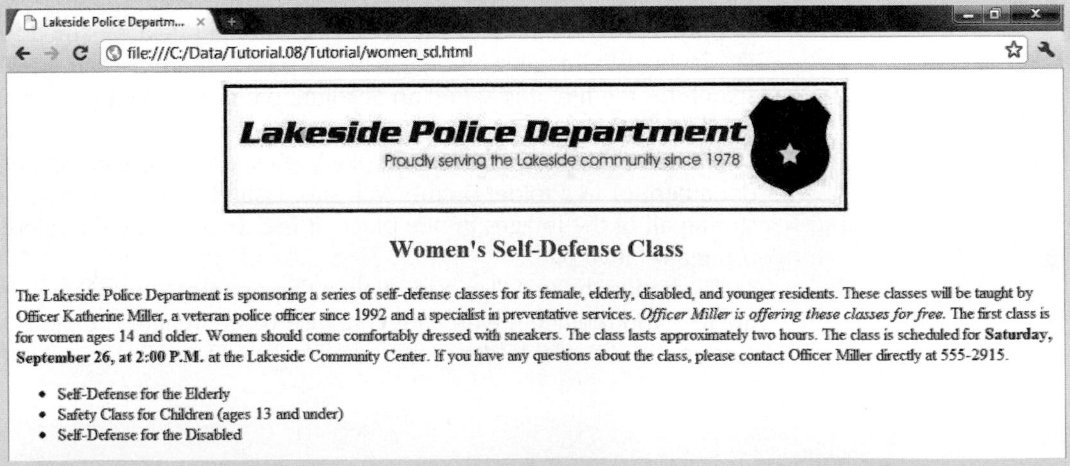

© Google

Trouble? If you see the alternate text (in Firefox) or a broken link like the one shown in Figure 8-13 instead of the image shown in Figure 8-12, your HTML document (women_sd.html) and the lpd_logo.jpg file are stored in different locations. To correct this problem, copy the lpd_logo.jpg file from the Tutorial.08\Tutorial folder into the same folder as the HTML document, or move the HTML document into the Tutorial.08\Tutorial folder. If you move the HTML document, you will need to open the file in the browser from its new location. If you move the lpd_logo.jpg file, you will need to refresh the page in the browser.

Figure 8-13	Broken link displayed in Internet Explorer

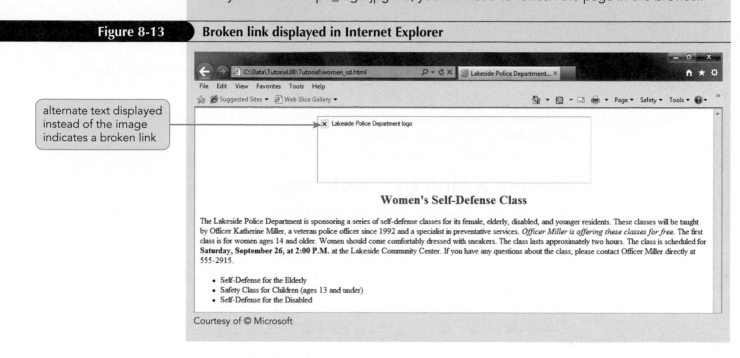

alternate text displayed instead of the image indicates a broken link

Courtesy of © Microsoft

Using Anchors

Throughout this book, you have used hyperlinks to navigate the pages in a Web site. The HTML tag that creates a hyperlink is the **anchor tag** (<a>). The most common use of a hyperlink is to connect the different Web pages in a Web site together. When connecting Web pages with a hyperlink, the page that opens when the hyperlink is clicked is called the hyperlink's **target** or **target page**. The Web page that contains the hyperlink is called the **source page**. The syntax of a hyperlink that connects a source page with a target page is as follows:

```
<a href="default.html">Home Page</a>
```

TIP

Most browsers let users customize the display of hyperlinks, so your hyperlinks might look different depending on your browser settings.

The <a> tag is a two-sided tag that includes the href attribute, which specifies the filename of the target page. The text "Home Page" indicates the text that will appear as a link in the source page. Most browsers underline hyperlinks and display them in a blue font so they are easy to identify in a Web page. When you click the "Home Page" link, the browser opens the page named "default.html."

A hyperlink can include a URL to another Web site in the href attribute. When a hyperlink connects to a target page on the Web, the href attribute includes the complete URL, including the HTTP protocol, as follows:

```
<a href="http://www.cengage.com">Cengage Learning</a>
```

In this example, clicking the "Cengage Learning" link on the page causes the browser to open the home page at the URL for that company.

You can also use the <a> tag to include a hyperlink to a location in the same page. When a hyperlink is used in this way, it is sometimes called a **bookmark**. A bookmark uses the id attribute to identify locations in a document so that you can create hyperlinks to those locations. A common use of a bookmark is to provide a way of scrolling a long Web page to a specific location, or to provide a link that scrolls a Web page to the beginning of the page. Creating a bookmark requires two steps. The first step is to use the id attribute to name a section in a Web page. For example, you might name the image at the top of the women_sd.html page so that it becomes the "top" of the page. To accomplish this task, you would change the existing <img /> tag as follows to add the id attribute to it:

```
<img id="#top" src="lpd_logo.jpg" alt="Lakeside Police Department
logo" />
```

To create a hyperlink to the named location, you would insert the following code:

```
<a href="#top">Back to top</a>
```

The text for the hyperlink can be anything you choose; in this case, "Back to top" is the text that is displayed in the page.

Adding a Link to a Web Page

You can create a hyperlink at any time when developing a Web page. The trick is to make sure that the page is stored in the correct location. For example, if you include a link to a filename without a path to the file, the browser will look in the current folder for that file. If the file is stored anywhere else, the browser won't be able to open it. This situation represents a common problem when creating hyperlinks. A good way to avoid problems is to test the hyperlink by opening the source page in a browser, and then clicking the hyperlink to make sure that it opens the correct page. After you publish the HTML document to the server, you should do the same testing to make sure that the page still opens correctly.

Chief Silva created the page for the self-defense for the elderly class, and now you want to create a hyperlink that links your page to her page. The file containing the Web page for the self-defense for the elderly class is saved in the Tutorial.08\Tutorial folder.

To create a hyperlink to a file:

1. Switch to your text editor.

2. Click the insertion point to the right of the first opening <li> tag in the bulleted list, and then type the opening tag for the hyperlink, which includes a hyperlink to the file elder_sd.html:

   ```
   <a href="elder_sd.html">
   ```

3. Click to the right of the word "Elderly" on the same line, and then type the closing tag for the hyperlink, **</a>**. Figure 8-14 shows the HTML document.

Figure 8-14   **Hyperlink added to the HTML document**

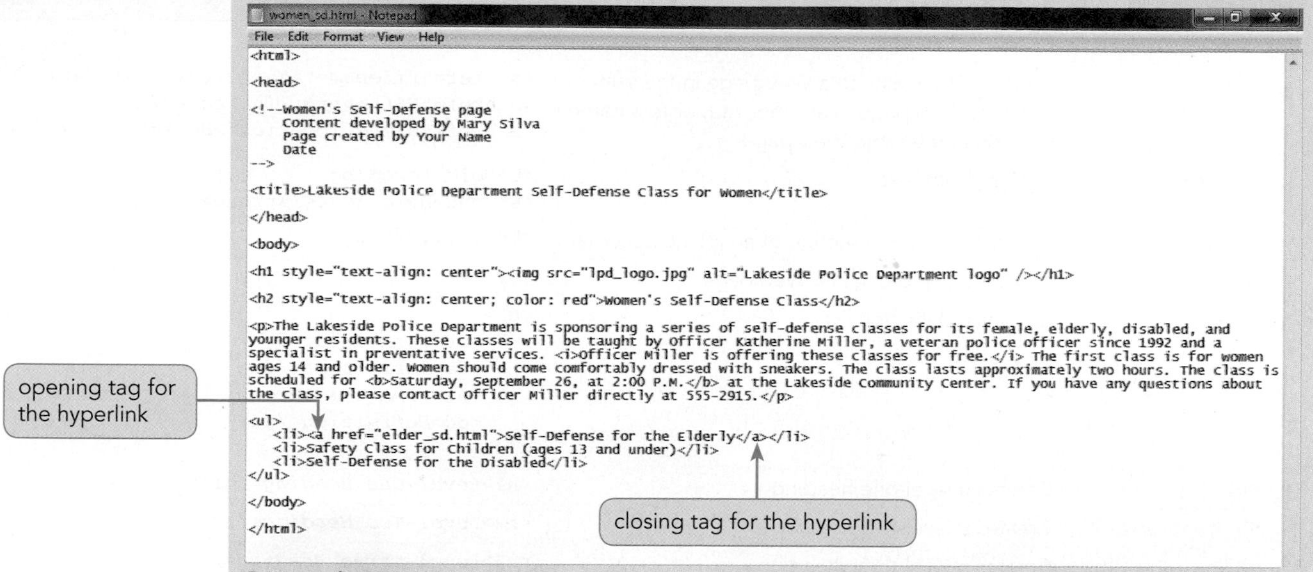

opening tag for
the hyperlink

closing tag for the hyperlink

Courtesy of © Microsoft

4. Save the file, switch to your browser, and then refresh the page. The first item in the bulleted list is formatted as a hyperlink. For most browsers, the default formatting for a hyperlink is underlined, blue text.

5. Click the **Self-Defense for the Elderly** link. The Self-Defense for the Elderly page opens in your browser.

Trouble? If the elder_sd.html page does not open, then the files for the target and source pages are not stored in the same folder. Move the files into the same folder, reopen the source page (women_sd.html) in your browser, and then click the hyperlink.

6. Click your browser's **Back** button to return to the women_sd.html page.

7. If you enabled the display of the menu bar in Internet Explorer or Firefox earlier in this session, right-click the menu bar to open the shortcut menu, and then click **Menu bar** (in Internet Explorer) or **Menu Bar** (in Firefox) to hide the menu bar.

8. Close your browser and your text editor.

Figure 8-15 summarizes the tags that you learned in this session.

Figure 8-15   Tag summary

Tag	Description	Syntax
`<!-- -->`	Creates an HTML comment tag	`<!-- comment -->`

`<a>`	Creates a hyperlink to a Web page in the same site, to a Web page in another site, or to a named location in the same Web page	`<a href="filename">hyperlink text</a>`
		`<a href="URL">hyperlink text</a>`
		`<a href="named location">bookmark text</a>`

`<b>` or `<strong>`	Creates bold text	`<b>Bold text</b>` `<strong>Bold text</strong>`
`<body>`	Identifies the body section of an HTML document	`<body>...</body>`
` `	Creates a line break in a Web page	` `

`<dl>`	Creates a definition list	`<dl>`
		`    <dt>Item 1</dt>`
		`    <dd>Definition</dd>`
		`    <dt>Item 2</dt>`
		`    <dd>Definition</dd>`
		`</dl>`

`<h1>`	Creates a level-one heading	`<h1>Level-One Heading</h1>`
`<h2>`	Creates a level-two heading	`<h2>Level-Two Heading</h2>`
`<h3>`	Creates a level-three heading	`<h3>Level-Three Heading</h3>`
`<h4>`	Creates a level-four heading	`<h4>Level-Four Heading</h4>`
`<h5>`	Creates a level-five heading	`<h5>Level-Five Heading</h5>`
`<h6>`	Creates a level-six heading	`<h6>Level-Six Heading</h6>`
`<head>`	Identifies the head section of an HTML document	`<head>...</head>`
`<html>`	Identifies the file as an HTML document	`<html>...</html>`
`<i>` or `<em>`	Creates italic text	`<i>Italic text</i>` `<em>Italic text</em>`
`<img />`	Inserts an image	`<img src="filename.ext"` `alt="alternate text" />`

`<input />`	Creates an object (check box, option button, text box, or button) in a form that accepts input from the user in a Web page	`<input type="checkbox" name="check box name"`
		`value="default value" />`
		`<input type="radio" name="option button`
		`group name" value="value" />`
		`<input type="text" name="text box name"`
		`size="width in characters" />`
		`<input type="button" name="button name"`
		`value="button label" />`

`<ol>`	Creates a numbered list	`<ol>`
		`  <li>Item 1</li>`
		`  <li>Item 2</li>`
		`</ol>`

`<p style="color: value">`	Changes text color to value	`<p style="color:` `color name or value"> ... </p>`

`<p style="textalign: value">`	Changes paragraph alignment to value (center, left, right, or justified)	`<p style="text-align: center"> ... </p>`
		`<p style="text-align: left"> ... </p>`
		`<p style="text-align: right"> ... </p>`
		`<p style="text-align: justify"> ... </p>`

`<p>`	Creates a paragraph with the default alignment (left-justified)	`<p> ... </p>`

`<ul>`	Creates a bulleted list	`<ul>`
		`  <li>Item 1</li>`
		`  <li>Item 2</li>`
		`</ul>`

In this session, you learned how to create an HTML document and view it in a browser. The HTML document that you created is very simple; if you are interested in learning more about HTML and XHTML, you can explore the links in the Additional Information section of the Tutorial 8 Weblinks page or take a separate class on HTML or XHTML to further your studies. In the next session, you will learn how to plan and prepare to publish a Web site.

Session 8.1 Quick Check

1. What is HTML? How was it developed?
2. What person or organization establishes specifications for HTML?
3. What is XML and how is it used?
4. What is XHTML and how is it used?
5. How are XHTML and HTML similar and how are they different?
6. Define tags and attributes as used in HTML.
7. How do you insert an image in a Web page?
8. How do you link Web pages to each other?

REVIEW

SESSION 8.2 VISUAL OVERVIEW

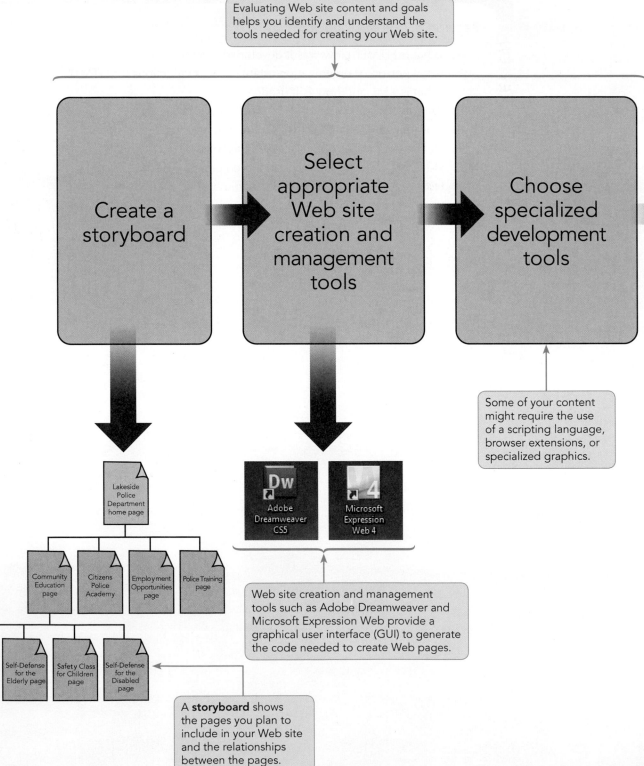

Evaluating Web site content and goals helps you identify and understand the tools needed for creating your Web site.

Create a storyboard

Select appropriate Web site creation and management tools

Choose specialized development tools

Some of your content might require the use of a scripting language, browser extensions, or specialized graphics.

Lakeside Police Department home page

Community Education page

Citizens Police Academy

Employment Opportunities page

Police Training page

Womens Self-Defense page

Self-Defense for the Elderly page

Safety Class for Children page

Self-Defense for the Disabled page

Adobe Dreamweaver CS5

Microsoft Expression Web 4

Web site creation and management tools such as Adobe Dreamweaver and Microsoft Expression Web provide a graphical user interface (GUI) to generate the code needed to create Web pages.

A **storyboard** shows the pages you plan to include in your Web site and the relationships between the pages.

CREATING A WEB SITE

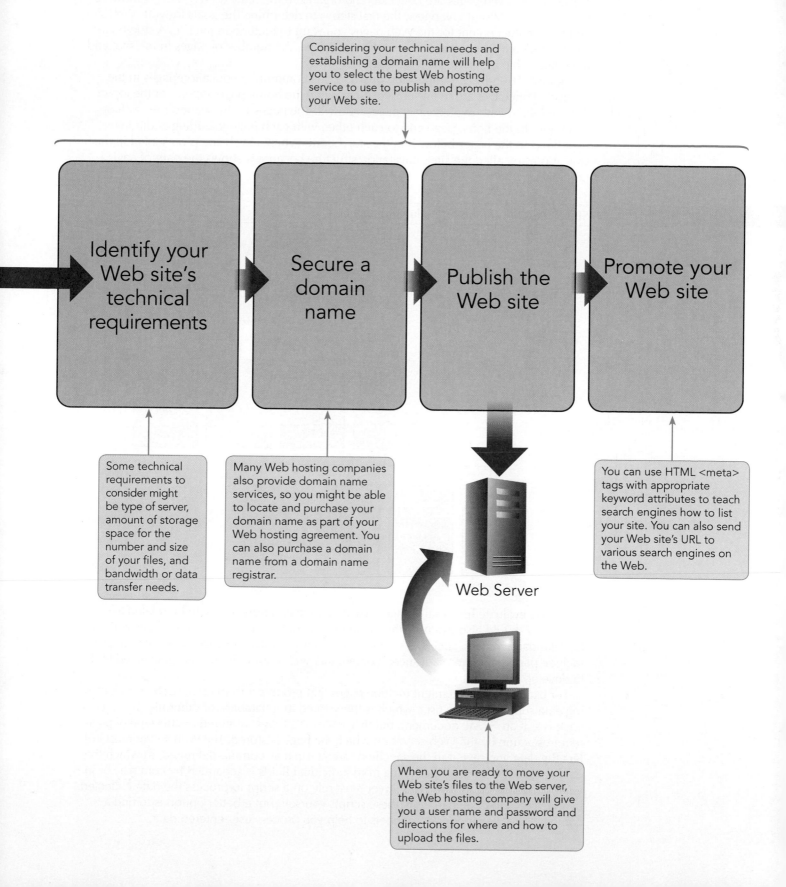

Considering your technical needs and establishing a domain name will help you to select the best Web hosting service to use to publish and promote your Web site.

Identify your Web site's technical requirements

Secure a domain name

Publish the Web site

Promote your Web site

Some technical requirements to consider might be type of server, amount of storage space for the number and size of your files, and bandwidth or data transfer needs.

Many Web hosting companies also provide domain name services, so you might be able to locate and purchase your domain name as part of your Web hosting agreement. You can also purchase a domain name from a domain name registrar.

You can use HTML <meta> tags with appropriate keyword attributes to teach search engines how to list your site. You can also send your Web site's URL to various search engines on the Web.

Web Server

When you are ready to move your Web site's files to the Web server, the Web hosting company will give you a user name and password and directions for where and how to upload the files.

Evaluating Web Site Content

Now that you understand some basic tags used to create HTML documents, you need to consider how Web pages are collected and organized to create a Web site. As shown in the Session 8.2 Visual Overview, the first step is to determine the goals for your Web site and to plan the content for the Web pages you want to include in the site. A storyboard can help identify the general content for each page, the number of pages in the site, and the relationship between the site's pages.

Figure 8-16 shows a sample storyboard for the community education pages in the Lakeside Police Department Web site. Notice that the home page appears at the top of the storyboard with two levels of pages below it. The pages in the second row include hyperlinks to the home page and to each other, with each page including additional hyperlinks to the pages below it in the storyboard. When a Web site is presented in this way, it is also called the site's navigation structure because it shows the path of navigation through the site.

Figure 8-16	Storyboard for community education pages

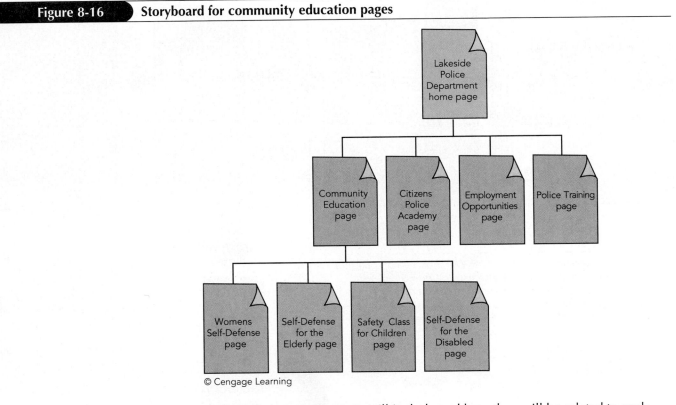

© Cengage Learning

As you evaluate how many pages you'll include and how they will be related to each other, you should also examine the planned content for each page. Most pages will contain standard content, such as images, text, and hyperlinks. However, your plan might include pages with more advanced content that will require the use of specialized tools to develop.

For example, the site might include pages that process information, such as collecting data supplied by the user, which is then stored in a database or other file. The Web page is still an HTML document, but the processing that is required by this type of page requires action by the Web server on which the page is stored. The Web server must collect the data and save it in the specified format (such as comma-delimited, in which the data is stored in a text file and data from individual fields is separated by commas, or in a table in a database). The Web server must rely on a script to process the data collected by the Web page. You can write these scripts yourself, but a better option is to find a company that provides code snippets to help you process user-entered data.

Using a Web Site Management Tool

You could use a text editor to create all of the pages in a Web site. In this case, you would need to have a thorough understanding of how to write all of the tags and attributes that are required to complete your site. Although it is possible to create an entire Web site, regardless of its complexity, using just Notepad and HTML, Web developers rely on other options for creating Web sites. Microsoft Expression Web and Adobe Dreamweaver are two Web site creation and management tools. These stand-alone programs use a graphical user interface (GUI) to generate the HTML documents necessary to produce Web pages.

Figure 8-17 shows the Web page that you created in Session 8.1 after creating it in Expression Web. Notice that the page looks the same as it would in a Web browser. The toolbars and panels include tools that let you format text, create hyperlinks, and perform other tasks that are supported by HTML and XHTML.

| Figure 8-17 | Web page created using Microsoft Expression Web |

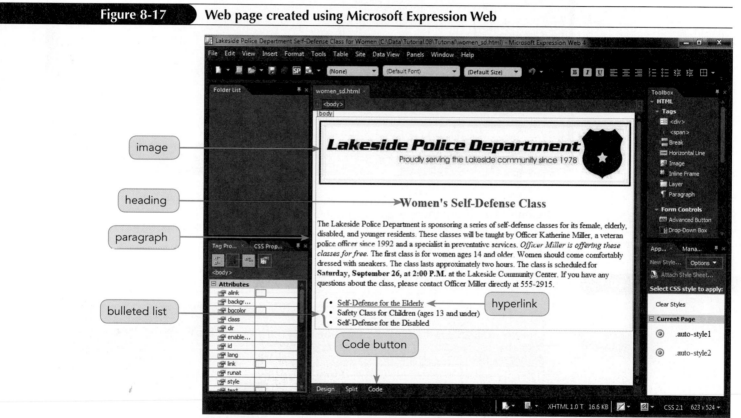

Courtesy of © Microsoft

By clicking the Code button at the bottom of the Expression Web window, you can see the HTML document for the current Web page. Figure 8-18 shows the HTML document that Expression Web generated to produce the page shown in Figure 8-17. Notice that Expression Web uses styles to define text formatting, instead of the tags that you used in the HTML document you created in Notepad. A **style** is a collection of formatting instructions that the Web browser applies to text. The code generated by Expression Web is slightly different from what you entered in your HTML document, but it produces the same result. The main difference is that the generated code is XHTML compatible.

Figure 8-18 **HTML document generated by Expression Web**

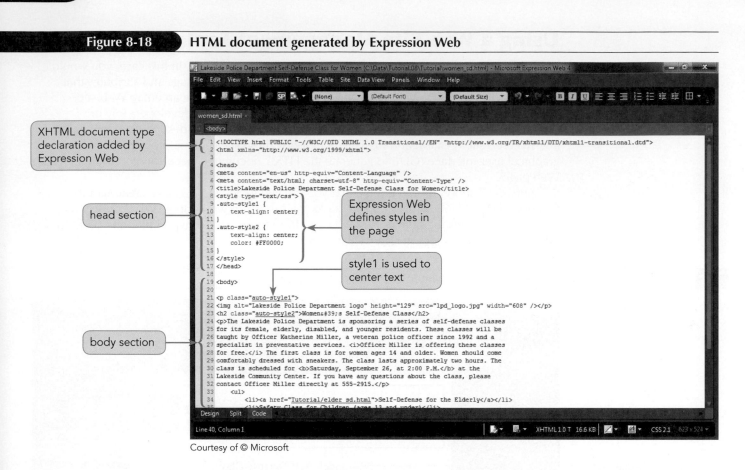

XHTML document type declaration added by Expression Web

head section

Expression Web defines styles in the page

style1 is used to center text

body section

Dreamweaver is another program with a GUI that you can use to create Web pages and then view the HTML documents that the program generated. Figure 8-19 shows the Web page you created in Session 8.1 in Dreamweaver.

Figure 8-19 **Web page created using Adobe Dreamweaver**

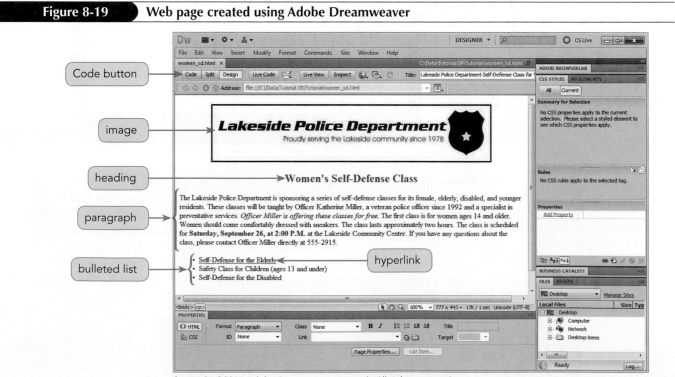

Code button

image

heading

paragraph

hyperlink

bulleted list

Clicking the Code button at the top of the document window in Dreamweaver shows the HTML document that Dreamweaver generated for the Web page shown in Figure 8-19. Figure 8-20 shows that Dreamweaver also generates code that is compatible with XHTML 1.0—for example, the beginning of the HTML document includes a document type declaration, and one-sided tags are closed with a space and a slash. In addition, notice that the <i> tags are replaced by <em> (for "emphasis") tags and the <b> tags are replaced by <strong> tags. These tags are used in anticipation of the deprecation of the current HTML 4.01 tags for creating italic and bold text.

Figure 8-20   **HTML document generated by Dreamweaver**

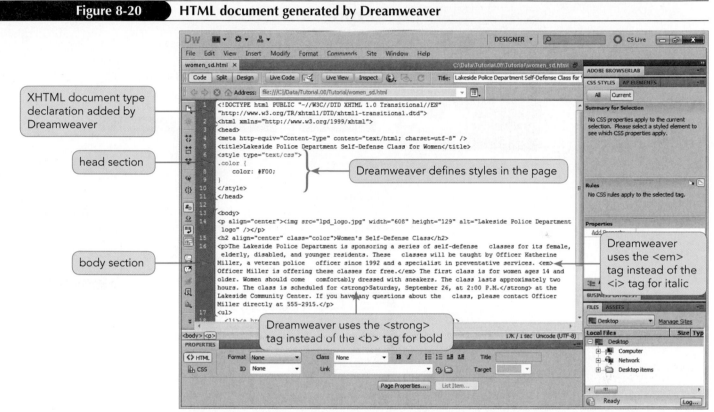

Using a Web site management tool such as Expression Web or Dreamweaver reduces the need for the developer to understand the syntax of all the tags and attributes that create Web pages. These tools also provide other benefits by simplifying some of the tasks needed to complete a Web site. Both programs simplify the process of adding multimedia, such as animation, movies, and sound, to your Web pages by incorporating drag-and-drop interfaces that let you place the multimedia object in a page and automatically generate the necessary code to support it. These programs also include code snippets that create animations in your Web pages and tools that let you check the entire Web site for broken links and other problems. Next, you'll explore the product pages for Expression Web and Dreamweaver to get a better sense of the features available in these powerful programs.

To learn more about Expression Web and Dreamweaver:

1. Start your Web browser, go to **www.cengagebrain.com**, open the Tutorial 8 Weblinks page, and then click the **Session 8.2** link.

2. Click the **Microsoft Expression Web** link to open the Microsoft Expression Web home page shown in Figure 8-21.

Figure 8-21 Microsoft Expression Web home page

Courtesy of © Microsoft

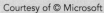 **3.** Use the links on the Expression Web home page to learn more about Expression Web. For example, you might use the links to learn more about the product, Web site design tips, or code support.

4. Return to the Tutorial 8 Weblinks page, and then click the **Adobe Dreamweaver** link to open the Dreamweaver page.

5. Use the links on the Dreamweaver page to learn more about Dreamweaver's features, and to read reviews and other information to better understand the features this program offers Web site developers.

6. Return to the Tutorial 8 Weblinks page.

Both Expression Web and Dreamweaver offer free trial versions of the software that you can download and use before purchasing a license. These trial programs are a good way to decide which program will best help you manage your Web site, and which will be the easiest for you to use.

Choosing Other Development Tools

Some Web pages include content that is beyond the capabilities of HTML. For example, you learned in Session 8.1 that an HTML document cannot store an image, but it can include a reference to an image and display it. The HTML tag and its attributes identify the location of the image file and, optionally, its height and width dimensions, border size, and alternate text.

Other nontext content that you see in a Web page is called by the browser in a similar way. Some Web pages include dynamic content—content that changes when you view the page—that is also beyond the capabilities of HTML. This dynamic content might be an image that represents the number of times a page has been viewed, an animated graphic, or an interactive product display. This type of Web page content requires more than just HTML to produce. Because Chief Silva might want to include interactive features in the police department's Web pages, you will explore some of the technology required to produce more complicated Web pages, such as those that include programming, image editing, and animation.

Programming with JavaScript

JavaScript is a scripting language that was originally developed as "LiveScript" by Brendan Eich while he was working as a programmer at Netscape Communications Corporation. A **scripting language** is a programming language that is executed by a Web browser. To process the script, the browser must have a feature called a **scripting engine**. The browser's scripting engine translates the code in the script into a format that the browser can execute.

JavaScript was originally available as part of the Netscape Navigator browser. At the same time, Microsoft created a compatible language called JScript, and subsequently, the language VBScript, both of which are processed by Internet Explorer. Because JavaScript is interpreted by most browsers, and because only the Internet Explorer browser can process scripts written in VBScript, most developers choose JavaScript to extend the functionality of a Web page.

The most common use of JavaScript is to perform tasks that are not possible in the static world of HTML documents. For example, a Web page might use a very simple JavaScript program to greet visitors depending on the time of day they view the page. Figure 8-22 shows the result of a JavaScript program that greets the user. The script uses the page title from the HTML document and a greeting of "Good morning!" because the visitor loaded the page in the morning.

Figure 8-22	Web page that contains a script

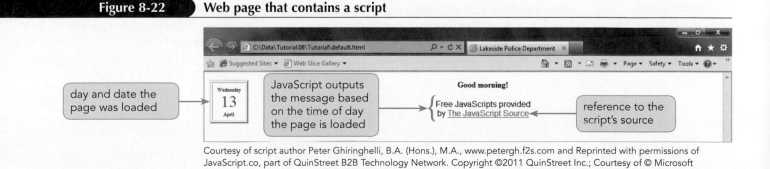

Courtesy of script author Peter Ghiringhelli, B.A. (Hons.), M.A., www.petergh.f2s.com and Reprinted with permissions of JavaScript.co, part of QuinStreet B2B Technology Network. Copyright ©2011 QuinStreet Inc.; Courtesy of © Microsoft

Figure 8-23 shows the HTML document for the page shown in Figure 8-22. The HTML document includes a script that provides the greeting, the date, and the day of the week. The script itself is embedded in the body section of the HTML document. When you view the HTML document in a Web browser, the browser executes the script and displays the result of the script in the Web page. Most scripts are embedded in an HTML document in this way. When a browser cannot execute the script (because it does not have a scripting engine to process the script), it simply displays the contents of the script as text. To avoid this situation, most scripts are enclosed in HTML comment tags so browsers that cannot execute the script will ignore the script as if it were really a comment. If the browser has a compatible scripting engine, the scripting engine ignores the HTML comment tags and processes the script.

| Figure 8-23 | **HTML document that contains a script** |

Courtesy of script author Peter Ghiringhelli, B.A. (Hons.), M.A., www.petergh.f2s.com and Reprinted with permissions of JavaScript.co, part of QuinStreet B2B Technology Network. Copyright ©2011 QuinStreet Inc.; Courtesy of © Microsoft

---

TIP

The Tutorial 8 Weblinks page includes a link to this and other resources that offer free scripts that you can use in your Web pages.

Although you can take courses to learn JavaScript and other languages, many Web sites include resources for downloading and using free scripts written in JavaScript in your Web pages. In return for the use of the script, some sites ask you to include a link to the developer's Web site in lieu of payment. Other Web resources that provide more complex scripts require payment for their use. Figure 8-22 includes a link to The JavaScript Source, a resource that includes more than 1,400 free scripts that you can use in your Web pages. You'll explore these resources next and view some scripts.

To view scripts written in JavaScript that are available on the Web:

1. In the Session 8.2 section of the Tutorial 8 Weblinks page, click a link in the JavaScript Resources section to open the home page for that site. Most sites that provide free scripts organize the scripts by topic or category. Figure 8-24 shows the JavaScript page for ScriptSearch.com.

Figure 8-24	JavaScript page on ScriptSearch.com

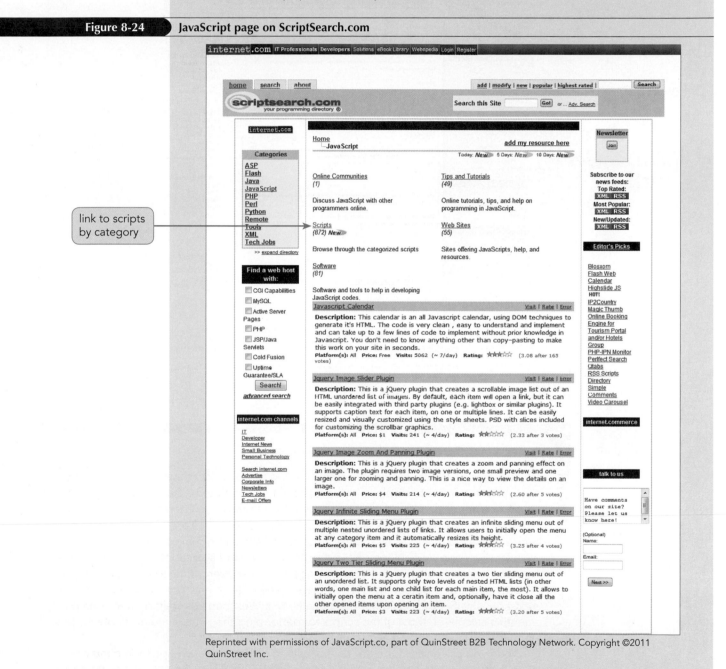

Reprinted with permissions of JavaScript.co, part of QuinStreet B2B Technology Network. Copyright ©2011 QuinStreet Inc.

2. Explore the different categories of scripts available at the site you selected, and use the Web pages to execute some of the scripts. Figure 8-25 shows the result of a script that adds a diagonal banner with custom text across the upper-left corner of the Web page. The page includes a scrollable window with detailed directions for inserting the script in an HTML document and the actual content of the script.

Figure 8-25 Script that adds a banner to a Web page

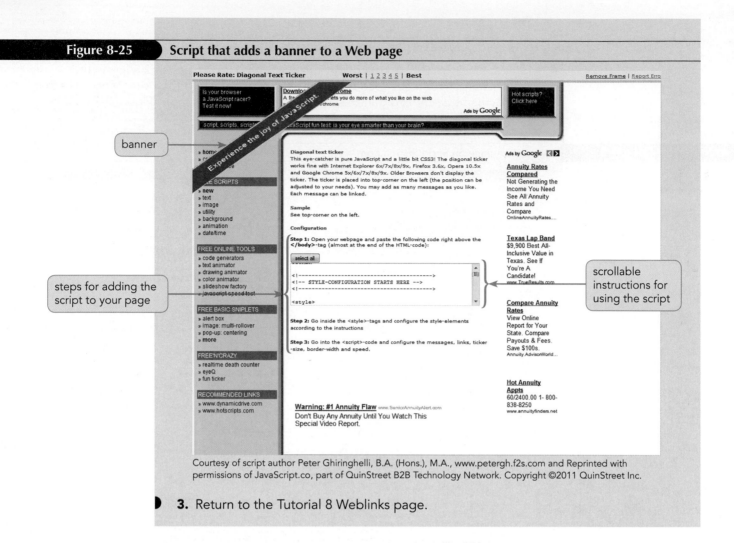

Courtesy of script author Peter Ghiringhelli, B.A. (Hons.), M.A., www.petergh.f2s.com and Reprinted with permissions of JavaScript.co, part of QuinStreet B2B Technology Network. Copyright ©2011 QuinStreet Inc.

3. Return to the Tutorial 8 Weblinks page.

INSIGHT

Using JavaScript to Enhance a Web Page

What can you do with JavaScript without having to learn how to write your own scripts? You can use a script to display a greeting based on the time of the day, the day of the week, or a special occasion. You can display a calendar or an interactive calendar that lets the user pick a date. You can also display the current date and time, or a countdown until a specific day and time, such as a holiday or a grand opening. You can also use JavaScript to display scrolling text, a drop-down menu of selections, or animated buttons that change color or display a message when the user points to or clicks a button. A script might also detect the user's browser version or open a pop-up window with a message. JavaScript adds other functionality to a Web page as well, such as a simple or scientific calculator. Most of the scripts for performing these tasks are available for free on the Web.

When you use a script to add functionality to a Web page, you provide content in your Web page that is beyond the basic capabilities of HTML. You also provide your page's users with tools that enhance their interaction with your Web site.

If you want to do more with JavaScript, you can take additional courses and learn the JavaScript programming language to write your own scripts.

Creating Animated Content

Although JavaScript can add some interactivity to your Web pages, you might be wondering how some Web sites are able to animate more than just text or buttons. The early versions of Web browsers displayed only text and simple images. As commercial use of the Internet flourished, Web site developers needed a way to include more features, such as sound and animation, in their Web pages. Because of HTML limitations, companies developed their own software to enhance the capabilities of Web browsers. These enhancements, generally called **browser extensions**, allow a Web browser to perform tasks it was not originally designed to perform.

There are three types of browser extensions. One type is called a **plug-in**; in this category, you will find integrated browser software that the browser uses to display or play a specific file that you request. Other browser extensions are called **helper applications**, or programs installed on the user's computer that the browser starts and uses to "help" display or play a file. The third category, **add-ons**, includes tools that enhance your browsing experience, such as toolbars that let you access a search engine without opening its Web site, or programs that block pop-up ads and other windows from opening when you view a Web site.

Plug-ins differ slightly from helper applications in the way they run. Helper applications are independent programs that are stored on your computer and are useful on their own. They are activated automatically by a browser when needed. For example, when a browser starts a spreadsheet program to display a spreadsheet, the spreadsheet program is functioning as a helper application; when a browser encounters a sound file, the browser might start a media player that acts as a helper application to play the file. Your computer probably has many helper applications already installed on it that your browser uses to display a variety of file formats that you encounter as you browse the Web.

Plug-ins, on the other hand, do their work inside the browser and do not activate a stand-alone program that is stored on your computer. Unlike helper applications, plug-ins are not independent programs; they can start only from within a browser. As Web developers started including different multimedia files in their Web sites, Microsoft and Mozilla began integrating plug-ins with their browsers so users could access and display files without needing a separate program.

Figure 8-26 lists some commonly used browser extensions on the Web.

Figure 8-26   **Commonly used browser extensions**

Browser Extension	Developer	Description
Adobe Reader	Adobe	Displays formatted document files saved in PDF format
Flash Player	Adobe	Displays simple animations, user interfaces, images, movies, sound, and text
QuickTime Player	Apple, Inc.	Plays audio and video files
RealPlayer	RealNetworks	Plays files in various audio and video media formats
Shockwave Player	Adobe	Displays animations, 3D interfaces, interactive advertisements and product demonstrations, multiuser games, streaming CD-quality audio, and video
Silverlight	Microsoft Corporation	Delivers high-definition video, high-resolution graphics, and interactive applications to various browsers, platforms, and devices
Windows Media Player	Microsoft Corporation	Plays files in various audio and video media formats

© Cengage Learning

Two widely used plug-ins for viewing animated content are Flash Player and Shockwave Player. Both players are free from the Adobe Web site, and they work seamlessly with most browsers. **Flash Player** lets your Web browser display simple animations, user interfaces, images, movies, sound, and text that was created using Adobe Flash software. Flash content usually appears in the same browser window as the page you are viewing. According to Adobe, more than 98% of all Internet-enabled desktop computers in the United States have Flash Player installed and can use Flash Player to view enhanced content on the Web. Because Flash Player is the world's most widely installed plug-in for playing enhanced, interactive content on the largest number of computer and mobile devices, many Web developers regularly use Flash to develop content that is more visually interesting and appealing to their site visitors.

Shockwave Player is a more fully featured browser plug-in. Shockwave Player lets you view animated, three-dimensional interfaces, interactive advertisements and product demonstrations, multiuser games, streaming CD-quality audio, and video that was created using Adobe Director software. Because Shockwave uses streaming technology, you do not need to wait for an entire file to download before playing it—the animation or sound plays almost immediately. (Remember from Tutorial 4 that streaming is a technology that delivers a continuous flow of information from the server to your browser and allows you to play the information, such as audio or video, before the entire file has been downloaded to your computer. Streaming can reduce the time required to begin playing a file from several minutes to several seconds.) Shockwave content usually appears in a new browser window. Some instructors use Shockwave to deliver audio instruction and interact with students over the Internet just as they would in the classroom. Shockwave is a very popular plug-in; according to Adobe, more than 450 million Internet users enhance their Internet experience using Shockwave Player to play games and view animated content.

You can purchase the Adobe Director program to create Shockwave files and the Adobe Flash program to create Flash files. Chief Silva might want to use animations in the Lakeside Police Department's Web site, so you will explore these resources to get a sense of what Flash and Shockwave can do.

To view Flash and Shockwave demos:

1. In the Session 8.2 section of the Tutorial 8 Weblinks page, click a link in the Flash Demos section, and watch the Flash animation. Many Web sites use Flash to animate content that users can interact with. Figure 8-27 shows an example of a Web site that uses Flash to animate the characters in a story and provides tools that let children interact with the story's characters.

| **Figure 8-27** | **Interactive Web site that uses Flash Player** |

© 2011 Made in Me

Trouble? If your browser does not have Flash Player installed, follow the on-screen instructions to install it.

2. Return to the Tutorial 8 Weblinks page and explore one or two of the other Flash animations. Notice the use of animated text, sound, and other images. Think about how these features make the Web site more inviting and appealing than if the same content appeared as just regular text.

3. Return to the Tutorial 8 Weblinks page, and then click one of the links in the Shockwave Demos section. As you explore these demonstrations, notice the kind of interaction that Shockwave creates. You can interact with a product, play a game, or direct some type of action on the screen.

   Trouble? If your browser does not have Shockwave Player installed, follow the on-screen instructions to install it.

4. Return to the Tutorial 8 Weblinks page, and then choose one or two other links to examine some additional Shockwave files.

5. Return to the Tutorial 8 Weblinks page.

Decision Making: Deciding When to Use Director and Flash

From your exploration of the demos, you probably already noticed a few differences between Flash and Shockwave. The first difference that you might have noticed is that Flash is used on a smaller scale, for items such as simple animations or games with sound and images. Shockwave is used for more complex applications, such as playing a multi-featured, interactive game or running a kiosk you might find at a mall. Second, you might have noticed that Flash animations load quickly in a browser because Flash outputs much smaller files than Director. Several other differences that you might not have seen from the demos are that Flash is a simpler program to learn and use than Director, Flash is much less expensive to purchase than Director, and Flash Player is a much more widely distributed plug-in than Shockwave Player.

Because Flash Player is installed on most desktop computers and mobile devices, Web developers know that most of their site's users will be able to view animations created using Flash. When deciding to use Flash or Shockwave, this is perhaps one of the most important considerations because you want to make sure that people can view your Web site content.

If Flash is well suited for many Web applications, when would you decide to use Director? Flash and Director share many features, but Director includes many more robust features that are required for creating larger, more interactive applications. You will need to use Director when your application requires more than just simple animation with video, sound, and images. Director is a multimedia authoring tool that can be used to create interactive content for the Internet, CDs, DVDs, and kiosks that include photo-quality images, digital video, animation, three-dimensional presentations, text content, hyperlinks, and Flash content. You might use Flash to bring a home page in a Web site to life; you would use Director to create a game for the Internet or to create full-featured product demonstrations that let users control the animation, sound, and video that they are viewing.

Creating content using Flash and Director is both fun and easy. If creating this type of content appeals to you, you might take a course in Flash animation or a general course in Web site animation.

Choosing Image Editing and Illustration Programs

You learned in Session 8.1 that you can insert an image into an HTML document by storing the image in a file and using the <img /> tag to insert the file into the Web page. An image can be any picture, including one you take with a digital camera or create using a drawing or illustration program. Computer-generated graphics come in two basic varieties: raster (also called bitmap) and vector. The main difference between the two graphics types is that **raster graphics** are composed of pixels, and **vector graphics** are composed of paths. Figure 8-28 shows the letter "S" that was created using Paint, a program that is installed with the Windows operating system. Paint is an example of a program that creates raster graphics, also called bitmap images.

| Figure 8-28 | Graphic created using Paint |

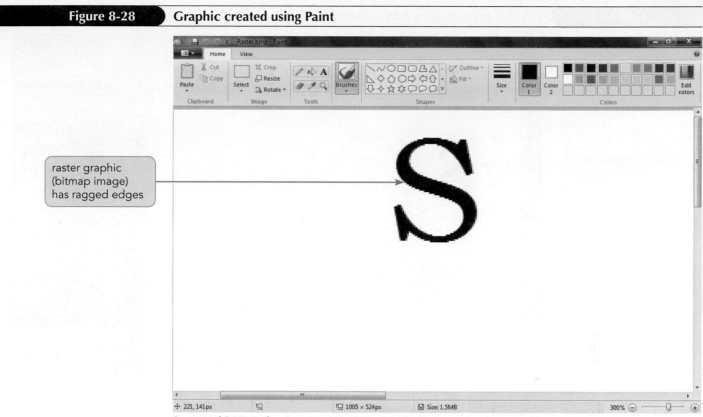

raster graphic
(bitmap image)
has ragged edges

Courtesy of © Microsoft

Raster graphics use the filename extensions .bmp, .gif, .jpg, .png, and .tif. Graphics with these filename extensions are created using a variety of programs, including Paint, Adobe Photoshop, Adobe Fireworks, and Corel PaintShop Photo Pro. In addition, any image that you take using a digital camera or make using a scanner is a raster graphic. Because raster graphics are made up of pixels, it is not possible to create layers of content. If you draw a circle using a raster graphics program, and then use a text tool to add a word on top of the circle, the pixels in the text *replace* the ones in the circle. If you later decide to cut the text out of the circle, you'll be left with a hole where the text once was, not the original circle that you drew. In addition, raster graphics are not scalable; if you zoom in on an image created using a raster graphics program, you'll see ragged edges on the image because you cannot change the size of the pixels in the image.

Figure 8-29 shows the letter "S" that was created using Adobe Illustrator. Illustrator is an example of a program that creates vector graphics.

Figure 8-29   **Graphic created using Adobe Illustrator**

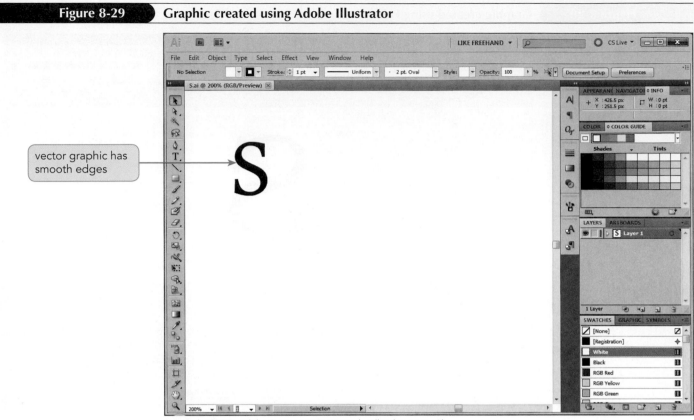

vector graphic has smooth edges

Vector graphics use the filename extensions .ai, .wmf, .cdr, and .dxf. Graphics with these filename extensions are created using programs such as Illustrator, CorelDRAW, and AutoCAD. Vector graphics are scalable, which means that their edges are smooth at any resolution. In addition, you can layer content in a vector graphic. In the same example using a circle with text on top of it, the text is a *layer* on top of the circle. In other words, the circle exists separately from the text, and vice versa. Because of this difference, vector graphics are best suited for drawing objects. Each object on a canvas has a certain dimension and color, and the program makes the distinction between the different objects on a canvas for you.

Why is this difference important? Depending on the type of image that you want to create, you might need to select a program specifically designed for that purpose. Raster graphics are the choice for photographs and images with different levels of shading. Vector graphics are the choice when you need to create drawings that require lines and curves to form different shapes. For these reasons, raster graphics require the use of a category of programs called **image editing programs**, and vector graphics require the use of a category of programs called **illustration software**. Some programs, such as Fireworks and Photoshop, do both, but most programs are geared primarily toward one category of graphic or the other.

Most beginning Web page developers can use a simple program such as Paint to draw basic images and create simple logos. An image editing program such as Adobe Photoshop is a good choice for someone who takes a lot of digital pictures and frequently needs to resize, crop, and retouch the images. Most image editing programs include a basic tool palette that lets you perform simple tasks that are common to creating and editing images. Learning how to use illustration software, however, usually requires a more thorough understanding gained from taking a course. The Tutorial 8 Weblinks page includes links to the programs discussed in this section and other resources for working with images.

Choosing a Web Hosting Service

After you have evaluated your Web site goals, planned your content, and determined the tools you will use to manage and create the Web site, you are ready to choose a Web hosting service or a Web presence provider to host your Web site. Some Web sites are hosted by private (dedicated) Web servers that are managed and maintained by the organization that creates the site. However, many Web sites are hosted by independent ISPs that sell server space to small- and medium-sized businesses. If you decide to use your own servers to host and maintain your Web site, it is important to have a thorough understanding of what is involved in upgrading your server space and services in case your initial plan changes over time.

If you decide to use a Web hosting service or Web presence provider, it is a good idea to select a Web hosting service *before* you begin work on actually creating the Web site's pages. The choice of a Web hosting service is more than just one of affordability—it is important to understand the types of Web servers the company uses, the software it uses to run the servers, and what services the company offers. You can then determine if the company's services and technology meet the requirements of your Web site's content.

Understanding Types of Web Servers

The type of Web server the Web hosting company uses can be important. Some types of pages that you might want to include in a Web site require a certain kind of server to process them. For example, if your site uses Active Server Pages (ASP), which are dynamic Web pages based on the content stored in a database, you'll need to store the site on a Windows-based Web server because the UNIX and Linux Web servers do not support ASP. It is important to identify the technologies that you'll use in your site to make sure that the company's Web server supports them. You don't want to create a Web site and later find out, for example, that your Web hosting company's Web server doesn't support the types of pages you created.

If any of your site's pages require users to supply information that is personal or confidential in nature, then you will need a secure server. A **secure server** encrypts data, which changes it into a format that prevents unauthorized parties from being able to read or use it. Some common situations that require a secure server are credit card transactions and forms that require a user to enter a Social Security number or other private data. When you need a secure server, the Web hosting service will require you to purchase and use a dedicated server. A **dedicated server** is a Web server that hosts only one site, compared to a **shared server**, which hosts several sites. A dedicated server is more expensive to operate. You will also need to install a server certificate as a method of proving your site's security features to its users.

Understanding the Site's File Size and Transfer Requirements

Because they are text files, most Web pages are small in terms of file size. However, a Web site can be very large if it contains many digital pictures, images, and supporting files such as a database or Shockwave or Flash files. For example, if you are a real estate agent, your site might include hundreds of digital photographs and virtual video tours of the homes that you have listed for sale. These files will require a lot of storage space. In addition, you need to consider the amount of traffic your site will receive and the sizes of the files that users will download from the Web server. The HTML document for a property listing might be 1,000 bytes (which is very small). But the pictures of the house and the video files of the main living areas might be several megabytes each. When a user downloads the Web page, the user's browser must also download the image and video files, resulting in the transfer of several megabytes of data.

The amount of data that is transferred from the Web server is known as the site's **bandwidth** or **data transfer**. Most companies sell server space based on a file size limit and a daily or monthly data transfer limit. When you exceed either of these limits, you might incur extra fees from the Web hosting service. In addition, your Web hosting service might not be able to increase your Web site's server space or bandwidth, which means that you would need to transfer your Web site to another company that can handle your site's file size and bandwidth requirements. Moving a Web site isn't an easy task, so you'll want to make sure that your Web hosting service can handle not only your current needs, but your anticipated needs for the future, as well.

Evaluating Other Services Offered by a Web Hosting Service

Finally, you should evaluate other useful services offered by the Web hosting service, such as site statistics, email accounts, Web site templates, Web site construction tools, database software, domain name management services, and technical support. You might need to pay an extra fee to obtain detailed site traffic reports, but this information is helpful when analyzing who is visiting your site and which pages they are viewing. You can use a traffic report to get detailed information, such as how many visitors used the site each day, how many pages the visitors viewed, which pages visitors used to enter and exit the Web site, what search strings were entered into the Web site's search feature, and so on. Analyzing a site's traffic is an important way of understanding who is using the site and what information they are seeking. If you use this information correctly, you'll be able to understand the site's visitors, and organize and design the site to better serve them.

You can use a registrar such as Network Solutions, whose home page is shown in Figure 8-30, or a similar registrar to enter your proposed domain name and check its availability.

Figure 8-30 | Network Solutions home page

enter a domain name here to check its availability

links to other services provided by the registrar

Figure reproduced with permission of Network Solutions LLC

If the domain name you want is available, you can purchase it directly from the registrar, or some Web hosting services will purchase the domain name for you. If you purchase your domain name from the Web hosting service that you decide to use, when you renew your Web site hosting agreement, the Web hosting service might automatically renew your domain name for you. This convenience saves you a step and ensures that your domain name does not expire and become eligible for sale to another entity if you forget or neglect to renew it.

You might also want to make sure that the company you select to host your site has technical support services available to you when you need them, especially if you are a new Web site developer. When you talk to people at the Web hosting service, try to get a sense of the level of support and service that it provides. For example, you can ask questions about the amount of server downtime it has experienced in the past month, how many hours a day and days a week that technical support personnel answer the phone, and any online resources that the company provides. When you view the online help resources, you can get a sense of the company's intended audience and whether it will assist you with future questions. If everything is written for advanced programmers, then you'll have to get more outside help than you would if the pages include basic information that is written in a clear and concise way for beginners.

You'll examine a few Web hosting services next to get a sense of the types of services and plans that they offer so you can report back to Chief Silva and recommend a choice.

To review Web hosting services:

▶ **1.** In the Session 8.2 section of the Tutorial 8 Weblinks page, click one of the Choosing a Web Hosting Service links.

▶ **2.** Review the site's home page, and then open a page that lists different Web hosting companies by name.

▶ **3.** Click a link to a company, and then examine the services that the Web hosting service provides. Figure 8-31 shows the home page for IPOWER.com, a company that provides Web hosting solutions for companies and individuals with different needs. As you are examining the hosting agreements, keep in mind the information you've learned about Web hosting. For example, be alert for different levels of service and whether the company lets you upgrade your server space and data transfer limits. Also, explore the site's technical support pages to see if they are written in a way that is easy for you to understand, so that you can diagnose and correct any problems that you have. Finally, see if the company offers domain name and renewal services for new accounts.

Figure 8-31   **IPOWER home page**

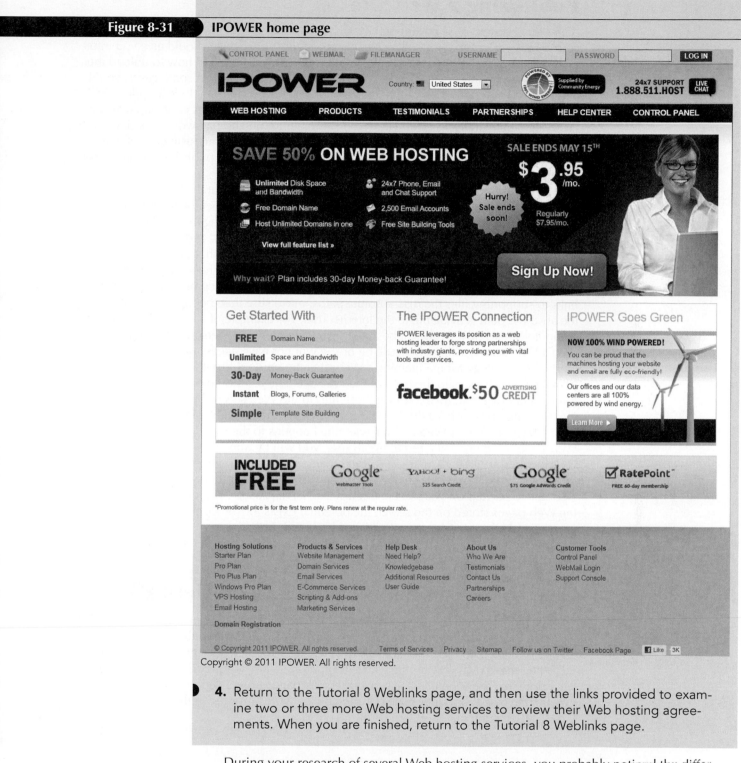

Copyright © 2011 IPOWER. All rights reserved.

4. Return to the Tutorial 8 Weblinks page, and then use the links provided to examine two or three more Web hosting services to review their Web hosting agreements. When you are finished, return to the Tutorial 8 Weblinks page.

During your research of several Web hosting services, you probably noticed the different levels of accounts each company offers and the services provided. You can also read reviews of different Web hosting services to understand the types of organizations they work with, and compare those organizations to your own to get a sense of the company's primary market.

Publishing a Web Site

After you choose a Web hosting service to host your Web site, the next step is to move your files to the company's Web server. Your Web hosting service should give you information about what user name and password to use, and where and how to upload the files. Most companies will ask you to use FTP to move your files. In some cases, you'll need an FTP program to make the transfer; but some companies include a built-in FTP interface that you access as part of your Web site's control panel. (A **control panel** is a Web page that you access with your Web site's user name and password; it includes all the tools you need to access and manage your Web site.) If you are using a Web site management program, you might be able to use the program to publish your site by setting up a remote Web site at the location of your Web server.

When you move your Web site's files to the Web server, be sure to include all of the folders and supporting files, not just the Web site's HTML documents. A common mistake made by many beginning Web site developers is omitting the Web site's supporting files, such as images, backgrounds, custom bullet characters, and multimedia files. If your HTML documents contain hyperlinks to supporting files that use relative paths, be certain to include the supporting files in the same folders as the HTML documents, or the links will be broken in your Web pages. If your HTML documents contain hyperlinks to supporting files that use absolute paths, make sure that the location of the file in the absolute path is available to the Internet user. For example, if a linked file is on your computer's hard drive, you will be able to view the file, but a person accessing the page from a Web server will not because he or she will not have access to your computer.

The best strategy for maintaining a Web site after you publish it for the first time is to make your changes to the copy of the Web site that you stored on your hard drive or other local drive, and then to move those files to the Web server. By having a copy of the Web site on your hard drive or other local drive (often called a **local Web site**), you have a backup of your Web site. If something happens to the Web site stored on the Web server (often called a **remote Web site**), you will be able to publish the files from your local Web site back to the server to repair any damaged or lost files. It is possible to make changes directly to the pages on the Web server, but then you would not have a complete backup on your local hard drive or server. Also, if you do make changes to the Web pages stored on the server, the potential exists for someone to be viewing the pages—and having problems with broken links and other issues—while you are editing the pages.

Search Engine Submission and Optimization

The last major task in publishing a Web site is promoting it. You can publish your pages and wait for search engines to perform crawls and add your site to their indexes. Or, you can be proactive and use <meta> tags to teach the search engines how to list your site by including the HTML <meta> tag with the appropriate keywords attribute to define your site's primary focus. Figure 8-32 shows the Web page you created in Session 8.1, with <meta> tags for a description of your site and keywords inserted in the head section of the HTML document.

Figure 8-32	Meta tags added to the Web page

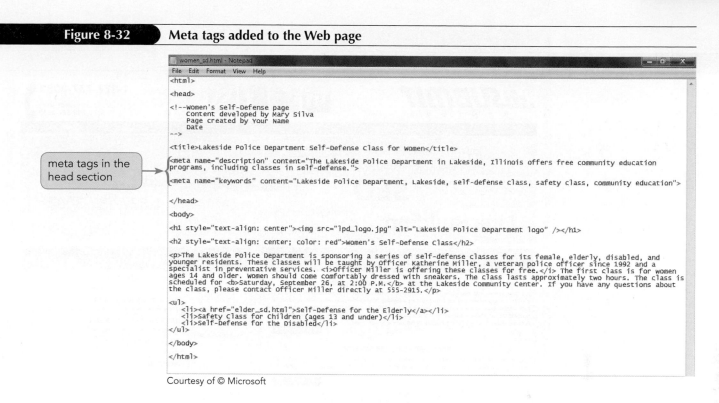

meta tags in the head section

Courtesy of © Microsoft

The description <meta> tag is a summary of the page's contents that a search engine might include in its search results. A search engine examines the keywords in an HTML document's <meta> tags to index the page and identify the search expressions that users might type to locate the page. For example, a user who types "Lakeside Police Department community education" into a search engine might see a link to the page in the search engine's results based on the keywords stored in the <meta> tag.

Using <meta> tags is a good way to help search engines list your site, but the search engines still need to find the site. To properly promote your site, you can send it to the various search engines on the Web. **Search engine submission** is the process of submitting your site's URL to one or more search engines so they will list your site in their indexes. **Search engine optimization (SEO)** is the process of fine-tuning your site so that it ranks well in a search engine's results when a user searches the Web using your site's keywords.

Your Web hosting service might include a resource for search engine submission. In this case, you'll need to create the <meta> tags that describe your site. You'll explore some resources for search engine submission and optimization next. Promoting the Web site for the Lakeside Police Department is an important step toward getting people to use it.

To explore resources for search engine submission and optimization:

1. In the Session 8.2 section of the Tutorial 8 Weblinks page, click the **Submit Express** link.

2. Explore the links on the Submit Express home page to learn more about search engine optimization and search engine submission. Use the links on the SEO tab to learn more about frequently asked questions, SEO, and how the service works. Figure 8-33 shows the home page, which includes links to articles and blog posts that Web developers might find helpful.

Figure 8-33 Submit Express home page

▶ **3.** Return to the Tutorial 8 Weblinks page, and then click the **Meta tags generator** link. Read the information in the page to learn more about <meta> tags, and examine the page to learn how to use it to generate <meta> tags for a Web site. (Do not generate any <meta> tags at this time.)

▶ **4.** Close your browser.

You can use the Additional Information section of the Weblinks page for Tutorial 8 to learn more about Web site development. If you have further interest in a specific area of Web page or Web site development, ask your instructor about courses that can help you to increase your understanding and knowledge of specific topics.

Session 8.2 Quick Check

REVIEW

1. Why is it important to create a storyboard of a Web site's content before deciding on the best ISP to host the Web site?
2. What is JavaScript, and what are some things that it can do?
3. How does a browser display content that is not written in HTML?
4. Which programs would you use to create Flash and Shockwave files for use on the Web? What kinds of files can you create using each program?
5. What is the difference between a raster graphic and a vector graphic? Which type of program would you use to create each type of graphic?
6. What features does a Web site management tool provide?
7. What is a secure server?
8. What are some important services that you should look for in an ISP besides Web site hosting plans and domain name and renewal services?
9. What is the difference between search engine submission and search engine optimization?

Practice the skills you learned in the tutorial using the same case scenario.

PRACTICE

Review Assignments

Data Files needed for the Review Assignments: academy.html, goals.txt, lpd_home.html, lpd_logo.jpg

Chief Mary Silva of the Lakeside Police Department asks you to help her with the content in the Citizen's Police Academy page in the Web site. This page will include information about an upcoming series of classes that trains citizens to help the police force in various ways. She also asks you to prepare a report on your findings, outlining the types of pages that the department should include in its Web site. Complete the following steps:

1. Start Notepad or your text editor, and then open the **academy.html** file from the Tutorial.08\Review folder included with your Data Files.
2. Make the following changes to the document:
   a. In the head section, replace the "[Your Name]" and "[Today's Date]" placeholder text with your name and today's date, respectively.
   b. Create a new paragraph in the body section by typing the opening and closing tags for a paragraph. Copy the text stored in the goals.txt file included in the Tutorial.08\Review folder and paste it between the paragraph tags.
   c. Insert paragraph tags so the sentence that begins "Interested participants…" appears in its own paragraph.
   d. Insert a heading at the beginning of the body section with the text **Citizen's Police Academy** and that displays the text in the largest font available for a heading.
   e. Change the color of the heading you inserted in Step 2d to blue and center it.
   f. Change the sentence that begins "Participants must be 21 years of age…" to italic and bold.
   g. Create a new paragraph above the heading in the body section. Then insert the image file lpd_logo.jpg, which is stored in the Tutorial.08\Review folder, in the paragraph. Include appropriate alternate text for the logo. Change the paragraph's alignment to center so the image will be centered on the page.
   h. Create a new paragraph at the bottom of the body section. In this paragraph, format the text **Return to home page** as a hyperlink that opens the Lakeside Police Department home page, which is saved as lpd_home.html in the Tutorial.08\Review folder.
3. Save the file and then preview it in a browser. If necessary, return to your text editor and make any changes.
4. Start your Web browser, and then use your favorite search engine or directory to search for police department Web sites in small metropolitan areas. Examine the sites to understand the type of information they contain. Also, review the contents of each page to look for different Web technologies such as scripts, images, and animations so you can develop a plan for the Lakeside Police Department. In your plan, identify the type of content you want to include.
5. Open the Tutorial 8 Weblinks page at www.cengagebrain.com, and then click the Review Assignments link. Use the links in the Review Assignments section to conduct sufficient research to recommend a Web hosting service for the Lakeside Police Department. (You should assume that the police department does not have access to a private dedicated server.) Make sure that the Web hosting service you recommend can process the pages you plan to include in the Web site (Step 4). Print the page that describes the services provided by the Web hosting service and the cost of the plan that you recommend.

6. Write a memo to Chief Silva explaining what technologies you have planned and which Web hosting service you recommend that the police department use to host its Web site. Be sure to support your recommendations with information you obtained through your research.

7. Close your Web browser.

Apply what you learned to create a Web page that links to a Web site.

APPLY

Case Problem 1

Data Files needed for this Case Problem: invitation.txt, swim.jpg

Storm Relief Fundraiser   Alyssa Cruze is managing a fundraiser to collect donations to help victims of flooding and other weather-related disasters in the United States. She has asked members of her swim team to teach swim lessons to younger participants in exchange for donations to the American Red Cross and for community service hours. She needs your help to create a Web page for the team's Web site that will contain some basic information about the fundraiser. The page will also include a link to the American Red Cross home page. To help Alyssa create the Web page, complete the following steps:

1. Start Notepad or your text editor.

2. Type the HTML structure tags in the document to create the HTML document, the head section, and the body section.

3. Add the page title **Storm Relief Fundraiser** to the page.

4. Copy the paragraphs stored in the **invitation.txt** document in the Tutorial.08\Cases folder included with your Data Files, and paste them into the body section of the HTML document.

5. Add the necessary HTML tags to the paragraphs that you pasted in Step 4.

6. Change the sentence "There is no charge for these swim lessons." in the first paragraph to italic.

7. Change the text "donation to the American Red Cross" in the first paragraph to bold.

8. Create a new, centered paragraph at the beginning of the body section, and then insert the image saved as **swim.jpg** in the Tutorial.08\Cases folder. Add appropriate alternate text to the image and make sure that you include a space before the ending slash in the <img> tag.

9. Change the text "American Red Cross" in the last sentence in the first paragraph to a hyperlink that opens the Web site at **http://www.redcross.org**. (Be sure to include the http:// in the URL or your link will not work correctly.)

10. Change the paragraph that begins "Space is limited…" to bold and red.

11. Save the file as **fundraiser.html** in the Tutorial.08\Cases folder.

12. Open the HTML document in a Web browser. If necessary, return to your text editor and make any changes, save the HTML document, and then refresh the page in the browser. Be sure to test the hyperlink you created (use the Back button to return to your Web page). Print the Storm Relief Fundraiser Web page.

⊕ **EXPLORE** 13. Use your browser to view and print the HTML document. (*Hint*: If you are using Internet Explorer, right-click a blank area on the page, and then click View source. If you are using Firefox, right-click a blank area on the page, and then click View Page Source on the shortcut menu. If you are using Chrome, right-click a blank area on the page, and then click View page source on the shortcut menu.)

14. Close your browser and your text editor.

Determine the best Web site creation and management tool for a local deli to use to create a Web site that accepts online orders.

RESEARCH

Case Problem 2

There are no Data Files needed for this Case Problem.

Shayla's Deli   Shayla Robinson owns and operates a deli that serves breakfast and lunch and caters local events. Because customers who call in their orders and pick them up constitute a large percentage of the deli's business, Shayla's employees spend a lot of time on the phone. Shayla wants to create a Web site on which she can post the menu and daily specials so customers can use it to place orders. Shayla wants to use a Web site creation and management tool to create the Web site. The Web site will contain many pages and images, and it will require forms that allow customers to place pick-up orders for breakfast and lunch and to place orders for catering services. She wants to accept credit card orders on the Web site so customers can pay the required deposit for catering orders. To help identify the best Web site creation and management tool for the deli's Web site, complete the following steps:

1. Start your Web browser, go to www.cengagebrain.com, open the Tutorial 8 Weblinks page, and then click the Case Problem 2 link. Click the Microsoft Expression Web link and wait while the browser loads the page.

⊕ **EXPLORE**

2. Use the resources on the Expression Web site to find information about Microsoft Expression Web that will assist you in making a recommendation for using Expression Web to create the Shayla's Deli Web site. Pay particular attention to the user interface, online help and tutorials, server issues, cost, and implementation. As you are gathering information, try to get a sense of how easy or difficult it would be for a beginner to use the program. In addition, learn about the tools that Expression Web includes for publishing a Web site and for creating simple images, such as logos.

⊕ **EXPLORE**

3. Return to the Tutorial 8 Weblinks page, and then click the Adobe Dreamweaver link. Use the guidelines in Step 2 to gather information about Dreamweaver, paying particular attention to what Shayla needs for her Web site.

⊕ **EXPLORE**

4. When you are finished, write a memo addressed to Shayla Robinson that includes a table identifying the pros and cons of using each program to create the deli's Web site. Below the table, write a paragraph in which you recommend the use of one program over the other. Be sure to support your recommendation with specific information.

5. Close your browser.

Use JavaScript to enhance a Web page.

CREATE

Case Problem 3

There are no Data Files needed for this Case Problem.

Point Blanke Airpark   Joe Fehrenbach is the president of the Point Blanke Airpark in Point Blanke, Colorado. The airpark is home to 50 small and medium-sized aircraft, mostly belonging to retired military officials and pilots. The airpark is a not-for-profit organization; and as such, it relies on dues and fundraising efforts to pay for maintenance and renovations to the airpark's small terminal and for other capital expenditures. The board recently voted to conduct a fundraiser in which corporations sponsor the airpark based on the mileage their employees travel and based on the mileage traveled by the aircraft at the airpark. To help compute the nautical miles and the donations, Joe needs to create a Web page with a mileage calculator and a calculator that computes the donation. To create the page for Joe, complete the following steps:

1. Start your Web browser, go to www.cengagebrain.com, open the Tutorial 8 Weblinks page, and then click the Case Problem 3 link.

2. Use the links to select a site that provides free JavaScript programs.

3. Search the site for a calculator that computes the mileage between airports in the United States. When you find a resource, examine the instructions for using the script and any requirements for its use (such as posting a link to the provider's Web site on your Web page).

4. Start Notepad or your text editor and create an HTML document using the required document structure.

5. Add an appropriate title to the HTML document using the <title> tags.

✛EXPLORE   6. Create a heading for the Web page and one or two paragraphs about the fundraiser and its objectives. Use your knowledge of HTML to enhance the content you provide to make it visually appealing.

7. Save the page as **airpark.html** in the Tutorial.08\Cases folder included with your Data Files.

✛EXPLORE   8. Follow the instructions on the Web site you located in Step 2 to insert the script into the HTML document. Make sure that your page contains information required by the provider in exchange for your use of the script.

9. Save the HTML document, and then open the file in a browser. Test the script. If necessary, return to the HTML document to make changes.

✛EXPLORE   10. Return to the Web site you located in Step 2 and search for a script that creates a simple calculator that performs basic calculations. Add the script to your HTML document. In addition, add supporting text to indicate that the donor can use the calculator to compute the per-mile donation based on the mileage computed by the airport calculator. (For example, if the donation is 10 cents per mile, the donor would use the calculator to multiply the nautical mileage between airports by 10 cents, or .10.)

11. Save the HTML document, and then refresh the page in your Web browser. Use the airport calculator to compute the mileage between Denver, Colorado and Miami, Florida. Then use the calculator to compute the donation based on 10 cents per mile. (*Note:* If you are using Internet Explorer and a warning opens at the bottom of the window, click the Allow blocked content button to display the result of the script. If you are using Firefox and nothing happens when you click the button to calculate the distances, press the Alt button if necessary to display the menu bar, click Tools on the menu bar, click Options, click the Content icon, click the Enable JavaScript check box to select it, click the OK button, and then try again.) Print the page.

12. Close your browser and Notepad.

Review the characteristics of good and bad Web sites using resources on the Web.

RESEARCH

Case Problem 4

There are no Data Files needed for this Case Problem.

The Best and Worst of the Web   You are an editorial assistant for a magazine whose core subscription base consists of Web site developers and programmers. As part of the annual "Best and Worst of the Web" issue, your editor, Chloe Hughes, has asked you to conduct some research to identify Web sites that rank other Web sites based on their content, presentation, and layout. Chloe asks you to use the information you find to write a sidebar feature about what makes a Web site great. Complete the following steps:

1. Start your Web browser, go to www.cengagebrain.com, open the Tutorial 8 Weblinks page, and then click the Case Problem 4 link. Choose a Web site that lists the "best" sites, and then wait while the browser loads the home page of the site you selected.

⊕ EXPLORE 2. Review the site's information to learn how it is organized and then examine the site's selection of "best" Web sites. As you are viewing the sites, take note of whether you agree with the site's "best" ranking. Print the home pages for at least three sites that you visit.

⊕ EXPLORE 3. Return to the Tutorial 8 Weblinks page, and then choose a link to a site that lists the "worst" Web sites. Review the site's information to learn how it is organized and then examine the site's selection of the "worst" Web sites. As you are viewing the sites, take note of whether you agree with the site's "worst" ranking. Print the home pages for at least three sites that you visit.

⊕ EXPLORE 4. Write a brief report to your instructor in which you identify three characteristics of good Web sites and three characteristics of bad Web sites. Be sure to back up your ideas with documentation or examples you found in the Web sites that you reviewed in Steps 2 and 3.

5. Close your browser.

Evaluate Web sites in a specific industry to help plan a new Web site.

CHALLENGE

Case Problem 5

There are no Data Files needed for this Case Problem.

Hilltop Custom Pools   John Davidson is the owner of Hilltop Custom Pools, a custom residential pool construction company in northern California. John wants you to conduct some research to help him plan the storyboard for his company's Web site. He wants you to look at the Web sites for other custom pool companies, and evaluate the resources they use to design their sites and the <meta> tags that they use to increase the effectiveness of their site's ranking in search engines. To help John plan his company's Web site and develop effective <meta> tags, complete the following steps:

1. Start your Web browser and then use your favorite search engine or directory to search for swimming pool contractors in northern California or in any other city, or for custom pool builders that you might already know by name. Evaluate the links and choose one to a specific construction company. Click the link to open the home page to the contractor's Web site, and then print the home page.

⊕ EXPLORE 2. Evaluate the contractor's Web site and take note of any technologies that you can identify, such as information presented in an animation or a script. If you notice the use of any of these technologies, evaluate their effectiveness.

⊕ EXPLORE 3. Click the links on the contractor's home page to explore the site and take note of the type of information it contains. Evaluate the Web site as if you were a customer by considering the information provided, the ease with which you can navigate the site, the attractiveness of the layout and design, and any other issues that you deem important to the overall success of the Web site.

4. Look for weaknesses in the Web site's presentation and design. Would you change anything? If so, why? Be specific.

⊕ EXPLORE

5. Examine the <meta> tags that the site uses by viewing the source document for the site's home page. (*Hint*: If you are using Internet Explorer, right-click a blank area on the page, and then click View source. If you are using Firefox or Chrome, right-click a blank area on the page, and then click View Page Source [Firefox] or View page source [Chrome] on the shortcut menu.) Evaluate the effectiveness of the <meta> tags used in the home page.

6. Return to your search results and evaluate another contractor's Web site using the guidelines presented in Steps 2 through 5. Print the contractor's home page.

7. When you have finished evaluating the two Web sites, close your browser.

⊕ EXPLORE

8. Write a one-page report addressed to your instructor. In your report, provide specific feedback on how you would use the information you found to recommend a presentation, a layout, and <meta> tags for the Hilltop Custom Pools Web site.

ENDING DATA FILES

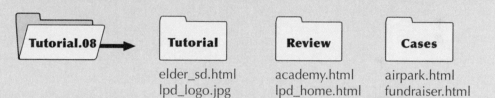

Tutorial.08 ➡

Tutorial
elder_sd.html
lpd_logo.jpg
women_sd.html

Review
academy.html
lpd_home.html
lpd_logo.jpg

Cases
airpark.html
fundraiser.html
swim.jpg

TUTORIAL 9

Electronic Commerce

Doing Business on the Internet

OBJECTIVES

Session 9.1
- Understand the basics of e-commerce
- Explore Web sites that conduct e-commerce
- Learn how companies generate revenues online by selling products, subscriptions, and services
- Determine how companies generate revenues online through advertising and marketing
- Learn how consumers pay for e-commerce purchases
- Learn about consumer concerns about transaction security and privacy
- Understand international and legal concerns related to e-commerce

Case | *Omega Group*

Omega Group is a human resources consulting firm that offers a full range of services to midsized and large companies. Omega's services include recruiting, compensation and benefits, training, and compliance. The recruiting division helps companies fill managerial, executive, administrative support, and technical professional positions. The compensation and benefits division helps Omega's clients maintain competitive pay scales and benefits packages, and provides administration services for medical, dental, retirement, and other employee benefit plans. The training division plans and monitors employee training, develops and sells training programs. The compliance division educates clients on human resources–related laws and regulations.

The Omega Web site contains information about the firm and its services, but does not offer visitors the opportunity to buy any products or services. Omega's managing director, Steven Boyce, is interested in selling Omega's current and upcoming new products and services online. You will explore these possibilities and analyze their potential for Omega by finding out more about e-commerce and how Omega might use its Web site to increase sales to current clients and to identify new opportunities: new services and products, new clients, or both.

STARTING DATA FILES

There are no starting Data Files needed for this tutorial.

SESSION 9.1 VISUAL OVERVIEW

Activities undertaken by a company to sell goods or services to individuals are called **business-to-consumer (B2C)** e-commerce.

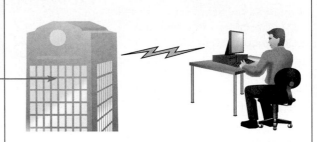

Business-to-Consumer (B2C)

- Subscription services
- Content providers
- Transaction brokers
- Service providers
- Portals

E-commerce, or electronic commerce, refers to the process of developing, marketing, selling, delivering, servicing, and paying for products and services online.

Activities undertaken by a company to sell goods or services to other businesses or nonprofit organizations are called **business-to-business (B2B)** e-commerce.

Business-to-Business (B2B)

- Online retailers
- Liquidation brokers
- Business service providers

E-COMMERCE CATEGORIES

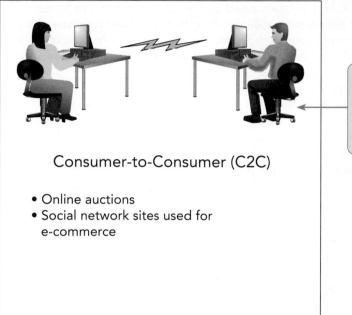

Online business transactions undertaken by individuals who are not operating a formal business are called **consumer-to-consumer (C2C)** e-commerce.

Consumer-to-Consumer (C2C)

- Online auctions
- Social network sites used for e-commerce

Using Internet technology to perform transactions with the government such as filing tax forms is called **business-to-government (B2G)** e-commerce.

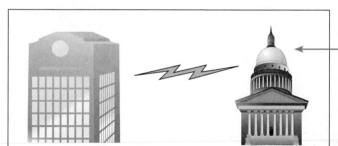

Business-to-Government (B2G)

- Tax filings
- Tax payments
- Financial reporting to government agencies

Buying and Selling over the Web

TIP

Mobile e-commerce (or m-commerce) is when e-commerce takes place on a mobile device.

In its simplest form, the term "commerce" refers to the buying and selling of products, services, or something of value. Electronic commerce, or e-commerce, refers to the buying and selling of these products and services over the Internet and the Web. E-commerce, also referred to as etail, can be grouped into different sectors or categories based on who is involved in this exchange of goods and services. The Visual Overview for Session 9.1 describes four sectors into which e-commerce is commonly categorized.

All businesses—no matter where they are located and what they sell—try to generate revenues (income) and pay the costs associated with generating those revenues. The **revenue model** is the process or processes that a company uses to find new customers, make sales, and deliver the goods or services it sells. The most common revenue model is direct sales of products and services.

Businesses take a variety of approaches to generating revenue on the Web. These approaches include the use of online sales of goods and services, subscriptions, and direct fees. The chart in Figure 9-1 shows the dramatic rise of e-commerce retail sales in the United States from 1998 to 2010 as compiled by the U.S. Census Bureau. Also, businesses use marketing strategies such as affiliate marketing and targeted advertising to generate revenue to support their online presence. Many companies also use a combined approach, such as charging direct fees for services or access to specific information as well as selling advertising and charging subscription fees for access to information. For more information about e-commerce, visit the links under the E-Commerce Information heading in the Additional Information section on the Weblinks page for Tutorial 9.

Figure 9-1 | **E-commerce retail sales in the United States**

Courtesy of www.USA.gov

Steven wants to learn more about how Omega might use e-commerce. You'll look at ways other companies are doing business over the Web.

Buying and Selling Goods

The most common form of e-commerce is **online retail**, which refers to selling physical products on the Web. The items are located, reviewed, and purchased on the Web, and then shipped to the buyer. In effect, this is an updated form of buying from mail order catalogs.

Companies have been selling goods through mail order catalogs since the late 1800s. Probably the most notable of these are Sears and Montgomery Ward. Originally, potential customers received catalogs in the mail, placed their order by mail, and then received their items by mail. When the telephone became commonplace, these companies began accepting telephone orders. In the mail order catalog model, the seller creates a brand image that conveys quality and a specific price point, and then uses the strength of that image to sell through its printed catalogs. Retailers that have successfully used mail order catalogs include sellers of consumer goods items such as clothes, computers, electronics, housewares, and gifts. Today's online retail is based on this time-tested mail order catalog model.

In the online retail model, a company replaces or supplements its printed catalogs and/or brick-and-mortar store with a Web site. Customers can place orders through the Web site as well as by telephone, by mail, or in the store. In some stores, sales staff can place a Web order for a customer, or customers can use computers that are available for accessing the store's Web site right in the physical store. Customers can also sometimes order an item on the Web site and then pick it up in a retail location near them. Some companies make certain products available only online and do not offer them for sale in their retail locations (or vice versa).

Some companies, such as Amazon.com, CafePress, and Zappos.com, sell only on the Web. Individuals who have a specialty item to sell might also sell their items only on the Web, such as crafters of knitted goods, chicken coop designers, and musicians. These Web-only businesses are sometimes called **dot-com** or **pure dot-com** companies. However, most companies doing business on the Web today are not pure dot-com companies, but instead use the Web to extend their existing businesses.

Adding a Web site to reach potential customers creates an additional **sales channel**, which is a way that a company supplies its products or services to customers. Companies that use both a physical store and the Web to sell their products and services are sometimes referred to as **bricks and clicks** (combining "bricks" from the bricks and mortar of a traditional retail outlet and "clicks" from the action of selecting items on a Web page; sometimes called "clicks and mortar"). Brick-and-click companies abound—from national chain stores such as Target, Kohl's, Toys"R"Us, OfficeMax, and Costco; to grocery stores such as Safeway, Whole Foods, and Albertsons; to manufacturers such as Hewlett-Packard and Apple; to banks and the U.S. Postal Service; to small, independent businesses such as baby clothing boutiques and comic book sellers.

To learn more about online retailers, you will visit Web sites operated by different types of businesses.

TIP

David Pottruck, former co-CEO of Charles Schwab & Co., coined the term "bricks and clicks" in a July 1999 speech at an Internet conference to describe the brokerage's success at integrating online access with its traditional face-to-face services.

To learn more about online retailers:

1. Start your Web browser, go to **www.cengagebrain.com**, open the Tutorial 9 Weblinks page, and then click the **Session 9.1** link.

2. Click one of the links in the Web-Only Retailers section to open that site's home page.

3. Explore the Web site by selecting a product to view. Zoom in on the product, and then watch a video about the product if one is available. Determine the shipping policies and payment options available for that product. Figure 9-2 shows a product page for CafePress, which is a Web-only retailer that sells customized items geared mainly toward consumers.

Figure 9-2 CafePress product page

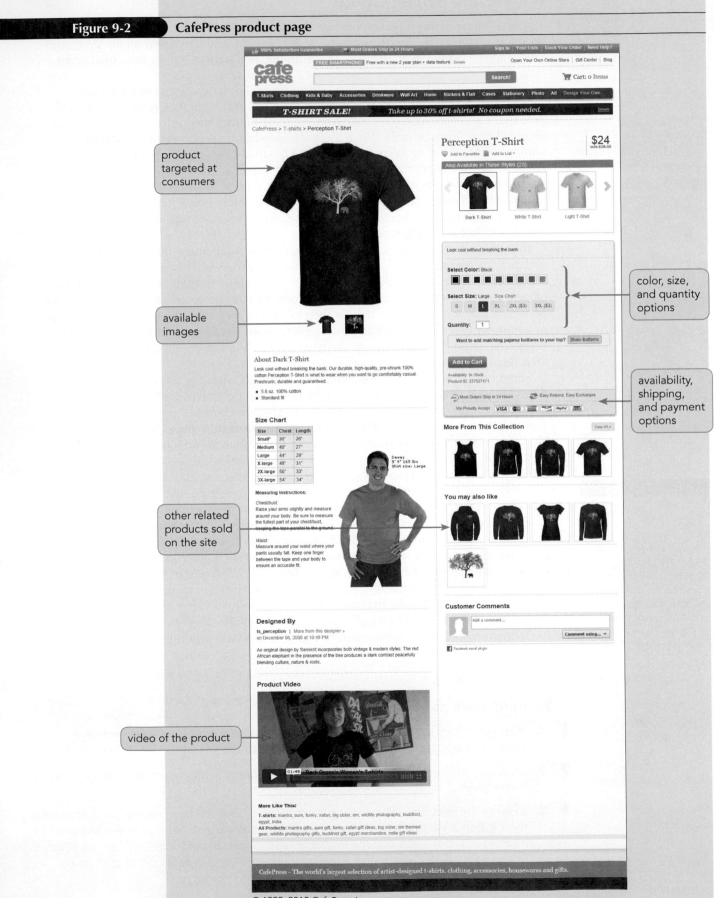

product targeted at consumers

available images

other related products sold on the site

video of the product

color, size, and quantity options

availability, shipping, and payment options

▶ **4.** Using the links at the bottom of the page, open the page that describes the site (labeled About Us, Company Info, FAQs, or something similar) to learn about the company's products and services available online and the company's goal for its Web storefront.

▶ **5.** Return to the Tutorial 9 Weblinks page for Session 9.1, click one of the links in the Print Catalog Retailers section, and then repeat Steps 3 and 4 to explore the Web site.

▶ **6.** Return to the Tutorial 9 Weblinks page for Session 9.1, click one of the links in the Storefront and Online Retailers section, and then repeat Steps 3 and 4 to explore the Web site.

▶ **7.** Click the store locator link at the top or bottom of the page (often labeled Store Locations, Find Store, or Locate Store), enter your city and state or zip code (as indicated on the page) to determine whether the company has a store in your area, and then find out whether the product you viewed can be ordered through the Web site but picked up in a retail store and how this impacts shipping charges.

▶ **8.** Return to the Tutorial 9 Weblinks page for Session 9.1, click one of the links in the B2B Online Retailers section, and then repeat Steps 3 and 4 to explore the Web site.

▶ **9.** Return to the Weblinks page for Tutorial 9.

As you can see, there is a wide variety of online retail Web sites. Even though the products for sale vary greatly, the sites provide similar types of information to aid consumers in their purchasing decisions. You might also have noticed that some business-oriented sites require a larger quantity purchase than consumer-oriented sites.

INSIGHT

Consumer Benefits and Drawbacks of Online Retail

Online retail has many benefits to consumers. You can shop at any time of the day or night. You can avoid crowds. It's simple to compare prices for the same item at different retailers. It can be easier to find items, particularly specialty items, by conducting a Web search. Many item listings include multiple images of the product that can be magnified to see greater detail and rotated to get additional views. In addition, a video demonstrating the product is often available. Reviews by media and other consumers are included, so you can get a quick overview of what other people liked and didn't like about that item. For smaller businesses and niche businesses that can't afford a storefront or national ads to compete with established and large retailers, selling items online somewhat levels the playing field.

There are also some drawbacks to online retail. You cannot see or hold the product to determine the quality or confirm that its color matches the color displayed on their monitor. Although people sometimes visit a brick-and-mortar store to evaluate the product but then purchase the item online when they can find it for a cheaper price. After purchasing an item, it can take up to a week to receive the item, depending on the shipping method selected. Also, the shipping often adds extra cost to the price. Finally, although you might find it convenient to view and purchase items on your computers or mobile devices, it can lead to more impulse purchases because you can purchase the item immediately without taking time to consider whether you really want that item.

Buying and Selling Subscriptions

Other businesses derive their revenue only from subscription fees. A **subscription** is an amount that users pay in order to access the site's content. The subscription charge might be payable on a recurring basis such as monthly, or allow access during a specific time frame such as a year. This subscription-only model has been used successfully by some magazines that include no advertising as a matter of policy as well as some cable television stations.

Entertainment sites that feature online games, music, movies, and books are often subscription based. Netflix, one of the most popular subscription-only Web sites, offers movies and TV episodes that can be viewed on demand online as streaming video as do Amazon, Crackle, Hulu, Walmart.com, YouTube, and a host of other online companies. The fees range from monthly subscription fees for limited or unlimited access to pay-per-view. In order to stream video, you need an Internet-connected device such as a gaming system, an HDTV, a smartphone, a tablet, or a streaming player.

Many gaming sites such as GameHouse and EA Games and portal sites such as Yahoo! Games and MSN Games represent another example of subscription-based sites. They offer free online games to attract visitors as well as premium games that visitors must pay to play either by buying and downloading software to install on their computers, or by paying a subscription fee to enter the premium games area on the site.

However, it's more common to see sites that charge a subscription fee as well as include advertising. Many newspaper and magazine sites use a combination of advertising and subscription revenue. These sites offer some content free of charge, but most of the content is available only to subscribers. For example, *The Economist* and *The Wall Street Journal* provide some free content on their Web sites (including article excerpts or summaries and classified ads) but charge a subscription fee to access the full articles and additional content. *The Economist* also publishes content in the subscriber section of its Web site before the printed magazine is delivered to subscribers or sold on newsstands. Other newspapers, including *The Washington Post*, *The New York Times*, and the *Los Angeles Times*, offer most of their current stories free of charge on their Web sites but require visitors to pay for articles retrieved from their archives.

Omega's benefits, training, and compliance divisions all publish newsletters and reports of various types. Omega sends some of these publications to clients and potential clients at no charge. Other publications are sold for a flat fee or by subscription. Next, you will examine Web sites that employ combinations of subscription and advertising to support their revenue streams.

> **TIP**
> Many subscription-based Web sites also display ads to their subscribers.

> **TIP**
> Many subscription-based Web sites offer a free trial period so you can preview the site and then decide whether to join.

To examine subscription sites:

1. On the Tutorial 9 Weblinks page for Session 9.1, click one of the links in the Subscription-Based Sites section.

2. Explore the Web site to determine what types of content the site offers, the cost and terms for the subscription, and whether or not the site offers a free trial period. Also, determine if some of the site's content is available without subscribing. Figure 9-3 shows the home page for Angie's List, a customer review service that is supported by membership subscription fees as well as business advertisements.

Figure 9-3 Angie's List home page

click this button to pay a subscription fee to join

3. Return to the Weblinks page for Session 9.1, and then repeat Step 2 for two other sites in the list of links in the Subscription-Based Web Sites section.

As you have seen, subscribers or advertisers (or both) pay to allow themselves or site visitors to access the content on a business's Web site. Steven will explore the potential of using these options to sell some of Omega's print publications. However, most of Omega's revenue is generated by professional services provided to clients by its recruiting and benefits divisions. Steven asks you to investigate Web sites that provide services for which they charge a fee.

Buying and Selling Services

Some businesses offer services for which they charge a fee. The fee can be based on the specific service provided, or it can be based on the number or size of the transactions processed. Fees charged to consumers include brokerage fees, sales commissions, and the costs of information search and acquisition. A wide range of businesses on the Web use this service fees revenue model—from professional services such as tax planning and legal advice to intermediaries such as travel services and brokers.

Professional services sites charge fees for their services. For example, users can prepare their tax returns online at the H&R Block or TurboTax sites. LegalShield offers legal services on its Web site. Individual law and accounting firms also offer various professional services on the Web.

Another type of services sold on the Web is broker and intermediary services. An intermediary is a person or an organization that acts as a mediator or an agent between two parties to effect a transaction or an agreement. For example, when planning a vacation, you might use a travel agent to book your flight, reserve your hotel, and secure a rental car. In this case, the travel agent is the intermediary. Travel agents earn a commission on each airplane ticket, hotel reservation, auto rental, cruise, or vacation package that they book. In most cases, the transportation or lodging provider pays these commissions to the travel agent. Online travel sites such as Expedia and Travelocity also earn commissions from transportation and lodging providers in the form of fees for each reservation made through their Web site.

Stock brokerage firms also typically charge fees for transactions. Customers pay a commission to the brokerage firm for each trade executed. Online brokers such as E*TRADE and TD Ameritrade are threatening traditional brokerage firms by offering trading over the Web with lower fees and commissions. In addition, customers can manage their trading accounts anytime, though transactions are posted only when the market is open. Other companies that offer intermediary or brokering services for a fee on the Web include event ticket agencies, mortgage lenders and brokers, banks, and insurance brokers.

INSIGHT

Disintermediation and Reintermediation

E-commerce has led to disintermediation in some markets, including the travel industry, automotive sales, and stock brokerages. **Disintermediation** is when an intermediary from an industry, such as the traditional travel agencies, is no longer needed for the consumer to obtain the goods and services from the industry. In the case of travel agents, consumers began doing their own research and purchasing of airline tickets, hotels, and rental cars, often saving money in the process. In many cases, however, the original intermediary is replaced by a new liaison, who then receives the commission for providing information and facilitating the purchase of the transaction. The introduction of a new intermediary into an industry is called **reintermediation**. In the travel industry, the new intermediaries are the Web-based travel agencies such as Travelocity, Expedia, Priceline.com, Hotels.com, and Orbitz that specialize in finding and making available the best travel resources for consumers.

The automotive sales industry has also encountered disintermediation. Traditionally, auto dealers buy cars from the manufacturer and sell them to consumers. They provide showrooms and salespeople to help customers learn about product features, arrange financing, and make a purchase decision. Autobytel.com, Cars.com, and other online firms specialize in locating dealers in the buyer's area who are willing to sell cars for a small premium over the dealer's nominal cost. The buyer can purchase the car from the dealer without negotiating its price with a salesperson. Autobytel charges participating dealers a fee for this service. Autobytel is disintermediating the salesperson and reintermediating itself. The consumer spends less time buying the car and often pays a lower price while avoiding the negotiation process; the dealer pays a lower fee to Autobytel than the commission it would otherwise pay to its salesperson.

An auction is another example of an intermediary transaction. Auctions are an efficient way for businesses to clear out old and slow-moving inventory. In the past, companies would hire a liquidation broker to help dispose of unwanted inventory by holding an auction. A **liquidation broker** is an intermediary who matches sellers of obsolete inventory with purchasers who are looking for bargains. Liquidation brokers and companies that were large enough to arrange their own liquidation sales often found it expensive to set up a physical auction for obsolete inventory. The greatest expenses were leasing a place to hold the auction and mailing notices of the auction to a sufficient number of people to create a decent-sized bidding pool. It was also difficult to accumulate a wide enough variety of items to attract bidders. Bidders who were interested in only one or two items would be reluctant to attend the auction. As a result, inventory sold this way seldom returned more than 10% of its cost.

Today, many liquidation brokers are opening Web auctions to obtain a better range of bids. Auctions are a good way for sellers to obtain the highest possible price if the pool of bidders is large enough. An auction on a Web site can attract bidders from all over the world and these bidders can select the specific item on which they want to bid.

Most online auction sites offer merchandise that is the property of others, much as an auctioneer would at a public auction. The items being auctioned might be surplus inventory, refurbished items, returns, discontinued items, packaging changes, and so forth. Each online auction site establishes its own bidding rules. Auctions can remain open for a few days or a week. Some sites are providing Webcasts so that bidders can attend a live auction via computer. Some sites provide automated software agents that bidders can instruct to place bids as needed to win the auction, subject to a maximum limit set by the bidder. Because bidders face a significant risk of buying a misrepresented product in a sight-unseen online auction, some auction sites offer mediation or **escrow services** that hold the buyer's payment until he or she is satisfied that the item matches the seller's description. Escrow services fees range from 1% to 10% of the item's cost, with a minimum fee of between $5 and $10. The advantages of conducting online auctions include a large pool of potential bidders, 24-hour access, and the ability to auction hundreds of similar items simultaneously.

Some companies are too small to operate their own liquidation sites or to attract the interest of liquidation brokers. These companies have found eBay and similar consumer-oriented auction sites to be useful tools for selling their excess inventory and used equipment.

As you learned in Tutorial 4, eBay, one of the first auction Web sites, has become the premier choice for many people who want to participate in auctions. Both buyers and bidders benefit from the large marketplace that eBay has created. As discussed in Tutorial 4, sellers and buyers must register with eBay and agree to the site's basic terms of doing business. Sellers pay a listing fee and a percentage of the final selling price. Buyers pay nothing to eBay. In addition to the basic fees, sellers can choose from a variety of enhanced and extra-cost services, including having their auctions listed in bold type or included as featured auctions that appear at the top of bidders' search results pages. In an attempt to address bidder concerns about seller reliability, eBay identifies sellers who have received high ratings from buyers for excellent customer service with an eBay Top-rated seal. Also, if a buyer doesn't receive the item purchased or believes that the received item is different from what was described in the listing, eBay Buyer Protection helps the buyers and sellers resolve the dispute.

These types of professional and intermediary services are similar to Omega's offerings. You will examine some of the different services provided on e-commerce sites next: professional services as well as broker and intermediary services.

> **TIP**
>
> Online auctions are an example of C2C e-commerce because one person auctions an item to another person. They can also be considered B2C e-commerce even if a seller is not operating a formal business.

To examine e-commerce sites that sell services:

1. Return to the Tutorial 9 Weblinks page for Session 9.1, and then click one of the links in the Professional Services section.

2. Explore the Web site by locating information about the services offered and the fees charged for those services. Figure 9-4 shows the home page for H&R Block Tax Services, on which the services and fees are described.

> **TIP**
>
> Some sites require visitors to create an account and log in before subscription fees are disclosed.

Figure 9-4   H&R Block home page

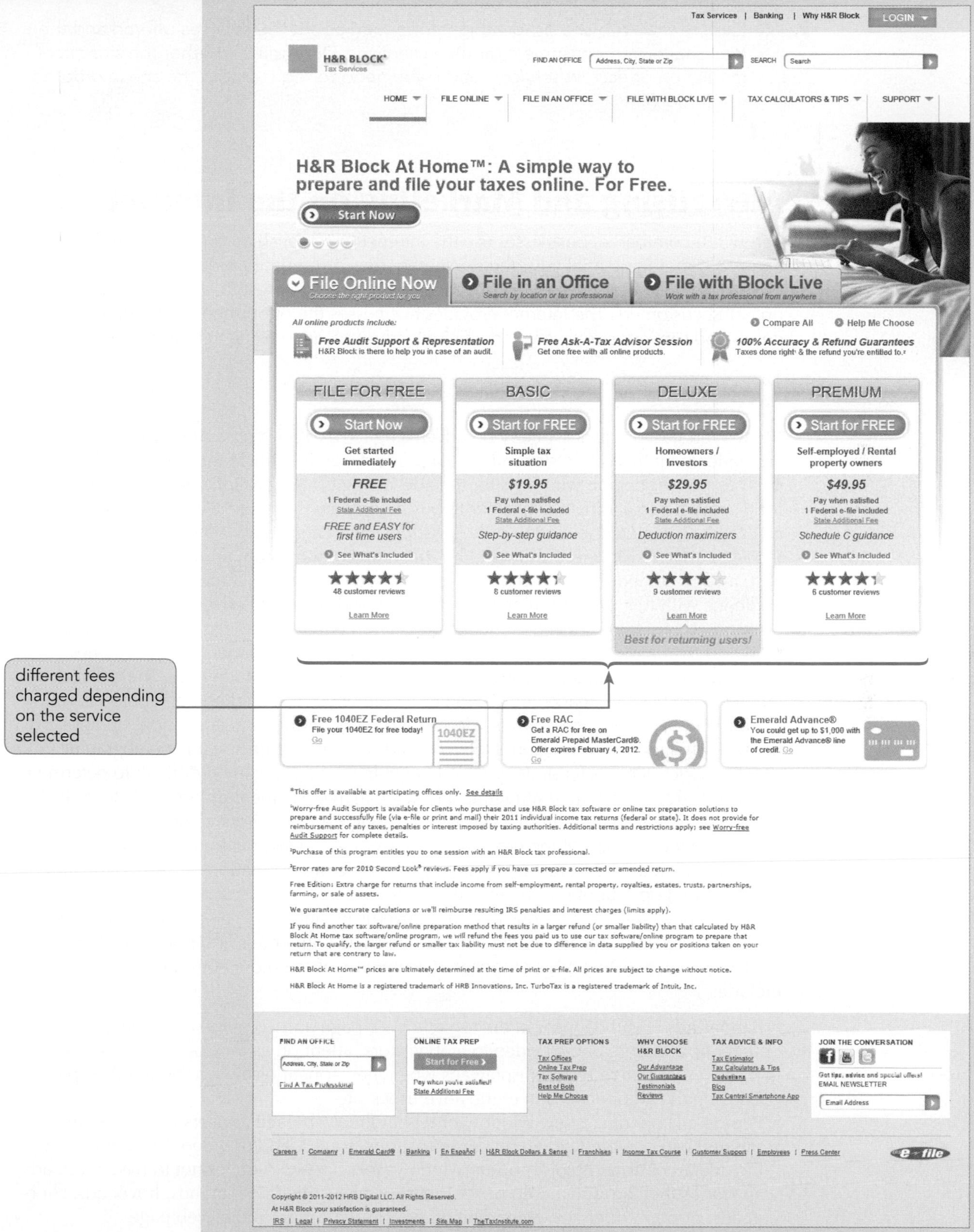

different fees charged depending on the service selected

© 2011–2012 HRB Digital LLC. All Rights Reserved.

3. Return to the Tutorial 9 Weblinks page for Session 9.1, and then click one of the links in the Broker and Intermediary Services section.

4. Explore the Web site by locating information about the services offered and the fees charged to consumers for those services. Determine whether the site offers mediation or escrow services, and if you need to register with the site in order to use its services.

Advertising and Marketing on the Internet

Through e-commerce, businesses use the Internet to establish an online marketplace and reach more potential customers. Whether they are selling products, subscriptions, or services on the Internet, businesses need to generate interest to effectively reach these potential customers. The Internet provides businesses the opportunity to promote their goods and services effectively and efficiently through advertising and marketing.

Advertising

Many Web-based businesses rely on advertising to pay their costs. **Advertising** is a paid announcement that attracts attention to a product, service, business, person, or idea. The business or person who pays for the advertising is trying to influence an audience; for example, persuading a consumer to buy a company's product. An ad that appears on a Web site is targeted toward that site's visitors, who can usually access some or all of the site's content for free. This model has been used successfully for television, broadcast, and print media. For example, television networks in the United States provide an audience with free programming that is interspersed with paid advertising messages. For Web-based businesses, some of the most common types of sites that support themselves with advertising are search engines, portals, and online newspapers and magazines.

The most successful advertising is directed at very specific audiences. The collection of characteristics that marketers use to group audiences is called demographic information and includes such traits as address, age, gender, income, education, hobbies, political affiliation, and religion. Delivering ads to outlets with specific demographic characteristics is part of a strategy called target marketing. It can be difficult to determine whether a given Web site is attracting a specific market segment unless that site collects demographic information from its visitors. Although some visitors voluntarily supply this information as part of the process for registering and signing in to a site, others are becoming increasingly reluctant to provide this type of information because of privacy concerns and opt out of sharing this information.

As you have seen in previous tutorials, advertising appears in a variety of different forms on Web sites. Some are very obvious, such as banner ads and pop-ups. Others are less so, such as text ads or sponsored ads. Some of the more common types of ads include:

- **Banner ads** usually appear at the top of a Web page and combine text, images, animation, sound, and/or video to grab visitors' attention as they open a Web page. These ads are often called display ads when they appear elsewhere on the Web page. Clicking the ad opens a link to the advertiser's site.
- **Pop-up ads** open in a new window or within the Web page as users browse a Web site and can contain text, graphics, animations, sound, and/or video. Browsers often include an option to block pop-up windows for users who prefer not to have these ads appear as they browse a Web page. These are also called floating ads, hover ads, slide-in ads, or pop-under ads depending on how they pop-up in the Web page.

- **Text ads** are simple text-based links that appear within the body of a Web page and are related to the content. These are also sometimes called inline ads.
- **Contextual ads** change based on the content you are viewing or searching. They can be any type of ad, including banner ads, text ads, and pop-up ads. These are most commonly seen on the results pages of a search engine.
- **Sponsorship ads** are often a logo or simple statement that the content being viewed was paid for by a company. They often appear on a separate Sponsors page or area of the Web site.
- **Video ads** are ads in a video format that appear at the beginning of online videos such as newscasts, within a video, or on their own when browsing or viewing related content such as on YouTube.
- **Interstitial ads** appear as visitors browse from one Web page to another and often contain rich media, streaming video, or large graphics. These ads might appear when you click a link in an excerpt of a news story to view the entire story.
- **Advertorials** are paid editorial ads that contain objectively written opinions about a product or service.
- **Classified ads** are descriptions of items for sale such as a car, boat, motorcycle, house, or airplane, or something someone is looking for, such as a job.

Affiliate Marketing

Affiliate marketing is an arrangement in which one company performs some business processes for another company in exchange for money or the sharing of expertise or access to customers. These arrangements can take many forms, such as when one company offers another company's products for sale in return for a share of the revenue, or when one company receives a payment for generating a lead, referring a new member, or getting someone to request a catalog or sign up for a newsletter. Affiliate marketing can also be called a **strategic alliance** (or a **strategic partnership**). Amazon.com, Dell, PriceGrabber, and Upromise are just a few examples of companies that use affiliate marketing in e-commerce.

Amazon has a variety of affiliate programs. When other Web sites and blogs suggest a book, they often include a link to the Amazon page for that book. Although the customer purchases the book directly through Amazon as usual, the site from which the customer linked to Amazon receives a small commission for helping to prompt the sale. Amazon also provides another affiliate program to companies such as Sears, Macy's, and Lands' End by allowing these companies to use Amazon as a sales channel for selling their products on the Web.

PriceGrabber, a comparison shopping service site, provides another example of affiliate marketing. Shoppers can use the site to compare the cost of items for sale at different stores, both large, national chains and smaller, Web-only businesses. Depending on the program that merchants select, they pay PriceGrabber a fee whenever a shopper clicks a link to one of their product offers, which brings shoppers to the merchant's Web site; or merchants pay PriceGrabber a commission (or a share of the revenue) whenever a shopper purchases an item from the PriceGrabber Web site. Other comparison shopping services include Buy.com, mySimon, Nextag, Pricewatch, and Shopzilla.

Upromise by Sallie Mae is a rewards program that provides members with a way to save money for college when shopping online, eating out, and purchasing groceries at participating retailers. These partner retailers, restaurants, and merchants are highlighted on the Upromise Web site, providing exposure to potential customers. These partners give a percentage of the total purchase price to the member's Upromise account in exchange for the business. Family and friends can also make purchases linked to a member's account to contribute to the member's savings.

You'll look at some affiliate marketing programs being used on the Web to see if there are any possibilities for Steve to incorporate this type of partnership with other companies.

To examine Web sites that use affiliate marketing:

1. Return to the Tutorial 9 Weblinks page for Session 9.1, and then click one of the links in the Affiliate Marketing section.

2. Explore the Web site, looking for ways that the site uses affiliate marketing.

3. Look for a link to information about the site's affiliate marketing programs. This link is often at the bottom of the page and includes the word "affiliate," "partner," or "about us" in the link text. Figure 9-5 shows the affiliate program page for Upromise.

Figure 9-5	Upromise's affiliate program page

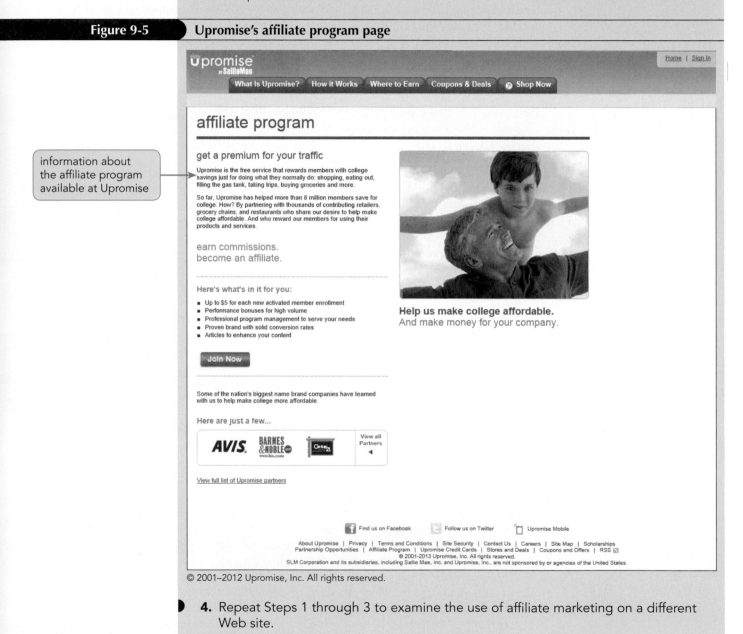

information about the affiliate program available at Upromise

© 2001–2012 Upromise, Inc. All rights reserved.

4. Repeat Steps 1 through 3 to examine the use of affiliate marketing on a different Web site.

Social Media Marketing

Social media marketing is the process of using social media Web sites such as Facebook, Twitter, and YouTube to attract attention to an idea, product, Web site, store, and so forth. Because of its personal nature, social media leads to word-of-mouth advertising between consumers. Businesses are tapping into social media as a way to attract new customers, perform market research, and address consumer concerns. As a consumer, be aware that a blog, tweet, or Facebook page could be created by a business to influence you. It might not be as blatant as other ads, so the effect is more insidious. Also, because of the amount of personal information that individuals tend to disclose on social media, advertisements can be displayed that match closely with each person's stated preferences.

Paying for E-Commerce Purchases

After selecting a product or service online, consumers need to pay for it. Although most e-commerce sites accept credit card payments, other forms of payment that are processed in real time are available as well, including online payment services and digital wallets.

Consumers can use a digital wallet to pay for their e-commerce purchases. A **digital wallet** (also called an **electronic wallet** or **e-wallet**) is an electronic device with software (or software that runs on a computer or phone) that enables the user to make a purchase online. The digital wallet stores a user's payment information such as bank account and credit card numbers, a digital certificate to identify the user, and information that the user provides such as shipping information to speed up Internet transactions. The consumer's information is encrypted to protect against identity theft and other forms of online piracy. During checkout at an e-commerce site, the digital wallet can automatically enter the user's information in the online form after the user enters a password. These online payment services provide consumers with a way to make online purchases easily and securely. E-commerce sites process transactions through an online payment gateway, which connects to their credit card processing account and enable automated, secure, online transactions to occur.

Originally, digital wallets were stored only on the user's computer. More often, mobile phones and other wireless devices are now used as digital wallets and stored on a server owned by a digital wallet vendor or an ISP. A digital wallet that an organization creates and maintains on its servers for consumers is sometimes called a **thin wallet**. A digital wallet vendor can charge a commission to a retailer on every purchase made with its wallet, or the merchant can pay a flat fee to the digital wallet vendor to use its wallets in transactions. Both the business and the consumer must use compatible digital wallets in order for the payment to be accepted. This is similar to how merchants choose which credit cards to accept for payment; for example, you cannot use an American Express card at a retailer that accepts only Visa and MasterCard.

Although digital wallets make e-commerce transactions easier, faster, and more secure, there are some things to consider before using one. Using a digital wallet enables a merchant to collect data about you and your shopping habits, including your name, address, gender, and age, as well as how many times you visit that merchant. Although this provides a quick way to verify the age of someone who is purchasing alcohol, for example, collecting personal data that can be sold to advertisers or used to attract advertisers to a site benefits only the merchant or digital wallet vendor.

TIP

Digital wallet transactions can occur online via a computer as well as in stores via a smartphone or other mobile device.

INSIGHT

Making Payment Transactions with PayPal

As more business transactions occurred on the Internet, people needed a safe and secure way to send and receive payments. PayPal was created to address this need. Peter Thiel and Max Levchin developed the first digital wallet in 1998. Their original company, Fieldlink, enabled users to store encrypted information on their handheld devices such as Palm Pilots. They believed these digital wallets were safer than cash because they couldn't be stolen. A year later, their company, then called Confinity, expanded on the concept to create PayPal, which allowed people to email payments. PayPal started to evolve into an online payment system. By 2000, eBay buyers and sellers were requesting each other to use PayPal to send and receive payments. Two years later, in response, eBay acquired PayPal. Since then, PayPal has continued to develop more advanced online applications and services, implement enhanced security and fraud systems, and expand purchase protection to buyers and sellers while becoming a global company. PayPal promoted e-commerce and instigated growth because it provided a safe avenue for exchanging payments, which helped people to feel more comfortable when making purchases online.

In addition to PayPal, other digital wallets include Google Wallet, V.me, Discover Money Messenger powered by PayPal, and Sprint Mobile Wallet. The Additional Information section of the Tutorial 9 Weblinks page includes links under the heading Digital Wallets that you can use to explore these sites.

The rise of mobile technology combined with near field communication technology means that more companies will be able to create smartphones that can act as digital wallets. **Near field communication (NFC)** is a standards-based, short-range wireless technology that allows electronic devices to interact over a couple of inches. NFC-enabled smartphones include chips that can store all the information from a physical bank, credit cards, and identification cards, and then transmit the payment or ID data wirelessly over a short distance when the phone is close to a compatible receiver. NFC-enabled smartphones are currently available through Sprint and AT&T; many others are expected to follow soon.

You'll learn more about PayPal to see how Omega might use the global online payment company in its e-commerce activities.

To explore how PayPal works:

1. Return to the Tutorial 9 Weblinks page for Session 9.1, and then click the **PayPal** link in the Online Payment Service section. The PayPal home page opens, as shown in Figure 9-6.

Figure 9-6 PayPal home page

click to learn more about how PayPal works

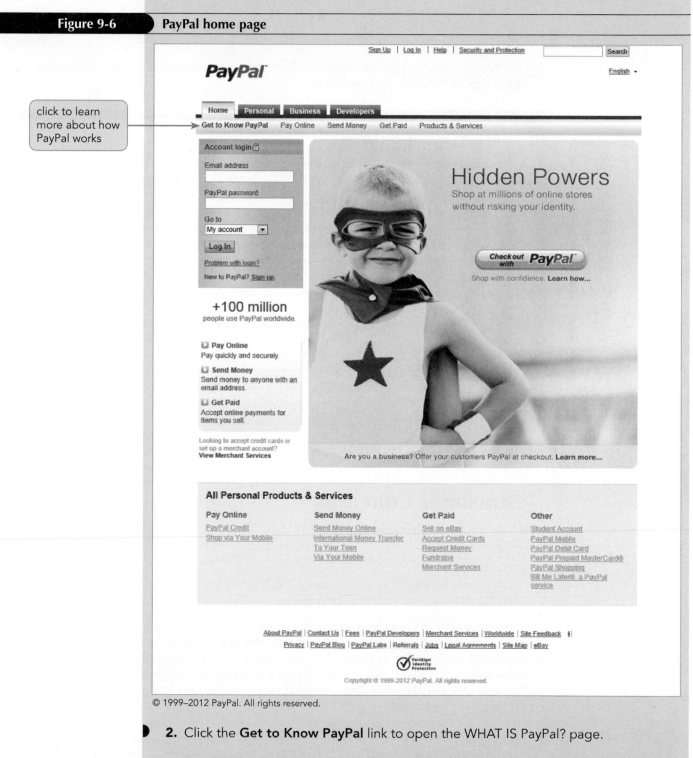

© 1999–2012 PayPal. All rights reserved.

2. Click the **Get to Know PayPal** link to open the WHAT IS PayPal? page.

Trouble? If you don't see the Get to Know PayPal link, the site might have been redesigned. Examine the PayPal home page to find links to information about PayPal and how it works, and locate a demo link.

3. Click the **View Demo** link next to the How Does PayPal Work? heading to open a new window and watch the video that provides an overview of how PayPal works.

4. When the video is finished, close the What Is Paypal window and return to the WHAT IS PayPal? Web page on the PayPal site.

5. Use the links on the page to locate information about why you would use PayPal, how to use PayPal, and the steps required to set up an account.

Although many companies accept PayPal to complete transactions, most companies also accept credit cards for payments.

INSIGHT

Shipping Purchased Items

One major difference between shopping at a physical store and shopping online is when you have the item you purchased in hand. When shopping at a physical store, you usually take the item with you for immediate use. When shopping online, the item must be shipped to you. This adds time as well as cost to the purchase. Some sites charge separately for shipping, others include the cost in the purchase price, and some provide free shipping when the cost of your purchase exceeds a specific amount. In addition, shipping costs can be based on the number of items or the total weight of the shipment as well as the shipping service selected. Usually shipments can most inexpensively travel through the U.S. Postal Service with delivery occurring up to a week later. Faster options include two- or three-day shipping or overnight shipping, which all cost more. The major private shipping companies in the United States include FedEx, UPS, and DHL.

Most successful small online businesses that sell products have inventory items with one common characteristic: a high value-to-weight ratio. The **value-to-weight ratio** is the price of the item divided by its weight. Large, heavy products that have a low price (for example, gravel, coal, or lumber) are difficult to sell online because the shipping costs exceed the profit on the item. Items that are small, light, and relatively expensive (such as jewelry, computer chips, or designer shoes) can be shipped at low cost and often generate enough profit to cover even next-day shipping costs.

Consumer Concerns

E-commerce leads to two major concerns: transaction security and privacy. Potential customers of any business worry about the same issues; however, the virtual nature of an e-commerce site increases these concerns.

Transaction Security Concerns

Consumers often do not know who is operating a Web site from which they want to make a purchase. They might wonder whether the firm is a real company that will deliver the merchandise ordered. Or, they might want to know if the company will replace defective merchandise or refund the purchase price within a reasonable period. Online customers also want assurance that the payments they make for goods purchased over the Internet are secure. Potential customers are concerned about the security of their credit card numbers as those numbers travel over the Internet.

INSIGHT

E-Commerce Customer Service

When customers have a question or problem with an online purchase, how can they get the information or help they need? Brick-and-mortar stores usually have a customer service desk or sales staff that customers can turn to. Online stores and companies provide this help using the Internet communication technologies you learned about in earlier tutorials, including chat, texting, email, and FAQs pages. In addition, some online businesses provide a phone number that customers can call to talk directly with an employee or customer service agent, and others offer a callback service to have a staff member contact the customer.

Privacy Concerns

Many potential customers of Web-based businesses are also concerned about their privacy. Web sites can collect a great deal of information about customers' preferences, even before they place an order. By recording a user's **clickstream** (a record of the links clicked by a user while visiting a Web site), the Web server can gather extensive knowledge about that visitor and use it for marketing purposes, or share it with other companies without the customer's knowledge. For example, many Web sites use clickstream information to display different banner ads to different visitors. Sites regularly use cookies to store personal information about visitors. Cookies can speed up the login process for a returning visitor, but they also enable the site to provide targeted ads based on the personal information provided.

A greater concern for many consumers is how e-commerce Web sites store their personal information. Many sites offer customers the option to store their credit card numbers so that customers do not have to type the card numbers every time they visit the site to buy something. Of course, the computer that stores these card numbers is connected (directly or indirectly) to the Internet. Any computer that is connected to the Internet is subject to attack from persons outside the company. There have been a number of widely reported cases in which an intruder has broken into an e-commerce site's computer and stolen names, addresses, and credit card information. Sometimes these individuals have even posted the stolen credit card information on the Internet.

Because online businesses want to attract customers, it is in their best interest to ensure both transaction security and buyer privacy on their sites. To ensure that the transactions conducted on their sites are secure, legitimate e-commerce Web sites use the SSL protocol to protect sensitive information as it travels over the Internet to and from their sites. Recall from Tutorial 6 that the SSL security protocol encrypts information flowing between a Web server and a Web client. When a Web site is using SSL, the site's URL in the Location or Address bar begins with https:// instead of http:// and is highlighted in green or a padlock icon appears in the status bar. You can click the green bar or the padlock icon to open a window with more information about the site's security certification.

Several assurance providers have started offering various kinds of certifications for Web site transaction security and privacy policies. As you learned in Tutorial 6, an assurance provider is a third party that, for a fee paid by the e-commerce Web site, will certify that the site meets some criteria for conducting business in a secure and privacy-preserving manner. Web sites can purchase these certifications and display the logo or seal of the assurance provider on the Web site for potential customers to examine before making any purchases. Most of these logos are hyperlinks to the assurance provider's site, at which customers can find more information about the nature of the specific assurances given by that provider. Currently, the four major assurance providers are the Better Business Bureau (BBB), TRUSTe, Norton Secured Seal (formerly VeriSign), and WebTrust.

No general standards currently exist in the United States for maintaining confidentiality regarding clickstream information or general identifying information about Web site visitors and customers. However, the Children's Online Privacy Protection Act of 1998 (often referred to as COPPA) does make it illegal for Web sites to collect identifiable information from children under the age of 13 without first obtaining their parents' consent. Many business Web sites include statements of privacy policy directed at concerned customers, but no U.S. laws exist requiring such statements or policies.

You will look at the privacy statements for several e-commerce sites next.

To review privacy statements for e-commerce sites:

1. Return to the Tutorial 9 Weblinks page for Session 9.1, click one of the links in the Privacy Statements section, and then locate and read the privacy statement for that site. Notice the types of information the site collects and how that information is collected and stored, what it uses that information for, and the methods the site uses to secure the information.

2. Repeat Step 1 for two more sites.

The Electronic Communications Privacy Act (ECPA) of 1986, which was enacted before most people were using the Internet, does not include rules specifically designed to protect the privacy of persons using Web sites to conduct transactions. Many people and organizations believe the ECPA needs to be updated to reflect advances in technology. For more information about the Electronic Communications Privacy Act and the Children's Online Privacy Protection Act, use the links in the Additional Information section of the Tutorial 9 Weblinks page.

PROSKILLS

Decision Making: Evaluating E-Commerce Sites and Transactions

Shopping online involves making a series of decisions. Decision making is the process of choosing between possible alternatives. The choice made is the actual decision. Some of the decisions you need to make as an online consumer include the following:

1. Should you purchase the item online or at a store? Consider things such as when you need the item, the selection available at a store versus online, how much the item costs, and the shipping costs and delivery time. Be sure you can wait for the item or are willing to pay more to have the item shipped overnight.
2. From what site should you purchase the item? Before purchasing an item, comparison shop to determine the prices being charged by different etailers. You can do this by visiting different online vendors and by using comparison shopping sites such as Pricewatch and Buy.com.
3. Is the site secure? Before you make a purchase, check the site for a logo from an assurance provider such as BBB, TRUSTe, Norton Secured Seal (VeriSign), or WebTrust. See whether the site offers HTTPS (secure HTTP) by checking whether its URL begins with https://. Find out what the site's payment processes are, and select how you want to pay (credit card, digital wallet, etc.).
4. What are your options if the item is not what you expected or doesn't arrive? Check the business's policies for returns and exchanges. See what protection plans it offers for shipping. You can also search the Web for customer reviews of the site.

If you take the time to evaluate a Web site and its policies, and research what others have to say about the merchant, your e-commerce experiences will be more positive.

International E-Commerce Issues

The Internet brings people together from every country in the world. E-commerce has an unprecedented geographic reach. When using a Web site to purchase products, subscriptions, or services, customers might be doing business with companies located anywhere around the globe. For example, customers in the United States might be doing business with a company in India, and vice versa. This international reach introduces special challenges for e-commerce.

Cultural and Language Issues

When visiting a Web site that originates in another country, you might see icons, phrasing, and colors that are different from what you've usually seen on other sites. This is because cultural conventions differ from country to country. Consider some examples: In the United States, people use a hand signal (the index finger touching the thumb to create a circle) that indicates "OK"; but in countries such as Brazil, this hand signal is an obscene gesture. In India, using the image of a cow in a cartoon or other comical setting is inappropriate. Customers in Muslim countries could be offended by an image that shows human arms or legs uncovered. Even colors or Web page design elements can be troublesome. For example, white denotes purity in Europe and the Americas, but is associated with death and mourning in many Asian countries. A Web page that is divided into four segments could be offensive to a Japanese visitor because the number four is a symbol of death in that culture.

Also, although the predominant language on the Web is English, sites in other languages and in multiple languages are becoming more common. To address the language issue, many companies hire a translation firm to translate their existing Web pages into other languages. Human translators can make adjustments for local versions of a language and can help ensure that the Web site is translated in a way that does not violate local customs. Translation that takes into account the culture and customs of the country is called **localization**. Once a business overcomes the language barrier, it can conduct e-commerce with any other business or consumer, anywhere in the world.

For more information about the international challenges of e-commerce, visit the links under the International E-Commerce Issues heading in the Additional Information section of the Tutorial 9 Weblinks page.

Well-designed Web sites are accessible and effective for users no matter what country they are located in and what language they speak. To accomplish this, companies that have a large global presence often have each visitor specify his or her country of origin or language so that the next Web pages that appear reflect that customer's geographic location and culture. Other companies create specific sites for each country in which they do business, such as Amazon.com, Disney, eBay, and Expedia.

For example, Amazon has different sites for Canada (www.amazon.ca), China (www.amazon.cn), France (www.amazon.fr), Germany (www.amazon.de), Italy (www.amazon.it), Japan (www.amazon.co.jp), Spain (www.amazon.es), and the United Kingdom (www.amazon.co.uk). Each site is customized to reflect the country it serves, using the appropriate language, currency, icons, and phrasing for that country. For example, customers on the Amazon United Kingdom and Amazon Canada sites store their items in a "Basket" rather than a "Cart" as customers on the Amazon United States site do. This is because many Europeans use shopping baskets when they go to a store and might be unfamiliar with the term "shopping cart," which is commonly used in the United States.

You'll look at how one company created different versions of its site to address the cultural and language issues. This will give Steve a good idea of how Omega might use different versions of its site to attract international customers for its new e-commerce ventures.

To review different versions of one company's e-commerce site:

1. Return to the Tutorial 9 Weblinks page for Session 9.1, and then click the **Amazon United States** link in the International E-Commerce Sites section.

2. Open a new page tab in your Web browser, return to the Tutorial 9 Weblinks page for Session 9.1, and then click the **Amazon United Kingdom** link in the International E-Commerce Sites section.

3. Open a new tab, return to the Tutorial 9 Weblinks page for Session 9.1, and then click the **Amazon Italy** link in the International E-Commerce Sites section.

4. Switching between the page tabs, compare the Amazon home pages for the three different countries. Notice the different currency, language, and icons used, though the basic layout remains consistent for each country's Amazon site. Figure 9-7 shows the home page of the Amazon United Kingdom site.

Figure 9-7   **Amazon United Kingdom home page**

page has the same basic layout as Amazon page for other countries

all Amazon sites use the same icon but the label changes to reflect the country's language

prices reflect the country's currency

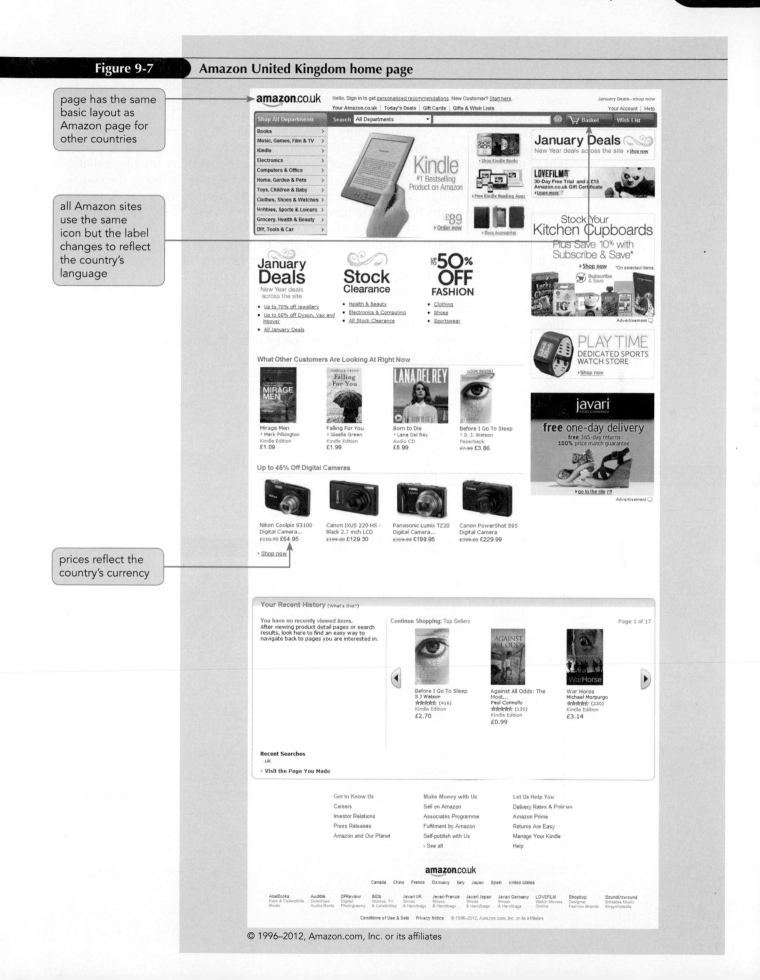

Legal Issues

Businesses that conduct e-commerce have the opportunity to participate in international commerce. Currency conversions, tariffs, import and export restrictions, local business customs, and the laws of each country in which a trading partner resides can each make international electronic commerce difficult. Many of the international issues that arise relate to legal, tax, and privacy concerns. Each country has the right to pass laws and levy taxes on businesses that operate within their jurisdictions. Countries that are members of the European Community (EC), for example, have adopted very strict laws that limit the collection and use of personal information that companies gather in the course of doing business with consumers. U.S. companies that do business in the EC must comply with these laws, which are much more restrictive than the laws in the United States. Within the United States, individual states and counties have the power to levy sales and use taxes on goods and services. In other countries, national sales and value-added taxes are imposed on an even more comprehensive list of business activities.

Complying with all of these laws and regulations can be difficult for small businesses that want to operate e-commerce Web sites. Therefore, many smaller sites restrict the countries to which they will deliver merchandise or in which they will provide services. These Web sites can place terms of service statements on their sites to protect themselves from laws and regulations of which they might be unaware. A **terms of service (TOS) statement** can include rules for site visitors and a statement of copyright interest in the site design and content, and can restrict the types of business that a visitor can conduct with the site. Most sites place their terms of service statements on a separate Web page and provide a link to it from the site's home page. These links are typically titled "Terms of Service," "Terms of Use," "Conditions of Use," "User Agreement," or something similar. Figure 9-8 shows the TOU statement for Cengage Learning, the publisher of this book.

Figure 9-8   **Cengage Learning's TOU statement**

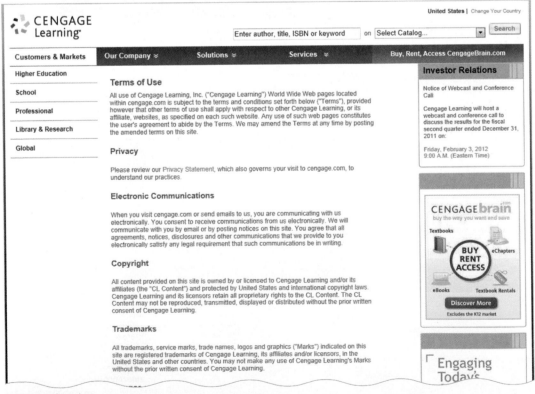

© Cengage Learning

You'll look at the TOS statements for several e-commerce sites.

To review TOS statements for e-commerce sites:

▶ **1.** Return to the Tutorial 9 Weblinks page for Session 9.1, click one of the links in the Terms of Service Statements section, and then locate and read the TOS statement for that site.

▶ **2.** Repeat Step 1 for two more sites.

▶ **3.** Close your browser.

You can learn more about the legal environment of e-commerce by exploring the links that are included in the Additional Information section under the Law and Government Regulation Sites heading on the Tutorial 9 Weblinks page.

The combination of the Web's interface and the Internet's extension of computer networking has created new opportunities for e-commerce. Businesses that once sold retail goods to consumers through catalogs using mail or telephone orders now use the Web to make shopping more convenient. Other retailers, such as booksellers, can use large-volume buying power to provide online shoppers with low prices and a wide variety of products. Information providers, such as newspapers, magazines, and newsletters, find that the Internet offers new ways to sell existing publications and platforms on which to deliver entirely new publications. Software manufacturers see that the Internet is an excellent vehicle for distributing new products, delivering upgrades to existing products, and providing low-cost support to users. The immediacy of the medium offers businesses, such as stockbrokers and travel agencies, an attractive way to interact with their customers.

Session 9.1 Quick Check

REVIEW

1. Define the term "e-commerce."
2. What is m-commerce?
3. What is disintermediation?
4. Explain what the term "bricks and clicks" means.
5. List some of the common types of ads that you see on Web sites.
6. Describe affiliate marketing.
7. Explain what a digital wallet is.
8. Name two concerns that potential customers often have about making a purchase from a Web site.
9. What are three international e-commerce issues?

Practice the skills you learned in the tutorial using the same case scenario.

PRACTICE

Review Assignments

There are no Data Files needed for the Review Assignments.

Steven wants you to develop a competitive analysis of Web sites operated by other firms in Omega's industry. You will explore several Web sites, and then write a report that summarizes your findings.

Complete the following steps:

1. Start your Web browser, go to **www.cengagebrain.com**, open the Tutorial 9 Weblinks page, and then click the Review Assignments link.
2. Click one of the links to explore the Web site of one of Omega's potential competitors and review its elements.
3. As you review the site, find out the following information:
   a. Determine how the site conducts business over the Web.
   b. Identify all of the ways the company uses the site to generate revenue (e.g., online retail, subscription, fees, affiliate marketing, advertising).
   c. Consider who the target audience is.
   d. Identify what e-commerce sector is being targeted.
4. What types of payment options are provided? How does the site address consumer concerns about transaction security and privacy?
5. How does the site address potential international issues related to culture, language, or legal issues?
6. Return to the Tutorial 9 Weblinks page, and then repeat Steps 2 through 5 for at least three other links in the Review Assignments section.
7. Write a short report to your instructor that summarizes your findings. Be sure to include the URL of each Web site you visited.
8. Close your Web browser.

Apply the skills you learned in this tutorial to shop for a Bluetooth headset on the Web.

APPLY

Case Problem 1

There are no Data Files needed for this Case Problem.

Dave Baker's New Bluetooth Headset   Your friend Dave Baker wants a Bluetooth headset to use with his smartphone. Dave asks you to help him comparison shop on the Web for the new headset.

Complete the following steps:

1. Start your Web browser, go to **www.cengagebrain.com**, open the Tutorial 9 Weblinks page, click the Case Problem 1 link, and then click one of the links to open the home page for a comparison shopping Web site.
2. Type **Bluetooth headset** in the site's search box, and then click the search button. The search results show Bluetooth headsets that are for sale along with their names, prices, current availability, and user ratings.
3. Click a Bluetooth headset name link to open a page with more information about that particular model. Record the information you find, including the product brand name and model number, purchase price, shipping cost, user or customer rating, seller name, seller rating, and return policy. (*Hint:* On some comparison shopping sites, you can select two headsets to compare in the search results.)
4. Return to the search results, and then repeat Step 3 for another headset.

5. Answer the following questions about the site:

   a. Is the site easy to use? Why or why not?

   b. Does the site display product information that was easy to understand? Explain your answer.

   c. Would you use this site to purchase items online? Why or why not?

6. Return to the Tutorial 9 Weblinks page for Case Problem 1, and then click another link to open the home page of a different comparison shopping Web site.

7. Repeat Steps 2 through 4 to find information about two Bluetooth headset models on that site. If possible, use the same headset models that you selected for the first site.

8. Write a short report to your instructor that summarizes your findings.

9. Close your Web browser.

Research and compare the services and prices of competing photo printing Web sites.

RESEARCH

Case Problem 2

There are no Data Files needed for this Case Problem.

Sagmore Community College Retirement Gala   A popular professor is retiring after teaching at Sagmore Community College for 40 years. As part of the celebration gala, the professor will be presented with one photo book for each decade he taught at the college, filled with pictures provided by former students and colleagues. You are in charge of collecting the photographs and creating the photo books. The books should be hardcover, be at least 8 × 11 inches in size, include both color and black-and-white photographs, and be customizable so you can include captions and choose backgrounds and layouts.

You need to research different photo printing sites and decide which site provides the best service, quality, and price for the books. Some photo printing sites started as retail services that expanded to an e-commerce format; others have been entirely e-commerce sites. Regardless of how the business originated, you must evaluate each company's Web site to determine the best option for your needs.

Complete the following steps:

1. Start your Web browser, go to **www.cengagebrain.com**, open the Tutorial 9 Weblinks page, and then click the Case Problem 2 link.

2. Click one of the photo printing Web site links to open the company's home page. Explore the site to find out the following information:

   a. Does it have the photo book options you need?

   b. Are there clear instructions on how to upload the photos, create layouts, select backgrounds, and include captions?

   c. What does a photo book cost?

   d. What payment methods are accepted?

   e. What are the shipping costs?

   f. Does the site have an assurance seal? If so, which one(s)?

   g. What is the site's return and refund policy?

   h. How easy is the site to navigate and use?

3. Return to the Tutorial 9 Weblinks page for Case Problem 2, and then repeat Step 2 for two more photo printing sites.

4. Based on your examination of the three Web sites, write a report for your instructor that summarizes your findings. Be sure to include a paragraph that states which site you would select and why.

5. Close your Web browser.

Research how to sell items in an auction on eBay.

RESEARCH

Case Problem 3

There are no Data Files needed for this Case Problem.

Nessie Cervante's Auction   Your friend Nessie Cervante recently inherited a house from her elderly aunt. While exploring the house, Nessie found that the basement is filled with items that her aunt collected during her lifetime. Nessie has been sorting through the items, and has come up with a lot of items that she wants to sell. She thinks her best bet is to use eBay to auction the items. She asks you to help her figure out how to go about setting up an eBay auction.

Complete the following steps:

1. Start your Web browser, go to **www.cengagebrain.com**, open the Tutorial 9 Weblinks page, and then click the Case Problem 3 link.
2. Click the eBay Seller Information Center link, and then explore the Seller Information Center to learn more about how to sell items on eBay. Gather the following information:
    a. How do you set up a seller account? Is this different from a buyer account? Do you need a PayPal account?
    b. How do you create a listing for an item? What information is required in a posting? Are photos allowed? How do you decide on pricing and shipping costs?
    c. What payment methods are accepted? How do you get paid?
    d. How does shipping work?
    e. What should you do if your item doesn't sell?
    f. What fees do you pay to sell an item in an auction?
    g. What is eBay Seller Protection?
    h. How easy is the site to navigate and use?
3. Write a report to your instructor that summarizes your findings. Be sure to include whether you would recommend that Nessie sell her items on eBay, and explain why or why not.
4. Close your Web browser.

Research the package shipping services of three major overnight delivery companies.

RESEARCH

Case Problem 4

There are no Data Files needed for this Case Problem.

Jordan's Glass Works   Jordan Esquivez is a talented glassblower who creates original ornamental and functional glassware, from knickknacks to drinking glasses. Jordan has been selling her items at a local craft fair, which is open only several months during the year. She wants to create an e-commerce site to sell her products year round, and she needs to research shipping options. She asks you to compare the services and prices of the major carriers and recommend which carrier to select.

Complete the following steps:

1. Start your Web browser, go to **www.cengagebrain.com**, open the Tutorial 9 Weblinks page, and then click the Case Problem 4 link.
2. Click the FedEx link. Examine the services provided on the FedEx Web site for overnight shipments. Record the information you find about package tracking, rates, and pickup and delivery services.
3. Return to the Tutorial 9 Weblinks page for Case Problem 4, and then click the UPS link. Examine the services provided on the UPS Web site for overnight shipments. Record the information you find about package tracking, rates, and pickup and delivery services.

4. Return to the Tutorial 9 Weblinks page for Case Problem 4, and then click the DHL link. Examine the services provided on the DHL Web site for overnight shipments. Record the information you find about package tracking, rates, and pickup and delivery services.

5. Write a report to your instructor that summarizes the information you found. Include a comparison of how easy each company's site was to use as you searched for the information you needed.

6. Close your Web browser.

Research different online payment methods.

RESEARCH

Case Problem 5

There are no Data Files needed for this Case Problem.

Custom Cases   You have decided to start a company called Custom Cases to sell custom-made cell phone cases on the Web. You have a variety of designs ready to go, your Web site is under development, your pricing structure is in place, and the shipping methods are selected. You are still debating what forms of payment to accept. You need to explore the different options, including credit cards, PayPal, and digital wallets.

Complete the following steps:

1. Start your Web browser, go to **www.cengagebrain.com**, open the Tutorial 9 Weblinks page, and then click the Case Problem 5 link.

2. Click one of the links and explore the payment method. Be sure to determine how much that method will cost you as the merchant, including any setup fees, monthly fees, and transaction fees.

3. Return to the Tutorial 9 Weblinks page for Case Problem 5, and then repeat Step 2 for two other payment methods.

4. Write a report to your instructor that summarizes the information you found. Be sure to evaluate the pros and cons of the different payment methods you evaluated.

5. Close your Web browser.

ProSkills

✔ Written Communication

Communicating Effectively in E-Commerce

Written communication is the ability to convey information from one person to another in written form. The information exchange may involve any combination of thoughts, opinions, facts, or quantitative values with the intention to motivate, inform or influence behavior. This is especially important when communicating on the Internet, including planning and writing the content of Web pages, promotional ads, business plans, and security plans.

Communication Fundamentals

The fundamental model for all communication processes consists of three parts: sender, channel, and receiver. The sender creates the message to be transmitted, preparing it in the appropriate format and sending it along the communication channel. The channel is the mechanism along which the message travels, such as in an email message or on a Web page. The receiver accepts the message, decodes and understands the message, and offers feedback, as needed, to the sender. Along the way, noise may interfere with the transmission and receipt of communications. For example, the sender's message might be unclear, such as a poorly written Web page.

Strategies for Effective Written Communication

Precision writing is important, especially in electronic documents such as Web pages, email, and text messages because they are often copied or forwarded to people you won't know, and who won't know the circumstances under which you wrote your communication. Also, most recipients of business communications are busy, and will take time to read only what is important and relevant to them at that moment. This means you must be succinct and to the point to effectively convey your message. Keep in mind the following strategies as you formulate your business communication:

- **Know your audience.** Who will read what you write? What knowledge do they already possess, and what attitudes might they have about your subject?
- **Determine the purpose of your writing.** Are you writing to inform, or do you want action to be taken? Do you hope to change a belief or simply state your position?
- **Research your topic.** Provide all the necessary information the receiver will need to make a decision or take action. If facts are included, be sure you can substantiate them.
- **Use proper grammar and spelling.** Most word processing programs and email programs provide tools for checking spelling and grammar. Keep in mind that spell-checking doesn't catch every error, so be sure to review your work carefully.
- **Consider the tone and language.** In formal documents, such as a business Web site, carefully consider the "tone" of your written communication so you don't unintentionally offend your readers. Using contractions is usually acceptable, but it is never acceptable to use offensive language. A friendly tone is usually welcome in the workplace, as is a positive one, but be careful not to be overly familiar.
- **Rewrite or revise as needed.** Have someone else read the final content so you can determine whether your meaning is clear.

ProSkills

Plan and Create an eBay Listing

The practice of buying and selling items online has remained popular with e-commerce sites such as eBay. Effective written communication is very important to eBay sellers because they will almost exclusively interact with potential buyers through written communication. In this exercise, you will use the skills presented in Tutorials 5 through 9 to research how to become an eBay seller. You will locate and document how to create a seller's account and set up a listing. You will also determine how to best convey in writing the information potential buyers will need to know about the item and your selling policies. Additionally, you will select a wireless device for checking your listing while away from home, and communicating effectively with potential buyers. You will then prepare a report that documents your findings and includes a fictional listing that clearly communicates the relevant information to buyers.

Note: Please be sure *not* to include any personal information of a sensitive nature in the documents you create to be submitted to your instructor for this exercise. Later on, you can update the documents with such information for your own personal use.

1. Start your Web browser, and go to the eBay site. Explore the site to research how to become an eBay seller, the difference between being an eBay seller and an eBay business seller, and which type of seller you would want to be. Find out how to create an account to become an eBay seller or an eBay business seller.

2. Select an item that you might want to sell on eBay. Search for similar items on eBay and review at least two listings you find.

3. Evaluate the different types of listing formats and determine which format is best to use for selling your item. What information will you include about the item in the listing? Will you include photographs to show the item; if so, how many? Create a storyboard that shows how the information in your listing will be organized.

4. Consider the possible shipping methods and costs and select an appropriate method. How do you determine the shipping costs? Who will pay the shipping costs? How will you communicate the shipping method and cost to potential buyers? What can you do to ensure that the item reaches its destination and avoid possible disputes with the buyer?

5. Assess the different payment methods. What are the advantages and disadvantages of each method? Is each method safe and secure for both you and the buyer? Which method seems most secure? Which payment method(s) will you offer in your listing, and why? How will you communicate the payment method you select to potential buyers?

6. Determine your return policy. Do you need to include a return policy? Must you accept returns? Who will pay the return shipping costs? How will you communicate your return policy to potential buyers?

7. Research how you can communicate with potential buyers on eBay. What are some guidelines you can follow in your interactions with potential buyers? What types of communication does eBay's member-to-member contact policy prohibit and allow? Why does eBay have such a policy?

ProSkills

8. How can you as the seller and potential buyers use Feedback scores and stars to evaluate each other and decide whether to do business together? Can you block a particular buyer from bidding on your listing? If so, how?

9. Prepare a fictional listing that you might place on eBay to sell the item you selected. The listing should include the format you selected, specific information about the item, the shipping method(s) and cost, the payment options, the return policy, and any other details you believe would help make the item you want to sell appeal to potential buyers.

10. Research a wireless device that you could use to check your postings and auctions while not at home. In your report, document the device you selected, and explain why you selected it.

11. Prepare a report for your instructor that documents the information you collected about becoming an eBay seller, the storyboard you created, and the fictional listing.

12. Submit the report to your instructor and close your browser.

The Internet and the World Wide Web

History, Structure, and Technologies

- Understand computer networks and connectivity
- Learn about domain names and Uniform Resource Locators (URLs)
- Explore the history of the Internet and the World Wide Web

In this Appendix, you will learn how computers are connected to each other in networks, how computers are identified on a network using IP addresses and domain names, and the origin of the network known as the Internet.

STARTING DATA FILES

There are no starting Data Files needed for this appendix.

Computer Networks

Computers that are connected to each other form a network. Each computer on a network uses a network interface card to create the network connection. A **network interface card** (often called a **NIC** or simply a network card) is a circuit board card or other device used to connect a computer to a network of other computers. Most computers and mobile devices have a network card built into them; for older devices, you might need to install a network card to connect the device to a network. These cards are connected to servers using cables or wireless signals. A **server** is a general term for any computer that accepts requests from other computers that are connected to it and shares some or all of its resources, such as printers, files, or programs, with those computers.

A server runs software that coordinates the information flow among the other computers in the network, which are called **clients**. The software that runs on the server is called a **network operating system**. Connecting computers this way, in which one server computer shares its resources with multiple client computers, is called a **client/server network**. Client/server networks commonly are used to connect devices in a **local area network (LAN)**, which is a network configuration in which devices that are located in close proximity to each other, such as in a home or small business, are connected to each other. Figure A-1 shows a typical client/server LAN.

| Figure A-1 | Client/server LAN |

© Cengage Learning. © AAGAMIA/Getty Images.

Each computer, printer, or other device attached to a network is called a **node** or **network node**. The server can be a personal computer (PC) or a larger, more powerful computer. Most of these larger computers are called "servers" to distinguish them from desktop or laptop computers. Companies that need substantial computing power to run their applications and manage their businesses often connect hundreds or even thousands of large PCs together to act as servers.

Like any computer, servers have operating systems; however, they also can run network operating system software. Although network operating system software can be more expensive than the operating system software for a stand-alone computer, having computers connected in a client/server network can provide cost savings. For example, by connecting each client computer to a server, all of the computers can share the server-installed network printer and the media used for creating computer backups.

Most personal computer operating systems, including current versions of Microsoft Windows and Macintosh operating systems, have built-in networking capabilities. Also, some personal computer operating systems that can serve as network operating systems, such as Linux, are available on the Internet and can be downloaded and used at no cost.

Connecting Computers to a Network

Not all LANs use the same kind of cables to connect their computers. The oldest cable type is called **twisted pair cable**, which telephone companies have used for years to wire residences and businesses. Twisted pair cable has two or more insulated copper wires that are twisted around each other and are enclosed in another layer of plastic insulation. A wire that carries an electric current generates an electromagnetic field around itself. This electromagnetic field can induce a small flow of electricity in nearby objects, including other wires. This induced flow of unwanted electricity is called **electrical interference**. In twisted pair wiring, the wires are twisted because wrapping the two wires around each other reduces the amount of electrical interference that each wire in the pair might pick up from other nearby current-carrying wires. The type of twisted pair cable that telephone companies have used for years to transmit voice signals is called **Category 1 cable**. Category 1 cable transmits information more slowly than the other cable types, but it is also much less expensive.

Coaxial cable is an insulated copper wire encased in a metal shield that is enclosed in plastic insulation. The signal-carrying wire is completely surrounded by the metal shield, so it resists electrical interference much better than twisted pair cable. Coaxial cable also carries signals about 20 times faster than Category 1 twisted pair; however, it is considerably more expensive. Because coaxial cable is thicker and less flexible than twisted pair, it is harder for installation workers to handle and thus is more expensive to install. You probably have seen coaxial cable because it is used for most cable television connections. You might hear this type of cable called "coax" (pronounced "koh-axe") by network technicians.

Over time, cable manufacturers have developed better versions of twisted pair cable. The current standards for twisted pair cable used in computer networks are Category 5, Category 5e, Category 6, and Category 7 cable. **Category 5 cable** carries signals between 10 and 100 times faster than coaxial cable and is just as easy to install as Category 1 cable. **Category 5e cable** (the "e" stands for "enhanced"), **Category 6 cable**, and **Category 7 cable** are three newer versions of twisted pair cable that look exactly like Category 5 cable, but are constructed of higher quality materials so they can carry more signals up to 10 to 100 times faster than Category 1 cable. Many businesses and schools have Category 5 cable installed, but they are replacing it with Category 5e, Category 6, or Category 7 cable as they upgrade their network hardware to handle the highest LAN speeds available today. You might hear these cable types called "Cat-5," "Cat-6," or "Cat-7" cable by network technicians.

The most expensive cable type is fiber-optic cable, which does not use an electrical signal at all. **Fiber-optic cable** (sometimes called "fiber" by network technicians) transmits information by using lasers to pulse beams of light through very thin strands of glass. Fiber-optic cable transmits signals much faster than either coaxial cable or any category of twisted pair cable. Because it does not use electricity, fiber-optic cable is completely immune to electrical interference. Fiber-optic cable is lighter and more durable than coaxial cable, but it is harder to work with and more expensive than either coaxial cable or Category 5 or higher twisted pair cable. The price of fiber-optic cable and the laser sending and receiving equipment needed at each end of the cable has dropped dramatically over time. Thus, companies are using fiber-optic cable in more networks as the cost becomes more affordable; however, its main use today remains connecting networks to each other rather than as part of the networks themselves. Figure A-2 shows these three types of cable.

Figure A-2	Twisted pair, coaxial, and fiber-optic cables

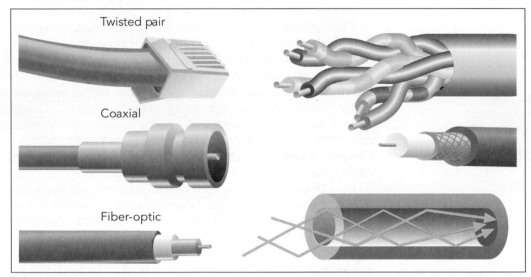

© Cengage Learning

Perhaps the most liberating way to connect computers in a LAN is to avoid using cables completely. **Wireless networks** use wireless transmitters and receivers that plug into or replace network cards to connect devices to a network without using cables. Wireless LANs are used to provide network services in many types of buildings, on school campuses, in retail outlets, and in homes and businesses. Figure A-3 shows the physical layout of a small wireless network that might be useful in a small office or a home. Connected to the wireless network are two desktop computers, two laptop computers, a shared printer, and two mobile devices. The only cable used in this configuration is the one that connects the wireless router to the Internet connection.

Figure A-3   **A small wireless network**

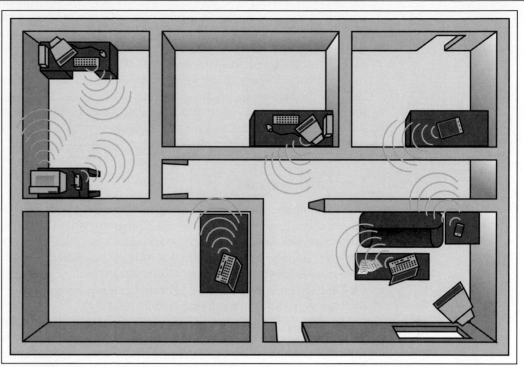

© Cengage Learning

All of these connection types—twisted pair, Category 1, coaxial, Category 5, Category 5e, Category 6, Category 7, fiber-optic, and wireless—are options for creating LANs. These LANs can, in turn, be connected to the Internet or to other, larger networks.

Understanding IP Addresses and Domain Names

Each computer on the Internet has a unique identification number, called an **IP (Internet Protocol) address**. IP addressing uses a unique number, such as 192.168.0.1, to identify each computer on the Web. Most people, however, do not use an IP address to locate a Web site. Instead, they use a domain name.

IP Addressing

Until 2011, the IP addressing system used on the Internet was called **IP version 4 (IPv4)**. IPv4 uses a 32-bit number to label each address on the Internet. The 32-bit IP address is usually written in four 8-bit parts. In most computer applications, an 8-bit number is called a **byte**; however, in networking applications, an 8-bit number is often called an **octet**.

In the binary (base 2) numbering system, an octet can have values from 00000000 to 11111111; the decimal equivalents of these binary numbers are 0 and 255, respectively. Each part of a 32-bit IP address is separated from the previous part by a period, such as 106.29.242.17. You might hear a person pronounce this address as "one hundred six dot twenty-nine dot two four two dot seventeen." This notation is often called **dotted decimal notation**. The combination of these four parts provides 4.2 billion possible addresses ($256 \times 256 \times 256 \times 256$). Because each of the four parts of a dotted decimal number can range from 0 to 255, IP addresses range from 0.0.0.0 (which would be written in binary as 32 zeros) to 255.255.255.255 (which would be written in binary as 32 ones).

In the mid-1990s, the accelerating growth of the Internet created concern that the world could run out of IP addresses within a few years. Originally, the 4.2 billion addresses provided by the IPv4 rules seemed sufficient for an experimental research network. However, by 2011, the supply of IP addresses was gone.

The IETF worked on several new protocols that could solve the limited addressing capacity of IPv4 and, in 1997, approved **IP version 6 (IPv6)** as the protocol that would replace IPv4. The new IP version was implemented gradually over a 20-year period because the two protocols are not directly compatible. However, network engineers have devised ways to run both protocols together on interconnected networks. The major advantage of IPv6 is that the number of addresses is more than a billion times larger than the 4.2 billion addresses available in IPv4.

Domain Names

A **domain name** is a unique name associated with a specific IP address by a program that runs on an Internet host computer. This program, which coordinates the IP addresses and domain names for all computers attached to it, is called **DNS (Domain Name System) software**, and the host computer that runs this software is called a **domain name server**. For example, the domain name "cengage.com" is the computer connected to the Internet for Cengage Learning, which is a commercial institution (.com). No other computer on the Internet has this same domain name.

Domain names have a hierarchical structure that you can follow from top to bottom as you read the domain names from right to left. The last part of a domain name is called its **top-level domain (TLD)**. For example, DNS software on the Internet host computer that is responsible for the .com domain keeps track of the IP addresses for all of the institutions in its domain, including "cengage." Similar DNS software on the "cengage" Internet host computer would keep track of the company's other computers in its domain.

Since 1998, the **Internet Corporation for Assigned Names and Numbers (ICANN)** has been responsible for managing domain names. In the 1980s, six TLDs were created (.com, .edu, .gov, .mil, .net, and .org). Domains registered using the .com, .net, and .org TLDs have no restrictions; however, domain names that use the .edu, .gov, and .mil TLDs are restricted to certain types of organizations and for limited purposes.

In addition to these original TLDs, ICANN created and manages additional TLDs, called **general TLDs (gTLDs)**, to expand the number of TLDs. Some of the gTLDs include ones for specific countries, such as .us, which is approved for general use by any person or organization within the United States. However, the .us domain is most frequently used by state and local government organizations in the United States and by U.S. primary and secondary schools (because the .edu domain is reserved for post-secondary educational institutions). Internet host computers outside the United States often use two-letter country domain names instead of, or in addition to, the six general TLDs. For example, the domain name uq.edu.au is for The University of Queensland (uq), which is an educational institution (.edu) in Australia (.au).

The four gTLDs introduced in 2000 included .biz (for business organizations), .info (for an informational Web site created by an individual or organization), .name (for individuals), and .pro (for licensed professionals, such as accountants, lawyers, and physicians).

ICANN also created other TLDs, called **sponsored TLDs (sTLDs)**, which are maintained by a sponsoring organization other than ICANN. The three sTLDs introduced in 2000 that are sponsored by various industry organizations are .aero (for airlines, airports, and the air transport industry), .coop (for cooperative organizations), and .museum (for museums). Each of these domains is maintained by its sponsoring organization, not by ICANN. For example, the .aero domain is maintained by SITA, an air transport industry association.

Figure A-4 shows a list of the original TLDs, and some of the country and general TLDs you'll find today.

Figure A-4	Commonly used domains

Original TLDs		Country TLDs		General TLDs Added Since 2000	
TLD	Use	TLD	Country	TLD	Use
.com	U.S. Commercial	.au	Australia	.asia	Companies, individuals, and organizations based in Asian-Pacific regions
.edu	U.S. Post-secondary educational institution	.ca	Canada	.biz	Businesses
.gov	U.S. Federal government	.de	Germany	.info	General use
.mil	U.S. Military	.fi	Finland	.int	International organizations and programs endorsed by a treaty between or among nations
.net	U.S. General use	.fr	France	.name	Individual persons
.org	U.S. Not-for-profit organization	.us	United States	.pro	Professionals (such as accountants, lawyers, and physicians)

Internet Assigned Numbers Authority Root Zone Database, http://www.iana.org/domains/root/db/

Origins of the Internet

In the early 1960s, the U.S. Department of Defense undertook a major research project. Because this was a military project and was authorized as a part of national security, the true motivations are not known with certainty; but most people close to the project believe it arose from the government's concerns about the possible effects of nuclear attack on military computing facilities. The Department of Defense realized that the weapons of the future would require powerful computers for coordination and control. The powerful computers of that time were all large mainframe computers, so the Department of Defense began examining ways to connect these computers to each other and to weapons installations that were distributed all over the world.

The agency charged with this task was the **Advanced Research Projects Agency (ARPA)**. During its lifetime, this agency has used two acronyms: ARPA and DARPA. This book uses its current acronym: **DARPA**, for **Defense Advanced Research Projects Agency**. DARPA hired many of the best communications technology researchers, and for many years funded research at leading universities and institutes to explore the task of creating a worldwide network of computers. A photo of these dedicated computer networking pioneers appears in Figure A-5.

Courtesy of Raytheon BBN Technologies

DARPA researchers soon became concerned about computer networks' vulnerability to attack because networks at that time relied on a single, central control function. If the network's central control point was damaged or attacked, the network would be unusable. Consequently, they worked hard to devise ways to eliminate the need for network communications to rely on a central control function.

Connectivity: Circuit Switching vs. Packet Switching

One of the first networking-related topics to be researched by the DARPA scientists was connectivity, or methods of sending messages over networks. The first computer networks were created in the 1950s. The models for those early networks were the telephone companies because most early wide area networks (WANs) used leased telephone company lines to connect computers to each other. In telephone company systems of that time, a telephone call established a single connection between sender and receiver. Once the connection was established, all data then traveled along that single path. The telephone company's central switching system selected specific telephone lines, or circuits, that would be connected to create the single path. This centrally controlled, single-connection method is called **circuit switching**.

Although circuit switching is efficient and economical, it relies on a central point of control and a series of connections that form a single path. This makes circuit-switched communications vulnerable to the destruction of the central control point or any link in the series of connections that make up the single path that carries the signal.

Packet switching is an alternative means for sending messages. In a packet-switching network, files and messages are broken down into packets that are labeled electronically with codes for their origin and destination. The packets travel from computer to computer along the network until they reach their destination. The destination computer collects the packets and reassembles the original data from the pieces in each packet. Each computer that an individual packet encounters on its trip through the network determines the best way to move the packet forward to its destination.

Computers and other devices that perform this function on networks are often called routing computers, or **routers**, and the programs they use to determine the best path for packets are called **routing algorithms**. Thus, packet-switched networks are inherently more reliable than circuit-switched networks because they rely on multiple routers instead of a central point of control, and because each router can send individual packets along different paths if parts of the network are not operating.

By 1967, DARPA researchers had published their plan for a packet-switching network; and in 1969, they connected the first computer switches at four locations: the University of California at Los Angeles, SRI International, the University of California at Santa Barbara, and the University of Utah. This experimental WAN was called the **ARPANET**.

The ARPANET grew over the next three years to include more than 20 computers. The ARPANET used the **Network Control Protocol (NCP)** to enable each of those computers to communicate with other computers on the network. A **protocol** is a collection of rules for formatting, ordering, and error-checking data sent across a network.

Open Architecture Philosophy

As more researchers connected their computers and computer networks to the ARPANET, interest in the network grew in the academic community. One reason for increased interest in the project was its adherence to an **open architecture** philosophy; that is, each network could continue using its own protocols and data-transmission methods internally. The open architecture philosophy includes four key points:

- Independent networks should not require any internal changes to be connected to the Internet.
- Packets that do not arrive at their destinations must be retransmitted from their source network.
- Router computers do not retain information about the packets they handle.
- No global control will exist over the network.

This open architecture philosophy was revolutionary at the time. Most companies that built computer networking products at that time, including IBM and Digital Equipment Corporation, put considerable effort into making their networks incompatible with other networks. These manufacturers believed that they could lock out competitors by not making their products easy to connect with products made by other companies. The shift to an open architecture approach is what made the Internet of today possible.

In the early 1970s, Vinton Cerf and Robert Kahn developed a set of protocols that implemented the open architecture philosophy better than the NCP. These new protocols were the **Transmission Control Protocol** and the **Internet Protocol**, which usually are referred to by their combined acronym, **TCP/IP**. TCP includes rules that computers on a network use to establish and break connections; IP includes rules for routing of individual data packets. TCP/IP continues to be used today in LANs and on the Internet. The term "Internet" was first used in an article about TCP written by Cerf and Kahn in 1974. The importance of TCP/IP in the history of the Internet is so great that many people consider Vinton Cerf to be the father of the Internet.

A number of TCP/IP-based networks—independent of the ARPANET—were created in the late 1970s and early 1980s. The National Science Foundation (NSF) funded the **Computer Science Network (CSNET)** for educational and research institutions that did not have access to the ARPANET. The City University of New York started a network of IBM mainframes at universities called the **Because It's Time** (originally, "Because It's There") **Network (BITNET)**.

New Uses for Networks

Although the goals of the ARPANET were still to control weapons systems and transfer research files, other uses for this vast network began to appear in the early 1970s. In 1972, an ARPANET researcher named Ray Tomlinson wrote a program that could send and receive messages over the network. Email had been born and rapidly became widely used in the computer research community. In 1976, the Queen of England sent an email message over the ARPANET. The ARPANET continued to develop faster and more effective network technologies; for example, the ARPANET began sending packets by satellite in 1976.

By 1981, the ARPANET had expanded to include more than 200 networks. The number of individuals in the military and education research communities who used the network continued to grow. Many of these new participants used the networking technology to transfer files and access computers remotely. The TCP/IP suite included two tools for performing these tasks. **File Transfer Protocol (FTP)** enabled users to transfer files between computers, and **Telnet** let users log in to their computer accounts from remote sites. The first mailing lists also appeared on these networks. A mailing list is an email address that takes any message it receives and forwards it to any user who has subscribed to the list.

Although file transfer and remote login were attractive features of these new TCP/IP networks, their improved email and other communications facilities attracted many users in the education and research communities. Mailing lists (such as BITNET's LISTSERV), information posting areas (such as the User's News Network, or Usenet newsgroups), and adventure games were among the new applications appearing on the ARPANET.

Although the people using these networks were developing many creative applications, relatively few people had access to the networks. Most of these people were members of the research and academic communities. From 1979 to 1989, these new and interesting network applications were improved and tested with an increasing number of users. TCP/IP became more widely used as academic and research institutions realized the benefits of having a common communications network. The explosion of PC use during that time also helped more people become comfortable with computing.

Interconnecting the Networks

The early 1980s saw continued growth in the ARPANET and other networks. The **Joint Academic Network (JANET)** was established in the United Kingdom to link universities there. Traffic increased on all of these networks; and in 1984, the Department of Defense split the ARPANET into two specialized networks: The ARPANET would continue its advanced research activities, and the **MILNET** (for **Military Network**) would be reserved for military uses that required greater security.

By 1987, congestion on the ARPANET caused by a rapidly increasing number of users on the limited-capacity leased telephone lines was becoming severe. To reduce the traffic load on the ARPANET, a network run by the NSF, called NSFNET, merged with another NSF network, called CSNET, and with BITNET to form one network that could carry much of the network traffic that had been carried by the ARPANET. The resulting NSFNET awarded a contract to Merit Network, Inc., IBM, Sprint, and the state of Michigan to upgrade and operate the main NSFNET backbone.

A **network backbone** includes the long-distance lines and supporting technology that transport large amounts of data between major network nodes. By the late 1980s, many other TCP/IP networks had merged or established interconnections. Figure A-6 summarizes how the individual networks described in this section combined to become the Internet as it is known today.

Figure A-6	Networks that became the Internet

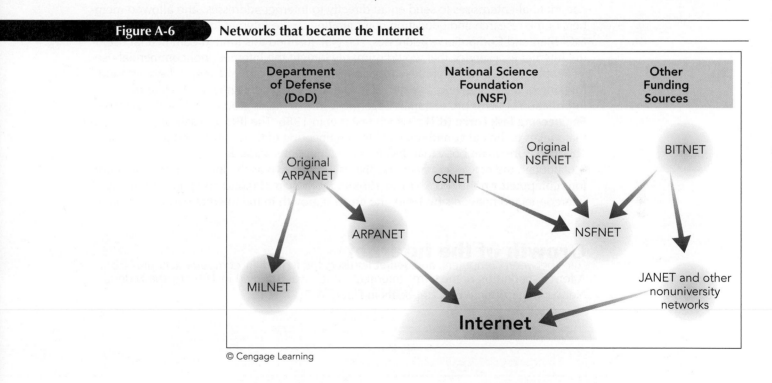

© Cengage Learning

Network Use in Business

As PCs became more powerful, affordable, and readily available during the 1980s, companies increasingly used them to construct LANs. Although these LANs included email software that employees could use to send messages to each other, businesses wanted their employees to be able to communicate with people outside their corporate LANs. The NSF prohibited commercial network traffic on the networks it funded, so businesses turned to commercial email services. Larger firms built their own TCP/IP-based WANs (wide area networks) that used leased telephone lines to connect field offices to corporate headquarters.

Today, people use the term **intranet** to describe LANs or WANs that use TCP/IP but do not connect to sites outside a single organization. Although most companies allow only their employees to use the company intranet, some companies give specific outsiders—such as customers, vendors, or business partners—access to their intranets. These outside parties agree to respect the confidentiality of the information on the network. An intranet that allows selected outside parties to connect is often called an **extranet**.

In 1989, the NSF permitted two commercial email services—MCI Mail and CompuServe—to establish limited connections to the Internet that allowed their commercial subscribers to exchange email messages with the members of the academic and research communities who were connected to the Internet. These connections allowed commercial enterprises to send email directly to Internet addresses, and allowed members of the research and education communities on the Internet to send email directly to MCI Mail and CompuServe addresses. The NSF justified this limited commercial use of the Internet as a service that would primarily benefit the Internet's noncommercial users.

People from all walks of life—not just scientists and academic researchers—started thinking of these networks as a global resource that we now know as the Internet. Information systems professionals began to form volunteer groups such as the **Internet Engineering Task Force (IETF)**, which first met in 1986. The IETF is a self-organized group that makes technical contributions to the engineering of the Internet and its technologies. The IETF is the main body that develops new Internet standards.

Although the network of networks that is now known as the Internet had grown from four computers on the ARPANET in 1969 to more than 300,000 computers on many interconnected networks by 1990, the greatest growth in the Internet was yet to come.

Growth of the Internet

A formal definition of the term "Internet," which was adopted in 1995 by the Federal Networking Council (FNC), appears in Figure A-7.

| Figure A-7 | The FNC's October 1995 resolution to define the term "Internet" |

RESOLUTION: The Federal Networking Council (FNC) agrees that the following language reflects our definition of the term "Internet"

"Internet" refers to the global information system that—

(i) is logically linked together by a globally unique address space based on the Internet Protocol (IP) or its subsequent extensions/follow-ons;

(ii) is able to support communications using the Transmission Control Protocol/Internet Protocol (TCP/IP) suite or its subsequent extensions/follow-ons; and/or other IP-compatible protocols; and

(iii) provides, uses or makes accessible, either publicly or privately, high level services layered on the communications and related infrastructure described herein.

Courtesy of http://www.nitrd.gov/fnc/Internet_res.html

The researchers who had been so involved in the creation and growth of the Internet accepted it as part of their working environment, but people outside the research community were largely unaware of the potential offered by a large interconnected set of computer networks until the 1990s. Realizing that the Internet was becoming much more than a scientific research project, the U.S. Department of Defense finally closed the research portion of its network, the ARPANET, in 1995. The NSF also wanted to turn over the Internet to others so it could return its attention and funds to other research projects.

The process of shutting down the ARPANET and privatizing the Internet began in 1991, when the NSF eased its restrictions on Internet commercial activity. Businesses and individuals continued to connect to the Internet in ever-increasing numbers. Although nobody really knows how big the Internet is, one commonly used measure is the number of Internet hosts. An **Internet host** is a computer that connects a LAN or a WAN to the Internet. Each Internet host might have any number of computers connected to it. Figure A-8 shows the rapid growth in the number of Internet host computers. As you can see, the growth has been dramatic.

Figure A-8   **Growth in the number of Internet hosts**

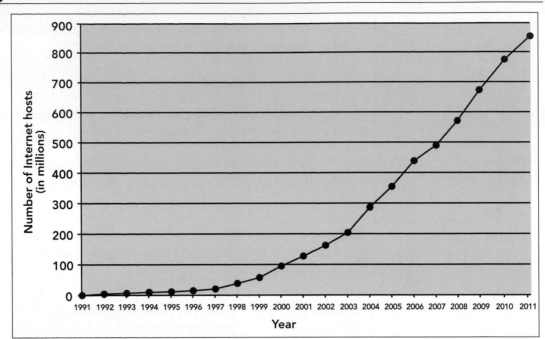

Adapted from Internet Systems Consortium (https://www.isc.org/) and other sources

The numbers in Figure A-8 probably underestimate the true growth of the Internet in recent years for two reasons. First, the number of hosts connected to the Internet includes only those computers that are directly connected to the Internet. In other words, if a LAN with 100 PCs is connected to the Internet through only one host computer, those 100 computers appear as one host in the count. Because the number and size of LANs have increased in recent years, the host count probably underestimates the growth in the number of all computers that have access to the Internet. Millions of mobile devices have features that allow them to connect to the Internet. These devices are connected through a relatively small number of Internet hosts at their wireless service providers, which is another reason why the number of devices connected to the Internet is probably underestimated.

Second, the number of computers is only one measure of growth. Internet traffic now carries more files that contain graphics, sound, and video, so Internet files have become larger. A given number of users sending video clips will use much more of the Internet's capacity than the same number of users will use by sending email messages or text files.

No one knows how many individual email messages or files travel on the Internet, and no one really knows how many people use the Internet today because the Internet has no central management or coordination, and the routing computers do not retain copies of the packets they handle. However, some companies and research organizations estimate the number of regular Internet users today to be nearly 2 billion.

The opening of the Internet to business enterprise helped increase its growth dramatically; however, another development worked hand in hand with the commercialization of the Internet to spur its growth. That development was the technological advance known as the World Wide Web.

The Evolution of the Web

Two important innovations played key roles in making the Internet easier to use and more accessible to people who were not research scientists. The first innovation, hypertext, connected the content stored on the networks and made that content more accessible. The second innovation was the Web browser itself, which provided users with a tool that made it possible to find and access that content.

Origins of Hypertext

In 1945, Vannevar Bush, who was the director of the U.S. Office of Scientific Research and Development, wrote an *Atlantic Monthly* article about ways that scientists could apply to peacetime activities the skills they learned during World War II. The article included a number of visionary ideas about future uses of technology to organize and facilitate efficient access to information. Bush speculated that engineers eventually would build a machine that he called the **Memex**, a memory extension device that would store all of a person's books, records, letters, and research results on microfilm. Bush's Memex would include mechanical aids to help users consult their collected knowledge fast and in a wide variety of ways.

In the 1960s, Ted Nelson described a similar system in which text on one page links to text on other pages. Nelson called his page-linking system **hypertext**. Douglas Engelbart, who also invented the computer mouse, created the first experimental hypertext system on one of the large computers of the 1960s. In 1976, Nelson published a book, *Dream Machines*, in which he outlined project Xanadu, a global system for online hypertext publishing and commerce. Figure A-9 includes photos of Bush, Nelson, and Engelbart—three forward-looking thinkers whose ideas laid the foundation for the Web.

Figure A-9	Left to right: Vannevar Bush, Ted Nelson, and Douglas Engelbart

© Getty Images; © 2011 Samuel Dietz; Courtesy of Doug Engelbart Institute

In 1989, Tim Berners-Lee and Robert Cailliau were working at CERN—the European Laboratory for Particle Physics. Berners-Lee and Cailliau were trying to improve the laboratory's research document-handling procedures. CERN had been using the Internet for two years to circulate its scientific papers and data among the high-energy physics research community throughout the world; however, the Internet did not help the agency display the complex graphics that were important parts of its theoretical models. Independently, Berners-Lee and Cailliau each proposed a hypertext development project to improve CERN's document-handling capabilities.

Over the next two years, Berners-Lee developed the code for a hypertext server program and made it available on the Internet. A **hypertext server** is a computer that stores files written in the hypertext markup language, and lets other computers connect to it and read the files. Berners-Lee, who was familiar with **Standard Generalized Markup Language (SGML)**—a set of rules that organizations have used for many years to manage large document-filing systems—began developing a subset of SGML that he called Hypertext Markup Language (HTML).

HTML, like all markup languages, includes a set of codes (or tags) attached to text. These codes describe the relationships among text elements. For example, HTML includes tags that indicate which text is part of a header element, which text is part of a paragraph element, and which text is part of a numbered list element. One important type of tag is the hypertext link tag. A hypertext link, or hyperlink, points to another location in the same or another HTML document. HTML documents can also include links to other types of files, such as word-processing documents, spreadsheets, graphics, audio clips, and video clips.

An HTML document differs from a word-processing document because it does not specify *how* a particular text element will appear. For example, you might use word-processing software to create a document heading by setting the heading text font to Arial, its font size to 14 points, and its position to centered. The document displays and prints these exact settings whenever you open the document in the word processor. In contrast, an HTML document surrounds the text with a pair of **heading tags** to indicate that the text should be considered a heading. Many programs can read HTML documents. The programs recognize the heading tags and display the text in whatever manner that program normally displays headings. Different programs might display the heading text differently.

Like the Internet itself, standards for HTML are not controlled by any central managing organization. Standards for technologies that are used on the Web (including HTML) are developed and promulgated by the World Wide Web Consortium (W3C), an international organization formed in 1994 and sponsored by universities and businesses from around the world. Berners-Lee was appointed director of the W3C when it was formed and continues in that position today.

Evolution of Web Browsers

A Web browser displays an HTML document in an easy-to-read format in its graphical user interface. A **graphical user interface** (**GUI**, pronounced "gooey") is a way of presenting program output using pictures, icons, and other graphical elements instead of just displaying text. All personal computers now use a GUI. The GUI presented in Web browsers played an important part in the rapid growth of the Web. The first Web browsers were text-based and lacked the graphical elements, such as buttons, that make today's browsers so easy to use. Figure A-10 shows a Web page displayed in Lynx, a text-based browser that was commonly used in the early days of the Web. As you can see, it does not look very much like the Web pages displayed by Web browsers today.

| Figure A-10 | Web page rendered in a text-based browser |

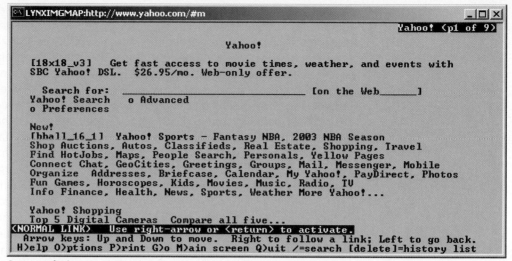

Courtesy of Yahoo! Inc. © 2011 by Yahoo! Inc. YAHOO! and the YAHOO! logo are trademarks of Yahoo! Inc.

In 1993, a group of students led by Marc Andreessen at the University of Illinois wrote Mosaic, the first GUI program that could read HTML and use hyperlinks to navigate from page to page on computers anywhere on the Internet. Mosaic was the first Web browser that became widely available for PCs. Figure A-11 shows a Web page from 1993 displayed in an early version of the Mosaic Web browser.

| Figure A-11 | Mosaic, the first widely available Web browser |

Courtesy of Pär Lannerö; Source: http://www.dejavu.org/emulator.htm

In 1994, Andreessen and other members of the University of Illinois Mosaic team joined with James Clark of Silicon Graphics to found Netscape Communications. The university was not happy when the team decided to leave the school and develop a commercial browser. The university refused to allow the team to use the name "Mosaic." Netscape's first browser was called the "Mosaic Killer" or "Mozilla." Soon after its release, the product was renamed Netscape Navigator. The program was an instant success. Netscape became one of the fastest growing software companies at the time.

Microsoft created its Internet Explorer Web browser and entered the market soon after Netscape's success. Microsoft offered its browser at no cost to computer owners using its Windows operating system. Within a few years, most users had switched to Internet Explorer and Netscape was unable to earn enough money to stay in business.

Microsoft was accused of wielding its monopoly power to drive Netscape out of business; these accusations led to the trial of Microsoft on charges that it violated U.S. antitrust laws. The charges were settled in a consent decree, but other violations by Microsoft led to a second trial in which the company was found guilty. Parts of Netscape were sold to America Online, but the browser became open-source software.

Open-source software is created and maintained by volunteer programmers, often many of them, who work together using the Internet to build and refine a program. The program is made available to users at no charge. The open-source release of Netscape is called Mozilla, which recalls the name of the original Netscape product. In an interesting turn of Web history, the Netscape Navigator browser available today is based on the Mozilla open-source software.

The proliferation of tools to make the Internet more usable led to an explosion in the amount of information stored online. The number of Web sites has grown more rapidly than the Internet itself. Figure A-12 shows the growth in the Web during its lifetime.

| Figure A-12 | Growth of the Web |

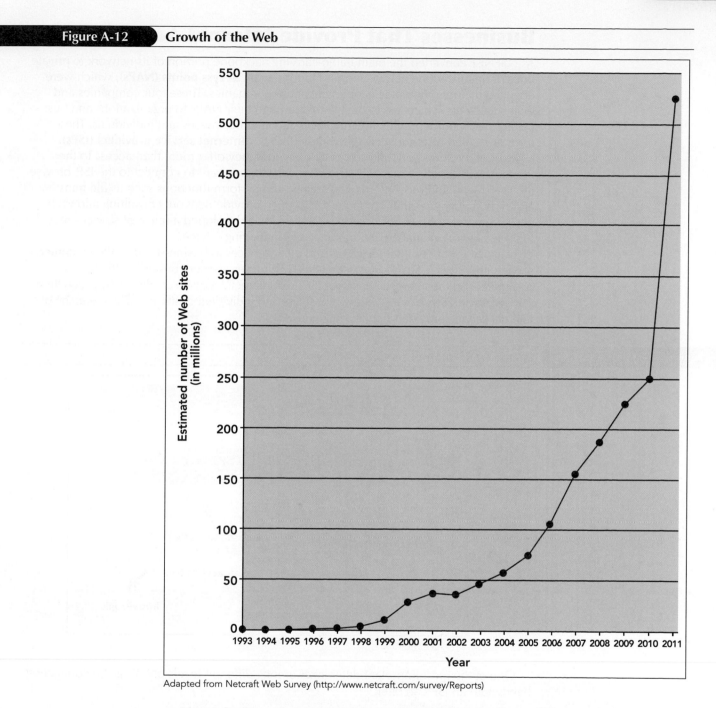

Adapted from Netcraft Web Survey (http://www.netcraft.com/survey/Reports)

After a dip between 2001 and 2002, growth in the number of Web sites resumed at its rapid rate. As individual Web sites become larger, they include many more pages. Experts agree that the number of pages available on the Web today exceeds 1 trillion, and that number is increasing faster than ever. As more people have access to the Web, commercial uses of the Web as well as its nonbusiness uses will continue to increase.

Businesses That Provide Internet Access

As NSFNET converted the main traffic-carrying backbone portion of its network to private firms, it organized the network around four **network access points (NAPs)**, which were operated by four different telecommunications companies. These four companies and their successors sell access to the Internet through their NAPs to organizations and businesses that, in turn, provide Internet access to other businesses and individuals. These firms are called **Internet access providers (IAPs)** or **Internet service providers (ISPs)**.

Most of the firms call themselves ISPs because they offer more than access to the Internet. ISPs usually provide their customers with software to connect to the ISP, browse the Web, send and receive email messages, and perform functions such as file transfer and remote login to other computers. ISPs often provide network consulting and Web design services to their customers. Some ISPs have developed a range of services that include network management, training, and marketing advice.

Large ISPs that sell Internet access and other services to businesses are called **commerce service providers (CSPs)** because they help businesses conduct business activities (or commerce) on the Internet. The larger ISPs sell Internet access to smaller ISPs, which then sell access and services to their own business and individual customers. The hierarchy of Internet service providers appears in Figure A-13.

| Figure A-13 | Hierarchy of Internet service providers |

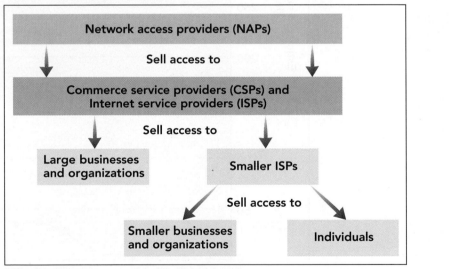

© Cengage Learning

One of the most important differences among different levels of ISPs is the connection bandwidth an ISP can offer.

Bandwidth and Types of Connectivity

Bandwidth is the amount of data that can travel through a communications circuit in one second. The bandwidth an ISP can deliver depends on the connection it has to the Internet and the connection you have to the ISP.

The available bandwidth for any type of network connection between two points is limited to the narrowest bandwidth that exists in any part of the network. For example, if you connect to an ISP through a regular telephone line, your bandwidth is limited to the bandwidth of that telephone line, regardless of the bandwidth connection that the ISP has to the Internet. Bandwidth for Internet connections is measured the same way as bandwidth for connections within networks, in multiples of **bits per second (bps)**. Common terms are **kilobits per second (Kbps)**, which is 1,024 bps; **megabits per second (Mbps)**, which is 1,048,576 bps; and **gigabits per second (Gbps)**, which is 1,073,741,824 bps.

Sometimes computer users are confused by the use of bits to measure bandwidth because file sizes are measured in bytes. As explained earlier, a byte is eight bits; it is abbreviated with an uppercase "B." A **kilobyte (KB)** is 1,024 bytes, or 8,192 bits. A **megabyte (MB)** is 1,048,576 bytes (or 8,388,608 bits), and a **gigabyte (GB)** is 1,073,741,824 bytes (or 8,589,934,592 bits).

Most LANs today run either Fast Ethernet, which operates at 100 Mbps, or Gigabit Ethernet, which operates at 1 Gbps. Some older LANs use an earlier version of Ethernet that operates at 10 Mbps. The effective bandwidth of wireless LANs depends on the distance between computers and what types of barriers the wireless signals must pass through (for example, wireless signals travel more easily through glass than steel). Most wireless LANs achieve an operating bandwidth of between 2 Mbps and 10 Mbps, although newer wireless devices with more than 100 Mbps are available. Figure A-14 shows examples of typical times required to send different types of files over different types of LANs.

| Figure A-14 | Typical file transmission times for various types of LANs |

Type of File	Typical File Size	Wireless (7 Mbps)	Ethernet (10 Mbps)	Fast Ethernet (100 Mbps)	Gigabit Ethernet (1 Gbps)
One-paragraph text message	5 KB	Less than .1 second	Less than .1 second	Less than .1 second	Less than .1 second
Word-processing document, 20 pages	100 KB	.1 second	Less than .1 second	Less than .1 second	Less than .1 second
Web page containing several small graphics	200 KB	.2 second	.2 second	Less than .1 second	Less than .1 second
Presentation file with 20 slides and several large graphics	800 KB	1 second	.7 second	Less than .1 second	Less than .1 second
Color brochure, five pages with several color photos	2 MB	3 seconds	2 seconds	.2 second	Less than .1 second
Compressed music file (MP3 format) containing a four-minute song	5 MB	6 seconds	4 seconds	.4 second	Less than .1 second
Uncompressed music file containing a four-minute song	60 MB	1 minute	50 seconds	5 seconds	.5 second
Compressed video file containing a 10-minute interview	200 MB	4 minutes	4 minutes	17 seconds	2 seconds
Compressed video file containing a feature-length film	4 GB	1.5 hours	1 hour	6 minutes	35 seconds

© Cengage Learning

When you extend your network beyond a local area, either through a WAN or by connecting to the Internet, the speed of the connection depends on the type of connection. One way to connect computers or networks over longer distances is to use regular telephone service (sometimes referred to as **dial-up**, **POTS**, or **plain old telephone service**). Regular telephone service to most U.S. residential and business customers provides a maximum bandwidth of between 28.8 Kbps and 56 Kbps. The rates vary because the United States has different telephone companies that do not all use the same technology.

When you connect your computer, which communicates using digital signals, to another computer through a telephone line, which uses analog signals, you must convert the signals from one form to the other. The device that performs this signal conversion is a **modem**, which is short for "modulator-demodulator." Converting a digital signal to an analog signal is called **modulation**; converting that analog signal back into digital form is called **demodulation**. A modem performs both functions; it acts as a modulator and a demodulator.

Some telephone companies offer a higher grade of service that uses one of a series of protocols called **Digital Subscriber Line (DSL)** or **Digital Subscriber Loop (DSL)**. The first technology that was developed using a DSL protocol is called **Integrated Services Digital Network (ISDN)**. ISDN service has been available in various parts of the United States since 1984. Although considerably more expensive than regular telephone service, ISDN offers bandwidths of up to 256 Kbps. ISDN is much more widely available in Australia, France, Germany, Japan, and Singapore than in the United States because the regulatory structure of the telecommunications industries in those countries encouraged rapid deployment of this new technology.

All technologies based on the DSL protocol require the implementing telephone company to install new equipment at its switching stations, which can be very expensive. New technologies that use the DSL protocol are currently being implemented around the world. One of those, **Asymmetric Digital Subscriber Line** (**ADSL**, also abbreviated **DSL**), offers transmission speeds ranging from 16 to 640 Kbps from the user to the telephone company, and from 1.5 to 9 Mbps from the telephone company to the user.

Businesses and large organizations often obtain their Internet connection by connecting to an ISP using higher-bandwidth telephone company connections called **T-1** (1.544 Mbps) and **T-3** (44.736 Mbps) connections. (T-1 and T-3 were originally acronyms for Telephone 1 and Telephone 3, respectively, but few people use these terms any longer.) Companies with operations in multiple locations sometimes lease T-1 and T-3 lines from telephone companies to create their own WANs to connect their locations to each other.

T-1 and T-3 connections are much more expensive than POTS or ISDN connections; however, organizations that must link hundreds or thousands of individual users to WANs or to the Internet require the greater bandwidth of T-1 and T-3 connections. Smaller firms can save money by renting access to a partial T-1 connection from a telephone company. In a partial T-1 rental, the connection is shared with other companies.

The NAPs operate the Internet backbone using a variety of connections. In addition to T-1 and T-3 lines, the NAPs use newer connections with bandwidths of more than 1 Gbps—in some cases exceeding 10 Gbps. These connection options use fiber-optic cables, and are referred to as OC3, OC12, and so forth. **OC** is short for **optical carrier**. NAPs also use high-bandwidth satellite and radio communications links to transfer data over long distances.

A group of research universities and the NSF now operate a network called **Internet2** that has backbone bandwidths greater than 10 Gbps. The Internet2 project continues the tradition of the DARPA scientists by sponsoring research at the frontiers of network technologies.

A connection option available in the United States and some other countries is to connect to the Internet through a cable television company. The cable company transmits data in the same cables used to provide television service. Cable can deliver up to 10 Mbps to a user and can accept up to 768 Kbps from a user. Cable connections usually deliver speeds between 500 Kbps and 3 Mbps, although some cable companies offer guarantees of higher speeds (for higher monthly fees). These speeds far exceed those of existing POTS and ISDN connections, and are comparable to speeds provided by the ADSL technologies currently implemented by telephone companies and other companies that rent facilities from the telephone companies.

Another option that is commonly used in remote geographic areas where cabled connections are more difficult to install is connecting by satellite, which uses satellites orbiting the earth to send and receive signals from dishes mounted on rooftops. Using a satellite-dish receiver, users can download at a bandwidth of approximately 400 Kbps. In the early days of satellite Internet access, users could not send information to the Internet using a satellite-dish antenna, so they needed to also have an ISP account to send files or email. Today, most satellite ISPs install transmitters on the dish antenna. This allows two-way satellite connections to the Internet. Because satellite connections are affordable and easy to install, they are used now throughout the world, and not just in remote geographic areas.

The actual bandwidth provided by all these Internet connection methods varies from provider to provider and with the amount of traffic on the Internet. During peak operating hours, traffic on the Internet can become congested, resulting in slower data transmission. The bandwidth achieved is limited to the lowest amount of bandwidth available at any point in the network. To picture this, think of water flowing through a set of pipes with varying diameters, or traffic moving through a section of highway with a lane closure. The water (or traffic) slows to the speed it can maintain through the narrowest part of its pathway.

Figure A-15 shows typical file transmission times for various types of Internet connection options. The speeds shown are examples of what a user can expect on average during download operations. Faster Internet connections cost significantly more money than slower connections.

Figure A-15	Typical file transmission times for various types of Internet connections

Type of File	Typical File Size	POTS (25 Kbps)	ISDN or Satellite (100 Kbps)	Residential Cable or DSL (300 Kbps)	Business Leased T-1 (1.4 Mbps)
One-paragraph text message	5 KB	2 seconds	.4 second	.2 second	Less than .1 second
Word-processing document, 20 pages	100 KB	33 seconds	8 seconds	3 seconds	Less than .1 second
Web page containing several small graphics	200 KB	1 minute	16 seconds	6 seconds	Less than .1 second
Presentation file with 20 slides and several large graphics	800 KB	4 minutes	1 minute	22 seconds	Less than .1 second
Color brochure, five pages with several color photos	2 MB	11 minutes	3 minutes	1 minute	Less than .1 second
Compressed music file (MP3 format) containing a four-minute song	5 MB	28 minutes	7 minutes	2 minutes	Less than .1 second
Uncompressed music file containing a four-minute song	60 MB	6 hours	1.5 hours	28 minutes	.4 second
Compressed video file containing a 10-minute interview	200 MB	19 hours	5 hours	2 hours	1 second
Compressed video file containing a feature-length film	4 GB	16 days	4 days	30 hours	25 seconds

© Cengage Learning

Figure A-16 summarizes the bandwidths, costs, and typical uses for the most common types of connections currently in use on the Internet. Some companies offer **fixed-point wireless** connections, which use technology similar to wireless LANs. Although fixed-point wireless service is not yet widely available, some companies are offering it to both business and residential customers.

Figure A-16   Types of Internet connections

Service	Upstream Speed (Kbps)	Downstream Speed (Kbps)	Capacity (Number of Simultaneous Users)	One-Time Start-up Costs	Continuing Monthly Costs
Residential-Small Business Services					
POTS	28–56	28–56	1	$0–$20	$9–$20
ISDN	128–256	128–256	1–3	$60–$300	$50–$90
ADSL	100–640	500–9,000	1–20	$50–$100	$40–$500
Cable	300–1,500	500–10,000	1–10	$0–$100	$40–$300
Satellite	125–150	400–500	1–3	$0–$800	$40–$100
Fixed-point wireless	250–1,500	500–3,000	1–4	$0–$350	$50–$150
Business Services					
Leased digital line	64	64	1–10	$50–$200	$40–$150
Fixed-point wireless	500–10,000	500–10,000	5–1,000	$0–$500	$300–$5,000
Fractional T-1 leased line	128–1,544	128–1,544	5–180	$50–$800	$100–$1,000
T-1 leased line	1,544	1,544	100–200	$100–$2,000	$600–$1,600
T-3 leased line	44,700	44,700	1,000–10,000	$1,000–$9,000	$5,000–$12,000
Large Business, ISP, NAP, and Internet2 Services					
OC3 leased line	156,000	156,000	1,000–50,000	$3,000–$12,000	$9,000–$22,000
OC12 leased line	622,000	622,000	Backbone	Negotiated	$25,000–$100,000
OC48 leased line	2,500,000	2,500,000	Backbone	Negotiated	Negotiated
OC192 leased line	10,000,000	10,000,000	Backbone	Negotiated	Negotiated

© Cengage Learning

OBJECTIVES

- Use and expand the skills you learned in Tutorials 3 and 4
- Visit Web sites to find information about a disease or medical condition
- Evaluate the resources you find
- Examine the resources provided by a credentialing site to evaluate health care information on the Web

Locating and Evaluating Health Care Information on the Internet

Some Web sites provide information about medical care, prescription drugs, and related health topics. Many doctors and other health care professionals have concerns about the quality of medical and health resources available on the Internet because anyone can post anything on the Web—there are no requirements for or restrictions on giving medical advice in this manner. Many health information Web sites include incorrect or incomplete information about health issues.

When you need information about a specific disease or medical condition, you can use one of the many sites on the Internet to conduct your research. In some cases, you might visit sites that are associated with credible research institutions, medical facilities, and universities. Sites in these categories include the Medical College of Wisconsin HealthLink, WebMD, and the Mayo Clinic. When you visit the sites of these organizations, you can read about the specific disease or medical condition that interests you, and often you will find links to other sites that provide more information. For example, if you are trying to learn about emphysema, a condition commonly associated with smoking cigarettes, one of these sites might provide information about the condition and links to other Web sites, such as the American Lung Association, where you can get more detailed information.

Just like any other Web site, you must carefully evaluate the quality of the resources and the information it provides. Sometimes you can make these determinations easily. For example, the American Lung Association is a well-known health organization that was founded

STARTING DATA FILES

There are no starting Data Files needed for this assignment.

in 1904 to fight tuberculosis and other lung diseases using donations and resources from public and private sources, foundations, and government agencies. Other resources, however, might be more difficult to evaluate because you might not be familiar with them. Fortunately, accrediting agencies that evaluate health information sites have their own Web sites that provide information about medical sites. Two of these sites are the Health on the Net (HON) Foundation and the URAC Health Web Site Accreditation. You can use the resources at these sites and other credentialing sites to evaluate health resources you find on the Internet. In some cases, the credentialing site might let you search its database to locate sites that it has already deemed credible using its own sets of rules, guidelines, and quality standards.

In this assignment, you will select a specific disease or medical condition that interests you (or your instructor might provide one for you to use), find information about it, and then use a credentialing site to evaluate its resources.

1. Visit at least two health information sites to obtain information about the disease or medical condition you selected. You can use your favorite search engine or directory to find the sites. Gather the information and evaluate the quality of the information and the quality of the Web site from which you obtained it.

2. Visit at least one credentialing or accreditation site and review its contents. Write a summary that describes how the site operates and evaluate whether the site accomplishes its goals.

3. Visit a site maintained by the U.S. government that offers health care information, such as the U.S. Centers for Disease Control and Prevention (CDC) or the U.S. National Institutes of Health MedlinePlus. Explore the site you selected and then write a review of the site in which you describe how the government-sponsored site is different from the privately operated sites you already visited. Provide your responses in a report for your instructor.

INTERNET

OBJECTIVES

- Use and expand the skills you learned in Tutorials 3, 4, and 5
- Explore the content requirements and processes for published encyclopedia resources
- Examine the content of and quality controls for a collaborative encyclopedia Web site
- Evaluate encyclopedia resources available on the Web and their role in research

Evaluating Encyclopedia Resources on the Internet

In Tutorials 3, 4, and 5, you learned techniques for locating and evaluating information on the Internet. When evaluating the information, you learned methods to ensure that it is complete, thorough, unbiased, and free from security threats such as viruses. As you search for information, you must assume responsibility for interpreting and analyzing the information you collect to make sure that it meets these criteria.

When you use Google or another search engine to search for information about a topic, chances are very good that your search results will include links to information that is posted on Wikipedia. Wikipedia, which began in 2001, is a much younger "encyclopedia" than its published counterparts, such as *World Book Encyclopedia* (which is more than 95 years old) or *Encyclopedia Britannica* (which is more than 220 years old). *World Book Encyclopedia* and *Encyclopedia Britannica* have established standards for research and information that rely on accredited and credentialed authors for content, subject matter experts for thorough reviews of that content, and editorial boards of experts in various fields to set standards for content. This established process of writing and reviewing greatly reduces problems related to bias or inaccuracies.

Wikipedia, on the other hand, does not apply these same types of standards to its content. The content that you find in Wikipedia might be written and reviewed by a casual user or an expert. According to the Wikipedia Web site, since its creation in 2001, over 82,000 people have actively contributed to more than 19 million articles in more than 270 languages. As a result of this collaboration, Wikipedia is one of the largest resource sites on the Internet. This collaboration of individuals has resulted in an enormous accumulation of knowledge. However, because material is freely contributed by people who might *not* be subject matter experts, and edited and reviewed by people with their own unique perspectives and biases, Wikipedia's content is subject to different quality standards than you might find in other publications.

STARTING DATA FILES

There are no starting Data Files needed for this assignment.

In this assignment, you will explore some of the pros and cons of using a collaborative site such as Wikipedia as a resource when conducting research.

1. Use your favorite search engine or directory to find the Web site for *World Book Encyclopedia*, and then use the "About Us," "Board," "Reviews," or other similarly named links on the publisher's Web site to learn about its contribution requirements and other quality assurance policies. (You might need to review several pages at the site to get a full picture of the encyclopedia's quality assurance standards.) Pay particular attention to author and reviewer credential requirements, review processes that ensure quality content, and any processes listed for making corrections to the published works.

2. Return to your search engine, and then find the Web site for *Encyclopedia Britannica*. Use the guidelines in Step 1 to evaluate the contribution requirements and quality assurance policies for this Web site.

3. Return to your search engine, and then search using the term **Wikipedia quality issues** and explore the links to learn about some controversies that have arisen as a result of Wikipedia's collaborative nature. Be sure to review material that details specific problems that have occurred and try to understand, what, if any, measures Wikipedia has taken to resolve these problems.

4. Referring back to the information you gathered in Steps 1 and 2 and the research you did in Step 3, what is your opinion of the use of traditional encyclopedias such as *World Book Encyclopedia* or *Encyclopedia Britannica* when compared to an online collaborative project such as Wikipedia? What role does each encyclopedia play in the field of research? How would you use each of these sources when conducting research? What level of confidence do you place in each source, and why? Provide your responses in a report for your instructor.

OBJECTIVES

- Use and expand the skills you learned in Tutorials 3, 4, and 5
- Learn about the Mars Student Imaging Project
- Find distance learning programs at your school or in your area
- Consider ways that distance learning can enhance education

Advances in Distance Learning

The Internet has enhanced the way that students in grades kindergarten through 12 learn about and participate in scientific research. The National Aeronautics and Space Administration (NASA) began its historic Mars Exploration Rover Mission, which is a long-term robotic exploration of the planet Mars, in June, 2003 and successfully landed a rover on the planet surface in January, 2004. NASA teamed with the Mars Education Program at Arizona State University to offer students in the United States the opportunity to participate in the Mars Student Imaging Project (MSIP). MSIP lets students in grades 5 through college sophomore level work in teams with scientists on the Mars project and choose a site on the Mars planet that they would like to map (photograph) from an orbiting rover. Archived data is also available for students to use in research projects. Students participate in the project through distance learning, which is made possible through video conferencing, chats, and teleconferencing. Students complete their projects by writing and submitting a final scientific report for publication in the online MSIP Science Journal.

STARTING DATA FILES

There are no starting Data Files needed for this assignment.

In this assignment, you will explore the Mars Student Imaging Project site and other distance learning sites that you find on the Internet. Then you will consider the future of using distance learning to enhance the education of grade school and college students.

1. Use your favorite search engine to locate the Mars Student Imaging Project Web site, and then explore the site to learn more about the project. Which Internet technologies make this project possible for students located in the United States?

2. Use your search engine to explore distance learning opportunities at your own school or at other colleges and universities in your area. How do these programs compare to the Mars Student Imaging Project? Which Internet technologies make these programs possible? Are all students able to participate in distance learning programs? Why or why not?

3. Based on your findings, determine other ways schools can use the Internet to enhance the education of grade school and college students. Are there technological impediments that prevent this method of learning? If so, what are they? What advantages do these types of programs offer students and educators? Provide your responses in a report for your instructor.

The Future of the Semantic Web

OBJECTIVES

- Use and expand the skills you learned in Tutorials 1, 3, and 4
- Review Web sites with information about the Semantic Web
- Use the skills you learned in this book to evaluate the resources you find
- Draw conclusions about the future of the Semantic Web based on your research

Tim Berners-Lee, widely regarded as the founding father of the Web, has been active in promoting and developing a project that blends technologies and information to create a next-generation Web, which he calls the **Semantic Web**. Today, people are the primary users of the Web as a communication medium. An increasing portion of the traffic on the Internet, however, is computers communicating with other computers. The Semantic Web is intended to facilitate automated computer-to-computer communication that can support all types of human activity.

The Semantic Web project, as currently conceived, would result in words on Web pages being tagged with their meanings (the meanings of words are called **semantics**, thus the name "Semantic Web"). These tags would turn the Web into a huge computer-readable database. People could use intelligent programs called **software agents** to read the Web page tags to determine the meaning of the words in their contexts. For example, a software agent could be given an instruction to find an airline ticket with certain terms (such as a specific date, destination city, and a cost limit). The software agent would launch a Web search and return an electronic ticket that meets the criteria. Instead of a user having to visit several Web sites to gather information, compare prices and itineraries, and make a decision, the software agent would automatically do the searching, comparing, and purchasing.

The key elements that must be added to Web standards so that software agents can perform these functions (and thus create the Semantic Web) include a well-defined tagging system and a set of standards. Many researchers working on the Semantic Web project believe that Extensible Markup Language (XML) could work as a tagging system. Unlike HTML, which has a common set of defined tags (for example, <h1> is the tag for a level-one heading), XML tags are defined by users. Different users can create different definitions for the same XML tag. If a group of users agrees on a common set of definitions, they can all use the same XML tags. For the Semantic Web to work, everyone must agree on a common set of XML tags that will be used on the Web. Semantic Web researchers call this common set of tag definitions a **resource description**

STARTING DATA FILES

There are no starting Data Files needed for this assignment.

framework (RDF). An **ontology** is a set of standards that defines, in detail, the relationships among RDF standards and specific XML tags within a particular knowledge domain. For example, the ontology for cooking would include concepts such as ingredients, utensils, and ovens; however, it would also include rules and behavioral expectations, such as identifying ingredients that can be mixed using utensils, the resulting product that can be eaten by people, and ovens that generate heat within a confined area. Ontologies and the RDF would provide the intelligence about the knowledge domain so that software agents could make decisions as humans would.

In this assignment, you will search for information about the Semantic Web and evaluate its potential for future use.

1. Use your favorite search engine to find sites with information about the Semantic Web, XML, RDF, and the term "ontology" as it is used in this area of research (the term "ontology" is used in philosophy and other disciplines, so you will need to use some of the techniques you learned in Tutorial 3 to narrow your results). Prepare a report that summarizes your findings on each of the four topics. Include citations for at least two Web pages for each of the four topics in your report.

2. For each of the eight (or more) Web pages you cited in the report required by the previous step, evaluate the quality of the information you obtained and evaluate the overall quality of the Web site from which you obtained it. Summarize your evaluations in your report. Be sure to include the reasons for your evaluations and explain how you performed the evaluations.

3. Using the information you have gathered about the Semantic Web, evaluate the likelihood that it will become a useful part of the Web within the next 10 years. Include a summary of your evaluation in your report and cite the Web sources that support your arguments.

OBJECTIVES

- Use and expand the skills you learned in Tutorials 4 and 9
- Use a Web site to translate statements into another language and then back into English
- Evaluate the quality of the translation
- Evaluate the effectiveness of using machine translation in business

Using a Web Site to Translate Business Correspondence

The Internet began as a series of research projects, mostly funded by the U.S. government. As the Internet expanded, people around the world started using the Internet for research and, eventually, for general information, entertainment, and to conduct online business activity.

The Internet contains resources that are written in languages from around the world. Because an important function of the Internet is to enhance communication, the global nature of the Internet often introduces and connects people who do not speak the same language. The need to translate email messages and the content of Web pages from one language to another has become very important.

Hiring human translators to do this work can be expensive. One solution for some applications is machine translation, in which a computer does a rough translation. Some Web sites that offer free machine translation tools are Yahoo! Babel Fish, Bing Translator, Google Translate, and SDL FreeTranslation.com.

The success of machine translation depends greatly on the type of information being translated. One way to check the quality of a translation (human or machine) is to take the result of the translation and translate it back into the original language. This process is called back-translation.

STARTING DATA FILES

There are no starting Data Files needed for this assignment.

In this assignment, you will evaluate the quality of online machine translation by translating several business-related statements into a foreign language, and then translating them back into English.

1. Use a search engine to locate one of the previously mentioned Web sites that provides online translation tools. Use the site to translate each of the following statements into another language of your choice, and then translate the result back into English.

   a. The scheduled arrival date of your order will be delayed.

   b. The crane operators' union at the port of embarkation has walked out on strike. This will delay the shipment of your order until at least one week after the work stoppage has been resolved. We will keep you apprised of developments.

   c. We appreciate the opportunity to bid on your project. To create a bid, we will need the detailed mechanical drawings by next Thursday, along with the supervising engineer's specifications list for all key parts.

   d. Our current catalog offers the hottest discounts on all in-stock items. We can meet all of your office furniture needs promptly. With our everyday low pricing, we can beat anybody in the business. Our extended warranties and service plans make us the top dog when it comes to wrapping up the job.

2. Evaluate the success of the machine translations of these four statements. In particular, identify the elements in each statement that were troublesome for the translation tool you used, and explain why you believe they were troublesome.

3. Provide an overall evaluation of the usefulness of machine translation technology in business communication on the Internet. Describe one specific situation in which you would use an online translation tool, and then describe a second specific situation in which you would be reluctant to use such a tool. Provide your responses in a report for your instructor.

Using Short Message Service

OBJECTIVES

- Use and expand the skills you learned in Tutorials 2 and 7
- Learn more about Short Message Service
- Examine the costs of sending messages
- Consider ways to improve text messaging services

Short Message Service (SMS), more commonly called text messaging, is a technology that allows the transmission of text messages between mobile devices, such as smartphones. Unlike email messages, text messages are limited in size (currently 160 characters) and cannot include graphics or photographic images. Some services allow you to send longer messages, but they automatically break the messages into smaller units (so they do not exceed the 160-character limit) and send them as separate messages.

Text messaging use has grown rapidly and is useful for sending short messages, such as "Am running late, see you in 30 minutes." Many wireless service providers offer SMS service as part of their cellular or broadband service packages. Some providers charge for SMS service by the message, but most carriers offer plans that include a certain number of messages (or unlimited messages) for a fixed monthly fee. Some wireless service providers also offer separate messaging functions (in addition to SMS) that allow you to send picture and video messages.

Because text messages use much less bandwidth than voice transmissions, they can be useful for communicating when wireless circuits become overloaded with unusually large amounts of traffic, which can happen any time many people want to send a quick communication to others. Thus, text messaging can be an important function when a natural disaster strikes and communications systems become overwhelmed. It can also be useful in less pressing circumstances, such as at midnight on New Year's Eve, when many people want to send a greeting at the same time.

STARTING DATA FILES

There are no starting Data Files needed for this assignment.

In this assignment, you will use your browser to visit a wireless service provider that offers SMS services to gather information you can use to answer the questions in the following steps. Summarize your findings in a report to your instructor.

1. Use your favorite search engine to search for wireless service providers that offer text messaging services and devices. Some examples are AT&T Wireless, Verizon Wireless, and TMobile. Choose one of these sites to answer the questions in Steps 2 through 6.

2. What is the cost to send and receive text messages using the service you selected? Does the provider offer unlimited text messaging at a fixed cost per month?

3. Are there any limits on the use of text messaging?

4. Can you send pictures using the provider's text messaging service? If so, is there an additional fee for this service?

5. How easy was it to find this information on the site you visited?

6. What kinds of devices are required to send and receive text messages? Do some devices provide an easier interface for composing and reading text messages? What is the general cost difference when comparing devices with more user-friendly interfaces to those with more difficult to use interfaces?

INTERNET

OBJECTIVES

- Use and expand the skills you learned in Tutorial 5
- Visit blogs to evaluate their content
- Consider ways to use blogs in business to enhance communication
- Consider some of the advantages and disadvantages of using blogs

Evaluating the Use of Blogs in Business

In this book, you learned how to use email messages to communicate with another person, a group of people, or a mailing list. You also learned about newsgroups and how to use them to obtain information about a specific topic, and how to use instant messaging, text messaging, blogs, and microblogs to communicate with another person or with groups of people. Each of these methods of communication requires different levels of participation from the user. For example, to use instant messaging software, you must install a program on your computer or wireless device; to join a mailing list or a discussion group, you must use your email program or a newsreader to obtain the messages. To write a blog or microblog, you need access to the Internet and software that publishes and distributes your postings.

Although blogs have been around since 1996, the availability of automated blog publishing systems from Web sites such as Blogger, WordPress, and LiveJournal gave them the boost they needed to become commonplace on the Web. Media attention increased their popularity in the 2004 presidential campaign when Howard Dean, who pursued but eventually lost the Democratic nomination for president, was the first presidential candidate to use a blog to rally his supporters across the country, to provide updates from his campaign, and to let people join discussions about current topics. By the 2008 presidential campaign, virtually all of the major candidates used blogs. There are hundreds of thousands of blogs on the Web related to all kinds of topics. Some directories, such as Google, identify blogs based on their category, such as news, arts, or sports.

Users need minimal expertise to create or contribute to a blog, and there is little or no expense associated with the technology. Most sites that offer automated publishing systems offer free or inexpensive accounts that new bloggers can use to set up their own blogs, making it easy for anyone to publish their thoughts on the Web. Specific features vary by company, but all automate the process of publishing chronologically arranged postings.

STARTING DATA FILES

There are no starting Data Files needed for this assignment.

Although individuals maintain most blogs, new bloggers include corporations, attorneys, and educators who have discovered the appeal of this technology for making information available to clients, building a practice, or creating academic knowledge communities.

In this assignment, you will learn more about automated blog publishing systems and consider ways to use this technology to enhance communication and develop business relationships. Summarize your findings in a report to your instructor.

1. Most blogs are collections of an individual's personal posts, but blogs can also allow a group of people to engage in a collaborative discussion. Use Google Blogs to find a categorical listing of blogs. Evaluate a couple of blogs in business-related categories, such as library science, news, or science. How does the information provided in the blog compare to using email, instant messaging, chat, or newsgroups as a communication tool? What value does a blog add to the topic? Can you identify any unique advantages of communicating using blogs that you cannot gain from other types of Internet communication?

2. Find a political candidate's blog and evaluate its content. What types of information are included in the blog? How does it differ from information presented elsewhere on the candidate's Web site? What is the impact, if any, on traditional news media outlets of the dissemination of political news through blogs?

3. Find a corporate blog and assess its content. What competitive advantages can blogs offer companies?

4. Some blogs that are affiliated with faculty members of colleges and universities. Locate a blog written by a faculty member at a university. Do blogs authored by faculty members differ from other blogs you have found? Do educators have a greater responsibility to control the content of postings at their sites? Do you feel that blogs belong in academic settings? Why or why not? Provide your responses in a report for your instructor.

Reintermediating Travel Services

OBJECTIVES

- Use and expand the skills you learned in Tutorials 4, 5, 8, and 9
- Develop ideas for the design of a surf travel Web site
- Use the skills you learned in this book to design a home page for a travel agency
- Outline the features for a social networking site that would lead to travel sales
- Choose Web sites that would be good locations on which to place advertising for the travel agency

The travel agency business has changed dramatically over the years as Web sites selling travel-related services, such as airline tickets, rental cars, and hotel reservations have replaced businesses that employed travel agents to locate these services and sell them to recreational and business travelers. In the past, travel agencies earned revenues from commissions on airline tickets, but airlines have mostly eliminated these commissions. Many travel agents (including online travel sites) now charge their customers a flat fee for booking flights; however, many customers object to paying such fees. This disintermediation has affected all travel agents, but small travel agencies that do not have Web sites have been hurt the most.

One way to address the revenue problems caused by disintermediation is for travel agencies to explore reintermediation opportunities. One reintermediation strategy for a small travel agency is to create a Web site that serves as an online meeting area for people desiring information about a specific travel opportunity, such as vacations involving surfing. The stereotypical surfer of the past was a young, unemployed male. Surfers today come from a broader demographic. Many surfers have significant financial resources and enjoy surfing in many worldwide locations. Web sites such as WaveHunters.com and WannaSurf.com have followed a reintermediation strategy and cater to this highly specialized market in ways that general travel agents have not.

STARTING DATA FILES

There are no starting Data Files needed for this assignment.

In this assignment, you will assume the role of a travel agency that is seeking to design a Web site that caters to surfers. You will examine surfing Web sites, consider ways to build a social network that will draw surfers to a Web site, and identify Web sites that a travel agency should consider using in its online advertising campaigns.

1. Use your favorite search engine to find at least two sites that offer surf vacation packages for sale, such as WaveHunters.com and WannaSurf.com. For each of the two sites you find, list at least four Web site elements that you believe a new travel agency could use on its Web site. Also list at least two Web site elements that the travel agency should avoid using. For each item on your lists, explain why you classified it the way you did.

2. Create a sketch to design a home page for a new travel agency that includes the four elements you included in Step 1. After completing your sketch, write a summary of each element that you plan to use and describe the technologies that you need to implement them.

3. Describe how you would use social networking sites to attract people who are interested in exotic surf vacations to the new Web site. Explain how your ideas would contribute to the overall goal of reaching people who are likely to buy travel services.

4. Use your favorite search engine to find surfing interest Web sites on which the new travel agency could purchase advertising space. Choose three specific sites that you believe are good choices. For each site you select, explain your rationale for choosing that site. Provide your responses in a report for your instructor.

GLOSSARY/INDEX

1G wireless. *See* first-generation (1G) wireless networks
2.5G wireless network A wireless network that transfers data at rates up to 144 to 384 Kbps. WEB 355
2G wireless. *See* second-generation (2G) wireless networks
3.5G wireless network A wireless network that provides network connections of up to 10 Mbps. Also called mobile broadband. WEB 355
    choosing provider, WEB 372
    wireless connections, WEB 366
3G wireless. *See* third-generation (3G) wireless networks
4G wireless. *See* fourth-generation (4G) wireless networks
802.11a, 802.11b standards, WEB 357

A

About.com Web directory, WEB 151
Abrams, Jonathan, WEB 268
absolute path A path that provides a file's location with absolute precision; there is no reference to the current file. WEB 415
access point A hardware device with one or more antennae that permits communication between wired and wireless networks so wireless clients can send and receive data. WEB 357
    installing wireless, WEB 382
accounts, setting up Hotmail, WEB 95–99
accuracy, evaluating Web resources, WEB 172
acronyms
    chat, WEB 266
    commonly used, WEB 82
active content A general term used to describe programs, such as Java, JavaScript, and ActiveX components, that travel with applications to a browser and are executed on a user's computer. WEB 322
ActiveX control Microsoft's technology for writing small applications that perform specific actions in Web pages and that have access to a computer's file system. WEB 322
add-on A general classification of browser extensions that includes tools to enhance the browsing experience, such as toolbars that are used to access a search engine without opening its Web site, or programs that block pop-up ads. WEB 433
Address bar (IE), WEB 7–8
addresses
    email. *See* email addresses
    IP, WEB A5
Adobe Director, WEB 434, WEB 436
Adobe Dreamweaver, WEB 402, WEB 422, WEB 425–429
Adobe Illustrator, WEB 438
Adobe Photoshop, WEB 438
Adobe Reader, WEB 433
ADSL (Asymmetric Digital Subscriber Line), **WEB A22**
Advanced Research Projects Agency (ARPA), **WEB A7**

ADSL. *See* Digital Subscriber Line (DSL)
Advanced Research Projects Agency (ARPA) The agency charged with the task of connecting Department of Defense computers to each other and to weapons installations distributed all over the world. Also called Defense Advanced Research Projects Agency (DARPA). WEB A7
advertisements
    adware, WEB 328
    on directories, WEB 201
    revenues from social networks, WEB 269–270
    search engines and, WEB 143
    spam. *See* spam
    targeted, in Webmail, WEB 93
    types of online, WEB 468–469
    in unmoderated lists, WEB 248
advertising A paid announcement that attracts attention to a product, service, business, person, or idea. WEB 468
    on the Internet, WEB 468–471
advertorials, WEB 469
adware A term that means "ad-supported software" and describes software that includes advertisements to help pay for the program in which they appear. WEB 328
affiliate marketing A arrangement in which one company performs some business processes for another company in exchange for money or the sharing of expertise or access to customers. Also called a strategic alliance or a strategic partnership. WEB 469
    types of programs, WEB 469–471
aggregators, WEB 249
AirTight Networks home page, WEB 383
algorithm A formula or set of steps that solves a particular problem. WEB 301
Amazon.com, WEB 204–205, WEB 255, WEB 469, WEB 478–479
American Psychological Association (APA) Web page citation standards, WEB 216
anchor tag An HTML tag that creates a hyperlink. WEB 417, WEB 418
AND Boolean operator, WEB 160–161, WEB 163–164
Andreessen, Marc, WEB A17, WEB A18
Angie's List, WEB 462–463
animated content, creating, WEB 433–436
Anti-Phishing Working Group (WPWG), WEB 305
antivirus program A software program that detects and eliminates viruses. WEB 88
    and firewalls, WEB 335
AOL Instant Messenger (AIM), WEB 264
APIs (application programming interfaces), **WEB 255**
    viewing those available on Web, WEB 258–260
Apple Apps Store, WEB 387
Apple iOS, WEB 386
API. *See* application programming interface (API)
app An application that runs on a smartphone. WEB 386
    security risks with smartphone, WEB 386–390

application programming interface (API) A means of communication with an operating system or some other program that is written by a programmer or developer with a specific goal in mind, such as displaying content on a screen or accessing a file system. WEB 255
    viewing those available on Web, WEB 258–260
APWG (Anti-Phishing Working Group), WEB 305
Arctic Monkeys, WEB 269
ARPA. *See* Advanced Research Projects Agency (ARPA)
ARPANET The experimental wide area network (WAN) created by DARPA in 1969 that grew to become the Internet. *See also* Advanced Research Projects Agency (ARPA). WEB A9, WEB A11
article A message posted in a newsgroup. WEB 248
assurance provider A third party that verifies the business practices of an organization and then issues the right to use the assurance provider's seal on a Web site that meets the specified criteria for conducting safe transactions and ensuring privacy. WEB 339
asterisk (*) wildcard character, WEB 162–163
Asymmetric Digital Subscriber Line (ADSL or DSL). *See* Digital Subscriber Line (DSL)
asymmetric encryption. WEB 302. *See also* public-key encryption
at sign (@) in email addresses, WEB 76
Atom A feed format that is used to syndicate (distribute) published content from one site to another. WEB 249
attachment A file encoded so that it can be sent with an email message over a network. WEB 79
    sending, viewing, WEB 79–80
    sending Hotmail, WEB 102–103, WEB 105
attribute The part of an HTML tag that specifies additional information about the content to be formatted by the tag. Some attributes are required; others are optional. WEB 402
auction sites, online, WEB 465
AuctionWeb, WEB 205
audio files
    finding on the Web, WEB 229–232
    formats (fig.), WEB 230
authentication A general term used to describe the process of verifying the identity of a person, computer, or server with a high degree of certainty. WEB 335
authorship, evaluating Web resources, WEB 171
AutoCAD, WEB 438
autoconnect A feature that lets a mobile device automatically connect to a Wi-Fi network when it is in range of the network. WEB 388

B

B2B. *See* business-to-business (B2B) e-commerce
B2C. *See* business-to-consumer (B2C) e-commerce
B2G. *See* business-to-government (B2G) e-commerce
Back button (IE), WEB 11–12

bandwidth The amount of data that can travel through a communications circuit in one second. WEB A20, WEB A23

banks' use of multifactor authentication, WEB 336

banner ad Advertising that appears in a box on a Web page, usually at the top, but sometimes along the side or at the bottom of the page and usually includes graphical elements including to the text in the ad. WEB 143, WEB 468

Bartleby.com, WEB 218

Bcc. *See* blind courtesy copy (Bcc)

Because It's Time Network (BITNET) A network of university computers that eventually became part of the Internet. WEB A10

BBB Accredited Business Seal, WEB 339–340

Berners-Lee, Tim, WEB 400, WEB A15, WEB A16

Bezos, Jeff, WEB 204

Better Business Bureau (BBB), WEB 339–340, WEB 476

Bing search engine, WEB 139–140

bitmaps, WEB 436

BITNET. *See* Because It's Time Network (BITNET)

bits per second (bps) The basic increment in which bandwidth is measured. WEB A20

BlackBerry OS, WEB 386

blind courtesy copy (Bcc) The copy of an email message sent to a recipient without that recipient's address appearing in the message so that the message's other recipients are unaware that the Bcc recipient received the message. WEB 78

blog A frequently updated Web site that expresses the opinions of the author(s), with frequently updated content that is focused on a specific topic or category of information. Also called a Weblog or Web log. WEB 189, WEB 262

    overview, WEB 276–278

    searching for, WEB 278–279

bluebugging An attack on a Bluetooth-enabled device that occurs when a hacker gains access to the device and its functions without the owner's consent. WEB 386

bluejacking An attack on a Bluetooth-enabled device in which a person called a bluejacker sends an anonymous message in the form of a phone contact displayed as a text message in an attempt to surprise the owner, express an opinion, or make a social connection. Web 385

bluesnarfing An attack on a Bluetooth-enabled device that occurs when a hacker with special software is able to detect the signal from a Bluetooth-enabled device and gain access to its data without the owner's knowledge. WEB 386

Bluetooth A wireless technology that uses short-range radio waves for communication between compatible devices in a personal area network. WEB 362

    overview, WEB 362–365

    security threats to, WEB 385–386

Bluetooth SIG Web site, WEB 362–363

body section The required section of an HTML document that includes the content of the Web page along with the tags needed to format that content. WEB 398

bold HTML tag, WEB 4

Boingo Wireless home page, WEB 374

bold heading tags, WEB 402

bookmark A hyperlink whose target is a location in the same page in which the hyperlink appears. WEB 418

    creating, organizing, WEB 47–50

    deleting from Library, WEB 53

    moving into folders, WEB 51

    saving, WEB 52

Bookmarks toolbar In Firefox, a toolbar of buttons that provide links to saved shortcuts to Web pages that you visit frequently. WEB 35

books, searching online for, WEB 204–205

Boole, George, WEB 160

Boolean algebra A branch of mathematics and logic in which all values are reduced to one of two values; in most practical applications of Boolean algebra, these two values are true and false. WEB 160

Boolean operator In Boolean algebra, an operator that specifies the logical relationship between the elements it joins, just as the plus sign arithmetic operator specifies the mathematical relationship between the two elements it joins. Most search engines recognize three basic Boolean operators: AND, OR, and NOT. Also called logical operator. WEB 160, WEB 161–162

bps. *See* bits per second (bps)

brands4friends, WEB 205

bricks and clicks Companies that use both a physical store and the Web to sell their products and services. WEB 459

Broadcast Communications, Ltd., WEB 368

broken links, fixing, WEB 417

broker services, WEB 464

browser. *See* Web browser

browser extension A plug-in, helper application, or add-on that allows a Web browser to perform tasks it was not originally designed to perform, such as playing audio and video files. WEB 433

browsing, private Web, WEB 24–25

browsing history, erasing, WEB 22

brute force attack An attack in which a program enters different character combinations of user names and passwords in a system with the goal of breaking into that system. WEB 336

bulleted list An HTML format in which a bullet character is displayed next to each item in the list. Also called an unordered list. WEB 412

    creating, WEB 413–414

Bush, Vannevar, WEB A15

business-to-business (B2B) e-commerce A category of e-commerce that includes activities undertaken by a company to sell goods or services to other businesses or nonprofit organizations. WEB 456

business-to-consumer (B2C) e-commerce A category of e-commerce that includes activities that a company undertakes to sell goods or services to individuals. WEB 456

business-to-government (B2G) e-commerce A category of e-commerce that that includes using Internet technology to perform transactions with the government such as filing tax forms. WEB 457

business communications

    correspondence guidelines, WEB 104

    email format, WEB 80–81

businesses

    Internet connection types (fig.), WEB A24

    network use in, WEB A12

    searching for, WEB 200–203

    that provide Internet access, WEB A20–A23

byte The basic increment in which file sizes are measured; it contains 8 bits. WEB A5

C

C2C. *See* consumer-to-consumer (C2C) e-commerce

CA. *See* certificate authority (CA)

cable

    Internet access, WEB A20–A24

    types, WEB A3–A5

Caesars Palace, WEB 256

café latte attack. *See* evil twin attack

CafePress product Web page, WEB 459–460

Calendar page A page in Windows Live Hotmail that contains options for organizing scheduled appointments and a daily calendar. WEB 101

Calliau, Robert, WEB 400, WEB A15

CAN-SPAM Act, WEB 90

CAPTCHA A feature on a Web page that asks the user to enter a displayed set of alphanumeric characters to verify that a person is using the form, and not a computer. CAPTCHA is an acronym for "Completely Automated Public Turing test to tell Computers and Humans Apart." WEB 98

Category 1 cable A type of twisted pair cable that telephone companies have used for years to carry voice signals; Category 1 cable is inexpensive and easy to install but transmits information much more slowly than other types of cable. WEB A3

Category 5 (Cat-5) cable A type of twisted pair cable developed specifically for carrying data signals rather than voice signals; Category 5 cable is easy to install and carries signals between 10 and 100 times faster than coaxial cable. WEB A3

Category 5e (Cat-5e) cable An enhanced Category 5 cable that is constructed of higher quality materials so it can carry signals faster than regular Category 5 cable. WEB A3

Category 6 (Cat-6) cable A type of twisted pair cable that is constructed of higher quality materials than Category 5e cable so it can carry signals faster. WEB A3

Category 7 (Cat-7) cable A type of twisted pair cable that is constructed of higher quality materials than Category 6 cable so it can carry signals faster. WEB A3

category An address book entry that consists of two or more email addresses. Also called a group. WEB 78

    creating contact list, WEB 117–119

    email address, WEB 78

Cc. *See* courtesy copy (Cc)

cell phones. *See* smartphone

Cellular, WEB 356

Cengage Learning, WEB 275

Cengage Learning's TOS statement (fig.), WEB 480

Cerf, Vinton, WEB A10

CERN, and hypertext, WEB A15–A16

certificate authority (CA) A trusted third party that verifies and attests to the identity of a person or organization as part of the process of issuing a digital certificate. WEB 337

chat A general term for real-time communication that occurs over the Internet using a Web site or a chat program. Chats can include text, voice, or video, depending on the type of chat and the equipment used. WEB 262
  acronyms, WEB 266
  types, overview, WEB 266
Children's Online Privacy Protection Act, WEB 476
Chrome browser
  encryption indicator (fig.), WEB 342
  SSL-EV indicator (fig), WEB 343
  strengthening security in, WEB 325–327
chat room The area of a chatting Web site where users could send text-only messages in real time with their Web browsers to other users in the chat room. WEB 264
cipher text A general term used to describe encrypted information. WEB 301
circuit switching A centrally controlled, single-connection method for sending information over a network. WEB A8
citing Web resources, WEB 215–217
city guide A Web site that provides information on hotels, restaurants, entertainment, cultural activities, and other things to do in a destination city. WEB 185
Clark, James, WEB A18
classified ads, WEB 469
clear GIF. See Web bug
clearinghouse. See Web bibliography
Cleveland Orchestra, WEB 211
clicking links, WEB 10, WEB 42
clickstream A record of the links clicked by a user while visiting a Web site. WEB 475
client A computer connected to a server and sharing its resources. WEB A2
client/server network A way of connecting multiple client computers to a server so the clients can share the server's resources, such as printers, files, and programs. WEB A2
closed list A mailing list in which the list's administrator approves requests for membership. WEB 247
closing Page tags, WEB 13–14
cloud A group of technologies and services that provide computing over the Internet so people can interact with programs and data using any device that can access the Internet, including computers, tablets, and smartphones. WEB 232
coaxial cable An insulated copper wire encased in a metal shield and then enclosed in plastic insulation; coaxial cable carries signals about 20 times faster than Category 1 twisted pair cable, but is considerably more expensive. WEB A3, WEB A4
colors
  changing font, WEB 409–410
  Web-safe color palette, WEB 403
.com domain name, WEB A7
Command bar In Internet Explorer, the toolbar that includes buttons and menu options for working safely and effectively in the browser and includes options for printing. WEB 3
comment tag The HTML tag that lets you insert a comment in an HTML document. WEB 398
comments, adding to HTML documents, WEB 408

commerce service provider (CSP) A large ISP that sells Internet access and other services to businesses to help them conduct business activities on the Internet. WEB A20
common key In private-key encryption, the private key is sometimes called a common key because it is known to both the sender and receiver of a message. WEB 301
comparison shopping sites, WEB 469
CompuServe, WEB A12
Computer Science Network (CSNET) An internet funded by the NSF for educational and research institutions that did not have access to the ARPANET. WEB A10
computer security. See logical security
Congressional Record, WEB 225
connections
  Internet types (fig.), WEB A24
  Wi-Fi and Bluetooth standards compared (table), WEB 364
  wired, wireless, WEB 354
consumer-to-consumer (C2C) e-commerce A category of e-commerce that includes online business transactions undertaken by individuals who are not operating a formal business. WEB 384
contact list The collection of email addresses and other contact information maintained by an email program or Webmail provider. Also called an address book or a contact manager. WEB 77
  creating categories, WEB 117–119
  maintaining, WEB 115–119
contact manager. See contact list
Contacts page A page in Windows Live Hotmail that contains options for managing information about the user's contacts. WEB 101
content, blocking inappropriate, WEB 283
control panel A password-protected Web page that includes tools that let a Web site administrator maintain and manage a Web site. WEB 444
conversation. See thread
cookie A small text file that a Web server saved on the hard drive of a user's computer that is running a Web browser; the Web server reads the cookie when the user revisits the Web site. WEB 22, WEB 55
  blocking, WEB 22
  managing, deleting IE, WEB 22–23
  managing, viewing in Firefox, WEB 55–57
  and Web bugs, WEB 333
copying
  See also copyright
  text from Web pages, WEB 29–30, WEB 62–64
copyright The legal right granted by a government to the author, creator, or other owner of an original work to control the reproduction, distribution, and sale of the tangible form of that work for a specific length of time as provided in the copyright law. WEB 29, WEB 62
  and fair use, WEB 210–211
  overview, WEB 210
  and plagiarism, WEB 214–215
  protecting materials with digital watermarks, WEB 307–309
  public domain works, WEB 211–214
CorelDRAW, WEB 438

countermeasure A physical or logical procedure that recognizes, reduces, or eliminates a threat. WEB 300
courtesy copy (Cc) An email message sent to other people in addition to the primary recipient(s). WEB 78
cracker. See hacker
craigslist, WEB 206, WEB 268
cryptography The study of ways to secure information. WEB 301
CSNET. See Computer Science Network (CSNET)
CSP. See commerce service provider (CSP)
cultural e-commerce issues, WEB 477–479
current news, information, searching for, WEB 186–193
customer service, online, WEB 475
cyberbullying Using Internet communication such as email, text and instant messages, blogs, microblogs, or social networks to harass, threaten, or intimidate someone. WEB 283

D

DARPA (Defense Advanced Research Projects Agency). See Advanced Research Projects Agency (ARPA) WEB A7, WEB A8–A9
data
  encrypting with WEP, WEB 378–379
  protecting integrity of electronic, WEB 302–307
data transfer. See bandwidth
databases
  accessing periodical, WEB 221–222
  library, searching, WEB 160
  search engine, WEB 145
dates, filtering search results by, WEB 187–189
DDoS attack. See distributed denial-of-service (DDoS) attack
dead link A hyperlink to a Web page that no longer exists or has been moved to another URL. WEB 143
decryption The process of converting encrypted text back into a readable form. WEB 301
dedicated server A Web server that hosts only one site. WEB 439
deep Web Information contained in the databases that some Web sites use to generate their dynamic Web pages. WEB 169–170
DeepPeep search engine, WEB 169–170
Defense Advanced Research Projects Agency (DARPA). See Advanced Research Projects Agency (ARPA) WEB A7, WEB A8–A9
definition list An HTML format in which each item in a list consists of a term followed by its definition. WEB 412, WEB 413
Deleted folder The folder in Windows Live Hotmail that temporarily stores deleted messages until you or the Hotmail server permanently deletes them. WEB 92
demodulation The process of converting an analog signal to a digital signal. WEB A21
demographic data, accessing, WEB 226–227
denial-of-service (DoS) attack A security attack that occurs when an attacker floods of computer, server, or network with messages with the goal of consuming the network's bandwidth resources and disabling its services and communications. WEB 309
  and active content, WEB 322
  preventing, WEB 309–311

denial-of-service (DoS) filter A computer or software that monitors communication between a Web server and a router and identifies potential DoS attacks by watching for patterns of incoming page requests or for specific repeating elements in the page request messages. WEB 311

deprecated An HTML feature that is being or has been replaced or phased out by a new or future HTML specification and that might not be supported by future browsers. WEB 401

destination information, searching for, WEB 196–200

detaching The process of saving an email attachment to a file location. WEB 80

detecting malware, WEB 327–332

devices
    Bluetooth-enabled, WEB 362–364
    PAN, WEB 362
    Wi-Fi certified, WEB 358
    wireless. *See* wireless devices

dial-up The standard telephone service provided by telephone companies to business and individual customers for voice communications that allows users to transmit data by using a modem at a bandwidth of between 28.8 Kbps and 56 Kbps. Also called plain old telephone service (POTS). WEB A21

Dickens, Charles, WEB 211

digital audio books, WEB 231

Digital Millennium Copyright Act (DMCA), WEB 212

digital certificate An encrypted and password-protected file that contains sufficient information to authenticate and prove a person's or organization's identity. WEB 336
    using, WEB 336–339

digital ID An electronic file that an individual can purchase from a certificate authority and install into a program that uses it, such as an email program or Web browser, to provide proof of their identity when sending electronic messages. WEB 337

Digital Impact Group, WEB 359

Digital Millennium Copyright Act (DMCA), WEB 212

digital object identifier (DOI) A unique alphanumeric identifier that identifies digital intellectual content and provide a persistent link to its location as long as the content exists somewhere on the Internet. WEB 216

digital rights management (DRM) A system of encoding that restricts the copying, use, or conversion to other formats of the contents of digital files. WEB 231

digital signature An electronic signature that provides verification of the contents of a file and identifies the file's author or developer. WEB 322

Digital Subscriber Line A type of broadband connection provided by a telephone company that provides transmission speeds of 16 to 640 Kbps from the user to the telephone company and transmission speeds of 1.5 to 9 Mbps from the telephone company to the user. Also called Asymmetric Digital Subscriber Line (ADSL). WEB A22

digital wallet An electronic device with software that enables the user to make a purchase online. Also called an electronic wallet or e-wallet. WEB 471, WEB 472

Digital Watermarking Alliance, WEB 308

digital watermark A process that inserts a digital pattern containing copyright information into a digital image, animation, or audio or video file. The watermark is inserted into the file using a software program so that it is invisible and undetectable. To view the digital watermark, a software program unlocks the watermark, retrieving the information it stores. WEB 307
    protecting materials with, WEB 307–309

directories
    exploring podcast, WEB 253–255
    funding of, WEB 201
    Web, WEB 148–153
    yellow and white pages, WEB 185

disabling
    autoconnect feature, WEB 388
    SSID broadcast, WEB 381

disintermediation The elimination of an intermediary that is no longer needed from an industry. WEB 465

displaying
    Firefox toolbars, WEB 38–39
    Internet Explorer toolbars, WEB 5–6
    See also viewing

distributed database A database that is stored in multiple physical locations, with portions of the database replicated in different locations. WEB 247

distributed denial-of-service (DDoS) attack A denial-of-service (DoS) attack in which an attacker takes control of one or more computers without the owner's permission and uses those computers to launch a DoS attack on other computers, servers, or networks. WEB 309

DNS (Domain Name System) software A program on an Internet host computer that coordinates the IP addresses and domain names for all computers attached to it. WEB A7

document type declaration (DTD) A one-sided tag that tells a browser which syntax version of a markup language a document uses. WEB 406, WEB 427

documents
    described, WEB 4
    HTML, WEB 4, WEB 36

Dogpile metasearch engine, WEB 154

DOI. *See* digital object identifier (DOI)

domain name A unique name associated with a specific IP address. WEB A6
    acquiring, WEB 441–442
    commonly used (fig.), WEB A7
    securing, WEB 423

domain name server The Internet host computer that runs DNS software to coordinate the IP addresses and domain names for every computer attached to it. WEB A7

domain name system software. *See* DNS (Domain Name System) software

DoS attack. *See* denial-of-service (DoS) attack

DoS filter. *See* denial-of-server (DoS) filter

dotted decimal notation A method of writing the parts of a 32-bit IP address as four decimal numbers separated by periods. WEB A7

dot-com A business that makes all its sales on the Web and has no physical stores; also called pure dot-com. WEB 459

DoubleClick, WEB 333–334

Dougherty, Dale, WEB 246

downloading
    Hotmail attachments, WEB 107–109
    plug-ins, WEB 230

Drafts folder Stores email messages that have been written, but that have not yet been sent. WEB 92

Dream Machines (Nelson), WEB A15

DRM. *See* digital rights management (DRM)

DSL. *See* Digital Subscriber Line

DTD. *See* document type declaration (DTD)

dual band access point An access point that accepts connections from wireless devices configured for two different Wi-Fi standards. WEB 357

Duff, Hilary, WEB 269

dynamic Web page A Web page created on the fly in response to a user's query from information stored in a database maintained by the Web site. WEB 169

E

eBay, WEB 466, WEB 472

Economist, The, WEB 462

e-commerce (electronic commerce) The process the process of developing, marketing, selling, delivering, servicing, and paying for products and services online. Also called etail. WEB 456
    advertising, marketing on Internet, WEB 468–471
    buying and selling over the Web, WEB 458–467
    categories: visual overview (fig.), WEB 456–457
    consumer concerns, WEB 474–477
    customer service, WEB 475
    disintermediation, reintermediation, WEB 465
    evaluating Web sites, WEB 477
    international issues, WEB 477–481
    legal issues, WEB 480–481
    paying for purchases, WEB 471–474
    shipping purchased items, WEB 474

editing bookmarks, WEB 48–49

Electronic Communications Privacy Act (CPA) of 1986, WEB 476

electronic data interchange (EDI) certification, WEB 341

electronic mail. *See* email

electronic wallet (e-wallet). *See* digital wallet

email A form of communication in which electronic messages are created and transferred between two or more devices connected to a network. WEB 76
    acronyms, commonly used, WEB 82
    messages. *See* email messages
    netiquette, WEB 81
    process described, WEB 74–77
    programs. *See* email programs
    protecting online privacy, WEB 249
    Webmail, WEB 93

email address A unique identifier consisting of a user name and a domain name that represents an individual's or organization's email account on a specific mail server. WEB 76
    Hotmail, WEB 96
    managing multiple, WEB 77

email messages
    common features of, WEB 77–81
    dealing with unsolicited, WEB 89
    deleting, managing, WEB 87
    forwarding, WEB 85
    guidelines, WEB 83
    replying to, WEB 86
    sending, receiving, printing, WEB 84
    sending Hotmail, WEB 102–106
email program. *See also* mail client software
    common features of, WEB 84–87
    overview, WEB 83–84
email-based communication, WEB 247–249
emoticon A group of keyboard characters that when viewed together represent a human expression; used in email and other electronic correspondence to convey emotions. WEB 82, WEB 266
    "emphasis" tags, WEB 427
eMusic home page, WEB 231–232
encryption The process of coding information using an algorithm to produce a string of characters that is unreadable, which secures the information during transit over a network. WEB 301
    digital and server certification, WEB 336–339
    MAC address filtering, WEB 380
    protecting against security threats using, WEB 300–302
    Wi-Fi Protected Access (WPA), WEB 379–380
    Wired Equivalent Privacy (WEP), WEB 378–379
Engelbart, Douglas, WEB A15
e-readers, WEB 217
escrow service A third-party service that holds a buyer's payment until he or she receives and is satisfied with a purchased item; often used in online auctions. WEB 466
etail. *See* e-commerce (electronic commerce)
Ethernet, WEB A21
evil twin attack An attack in which a hacker gathers information about an access point and then uses that information to set up his own computer to impersonate the real access point and use its signal to attempt to steal information from the wireless devices that connect to the spoofed access point. Also called café latte attack. WEB 384
e-wallet. *See* electronic wallet
Exalead search engine, WEB 163–164
expertise, evaluating Web resources, WEB 171
exploratory question An open-ended question that can be difficult to phrase and for which it can be difficult to determine when you find a good answer. WEB 134
    effective Web search strategies for, WEB 137–139
    finding answers to, WEB 135–136
    using Web bibliographies, WEB 157
Extensible Hypertext Markup Language (XHTML) A stricter version of HTML designed to confront some of the problems associated with the different and competing versions of HTML, and to better integrate HTML with XML. WEB 400
    vs. HTML syntax requirements (fig.), WEB 401
Extensible Markup Language (XML) A markup language that uses customizable tags to describe data and its relationship to other tags. WEB 400
extranet An intranet that permits access by selected outside parties. WEB A12

F

Facebook, WEB 317, WEB 471
fair use A provision in the U.S. copyright law that allows a limited amount of copyrighted information to be used for such purposes as news reporting, research, and scholarship. WEB 29, WEB 62
    determining, WEB 210–211
Fashion Outlet virtual mall, WEB 205
Fast Ethernet, WEB A21
favorite In Internet Explorer, a stored shortcut containing the URL of a Web page so you can return to the page later without having to remember the URL or search for the page again. WEB 2, WEB 16
    creating, organizing, WEB 16–20
Favorites bar In Internet Explorer, a toolbar that includes buttons that provide links to saved shortcuts to Web pages that you visit frequently. WEB 2
Favorites Center In Internet Explorer, a pane that you use to organize and display links to your preferred Web sites, RSS feeds, and recently visited sites. WEB 2
    creating, organizing favorites, WEB 16–20
    deleting favorites, folders, WEB 20
    overview, WEB 15–16
Federal Communications Commission (FCC) blog page, WEB 276–277
Federal Trade Commission
    Identity Theft site, WEB 314
    Spam page, WEB 90
feed Technology that sends subscribed users frequently updated content from a news sources, blog, podcast, or other network on a schedule that the user specifies. Also called a newsfeed or a Web feed. WEB 244, WEB 249
femtocell In an LTE network, a base station that uses minimal power to transmit the LTE signal from a wired connection, such as a cable or DSL modem, to an LTE device within its range to increase its speed. WEB 370
fiber-optic cable A type of cable that transmits information by pulsing beams of light through very thin strands of glass; fiber-optic cable transmits signals much faster than coaxial cable does, is immune to electrical interference, and is more durable than coaxial cable, but it is harder to work with and is more expensive. Also called fiber. WEB A4
file transfer protocol (FTP) That part of the TCP/IP protocol set that includes rules for formatting, ordering, and error-checking files sent across a network. WEB 7, WEB 39, WEB 444, WEB A10
files
    See also specific type
    protocols for transferring, WEB 7
    read-only, WEB 80
    sharing using SkyDrive, WEB 119–122
    signature, WEB 80–81
    size, and Web site's transfer requirements, WEB 439–440
    storing in the cloud, WEB 232
    typical file transmission times for various LANs (fig.), WEB A21
filtering search results by date, WEB 187–189

filter A feature in an email program that examines the content of an email message and then moves that email message into a specific folder or deletes it automatically based on the content of the message. WEB 84, WEB 311
Firefox
    encryption indicator (fig.), WEB 342
    browsing history, erasing, WEB 55
    changing default home page, WEB 44–45
    components and features (fig.), WEB 2–3
    cookies, handling, WEB 55–57
    customizing window, WEB 38–39
    Help, getting, WEB 59–60
    MedlinePlus page showing syndicated content (fig.), WEB 250
    Private Browsing mode, WEB 57–59
    returning to home page, WEB 44
    SSL-EV indicator (fig), WEB 343
    starting, WEB 37–38
    strengthening security in, WEB 324–325
    using Page tags, WEB 45–47
Firefox button A button at the top of the Firefox program window that opens a menu with options for all the main functions and features in the Firefox browser. WEB 34, WEB 37, WEB 53
firewall A hardware device or software program that protects networks and attached network devices by preventing unauthorized communications. Web 299
    blocking communication using, WEB 334–335
Fireworks, WEB 438
first-generation (1G) wireless network The first wireless network, which transmitted voice data only using analog signals. WEB 352, WEB 354
first-party cookie A cookie placed on a user's computer by the Web site being visited. WEB 22, WEB 55
fixed-point wireless A technology for wireless connections to a network that uses technology that is similar to wireless LANs. WEB A23
Flash Player A browser plug-in that displays simple animations, user interfaces, images, movies, sound, and text that was created using Adobe Flash software. WEB 433, WEB 434, WEB 436
Flickr, WEB 228, WEB 272–274
folders
    creating for favorites, WEB 16–20
    deleting, WEB 20
    deleting from Library, WEB 53
    deleting Hotmail, WEB 114–115
    filing Hotmail messages in, WEB 112–113
    moving bookmarks into, WEB 51
    for Web site's images, WEB 415
follower In microblogging, the term given to a person or an organization who is receiving updates from a microblogger. WEB 280
fonts
    color, changing, WEB 409–410
    creating headings with smallest size, WEB 408
    installed with Windows, WEB 404
    using in Web pages, WEB 404
    and Web-safe color palette, WEB 403
formatting paragraphs, WEB 410–412

formats
   audio file (fig.), WEB 230
   video, WEB 233–234
forums (newsgroups), WEB 247
forward The process of sending a copy of a previously sent or received email message to another recipient. WEB 85
Forward button (IE), WEB 11–12
forwarding
   email messages, WEB 85
   Hotmail messages, WEB 109–112
fourth-generation (4G) wireless network A wireless network that transfers data at rates of 50 to 100 Mbps and delivers high quality audio and video to connected devices. WEB 355
Friendster, WEB 268
From line The part of an email message header containing the email address of the message's sender. WEB 79
Frommer's Travel Guides, WEB 199–200
FTP. *See* file transfer protocol (FTP)
Full Screen mode The browser view in Firefox that temporarily hides the program window—the Firefox button, the Navigation toolbar, and any toolbars as well as the Windows taskbar—leaving only the Web page visible on the screen. WEB 38, WEB 39
Full screen mode The browser view in Internet Explorer that temporarily hides the program window—the title bar, the Navigation bar, the menu bar, and any toolbars as well as the Windows taskbar—leaving only the Web page visible on the screen. WEB 6
full text indexing A method used by some search engines for creating their databases in which the entire content of included Web pages is stored in the database. WEB 146

G

gaming sites, subscription-based, WEB 462
GB. *See* gigabyte (GB)
Gbps. *See* gigabits per second (Gbps)
general TLD (gTLD) A top-level domain (TLD) that is maintained by ICANN. WEB A7
Getty Images, WEB 228
GIF files, and Web bugs, WEB 333
Gigabit Ethernet, WEB A21
gigabits per second (Gbps) A measure of bandwidth; 1,073,741,824 bits per second (bps). WEB A20
gigabyte (GB) A unit of measure for file sizes; it is 1,073,741,824 bytes or 8,589,934,592 bits. WEB 21
Gmail visual overview (fig.), WEB 74–75
Google, WEB 274
Google AdSense, WEB 258
Google Advanced Search, WEB 164–167, WEB 186–189
Google Android, WEB 386
Google Blog Search, WEB 278–279
Google Groups home page (fig.), WEB 248
Google Images, WEB 228–229
Google Maps, WEB 196–199
Google Maps API, WEB 255, WEB 256
Google search engine, WEB 140, WEB 142, WEB 155–156
Google Videos, WEB 234–235
Gottfried, Gilbert, WEB 282

government Web sites, WEB 225–228
GPS tracking, WEB 390
grammar-checking, WEB 224
graphic images, WEB 228
graphical user interface (GUI) A way of presenting program output that uses pictures, icons, and other graphical elements instead of just displaying text. WEB A16
graphics, raster and vector, WEB 436
group. *See* category
grouping operator. *See* precedence operator
gTLD. *See* general TLD (gTLD)
GUI. *See* graphical user interface (GUI)

H

H&R Block site, WEB 464, WEB 467
hacker A term sometimes used to describe a person who uses his knowledge of computers and programming to gain unauthorized access to a computer for the purpose of stealing or altering data. Also called cracker. WEB 301
Half.com, WEB 205
hashtag In a microblogging site, the name given to a user-defined keyword that creates the topical categories that link messages together across the network. A hashtag begins with a pound sign (#) and includes one to several words, which are typed without any space characters. WEB 281
head section A required section in an HTML document that includes the <head> tag, general information about the document, optional tags that identify the document's content for search engines, optional comments about the document's creator or the date on which the document was last updated or created, and the nested <title> tag, which identifies the title of the Web page so the browser can display it in the title bar. WEB 390, WEB 407
heading tag An HTML tag that instructs a Web browser to display the text enclosed in the tag as a heading. WEB 398, WEB 402, WEB 403, WEB 416, WEB A16
heading tags, WEB 398, WEB 402, WEB 403, WEB 416
headings, creating with smallest font size, WEB 408
Help
   Facebook, WEB 269–270
   Firefox, WEB 59–60
   Internet Explorer (IE), WEB 25–26
helper application A program installed on a user's device that a browser starts and uses to "help" display or play a file. WEB 433
hidden Web. *See* deep Web
hiding Internet Explorer toolbars, WEB 6
history, erasing browsing, WEB 22, WEB 55
History list
   navigating Web pages using, WEB 53–54
   viewing, WEB 54–55
History tab, Favorites Center, WEB 21
hit A Web page that is indexed in a search engine's database and contains text that matches the search expression entered into the search engine. Search engines provide hyperlinks to hits on results pages. WEB 143
Holiday Inn, WEB 358

Home button
   Firefox, WEB 35
   Internet Explorer, WEB 12–13
home networks, disabling SSID broadcasts, WEB 381
home page (1) The main page that all of the pages on a particular Web site are organized around and to which they link back; (2) the page that opens when you start a Web browser program; (3) the page that a particular Web browser loads the first time it is run. Home pages under the second and third definitions also are called start pages. *See also* start page. WEB 3
Hotmail. *See* Windows Live Hotmail
Hotmail
   accessing Windows Live account, WEB 99–101
   adding contacts, WEB 115–117
   creating Windows Live ID, WEB 95–99
   deleting messages, folders, WEB 114–115
   filing messages in folders, WEB 112–113
   Internet Explorer settings, WEB 12–13
   loading, WEB 8–9
   moving to Favorites bar (IE), WEB 19–20
   printing messages, WEB 112–113
   receiving, opening messages, WEB 106–107
   replying, forwarding messages, WEB 109–112
   sending messages using, WEB 102–106
   and start pages, WEB 8, WEB 41
   viewing, saving attachments, WEB 107–109
   visual overview (fig.), WEB 74–75, WEB 92–93
hotspot An area of network coverage in a wireless network. WEB 356
   MiFi, WEB 360
   public, using safely, WEB 385
.html, WEB 405
HTML (Hypertext Markup Language), WEB 4, WEB 36, WEB 400
   vs. XHTML syntax requirements (fig.), WEB 401
HTML anchor tag A tag that enables Web designers to link HTML documents to each other. WEB 4, WEB 36
HTML document A text file that includes HTML tags that indicate how a Web browser should format the text. WEB 4, WEB 36, WEB A16
   adding comments to, WEB 408
   creating, WEB 405–414
   example of, WEB 398–399
   hyperlinks added to (fig.), WEB 419
   naming, saving as .html, WEB 405–406
   planning, WEB 402–404
   using images in, WEB 414–417
   with Web bugs, WEB 333
   Web pages. *See* Web page
HTML tags, summary (fig.), WEB 420
HTTP. *See* hypertext transfer protocol (HTTP)
hybrid search engine directory A Web site that combines the functions of a Web search engine and a Web directory. WEB 150
hypertext A system in which text on one page links to text on other pages. WEB A15
hypertext link A text or graphics object on a Web page that contains instructions to connect to and display another place on the Web page or another Web page entirely. Also called hyperlink or link. WEB 3, WEB 5, WEB 35, WEB 36
   anchor tags. *See* anchor tag
   clicking, WEB 10, WEB 42

dead links, WEB 143
to files, creating, WEB 418–419
in HTML, WEB A16
in HTML documents, WEB 4–5
hypertext, WEB 5
inbound, WEB 146
positioning, organizing, WEB 9
and phishing, spoofing attacks, WEB 303–307
tag, WEB 398
Hypertext Markup Language (HTML) A programming language used to format documents containing text and images to they can be viewed in a Web browser. WEB 2, WEB 36, WEB 400, WEB A16
viewing code for Web pages, WEB 425–426
hypertext server A computer that stores HTML documents and lets other computers connect to it and read those documents. WEB A15
hypertext transfer protocol (HTTP) The communication protocol used to transfer Web pages from a Web server to a Web browser. WEB 7, WEB 39

I

IAP (Internet access provider). *See* Internet service provider (ISP)
ICANN. *See* Internet Corporation for Assigned Names and Numbers (ICANN)
ICQ Short for "I seek you," the first instant messaging program on the Internet, which later became AOL Instant Messenger and later, AIM. WEB 264
identity theft A crime in which a thief obtains an individual's personal information and then uses that information to open bank accounts, obtain new credit cards, and purchase items using credit cards, often damaging the victim's credit rating in addition to making transactions for which the victim is responsible. WEB 312
preventing, WEB 311–315
recovering from, WEB 315
IETF. *See* Internet Engineering Task Force (IETF)
illustration software A software program that is used to create and edit vector graphics. WEB 438
image In HTML, any file that contains a picture, such as a photograph, logo, or computer-generated file. WEB 414
in HTML documents, WEB 414–417
saving Web page, WEB 28–29, WEB 61–62
sharing pictures on the Web, WEB 272–274
stock, WEB 228
See also photos
image editing program A software program that is used to create and edit raster graphics. WEB 438
IMAP (Internet Message Access Protocol) A protocol for retrieving email messages from a remote mail server or messages that are stored on a large local network. WEB 76
inbound link Connection to a Web page formed by other Web pages' hyperlinks pointing to it.
Inbox The folder in which email messages received from the mail server are stored. WEB 146
inclusion operator. *See* precedence operator

information
finding current or specific on Internet, WEB 186–189
on the Internet, visual overview (fig.), WEB 184–185
useful vs. tangential, WEB 136
infrared A wireless technology that uses infrared light rays to allow communication between compatible devices. WEB 362
Infrared Data Association (IrDA) A group dedicated to developing low-cost, high-speed wireless connectivity solutions using infrared technology. WEB 362
InPrivate Browsing mode A browsing mode in Internet Explorer in which the user's browsing history, cookies, or copies of Web pages that were visited are not stored on the computer, helping to protect the user's privacy and security. WEB 24, WEB 25–26
inserting
images in HTML documents, WEB 416–417
paragraphs, WEB 410–412
instant message A message sent in real time between users who are chatting over a network and using network-connected devices. Instant messaging usually occurs over an Internet connection using computers or over a cellular network using mobile devices. WEB 262
and Internet chat communication, WEB 264
insurance, identity theft, WEB 313
Integrated Services Digital Network (ISDN) A type of DSL that allows data transmission at bandwidths of up to 256 Kbps. WEB A22
integrity threat A threat that results in unauthorized data modification. WEB 300
Intel WiMAX technology Web page, WEB 369
intellectual property All creations of the human mind, such as original ideas and creative works presented in a form that can be shared or that others can recreate, emulate, or manufacture. *See also* copyright. WEB 210
interconnected network The system when networks are connected to each other. Also called internet. WEB 4, WEB 36
intermediary services, WEB 464, WEB 465
Internet A specific interconnected network that connects computers all over the world using a common set of interconnection standards. WEB 4, WEB 36
accessing with wireless devices, WEB 372–375
connection types (fig.), WEB A24
and evolution of the Web, WEB A15–A19
growth of, WEB A12–A14
origins of, WEB A7–A12
overview, WEB 4–5
term's origin, WEB A10, WEB A12
and the Web, WEB 36–37
vs. Web 2.0, WEB 246
Internet access provider (IAP). *See* Internet service provider (ISP)
Internet Archive's Wayback Machine, WEB 219
Internet chat communication
exploring Windows Live Messenger, WEB 265–266
overview, WEB 264
Voice over Internet (VoIP) protocol, WEB 266–267
Internet Corporation for Assigned Names and Numbers (ICANN) The organization that since 1998 has been responsible for managing domain names on the Internet. WEB A7

Internet discussion group. *See* newsgroup
Internet Engineering Task Force (IETF) A self-organized group that makes technical contributions to the engineering of the Internet and its technologies. It is the main body that develops new Internet standards. WEB A12
Internet Explorer (IE)
components and features (fig.), WEB 2–3
cookies, handling, WEB 22–23
customizing window, WEB 6–7
encryption indicator (fig.), WEB 341
Help, getting, WEB 25–26
home page settings, WEB 12–13
InPrivate Browsing mode, WEB 24–25
Page tags, using, WEB 13–14
starting, WEB 5–6
SSL-EV indicator (fig), WEB 342–343
strengthening security in, WEB 322–324
and VBScript, WEB 429
Internet hoaxes, WEB 112
Internet host A computer that connects a LAN or WAN to the Internet. WEB A13, WEB A14
Internet Message Access Protocol. *See* IMAP (Internet Message Access Protocol)
Internet Protocol (IP) A part of the TCP/IP set of rules for sending data over a network. WEB A10
Internet Relay Chat (IRC) A multiuser program that allows users to exchange short messages over the Internet. WEB 264
Internet security software Software that detects and eradicates viruses and other common security threats on the Internet. WEB 288
Internet service provider (ISP) A firm that purchases Internet access from network access points and sells it to businesses, individuals, and smaller ISPs. Also called an Internet access provider (IAP). WEB A20
internet. *See* interconnected network
Internet2 A network developed by a group of research universities and the NSF that has backbone bandwidths that exceed 10 Gbps. WEB A22
interstitial ads, WEB 469
intranet A LAN or WAN that uses the TCP/IP protocol but does not connect to sites outside a single organization. WEB A12
invisible Web. *See* deep Web
IP (Internet Protocol) address A series of four numbers separated by periods that uniquely identifies each computer connected to the Internet. WEB A5
IP version 4 (IPv4) An IP addressing system that uses a 32-bit number to label each address on the Internet. WEB A5
IP version 6 (IPv6) An IP addressing system approved in 1997 as the protocol that replaces IPv4; IPv6 generates a billion more addresses than IPv4. WEB A6
IP. *See* Internet Protocol (IP)
ip11 virtual library, WEB 222–223
iPOWER.com, WEB 442–443
IRC. *See* Internet Relay Chat (IRC)
IrDA. *See* Infrared Data Association (IrDA)
ISDN. *See* Integrated Services Digital Network (ISDN)
ISP. *See* Internet service provider (ISP)

J

jailbreaking The practice of unlocking the operating system on an Apple device so it can run apps created for other operating systems. WEB 388

JANET. *See* Joint Academic Network (JANET)

Java applet A program written in the Java programming language. WEB 322

JavaScript A scripting language that is used to perform tasks that are not possible in static HTML documents, such as animating buttons or making simple calculations. WEB 429
    enhancing Web pages using, WEB 432
    programming with, WEB 429–433

JavaScript program A program written in JavaScript that a compatible browser can execute without first compiling it into computer-readable codes. WEB 322

Joint Academic Network (JANET) An early network established by U.K. universities. WEB A11

JScript, WEB 429

Junk folder A folder in Windows Live Hotmail that stores email messages from senders that you or Hotmail have identified as spam. WEB 92

junk mail Unsolicited email messages, usually advertising or selling an item or service. Also called spam. WEB 84, WEB 89

K

Kahn, Robert, WEB A10

key A fact used by an encryption algorithm as part of its encryption formula. WEB 301

Key, Francis Scott, WEB 211

keywords
    and hashtags, WEB 281
    and meta tags, WEB 145, WEB 423
    search engine, WEB 133

KB. *See* kilobyte (KB)

Kbps. *See* kilobits per second (Kbps)

kilobits per second (Kbps) A measure of bandwidth; 1,024 bps. WEB A20

kilobyte (KB) A unit of measure for file sizes; it is approximately 1,000 characters, 8,192 bits, or 1,024 bytes. WEB 79, WEB A21

L

LAN. *See* local area network (LAN)

languages, e-commerce issues, WEB 477–479

Lavasoft Ad-Aware Free, WEB 331

layering content in vector graphics, WEB 438

LearnOutLoud.com Podcast Directory page, WEB 254

Lee, Congressman Christopher, WEB 282

legal issues, e-commerce, WEB 480–481

letters, business correspondence guidelines, WEB 104

libraries, online and virtual, WEB 222–224

Library (Firefox) The area in Firefox that stores, organizes, and displays links to your preferred Web sites and view the History list. WEB 34
    using, WEB 47–53

library databases
    accessing, WEB 217
    searching, WEB 160

link rot A term that defines Web pages or sites that have a number of dead links. WEB 143

LinkedIn, WEB 270–271

links
    adding to Web pages, WEB 418–419
    broken, fixing, WEB 417
    creating shortened URL for, WEB 317–318
    See also hyperlink

liquidation broker An intermediary who matches sellers of obsolete inventory with purchasers who are looking for bargains. WEB 465

list moderator The person or group that monitors messages sent to a moderated mailing list and discards inappropriate content. WEB 247

list server A server that runs email list software to manage the functions of a mailing list. WEB 247

lists, contact. *See* contact lists

list tags, WEB 398

lists
    contact. *See* contact list
    creating, WEB 412–414
    HTML supported (fig.), WEB 413

local area network (LAN) Any of several ways of connecting computers to each other when the computers are located close to each other (no more than a few thousand feet apart). WEB A2
    file transmission times for various (fig.), WEB A21

local Web site A copy of a Web site that is stored on a hard drive or other local drive to provide a backup of a Web site. WEB 444

localization Translation that takes into account the culture and customs of the country. WEB 478

Location bar (Firefox), WEB 40–41

location operator A Web search engine operator that lets you search for terms that appear close to each other in the text of a Web page. The most common is the NEAR operator. Also called proximity operator. WEB 162

logging in to Hotmail, WEB 99–101

logical operator. *See* Boolean operator

logical security The protection of assets using nonphysical means. Also called computer security. WEB 298

logins
    auction sites, online, WEB 466
    changing default, WEB 381
    smartphone app risks, WEB 388–390
    using public hotspots safely, WEB 385

Long Term Evolution (LTE) A wireless standard that creates a 4G wireless broadband network in metropolitan areas using radio waves broadcast in the 700 Mhz spectrum. WEB 370, WEB 371–372

LTE. *See* Long Term Evolution (LTE)

lurking The practice of reading messages posted to a chat room, mailing list, or newsgroup and not contributing to the discussion. WEB 264

M

MAC address. *See* Media Access Control address

magazines, accessing periodical databases, WEB 221–222

MagPortal.com, WEB 221–222

mail client software Software that requests mail delivery from a mail server to a user's device. Also called email program. WEB 76

mail server A hardware and software system that determines from the recipient's email address one of several electronic routes on which to send the message. WEB 74

mailing list A list of names and email addresses for a group of people who share a common interest in a specific or broad subject or topic and exchange information by subscribing to the list. WEB 244, WEB A11

malware A term that means "malicious software" and describes any software that is installed without the user's consent, usually through a hidden program in an email attachment or from a file downloaded from a Web site, with the goal of spreading a virus, Trojan horse, worm, or posing any security threat to the user's device. WEB 327
    detecting, removing, WEB 327–332

MAN. *See* metropolitan area network (MAN)

managing Web sites, tools for, WEB 425–429

man-in-the-middle attack (MITM attack) An attack in which messages sent between two devices are intercepted by an unauthorized third party, who eavesdrop on the conversation, gathers information from the messages, or alters the messages in some way. WEB 384

man-in-the-middle exploit An integrity violation in which a third party alters the contents of a message in a way that changes the message's original meaning. WEB 303

MapQuest, WEB 196

maps, searching for, WEB 196–200

marketing
    affiliate, WEB 469–470
    social media, WEB 471
    See also advertising, advertisements

markup language A general term that indicates the separation of the formatting of a document and the content of a document. *See also* Hypertext Markup Language (HTML). WEB 400
    examples of, WEB 398–399

mashup A Web site that combines the data from different Web resources to create a new Web site that is updated by these resources. WEB 245

MB. *See* megabyte (MB)

Mbps. *See* megabits per second (Mbps)

McAfee antivirus, WEB 88

McAfee security products, WEB 329–331

MCI Mail, WEB A12

m-commerce, WEB 458

Media Access Control address A unique number assigned to a network interface card by its manufacturer that is used on a network to identify the device. Also called a MAC address. WEB 380

MedlinePlus, WEB 249–250

megabits per second (Mbps) A measure of bandwidth; 1,048,576 bps. WEB A20

megabyte (MB) A unit of measure for file sizes; it is 1,048,576 bytes or 8,388,608 bits. WEB A21

Melville, Herman, WEB 218

Memex A memory extension device envisioned by Vannevar Bush in 1945 that stored all of a person's books, records, letters, and research results on microfilm; the idea included mechanical aids to help users consult their collected knowledge fast and in a wide variety of ways. WEB A15

message body The content of an email message. WEB 77, WEB 78, WEB 80–81

message header The part of an email message containing information about the message's sender, recipient(s), and subject. WEB 77

meta tag An HTML element that a Web page creator places in a Web page header to inform Web robots about the page's content. WEB 145

Meta tags generator, WEB 448

metalanguage A language used to create other languages. WEB 400

metasearch engine A tool that accepts a search expression and transmits it to several search engines that run the search expression against their databases of Web page information and return results that the metasearch engine consolidates and reports. WEB 154, WEB 155

metropolitan area network (MAN) A network that provides wireless broadband Internet service to large geographical areas, usually in hotspots of several square miles each, and connects these hotspots using technology similar to cellular service to create a very large area of network coverage. The two competing MAN standards are WiMAX and LTE. WEB 366

    Long Term Evolution (LTE), WEB 370–371

    WiMAX, WEB 366–369

microblog A form of blogging in which users send short messages (usually 140 characters or less) on a very frequent schedule. WEB 262

    overview, WEB 279–281

Microsoft and 'browser wars,' WEB A18

Microsoft Encarta, WEB 217

Microsoft Excel Web App, WEB 120–122

Microsoft Expression Web, WEB 402, WEB 422, WEB 425–429

Microsoft Internet Explorer, WEB 1

    See also Internet Explorer (IE)

Microsoft Safety & Security Center, WEB 306

MIDI audio format, WEB 230

MiFi A small wireless router that provides a battery-operated, mobile, personal hotspot for connecting Wi-Fi devices to the Internet using a broadband service provider. WEB 360

MILNET (Military Network) That part of ARPANET, created in 1984, reserved for military uses that required high levels of security. WEB A11

Milo.com, WEB 205

MIME (Multipurpose Internet Mail Extensions) A protocol specifying how to encode nontext data, such as graphics and sound, so you can send it over the Internet. WEB 76

MindTap, WEB 275

MITM attack. *See* man-in-the-middle attack (MITM attack)

mobile broadband. *See* 3.5G wireless network

Mobile e-commerce (m-commerce) E-commerce that takes place on a mobile device. WEB 458

modem A device that converts a computer's digital signal to an analog signal (modulation) so it can travel through a telephone line, and also converts analog signals arriving through a telephone line to digital signals that the computer can use (demodulation). WEB A21

moderated list A mailing list that has a list moderator who is responsible for discarding inappropriate content. WEB 247

Modern Language Association (MLA) Web page citation standards, WEB 216

modulation The process of converting a digital signal to an analog signal. WEB A21

Mosaic Web browser, WEB A17–A18

Mozart's works, WEB 211

Mozilla, WEB A18

Mozilla Firefox. *See* Firefox

MP3

    finding audio files on the Web, WEB 229–232

    format described, WEB 252

MSN Messenger, WEB 264

multifactor authentication A method of authenticating a user that requires more than one factor, such as requiring the user to present a debit card and enter a PIN to conduct a transaction. WEB 336

multimedia Anything you can see or hear, including text, pictures, audio/sound, videos, films, or animations. WEB 228

    finding images, audio, video on the Web, WEB 228–236

multiple band access point An access point that makes it possible to connect any wireless device to the same access point. WEB 357

multiple layers of control A method of authenticating a user that requires more than one authentication method, such as entering a username and password and answering a challenge question. WEB 336

Multipurpose Internet Mail Extensions. *See* MIME (Multipurpose Internet Mail Extensions)

municipal broadband The name given to a wireless network with sufficient network coverage to create a hotspot the size of a municipal area such as a city. Also called Muni Wi-Fi or a Muni-Fi network. WEB 359

Muni-Fi network. *See* municipal broadband

Muni-Wi-Fi. *See* municipal broadband

music files, finding on the Web, WEB 229–232

Myspace, WEB 269

N

naming HTML documents, WEB 406

NAP. *See* network access point (NAP)

natural language query interface An interface that allows users to enter a question exactly as they would ask a person that question. The search engine analyzes the question using knowledge it has been given about the grammatical structure of questions and converts the natural language question into a search query. WEB 147

navigating

    among visited Web pages, WEB 11–12

    Web pages, WEB 39–47

    Web pages using history list, WEB 21–22

    Web pages using links, WEB 10

    Web pages using Page tabs, WEB 13–15

    Web pages using URLs, WEB 7–9, WEB 39–41

Navigation bar A toolbar in Internet Explorer used to open and move among Web pages as well as access favorites and commands for saving and printing. WEB 2

Navigation toolbar A toolbar in Firefox that is used to open and move among Web pages and search for Web pages. WEB 34, WEB 37

NCP. *See* Network Control Protocol (NCP)

near field communication (NFC) A standards-based, short-range wireless technology that allows electronic devices to interact over a couple of inches. WEB 472

NEAR operator, WEB 162

necessity threat A threat that causes data delays (which slow down the transmission of data) or denials (which prevent data from getting to its correct destination). WEB 300

Nelson, Ted, WEB A15

nested tag An HTML tag included within another HTML tag. WEB 401, WEB 404

netiquette The set of commonly accepted rules that represent proper behavior on a network. WEB 81

Netscape Navigator, WEB 429, WEB A18

Network Solutions, WEB 440–441

network A configuration that connects computers and other devices together. WEB 4, WEB 36

    connecting computers to, WEB A3–A5

    IP addresses, domain names, WEB A4–A7

    online business, WEB 270–271

    online social. *See* online social network

    overview of computer, WEB A2–A3

    that became the Internet (fig.), WEB A11

    wireless, WEB A4

    wired vs. wireless (fig.), WEB 357

network access point (NAP) The point at which local portions of the Internet connect to its main network backbone. WEB A20

network backbone The long-distance lines and supporting technology that transport large amounts of data between major network nodes. WEB A11

Network Control Protocol (NCP) A set of rules for formatting, ordering, and error-checking data used by the ARPANET and other early forerunners of the Internet. WEB A9

network interface card (NIC) A card or other device inserted into or attached to a computer that allows it to be connected to a network. WEB A2

network node. *See* node

network operating system Software that runs on a server and that allows clients to be connected to it and share its resources. WEB A2

Newmark, Craig, WEB 206, WEB 268

news, searching for current, WEB 189–193

news aggregation Web site A Web site that collects and displays content from a variety of online news sources, including wire services, print media, broadcast outlets, and even blogs, and displays it in one place. WEB 190

news feed. *See* feed

news server The server that stores a Usenet newsgroup. WEB 247

newsgroup A discussion group that occurs over a computer network with many users contributing to a specific topic. Also called an Internet discussion group. WEB 244

newspapers, accessing online, WEB 223

newsreader A program that handles the communication between a client and a news server. WEB 248

NIC. *See* network interface card (NIC)

nickname An abbreviated name, such as "Mom," that represents an email address in an address book for an email program. WEB 77

Nielsen, Dr. Jakob, WEB 175

node Each computer, printer, or other device that is attached to a network. Also called a network node. WEB A2
    wireless, WEB 361

Norton Secured Seal, WEB 339–340, WEB 341, WEB 476

Norton security products, WEB 328–329

NOT Boolean operator, WEB 160–161

Notepad, WEB 403
    creating HTML documents using, WEB 405–414

Novatel, WEB 360

NPR News page, WEB 251

numbered list An HTML format in which a sequentially ordered number or letter is displayed next to each item in the list. Also called an ordered list. WEB 412, WEB 413

O

objectivity, evaluating Web resources, WEB 171–172

OC. See optical carrier (OC)

octet In networking applications, the term given to represent an 8-bit number. WEB A5

Oikarinen, Jarkko, WEB 264

Omidyar, Pierre, WEB 205

online business networks, WEB 270–271

online references, WEB 217–220

online retail The selling of physical products on the Web; the most common form of e-commerce. WEB 459
    consumer benefits, drawbacks of, WEB 461

online social network A site at which people can discuss issues and share information using the Internet or cellular networks. WEB 247
    advertising revenues, WEB 269–270
    creating profiles on, WEB 283
    overview, WEB 268–269
    protecting privacy, identity on, WEB 283
    protecting your reputation, WEB 284–285

open architecture An approach that allows each network in an internet to continue using its own protocols and data transmission methods for moving data internally. WEB A10

Open Directory Project, WEB 150–151, WEB 175

open list A mailing list in which membership is automatic. WEB 247

open-source software Software that is created and maintained by volunteer programmers; the software is made available to users at no charge.

opening tags, WEB 406

operators
    logical, WEB 160–161
    search expression, WEB 161–162

optical carrier (OC) A type of fiber-optic cable. WEB A22

optimizing, WEB 444–447

OR Boolean operator, WEB 160–161, WEB 163–164

O'Reilly, Tim, WEB 246

ordered list. See numbered list

over-the-shoulder attack An attack in which an unauthorized person uses his or her physical proximity to a user's device to attempt to get login information, passwords, or other sensitive data while the user is working. WEB 384

P

packet sniffer A network software tool that examines the structure of the data elements that flow through a network. WEB 311

packet switching A method for sending information over a network in which files and messages are divided into packets that are labeled electronically with codes for their origins and destinations, sent through the network, each possibly by a different path, and then reassembled at their destination. WEB A8

Paint, WEB 438

PAN device A device that works in a personal area network. WEB 362

PAN. See personal area networking

page ranking A method used by search engines to grade (rank) Web pages by the number of other Web pages that link to them so that the URLs of Web pages with high rankings can be presented first on the search results page. WEB 146

Page Setup dialog box, WEB 31

page tab A way of showing multiple Web pages open at once in a browser, and to easily navigate among the open pages. WEB 13–14, WEB 34, WEB 45–47

paid placement The right to have a link to a Web site appear on a search engine's results page when a user enters a specific search term. WEB 143

paragraph tag, WEB 398

paragraphs, inserting and formatting, WEB 410–412

parsing The work that a search engine does when it analyzes a natural language query to convert it into a search query. The search engine uses knowledge it has been given about the grammatical structure of questions to perform the parsing task. WEB 147

passphrase A user-entered key that is used to encrypt data that is sent to and received from a wireless network that uses WEP. WEB 378

password manager A program that stores login information in an encrypted form on a user's device. WEB 335

passwords
    and brute force attacks, WEB 336
    changing default login, WEB 381
    and communication channel security, WEB 335–336
    Hotmail, creating, WEB 97
    and security risks with smartphones, WEB 389
    for uploading to Web sites, WEB 423

paths
    absolute, WEB 415
    in vector graphics, WEB 436

PayPal, WEB 205, WEB 260, WEB 303–307, WEB 472, WEB 473

PCS. See Personal Communication Service (PCS)

PDF files as email attachments, WEB 79

PDA. See personal digital assistant (PDA)

people, searching for, WEB 200–203

periodical databases, accessing, WEB 221–222

personal area networking (PAN) A wireless network that connects personal devices to each other in a Bluetooth or an infrared network. WEB 362, WEB 363–365
    overview, WEB 362–365

Personal Communication Service (PCS) A digital wireless network that transfers voice and text data at a rate of up to 14.4 Kbps. WEB 354

personal digital assistant (PDA) A handheld computer that can send and receive wireless telephone and fax calls, act as a personal organizer, perform calculations, store notes, and display Web pages from the Internet. WEB 354

phishing An integrity violation in which email messages claiming to be from a legitimate sender direct recipients to a spoofed Web site where the recipient is asked to provide sensitive information so the spoofed Web site can steal the recipient's personal information. WEB 303
    structure of, WEB 303–307

photos, sharing using SkyDrive, WEB 119–120

photo-sharing site A Web site that lets users create accounts into which they can upload photos with the option of making them available so other users can view them. WEB 262, WEB 272–274

pictures
    sharing on the Web, WEB 272–274
    sharing using SkyDrive, WEB 119–120
    See also image

physical security The protection of assets using physical devices, such as vaults, safes, and fire-proof devices, from different types of security threats, such as burglaries and fires. WEB 298

piconet A collection of two to eight devices connected in a personal area network using Bluetooth. WEB 364

pictures, using in Web pages, WEB 414

piggybacking A term used to describe a person who gains access to and uses a wireless network, sometimes by wardriving.

pixel A single point in an image; used to describe an image's width and height. WEB 415
    in raster graphics, WEB 436

plagiarism Use of material (whether it is in the public domain or is protected by copyright) without crediting the source of that material. WEB 214

plain old telephone service (POTS). See dial-up

plain text A general term used to describe unencrypted information. WEB 301

plug-in A program that extends the functionality of a Web browser to display or play files. WEB 433

podcast An audio or video broadcast that is created and saved in a digital format and then saved on a computer or server. WEB 244

podcasting A digital audio or video feed that a user listens to or watches at the user's convenience on a compatible device, which might include the user's computer, or a mobile device such as an iPod or a cell phone. WEB 252
    exploring podcast directories, WEB 253–255
    overview, WEB 252–253

podcatcher Software that manages the schedule for downloading podcast files to a user's device. WEB 252

POP (Post Office Protocol) An Internet protocol that handles incoming email messages. WEB 75

POP message A message that is routed through an Internet domain using the POP protocol. Also called POP3 message. WEB 83

POP3 message. See POP message

pop-up ads, WEB 468

port A virtual door on a computer that permits traffic to enter and leave the computer. Different ports handle different forms of communication between a computer and a network or devices, such as a printer. WEB 334

port scan The process that occurs when one computer tests all or some of the ports of another computer to determine whether its ports are open (traffic is not filtered and the port permits entry through it), closed (the port does not accept traffic, but a cracker could use this port to gain entry to and analyze the computer), or stealth (the port might be open or closed, but permits no entry through it). WEB 335

portal site A Web site that provides a gateway or entry to other sites on the Web. WEB 222

Post Office Protocol. *See* POP (Post Office Protocol) posting content using microblogs, WEB 280–281

POTS. *See* dial-up

Pottruck, David, WEB 459

precedence operator An operator that clarifies the grouping within complex search expressions, usually indicated by parentheses or double quotation marks. Also called inclusion operator or grouping operator. WEB 161, WEB 163–164

preventing
    denial-of-service (DOS) attacks, WEB 309–311
    identity theft, WEB 311–315

previewing Web pages before printing, WEB 31–32, WEB 64–66

PriceGrabber, WEB 469

print resources, accessing online, WEB 217–227

printing
    email messages, WEB 84
    Hotmail messages, WEB 93, WEB 112–113
    Web pages, WEB 30–33, WEB 64–66

privacy
    e-commerce concerns, WEB 475
    Internet Explorer cookie settings, WEB 22–23
    protecting on social networks, WEB 283
    protecting online, WEB 249
    protecting your online reputation, WEB 284–285
    social media sites, WEB 282
    statements, WEB 476

Private Browsing mode A browsing mode in Firefox in which the user's browsing history, cookies, or copies of Web pages that were visited are not stored on the computer, helping to protect the user's privacy and security. WEB 57
    starting, using, WEB 57–59

private key A key used as part of an algorithm that encrypts messages in private-key and public-key encryption. WEB 301, WEB 302

private-key encryption A form of encryption that uses a single, private key that is known by both the sender and receiver, or by the programs that the sender and receiver are using, to encrypt messages. Also called symmetric encryption. WEB 301

private Web browsing, WEB 24–25

Procter & Gamble, WEB 269

products, searching online for, WEB 203–207

professional services sites, WEB 464

profiles, creating online social network, WEB 283

ProgrammableWeb.com, WEB 258–261

Project Gutenberg, WEB 218

ProQuest Dialog, WEB 217

protocol The rules for formatting, ordering, and error-checking data sent across a network. WEB A9
    email, WEB 74

proximity operator. *See* location operator

public domain Copyrighted works or works that are eligible for copyright protection whose copyrights have expired or been relinquished voluntarily by the copyright owner. Anyone can copy text, images, and other items in the public domain without obtaining permission. WEB 211

public key A key used as part of an algorithm that encrypts messages using public-key encryption. WEB 302

public-key encryption A form of encryption that uses two different keys that work as a pair to encrypt messages. The private key is known only to one party, and the public key is known to everyone. Also called asymmetric encryption. WEB 302

publishing Web sites, WEB 444

pull technology A communications model that downloads content to users' computers on a schedule or when they request it. WEB 246
    visual overview (fig.), WEB 244–245

pure dot-com A business that makes all its sales on the Web and has no physical stores. Also called dot-com. WEB 459

push technology A communications model that sends content to users' devices on a schedule set up by the user. WEB 246
    visual overview (fig.), WEB 262–263

Q

query. *See* search expression

questions, types of search, WEB 134–136

queued The status of an email message that has been temporarily held in a folder before being sent when the user exits the program or checks for new mail. WEB 84

QuickTime Player, WEB 433

quoted message That portion of the body of a sender's original message that you include in a reply to the sender, which might include your own comments. WEB 85

R

range In a wireless network, the physical distance between an access point and a wireless device. WEB 357
    Wi-Fi and Bluetooth standards compared (table), WEB 364

raster graphics Images that are composed of pixels. WEB 436, WEB 437, WEB 438

read-only A file whose contents you can view (read) but that you cannot change (edit). WEB 80

Really Simple Syndication (RSS) A feed format that is used to syndicate (distribute) published content from one site to another. WEB 249

RealPlayer, WEB 433

Refresh button A button on the Internet Explorer Address bar that loads a new copy of the Web page in the browser window. WEB 2, WEB 11–12

reintermediation The introduction of a new intermediary into an industry. WEB 465

relative path A path that describes the location of a file relative to the location of the current file. WEB 415

relevance, evaluating Web resources, WEB 172

Reload button A button on the Firefox Location bar that loads a new copy of the Web page that appears in the browser window. WEB 35

remote Web site A Web site stored on a Web server. WEB 444

remote wipe The action of remotely issuing a command to delete everything stored on a wireless device as a security precaution in the event of loss or theft of the device. WEB 388

removing malware, WEB 327–332

Rent.com, WEB 205

reply An email message sent in response to a previously received email message. WEB 86

replying
    to email messages, WEB 86
    to Hotmail messages, WEB 109–112

reputation, protecting your online, WEB 284–285

ReputationDefender, WEB 284–285

research
    evaluating Web sites, WEB 170–177
    summarizing results, WEB 224

resource list. *See* Web bibliography

resources, accessing online text-based, WEB 217–227

restoring
    Firefox toolbars, WEB 38–39
    Internet Explorer toolbars, WEB 6

results page Web pages generated by a Web search engine containing hyperlinks to Web pages that contain matches to the search expression entered into the search engine. WEB 141

retail sales, e-commerce, WEB 458–459

retweet The act of forwarding a message in a microblog to other users to share its content with new followers. WEB 281

revenue model The business processes that a company uses to find new customers, make sales, and deliver the goods or services it sells. WEB 458

robots, WEB 133

rooting The process of unlocking the operating system on an Android device so it can run apps created for other operating systems. WEB 388

router A hardware device that accepts packets from other networks and determines the best way to move each packet forward to its destination. WEB A9
    installing wireless, WEB 382

routing algorithm The program on a router in a packet-switching network that determines the best path on which to send packets across the network. WEB A9

RSS. *See* Really Simple Syndication (RSS)

RSS feeds The display of content published by a Web site that is updated often. WEB 16, WEB 249
    getting information from, WEB 249–252

S

sales channel A way that a company supplies its products or services to customers, such as a Web site. WEB 459

Sallie Mae's Upromise site, WEB 469–470
Salon.com, WEB 189
satellite Internet access, WEB A22
saving
    bookmarks, WEB 52
    email messages, WEB 84–85
    files in the cloud, WEB 232
    Hotmail attachments, WEB 107–109
    HTML documents, WEB 405
    Web page content, WEB 27–30, WEB 60–64
    Web page images, WEB 28–29, WEB 61–62
scanners and raster graphics, WEB 437
scope, evaluating Web resources, WEB 172
ScreenTips, hyperlink, WEB 10, WEB 42
scripting engine The part of a browser that translates code in a script into a format that the browser can execute. WEB 429
scripting language A programming language that is executed by a Web browser. WEB 429
scripts, running, WEB 429–433
ScriptSearch.com, WEB 431
search
    Google filtered, WEB 164–167
    questions, types of, WEB 134–136
    repeating, WEB 139
    Web strategies, WEB 137–139
    Web tools, WEB 139–159
search engine A Web site (or part of a Web site) that finds other Web pages that match the text you typed in a search box. WEB 8, WEB 41, WEB 139
    features of, WEB 146–148
    filtering results by date, WEB 187–189
    hybrid, WEB 148–153
    and metasearch engines, WEB 154–155
    overview, WEB 139–145
    using different, WEB 141
    visual overview (fig.), WEB 132–133
    wildcard characters, using, WEB 162–163
search engine databases, WEB 145–146
search engine optimization (SEO) The process of fine-tuning a Web site so that it ranks well in a search engine's results when a user searches the Web using the site's keywords. WEB 445
    exploring resources for, WEB 445–447
search engine submission The process of submitting a Web site's URL to one or more search engines so they will list the site in their indexes. WEB 445
    exploring resources for, WEB 445–447
search expression The word or phrase that you enter into a Web search engine. WEB 139
    and different search engines, WEB 145
    using Boolean operators, WEB 161
search filter A Web search engine feature that allows you to eliminate Web pages from a search based on attributes such as language, date, domain, host, or page component (hyperlink, image tag, title tag). WEB 163
search question. See search expression
searches
    filtering techniques in complex, WEB 160–163
    performing complex, WEB 163–169
    using logical operators, WEB 160–161

searching
    for blogs, WEB 278–279
    for businesses, WEB 200–203
    for current news, WEB 189–193
    for current or specific information, WEB 186–189
    for current weather information, WEB 193–196
    library databases, WEB 160
    for maps, destination information, WEB 196–200
    for music agencies, WEB 201–203
    for people, WEB 200–203
    for products, services, WEB 203–207
    for Web sites that include feeds, WEB 250–252
Seattle's wireless network, WEB 359
second-generation (2G) wireless network A wireless network that transfers voice and small amounts of unformatted data at a rate of up to 14.4 Kbps. WEB 352, WEB 354
secrecy threat A threat that occurs when data is disclosed to an unauthorized party. WEB 300
secret key In public-key encryption, the term "secret key" is another name for the private key a sender uses to encrypt messages because the secret key is unknown to the message receiver. WEB 302
secure server A server that encrypts data to prevent unauthorized parties from being able to read or use it. WEB 439
Secure Sockets Layer (SSL) A widely used protocol that is used to establish secure, encrypted connections between Web browsers and Web servers. WEB 321, WEB 337–338, WEB 341
    using, WEB 341–344
Secure Sockets Layer-Extended Validation (SSL-EV) A set of stricter criteria than are used to verify applicants for SSL certificates and an assurance of consistent application of verification procedures that certification authorities use to establish the identity of Web site owners. WEB 342
    using, WEB 342–344
securing
    Chrome browser, WEB 325–327
    domain names, WEB 423
    Firefox, WEB 324–325
    Internet Explorer (IE), WEB 322–324
    Web clients, WEB 320
    Web servers, and transactions, WEB 321
    wireless devices, WEB 388–390
    wireless networks, WEB 378–383
security The protection of physical and logical assets from unauthorized access, use, alteration, or destruction. WEB 298
    basics of, WEB 300
    communication channel, WEB 335–341
    encryption. See encryption
    enhancing: visual overview (fig.), WEB 320–321
    physical and logical, visual overview (fig.), WEB 298–299
    social network concerns, WEB 315–318
    transactions online, WEB 474–477
    unsolicited email messages, WEB 84
    using public hotspots safely, WEB 385
    Web client, WEB 322–327
    wireless. See wireless security
sending email messages, WEB 84

Sent folder The folder in Windows Live Hotmail that stores copies of messages that have been sent. WEB 92
SEO. See search engine optimization (SEO)
server A computer that accepts requests from client computers that are connected to it and shares some or all of its resources, such as printers, files, or programs, with those client computers. WEB A2
    domain name, WEB A7
    hypertext, WEB A15
    list, WEB 247
    mail, WEB 74
    news, WEB 247
    preventing denial-of-service (DOS) attacks, WEB 310–311
    Web, WEB 4, WEB 36, WEB 439
server certificate An electronic file that is issued by a certificate authority and installed on a Web server to prove the identity of the server to Web clients that connect to it to conduct transactions. WEB 337
    using, WEB 336–339
service set identifier (SSID) A name broadcast by a wireless router or access point that wireless devices use to identify the network and connect to it. WEB 381
service statements, WEB 480
services, buying and selling online, WEB 464–468
session key A temporary key used to secure the connection made between a Web browser and a secure server during SSL or TLS connections. WEB 342
SGML. See Standard Generalized Markup Language (SGML)
shared server A server that hosts multiple Web sites. WEB 439
Shockwave Player A browser plug-in that displays animated, three-dimensional interfaces, interactive advertisements and product demonstrations, multiuser games, streaming CD-quality audio, and video that was created using Adobe Director software. WEB 433, WEB 434
shopping carts, electronic, WEB 478
Shopping.com, WEB 205
Short Message Service (SMS) On a wireless network, the feature that lets users send data in the form of text messages. WEB 352
shortcuts, favorites, WEB 16
signature An optional part of an email message that appears at the bottom of the message body and usually contains information about the sender, such as the sender's name and contact information. WEB 77, WEB 78
    formal, informal, WEB 80–81
    virus, WEB 88
signed ActiveX control An ActiveX control that uses a digital signature to identify the control's developer or source. WEB 322
sign-in. See logging in
signing out of Windows Live, WEB 122–123
Silverlight, WEB 433
simultaneous support A feature of 4G wireless networks that refers to a device's ability to process many tasks at the same time, such as talking on the phone and displaying Web pages, as a result of the network's connection speed. WEB 355

single-factor authentication A method of authenticating a user with a single factor, such as a username and a password, to access a system. WEB 336

SkyDrive A Windows Live service that lets users post files to a server and use a Windows Live Hotmail account to share access to those files with other users. WEB 119

sharing files using, WEB 119–122

Skype home page (fig.), WEB 267

Slate, WEB 189

smartphone A mobile device that combines the functionality of a cell phone with an operating system that performs functions such as displaying Web pages, playing audio and video files, sending and receiving email and other messages, and using applications to open, edit, and create documents and other files. WEB 354

examples of, WEB 355

security risks with apps, WEB 386–390

SMS. *See* Short Message Service (SMS)

SMTP (Simple Mail Transfer Protocol) An Internet protocol that determines which path an outgoing email message takes on the Internet. WEB 74

sniffer program A program that a hacker uses to illegally monitor activity on a wireless network in order to obtain personal information that is transmitted to it by its connected wireless devices. WEB 384

social media marketing The process of using social media Web sites such as Facebook, Twitter, and YouTube to attract attention to an idea, product, Web site, store, and so forth. WEB 471

social media sites, privacy and appropriateness, WEB 282

social network A general term that refers to any community of people who use the Internet to share information, which might include updates, business information, contacts, photos, videos, or links to other users or sites. WEB 262

security of, WEB 315–318

Social Security Numbers, WEB 312

sound files, finding on the Web, WEB 229–232

source page A Web page that contains a hyperlink. WEB 417

spam. *See* junk mail

specific question A question that can be phrased easily and one for which the answer is readily recognizable. WEB 134

effective Web search strategies for, WEB 137–139

finding answers to, WEB 143–145

specifications Sets of standards that identify how a browser interprets code. WEB 400

spell-checking, WEB 224

email messages, WEB 83

Hotmail messages, WEB 105

spider. *See* Web robot

sponsored link A link that appears on a search engine results page because an advertiser paid to have it placed there. WEB A7

sponsored TLD (sTLD) A top-level domain (TLD) that is maintained by a sponsoring organization (such as an industry trade group) rather than by ICANN. WEB A7

sponsorship ads, WEB 469

spoofing A type of integrity violation in which a Web site is designed to deceive visitors into believing that they are using a Web site for a legitimate business as part of a phishing scam that seeks to steal data and other assets from its victims. WEB 303

and phishing attacks, WEB 303–307

spyware Software that is installed without the user's knowledge and consent, either by itself or in conjunction with a program that the user did intend to install, and that produces ads or covertly monitors the user's computer activity for a third party. WEB 328, WEB 334

SSID. *See* service set identifier (SSID)

SSL. *See* Secure Sockets Layer (SSL)

SSL-EV. *See* Secure Sockets Layer-Extended Validation (SSL-EV)

SSL Web server certificates, WEB 337

Standard Generalized Markup Language (SGML) The document description language on which HTML is based. WEB A15

start page The page that opens when you start a browsing session or the page that a particular Web browser loads the first time it is run. *See also* home page. WEB 3, WEB 35

static Web page An HTML file that exists on a Web server computer. WEB 169

steganography A process that hides messages within different types of files. WEB 309

stemming The process of using the root form of a word to create variations on the word. WEB 146

use by search engines, WEB 147

stock brokerage sites, WEB 464

sTLD. *See* sponsored TLD (sTLD)

stock image A professional photograph, line drawing, or other graphic that is available for purchase and can be sold to multiple customers. WEB 228

stop word A common word, such as "and," "the," "it," or "by" that most search engines (even those that claim to be full-text indexed search engines) omit from their databases when they store information about Web pages. WEB 146

storing

email messages, WEB 84–85

files in the cloud, WEB 232

storyboard A diagram of a Web site's content and structure that shows all the pages in the site and the relationships between the pages. WEB 422

example of (fig.), WEB 424

strategic alliance. *See* affiliate marketing

strategic partnership. *See* affiliate marketing

streaming transmission A technique for transferring sound and video files on the Web in which a Web server sends the first part of a file to a Web browser or media player program, which uncompresses and plays the file immediately, and while the first part of the file plays, the server is sending the next segment of the file. WEB 232

strong key A general term that describes an encryption key that is at least 128 bits in length. WEB 302

style A collection of formatting instructions that a Web browser applies to text. WEB 425

changing font, WEB 411–412

subject guide. *See* Web bibliography

Subject line The part of an email message header that gives a brief summary of the message's content and purpose. WEB 79

subscribe The act of joining a mailing list or other feed resource. WEB 247

to feeds, WEB 249–250

subscription An amount that users pay in order to access the site's content. WEB 462

buying and selling, WEB 462–463

Superpages.com, WEB 201–203

Symantec antivirus (Norton), WEB 88

symmetric encryption. *See* private-key encryption

T

T-1 A high-bandwidth (1.544 Mbps) data transmission connection used as part of the Internet backbone and by large firms and ISPs as a connection to the Internet. WEB A22

T-3 A high-bandwidth (44.736 Mbps) data transmission connection used as part of the Internet backbone and by large firms and ISPs as a connection to the Internet. WEB A22

tabs, opening Web pages in new, WEB 13–14

tag (1) In Firefox, a label or keyword you create to help you identify your bookmarks; (2) A user-defined keyword that categorizes the content of a Web site, photo, post, video, podcast, or almost any other form of Web content based on the information it contains; (3) A code that tells the Web browser software how to display the text contained in an HTML document. WEB 4, WEB 36, WEB 47

and attributes, WEB 402

deprecated, WEB 401

examples of, WEB 398–399

heading, WEB A16

meta, WEB 145

nested, WEB 401

summary (fig.), WEB 420

tag cloud A cloud arrangement that displays user-defined keywords (tags) so that larger words in the cloud indicate more content in that category. WEB 260

Talk An early prototype of the IRC program that let users send short text messages to each other. WEB 264

tangential vs. useful information, WEB 136

target page. *See* target

target The page that is opened when a hyperlink is clicked. WEB 417

tax return services, online, WEB 464

TaxiWiz mashup site, WEB 257–258

TCP. *See* Transmission Control Protocol (TCP)

TCP/IP A combined set of rules for data transmission; TCP includes rules that computers on a network use to establish and break connections, and IP includes rules for routing of individual data packets. WEB A10

Telnet An Internet protocol that lets users log in to their computer accounts from remote sites. WEB A10

templates, for blogs, WEB 277

terms of service (TOS) statement A Web site policy that typically includes rules that site visitors must follow, a statement of copyright interest in the site design and content, and restrictions on the types of business that a visitor can conduct with the site. WEB 480 text ads, WEB 469

text chat Real-time communication in which users exchange typed messages. WEB 264

text message A type of instant message that is limited to 140 text characters in size that is sent over a cellular network between users who are connected to the network using cell phones or other mobile devices. WEB 266

text message A message with a maximum of 160 alphanumeric characters that is sent and received over a network using mobile devices. WEB 354

text messaging A commonly used name for sending and receiving text messages using SMS. WEB 354

Thawte Web site, WEB 337–338

thin wallet A digital wallet that an organization creates and maintains on its servers for consumers. WEB 471

third-generation (3G) wireless network A wireless network that transfers data at up to 2 Mbps. WEB 354

third-party cookie A cookie that is placed on a user's computer by a company other the company whose Web site is being visited. WEB 22, WEB 55

THOMAS legislative information site, WEB 225

thread (1) A series of messages in a mailing list or newsgroup that are replies to a single, original message posted to the list or newsgroup; (2) The name given to a group of related email messages, which are usually stacked in the Inbox so that a sender's original message and all related replies are grouped together. Also called a conversation. WEB 86, WEB 248

threat Any act or object that endangers an asset. WEB 300

TLS. *See* Transport Layer Security (TLS)

To line That part of an email message header containing the message recipient's email address. WEB 78

Tomlinson, Ray, WEB A10

toolbars, WEB 6
    displaying, hiding Internet Explorer, WEB 5–6
    displaying Firefox, WEB 38–39

top-level domain (TLD) The last part of a domain name, such as .com. WEB A7

TOS. *See* terms of service (TOS) statement

Towerstream, WEB 368

tracking devices, blocking, WEB 333–334

transactions
    assurance providers, WEB 339–340
    evaluating, WEB 477
    security concerns, WEB 474–477

transfer rate In a wireless network, the speed at which data is transmitted from an access point (or base station) to a wireless device. WEB 357
    file size, and Web site's transfer requirements, WEB 439–440
    Wi-Fi and Bluetooth standards compared (table), WEB 364

translation, and product localization, WEB 478

Transmission Control Protocol (TCP) A part of the TCP/IP set of rules for sending data over a network. WEB A10

transparent GIF. *See* Web bug

Transport Layer Security (TLS) The name given to the SSL version 3 protocol by the IETF and that is used to establish secure, encrypted connections between Web browsers and Web servers. WEB 341
    using, WEB 341–344

travel industry, disintermediation and reintermediation, WEB 465

Trojan horse A program hidden inside another program that is created with the intent of causing damage. WEB 327

Trojan horse programs, WEB 309

TRUSTe, WEB 339–340, WEB 341, WEB 476

network. WEB A10

tweet A common nickname for a microblog posting that references the popular microblogging site, Twitter. WEB 279

troubleshooting printing of Web pages, WEB 30

Turnitin anti-plagiarism Web site, WEB 214–215

tweeting A common nickname for the act of posting messages on a microblog site that references the popular site, Twitter. WEB 279

twisted pair cable The type of cable that telephone companies have used for years to wire residences and businesses; twisted pair cable has two or more insulated copper wires that are twisted around each other and enclosed in another layer of plastic insulation. WEB A3, WEB A4

Twitter, WEB 471

U

undiscoverable mode A setting on a Bluetooth-enabled device that makes its signal invisible (undetectable) to other devices. WEB 386

Uniform Resource Locator (URL) The four-part address for an HTML document that tells a Web browser which protocol to use when transporting the file, the domain name of the computer on which the file resides, the pathname of the folder or directory on the computer in which the file resides, and the name of the file. WEB 2, WEB 34
    entering in search engines, WEB 133
    navigating Web pages by, WEB 7–8, WEB 39–41
    shortened, WEB 317–318
    Web page citations, WEB 209, WEB 215–217

unmoderated list A mailing list in which there is no moderator. WEB 247

unordered list. *See* bulleted list

unsolicited email messages, WEB 89

updating antivirus programs, WEB 88

uploading files to SkyDrive, WEB 120–122

Upromise Web site, affiliate program, WEB 469–470

URL. *See* Uniform Resource Locator (URL)

Usenet News Service (Usenet) An information resource on the Internet originally founded to collect and store information by topic category. WEB 247, WEB 248

Usenet. *See* Usenet News Service

US-CERT Staying Safe on Social Network Sites page, WEB 316

user name A unique name that identifies an account on a server. WEB 76
    and authentication, WEB 335–336
    Windows Live ID, WEB 96

user-generated content, WEB 246

V

value-to-weight ratio The price of an item divided by its weight. WEB 474

VBScript, WEB 429

vector graphics Images that are composed of paths. WEB 436, WEB 438

Vegas Hotel Hunt page for Caesars Palace, WEB 256

VeriSign, WEB 476

Verizon Wireless, WEB 360

Verizon Wireless 4G LTE Web page, WEB 371

video ads, WEB 469

video chat Real-time communication over the Internet in which people use a Webcam to exchange messages with audio and video. WEB 264

video content that has a progression of visual images and can include audio as well. WEB 232
    finding on the Web, WEB 234–235
    sharing on the Web, WEB 274–276

video-sharing site A Web site that lets users create accounts into which they can upload videos with the option of making them available so other users can view them. WEB 262

virtual library A Web site that provides online access to library information services. WEB 222
    using, WEB 222–224

virtual ports, WEB 334

virtual team communications, WEB 261

virus A malicious program that causes harm to a computer's disk or files. WEB 88
    and malware, WEB 327–328

virus definition. *See* virus signature

virus pattern. *See* virus signature

virus signature A sequence (string) of characters that is always present in a particular virus. Also called a virus pattern or a virus definition. WEB 88

voice chat Real-time communication over the Internet in which users exchange audio messages. WEB 264

Voice over Internet protocol (VoIP) A type of data transmission that converts audio signals to digital packets which uses a person's Internet connection to make and receive local and long distance telephone calls. WEB 267, WEB 368

VoIP. *See* Voice over Internet protocol

W

W3C. *See* World Wide Web Consortium (W3C)

wardriving The term used to describe the process of driving through a neighborhood with a wireless device with the goal of locating houses and businesses that have wireless networks in order to gain access to them. WEB 381

Wave format (WAV) A file format jointly developed by Microsoft and IBM that stores digitized audio waveform information at a user-specified sampling rate and plays on any Windows computer that supports sound. WEB 230

weather, finding current information, WEB 193–196

Weather Channel, WEB 194–196

Web 2.0 A term that indicates a change in the way people use the Web, just like a version change in a software program indicates that a new release of the software that is better than the old version. WEB 246

Web bibliography A Web site that contains a list of hyperlinks to other Web pages that contain information about a particular topic or group of topics and often includes summaries or reviews of the Web pages listed. Also called resource list, subject guide, clearinghouse, or virtual library. WEB 155
    using, WEB 155–157

Web browser Software that allows your computer run as a Web client, allowing it to connect to, locate, retrieve, and display Web content. The most popular are Microsoft Internet Explorer, and Mozilla Firefox. WEB 2, WEB 4, WEB 36
    choosing, WEB 4, WEB 36
    evolution of, WEB A16–A19
    history lists, WEB 21–22
    home page settings, WEB 12–13, WEB 44–45
    plug-ins, WEB 230
    See also specific Web browser

Web. *See* World Wide Web (WWW)

Web bug A small, hidden graphic on a Web page or in an email message that is designed to work in conjunction with a cookie to obtain information about the person viewing the page or email message and to send that information to a third party. Also called clear GIF or transparent GIF. WEB 333

Web client A computer that uses an Internet connection to become part of the Web and runs Web browser software. WEB 4, WEB 36
    securing (checklist), WEB 320
    securing transactions (checklist), WEB 321
    security, WEB 322–327

Web directory A Web site that includes a listing of hyperlinks to Web pages organized into predetermined hierarchical categories. WEB 148
    using, WEB 148–153

Web feed. *See* feed

Web hosting agreements, WEB 423

Web hosting services
    overview, WEB 439
    search engine submission, optimization, WEB 444–447
    services offered by, WEB 440–442

Web page An HTML document and its associated files that are stored on a Web server and viewed in a Web browser. WEB 2, WEB 37, WEB 409–410
    adding links to, WEB 418–419
    citations. *See* Web page citations
    components and features (fig.), WEB 398–399
    copyright and fair use, WEB 29, WEB 62
    enhancing using JavaScript, WEB 432
    evaluating quality of, WEB 173–175
    fonts, using, WEB 404
    HTML documents, WEB 5
    and intellectual property, WEB 210–211
    links. *See* links
    moving among visited, WEB 11–12, WEB 43–44
    navigating, WEB 7–15, WEB 39–47, WEB 53–55
    opening in new tab, WEB 13–14
    previewing, WEB 31–32
    printing, WEB 30–33, WEB 64–66
    ranking, WEB 146–147
    saving content of, WEB 27–30, WEB 60–64
    saving images from, WEB 28–29, WEB 61–62

    searching for, WEB 139–145
    shortened URLs to, WEB 317–318
    static, and dynamic, WEB 169
    using pictures in, WEB 414
    viewing HTML code of, WEB 425–426
    with Web bugs, WEB 333–334

Web page citations
    APA, WEB 216–217
    citing Web resources, WEB 215–217
    and copyright. *See* copyright
    visual overview (fig.), WEB 208–209

Web page formatting software, WEB 132

Web research resources, evaluating, WEB 170–177

Web robot A program that automatically searches the Web to find new Web sites and update information about old Web sites that already are in the database. Also called bot or spider. WEB 141

Web search strategies, WEB 137–139

Web server A computer that is connected to other computers through the Web and contains HTML documents that it makes available to other computers connected to the Web. *See also* server. WEB 4, WEB 36
    securing (checklist), WEB 321
    types of, WEB 439
    in Web site creation process (fig.), WEB 423

Web services The process of organizations communicating through a network to share data, without any required knowledge of each other's systems. WEB 255

Web site development tools, WEB 429–438

Web site management tools, WEB 425–429

Web sites
    creating (visual overview), WEB 422–423
    creating animated content, WEB 433–436
    evaluating content, WEB 424
    evaluating Web research resources, WEB 170–177
    evaluation, visual overview (fig.), WEB 158–159
    file size, transfer requirements, WEB 439–440
    Flash Player, Web site using (fig.), WEB 435
    form, appearance, WEB 172–173
    government, WEB 225–228
    growth of the Web, WEB A18–A19
    home pages, start pages, WEB 8
    image editing and illustrations programs, WEB 436–438
    international issues, WEB 478–479
    news aggregation, WEB 190
    organization of, WEB 9
    ownership, and objectivity, WEB 171–172
    portals, WEB 222
    programming with JavaScript, WEB 429–433
    publishing, WEB 444
    push and pull technologies, WEB 246
    remote, local, WEB 444
    search engine submission, optimization, WEB 444–447
    searching for feeds, WEB 250–252
    selling using. *See* e-commerce
    verifying certification of, WEB 343–344

Web Slice, WEB 249

Web-based publications, WEB 189

Web-safe color palette A collection of 216 colors that all computers render in the same way. WEB 403

webcams, WEB 264

Webmail An email address that you get through a Webmail provider. *See also* Windows Live Hotmail. WEB 93

Webmail provider A Web site that provides free email addresses and other Web-based services to registered users along with the capability to use any Web browser with Internet access to send and receive email messages. *See also* Windows Live Hotmail. WEB 93

Weiner, Congressman Anthony, WEB 282

WEP. *See* Wired Equivalent Privacy (WEP)

white pages directory A Web site you use to locate people, and obtain their postal address, phone number, and email address. WEB 185

wide area networks (WANs), WEB A8

widget A set of tools included on a Web page that facilitate the process of reposting the page's content on other sites, such as social networking sites and blogs. WEB 277

wiki A Web site that is designed to allow multiple users to contribute new content and edit existing content, often anonymously. WEB 189

Wikipedia A Web site that hosts a community-edited set of online encyclopedias in more than a dozen different languages. WEB 175
    evaluating resources, WEB 175–177

wildcard character The character, usually the asterisk (*), used to indicate that part of the term or terms entered into a Web search engine has been omitted. WEB 162
    using with searches, WEB 162–163

Windows Live Calendar A Web-based service from Microsoft that lets users post appointments and other information to an individual or shared calendar. WEB 101

Windows Live Hotmail A Webmail provider from Microsoft that is used to send and receive email messages. *See also* Hotmail. WEB 74–75

Windows Live ID The user name for logging in to Windows Live services, such as Windows Live Hotmail. WEB 96, WEB 97–99, WEB 122–123

Windows Live Messenger, WEB 264–266

wire service An organization that hires reporters to gather and write news stories, which it then distributes to newspapers, magazines, broadcasters, Web sites, and other organizations that pay a fee to the wire service (also called a press agency or news service). WEB 193

wireless network A way of connecting computers in a network that uses radio signals for communication instead of cables. WEB A4

Wi-Fi The trademarked name of the Wi-Fi Alliance that specifies the interface between a wireless client and a base station, or between two wireless clients to create a hotspot, to create an area of network coverage. Also called wireless fidelity. WEB 356
    and Bluetooth standards compared (table), WEB 364
    subscription-based services, WEB 374–375
    using public hotspots safely, WEB 385

Wi-Fi Alliance, WEB 356

Wi-Fi Protected Access (WPA) A wireless network standard that uses a preshared key to encrypt data and individual data packets sent over the network. WEB 379–380

WiMAX A wireless network that uses the 802.16 standard to create a 4G wireless broadband network in metropolitan areas by creating network hotspots of up to 10 or more square miles each using radio waves broadcast by WiMAX transmitters. Also called Worldwide Interoperability for Microwave Access. WEB 366, WEB 372
    overview, WEB 366–368
Windows Media Player, WEB 433
Windows Mobile, WEB 386
Windows operating system
    installed fonts, WEB 404
    malware symptoms, WEB 332
wired connection The type of connection to a network in which devices use cables. WEB 354
Wired Equivalent Privacy (WEP) A security protocol for wireless LANs that works by encrypting data sent over the network. WEB 378–379, WEB 380
wireless connection The type of connection to a network in which devices use radio waves or infrared technology instead of cables. WEB 354
wireless devices
    accessing Internet with, WEB 372–375
    chronological timeline, WEB 352–353
    securing, WEB 388–390
    security threats to, WEB 384–388
wireless fidelity. *See* Wi-Fi
wireless local area network (WLAN) A network in which devices use high frequency radio waves instead of wires to communicate with a base station that is connected to the Internet. WEB 356
    overview, WEB 356–360
wireless mesh network A self-configuring wireless network that is comprised of wireless nodes that relay communication across the network. Only one of the nodes is wired to the Internet connection, and then it shares that connection with the other nodes in the network. WEB 360
    overview, WEB 360–362

wireless networks
    changing default login, WEB 381
    evolution of, WEB 354–356
    protecting using software, WEB 382–383
    security. *See* wireless security
    visual overview (fig.), WEB 352–353
Wireless Philadelphia, WEB 359
wireless security
    checklist for installing router, access point, WEB 382
    overview, WEB 376–378
    protecting networking using software, WEB 382–383
    risks with smartphone apps, WEB 386–390
    securing networks, WEB 378–383
    threats to wireless devices, WEB 384–388
    visual overview (fig.), WEB 376–377
wireless wide area networking (WWAN) A wireless network created by nationwide cellular phone carriers that provides network coverage to a large geographical area using 3G or 4G networks. WEB 365
WLAN. *See* wireless local area network (WLAN)
Wolfram Alpha search engine, WEB 147–148
workbook attachments, WEB 79
World Wide Web (Web) A collection of files that reside on computers called Web servers that are connected to each other through the Internet. WEB 4, WEB 36, WEB A14
    evolution of the, WEB A15–A19
    finding audio files on the, WEB 229–232
    multimedia on the, WEB 228–236
    overview, WEB 4–5
    search engines and, WEB 133
    sharing pictures on the, WEB 272–274
    sharing videos on the, WEB 274–276
World Wide Web Consortium (W3C) The organization that establishes standards and specifications that identify how a browser interprets code. WEB 400
Worldwide Interoperability for Microwave Access. *See* WiMAX

worm A self-replicating and self-executing program that sends copies of itself to other computers over a network with the goal of infecting other computers. WEB 327
WPA. *See* Wi-Fi Protected Access (WPA)
written communication
    business correspondence guidelines, WEB 104
    chatting acronyms, WEB 266
    email message guidelines, WEB 83
    media, Web sites as, WEB 9, WEB 41
    research, using Wikipedia, WEB 177
    summarizing research results, WEB 224
WWAN. *See* wireless wide area networking (WWAN)

X

XHTML. *See* Extensible Hypertext Markup Language (XHTML)
XML. *See* Extensible Markup Language (XML)

Y

Yahoo! Advanced News Search page, WEB 191–192
Yahoo! API, WEB 256
Yahoo! News, WEB 190–191
Yahoo! Web directory, WEB 149–150, WEB 152–153, WEB 157, WEB 210
Yammer microblog, WEB 281
yellow pages directory A Web site that provides information about businesses, such as a description, address, phone number, Web site address, and reviews. WEB 185
Yippy search engine, WEB 167–169
YouTube, WEB 274, WEB 275, WEB 471

Z

zombie. *See* bot
ZoneAlarm antivirus, WEB 88
ZoneAlarm firewall, WEB 335
Zuckerberg, Mark, WEB 268–269, WEB 270